The Course of
Russian
Fifth Edition
History

Red Square in Moscow, with Lenin's mausoleum (center) *and Saint Basil's Cathedral* (upper left) *adjacent to the outer fortress walls of the Kremlin* (right)

The Course of
Russian
Fifth Edition
History

Melvin C. Wren
late of The University of Toledo

Taylor Stults
Muskingum College

WAVELAND

PRESS, INC.

Prospect Heights, Illinois

For information about this book, write or call:
    Waveland Press, Inc.
    P.O. Box 400
    Prospect Heights, Illinois 60070
    847/634-0081

Credits

To Gwen, Nancy, and David

MCW

To my parents,
who taught me to keep an open mind

TS

About the Authors

Melvin C. Wren, a well-known historian and educator, was born in Iowa in 1910. He received his undergraduate and graduate degrees from the University of Iowa. He also did postgraduate work at the University of California, Berkeley. Professor Wren devoted over thirty years to education and research. He taught in Europe and Africa as well as the United States. The first edition of *The Course of Russian History* was published in 1958, with the completion of the fourth edition in 1979. Professor Wren also authored *Ancient Russia* (1965), *The Western Impact Upon Tsarist Russia* (1971), and many journal articles. Dr. Wren, who can be characterized as a true scholar, passed away in 1984.

Taylor Stults, born in Illinois in 1936, received his undergraduate degree in history from Antioch College and his graduate degrees from the University of Missouri. He has been a member of the History Department at Muskingum College since 1962. Professor Stults has made several trips to the former Soviet Union, and his research and writing on Russian topics have been published in many books and journals.

Table of Contents

Illustrations

Maps

Excerpts from the
Preface to the Fourth Edition

There are today hundreds of scholars of Russian history—competent, productive, forceful, and daring to disagree vigorously. As the popularity of college courses on Russia swept the country after World War II, those who were pressed into service to teach the courses generally were not graduates of Russian or Slavic programs, few of which existed before 1945. But with few exceptions those who today teach the history of Russia have received extensive education in Russian history and in collateral areas—Russian or Slavic languages, literature, and culture or civilization.

My concern has been to leave a substantial but not fully fleshed-out structure that instructors may develop along various lines to suit their own interests and needs. The essential facts are there. I have not involved the student in historical debates over issues that invite differences of interpretation. Some teachers may want to examine a few of these issues in a problem sort of approach. If so, the choice of which debates or problems to explore I leave to them. Of course history is a matter of interpretation, but I have little patience with the caution that "historians disagree about the meaning and importance of almost every occurrence we know of in Russia before 1600."

I have softened the approach to the nation's heroes and villains. Alexander Nevsky may have been a hero to the Russians whose city of Novgorod he defended, but he must also have been a villain to the Swedes and Germans whose lands he scourged. Ivan the Great may have been a hero, to some Russians at least, but surely not to the Poles and Lithuanians whose borders he ravaged. German soldiers were ruthless to Russians in World Wars I and II, but Russian troops were no less so to Germans, Poles, and others in the same wars.

I have taken certain liberties, common to many who write for English-speaking audiences, with the Russian language. The plurals of *zemstvo* and *duma* appear here as *zemstvos* and *dumas*, rather than in the Russian form, *zemstva* and *dumy*. And I have chosen the common Anglicizations *Alexis, Andrew, Leo, Michael, Peter, Trotsky*, and *Tolstoy*, rather than the Russian *Alexei, Andrei, Lvov, Mikhail, Pyotr, Trotskii*, and *Tolstoi*. However, I have clung to *Fedor, Ivan*, and *Vasily*, in preference to the Anglicizations *Theodore, John*, and *Basil*.

I am grateful to the trustees of the Harvard University Press for permission to quote from S. H. Cross's translation of *The Russian Primary Chronicle*.

I owe much to many who have helped me along the way. A few contributed immensely to my development. The late Joseph Kramer, Professor of Botany at the University of Montana, gave me my first lessons in the Russian language. His knowledge of the old Russia and his appreciation of Russian literature gave me a sense of Russia's past that I could have acquired from few others. The late Robert J. Kerner of the University of California was an inspiring mentor. Professor Oleg Maslennikov, Liudmilla Patrick, and the late Georgy Patrick, all of the Department of Slavic Languages at the University of California, were superb teachers.

Melvin C. Wren
1979

Preface to the Fifth Edition

Finding appropriate examples, images, and metaphors to describe Russia and its long history challenges both casual observers and Russian scholars. Winston Churchill, in 1939, expressed the dilemma of attempting to understand this land, its people, and its government. During the early weeks of World War II, he said that Russian behavior "is a riddle, wrapped in a mystery, inside an enigma." Others might reflect Pushkin's terse remark: "God, what a sad country our Russia is." A Western visitor in the 1850s wrote that Russia was an unfortunate society since its cultural leaders died all too young, "as though the branches of her culture are not yet strong enough to bear such fruits." On the other hand, the joy of Russian life can be found in the words of Tchaikovsky who loved the beauty of the Russian winter and delighted at searching for wild mushrooms in the summer.

Russia is a land rich in resources and talents. It is one of the older societies in world history and has played many roles in Europe, Asia, and beyond. Christianity has been part of Russian life for more than a thousand years, and Russian literature and music have expanded and enriched the cultural horizons of Western civilization. Russian literature deals with universal themes, as well as settings and values more uniquely Russian. As Dr. Wren noted about the literary heritage, "There is no surer way of catching the feel of the Russian land and the Russian people, of experiencing Russia's glories and her sufferings." Students are therefore encouraged to delve into the writings of such authors as Pushkin, Gogol, Goncharov, Turgenev, Dostoevsky, Tolstoy, Chekhov, Gorky, Sholokhov, Pasternak, Yevtushenko, Solzhenitsyn, Rasputin and Rybakov, among others. Their major works are available in English translation.

Those who study this nation develop their own themes and interpretations, and Melvin Wren shared his own synthesis with students in his readable and useful textbook, *The Course of Russian History*. Many Americans, when thinking about Russia, may be prone to believe that the Soviet period represents a distinct break with Russia's past and that understanding this nation requires consideration only of the years since 1917. This is only partially true, for these years reveal numerous ties to the Russian heritage antedating Lenin's rise to power. I agree with Dr. Wren when he wrote that "no serious student can be satisfied that he or she understands the Soviet Union without knowing the Russia of prerevolutionary times." I also share his perspective of examining Russia through its political development, assessing its leadership, seeing periods of integration and disintegration, and contemplating its growth into a leading military power. The interplay of the forces for change and continuity, and the uneven efforts for democratic reform, also provide a motif for our understanding of its long history.

Even the name of this nation may be something of a puzzle to observers. The title of this textbook correctly places emphasis on Russia even while it comprised a part of the larger nation, the Union of Soviet Socialist Republics, between the time of Lenin's Bolshevik Revolution and the end of the Soviet Union in December 1991. During the Communist period many referred to the entire USSR as "Russia," although this was technically incorrect. Yet even during the Soviet era, the Russian region dominated the other Soviet republics in land size, population, economy, military strength, and leadership. Moscow retained its role as the capital both of the Russian Republic and the Soviet Union. For that reason, the focus on Russia during its lengthy period of independence as well as for its existence as the central part of the Soviet Union is justified and also convenient for the reader to comprehend.

As a teacher of Russian history for more than three decades, I have used a variety of texts, including Professor Wren's. Students consistently found his work to be manageable in size and scope, clearly written, informative, and stimulating. It had the right balance for our classroom needs. However, the passage of time inevitably made the fourth edition (published in 1979) outdated for the contemporary period. Some teachers continue to use it for the long span of earlier Russian history, while others hoped for a revised edition bringing the story to the present. These considerations led me to inquire about undertaking a fifth edition, and I am pleased that Waveland Press responded positively. We jointly hope readers will agree that its utility has been renewed and strengthened.

Our common goal is to keep an established and reputable book in print for a wide student audience, and extensive revisions and additions have been made throughout the entire fourth edition to create the fifth edition, especially in chapters 19 and 20. Chapter 21 has been substantially expanded to cover the entire Brezhnev era, and chapters 22–23 are totally new. The reading suggestions at the end of every chapter have been extensively revised to take account of recent scholarship. The purpose of these lists is to assist students who are seeking more information on selected topics. The textbook continues to be directed to undergraduates with little or no background in Russian history and is intended as a point of departure for further inquiry.

In the fourth edition, Professor Wren called attention to important journals in the field, such as the *Russian Review* and the *Slavic Review*. I second his comments and also recommend the excellent multi-volume reference work, *The Modern Encyclopedia of Russian and Soviet History*. The entries are clear, authoritative and detailed, and provide a convenient source of information. For the more recent period, the weekly publication *Current Digest of the Soviet Press* (1949–1992) and *Current Digest of the Former Soviet Press* (starting in 1992) provide verbatim coverage in English translation of articles from Russian language newspapers, magazines and journals. This source enhances our understanding of the last four decades through the perspective of Soviet authors. Regarding spelling, Professor Wren noted his decision to use terms and names more commonly accepted or understood in the West. I have continued this practice, except for the use of Mikhail Gorbachev (rather than Michael).

Acknowledgements need to be made and appreciation expressed to the following: the German Information Office for permission to use the photograph of Mikhail Gorbachev; faculty members across the United States who are past and present users of this Wren text, for their helpful written comments to the publisher, which were considered in preparing this revision; my colleagues in Muskingum's History Department for their congeniality, friendship, and continued support, and to the hundreds of students enrolled in my Russian and Soviet courses over three decades, who have shared in our joint study of this nation; Professor Irwin Abrams who first exposed me to Russian history during my undergraduate years at Antioch College and whose affirmation of life and dedication to improving our understanding of the Russian people has been an inspiration to me over many years; Professor Roderick McGrew for his influence during my graduate studies at the University of Missouri, who set high academic and intellectual standards for his students and who continues his interest in my professional career; Laurie Prossnitz of Waveland Press for her assistance and interest in supporting a new and revised edition of Professor Wren's text; Jeni Ogilvie of Waveland Press for her outstanding contributions in suggesting and making improvements throughout this project. Grammar, style and content bear the mark of her excellent and diligent efforts in overseeing the revision; Judy Woodard whose expert secretarial skills on the bulk of this revision and my earlier research projects in previous years have been essential to their final appearance. Her capable efforts, unfailing cooperation and positive attitude make the process of writing and revising less onerous; my sons whose curiosity and interest about the people and regions of the world have led them to Europe and the Soviet Union for their own deeper understanding; and finally, my wife Jan for her unfailing good spirits and support which have expanded and enriched our common interests in America and beyond. Our journeys to many nations over the years included the Soviet Union on several occasions. Her contributions to my life are legion, and I am grateful for her partnership in our common odyssey.

Taylor Stults
1994

To the Student

One comparatively minor yet distracting situation that can confuse the student is the appearance of two calendar dating systems in Russia. The Julian calendar was used in Russia until 1918 while Western nations changed to the Gregorian calendar in the sixteenth century. A time gap exists between the two systems. The Julian (Old Style or O.S.) was eleven days behind the Gregorian system (New Style or N.S.) in the eighteenth century, twelve days behind in the nineteenth century, and thirteen days behind in the twentieth century.

That is why the revolution in the winter of 1917 may be dated as occurring either in February or March. According to the calendar then in use in Russia, the revolution began in late February while by the Western calendar it began in early March. Likewise, the Bolshevik coup d'état in the fall occurred in late October (O.S.) or early November (N.S.). For decades, the Soviet Union celebrated the "Great October Revolution" on November 7. Various sources, especially for the crucial political years of 1905 and 1917 use one or the other calendar system. To avoid confusion if the student consults other accounts for this period, both dates will be given for key events in those two years. "Bloody Sunday," for example, will be dated as January 9/22, 1905. The Russian Revolution coverage will show key dates such as February 24/March 9 or October 25/November 7, 1917. The purpose is to make clear that important events such as "Bloody Sunday" or the overthrow of Nicholas II occurred only once, not twice!

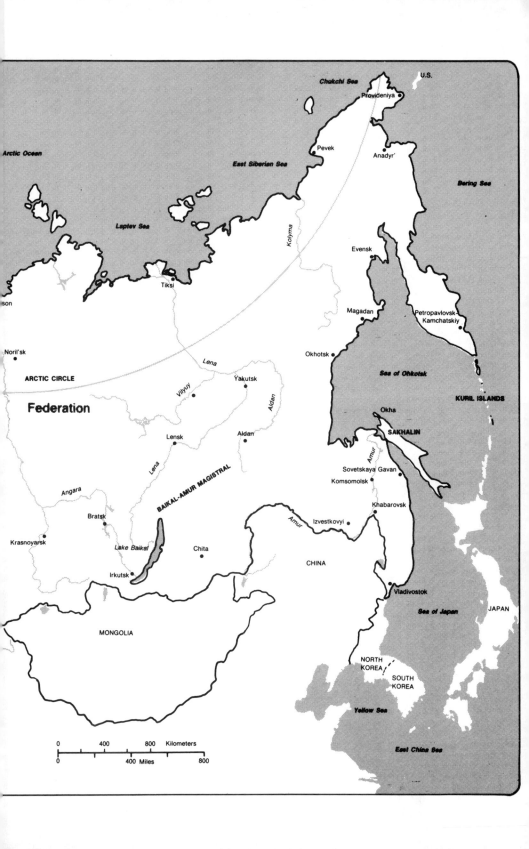

CHAPTER 1

The Land and Its Early Inhabitants

Geographical factors may strongly influence the development of a nation or a people. Insularity or the proximity of the sea and the familiarity that it breeds prompted the Phoenicians, Athenians, Romans, Portuguese, Spaniards, Dutch, English, and Japanese to exploit it as a bulwark of defense, an avenue of communication, and a source of food. Continentality may turn a people away from the sea, as it has done with the inhabitants of India, China, and to some extent Russia. Rivers may serve as boundaries, as the Rhine and the Danube served the Roman Empire; or as highways, as the Ohio, the Mississippi, and the Missouri have served the United States; or as means of irrigation, as the Nile serves Egypt and the Yangtze China. Climate may be stimulating, as it has been in the temperate zones, or enervating, as it has been in the tropics. Rich soil and adequate rainfall may encourage, and poor soil and drought may discourage, the investment of labor and capital in agriculture. Generous endowment of mineral resources may profit a people possessed of the technological skill to exploit it.

Topographical Setting

The modern Russian state is geographically isolated, for, except in the west, its borders rest on deserts, mountains, and closed seas. If one aspect of the

1

land leaves a stronger impression than any other it is the enormous area that the nation covers. To visitors, the effect of its overwhelming size has always been breathtaking. The boundaries of the Union of Soviet Socialist Republics in 1990 encompassed 8,700,000 square miles, or nearly one-sixth of the earth's land surface. Approximately thirty-eight thousand miles of land frontier, nine times that of the United States, bring many neighbors close up against its homeland. Larger than all North America, nearly three times the size of the continental United States, more than forty times the size of France and seventy times larger than the British Isles, Russia stretches nearly halfway around the globe.

European Russia consists of a vast plain, no part of which rises more than a thousand feet above sea level. Natural barriers, either seas or mountains, guard the plain except at the Polish border. Inside this perimeter of seas and mountains the monotony of the plain is broken only by the Ural Mountains, a chain too low to bar movement over and through it. The hills that line the west banks of the rivers that flow south to the sea and the Valdai Hills, only a thousand feet in elevation, provide little relief. This rolling plain has permitted an easy flow of population over the entire area and made difficult its defense once an enemy crossed its natural frontiers.

The Russian coastline is the longest of any nation but is of limited utility because the country is icelocked through much of the year. Most of Russia is far from the open sea. The nation's chief harbors lie on border seas—the Baltic, Black, and Caspian seas and the Seas of Okhotsk and Japan. Throughout history the exits from these seas have been controlled by foreign powers.

No country has been so bountifully provided with rivers as has Russia. They constitute an inexpensive if leisurely system of transportation, by boat in summer and by ski and sled in winter. In the Valdai Hills rise the headwaters of the Western Dvina, which flows into the Gulf of Riga; the Dnieper and Don, which enter the Black Sea; and the mighty Volga, with its many mouths opening on the Caspian. Except for the Amur, which empties into the Pacific, the great rivers of Siberia flow north into the Arctic. Because of the meandering length of the rivers of European and Asiatic Russia and their gradual drop to the sea, and because each gathers up many tributaries, the nation possesses a crisscross pattern of natural highways. The tributaries of one river system may rise within a mile of those of another, so that men and goods may move, over easy portage or more recently by canal, from one river system into another. Indeed, it always has been possible with slight inconvenience to travel by boat or by sled from the Baltic to the Black and Caspian seas or to the Arctic or Pacific. Moscow, now connected by canal to all the great rivers boasts of being a port of five seas.

Climate and Vegetation

Although four-fifths of the country lies in the temperate zone, Russia lies farther north than any other great power. St. Petersburg is in the same latitude as

Stockholm and Anchorage. Moscow is in the latitude of Edinburgh and Sitka. Kiev in south Russia is as far north as Calgary, and the Crimean resort of Yalta is as far north as Minneapolis.

Continentality, with its extremes of heat and cold, distinguishes the Russian climate. Because of the nation's distance from the Atlantic, and because the Scandinavian Mountains deflect the warm air of the Gulf Stream, temperatures are generally lower and winters longer in Russia than is the case elsewhere in the same latitudes. No protective mountains rise to keep back the cold air mass from the Arctic, and the icy blasts sweep out of the north unchecked over the plain. The result is that although there is considerable difference in temperature between west and east, there is remarkably little between north and south.

The growing season is short in nearly all of Russia. Less than two months are free of frost in northern Siberia, a hundred days in the northern half of European Russia, and six months in south Russia. The short summer forces the farmer to work prodigiously to beat the autumn frost. There can be little work outside in the low temperatures, the icy winds, and the few hours of daylight that come with winter. Travel is dangerous, and one goes on only the most urgent journeys during the bitterly cold months.

For various reasons—climate, topography, or soil—only one acre in eight or nine is arable. Most of this land lies inside a triangle whose base rests at St. Petersburg (renamed Leningrad between 1924 and 1991) and the mouth of the Danube and whose apex reaches just east of the Ob river in the direction of Lake Baikal. About 500 million acres were under cultivation in 1990, slightly under two acres for each of the 287 million inhabitants. Inadequate rainfall makes unfeasible the cultivation of wide expanses of land. In much of European Russia the annual precipitation is less than the twenty inches essential to profitable farming.

The arid region north and east of the Caspian receives less than ten inches, in places as little as three. So delicate is the balance between sufficient moisture and aridity that famine may result from a delay of spring rains in the lower valleys of the Dnieper, Don, and Volga. Rainfall is greatest in early summer. Erosion is a serious problem in the porous black soil of the steppe, and a hard spring rain may cut deep gashes in the fields. July and August may be very dry, with some of the great rivers threatening to dry up near their mouths. Dredging to remove the silt brought down by spring floods is necessary to keep open the mouths of the rivers that flow into the Black Sea.

Although precipitation is greatest in early summer, heavy snows in October and November lay a blanket that covers the ground for four to six months, but spring brings warm weather so quickly in south Russia that most of the winter's precipitation escapes in runoff and the farmer must have rain in the planting season to reap a crop.

In this huge country, which includes within its limits latitudes varying from subtropical to Arctic, there is a variety of vegetation found nowhere else in Eurasia. Distinct types of vegetation run in east-west bands across the face of Russia from the Arctic to the southern seas and mountains.

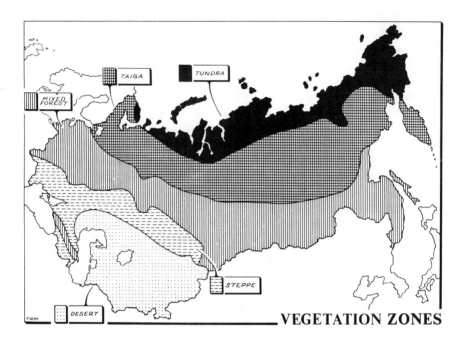

VEGETATION ZONES

Along the northern third of the Kola peninsula and in a widening span along the northern coast of Russia from the White Sea to the Bering Strait is the desolate waste known as the tundra. Nearly 15 percent of present-day Russia is tundra, and most of it is uninhabitable. Much of it is swampland, frozen most of the year. Little but moss and lichens grow in the northern tundra in summer. Farther south the tundra produces a scrawny scrub, heather, blackberry, and cranberry. Over much of this land the subsoil remains frozen the year round, and trees with their long roots cannot grow in it. South of the shrub zone, trees appear. Still farther south the trees rise in height as the tundra merges with the next vegetation zone, the taiga.

A fifth of the world's forests lie inside the former USSR. The taiga, the zone of the coniferous forest, stretches from Arkhangel and the Gulf of Finland in a band that widens to include the Central Urals and Lake Baikal and continues on across Siberia to the Sea of Okhotsk. Although the taiga is predominantly coniferous, mountain ash, poplar, birch, and aspen frequently appear.

South of the taiga is the zone of the mixed forest, where coniferous and deciduous trees appear interspersed. Forests of oak alternate with those of fir; elm, maple, ash, linden, lime, birch, and hornbeam splash brilliant color in the autumn. Much of the mixed forest zone west of the Urals has been cleared and brought under cultivation. The gray, acid soil of the region provides sufficient nourishment for flax and rye. Spring wheat has become popular, but the yield per acre remains low by Western standards. The forest—including the taiga and the mixed-forest zones—still covers over half of all Russia; it thins out south of a line connecting Kiev, Ryazan, and Kazan. A thin band, widening toward the Urals is the wooded steppe where grove and grassy meadow alternate.

Beyond the interval of the wooded steppe and running to the shores of the Black Sea is the true steppe, or prairie. The steppe is treeless, except in the river bottoms and in the shelter belts that the government has maintained for generations. The rick black soil makes the steppe, and particularly its western segment in the Ukraine, one of the finest agricultural areas in the world. The soil crumbles into fine powder when dry and rapidly absorbs water. This is a natural grassland. In the summer, however, the grass quickly parches, forcing early nomads to move their herds constantly in search of pasturage. Now the steppe is nearly all under the plow, for two-thirds of the cultivated land of Russia lies in this zone. Winter wheat has long been the chief crop, and the Ukraine has earned its reputation as the breadbasket of Europe. From Odessa on the Black Sea Russian wheat has moved to ports all over the world, at least when there was a surplus. Sugar beets are now an important crop, as are soybeans, potatoes, hay, and, locally, cotton and rice. So vital to the economy is the steppe and particularly the Ukraine that prolonged interference with the flow of its products may paralyze or seriously cripple the surrounding republics.

Northwest, north, and east of the Caspian Sea, and extending past the Aral Sea and Lake Balkhash to the foothills of the Pamir Mountains, is a vast expanse of desert and semidesert covering a sixth of the area of the former USSR. In the northern half of this region the clay soil of the semidesert nourishes patches of coarse grass and may become profitable to agriculture under irrigation.

The Black Sea littoral from the south slope of the Caucasus to the Turkish border, and the west shore of the Caspian south of Baku, enjoy a very humid subtropical climate where the annual rainfall may exceed eighty inches. The Crimea and the north slope of the Pamirs have a similar climate. The valleys of Turkmenia and southern Tadjikistan, where the climate is dry subtropical, receive very little rainfall but have blossomed under irrigation projects. The mountains along the southern rim of Russia and Siberia show wooded slopes up to varying altitudes, above which are alpine meadows whose rich grasses offer splendid pasture for sheep and goats.

Early Inhabitants

The north coast of the Black Sea and the steppe hinterland beyond it were significant in Greek and Roman times as an important source of food and raw materials and as a market for the products of Aegean and Mediterranean manufacturing centers. Indeed, the Greeks ventured into the Black Sea six or seven centuries before the Christian era in search of iron, gold, and fish, and established colonies that began as fishing villages and grew into thriving market centers. Into these Greek towns natives from the interior brought the products of the forest and steppe—hides, meat, grain, furs, honey, and wax—to trade for the manufactured goods of Greece—weapons, armor, tools, and luxury items. For a thousand years the Greeks, and the Romans who later took over the area, maintained this trade tie with south Russia.

The Greeks gave the name of Scythians to the people with whom they traded in their Black Sea colonies. The Scythians, an Iranian people, were nomads who entered the Russian steppe from Asia, following their herds westward in search

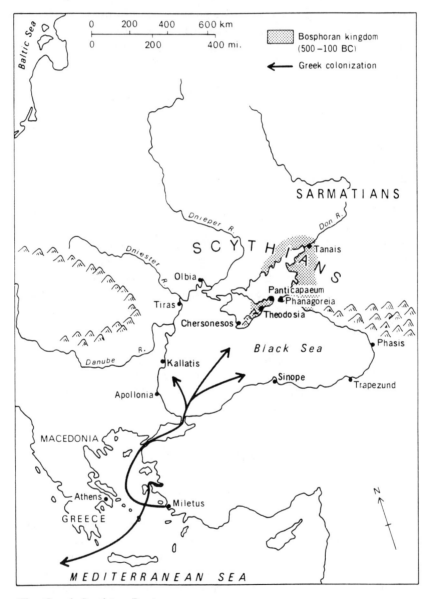

The Greek-Scythian Region

of better pasture. By the beginning of the sixth century B.C., Scythian power extended over the Black Sea littoral. This confederation of related tribes centered between the Dnieper and the Don and covered the entire steppe area of south Russia, reaching into the Kuban valley on the east and to the Carpathians on the west. Later the Scythian kingdom expanded into the Hungarian plain.

During the centuries of Scythian domination, these Iranian nomads ruled the peoples of south Russia under a military regime. For some time after their arrival on the steppe they continued the nomad's life of moving their tents and families to and fro over the grassland as they followed their herds to new pasture. Slaves tended the flocks and herds, and with the produce of their own animals the Scythians combined the agricultural and other products gathered as tribute from the subject population.

In the early part of the third century B.C. Macedonian attacks, the movement of Celts from the northwest into the Black Sea littoral, and the appearance of the Sarmatians out of the east, forced the Scythians to pull in their outposts and to concentrate between the Don and the Dnieper. Toward the end of the century the Sarmatians from the east, an Iranian people like the Scythians, crossed the Don and moved firmly against their cousins. Pressed on the north by Celts and Germans and on the east by Sarmatians, the Scythians surrendered or withdrew to the Crimean peninsula. The great Scythian kingdom disappeared, although some Scythian princes may have received permission to retain local authority as vassals to the Sarmatians.

The new conquerors controlled south Russia for four centuries after their appearance out of the Siberian grassland about 200 B.C. They were pushed out of their homeland in Central Asia and Turkestan by Mongols turned aside from an attack on China by the newly constructed Great Wall. At about the same time, the Celts moved into southeastern Europe from the north, and some of them pressed into the western Ukraine. These Celts, or Gauls, left their name in Galicia, but they made no serious effort to settle permanently in the Russian steppe.

The Ionian Greeks ventured into the Black Sea as early as the seventh century B.C. and found the area abundantly rewarding. Soon along the shores of the inland sea, there appeared towns built by the Greeks and maintained as colonies that shipped metals, grain, fish, furs, hides, meat, wax, honey, and other goods back to the homeland. In return the colonies received from Greece the weapons, armor, clothing, and luxury goods for which the natives were anxious to trade.

Population pressure in Scandinavia in the first century A.D. forced the Germanic people known as the Goths to emigrate to the valley of the Vistula. Toward the end of the second century these Goths moved southeast into the lower Dnieper, crossed the river near Kiev, and moved south into the Crimea and Kuban valley. Those who remained on the right or west bank continued down the river to its mouth. The name of Visigoths, or West Goths, came to attach to those tribes that settled between the Dniester and the Danube. The Ostrogoths, or East Goths, settled farther east along the north Black Sea shore.

By the year 250 the north coast of the Black Sea was under Gothic control.

Being pre-eminently a seafaring people, the Goths took full advantage of the Russian rivers and the Black and Aegean seas to plunder Roman settlements in the area. In 267 they even raided Athens. Their relations with Rome were frequently peaceful and commercial, however. The trade that had long focused in south Russia continued to flourish under the new masters of the steppe. Furthermore, early in the fourth century, the Goths accepted the religion of the Romans and became Christians.

The grassy steppeland of south Russia, extending from the Carpathians eastward nearly to the Altai-Sayan Mountains, was an inviting highway to nomadic herdsmen, and the Scythians and the Sarmatians in turn had followed it into the Black Sea area. Then in 380 came the Huns—Turkic peoples who had conquered various Mongol tribes in their progress westward and forced the vanquished to join the migration.

The great leader Attila later consolidated Hunnic power from the Caucasus to the middle Danube. He attacked Constantinople (formerly Byzantium until the fourth century) in 447 and laid it under tribute. The Roman emperor in the west sought his favor, and the Hunnic khan even considered marrying the emperor's sister. In 451, Attila attacked the Roman power in France. Near Troyes, a Roman force, strongly supported by Germans, defeated Attila, and he withdrew to the middle Danube from where he had come. The following year he invaded Italy, but the pope and the Roman emperor persuaded him to return to the Danube. With Attila's death in 453, the Hunnic empire dissolved. Some of the Huns settled in the Balkans; others withdrew east of the Carpathians. For another century they appeared from their headquarters between the Don and the Dnieper alternately as opponents of the Eastern, or Byzantine, Empire and as allies of the Roman emperor in his efforts to suppress uprisings among his German subjects.

In 558, a formidable force of Bulgars, a Turkic people who had recently settled in the Russian steppe, attacked Constantinople by land and by sea, and so likely seemed the prospect of the capital's fall that the emperor had to pay ransom to the invaders. Then the Bulgars hurried back to their home on the north coast of the Black Sea. Word had come that a new horde of nomads was pouring out of the east.

The Avar horde that moved into the Russian steppe in 558 consisted of Turkic and Mongolian tribes. Its fighting force may have numbered no more than twenty thousand, but the use of stirrups made the Avar horsemen difficult to unseat and consequently gave them an advantage over European horsemen. It was the Avar who introduced the stirrup into Europe.

The new force moved sternly against the Bulgars in the steppe; indeed, the Eastern emperor paid it to do so. In three years' time the Avars had brought the Bulgars under their rule and had pushed on to the Dniester and then to the Danube. They established their headquarters in the middle Danube, and from there they ruled over the entire area between the Volga and the Hungarian plain. During the last quarter of the sixth century and for the first quarter of the seventh, the Avars constituted the most serious threat to the security of Constantinople. Avar raids south of the Danube constantly threatened the emperor's hold on the Balkans.

Avar power reached its height in 626, when the Avars laid siege to Constantinople. An epidemic that decimated the attacking host forced its retirement to the camp on the Danube. The peoples whom the Avars had subjugated recovered their independence and the Avar state was swept away. There is a Russian saying, "They perished like the Avars," which refers to the complete vanishing of a sometime conqueror.

There was a momentary resurgence of Bulgar power in the Russian steppe after the withdrawal of the Avars, but with the death of the leader who had reunited the various tribes, the Bulgars again separated into independent communities and scattered. One group drifted into the middle Danube and there joined the remnant of the Avars. Another settled in northern Italy. A third moved to the lower Danube. Still another remained in the lower Don valley and accepted the overlordship of the new masters of the eastern steppe, the Khazars. From the viewpoint of the history of Russia, the most important segment migrated to the middle Volga and settled around the mouth of the Kama. There they gathered under their authority the loosely organized Finnish tribes of the area and gained control of western Siberia as well.

In the area between the Kuban valley and the lower Volga there appeared in the seventh century a new political power, the Khazars. They had once been part of the main Turkic nation centering in Turkestan but seceded and set up an independent state known as the Khazar kaganate, or khanate, on the north slope of the Caucasus and around the head of the Caspian. These nomads, like the many who had gone before, kept to the grassland where their herds could find pasturage, but by bringing firm rule and peace to all the area under their control, they set the conditions in which trade could prosper.

With the founding of the Mohammedan religion and the erection of the Arabian Empire, the Khazar state came under pressure from the crusading zeal of the Moslems. However, the rapid expansion of the Arab caliphate may have been of indirect service to the peoples on the north shore of the Black Sea. The Eastern Empire shrank to a modest size, limited to Asia Minor and the Balkans south of the Danube. In seeking to defend itself by fostering war among the various peoples of the steppe, the Eastern Empire had promoted perennial unrest in south Russia.

The Khazar state, which centered on the lower Volga, was in an admirable position to profit from the trade routes that crossed its territory. Arab merchants brought to the markets in Khazaria the riches of Persia and China and exchanged them for the food, horses, and forest products—wax, honey, and fur, particularly marten and sable—that came down the Volga from the Volga Bulgars. The trade along the Volga extended over its upper reaches even to the Baltic, from which the Vikings from Scandinavia had been exploring the Russian river system as early as the sixth century. The peace that the Khazar power brought to the lower Volga encouraged agriculture in the region, but the primary concern of the Khazar khan was to foster the trade that moved over the land and water routes threading his territory and to collect taxes from which he profited so richly.

Although the center of Khazar power rested between the Caucasus and the lower Volga, a loose hegemony extended over European Russia far to the north and west as far as the Dniester river. The various tribes in the western steppe and the disorganized bands of Finns in the Oka and the upper Volga enjoyed local autonomy but recognized the suzerainty of the Khazar state on which they depended for goods and markets. Khazar rule seems to have been particularly mild. Although the rulers embraced Judaism, they did not impose their religion on subject peoples. There were Christian churches, Moslem mosques, and Jewish synagogues in their cities. The Khazars maintained cordial relations with neighboring peoples—Byzantines in Constantinople, Turks in Turkestan, Moslems in Baghdad, and Volga Bulgars at the mouth of the Kama.

In the late seventh and early eighth centuries, the Khazars were at war with the Arabs who were seeking to cross the Caucasus into the Russian steppe at the same time that they were pushing across the Pyrenees into France. In the ninth century the Khazar state faced a threat from the Slavs, a new power in the steppe.

At the beginning of the Christian era some Slavic peoples were settled along the Vistula in what is now central Poland; others dwelt between the Carpathians and the middle Dnieper. By A.D. 500 the Slavs were moving out to the north, east, and west and occupying nearly every corner of what is now European Russia. Much of central Russia, particularly the Oka and middle and upper Volga valleys, also sheltered scattered tribes of Finns. The successive waves of control that passed over south Russia affected the lives of the natives only slightly. The people kept to their customs and worked the soil, in contact with the ruling foreigner only when the tax collector or the merchant came round. Occasionally, Slavs enlisted in the armies of the ruler. By and large the lives of the natives went on quite apart from those of the nomads who fought for the pasture, for control of the trade routes, and for the power to levy tribute on the peaceful farmers. There was some intermarriage, and each new wave of conquerors added its drop to the blood strain of the Slavs.

The Middle and East Slavs, then, are the ancestors of the Russians. At first these Slavic tribes lived chiefly along the northern edge of the steppe, with some small groups edging south into the grassland and others drifting north into the forest zone. Those who lived on rich soil tilled the land; those in the forest hunted and gathered honey and mushrooms and planted small patches in the clearings; those on the grassy steppe tended herds; all fished, for the Slavs settled along the rivers and traveled over them in canoes. In contrast to the nomads who ruled the steppe, the Russians were a river folk who kept to the banks and watersheds.

During the Scythian period the basic population of the fringe of the steppe and southern forest zone was Slav. Slav farmers tilled the soil and raised the produce, especially the wheat that in Scythian times went to Greece in great volume. The rulers levied taxes in kind on the farming population, and the grain found its way into the markets of the Greek colonies along the north shore of the Black Sea, and then by ship to Athens.

The Goths brought the East Slavs of the steppe under their rule and forced them to take part in some of their forays. In Slavic boats they mounted maritime raids against the Roman power in the Balkans and in the Aegean. For two centuries the East Slavs lived under the rule of various Gothic bands, culminating in the Gothic Empire that reached from the Black Sea to the Baltic.

The Hunnic invasion in 360 liberated the East Slavs and freed them from the possibility of being Germanized by the Goths who fled westward or entered Hunnic service. Slavs, too, were forced into the armies of the Huns, and in that service acquired military knowledge and experience.

With the collapse of Hunnic power after the death of Attila, Slav power surged forward. Slavs attacked the Roman Empire along the Danube and detachments of them broke through to the Aegean and the Adriatic. A Slav community appeared between the Dnieper and the Danube. At times, when relations with the Byzantine Empire were friendly, Slav soldiers served as mercenaries in imperial armies. At other times the Slavs conducted raids into the Balkans and on several occasions attacked Constantinople itself.

By the beginning of the Khazar period, the East Slavs—so-called to distinguish them from South Slavs who had migrated into the Balkans and from West Slavs who had settled in what is now central and western Poland—dwelt in great numbers in the steppe in south Russia, and many lived in the forest zone as well. The Slavs who settled in the forest zone mingled there with the Lithuanian and Finnish peoples native to central and northern Russia. In settling in the forest zone, the Slavs adapted themselves to the economic opportunities that the region afforded. They used the vast river system of central Russia to exploit the resources of the forest for the purpose of trade with the Volga Bulgars and with the Arab merchants who traveled the lower Volga. The peace in the Volga basin that the Khazar hegemony assured encouraged the Slavs of the steppe and forest to take full advantage of the opportunity to trade.

Under Arab pressure from the south in the eighth and ninth centuries, Khazar power steadily waned. When the Arabs overran the Kuban and Don valleys, they weakened Khazaria's trade ties with the steppe and forest zones. In the absence of any Arab effort to retain control of the area, the way lay open for the emergence of a new organizing force in Russia. The East Slavs would build a nation of their own.

Suggested Reading

BAGER, J. M., *The Soviet Scene: A Geographical Perspective* (London, 1989).
BORISOV, A. A., *Climates of the U.S.S.R.* (Edinburgh, 1968).
CHEW, A. F., *An Atlas of Russian History* (New Haven, 1970).
COLE, J. P., *Geography of the Soviet Union* (New York, 1971).
CRESSEY, G. B., *Soviet Potentials: A Geographical Appraisal* (New York, 1962).
DEWDNEY, J. C., *A Geography of the Soviet Union* (New York, 1971).
DUNLOP, D. M., *The History of the Jewish Khazars* (Princeton, 1954).
DVORNIK, F., *The Slavs in European History and Civilization* (New Brunswick, NJ, 1962).
HOOSON, D. J., *The Soviet Union: People and Regions* (London, 1966).

JORRÉ, G., *The Soviet Union: The Land and Its People* (New York, 1967).

KERNER, R. J., *The Urge to the Sea: The Course of Russian History* (Berkeley, 1946).

KOZLOV, V., *The Peoples of the Soviet Union* (Bloomington, IN, 1988).

LYDOLPH, P. E., *Geography of the U.S.S.R.* (New York, 1990).

MELLOR, R. E. H., *The Soviet Union and Its Geographic Problems* (London, 1982).

METROPOLITAN MUSEUM OF ART, *From the Lands of the Scythians: Ancient Treasures from the Museums of the U.S.S.R., 3000 BC–100 BC* (New York, 1975).

MILLER, M. O., *Archaeology in the U.S.S.R.* (New York, 1956).

MILNER-GULLAND, R., and N. DEJEVSKY, *Cultural Atlas of Russia and the Soviet Union* (New York, 1989).

MIROV, N. T., *Geography of Russia* (New York, 1951).

ROSTOVTZEFF, M., *Iranians and Greeks in South Russia* (Oxford, 1922).

SHABAD, T., *Geography of the U.S.S.R.; A Regional Survey* (New York, 1951).

SULIMIRSKI, T., *The Sarmatians* (New York, 1970).

SYMONS, L.; J. C. DEWDNEY; J. M. HOOSON; W. W. NEWEY; and R. E. H. MELLOR, *The Soviet Union: A Systematic Geography* (London, 1982).

VASILIEV, A. A., *The Goths in the Crimea* (Cambridge, 1936).

VERNADSKY, G., *Ancient Russia* (New Haven, 1943).

VUCINICH, W. S., *Russia and Asia: Essays on the Influence of Russia on the Asian Peoples* (Stanford, 1972).

CHAPTER 2

Kievan Russia

By the eighth century, the East Slavs were living in tribal clusters in the forest and wooded steppe zones of what is now European Russia. The Graeco-Iranian and German influences they had known since 1000 B.C. endowed them with some political and economic experience, and the waterways that crisscrossed their land prompted their interest in commerce. They succeeded to the urban trade centers along the Dnieper, Don, upper Volga, and Volkhov, and goods continued to move over the rivers of north and south Russia and over the great highway link with Central Asia and China. The towns in Russia continued to flourish and to enjoy the rich cultural advantages that commerce made possible. The Slavs who lived in rural areas followed a more primitive pattern of existence. Agriculture, apiculture, hunting, and fishing meant ceaseless toil and little reward, particularly as the profit from exchanging their products went chiefly to the city merchants and the tribute gatherers.

Slavic Russia in the eighth century was a confederation of city-states, each city controlling a surrounding area whose trade it dominated and from whose rural inhabitants it wrung taxes in kind. Each town governed itself by an assembly of its citizens, through a council of elders and elected administrative officials, the power probably resting in an oligarchy of its wealthier merchants. The organization of the countryside followed a loose, primitive tribal pattern and stood in sharp contrast to the political order that town life and trade promoted.

The conquerors who had entered the Russian land in successive waves for fifteen centuries had imposed a military-commercial rule over the area. A military minority of Scythians, Sarmatians, Goths, Huns, and Khazars had organized the land. Each in turn had maintained the peace that made possible the cultivation of the soil and the trade that flowed through the area over the natural highways that it possessed in such abundance.

A Scandinavian presence, of uncertain strength and influence, seems apparent in the eighth and ninth centuries along the south and east shores of the Baltic and even near the Black Sea. An interest in trade and the proximity of their homeland would account for exploration of the Russian river net by these Vikings, or Norsemen. The organizers of the first Slav state, indeed, bore Scandinavian names.

Early in the ninth century the East Slav peoples occupied scattered settlements over the forest and steppe between the Baltic, the lower Volga, and the Black Sea. They lived in tribes, each governing itself free from any higher Slav authority, although most of them lived in some degree of subjection, political or economic, to Khazaria or some other non-Slav power. They were primarily tillers of the soil; grain and vegetables provided food as they had done for eighteen centuries. Herds of horses and cattle fattened on the lush pasture as the Slavs followed the example of the many peoples who had preceded them in the steppe. Agriculture as well went on in the clearings of the forest, for most Slavs were farmers. Hunting, trapping, and agriculture added meat, furs, honey, and wax for those who lived in the forest zone. They practiced weaving and forged their own weapons and tools of iron. Some grew wealthy by trading raw materials for the luxury goods of the east and south. Their towns—Kiev, Smolensk, Chernigov, and Novgorod—contained many well-to-do Slav merchants as well as poor Slav craftsmen and laborers. East Slav civilization had already reached the point of social stratification.

The Building of the Kievan State

The founder of the first East Slav state was the heroic figure Oleg, "who set himself up as prince in Kiev" in 882. The title "grand prince" later identified the ruler from the lesser princes who accepted his authority.

Tradition has it that Oleg's predecessor was Rurik, a Norseman, or Norman, who led a band of his fellow Vikings—Russians called them Varangians—into the eastern Baltic to Novgorod in 862. The legend, immortalized by the chronicler, even insists that Rurik was invited into the land of "Rus" by Slavs who could not keep peace among themselves. According to the chronicler, the "calling of the Varangians" read: "Our land is great and abundant but there is no order in it; come rule and reign over us." The romantic tale is buttressed by the supposition that Oleg's successor, Igor, was in fact Rurik's son.

Kiev immediately became the administrative center and the base from which Oleg set forth to unite forest and steppe and to bring the native tribes under his control. The grand prince built forts and settled garrisons at strategic points and pushed the conquest of those Slav tribes who did not voluntarily submit. The Magyars—ancestors of modern Hungarians—who were in control of the mouth of the Dnieper, were driven out of south Russia and moved into the area of present-day Hungary. Their removal from the lower Dnieper cleared the "water road" from the Baltic to the Black Sea.

By the end of the ninth century, Oleg had made notable progress toward fulfilling the tasks that lay before him when he assumed the leadership of Russia. Many of the Slav tribes had come under his rule. Much of the forest and steppe had been united. The Dnieper lay open all the way to its mouth. By 907 Oleg had consolidated his position at Kiev sufficiently to be ready for his most ambitious undertaking—an attack against Constantinople, not necessarily with the idea of capturing it but of forcing the Byzantine Empire to open its markets to Kievan merchants. A flotilla of two thousand boats moved down the west coast of the Black Sea, while a cavalry force crossed the Danube and advanced toward Constantinople. Threatened with a serious defeat, the emperor accepted peace on Russian terms.

By the treaty of 907, the Byzantine emperor agreed to pay a sizable indemnity and to set aside funds to provide hospitality for Russian traders coming to Constantinople. They were to enjoy access to Byzantine markets without payment of customs and were to be provided for during their sojourn in the capital. They agreed to remain in a suburb during their stay, from which they were to be escorted inside the walls during trading hours. The emperor was to provision their boats for the voyage home.

Oleg's brilliant career set the Grand Principality of Kiev on firm foundations. By the time of his death in 913, he had cleared the water road from the Baltic to Constantinople and had provided the state with a trade axis that would assure its future prosperity. In addition, he had taken a long step toward uniting the Slavs of the forest and steppe under a government whose leaders had the vision to foresee the needs of the future.

Almost from the moment of its founding, the line of development of the new state on the Dnieper became clear. Its attention focused on Constantinople. Several factors contributed to this fascination with the capital of the Eastern Empire. Constantinople was geographically the obvious terminus of the water road that led from the Baltic to the Black Sea, "from the Varangians [Vikings] to the Greeks," as the chroniclers put it. And from the fifth century to the thirteenth, Constantinople, or Byzantium, was the most important city in the European world. Commercially, it was without a peer until the rise of the cities of northern Italy during the Crusades. Culturally, it was the transmitter of the heritage of Greece and Rome. Religiously, its leadership of the eastern Mediterranean faced no serious challenge until the eleventh century. Politically, the Byzantine Empire was the most important state in Europe until the sack of Constantinople by the Fourth Crusade. The city's position as an entrepôt of world trade, as a warehouse for the silks of China and the spices of India, and as a market where the raw materials of Russia found ready sale; its prominence as spiritual capital for millions whose chief shrine was the Church of St. Sophia; its influence as tutor to those whose only contacts with the wisdom of the ancients had to come through Byzantium or from the Arabs; its importance as capital of the state that mattered most in international affairs and whose diplomatic envoys commanded universal respect because of the power they represented—these things fascinated the rulers of Kievan Russia, who sought to turn Kiev and Novgorod into "little Constantinoples." The newly organized state on the Dnieper enjoyed indirect contact with the other great civilizing power of the period—the Arab—through Byzantium and through the Volga Bulgars, who were Moslem.

Oleg's Successors

Oleg was followed by his kinsman Igor, whose descendants occupied the princely throne of Kiev and later that of the tsardom of Moscow until the end of the sixteenth century. Igor spent his life warring against the Khazars, the Byzantines, and the Slavic tribes whom Oleg had left unconquered. He fought the Pechenegs, the wild Turkic nomads who had swarmed out of Asia in the ninth century to ravage the steppe and to harass the annual trade flotilla that passed down the Dnieper to Constantinople. When the Byzantine emperor broke the treaty that Oleg had forced on him, Igor led another attack against the great commercial capital and forced the Eastern Empire to restore its trade relations with Kiev. However, his ruthless collection of tribute from the subject tribes to support his military ambitions eventually caused his death. Igor was slain in 945 by resentful tribesmen who refused to meet his exorbitant demands for tribute.

Because Igor's son Sviatoslav was only a child at the time of his father's death, the child's mother, Olga, assumed power. Her first act was to put an end to the annual tax-gathering visitations to each subject tribe by the grand prince of Kiev and to replace it with a regular levy on tribes, to be collected by agents sent out from Kiev. Olga's most memorable act, and the one that immortalized her in the eyes of the monkish chronicler, was her acceptance of Christianity.

By the middle of the tenth century many Russians had probably received baptism. The intimate trade contact with Constantinople, by which scores of merchants annually visited the Byzantine capital and marveled at the splendor of its churches, was responsible for many conversions. Indeed, this contact paved the way for the eventual acceptance of Christianity by Kiev. Byzantine colonies in the Crimea—the Eastern Empire as successor to Rome had fallen heir to the Greek towns in the peninsula—had brought Russians in contact with Christianity a century before Olga's conversion. The Slavs of Moravia and Galicia, with whom Kiev traded, had long been Christian, and the Bulgars had been won over by 864. Missionaries from Moravia and from Constantinople had appeared in Kiev even before Oleg.

Missionaries from Constantinople baptized Olga in Kiev in 955. She probably accepted Christianity as a matter of state policy. She may have hoped that more cordial economic and political relations with the Eastern Empire would grow out of her baptism. The nation, however, did not follow her, nor did her son Sviatoslav.

Whether Oleg and Igor ever considered accepting Christianity is uncertain. There was good reason that they should not accept it, if they ever did give it serious thought. That reason lay in the fact that converts to the church headed by the patriarch of Constantinople must accept the authority of the patriarch in religious matters, and at the same time the Eastern emperor insisted upon recognition of his authority over the new converts in political matters. Whenever a pagan nation in the East accepted the new faith, there arose this question of religious and political subjection to Constantinople, the two going hand in hand. The only possibility of retaining political independence was through the patriarch's consent that the new converts might have their own autonomous church under an archbishop or a metropolitan bishop. The consent was never lightly given, and had to be wrung from the patriarch in each case. For example, the Bulgars for a time transferred their allegiance to the pope at Rome because the patriarch at Constantinople would not accede to their demands for an autonomous church. The patriarch acquiesced and the Bulgars received their own metropolitan bishop, whereupon they returned to the Eastern orbit.

This same problem of obtaining religious autonomy for Russia faced Olga after her conversion. She journeyed to Constantinople after her baptism to seek the appointment of a metropolitan bishop in Kiev, but her plea failed. She then resorted to the tactics the Bulgars had applied nearly a century earlier and asked the Holy Roman emperor, Otto I, to send priests and a metropolitan bishop to Kiev. Otto sent an ordinary bishop, with the implication that the Russian church in accepting him should accept a position subordinate to the German clergy. Olga would not agree to this and the status of the Russian church remained unsettled. Olga's toying with the idea of accepting a religious tie with the West must have been only a ruse. Cordial economic relations with Constantinople were too vital to the Kievan state to permit their being endangered by a religious alliance with the West.

Olga's efforts to work out a satisfactory religious settlement with Constantinople met with failure at the time. However, her own conversion must have given considerable impetus to the trend away from paganism, and the stubbornness with which she held out for her own terms must have impressed upon Constantinople the need to compromise when the question of religious administration came up again.

His mother's failure to obtain concessions from Constantinople brought into popularity Sviatoslav and the pagan party that opposed the acceptance of Christianity. Olga stepped aside and in 962 Sviatoslav, now grown to manhood, took over as grand prince of Kiev. Olga had carefully husbanded the resources of the state and had saved its manpower through nearly a generation of peace. For the next decade those reserves were available for use by her son in a succession of brilliant campaigns.

Sviatoslav set out to bring the lower Volga under his control and then to open the way to the Caspian and so to the trade of the Orient. He advanced against the Khazars, but to destroy Khazaria he must control the Volga, and to do that he must first subdue the Volga Bulgars. He sacked their capital and was ready to move down the Volga to strike at the heart of Khazaria when an envoy from Constantinople came to ask his help in curbing the Danubian Bulgars who were threatening the Eastern Empire. In return Sviatoslav apparently received a free hand in the territory of the Bulgar khan, whose lands extended on both sides of the Danube.

At the head of a huge force the grand prince of Kiev drove across the Danube and overran northern Bulgaria. The Bulgars appealed to the Pechenegs, whose main host was still in camp east of the Volga, for assistance against Sviatoslav. At about the same time the Khazars, fearful of the invincible Kievan prince, let down their defenses and invited the Pechenegs to move into the Russian steppe. The Pechenegs poured into Russia but, instead of proceeding against Sviatoslav, struck for Kiev and laid siege to his capital. Sviatoslav left part of his army in Bulgaria; with the rest he hurried back to Kiev and drove off its attackers.

To punish the Khazars for setting the Pechenegs upon him, Sviatoslav sent a powerful army against Khazaria. The Russians proceeded first to the middle Volga and once more plundered the capital of the Volga Bulgars. Then moving downriver they attacked the Khazars. The Khazar state collapsed, leaving the Volga frontier unguarded against later invasions from Central Asia.

Back in Kiev, Sviatoslav waited for news of the expedition against the Khazars. Once the campaign had come to a successful conclusion, Sviatoslav hoped to return to the Danube. So enamored of the Danube basin had the prince become that he made up his mind to shift his capital from Kiev to the lower Danube and to leave Russia to the vice-regency of his sons. "I do not care to remain in Kiev, but should prefer to live in Pereyaslavets on the Danube, since that is the center of my realm, where all riches are concentrated: gold, silks, wine, and various fruits from Greece, silver and horses from Hungary and Bohemia, and from Russia furs, wax, honey, and slaves." His mother died a few days later, and Sviatoslav set out for the Danube after dividing the land of Russia among his sons, expecting never to return to Kiev.

Sviatoslav went to Bulgaria and took up once more his successful raiding over the land south of the Danube. Now the Byzantines, seeing that Sviatoslav, not the Bulgars, posed the most serious threat to Constantinople, came to terms with the Bulgars and the two combined their forces against the Russians. Sviatoslav lost several engagements and finally agreed to withdraw from Bulgaria. With the bitter loss of the land that he preferred to his own, Sviatoslav set out for Kiev. The Bulgars sent word to the Pechenegs that the Russians were returning to the Dnieper, and the Pechenegs lay in wait at the cataracts in the lower river. In the battle that ensued Sviatoslav lost his life and the Pecheneg chieftain fashioned the victim's skull into a drinking cup.

The ten years of Sviatoslav's short reign were years of high adventure and tremendous achievement. The grand prince had enormously increased the state territory. He had seen the trade possibilities of the area perhaps more clearly than had any of the Kievan princes. He had united the entire Russian steppe, from the Volga and the Kuban to the Danube. He had added the Kama region and the valley of the lower Volga to the principality. Sviatoslav's successes were only temporary, however, and began to melt away even before his death. He quickly won the Danubian lands and as quickly lost them. Indeed, even the destruction of Khazaria later brought only grief, because its reduction left nothing to stem the flood of nomad invasion from the east.

Vladimir and the Russian Conversion

When Sviatoslav left Kiev to return to Bulgaria in 969, thinking to establish his capital permanently on the Danube, he turned over the administration of certain districts in Russia to three of his twelve sons. His death at the hands of the Pechenegs on his way back to Kiev left the land divided among the three. The eldest, Yaropolk, ruled in Kiev; Oleg administered the southwest; the youngest, Vladimir, received Novgorod.

For the next five years the brothers warred over the succession. Yaropolk slew Oleg in battle, and Vladimir fled to Scandinavia to gather troops for an attack on his oldest brother. Yaropolk's advisers urged him to call in the Pechenegs to back him, but he hesitated too long. Vladimir returned to Novgorod with a strong band of Varangians, enlisted Slavs in north Russia, and advanced down the Dnieper to Kiev. Yaropolk came out to negotiate with his brother and was struck down by some of Vladimir's followers. The question of the succession was settled, and Vladimir ruled Kiev from 980 to 1015.

Yaropolk, whose wife had been a nun, had seriously considered accepting Christianity. This put him at some disadvantage during the war with Vladimir, whose enthusiastic paganism brought him wide support among the people of Russia. Indeed, the religious issue may have provoked more interest among those who watched the war between the brothers than did the question of the succession.

Vladimir spent the decade after becoming grand prince on campaigning. Although he showed no disposition to pursue his father's interest in the Danube, he did attempt to push Kievan influence west of the capital for the purpose of improving trade relations with the Czechs in Central Europe. He advanced against the Poles, capturing a number of their cities in what is now western Ukraine. Then he moved into northern Poland and brought under his rule the Slavic tribes of the upper Niemen region. His concern here was to improve Russia's access to the Baltic. The way from Kiev into the Baltic by way of the Dnieper and the Niemen was considerably shorter than the other routes in use at the time over the Western Dvina or by way of the Lovat, Lake Ilmen, the Volkhov, Lake Ladoga, and the Neva.

Vladimir had won the title of Grand Prince of Kiev in the role of champion of paganism against the rising tide of Christianity that had been washing over the area from Constantinople, from Moravia and Central Europe, and from the Byzantine outpost on the Sea of Azov. Missionaries from the west and south had been at work in Kiev for a century. Some of Igor's *druzhina*, or bodyguard, had been baptized, and Olga had accepted the new faith. Many Russian merchants—the dominant class in a commercial state—had become Christian too. Indeed, there were few of Kiev's neighbors who had not forsaken their pagan gods. The Khazars were Jewish and the Volga Bulgars Moslem. Poland, Hungary, and Bulgaria had become Christian. Even the Vikings in their Scandinavian homeland were welcoming Christianity. The kings of Denmark and Norway accepted baptism shortly after Vladimir assumed power in Kiev. The pressures on Vladimir, then, were mounting to adopt a new faith and the new civilization that went with it.

After Vladimir's accession there had been a brief, violent reaction in favor of continuing pagan worship in Kiev. Contemptuous of the virtues proclaimed by the Christian missionaries, Vladimir took seven wives, one of them the widow of his murdered brother Yaropolk, and in addition kept many concubines.

After the brief orgy of paganism that opened the new reign, Vladimir went off on campaign. Everywhere he went, to west or to east, the grand prince came up against the fact that only Kiev was behind the times in still clinging to its old gods. During the negotiations to end his indecisive war with the Volga Bulgars, his recent antagonists urged him to accept Islam. Returning from that campaign, Vladimir decided to examine the various religions that surrounded pagan Kiev. Elders of the capital and members of the prince's bodyguard came together to discuss the merits of the various faiths, and it is not unlikely that missionaries from east, west, and south harangued the meetings. Those who spoke for affiliation with Constantinople could make the best case. They could remind the prince that his grandmother Olga had chosen the faith that emanated from the Eastern Empire's capital, and they could plead the advantages that must come from association with the greatest city of the Western world, the city on whose markets Kievan prosperity in large measure depended.

While the question of accepting one of the new religions was under discussion, envoys came to Kiev from the emperor in Constantinople to beg Vladimir's help in putting down a revolt in Asia Minor that threatened the capital. The envoys proposed as an inducement the offer that Vladimir might marry the emperor's sister, a signal honor from the head of so powerful a state. Vladimir, in turn, must accept Christianity before the marriage could take place. The prospect must have flattered him. The Christians in his entourage must have urged him to accept. Behind all the pressures of the moment, Vladimir must fully have realized that Russia's religious isolation had to end sooner or later, and he must have understood as well that the logic of Russia's geographical, economic, and political situation was overwhelmingly on the side of accepting the faith of Constantinople in preference to any other.

Vladimir was baptized early in 988. During the negotiations with the emperor's envoys, the grand prince surely received a promise that Kiev would have its own metropolitan bishop and that the Russian church would enjoy autonomy.

Remembering his grandmother's failure to settle the question of church government, and having before him the example of the Bulgarians in their struggle with the patriarch, it is inconceivable that Vladimir would have accepted the new faith without a full understanding that the Russian church would be autonomous. However, after the emperor had put down the revolt against him, which he managed with the aid of a Russian band of six thousand warriors, he seemed reluctant to follow through on his promises to Vladimir. His sister did not go to Russia for the marriage, nor was there any metropolitan bishop for Kiev.

Having taken the step of accepting Christianity, from which there could hardly be any turning back, Vladimir was determined to force a settlement of church government compatible with the independence of the Kievan state. He launched a campaign in the Crimean peninsula designed to restore the Kievan hegemony that his father had surrendered to the empire at the end of his Bulgarian disaster. Vladimir's chief concern, however, was to capture the imperial cities in the peninsula, some of which had their own bishops. When Vladimir captured the episcopal city of Korsun, the ancient Chersonese, the emperor gave in, at least partially, and sent his sister to become Vladimir's bride. After the marriage, Vladimir returned the city to the emperor as a gift.

Before concluding the marriage arrangements, Vladimir sent for envoys from the pope at Rome to discuss the possibility of Russia's affiliating with the church of the West. Presumably, the terms the pope offered did not satisfy Vladimir's demand for Russian religious autonomy. This act must have been a ruse to bring the emperor and the patriarch of Constantinople to terms, for all Russia's interests centered in the East. The authorities at Constantinople apparently were skeptical of the sincerity of Vladimir's dealings with Rome, for they did not agree to send a metropolitan to Kiev. The prince stayed in the Crimea a year waiting for a favorable settlement. Not obtaining it, he decided to build his own church, and he set off for Kiev with a number of priests and a supply of relics and icons in his baggage.

Upon his arrival in Kiev, Vladimir set to work with a vengeance to establish the faith that he had espoused. His men hurled down the pagan idols in the city and cast them into the Dnieper. At his order, the entire population of the city marched to the river to receive baptism from the priests who had come from the Crimea. Couriers rode off to the other cities of the realm to order similar measures. That very summer, construction began on the first of a number of stone cathedrals, and the prince assigned a tithe of his revenue to their maintenance. The chief Kievan cities—Novgorod, Chernigov, Polotsk, and Rostov—became episcopal centers. For many years the bishop of Tmutorokhan in the Crimea served as head of the Kievan church. Vladimir ignored the patriarch of Constantinople, and there was no direct contact between the Russian church and Constantinople until 1037. In that year the patriarch appointed the first metropolitan bishop of Kiev, who assumed the headship of the Russian church.

Christian churches were built all over Kievan Russia at Vladimir's command. Monasteries appeared, not only in Kiev but in the recesses of the forest. The church opened schools that trained recruits for the clergy, to which Vladimir ordered members of the upper classes to send their children. A regular system of charity was inaugurated under government auspices.

After the conversion, Vladimir never again went to war with his Christian neighbors. The increasing severity of Pecheneg raids into his territory, however, brought energetic measures of defense. Along the northern and eastern banks of the rivers of south Russia, Vladimir erected lines of forts to keep back the nomads; he sent settlers south to strengthen the defenses.

Toward the close of his reign, Vladimir divided the land of Kiev into districts, over each of which he placed a son as lieutenant. Yaroslav, who ruled in Novgorod, threatened to revolt against his father rather than pay the taxes imposed on him; the Novgorodians probably forced him to it. Just as Vladimir was gathering a force to move against his son, the old prince died in 1015, leaving the succession in question as his father had done before him.

The reign of Vladimir is pre-eminently important in the history of Kievan Russia. By his decision to embrace Christianity, although it could not for long have been forestalled, he brought a new civilization to Russia. A new code of morals, a sense of social justice, a group of literate clerics capable of keeping court records and of committing to writing the historical experience of the nation, a sense of the need for education, a school of art and architecture, an alphabet and a language, and a changed international position—all came to Russia with the new faith. Vladimir accepted the new religion without sacrificing his independence. The Russian church, from its very founding, was an intensely national church. Religiously, Russia was not lost in the anonymity that characterized Western Europe in medieval times. Indeed, there would be many times in later centuries when the most nationally conscious agency in the nation was the Russian church that Vladimir had established and whose chauvinistic direction he had done so much to inspire.

Yaroslav the Wise

Vladimir's death precipitated a civil war among his sons to decide the succession. An older son, Sviatopolk, seized Kiev and murdered three of his brothers who might have contested his action. The eldest son, Yaroslav, whom his father before his death had named to rule in Novgorod, brought in mercenaries from Scandinavia and recovered Kiev from Sviatopolk, who had enlisted the support of Pechenegs and Poles. The two remaining brothers, Yaroslav and Mstislav, divided the Russian land between them: Mstislav set up his capital in Chernigov and Yaroslav preferred Novgorod to Kiev. This shift of political focus away from Kiev reduced the commercial importance of the former capital. Some goods moving south from Novgorod may have been directed, instead, southeast through Mstislav's lands, over the rivers and portages east of the Dnieper. From there distribution to the Caspian and the east or to Constantinople and the west was easy. The lower Dnieper at this time was blocked by the Pechenegs, so that the shift in the trade route from Novgorod south was a matter

Yaroslav the Wise

of necessity. Mstislav's death without heirs in 1036 left Yaroslav in undisputed possession of the Russian land. His first act was to move his capital back to Kiev.

Shortly after his removal to Kiev, Yaroslav settled the question of Russia's relationship to the church at Constantinople. The patriarch ordained and sent to Kiev a metropolitan bishop, thus making the Russian church independent under the patriarch of Constantinople. Now Kiev was the religious as well as the political capital of the state. Yaroslav celebrated the settlement by building the beautiful cathedral of St. Sophia, and architects from Byzantium designed other churches modeled after those in Constantinople. Scribes took up the task of translating the holy books from Greek into Slavic, and the books and chronicles deposited then and subsequently in St. Sophia in time raised the church to the position of a national library.

Yaroslav added territory to the Kievan state, as had each of his predecessors before him. He pushed the boundary far to the west by attacking the Baltic lands and incorporating nearly the entire valley of the Western Bug, a tributary of the Vistula. He gave the Novgorodians a firmer hold on the Gulf of Finland by driving back the Finnish peoples on its northern shore. Earlier, while ruling jointly with his brother Mstislav, he had conquered the Estonians on the southern shore of the Gulf of Finland. He drove the Pechenegs away from the lower Dnieper and attacked Constantinople. He was the last of the Kievan princes to do so.

Yaroslav's war with the Pechenegs was decisive. Never again did they threaten the water road, nor were they ever again able to attack Kiev. The state won only temporary relief from the steppe-raiders, however. The Pechenegs soon gave way to a fresh nomad people out of Asia, the Polovtsy, or Cumans, whom the Arabs and Chinese called Kipchak.

Yaroslav married his sister to the king of Poland and three of his daughters to the kings of Norway, Hungary, and France. Kiev had long been a state of sufficient size and importance to merit international attention, but recognition in the form of marriage alliances with its ruling house would have been unthinkable before the Russian conversion.

Yaroslav set scholars to the task of assembling a collection of Russian laws, known as Russkaia Pravda, or Russian Justice. By doing so, he earned the title "the Wise," although the code that won him credit would continue to be in the process of development and refinement for generations. A combination of Varangian and Slavonic practice, softened by the Christian aversion to vengeance, the code shows the effects of the Russian conversion, particularly in the field of criminal procedure. Yaroslav also delineated the powers and jurisdiction of church courts to deal with all clergy and with those members of the laity charged with violating moral law.

The early Kievan princes had established a firm political organization in the Russian land. Their first concern had been to clear trade routes, and in this they enjoyed the wholehearted support of the merchants whose welfare had long depended on the free movement of goods in and through the area. One after another the grand princes had seen the vital need to keep open the water road and its tributaries, to marshal the full economic potential of the forest and steppe, and to bring the full political and commercial weight of the state to bear upon Constantinople in order to insure Kiev's prosperity and continued growth. It is significant that when military pressure—under Oleg, Igor, and Sviatoslav—failed to establish or to maintain intimate relations with Constantinople, the Kievan rulers—Olga, Vladimir, and Yaroslav—accepted religious and cultural ties with the eastern capital in the hope of establishing once and for all the firm contact without which Kiev could not live. The deliberate contemplation, by Vladimir and his druzhina and the leading citizens of Kiev, of the various religions seeking to win Russia's conversion in the tenth century indicates clearly that the choice was a matter of high state policy. Even the account of the conversion in the *Primary Chronicle*, written by monks in the eleventh century and still the best source for the early history of Kiev, shows that Vladimir's decision to embrace the faith of Constantinople was the result of cold calculation. Russian trade dictated Russian foreign policy, and religion became an aspect of that policy.

The strengthening of the tie with the Byzantine capital and the assurance of its full and continued support were not enough to keep open the water road and maintain the trade contact with Constantinople. From the time of the first Kievan prince, new hordes of nomads were coming into the steppe from east of the Volga. From Oleg's time on through the eleventh century, it was the Pechenegs, later followed by the Polovtsy and finally by the Mongol-Tatars. As the pressure mounted there was growing need for strong government and unity in Kiev to keep the trade routes open. The early princes with amazing energy had maintained that strong government and unity. After Yaroslav's death that strength and unity disappeared. Civil war over the succession, "the senseless brawlings of the princes," left Russia divided and weak and unable to beat back the nomads who threatened, and finally accomplished, the destruction of the Kievan state.

The Decline of Kiev

Yaroslav's death in 1054 brought an end to the early period of Kievan history and introduced another, in which the power of the state declined as precipitately as it had mounted during the early period. The reasons for the change were the confusion over the succession that set in very shortly after the end of the reign and the desolation of the land wrought by a new horde of steppe-raiders who appeared from out of the east in the very year of Yaroslav's passing.

The Succession

The old prince had seen the possibility of a dispute over the succession, even as he and his brothers had fought over the inheritance when Vladimir died, and he warned against it in his dying charge to his sons. The eldest, who might have succeeded to an undivided patrimony, had preceded his father in death. Because Yaroslav felt no confidence that any of the others could manage the entire realm, he willed that the rule of the Kievan state should descend to all his five sons as a group, the oldest son standing as leader and protector of the rest. The younger brothers were to govern as lieutenants over the towns and districts of the realm. The *Primary Chronicle* reports Yaroslav's deathbed disposition of the succession.

> "My sons (said Yaroslav), I am about to quit this world. Love one another, since ye are brothers by one father and mother. If ye dwell in amity with one another, God will dwell among you, and will subject your enemies to you, and ye will live in peace. But if ye dwell in envy and dissension, quarreling with one another, then you will perish yourselves and bring to ruin the land of your ancestors, which they won at the price of great effort. Wherefore remain rather at peace, brother heeding brother. The throne of Kiev I bequeath to my eldest son, your brother Izyaslav. Heed him as ye have heeded me, that he may take my place among you. To Sviatoslav I give Chernigov, to Vsevolod Pereyaslav, to Igor the city of Vladimir [in Volynia], and to Vyacheslav Smolensk." Thus he divided the cities among them, commanding them not to violate one another's boundaries, not to despoil one another. He laid upon Izyaslav the injunction to aid the party wronged, in case one brother should attack another. Thus he admonished his sons to dwell in amity.

The sons received not only the chief towns named in the testamentary admonition, the whole land was apportioned among them. So Izyaslav received Kiev and Novgorod, which gave him both ends of the water road; to Sviatoslav went the districts of Murom and Riazan in the northeast in addition to the province of Chernigov; Vsevolod received Suzdal, in the upper Volga, as well as Pereyaslav; and so on. It would seem that the old prince was not willing to trust his oldest son to provide for his younger brothers, and so assigned to each one a sufficient portion of the state territory to provide him an income proportional to his seniority. The older the prince, the better and richer was his allotted share. Thus the second oldest son received Chernigov, the next richest of the towns after Kiev and Novgorod, which both went to the oldest son; the third son obtained Pereyaslav, the third richest town; and so on.

Beyond the distribution of land to provide an income for each son, Yaroslav may have had in mind a definite order of succession. He may have thought that the princedom of Kiev should not descend according to the right of the first-born, but that each of his own sons should ascend the throne in order of seniority on the death of the next oldest. If the grand prince of Kiev, the oldest of the brothers, should die, the second oldest was to move up from Chernigov to take over Kiev, and the rest of the brothers were each to move up one notch in the scale: the third brother to the second city, Chernigov; the fourth brother to the third city, Pereyaslav; and the fifth brother to the fourth city, Smolensk. If anyone in the scale should die, each of those below him advanced one step. The death of any prince would leave the rule over the fifth city, Vladimir, vacant, and it was to go to the oldest son of Yaroslav's oldest son. He and his dependents would be required to move on to the next city when a death among those senior to him brought about his promotion. This complicated system of succession was called the "rota system." The underlying principle was that the power to rule over Kiev resided in the princely family of Yaroslav, and not in the line of any one of his descendants.

Whatever intentions and hopes for Russia the dead prince may have had, his sons ignored the old man's deathbed wishes. They would not allow the oldest, Izyaslav, to rule alone in Kiev, and a triumvirate of brothers insisted on managing the realm. After putting down the rebellion of a disgruntled nephew, the triumvirate broke down when two of the brothers joined to drive the oldest from the throne. As the brothers went to war over the succession, they solicited foreign aid. The Poles joined it at one time, the pagan Polovtsy at another. Izyaslav appealed to Emperor Henry IV of Germany and later to Pope Gregory VII, promising to bring Russia into the Western church in return for substantial assistance. The disgusting spectacle came to an end only when all but one of the brothers died, leaving the throne to Vsevolod, the weakest of the lot.

Among the more responsible of the descendants of Yaroslav there was deep respect for the system that the old prince had founded. The citizens of Kiev urged Vladimir Monomakh to take over the throne on his father's death in 1093, but his cousin Sviatopolk was senior to him, being the son of Yaroslav's oldest son. Monomakh refused to challenge the rota system, saying, "If I should seat myself upon the throne, then will there arise a feud between myself and Sviatopolk, seeing that his father sat thereon before my father.''

Although there was general acceptance of the principle that the Kievan throne should go to the oldest member of the generation nearest to Yaroslav, there was no such agreement over the disposition of the other districts into which Yaroslav had divided the realm. In the first place, the descendants were so numerous that it soon became impossible to determine precisely who was the senior successor. The early princes married young and died late, so that a nephew might be older than an uncle. Vladimir Monomakh had eight sons, the last three by a remarriage late in life. His fifth son once said to his sixth, ''I was already bearded when thou wert born.'' Under such circumstances the question often arose whether a man of a junior generation should precede a child of a senior generation, whether a bearded nephew should precede a toddling uncle. Every death in the princely family raised anew the question of succession. Occasionally, there was an amicable settlement in a conference of all the princes. More often there was civil war.

The strict order of succession to the towns and districts of the realm was further complicated by the fact that the perennial shifting of the princes from one province to another as they graduated up the scale permitted the towns to acquire more and more control over their own affairs at the expense of princely power in the town. This growth of local power reached the point where towns frequently insisted on raising a prince to rule over them regardless of whether he was entitled to the position under the rota system. Novgorod, particularly, time and again ignored the strict order of seniority and reached down for a junior prince to rule over the city. On one occasion, Novgorod took a younger son of a younger son and raised and trained him from childhood for the task of governing the city. When the father of the legitimate claimant stepped forward to demand the principality of Novgorod for his own son, the citizens answered, ''We desire neither thee nor thy son. Send thy son unto us only if he hath two heads. Already have we Mstislav, given unto us by Vsevolod his grandfather, and reared by us to rule Novgorod.''

The effect of the operation of the rota system was to divide the Kievan state dynastically and territorially. There continued to the end of the period, the myth of supreme authority of the grand prince and, until it was sacked by the Tatars, a degree of respect for Kiev as the political, as well as the religious, capital. Except for the land of Russia, for its unity, for its people, for its welfare, the princes showed no concern. Now and again a minor prince broke away from the rota system and managed to keep for himself and his line the province to which he had succeeded. This had the effect of dividing the land into semiautonomous and sometimes isolated units. Particularly was this tendency observable in small parts of districts lying a considerable distance from Kiev, far enough away to enjoy immunity from interference by the grand prince. From such a beginning the princes of Moscow after 1300 laid the basis for a new Russia.

The Polovtsy Devastate the Steppe

In 1093, the last of Yaroslav's sons died and the oldest son of his oldest son became grand prince of Kiev as Sviatopolk II. Throughout the twenty years of his reign he retained the loyalty of his cousin Vladimir Monomakh, but not all the cousins saw the need as did Vladimir to rally behind the central authority.

The tragedies that plagued the Kievan state after the death of Yaroslav were the princely feuds that sapped the nation's strength and the perennial attacks of the wild steppe nomads. Kiev had been subject to raids from the steppe from the very moment of the state's birth, but in the latter half of the eleventh century they became more frequent and more severe. Yaroslav had driven off the Pechenegs, but the Polovtsy, the cruelest of all the nomads, had taken their place. They first attacked Russia in earnest in 1061, and for the next fifty years their raids were an annual catastrophe. Each raid left its trail of burned villages, sacked cities, desecrated churches, and ruined farms. At one conference among the princes, called to plan a defense for the coming year, Vladimir Monomakh warned: "As soon as the peasant begins his plowing, the Polovtsy will come, shoot him down with his bolt, seize his horse, ride on into his village, and carry off his wife, his children, and all his property." The chronicler complained: "All our cities are desolate, our villages are laid waste. We traverse the fields where horses, sheep, and cattle once grazed in herds, and behold them desolate. The meadows are grown wild, and have become the lairs of wild beasts." The steppe-raiders denuded whole provinces, slaughtering the land's inhabitants or herding them off in long columns to the Crimea to be sold in the slave markets of Asia.

Sviatopolk fought relentlessly against the nomads of the steppe and was joined on every occasion by his cousin Vladimir Monomakh, who was at that time prince of Chernigov. Unfortunately, not all the princes were willing to risk life and fortune in the common defense, and some chose to remain neutral, perhaps hoping that deaths among the princes who led their men to battle might improve their own position in the rota. Although the war against the invader went on incessantly, the civil war among the princes flared up now and again, for the struggle for position in the chain of succession never came to an end. A number of princely conferences took place in an effort to reduce dissension in the family and to promote the unity so necessary to national survival. The first conference concluded with a grand resolution to live in peace: "Why do we ruin the land by our continued strife against one another? The Polovtsy harass our country in divers fashions and rejoice that there is war among us. Let us rather hereafter be united in spirit and watch over the land of Rus, and let each of us guard his own domain." Yet, the conference had hardly adjourned before the cousins were at it again.

Vladimir Monomakh and His Successors

The day after Sviatopolk's death in 1113, the *vieche*, or assembly, of Kiev met in clamorous convocation and demanded the accession of Vladimir

Monomakh, the prince of Chernigov. Once again the prince refused to accept. He was not yet senior in the rota system, and only a conference of the princes could set aside the regular succession.

When Vladimir's refusal became known in Kiev, riots broke out and the mob plundered the palaces and attacked the moneylenders. As the violence grew more desperate, the upper classes and the clergy began to fear for their own safety and frantically appealed to Vladimir to save the nation. This plea from the upper classes apparently convinced him, and he entered the capital to the cheers of the populace. With the appearance of the leader who had saved the state from its enemies, the riots came to an end.

Vladimir took steps to relieve the conditions that had produced the riots. He replaced Sviatopolk's appointees with officials whom he could trust not to misuse power. He placed a reasonable limit on interest rates and added a strict law against usury to the Russkaia Pravda. The code forbade landowners to make loans to their tenants and to enslave those unable to pay; it curtailed the right of the bankrupt and the pauper to sell themselves into slavery by restrictions that reduced the possibility of fraud.

Vladimir's election as grand prince of Kiev violated the rota system, because he was not the senior, by generation or by age, among the descendants of Yaroslav. The succession after him further violated the principle of seniority, which frequently was the only thread of loyalty that kept the princely family together. After Monomakh's death in 1125, the throne went not to his brothers, but to first one and then another of his sons. This destroyed all semblance of unity among the princes, although the succession of the Monomashichi, or descendants of Vladimir Monomakh, provoked no immediate opposition.

Mstislav I, the capable eldest son who had succeeded his father, Vladimir, won the acclaim of the citizens of Kiev. He had served as prince of Novgorod during his father's lifetime and, with the consent of the Novgorodians, left his son there to rule after him. During his reign there was relative harmony among the princes, and Mstislav did particularly well at keeping peace among his brothers, a problem not so ably handled by his successors.

After the death of Mstislav in 1132, the Kievan state rapidly disintegrated. The princes warred constantly among themselves, each trying to win the capital and with it the titular headship of the nation, but none had sufficient resources or managed to enlist enough allies to manage it. Sometimes the princes divided into two hostile groups to fight each other; occasionally, they came together to fight the Polovtsy; at other times the Polovtsy fought as allies of one or more of the princes. Kievan Russia split up into a number of principalities, each ruled by a prince who was practically free of control by a central government. The only unifying force was the church. Kiev's prestige grew out of the fact that the city was the seat of the metropolitan and was therefore the religious capital (not the political capital) of the nation. Yet, paradoxical as it may seem, the princely family never lost sight of the fact that the state belonged to the family as a group. Although there was constant disagreement over who in the family should head the nation and its divisions, there was never any thought that any outsider—Pole, Hungarian, Bulgar, or Byzantine—should rule in Kiev.

The civil war that wracked Kievan Russia after 1139 was not entirely a matter of princely pettiness or greed. For a prince to put an army into the field, he must have the support of the warrior class in his province, and more particularly he must have the financial backing of the merchant class in his territory. Once the commercial axis around which early Kievan Russia revolved broke down when the Polovtsy seized the steppes and the lower Dnieper, a struggle developed among the towns of Russia to reroute trade to their own advantage. Novgorod and Rostov sought to restore the trade with the Orient. Smolensk hoped to force through its own markets the commerce that passed between the Baltic and the Volga. Chernigov, Pereyaslav, and Kiev tried to develop trade between Galicia and Central Europe on the one hand and the forest zone of Russia on the other.

As Polovtsy control tightened over the Dnieper, Constantinople lost interest in the use of that waterway and in the trade with Kiev that earlier had been so profitable. In 1082 the Byzantine Empire arranged a treaty with Venice by which the Venetians agreed to serve as carriers and wholesalers of Byzantine trade. Finally, in 1204, the Fourth Crusade seized and sacked Constantinople, and the city fell under Venetian, and then under Genoese, domination. Between 1082 and 1204 the trade that had flowed north from Constantinople was rerouted through the Aegean and Mediterranean into northern Italy and through the Alpine passes into Europe.

For forty years after the end of the reign of Mstislav, Kiev was pulled one way and then another in the wars among the princes. The citizens of the capital preferred the rule of a descendant of Monomakh, and often managed to keep one on the throne in defiance of his junior position in the rota system. At other times the genealogical senior was able to seize the city and to drive the favorite into exile. In 1169, Prince Andrew of Suzdal captured Kiev and plundered and sacked it without mercy. What was left was of so little value that Andrew, whose conquest made him the chief among the princes, disdained to make it his capital and returned to his lands in the northeast.

The Rise of Suzdalia

The city of Suzdal, situated on a branch of the Kliazma, a tributary of the Oka, had grown to be one of the chief cities of the "Russian Mesopotamia" between the Oka and the Volga because of its favorable site for trade. Andrew, the grandson of Vladimir Monomakh, ruled the principality of Suzdalia, which straddled the upper Volga. He beat down opposition to his authority by treating his *boyars*, or nobles, as personal servants and allied princes as his vassals. To free himself of popular control through the town vieche, he moved his capital from Suzdal to Vladimir—the city founded by Vladimir Monomakh—which had no vieche. In 1169 he captured Kiev, sacked it without mercy, and then removed many holy icons and relics from the capital to his own city of Vladimir, where he erected several beautiful stone churches. His Cathedral of the Assumption was the finest in the region. In time, Vladimir became the religious center of northeast Russia. Toward the end of his life Andrew sought a more quiet life away from his new capital and built a palace in the village of Bogoliubovo, which inspired his nickname, Andrew Bogoliubsky.

The despotism Andrew practiced was benevolent. He always posed as the protector of the poor, and it was in their interest as well as his own that he reduced the power of his haughty boyars. He maintained peace in his principality and offered sanctuary to Russians fleeing the Polovtsy. He even welcomed Poles, Hungarians, Germans, and Volga Bulgars into his territory, and so its population swelled.

Andrew was a great warrior, wielding his sword with the best of his men, but he had no love for war as such, and felt only disgust at the suicidal conflict among the princes that left "the heathens" free to ravish Russia. As grand prince, he forced them to stop their "senseless brawlings." He was determined to prevent any such family strife in his own principality and drove his brothers and nephews from Suzdalia rather then see his land devastated and the power that he had built up drained away in civil war. He had a sentimental attachment to his capital of Vladimir, which he beautified and which he hoped to make a second Kiev.

A prince so sympathetic to strong monarchy had little patience with the citizens of Kiev, and Andrew turned the capital over to subordinate princes who were his agents. For five years Andrew was grand prince in Kievan Russia, but he remained the grand prince of Vladimir, not of Kiev. The former capital on the Dnieper had surrendered its position as chief among Russian cities. When Andrew was assassinated in 1174, his brother Vsevolod, called "Big Nest" because of his large family, succeeded as grand prince of Vladimir and ruler of the Russian nation.

Vladimir continued as capital of the principality and so in effect of the state. Its citizens swore allegiance to Vsevolod and to his sons after him. The other princes complained that he was setting aside the rota system, but he ignored their complaint. During his reign of thirty-five years, Vsevolod treated all other princes as mere underlings and forced them to remain at peace. He continued his brother's policy of encouraging immigration, and promoted trade by maintaining close commercial relations with the Volga Bulgars. He showed no concern for the fate of south Russia, and ignored pleas that he help to drive back the Polovtsy, whose raids against Kiev and the surrounding territory became more ferocious than ever.

When Vsevolod died in 1212, his sons and nephews fought over the succession, and, because none was strong enough to win full control, the province of Suzdalia split up into a number of nearly independent districts, each ruled by a descendant. The story of Kiev repeated itself all over again, but there were differences. Most of the cities of the principality of Suzdalia had no vieche to check the growth of princely authority, or if there were assemblies they had lost all power. The prince in each small region and town, then, ruled his territory as though it were his personal estate, or appanage. The rota system that had contributed so much

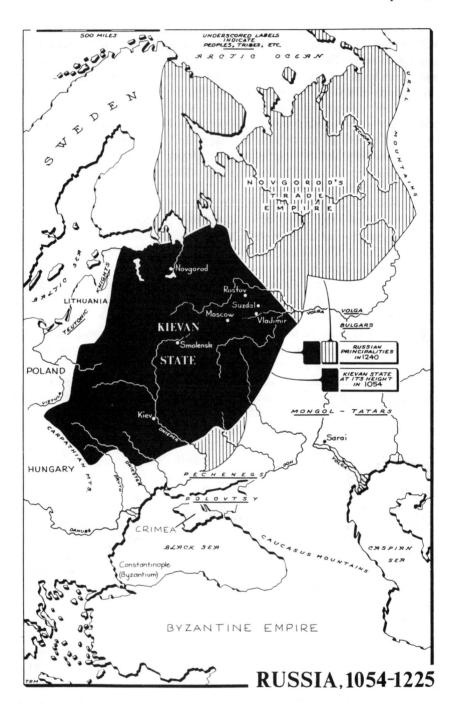

RUSSIA, 1054-1225

to the decline of the south was not allowed to apply in Suzdalia. After Vsevolod, the principality was divided into districts, each to go in perpetuity to its ruler. Upon the latter's death his district underwent further subdivision and soon the northeast had splintered into a number of infinitesimal hereditary lots. Thus north Russia invented its own weakness in trying to escape the weakness of the rota system that had sapped the strength of south Russia.

During the period of Suzdalian ascendancy, south Russia declined to impotence under the devastating raids of the Polovtsy. Although they showed no interest in organizing the steppe politically or economically, the Polovtsy annually scourged it, burning and plundering and seizing prisoners whom they sold to slave dealers from the Orient and from Venice, which had taken over the trade of Constantinople. The human and economic potential of south Russia fell victim to the combined efforts of the princes in their wars among themselves and of the Polovtsy whose attacks the princes were unable or unwilling to check.

The Tatar Invasion

During the eleventh century, the Mongols, whom Russians call Tatars, were living under Chinese hegemony in the area west and south of Lake Baikal. Shortly after 1200 they moved north, and in their new home the various tribes united under the leadership of Genghis Khan. The first step in the expansion that followed the unification of the Tatar tribes was against China, and Peking fell before their assault in 1215. Then they turned to the west, and incorporated Turkestan into the growing empire. After absorbing Turkestan Genghis Khan sent a strong, highly mobile army to explore the Caspian region. While circling the Caspian, this force came up against the Polovtsy, drove them back, and penetrated the Crimea.

The Polovtsian khans hurried messengers to the Russian princes to seek an alliance against the danger that threatened them all. "They have taken away our land today, and yours they will take tomorrow," the Polovtsy pleaded. The princes of Novgorod, Kiev, Chernigov, and Volynia agreed to march against the Mongols, but the prince of Suzdalia and others held back.

On the lower Dnieper the Russians encountered and routed an advance guard of the Mongols—a minor success that turned the heads of the Russian leaders. They decided to push on into the steppe to meet the invader, and with their Polovtsian allies they came up against the enemy's main body on the river Kalka, which flows south into the Sea of Azov. In the attack and the confusion that followed, the Russians lost heavily. After sacking border settlements and seizing many captives, the Mongol force withdrew, leaving the Russian land to survey its losses and count its dead.

The Mongol khan died in 1227, and a convention of tribal chieftains decided to advance against China, Persia, and Russia simultaneously. Batu, nephew of the new khan, led the assault against Russia. In the spring of 1237 he assembled a huge army on the east bank of the Volga and attacked and crushed forever the Volga Bulgars. Crossing the river he stormed the city of Vladimir and burned its cathedral. Driving on through the principality of Tver, Batu approached Novgorod, but turned south before reaching the city. He crossed Russia from north to south, scattering those Polovtsy he did not kill or enslave and set up headquarters at Sarai on the lower Volga. In 1240 he again moved against the Russian princes and conquered and pillaged Kiev, slaughtering the citizens who had dared to put up a stubborn defense.

Alexander Nevsky

After the Mongol-Tatar scourge had passed over the land for the second time, the grand prince of Vladimir undertook to restore order, rebuild his towns, bury the corpses that cluttered the roads, and provide for the refugees who fled to his territory from the border regions. The succession passed to Alexander—a grandson of Vsevolod and great-great grandson of Vladimir Monomakh—who was to become immortal as one of Russia's greatest heroes.

Alexander first won fame and recognition as prince of Novgorod. He built up the city's defenses and repulsed the pressure of neighboring tribes of Finns and Lithuanians that threatened to cut Novgorod's contact with the Baltic. Swedes, whom the pope had incited to undertake a crusade against Orthodox Russia, invaded Novgorodian territory in 1240. Alexander, with a handful of followers, met and routed the Swedes on the river Neva, an achievement that won him the name Nevsky, or "of the Neva." The clergy saw in the exploit a victory of Orthodoxy over the Roman Catholic Church of the West, and later canonized Alexander. Instead of showing their gratitude, however, the Novgorodians quarreled with the prince, as they did with so many, and Alexander left the city. He had been away less than a year when he received a frantic call to defend Novgorod against the Teutonic knights.

The Germans had moved into the eastern Baltic as early as the twelfth century. German traders brought along German missionaries seeking to convert the pagan Letts and Lithuanians to Roman Christianity and to make of them allies against Orthodox Novgorodians for control of the area. By the end of the twelfth century many Germans had settled in the region, a Roman Catholic bishop had arrived, and in 1201 the German city of Riga rose where the Western Dvina enters the Gulf of Riga. The crusading Order of Sword Bearers, the Livonian Order, led the German drive eastward. Within a decade the native Lett and Estonian tribes were paying tribute to the Germans. In 1224 the Germans took Iuriev, built two centuries earlier by Yaroslav the Wise, and renamed it Dorpat.

While the Livonian knights were winning success in the basin of the Western Dvina, the Teutonic Order received territory on the lower Vistula from which to move against the Prussians, a Lithuanian tribe that had resolutely resisted all Polish attempts to convert them to Christianity. The Teutons proceeded systematically against the Prussians, conquering one district after another and slaughtering or expelling its inhabitants. German colonists moved in and built castles and churches to impose German rule. In 1234, the pope granted the territory they had conquered to the Teutonic Order in perpetuity. Three years later, the Teutonic knights absorbed the Livonian Order, and the grand master became the formidable leader of German power in the southeastern Baltic. With the Prussians subdued, the Teutonic knights turned to new fields to conquer and began to press against Poland, Lithuania, and Russia.

It was the expanding drive of the knights that Alexander Nevsky was called back to Novgorod in 1241 to halt. The invaders had pressed to within twenty miles of the city and were besieging Pskov. Advancing against the Germans, Alexander met them on frozen Lake Peipus in April, 1242. The famous "iron wedge" of the knights broke through the Russian center, but the Russian flanks encircled the knights and the attacking force collapsed. The German defeat became a rout, and many of the knights were slain before reaching the shore to escape into the forest.

When his older brother died, Alexander Nevsky became grand prince of Vladimir and so titular head of the Russian nation. Understanding the hopelessness of opposing the Mongols in Russia's weakened condition, he accepted the inevitability of their rule and advised other princes to do likewise. Time and again Alexander made the long journey to Mongol headquarters to plead that various towns not suffer punishment for refusal to pay the taxes that the conquerors laid upon the land. On such a journey in 1263 Alexander died, ending his life as he had lived it, in the service of his people. The metropolitan, or head of the church in Vladimir, broke the news to the people: "Know that the sun of Russia has set."

The words of the metropolitan of Vladimir were prophetic. Alexander Nevsky was the last of the princes to work to hold together the land that had been Kievan Russia. He had urged princes and people not to court destruction by opposing the Mongol domination they had been powerless to prevent. He had saved the Russian people from possible inundation by the Teutonic knights. In accepting Mongol rule, he risked no danger that the Russians would lose their cultural identity because the Mongols never attempted to impose their customs and civilization on the conquered land. By the time of Alexander's death, Russians grudgingly accepted Mongol rule, but the unity was gone; the land was separated into principalities practically independent of each other. For a long time, the only cohesive force in the territory, aside from that of the church, was to be that imposed by the alien conqueror, until a descendant of Alexander Nevsky came forward to provide the leadership that would rid the land of foreign rule.

Suggested Reading

See "Suggested Reading" at end of Chapter 3.

Kievan Society

Russians have always felt a sentimental attachment for the history of Kiev, "the mother of Russian cities." This first capital of Russia has been the subject of romantic affection and has caught the popular fancy much more successfully than either of the later two capitals managed to do. The reason lies perhaps in the fact that popular attention has centered on the heroic figures from Oleg to Yaroslav, and has found relief from the dreary decline of Kiev in the careers of men like Vladimir Monomakh and Alexander Nevsky. The story glosses over much that was brutal and narrow and prosaic in Kievan life, and pays too much attention to the brave and daring and venturesome.

The Kievan experience produced certain sociopolitical attitudes to which the Russian people would cling throughout their history. The first of these was a deep sense of attachment to the Russian land. The concept of "Mother Russia" as a land meriting the love and respect of its people, quite apart from the administration or the prince who ruled over it, goes back to Kievan times. The Kievan period was indeed the cradle of Russian nationality.

The awareness of the unity of the Russian people developed soon after the founding of the state. The early princes of Kiev welded the various tribes of East Slavs firmly together so completely that they lost all sense of identity other than Russian. Pressure on the frontier from Swedes, Lithuanians, Poles, Germans, Bulgars, and steppe-raiders contributed to the feeling of individuality of the Russian people. The foreigner was an enemy whom the Russians must expel from the homeland. Here lies the key to the affection in which the people have always held Vladimir Monomakh and Alexander Nevsky.

Government

Until the birth of the Kievan state there was no central government in the sense of an administration for the entire land and an authority over the various groups of East Slavs. Each tribe governed itself in matters affecting its own local interest. Not until Oleg brought together both ends of the water road and went far toward uniting the East Slav tribes were the foundations present for building a national state. For nearly two centuries, all Russians regarded the state as a political unit to be ruled by one man and handed down inviolate from one ruler to another as a single heritage or patrimony. After Yaroslav, the nature of the executive changed radically. The ruler was not an individual but a family. Ruling out all such complications as nomad attacks and the decline of Constantinople, the change in the executive power alone was sufficient to destroy the likelihood that the ruler would continue to meet the responsibilities that were his.

There was never any thought in Kievan Russia that the power of the executive was absolute. After the conversion to Christianity, men accepted the principle that the prince must rule according to Christian precepts. They frowned on arbitrary rule, in violation of the new morality or without reference to the wishes of at least some segments of the population. A council of boyars limited the authority of the prince. The boyars, known collectively as his druzhina, attended the prince on campaigns or sat as a deliberative body to advise him. The Boyar Council that advised the grand prince of Kiev occupied somewhat the position of a baronial assembly for the state, but only because the grand prince was the ruler of Kievan Russia. Every prince had his own druzhina, who followed him to wars and advised him in the administration of his principality, no matter how small.

The council, or Duma, of boyars was a body possessing considerable power. The prince must accept its advice on any important matter and must have its approval of legislation and treaties with other nations. An inner circle or cabinet of a few members of the Boyar Duma attended the prince constantly, probably assisted him in administration, and advised him in the disposition of routine problems. Only a full session of the Boyar Duma, however, could decide important matters of state.

There was a second assembly exercising some vague limit upon princely authority—namely the town meeting, or vieche, of the capital city. Although the vieche concerned itself primarily with local problems, there were times when it raised its voice in national affairs. Each district capital had its own vieche that dealt with only local affairs, but that of Kiev frequently influenced national matters because of the pressure it occasionally was able to exert upon the grand prince.

By Oleg's time, the East Slavs had tended to gather around certain old tribal capitals and to build other towns when they moved into new territory. Theirs was a land of city-states. Throughout the Kievan period the major cities dominated the area surrounding them, each controlling certain trade routes. Each major city became a provincial capital, its position recognized by occupying a rank in the rota system. Minor towns of each area were bound to each capital by trade and administrative ties. The rural area associated with each capital was its *volost* or district.

The basic unit of local government, in town and country, was the commune, or *mir*, an assembly composed of the heads of all families in a neighborhood or town. In cities like Novgorod and Kiev there were many mirs, each representing a street or quarter that settled its own neighborhood problems. The citywide vieche included all the citizens of the town.

All freemen in the province who were heads of families could participate in vieche meetings. The ringing of the great bell or the chanting of criers sent through the streets called the citizenry together in the market place or in the cathedral square to voice approval or objection to matters put before the vieche by the prince or the mayor. The power of the city assembly varied from city to city, reaching its apogee in Novgorod and first losing its influence in Suzdalia. In none of the Russian cities did the vieche ever become representative, in the sense of containing elected delegates. Consequently, the larger the town grew, the more unwieldy became the assembly and the greater the tendency to circumvent it and to allow the accumulation of power by an oligarchy.

In late Kievan times, as many freemen in rural areas fell into slavery and as few merchants in the towns rose to commanding positions of wealth, there was a drift away from the democratic institutions of earlier days. Great landowners assumed political power in the country, and the manorial lord ruled over his great estate and over the slaves who cultivated it. The number of freemen declined sharply in the thirteenth century. Those who accumulated fortunes from trade won power in the cities.

The Appanage System

As the political power of Kiev ebbed in the twelfth century, the influence of the rota system, which focused princely attention on Kiev as the national capital, declined proportionately. Andrew Bogoliubsky, who became grand prince by dint of military power, scorned Kiev as a capital and preferred his city of Vladimir on the river Kliazma. This shift of political direction was a reflection of a population flow away from the steppe zone to escape the frustrating wars of the princes and the raids of the nomads. Andrew and his brother Vsevolod strove to reorganize Russia by subordinating the princes to the new power center. In the attempt, the rota system fell into abeyance as precipitately as the capital around which it revolved had declined in importance.

In the valley of the upper Volga, where the fleeing population of Kievan Russia found sanctuary, a new political order developed, based not on the idea of territorial unity but on the concept of individual princely ownership of a parcel of land. This system that sprang up in north central Russia is known as the appanage system.

Andrew Bogoliubsky was responsible for abolishing the rota system and for laying the foundations of the appanage system that replaced it. When he became grand prince, instead of removing to Kiev as his predecessors had done, he remained in his principality of Suzdalia. Suzdal, which along with Pereyaslav had been part of the heritage of Yaroslav's third son and therefore one of the stepping stones to the capital, thus withdrew from the rota system. The province of Suzdalia lost its family significance and became the inalienable property of its prince and his heirs. Andrew's successor, Vsevolod, did not bother to journey to Kiev to assume the title of grand prince but ruled the land of Russia, the grand principality, from his capital on the distant Kliazma River. The brothers Andrew and Vsevolod succeeded in taking the principality of Suzdalia out of the rota system and preserving it as a hereditary province in their own branch line.

The successors of Vsevolod "Big Nest" treated the province of Suzdalia as a heritage of private property. A father would will it to an only son. When there were several sons, he divided up the province among them, each receiving his portion outright to pass on as he chose. The next generation subdivided the subprovinces until each heritage was small and poor, but in each case the heritage passed down vertically from father to sons and not horizontally from brother to brother as under the rota system. Each inheritor under the new system looked on his heritage as his patrimony, or appanage, as his estate to will in turn to his heirs. With the appearance of the appanage system among the sons of Vsevolod, the movement of princes from one province to another that had characterized the rota system came to an end. The earlier view of the family heritage as possessing integrity and indivisibility gave way to the heir's concern to receive his share in absolute proprietorship.

The appanage system, recognizing the right of all sons to share a father's estate, was responsible for breaking down the new Russia of the upper Volga into scores of microscopic principalities. Vsevolod left five sons who raised twelve grandsons. Thus, in two generations' time the region of Suzdalia splintered into twelve appanages, one of which, incidentally, was Moscow. One of the twelve was split into twenty small parcels in a century's time. This atomization obviously impoverished the princes who succeeded to such an insignificant patrimony. One fifteenth-century prince entered a monastery in preference to sharing with several brothers an inheritance that consisted only of a manor house, a church, and a hamlet.

Another consequence of the appanage system was the complete estrangement of the family that descended from Vsevolod. The rota system, even in its worst days, had given the members of the princely family a sense of family solidarity. Even their fighting for place drew them together at the same time that it pitted them against each other. Seniority in the family, and how to enforce it or circumvent it, was always foremost in the minds of the princes of Kiev. But in Suzdalia the descendants soon forgot that they were "grandsons of one grandfather," and lost all contact with each other.

The appanage system had the effect of depriving the princes of all political significance and of reducing them to the position of simple landowners. In the best days of Kiev, the state on the Dnieper was a nation, bordering on other nations and having to defend itself against them. At that time it possessed a people, different, in language and custom, from other peoples who were aware of its individuality and jealous of its independence. Later, in the fourteenth century, the prince of a small appanage was no different from scores of others. He fenced off his lands from those of other princes no greater than himself. His people were the same in habit, tongue, dress, faith, work, and play as those of every other prince. He had no foreign relations, only the relations of one landowner to another. Indeed, he had no people, in the sense of being able to force the freemen of his territory to stay with him and serve him. Only his slaves were bound to him. The freemen who rented from him could leave to rent from another prince when their lease was up. Even his boyars were free to seek service where they chose. Many of them in the fourteenth century chose to serve the grand duke of Lithuania, who paid much better than a poor appanage prince. Many of them drifted to the court of the prince of Moscow, whose wealth and power were growing rapidly in the fourteenth century. The average small appanage prince had no feeling that anyone was his subject, for the reason that he did not consider himself a sovereign. It was not unusual for a boyar to own or lease land in one appanage and to take service under the prince of another. Holding land did not entail any service to the overlord as it did in Western Europe, and so there was no political similarity between the feudalism of the West and the appanage system of north Russia.

Finally, the appanage prince became independent of all other princes, and the only political hegemony over the land was that imposed by the Mongol-Tatar khan, whose capital at Sarai was far away on the lower Volga. All sense of territorial unity disappeared among the princes, to appear again only in the fifteenth century. The appanage system, which reduced the princes to impoverished small landowners, deprived them of all political awareness and all feeling of responsibility to the inhabitants of their small estates. When a strong leader appeared among them, anxious to reunite the land, he found little popular opposition to destroying the appanage princes, for there never had been any spirit of loyalty to them. The prince of Moscow found the work of reunification made easy by the fact that he encountered no political opposition in the system that he swept away.

The Economy

Oleg, founder of the Kievan state, brought most of the East Slavs under subjection and imposed an annual tribute on the various tribes. This tribute, paid in furs, wax, and honey, he personally collected each year on visits to the tribal capitals. Early in November the prince set out from Kiev with his retinue to call at the various cities in the land. In each city he collected the tribute and settled for a stay to be entertained by the tribal chief. The journey lasted through the winter, for the princely party did not return to Kiev until the ice had left the Dnieper. During the winter the Slavs trapped and hunted and built boats of hollowed logs in which the season's catch was shipped to Kiev when the rivers opened. In April they beached their boats near the capital and the prince and members of his druzhina came to the riverbank to buy the furs and other products that the tribes brought in and often to purchase their boats. This stock together with the tribute that the prince had collected—wheat brought in from the steppe farmers who had it to sell and slaves captured in the wars against enemy tribes—all were loaded into the boats for Byzantium. Then the prince and his warrior-merchants, joined by similar fleets of private merchants from Novgorod, Smolensk, Chernigov, and the other towns, dropped down the Dnieper to the Black Sea and continued onward to the great trading center on the Bosporus, Constantinople.

The Russian merchants spent the summer trading season in the eastern capital. Trading was by barter; the Russian furs, wax, honey, and slaves were exchanged for Byzantine wines, gold and silver ornaments, glassware, spices, fruit, and silks. At the end of the season, the emperor provided the ship's stores necessary for the return voyage, and the Russians set out for Kiev, arriving there shortly before the annual circuit began again in the fall. The prince and his druzhina stopped at Kiev, and the merchants from the other towns returned home for the winter to exchange in their own markets the Byzantine wares they had brought with them. At Novgorod the products of the East were sold to Scandinavian merchants who distributed them over the Baltic area and into Central Europe. Trade was of tremendous importance to the Kievan economy, and the exchange of goods between Novgorod and the Baltic region on the one hand and between the entire water road area and Byzantium on the other was vital to the prosperity of the state.

Along with Kievan commercial relations with foreigners, which were important and certainly spectacular, there was a considerable volume of interregional trade inside Russia itself. The products of the forest moved south over the Dnieper from Smolensk, and the grain and meat of the northern steppe moved north from Kiev over the same river. Novgorod received from the steppe the grain necessary to feed its large population and was as dependent on the water road for its own food supplies as for the exotic foreign wares its merchants displayed in their market stalls. Because of the early growth of cities there was always a lively local trade, as the farmers from outlying areas exchanged their produce for the tools, weapons, pottery, clothing, and leather goods that city craftsmen manufactured. Although many of the transactions were between the neighboring farmer or trapper and the local artisan, every city market welcomed merchants from other towns who sold wholesale to local distributors or who bought up quantities of goods to take back home to their own markets. Market day was a weekly event, usually held on Friday.

The fair was an annual event and often ran for weeks on end. In general, the fairs brought together the produce of wide areas and usually attracted foreign merchants. Smolensk and Novgorod held annual fairs visited particularly by

German and Scandinavian merchants. The trade of Novgorod in the tenth and eleventh centuries was in part a transit trade, for through it passed silks, spices, jewels, and carpets from the Orient and Constantinople to northern Europe. In addition, Novgorod and Smolensk were collecting stations for Russian goods that found ready sale in German markets. Russian merchants traveled abroad to buy and to sell, in Persia and Baghdad, until the Polovtsy put a stop to it, and in Visby and north German towns throughout the Kievan period.

Cultivation of the soil was common all over Russia. In the forest zone, the preparation of the land required a heavy investment of labor. The trees and brush had to be burned away before plowing and sowing. After three or four years the soil lost its strength, and the farmer and his family moved on to another patch, burned it off, and started anew. As population grew in northern and central Russia, the enlarged family of several generations occupied a greater holding, burning off one patch and tilling it for three or four years, then doing the same to another plot while the first rested and so could be used again when yields on the second declined. Thus a two-field or three-field system of rotation became necessary if the cultivator were to avoid the rapid impoverishment of the soil.

The rich black soil of the steppe was so fertile and of such fine texture that it needed plowing only once in several years. The quality of the soil made possible small farms, which were much more common in the south than in the north. Oxen- and horse-drawn plows with iron plowshares that turned the sod were in use long before Oleg's time. Although small family farms were common in the southern areas, there was a steady growth of great estates owned by princes, boyars, or the church. Although the church objected to slavery, armies of slaves tilled the estates of boyars and princes. Church lands were cultivated by monks or let out to tenants on a share or cash-rent basis.

Throughout Kievan times the Russians mined iron and made it into plowshares, hoes, rakes, nails, spears, arrowheads, and shields. They imported copper, tin, lead, gold, and silver from Central Europe, Asia Minor, the Caucasus, and the Urals, to make into household utensils, church bells and ornaments, coins, bridles, jewelry, and building materials.

Because of the plentiful supply of timber, the Russians made their houses of wood, even parts of them in the steppe, floating the timber down the rivers. Novgorod, famous for its carpenters, even paved its streets with timber. After the conversion, masons built cathedrals of stone, and lay princes aped those of the church by building palaces of brick and stone. The city of Vladimir, which Andrew Bogoliubsky did so much to endow with rich churches, came to be as famous for its masons as was Novgorod for its carpenters. In Novgorod, as in other cities, guilds set the standards of workmanship and controlled the enrollment of apprentices, as was true of medieval practices all over Europe. The guilds also controlled or strictly influenced city government.

Several items of exchange were popular in pre-Kievan times, including furs in the forest zone and cattle in the steppe. Silver bars of measured weights constituted the monetary standard, such bars being worth so many marten skins or so many cattle. Arabic, Persian, Roman, and Byzantine coins circulated freely, but there were no Russian coins until Vladimir's time.

The Russians learned credit and investment techniques from Constantinople, and merchants borrowed from a prince, from each other, and from associations. Interest rates in the period were surprisingly low, evidence of the fluidity and availability of investment capital. The law limited interest rates on long-term loans to 10 percent.

The princes managed to accumulate large holdings of gold and silver by selling more than they bought in Constantinople or by disposing of Byzantine goods to traders in Russian cities, by gathering plunder in war, and by the collection of tribute and taxes from the land. This reserve they invested in trading ventures, loaned out to merchants or injected into the economy as the government paid for the goods and services it needed. The boyars amassed smaller accumulations of treasure from trade and from their share in the booty yielded by war. The church soon found itself in possession of a respectable treasure through gifts from the princes and boyars, and from the tithe that Vladimir had assigned to it. However, church funds were seldom liquid, for the gold and silver that came to it went into church ornaments, or was quickly invested in land and buildings. After the decline of Kiev and the removal of the metropolitan to Vladimir and later to Moscow, gifts to the church were usually in the form of land, until the church became the greatest landowner in Russia. Much of the capital in later Kievan times was in the form of slaves, a highly liquid investment because of the ready market for them both at home and abroad. Merchants of the leading towns must have grown very wealthy, considering that several of them built churches entirely at their own expense.

Social Organization

Nearly eight million people were living in Kievan Russia immediately after Yaroslav's death. The draining of population through perennial Polovtsy raids and princely civil wars probably kept the figure stable through 1250. The awful desolation that followed the Mongol-Tatar invasion may have so depleted the population that there was no recovery through the thirteenth century. In the fourteenth century the Black Death struck Russia and then swept westward to decimate Europe. By 1500, the population of Russia had grown to nearly ten million. A century later it had risen to fifteen million.

A relatively high percentage of the population of Kievan Russia was urban, for the national economy had developed into something like commercial capitalism. City-dwellers numbered perhaps a million on the eve of the Tatar conquest, or a seventh of the national total. Kiev, Novgorod, and Smolensk together contained not less than four hundred thousand inhabitants. The percentage of urban to rural population in Kievan Russia was high in comparison to that found anywhere in Western Europe at the time.

Classes were clearly identifiable in Kievan society. The boyars, the aristocratic element, sprang from a number of roots. At the top of this class, and in early times separate from it, were the members of the princely family. Oleg and his successors down to the first generation after Yaroslav constituted a distinct class of royalty. However, by the time of the Tatar invasion, the family had multiplied to such an extent, and the land holdings of the junior princes had become so small, that royalty had merged with the princes, constituting a sort of upper stratum. The chief but not the only agency through which a man might become a boyar was the prince's druzhina, or retinue. The early druzhina was a heterogeneous lot. Some of its members were Slav tribal chieftains; some were of noble ancestry; others, occasionally even slaves, rose from humble origin through outstanding service to the prince. The senior members of the druzhina were the officers of the prince's army and leading servants in his household, such as the steward and the master of the house, whereas pages and common warriors made up the junior membership of the retinue. A man might rise to boyar rank without serving in a princely druzhina. Leading officials and merchants in the chief towns also held boyar status. The boyars before the decline of Kiev were becoming landowners, and it is their occupation of great estates that distinguishes them in a later period from other social classes.

The middle class in the cities contained upper and lower strata. Extremely wealthy merchants probably were not numerous, although some of the most prosperous families came to dominate city office and so rose into the class of city boyars. Small merchants and prosperous artisans made up the lower middle class, distinct from the laborers beneath them whom they employed. There was also a rural middle class, freemen who owned small estates but who were clearly distinct from the great landowning boyars above them and the landless peasants— free, half-free, or slave—beneath them. In south Russia, this rural middle class succumbed to Polovtsy raids and the Tatar invasion, but it reappeared in central Russia in the thirteenth century and never disappeared from Novgorodian territory. The laboring element in Kievan cities contained skilled, semiskilled, and unskilled workers. Many skilled craftsmen, no matter how modest their income, really belonged to the middle class in the sense that they did not work for others but owned their own shops.

There were three classes of agricultural workers in Kievan Russia: the state peasant, or *smerd*, who was a freeman; the *zakup*, who was half-free; and the slave, or *kholop*. Smerds tilled their own small farms, which fell to their sons when they died. This free peasant enjoyed the "privilege" of paying the tribute or tax and of furnishing horses to the state in time of war, whereas the half-free and unfree classes had no such privilege. The prince extended a special protection to the state peasant, who was free of arrest or punishment without the prince's consent. On the other hand, the prince could fine the smerd for infractions of the law, and the right to be fined was a distinction of free peasants.

Midway between the free peasant and the slave was the zakup. Once a freeman, the zakup was one who had fallen by debt into a period of indenture or who had voluntarily sold future labor for a sum of money. When the zakup paid the obligation the zakup again became a freeman. A small farmer or a town craftsman might borrow money for farm or business. If unable to repay the loan with interest at maturity, the zakup had to work it out by personally providing labor. The creditor was free to employ the debtor in any way the creditor chose. Most debtors became agricultural laborers. Zakups could not be sold as slaves, although they became slaves if they attempted to escape. Creditors were free to impose corporal punishment upon their indentured workers for just cause, but zakups could sue their lords for excessive cruelty or for unjust punishment. They could bear witness in court, the distinction of a freeman, but on the other hand they were not accountable for theft. Responsibility for theft by a zakup lay upon the master, who could then bind the culprit in complete slavery. Vladimir Monomakh took steps to protect the indentured worker from falling into slavery by fraud of a creditor and to fix interest rates at a fair level to prevent wholesale loss of freedom by the debtor class. Other half-free people were those who, during war or famine, voluntarily gave up their freedom and worked for a lord in return for protection and for food and shelter.

Slaves, or kholops, might lose their freedom only temporarily, as when they fell captive to the Polovtsy and were later ransomed, or were seized by the Poles and released at the end of a war. Civilians captured and sold to Byzantium could work out their freedom. Treaty arrangements between Kiev and the Eastern Empire set limits to the amount of ransom and provided specific lengths of time a member of each class might be worked before obtaining freedom. By far the largest number of slaves consisted of those who had permanently lost their freedom, that is, had descended into full slavery. A freeman might become a full slave by entering the service of another without a clear contractual understanding that the person should remain free, by marrying a female slave without the agreement of her lord that he should remain free, by selling oneself into slavery, or by condemnation to slavery as punishment for theft or robbery. An agreement to sell oneself into slavery was only binding if the seller received the minimum legal price and if the town clerk received the registration fee. To prevent fraud, the city official was assured that the sale was voluntary and that the new owner had paid the legal price. Once individuals descended into the kholop class, their owners could sell them with or without their families. The church frowned on traffic in slaves for speculative purposes, for it regarded the buying and selling of slaves for profit as sinful.

Slaves possessed no civil rights whatsoever. They could not appear in court, as suitors or even as witnesses. They could not own property or transact business, and if a slave did so surreptitiously, the other party could obtain redress for damages from the slave's owner. Their lords could kill them with impunity, although the church might force the lord to do penance for the crime. A master could put a kholop's labor to any use—in the field, in the stable, or about the house. Some slaves were trained in the crafts, and a few even became tutors to the master's children. Escape from slavery was only possible by running away, for which penalties were severe, or by being freed by the owner. The church constantly encouraged masters to free their slaves, and some masters provided for emancipation of their slaves in their wills.

Slavery existed throughout the Kievan period, and tended to become more widespread after the middle of the eleventh century. In the turbulent times that civil war and nomad raids produced, the individual tiller of the soil often despaired of being free and safe and sold freedom for protection or found it impossible to stay out of debt and so sank into slavery to a creditor. Vladimir Monomakh probably provided only a temporary stay to this drift by forbidding landowners to enslave tenants who could not repay loans and by restricting the right of the bankrupt to sell themselves into slavery.

Christianity in the Kievan Period

For a half century after Vladimir's conversion in 988, the relations of the Russian church with the parent church in Constantinople were irregular and cool. Russia's metropolitan bishop seems to have lacked patriarchal approval until 1037. Constantinople's concern by that time to improve relations with Kiev and to tie the Russian church into the Orthodox orbit is hardly surprising. Less than a generation after the settlement, a schism developed between the patriarchate of Constantinople and the Roman papacy. In 1054 the two excommunicated each other, the Western church henceforth claiming to be the Catholic or universal church, whereas the Eastern church held itself up as the Orthodox or only true church. The two rescinded the excommunications only in 1966. When the split between the two Christian churches developed, the Kievan church followed Constantinople, as the patriarch shrewdly had guessed it would when he won its favor by granting local autonomy under its own metropolitan. There was no serious question in Kiev, when the breach between East and West opened, as to which the Russian church should follow. In religious affairs, Russia went automatically and without dispute where the patriarch led.

The religious break between East and West produced consequences of vast importance to the history of Russia. After 1054, relations between the peoples who embraced the two faiths were frequently strained and always potentially hostile. Popes felt no more scruple in urging crusades against the Orthodox than in sending the faithful against pagans or Moslems. The Germans, intermittently at war with the Slavs since the time of Clovis in the sixth century, found in the schism an excuse for their *Drang nach Osten* (''Drive to the East''). Prussian secession from the Roman Catholic discipline in the sixteenth century had no effect on relations with the Orthodox Slavs, whose lands were the goal of German expansion down to 1945. On the other hand, the Russian clergy implied that Roman Catholics were not Christian when they spoke of Russians as Christians and Westerners as ''Latins,'' and they invariably preached a holy crusade when Russia went to war with Poles or Germans.

The estrangement between East and West after 1054 cut Russia adrift from the West European cultural stream. The stimuli that quickened the thought and life of Western peoples, such as the Renaissance and the Protestant Revolt, did not affect Russia. From this isolation Russia suffered an intellectual and technological handicap that placed it sometimes at a disastrous disadvantage. Russia's greatest leaders have been fully conscious of this backwardness and they undertook concerted efforts to overcome it.

When in 1037 the patriarch of Constantinople ordained and sent to Kiev the first metropolitan, Russia became a metropolitical diocese of the Byzantine church. With only two exceptions, all the metropolitans of the Kievan period came from Constantinople, as did perhaps half of the ordinary bishops. The Byzantines sent out to occupy the Russian bishoprics took with them a train of clerks and assistants, and each cathedral city became a center from which the culture of Constantinople spread over the land. At the time of the conversion, Russia received eight bishops for the principal cities of the realm. Two and a half centuries later the number of bishoprics had grown to fifteen. Although the metropolitan ordained all bishops, the selection of those not sent out from Constantinople was left to the grand prince or, as in the case of Novgorod, to the city vieche. These princes of the church—the bishops, whose authority and wealth contrasted so markedly with the position of the lower clergy—came from the monastic ranks, the so-called "black" clergy. The parish priests, or "white" clergy, took no vow of celibacy and were, in fact, selected from married men. Because each congregation nominated its own priest, whom the bishop then ordained, the lower clergy represented the class dominant in each particular parish. Most of them consequently sprang from the lower classes of society.

All monks in the Russian church belonged to one order, but not all followed the same pattern of life. In some monasteries the brothers lived, dined, and worked communally; in others each monk kept to his own cell. By the close of the Kievan period over fifty monasteries and a dozen convents had opened, all but one of them located in cities. The Monastery of the Caves in Kiev, which became the most famous in the land, did much to promote learning, and it was there that numerous monks wrote the *Primary Chronicle*.

The church, in its own courts over which the bishops presided, exercised complete legal jurisdiction over various categories of Russians who served it. Among these were the clerics and their families, sextons, caretakers, choristers, physicians, keepers of inns for pilgrims and homes for the aged, those freed from slavery who tilled church lands, and even the women who baked the wafers for use in the communion service. Furthermore, as in the West, all Kievans came under the authority of church courts in some cases, notably in those having to do with infractions of the moral law. Byzantine law spread quickly in Russia by its application in ecclesiastical courts. The church accepted responsibility for caring for the needy and for promoting education. It maintained schools for the education of recruits for the ranks of the clergy, and many graduates took service with lay princes. Monasteries operated hospitals, inns, and homes for the aged, and the church cared for the poor and recommended that laymen do so as well.

The adoption of Christianity brought vigorous stimulation to the pursuit of the fine arts. The new faith introduced choral music, and the Russians have excelled in it ever since. Following the Byzantine practice there was no instrumental music in the churches. In the eleventh century, however, the use of bells came in from the West, and in their casting Russians have remained unsurpassed. It was in the field of church architecture, however, that the conversion revealed its most pronounced effects. Vladimir began work on the Church of the Tithe in Kiev shortly after his baptism. The Cathedral of St. Sophia, with its richly painted walls and its central cupola surrounded by twelve smaller ones, must have been an imposing sight. Begun by Yaroslav and completed in 1100, it suffered badly from fires and desecrations during times of political instability. The stone cathedral of the same name in Novgorod, begun in 1045, survived until 1944. In the late twelfth century there developed in the north, centering in Vladimir, a new type of church building known as Suzdalian architecture. Andrew Bogoliubsky and Vsevolod imported Westerners to aid in the construction of a number of churches, and the peculiar type that resulted was a blend of Byzantine and Romanesque lines. The princes of Moscow later patterned their churches after those in the Suzdal period. The Eastern church frowned upon sculpture but encouraged painting and mosaics. Painted images were substituted for sculptured ones, and the icon corner, where pictures of the saints hung and candles burned before them on holy days, was prominent in every Russian home. In succeeding centuries, with the growth of Moscow and Muscovy, the steady increase of churches and other religious buildings created many opportunities for artists to visually express their faith. These places of worship were filled with icons and other religious art, works that today are regarded for their immense artistic and cultural importance. Andrei Rublev, who died in 1430, has the reputation of being the most famous of these creative talents in the medieval period.

Judaism and Roman Catholicism also existed in Kievan Russia, but chiefly among foreigners who came there to trade. Roman Catholic churches in Kiev, Novgorod, and Smolensk ministered to German and Scandinavian merchants, and there was even a Dominican monastery in the capital. Inside the Russian church the Bogomil heresy, emphasizing the struggle between good and evil or God and Satan and objecting to the accumulation of wealth by the Orthodox clergy, made some headway. This concept entered Russia from Bulgaria, and passed on to the west to appear in southern France as the Albigensian heresy.

Russian society in Kievan times developed a number of trends that extended through the Mongol period into the new Russia that was to emerge under the leadership of Moscow. Perhaps the strongest link between the old and the new was the church, which in times of chaos often seemed the only tie binding East Slavs together. A system of law, welding together Byzantine practice and East Slav custom, survived the decline of Kiev. A common language, given stability by the introduction of the cyrillic alphabet that permitted the tongue to be written as well as spoken, bound all Russians together. A literature handed down to succeeding generations the stories of the great deeds and of the sufferings of the people. A strong feeling of national unity and inviolability of the land, a feeling for "Mother Russia," continued through times when there was no nation in the political sense. Cultural homogeneity characterized the society of Kievan Russia and survived through the period of chaos that followed the collapse of the state, to be caught up again and given political leadership by the princes of Moscow.

Suggested Reading

ARBMAN, H., *The Vikings* (London, 1962).

BILLINGTON, J. H., *The Icon and the Axe: An Interpretive History of Russian Culture* (New York, 1966).

BLUM, J., *Lord and Peasant in Russia from the Ninth to the Nineteenth Century* (Princeton, 1961).

CHADWICK, N. K., *The Beginnings of Russian History: An Inquiry into Sources* (Cambridge, Eng., 1946).

CROSS, S. H. (ed.), *The Russian Primary Chronicle* (Cambridge, 1953).

DMYTRYSHYN, B., *Medieval Russia, A Source Book*, 900–1700 (New York, 1967).

DVORNIK, F., *The Slavs in European History and Civilization* (New Brunswick, NJ, 1962).

FEDOTOV, G. P., *The Russian Religious Mind: Kievan Christianity* (Cambridge, 1966).

GIMBUTAS, M., *The Slavs* (New York, 1971).

GREKOV, B., *Kievan Rus* (Moscow, 1959).

GROUSSET, R., *The Empire of the Steppes* (New Brunswick, NJ, 1947).

HALPERIN, C. J., *Russia and the Golden Horde: The Mongol Impact on Medieval Russian History* (Bloomington, IN, 1985).

HAMILTON, G. H., *The Art and Architecture of Russia* (New York, 1983).

KLIUCHEVSKY, V. O., *A History of Russia*, vol. I (London, 1911).

McGOVERN, W. M., *The Early Empires of Central Asia* (Chapel Hill, 1939).

MILIUKOV, P., C. SEIGNOBOS, and L. EISENMANN,, *History of Russia*, 3 vols. (New York, 1968).

MILIUKOV, P. N., *Outlines of Russian Culture*, 3 vols., (Philadelphia, 1943; Gulf Breeze, FL, 1974).

MITCHELL, R., and N. Forbes, *The Chronicle of Novgorod*, 1016–1471 (London, 1914).

PUSHKAREV, G. G., *A Source Book for Russian History from Early Times to 1917*, 3 vols. (New Haven, 1972).

VASILIEV, A. A., *History of the Byzantine Empire* (Madison, WI, 1929).

VERNADSKY, G., *Kievan Russia* (New Haven, 1948).

_____, *Medieval Russian Laws* (New York, 1948).

_____, *The Mongols and Russia* (New Haven, 1953).

Vikings in Russia: Yngvar's Saga and Eymund's Saga (New York, 1989).

VOYCE, A., *The Art and Architecture of Medieval Russia* (Norman, OK, 1967).

ZENKOVSKY, S. A. (ed.), *Medieval Russia's Epics, Chronicles, and Tales* (New York, 1963).

_____. *The Nikonian Chronicle*, 5 vols. (Princeton, 1984–1989).

CHAPTER 4

Novgorod and the Rise of Moscow

Pre-Kievan Russia was only a loose confederation of city-states. Because of their location near opposite ends of the Dnieper water road, two of these city-states, Kiev and Novgorod, towered above all the rest in importance. The former became the capital of the state that Oleg welded together, and so in a sense lost its identity, but Novgorod did not suffer by the prince's decision to set up his capital at the other end of the water road. Its economic and even its political importance continued through Kievan times, and indeed toward their close.

Novgorod

When the capital was falling into eclipse, Novgorod, the great city of the north, was at work building and developing a distinct economic empire of its own. Long before the end of the fifteenth century, when it came under the rule of the Muscovite state, Novgorod had extended its control over nearly a third of European Russia and was far larger than any of the other principalities.

The city of Novgorod straddled the river Volkhov a few miles downstream from where the river leaves Lake Ilmen. Near the town center the Great Bridge connected the two banks. On the eastern bank lay that portion of the city known as the commercial side, named for the principal market located near the bridge.

Adjoining the market was a great square called Yaroslav's Court, in the center of which stood a rostrum from which leaders addressed the citizens assembled in the vieche. Nearby rose the tower containing the great bell that called the people to meet in assembly in the square. This "commercial" side was the working-class district of Novgorod. Across the river lay the "Sophia," or Cathedral, side of the city, so named because near the bridge in an enclosed square stood the great Cathedral of St. Sophia. Here were the homes of the well-to-do merchants and boyars. The city proper which included both riverbanks, was divided into five "quarters," some of which originally had housed particular crafts or trades, such as the "potters' quarter" and the "carpenters' quarter." A rampart and ditch surrounded the five quarters. Outside these defenses lay the city's suburbs and a number of monastic communities, and beyond the suburbs extended a vast colonial territory, a tributary to the city.

Government

In the early Kievan period, the princes paid little attention to Novgorod, or perhaps took it for granted. Their attention was on Constantinople, and their energy concentrated on keeping open the lower Dnieper and winning Russian access to the markets of the great entrepôt on the Bosporus. After Yaroslav's death, Novgorod did not become a separate principality, as did Smolensk and Chernigov and Pereyaslav, but went along with Kiev to the senior member of the family. As grand prince, he kept to the capital on the lower Dnieper and delegated one of his sons to rule in Novgorod as his viceroy. None of the princes who ruled in Kiev after Vladimir Monomakh was sufficiently powerful to maintain his authority undiminished over the northern city. As the family feuds brought to Novgorod a rapid succession of princes, each a transient waiting for promotion in the rota system, the Novgorodian vieche won two important political victories: the right of the citizens to name their own administrative officers and the right to wring concessions from their prince by arranging a treaty with him before he assumed office. The city began referring to itself as "Lord Novgorod," indicating that, no matter what lord or prince might rule in Kiev or elsewhere, this giant of the north was its own master.

The famed Novgorodian freedom referred to the city's relative independence from higher authority; it arose from a combination of factors that distinguished Novgorod from the rest of Kievan Russia. The city and province were on the outer rim of the state both geographically and politically. It had no separate place in the rota system, and consequently was not a prize to be sought after as the princes struggled for position in the scale of succession. To serve as prince of Novgorod offered no attraction to members of the royal family, one of whom referred to its citizens as a "contemptible small company of carpenters." Furthermore, when the princely squabbles were at their worst, Novgorod had no need of strong leadership to protect it against powerful neighbors and could manage its own administration. Later, when it did sorely require the military leadership of a strong prince, it had already won the elements of that freedom that subordinated the prince to the city vieche. Finally, Novgorod was the economic hub of a vast empire so rich and powerful that its importance dwarfed that of any individual prince.

Soon after the death of Vladimir Monomakh, Novgorod won control over the selection of its own officials. Theretofore the prince of Novgorod, acting as the viceroy of the grand prince of Kiev whose son he usually was, ruled the city through two officials he brought with him from Kiev. These officials, invariably Kievans until 1126, were the mayor and the police prefect. When the prince of Novgorod died or moved into a spot in the rota system, his mayor and police prefect necessarily resigned, because the new prince would bring his own officials with him. During the time between the departure of one prince and the arrival of another, the city was without administrative officers; it developed the practice of choosing a temporary mayor and asking the new prince to make the selection permanent. This first happened in 1126, when the chronicler noted that "the men of Novgorod did award the office of mayor to one of themselves." The practice continued and it changed the pattern of relationships between the citizens and their prince. Henceforth the citizens in the public square chose the mayor and, instead of guarding the interests of the prince as he had previously done, the mayor represented the citizens who had elected him and who had the power to unseat him. Soon they were electing the police prefect. Finally, the citizens won the right to elect their own bishop from among the monks in the monasteries that rimmed the city and to send him to Kiev for investiture by the metropolitan.

The city had rid itself of princely domination over its officials. As the descendants of Yaroslav increased in number and made it possible for the city to choose its prince from among several rivals who had no principality, it became easy to accept a prince only after imposing further restrictions on his power in the city. One prince scorned the position, saying, "Talk not to me of Novgorod. Let it rule itself as best it may, and seek itself princes where it listeth." Soon the princely family recognized the city's right to choose its ruler from anyone in the royal family who would accept the position. The treatment often meted out to the prince suggests that the citizens were not easily satisfied. In 1136 the Novgorodians seized their prince, imprisoned him for a time, and finally expelled him—"showed him the road," as the chronicler expresses it. They kept his successor less than a year, and a third prince lasted less than two years. Between 1154 and 1160 the city tried out seven princes, all of whom fled in the night or were expelled.

The princes granted charters specifying the privileges of the city—the closest approximation to a constitution in the Kievan period. In approving the charter of 1265, the oldest still in existence, the prince agreed to rule and "maintain Novgorod according to the custom of ancient times." The charter named the prince as the supreme administrative and judicial head in Novgorod, but he was to exercise powers not as his will dictated but only with the consent of the elected mayor. Without the latter's presence, the prince could not hold court; without his approval, the prince could not appoint officials to minor administrative posts.

The vieche was to fill important offices by election. Only Novgorodians could hold appointive posts, and none could be dismissed without trial. The prince must reside in the city and carry out his administrative and judicial functions under the observation of the mayor. "Not from the land of Suzdal shalt thou administer Novgorod," one prince was warned.

The revenue of the prince of Novgorod was adequate but strictly limited. He received "tribute," or direct taxes, from the citizens, not in annual payments but in installments, only while he was present in the city. If he should leave the city, even only temporarily, perhaps to inspect his private estate elsewhere, the tribute stopped until he returned. He could not own property in Novgorod, lend money at interest, or engage in any business, for such income might free him from complete financial dependence upon his office. The prince was simply a defender of the city and protector of its trade, and the charter kept him from being anything else. He was the military leader, not the commander, of the citizen army, "alongside of whom the citizens may stand and fight." His residence lay some distance outside the walls. So completely did Novgorod circumscribe his power that in effect the city was a free commonwealth, even though it possessed a prince just as did other Russian cities.

The mayor and police prefect were elected and were paid from a tax on agricultural land. The two cooperated to maintain the peace and enforce the laws of the commonwealth. The prefect of police kept the watch and made arrests, and he and the mayor worked together in bringing criminals to justice. Both officials sat on a board to decide disputes between Novgorodian and foreign merchants. There was a confusion of courts—at the ward level and in each quarter, the prince's court, the bishop's court, the mayor's court, and police court. Court fees were an important source of revenue, and a right to a share in fees and fines was a much sought after perquisite.

In spite of the growth of the city and the unwieldy size of the assembly, the Novgorod vieche continued to include all heads of families in the city and its subject territory. In practice only inhabitants of the city proper attended its sessions, for the technique of representation never developed in early Russia. The power of the Novgorod vieche exceeded that of any assembly in Europe at the time. It could dismiss or imprison a prince and summon a new one. It elected and could recall the leading officials. It voted war and peace and decided all questions of foreign relations. It enacted all legislation affecting the city at large and approved all taxes. Finally, it acted as supreme court to punish all criminals whose offenses were serious enough to make them liable to death, exile, or confiscation of property.

Because of the size of the vieche, its lack of organization, and the fact that it did not hold regular meetings but came together to pass upon a given question, the Novgorodian assembly simply approved or rejected a proposal. The Novgorodian Council of Magnates formulated questions or laws for the vieche to decide. The archbishop, most wealthy citizens, and all who had ever held high office sat on the council, which numbered perhaps fifty members. It consisted exclusively of members of the great merchant families who dominated city office and gave city government the character of an oligarchy. A dozen different mayors, for example, came from a single family. Although the members of the Council of Magnates could not vote in the vieche, they could so word the propositions put before it as to obtain the action they sought.

Novgorod was a city on whose markets a large surrounding district depended, and the city had managed to impose control over a wide area. Some of its early princes had led the militia to further conquests, and the city had expanded in all directions. Its most notable strides were toward the northeast, where bands of armed traders pushed into the sparsely inhabited forests, founded settlements, levied fur tribute upon the natives, and gathered wax and honey in the forests. Such bands had settled east of the Northern Dvina in the eleventh century, and a century later had reached the Pechora and the north coast of the White Sea. By 1200 "Lord Novgorod the Great" was not just a city but a vast colonial empire stretching away to the Arctic Ocean and to the Urals and even beyond.

The city government divided that portion of this colonial area that was first acquired into provinces, or "fifths," and administered separately the towns and regions that were later brought under the city's control or shared with other principalities. Beyond the provinces lay the domains, or "lands," which were conquered last in Novgorod's insatiable drive for territory.

The administration of the fifths centered in Novgorod, although each enjoyed considerable latitude in controlling its own local affairs. Each of the fifths was assigned to one of the five quarters of the city. Residents of the provinces paid taxes to its parent city quarter, and could arrange contracts only with citizens of that quarter. Leading provincial officials were responsible to the vieche of the ward that confirmed their appointment. Serviceable men residing in the fifths must bear arms in the militia in time of need. Aside from these ties to the capital, the provinces were left very much to themselves. However, now and again a provincial town refused to pay taxes to Novgorod and was punished by the execution of some of the local inhabitants and the burning of part of the town. "Lord Novgorod the Great" could be a stern master.

Social Organization

Both urban and rural inhabitants of this great metropolitan empire of the north belonged to some class. At the top of urban society were the boyars, who insisted on the same social recognition that fell to those noble servants of the princes who attained boyar status through the druzhina and who developed into landowning gentry in late Kievan times. In Novgorod members of the wealthiest families, often moneylenders, who monopolized high office—the ward aldermen, mayors, and police prefects—came to refer to themselves and to be considered by the prince as boyars. Next to the boyars and closely allied to them was a small class of moderately wealthy merchants, not sufficiently wealthy and influential to be included in the closed circle of magnates from which the chief officials were selected, but towering over the class of small merchants and shopkeepers who stood below them. Members of this class owned spacious town houses; some had estates in the country. These were the great traders and wholesale merchants; as "capitalists of a secondary order," they stood midway between the investment banking and important office-holding class on the one hand and the small tradesmen on the other. The third class in society included retail merchants, the more prosperous of whom belonged to the "corporation of the Merchants of St. John," a guild that maintained mercantile standards and settled trade disputes. At the bottom of urban society were the skilled and unskilled wage laborers who worked for the merchants above them.

For the most part, agriculture operated under a system of great estates, the owner of which at times lived on the estate and supervised its operation but at others preferred to leave its management to a bailiff while following commercial interests in the capital. At the bottom of rural society were the slaves who had lost their freedom by debt or by capture. Slaves were numerous on privately owned estates, but the state lands of Novgorod were worked only by free peasants. Some free peasants also lived as sharecroppers on private lands, where they surrendered to the owner a third or a fourth of the harvest in return for the use of the land. Although the peasants who labored on Novgorodian state lands retained their freedom until Novgorod fell to Moscow, the status of those on private estates declined steadily until they were hardly distinguishable from slaves.

During the thirteenth and fourteenth centuries, the character of civil strife in Novgorod changed markedly. Now it was war between boyar merchant-citizens from the Cathedral side and workers and small shopkeepers from the commercial side of the Volkhov. As the lower classes became more and more liable to loss of freedom through debt and the heavy taxes that they could not manage to escape, some of them formed gangs, joined by runaway slaves, and roamed and pillaged the countryside, some operating as far east as the Volga. In 1386, according to the *Chronicle of Novgorod*, the city had to pay eight thousand rubles to the grand prince of Moscow "for the guilt of the Volga men," as the chronicler called such gangs. Others who could not escape rose up against their masters, surged over the Great Bridge, and beat or killed boyars and sacked their homes, only to suffer an awful vengeance when the boyars recovered and counterattacked. One boyar family came forward to lead the oppressed, and so managed to take over the administration when a working-class uprising unseated those who represented the wealthy. Because the lower classes produced no leaders from among their own ranks, through the thirteenth and fourteenth centuries, the mayor, police prefect, and ward aldermen continued to come from two or three great families, as they had in earlier centuries. However, the vieche became a mob whose meetings no boyar dared attend, except those of the renegade family that now led the popular uprising. The propertied classes organized their own assembly on the Cathedral side, and at times there was no central administration in the city.

The Economy

The economic base upon which Novgorod depended was the exploitation of natural resources. This explains the city's insatiable drive to extend the area under its control and to incorporate within the state ever new untouched expanses that its armed traders might develop. The availability of vast reaches of territory to the northeast, rich in the products of the forest and still lying beyond the borders of any Russian principality, made possible the steady expansion of Novgorod and with it a corresponding growth in the city's size and wealth.

The forest product that prompted this restless drive into the hinterland was fur, Novgorod's most important export commodity. The Novgorodians used every possible method of gathering furs. Armed expeditions went out each spring to levy tribute, payable in pelts, on the Finnish peoples native to the area. These military bands moved only into territory not yet brought firmly under Novgorodian authority. Occasionally, the natives on both slopes of the Urals rose and massacred the Russians who came to collect tribute. In domains where Novgorod maintained trading posts, the natives exchanged furs for axes, knives, and trinkets. From these trading posts traveling merchants visited the native villages, loaded on the out journey with articles the natives were willing to buy and weighted down on the return trip with a fortune in pelts. Here on the Russian frontier, the quest for fur consumed the energy of every Novgorodian in the area. So important was fur that it occupied the place of currency.

The pelts gathered on the northeastern frontier were brought into Novgorod, sorted, graded, baled, and sold wholesale to the German merchants of the Hanse who maintained warehouses in the city. From Novgorod the furs went to important markets in Western Europe—to Bremen, Hamburg, Lübeck, Ghent, Bruges, London, and even Italian cities. These shipments balanced imports from the West of such commodities as Ypres cloth, fine clothing, weapons, needles, iron, copper, tin, herring, wine, beer, and occasionally salt and grain. To buy up these products and to negotiate contracts for the sale of its own exports, Novgorod sent its own merchants into foreign ports on the eastern and southern shores of the Baltic. In Visby, on the island of Gotland, the colony of Russian merchants was of sufficient size to justify maintaining a parish church. Novgorodian exports moved into Western Europe chiefly through Hanseatic merchants. The city was the great fur center of the world, and it enjoyed a wide reputation for high quality fur.

Fur was not the only product of the colonial empire that Novgorod exploited, although it was by far the most important. The area produced a large quantity of honey, most of it for local consumption. Catholic Europe bought large quantities of wax and wax candles, although Orthodox Russia also used large amounts. Timber, always the primary building material of the north, was cut even in remote areas where it could be floated downstream to market. Clothing and leather goods were manufactured by city artisans, chiefly for the domestic market.

Novgorod, always pre-eminently a market rather than a production center, was dependent on trade for its very existence. The maintenance of its contact with the West was absolutely necessary to permit it to market the surplus that its colonial empire yielded and to receive in exchange the finished goods that Western Europe could provide. There was another aspect, however, of Novgorod's reliance upon the outside, which, if not as dramatic, was just as vital to it. This was its need to import food, particularly grain, from distant areas. Until the middle of the eleventh century the great city could rely on wheat brought up the water road from the steppe, but when the Polovtsy raids increased in frequency and severity, the Kiev area no longer produced a surplus for export. Occasionally, wheat was imported from Western Europe, but transportation costs ran high when grain was shipped such a distance in vessels that could carry only a few hundred tons of cargo. From the twelfth century on, Novgorod found a new source of food—the valley of the upper Volga, on which the city came more and more to rely for bread grain, notably rye. So completely did it come to depend on the valley that the city made itself dangerously vulnerable to attack by any power able to sever its contact with the Volga basin.

In 1471, when Ivan III of Moscow cut Novgorod's connection with the Volga, the city was starved out, and a rising of the population brought Ivan a speedy and costless victory. By mid-decade "Lord Novgorod the Great" and the fur empire that it had built fell almost without a struggle, a victim of its dependence on a distant source of food.

The Princes and External Relations

In periods of peace the prince was a shadowy figure, and at times many paraded through the princely office only to end a momentary career in dismissal or imprisonment. When outside danger threatened the city, however, the prince became invaluable, and those who led the citizens in defense of Novgorodian territory stand out in the chronicles in sharp contrast to the princes whose misfortune it was to sit in Novgorod in times of peace.

The first of these princes to rise above the anonymity that most of them shared was Vladimir, the founder of the Russian Orthodox Church. When Sviatoslav left to take up his permanent home on the Danube, he assigned Novgorod to the rule of his youngest son, Vladimir. At Sviatoslav's death, the three surviving sons disputed the succession, and Novgorod gave its active support, military and financial, to its own prince in his campaign to win the Kievan throne. Vladimir hired a band of troops from Scandinavia and, with an army of volunteers from Novgorod, won his father's throne by conquest and by murdering his elder brother.

Vladimir's son, Yaroslav the Wise, ruled as prince of Novgorod during the later years of his father's life and nearly went to war with the grand prince over the taxes assessed against his city. The initiative surely came from the Novgorodian vieche, and Yaroslav was only the spokesman for the merchants who refused to pay at the rate that Kiev demanded. When Vladimir died, his sons fought over the succession, and again the Novgorodians backed their prince to force the settlement. After his brother's death, Yaroslav became sole ruler of the land of Kiev and left Novgorod to return to the capital on the lower Dnieper. He continued, however, to support Novgorodian interests, and led a Kievan force to drive the Finns from the northeastern shore of the Gulf of Finland, thus improving still further Novgorod's control over the outlet to the Baltic.

For more than a century after the death of Yaroslav the Wise, Novgorod sought no favors of the princes and remained relatively free of their control. There was still no serious threat from the West, and the great city spent its energy in expanding with little opposition into the rich fur-producing lands to the northeast. During the wars over the succession Novgorod accepted its own princes only after obtaining concessions from them. This was the period of the founding of the "freedom of Novgorod."

Only Vladimir Monomakh saw the need to restore unity in the land of Russia, and during his short reign as grand prince, he held hostage in Kiev a number of Novgorodian citizens to force the giant of the north to accept his rule. When he died, the princes returned to their costly feuds, and Novgorod was free once more to impose its conditions upon the princes it condescended to admit inside its walls. Even Andrew Bogoliubsky was unable to bring the city completely to heel. Novgorod accepted "of its own free will" a prince nominated by Andrew, but only after his assurance that the city's "ancient" privileges would not suffer. Andrew's successor, Vsevolod, did manage to dominate the city, forcing it to accept the princes whom he delegated to rule in his stead. Novgorod's submission, however, lasted only until Vsevolod's death. His son was unable to hold the city in check.

In 1236 Novgorod received as prince Vsevolod's grandson Alexander. In the following spring the Mongol-Tatars crossed the Volga into Russia. A year later they were in the principality of Riazan, demanding a tenth of all valuables as the price of peace. "Only when none of us remains then all will be yours," the princes answered, and Riazan and the neighboring towns suffered mercilessly. The scourge drove to within seventy miles of Novgorod.

Hardly had this awful terror passed before Novgorod was threatened from the West. In 1240 the Swedes challenged the city's control of the Gulf of Finland. Novgorod's Prince Alexander led the city militia against the Swedes and almost annihilated them in their camp on the Neva. This brilliant victory won Alexander the title of Nevsky, immortality as defender of the homeland and canonization as a champion of Orthodoxy against the Latin West.

For some years the German knights had been pressing eastward from the Gulf of Riga, and in 1240, the year of Alexander's victory over the Swedes, the knights advanced southeast of Dorpat and captured Pskov. At this critical time, when the knights were pushing deep into Novgorodian territory, the citizens had quarreled with their prince and Alexander had left the city. Now, with the invaders so near, the townspeople pleaded for him to save them.

In 1241 Alexander led the militia against the Teutonic knights who had attacked the Neva area. He delivered the territory from the invader and drove the Germans back to the west. Then on April 5, 1242, the Russians caught up with the German main body and won a decisive victory on the ice of Lake Peipus. The enemy sued for peace and agreed to return to Dorpat. Once again Alexander had saved Novgorod.

Alexander became grand prince of Vladimir and titular leader among the princes in 1246. Even after his promotion he kept in close touch with Novgorod, giving the city his son as prince and coming himself to succor the citizens when the need arose.

Novgorod had been spared the sight of Mongol troops, but in 1257 the khan sent tax assessors to the city to demand payment of the tithe; the citizens refused. When the tax collectors returned in 1259, however, there was no escape. So incensed were the Novgorodians that Alexander had to provide a guard lest the khan's representatives be killed. Alexander saw the utter futility of opposing the Tatar power and urged the Novgorodians to submit to the tax that all Russia was forced to pay. Finally, the advice of this prince who had given the city so much prevailed over less cautious counsel, and the citizens agreed to the census.

It is too easy to characterize Alexander as the defender of a "Holy Russia" against greedy Swedes and Germans and cruel Mongols. Surely both Swedes and Germans were suffering Russian pressure to drive westward, and surely the Mongols were more fearful of Russian interest in Siberia and Eastern European Russia than of any threat they faced in middle or Eastern Asia. Alexander's heroics made him a Russian giant, but he was a powerful and crafty enemy to those he threatened.

Through the long, dismal period of Russian history from the twelfth to the fifteenth centuries, when the country first was torn asunder by nomad attacks and internal strife and then subjected to the Mongol yoke, Novgorod, by bribing Mongol leaders for some gentler treatment, stood forth as a reminder of a great Russian past and as a harbinger of greatness yet to come. The city managed to stand aloof from the petty brawls of the princes and to retain its independence while the rest of Russia groveled at the feet of the khan. The best of the early Kievan period lived on in Novgorod through the centuries of chaos and humiliation that lay between the death of Yaroslav and the lifting of the Mongol burden. What relative freedom Kievan cities had nurtured continued to flourish in the north. The spirit of enterprise that motivated early Kievan princes and merchants moved Novgorodians to the conquest of an empire. The foreign contact that had meant so much to Kiev and that faded away for most of Russia in the Mongol period was kept alive by Novgorod's ties with Central and Western Europe. The conquest of Novgorod by Grand Prince Ivan III of Moscow in 1478 destroyed the last remnant of the Kievan period and, by virtue of the city-empire's size and wealth, provided Moscow with a firm base on which to build a new Russia.

The Rise of Moscow

In 1147 the principality of Suzdalia was ruled by Yuri, called Dolgoruky, or "Long Arm," the youngest son of Vladimir Monomakh and father of Andrew

Bogoliubsky. In that year Yuri invited a neighboring prince to a "mighty feast" to be held at Moscow, one of Prince Yuri's country villas situated on a height overlooking the Moskva river. This is the first mention in the chronicles of the town that was one day to become the capital of a mighty nation.

Nine years later, Prince Yuri built a wall around the few buildings that crowned the hill on the river's bank, thus making the villa a walled town. This *kreml*, or fort, the original Kremlin, was strategically located near Suzdalia's border to protect it from the neighboring principalities of Chernigov and Riazan. The town grew, unnoticed again by the chronicler until 1237 when the Tatars sacked it on their way to Suzdal. Because its recent origin made it junior to other Russian towns, Moscow occupied a minor position and was assigned to junior princes. Indeed, for years on end it seems to have had no prince at all.

Early Moscow Princes

Before his death in 1263 Alexander Nevsky willed to his youngest son, Daniel, the principality of Moscow, which included only the Kremlin and a few neighboring villages. Daniel bequeathed to his successors an enlarged territory and a policy of expanding the principality by winning control of strategic rivers. From a childless nephew Daniel inherited the important town of Pereyaslavl-Zalieski, eighty miles northeast of Moscow, which placed his principality on a tributary of the Volga. From the prince of Riazan, who was taken prisoner and then murdered at Daniel's command, the prince of Moscow seized the town of Kolomna, located where the river Moskva empties into the Oka. His son Yuri (1304–1326), who had inherited his father's acquisitive proclivities, seized Mozhaisk from the prince of Smolensk. This gave the principality of Moscow control over the Moskva from its head waters to its mouth. Thus the "river policy" of the Muscovite princes and the later tsars of Russia originated with the very founders of the dynasty.

Ivan, the second son of Daniel, is known as Kalita, or "Money Bags," because of the use he made of his seemingly plentiful supply of money. His heritage consisted of only four or five town-districts and the peasant villages surrounding them, but it also included the considerable treasury that his predecessors had built by levying duty upon the trade that passed up and down the Moskva river.

Soon after succeeding his brother as prince of Moscow, Ivan became grand prince of Russia* and received from the Mongol-Tatar khan the *yarlik*, or official confirmation, without which he would have had no authority. Furthermore, the khan appointed Ivan his collector of tribute from the Russian lands. Ivan turned this thankless assignment to his own good use. Although Christian Russia was

---

* Technically, he became grand prince of Vladimir. The Grand Principality of Vladimir was the name for the East Slav state at this time, earlier, it had been the Grand Principality of Kiev. To the west lay the Grand Principality of Lithuania. The prince of Moscow could will his principality to his heirs, but the yarlik, or appointment as grand prince of Vladimir, might be give to any of the princely family whom the khan chose to name. As a matter of fact, the princes of Moscow after Ivan I were almost always appointed grand princes of Vladimir.

free of the humiliation of having Moslem Tatars visit every town each year to demand tribute, Ivan and his successors proved themselves to be as efficient and as merciless in gathering the levy as ever the conquerors could have been. They did not hesitate to resort to force if necessary. When the citizens of Tver revolted against payment of the tribute, Ivan led an army of Tatars, accompanied by a small band of his own Muscovites, against Tver and laid waste the entire principality.

Ivan employed the profit that he realized from serving the khan as tax collector to expand his own possessions. He bought Galich, far to the northeast beyond the Volga and close to the rich fur country that belonged to Novgorod. He found a bargain in the town-district of Beloozero, a spot even closer to Novgorodian territory. By the purchase of Uglich, north of Moscow, he obtained land on the mighty Volga itself. In all these cases he allowed the princes of those towns to stay on and govern in his name, and the districts fell to the principality of Moscow only in the reign of his grandson. Ivan married his daughters to the princes of Rostov and Yaroslavl, both near neighbors, and by so doing brought those princes under his influence even if he could not bring their lands under his control. Thus, by purchase of land and by marriage, Ivan and his sons contributed to the growing importance of Moscow. His grandson was not so patient and resorted to firm pressure and even to war when he could win territory in no other way.

Ivan Kalita ruled his principality like a landowner managing his estates. There were no town vieches to contest his authority or to embarrass him by rising against the Tatars. Indeed, the absence of a vieche or of any other check whatsoever on the authority of the prince, ordained that Moscow—principality now or tsardom or empire later—would develop as an autocratic state. From the moment of Ivan's accession, the chronicler maintains "there was thenceforth a great quietness throughout the Russian land, and the Tatars ceased fighting against the Russian land." Punitive expeditions against those who refused to pay tribute were sometimes necessary, but the prince of Moscow led them in the khan's name. Contemporaries must have considered Ivan a scoundrel and a renegade. Actually, he exhibited the same good sense that Alexander Nevsky had shown earlier in not risking the complete destruction of Russia by challenging the khan.

The "great quietness" that spread over his principality gave it the character of a sanctuary. Peasants from the south sought refuge there in the hope of tilling the land in peace, and found the well-to-do prince of Moscow willing to advance them money to buy seeds and tools. Boyars left the service of other princes to enlist under him, for there was more prestige and more promise of gain in serving the grand prince whom the khan trusted above all others. Ivan and his successors ransomed thousands of Russian captives from the Tatars and settled them in Moscow. This flow of population raised the productivity and the prosperity of Ivan's territory and brought into it additional taxpayers to fill the prince's coffers.

At the end of the thirteenth century, the then metropolitan of Kiev, alarmed that the population of south Russia was melting away and disappearing into the north to escape Tatar violence, left the city on the Dnieper and moved to Vladimir, the new capital of the grand principality on the river Kliazma. From his new home, however, it was necessary to visit the Kievan bishoprics periodically, and on such journeys the metropolitan often stopped to rest at Moscow. There his successor, Metropolitan Peter, developed a friendship with Ivan Kalita. Peter and Ivan worked together in founding the Cathedral of the Assumption in the Moscow Kremlin. The old metropolitan told Ivan that he wished to be buried in the new church and prophesied a great future for the prince of Moscow who had helped to found it. After Peter's death in 1326 a number of miracles conveniently transpired at the site of his tomb, and the spot soon became the goal of pilgrimages from all over Russia. Peter's successor moved the metropolitical seat permanently to Moscow. Peter's tomb became a national shrine, and the city in which it rested and from which Peter's successors ruled over the Russian church became the religious capital of the land.

When Ivan died in 1341, his son Simeon (1341-1353) was received with great cordiality by the khan and promptly won the appointment as grand prince. Because of his domineering attitude toward the other princes, Simeon was known as "the Haughty." To the Tatars he was subservient, assuring the khan that Russia was his "faithful province," but he urged the princes to stand together and accept his rule dutifully, for only if the land were firmly united would it some day be possible to throw off the alien yoke. Because the prince of Moscow had the power of the khan to enforce his commands, there was nothing the other princes could do but obey him.

Simeon, like his father, gave every encouragement to the church and received in return its staunch support. Foreign artists and native painters schooled in Constantinople came to cast bells for and decorate the cathedral churches of Moscow and Novgorod. Moscow, with its brilliantly adorned churches and its miracle-working tombs, was fast succeeding Kiev in the minds of the faithful as a sacred city. North of Moscow, St. Sergius founded the Monastery of the Trinity. It grew to be one of the richest and most venerated in the land, and the respect that the monastery achieved added much to the rapidly growing religious importance of the Moscow area.

Simeon the Haughty died of the plague. His brother Ivan II (1353-1359), called the Fair, ruled for six years as prince of Moscow and grand prince of Russia. Ivan's mild and gentle nature inspired only contempt from the other princes, who showed no respect for his authority and who warred among themselves and insulted even the grand prince himself with impunity. Anarchy reminiscent of the declining days of Kiev descended over the land. Even his own district governors were assassinated, and Ivan let the criminals go free. Then Metropolitan Alexis stepped forward to steady the government and carry out the tasks that Ivan should have shouldered. Alexis was highly respected by the Mongol-Tatars, to whose headquarters he journeyed often to mollify the khan. The khan's confidence in the wisdom and justice of this metropolitan of the Russian church must have been great, for he could not have supposed that the power would be exercised by the weak-willed Ivan II. When Ivan died in 1359, he left a minor to succeed him, and the metropolitan governed as regent and guardian until the young prince reached maturity.

Reasons for Muscovite Success

Alexander Nevsky's bequest of the insignificant principality of Moscow to his youngest son Daniel had produced unexpected results by the middle of the fourteenth century. Moscow by then had become the capital of Russia. Less than a century earlier it had been a small group of buildings serving as a resting station for the grand prince on his journeys from Vladimir to the Dnieper. A number of factors contributed to this transformation.

Moscow's geographical location gave the town a tremendous advantage. It lay on the Moskva river at the spot where the tributary Yauza flows into it, and the upper reaches of the Yauza approach very near to the Kliazma. This was a great trade highway long before the building of the Kremlin, for the river Kliazma flows east to join the Oka not far from Nizhni Novgorod on the Volga. From its source to its mouth the Volga was always an important avenue of communication. Moscow lay almost exactly in the center of the "Russian Mesopotamia," midway between the Volga and the Oka rivers. One could travel from Moscow to the Dnieper by going up the Oka and its tributary the Ugra, and then portaging directly to the Dnieper above the important trade town of Smolensk. At Smolensk the traveler was on the ancient water road "from the Varangians to the Greeks."

Moscow was ideally located, then, at the heart of a network of trade routes, both land and water, that could offer rich opportunity to the merchants who settled there. The early princes encouraged the flow of trade through Moscow, but they also taxed it. Merchants who stayed the night in Moscow paid for their shelter and care and for the security their boats or pack trains enjoyed. Moscow soon became an important market, and those who displayed their wares in its streets paid for the privilege. A steady flow of fees fed the treasury of the Moscow princes. They carefully invested the money—buying up land, endowing the church, bribing the khan—in ways that brought rich return to Daniel and his successors.

Moscow gained peace and security from the sheltered position in the very center of Russia. There was no problem of foreign relations, little need to fear foreign aggression. Although the grand prince of Lithuania might occasionally press eastward dangerously close to Moscow territory, it was the principalities lying to the west of Moscow, such as Tver and Smolensk, that took the blow. To the east the principalities of Rostov, Nizhni Novgorod, and Riazan absorbed the shock of Mongol fury when it came.

The prince of Moscow gained an enormous advantage over the other princes by winning and keeping in his family the yarlik, which set him apart as grand prince. He was much more an absolute ruler than the later princes of Kiev had been because the power of the khan backed up his authority. His absolutism may have been somewhat secondhand, but for all that no one dared question it. When Ivan the Fair received from the khan judicial authority over the other princes, all the rest had to look up to him, court his favor, beg his mercy, and respect his judgment. What the Russian princes may have gained, by having one of them for judge and by avoiding the long journey to Tatar headquarters, must at times have been offset by the fact that the prince of Moscow looked on every dispute, whether he himself was a party to it or not, from the point of view of his own interests. The early princes of Moscow assiduously courted the khan's favor. Princes of Tver or of Riazan might tempt disaster by rising against the Tatars, but those of Moscow saw clearly that they could only win over the khan by "peaceful cunning," by fawning servility, and by offering bribes. No prince more often went to pay his respects to the khan than did Ivan Kalita.

Moscow profited immeasurably from Ivan's foresight in currying the friendship of the metropolitan of the Russian Orthodox church. The tomb of the Metropolitan Peter became a national shrine, and he and the other early metropolitans of Moscow were beatified. The early Muscovite princes assured the church of their protection, built churches for its edification, and gave liberally to it from their treasuries. In return the princes received the church's support and blessing in their rise to power.

Members of the monastic orders gave support to the growing power of Moscow in their own way. They founded monasteries in the sparsely settled wilderness, and this prompted colonists to follow them. Thus, there was a steady flow of clergy and settlers to the north and east into the rich fur country, and Moscow was early able to contest the area's control by Novgorod. Missionaries from the Troitsky or Trinity Monastery crossed the Volga to the north of Moscow and built cloisters deep in Novgorodian territory. The settlements that soon grew up around them filled with Muscovites, giving a later prince of Moscow a claim to the land because his own people lived there.

An important factor in Moscow's rise to preeminence was the absence of dispute over the succession. This was only partly the result of the fortuitous scarcity of heirs. When a prince left more than one son, as did Daniel and Ivan Kalita, there was never any warring among the brothers. When Daniel's elder son Yuri succeeded him, the younger son Ivan accepted the settlement without question, and contented himself with serving as viceroy in Moscow while Yuri held forth at Vladimir as grand prince. Because Yuri left no sons, Ivan's turn came when his brother died. Kalita again left two sons, but there was no disagreement over the succession. Simeon ruled proudly over his brother as well as over the other princes, and the death of his sons before him precluded any contest over the principality when the plague struck him down. There was a single exception to this rule of uncontested succession, and the exception caused a flurry for less than two years. The reason for these peaceful successions lies in the fact that the princes of Moscow made testamentary provision for all sons, if there were more than one, but were careful always to leave the title and the bulk of the inheritance to the oldest son.

Daniel's original appanage consisted of less than five hundred square miles. A century and a half later the principality of Moscow had grown thirty times over to about fifteen thousand square miles. That phenomenal expansion, to which every one of the early princes made a contribution, was the result of a number of circumstances. Favorable location and good fortune certainly played their part. However, the political acumen of the early princes—careful stewardship of their estates, shrewd investment of treasure, keen understanding of the political milieu in which they lived, groveling before the conqueror when there was no force with which to oppose him—was responsible above all for the accumulation of power that ultimately enabled Moscow to contest Tatar domination.

The Polish-Lithuanian Challenge

Paralleling the growth of the Moscow state was the rise in the west of the grand principality of Lithuania, which by the fifteenth century had gained control over the basin of the Dnieper. Impelled by pressure from the Teutonic knights in the early thirteenth century, the various tribes of Lithuanians united under Prince Mindovg, seized Grodno, which became his capital, and drove east up the valley of the Niemen into Russian territory. Pressed on one side by Alexander Nevsky and on the other by the German knights, Mindovg embraced Roman Christianity in the hope that the knights would halt their crusade against his people. When this forlorn hope did not materialize, the prince returned to his pagan ways and wreaked stern vengeance on the Teutons.

Anarchy among the Lithuanians following Mindovg's rule ended in 1316 with the appearance of Prince Gedimin. Not only did he reunite the Lithuanians but he also added to the state twice as much Russian as Lithuanian land. From his new capital of Vilna, Gedimin ruled over a principality stretching from Polotsk on the Western Dvina to Kiev on the Dnieper. Not until the seventeenth century would Kiev return to Russian control. While he and his people kept to their pagan customs, Gedimin tolerated Orthodoxy, and Russian influence at the Lithuanian court was strong. Lithuanians and Russians lived together in peace and intermarried freely. The great threat to Lithuanian independence was the aggression of the German knights, and Gedimin took Mindovg's way of seeking to counteract it; he offered to embrace Roman Catholicism if the pope could persuade the knights to cease their attacks. This the pope was unable to do, and the missionaries were expelled. Gedimin received a pagan burial in 1345.

Gedimin's son, Olgerd, pushed the Lithuanian border far to the east and south. The seizure of Podolia on the Southwestern Bug from the Tatars carried the Lithuanian frontier to the shores of the Black Sea. Olgerd attacked Novgorod and encouraged its vassal Pskov in its efforts to win independence. He sought an alliance with Prince Simeon the Haughty of Moscow, but then attacked Simeon's nephew Dmitry and advanced almost within sight of the Kremlin.

Olgerd's successor, his son Yagailo, overwhelmingly defeated the Teutonic knights. His marriage to the Polish queen brought about the union of Poland

and Lithuania. Poland, suffering from internal dissension and the encroachments of its nobles upon the central authority, was under pressure on the east by the Lithuanians and on the north by the German knights. Polish leaders proposed to absorb the one enemy, Lithuania, and concentrate their combined strength on the other, the Teutonic Order. In 1386 Yagailo converted to Roman Christianity for the occasion, married Queen Jadwiga of Poland, changed his name to Wladyslaw II, king of Poland, and moved his capital to Krakow. Priests converted the Lithuanians to Christianity, and Polish nobles received estates in Lithuania.

Yagailo's attempt to force Polish customs, Polish landowners, and "Latinism" upon the Lithuanian and Russian people under his rule provoked bitter opposition. His nephew Vitovt united the dissident elements in the eastern districts and declared war on Yagailo and the Poles; the king of Poland was forced to give way. Vitovt became grand prince of Lithuania, technically subordinate to the Polish king but in effect completely independent. The union of Poland and Lithuania was purely dynastic, and the two might even have gone their separate ways again had it not been for external pressures that later forced them into a firmer union.

Vitovt set about to restore the former brilliance of Lithuania and to conquer new territory to the east and south. He seized the Russian principality of Smolensk, and so became next-door neighbor to the princes of Tver, Moscow, and Riazan. Only these lands and those of Novgorod and Pskov remained in Russian hands, and Vitovt had hopes that even they some day would be part of Lithuania. In the meantime he proposed to conquer the Golden Horde. The Mongol-Tatars on the lower Volga, known as the Golden Horde, had won their independence from the great khan in Central Asia, and this division of Tatar power gave Vitovt reason to hope for victory.

However, the Lithuanian prince soon ran into complications. A new conqueror, Tamerlane, became the great khan in Asia and determined to reunite all Mongol-Tatars and expand their empire. The rebellious khan of the Golden Horde was driven from his capital at Sarai and sought refuge with Vitovt. Ambitious himself to absorb the Golden Horde's territory and to add it, together with Moscow and the rest of Russia, to his expanding principality, Vitovt gathered a mighty army at Kiev in 1399. His Lithuanian force was joined by Polish troops sent by Yagailo, by detachments contributed by several Russian princes, by Mongols of the Golden Horde who had fled from Tamerlane, and even by five hundred Teutonic knights. On the banks of the river Vorskla, which enters the Dnieper above the cataracts, the formidable array met the Mongols. So fearsome was the western host that Tamerlane offered to arrange a peace, but Vitovt ordered the great khan to surrender. In the battle that ensued, Vitovt's army, outnumbered and outmaneuvered, was beaten and two-thirds of it was left on the field. The rest fled beyond the Dnieper, and Tamerlane laid a heavy indemnity upon Kiev.

After the disaster on the Vorskla, Vitovt gave up his plan to subdue the Golden Horde and conquer Russia. His greatest triumph still lay before him. When the Prussians, a Lithuanian people, rebelled against the oppression of the Teutonic knights who ruled over them, Vitovt went to their relief. Again a mighty army gathered under him, for his fame as a fighter won him widespread respect. Tatars came from the Golden Horde to serve with his Poles and Lithuanians, and Russians joined the host. Although technically Yagailo, or Wladyslaw II of Poland, commanded the force, it was Vitovt's leadership that was most responsible for the victory that followed. At the battle of Tannenberg in 1410, the Teutonic knights lost decisively and the grand master and many of the knights were slain. The Russians contributed to this great victory of Slav over German, and the power of the Teutonic Order collapsed.

The cooperation of Poles and Lithuanians at Tannenberg led to closer political ties between the two nations. Three years after the great victory, Vitovt led his Lithuanian nobles to a conference with Yagailo and his Polish lords to work out a union of their subjects. The terms provided that Lithuanian nobles who embraced Catholicism should enjoy the privileges of the Polish nobility and that a council of Polish and Lithuanian lords should settle common issues and elect Polish kings and Lithuanian grand princes. Vitovt later considered renouncing the agreement and seeking recognition as king of Lithuania, but the Poles with papal backing blocked the move. The old man died in 1430 at the age of eighty, and with his death Lithuania speedily declined. Finally, at the Union of Lublin in 1569, Lithuania and Poland became one, and soon thereafter hurled their combined strength once more against Russia. Their cooperation was less an effort to seize Russian territory than it was to brace themselves against the unrelenting Muscovite drive to the west. Efforts of tsarist and Soviet historians to color the operation as an attack on Russia are imaginative.

Dmitry Defies the Tatars

Ivan the Fair, prince of Moscow and grand prince of Russia, died in 1359 leaving two minor sons. The older, Dmitry, became prince of Moscow (1359–1389), and the metropolitan of Moscow ruled in his name as his guardian. However, a child of ten, even with the church's blessing, could not command the respect of all the Russian princes, many of whom had scorned the authority of the child's weak father. The prince of Suzdalia secured the yarlik for Moscow after the death of Ivan II and with it the title of grand prince. His own brother rebuked him for it, for many of the princes were certain that only under Moscow's leadership could Russia rid itself of the alien yoke. Now the metropolitan put the young Prince Dmitry of Moscow at the head of an army that marched on the capital city of Vladimir and literally captured the title of grand prince from the grasping prince of Suzdalia.

The Golden Horde was beginning to disintegrate in the latter half of the thirteenth century. Contests for the throne were frequent and there already were signs that segments might fall away and become independent, as the Golden Horde itself had become practically independent of the great khan in Asia. The Russians were quick to grasp the significance of this Tatar decadence, and by Dmitry's time, a number of Russian princes were ready to try their strength against the oppressor. The prince of Riazan gathered a small force and dared to punish the Tatars for having ravaged his principality. The prince of Nizhni Novgorod put to death the khan's envoys and fifteen hundred troops who accompanied them, although the Tatars sacked his capital the following year in retaliation. Dmitry himself defied the khan on a number of occasions. He attacked Kazan and withdrew only when the Tatars paid him to do so. In 1378 he tackled the khan's army with a large force and won a signal triumph. "Their time is past and God is with us!" Dmitry boasted after the victory.

To punish such insolence and to restore the payment of tribute that Dmitry now refused, Khan Mamai assembled a great army of Tatars, Turks, Polovtsy, and even Genoese from their trading towns in the Crimea. The prince of Riazan aided the cause of Russia's enemies by arranging an alliance between the khan of the Golden Horde and Yagailo, at that time grand prince of Lithuania. The two were to attack simultaneously, and Dmitry of Moscow would be crushed between them.

In August 1380, Dmitry led his army through the principality of Riazan to meet Mamai and his Tatars and beat them back from Moscow. Word came to him en route that the Tatars were turning westward to join forces with the Lithuanians, so Dmitry marched south to put himself between the two enemies. His army crossed the Don east of present-day Tula and lined up on a meadow known as Kulikovo Pole (the snipe field). The Mongol-Tatars attacked, but were quickly routed and fled. The chroniclers say that Mamai lost one hundred thousand men; Russian losses must have been equally severe.

Dmitry, henceforth called Donskoi ("of the Don [River]") in honor of his victory on the Don, became something of a hero all over Russia. He had proved that the Tatar was not invincible, and inspired his people to hope that the oppression might soon end. Unfortunately, the victory came only at a terrible cost. The khan could quickly refill his ranks, but Dmitry's loss was irreparable. It was his great misfortune to beat back the Golden Horde only to face a new threat. Tamerlane, engaged in reuniting the Tatars, welcomed the defeat of Mamai. He ordered Mamai executed, and the Golden Horde came once more under the authority of the great khan.

Now Tamerlane called on the Russian princes to appear at Sarai, but Dmitry refused. Marshaling another force, Tamerlane sent his finest general, Tokhtamysh, to punish the prince of Moscow. Dmitry left his capital to gather another army, but met only with indifference among the princes, who had had enough. While he was gone Tokhtamysh captured Moscow, razed the city, and slew twenty thousand inhabitants. Mozhaisk, Vladimir, and other towns belonging to the prince of Moscow received similar treatment. Unable to win support for another campaign, Dmitry could only resume payment of the Tatar tribute and admit the khan's sovereignty over the Russian land.

Dmitry Donskoi salved his disappointment by wreaking vengeance on the traitorous prince of Riazan. The prince managed to escape, but his capital was sacked as thoroughly as though the Tatars themselves had done it. The prince of Riazan fought back, but the abbot of the Trinity Monastery threatened him

Valiant Knights *by Apolinari Vasnetsov*

with anathema unless he arranged a peace with Dmitry. Kulikovo had so weakened Donskoi that he was unable to triumph even over the prince of Riazan.

He was more successful, however, in punishing Novgorod for the depredations of the "Volga men," those bands of Novgorodian outlaws who pillaged Muscovite settlements in the territory north of the Volga. In 1386, the grand prince led an army against the great republic, forced it to pay an indemnity, and laid it under an annual tribute to Moscow. By its refusal to join in the crusade against the Tatars and by the frequent enlistment of its boyars in the service of Lithuania, Novgorod had merited little sympathy. Less than a century of independence lay before it.

Dmitry's tilts with the Tatars are perhaps the most spectacular and dramatic events of his reign, but they do not tell the whole story. He continued his predecessors' policy of aggrandizement of his position and territory. He exalted his authority over the other princes and took the attitude that the succession to the grand principality was not open to question, that it must go as a matter of course to the prince of Moscow. With the exception of Tver and Riazan, the princes of north central Russia recognized him as "elder brother." He treated the territory of Vladimir, which went with the title of grand prince, as though it were part of his patrimony. Dmitry added more territory to the principality than he had received as his inheritance, and he continued the river policy of his predecessors by adding lands of strategic and commercial importance. Nearly the whole left bank of the Volga almost to Kazan came under his rule. The principality of Riazan was all but surrounded by Muscovite land, as were the principalities of Rostov, Suzdalia, and Nizhni Novgorod. Moscow even moved into the Don river system when Dmitry won control over the headwaters of its tributary, the Voronezh. His successors had simply to fill in the gaps in order to make the territory of Moscow contiguous and in absolute control of the strategically located river network of north central Russia.

The Growing Strength of Moscow

Dmitry left two sons of whom the elder, Vasily I (1389–1425), succeeded to the throne without dispute. He did not travel to the Horde to be confirmed, but took over his patrimony and his title of grand prince in full confidence that they were rightfully his and that his father had left no doubts about either one.

Soon after his accession Vasily set out to fill in the remaining gaps in his territory. In 1392 he went to Sarai, accompanied by a large band of attendants, and ceremoniously and with great pomp presented himself to the khan. With rich presents he prevailed upon the khan to grant him possession of the principalities of Suzdalia, Nizhni Novgorod, and Murom.

Dmitry Donskoi had decreed that "when my son Vasily dies, his territory shall go to the brother next after him." Vasily died in 1425, leaving a brother and a ten-year-old son. The brother, Yuri, insisted that Donskoi's will meant that he should become grand prince. By long tradition, ever since the time of the first prince of Moscow, however, the throne had descended from father to son when there was a son to receive it. For the time being Yuri was unable to gain the princely title because the dead Vasily's son, Vasily II (1425–1462), had as his guardian his maternal uncle, the powerful Vitovt, grand prince of Lithuania. When the guardian's death in 1430 left Vasily II to his own devices, envoys of both Yuri and the young prince went before the khan to settle the matter. By groveling flattery the grandson of Dmitry of the Don won the contest and was named grand prince. Yet, for the next twenty years there was civil war between Yuri and his sons and Vasily II over who should hold the title of grand prince.

During most of that time Vasily II ruled in Moscow, whose citizens gave him their unqualified support simply because he was his father's rightful heir and the interest of the state seemed to them to demand allegiance to him. For brief moments Vasily II lost his throne and his capital to his uncle or one of the uncle's sons. So divided was the territory of Moscow that Vasily could muster only fifteen hundred men against the Tatars when they raided his land and carried him away prisoner to the new Tatar city of Kazan on the middle Volga. The prince of Tver raided Muscovite territory when he chose, and armed bands of Lithuanians, Tatars, and Novgorodian outlaws roamed and plundered the land

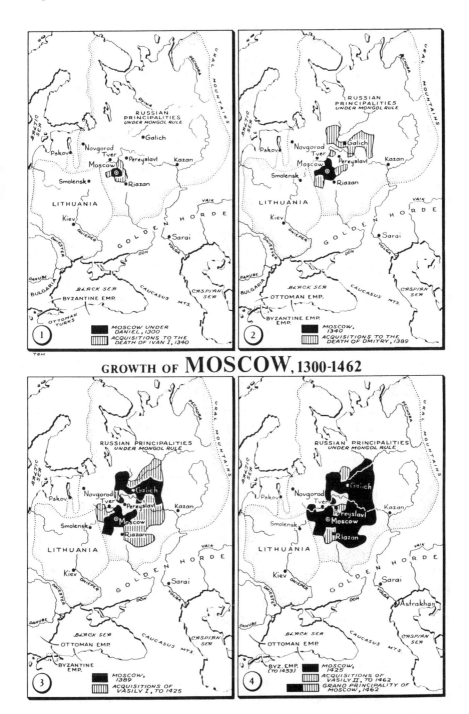

GROWTH OF MOSCOW, 1300-1462

at will. On one occasion Vasily was captured and blinded by Yuri's son, and came to be known as Vasily the Dark, or the Blind.

Yuri's son, petty, selfish, and utterly unscrupulous, so enraged the Muscovites by his complete disregard for the state's welfare that by 1450 he was driven into retirement and died soon after. Only then was Vasily the Dark free to take up the work of the earlier princes of Moscow. During the last twelve years of his reign he added much to the state territory. He ruthlessly dispossessed petty princes who still held small independent appanages and forced them into his service.

During the reign of Vasily II, the territory of Moscow expanded far to the northeast. The expansion went forward, not on the military exploits of the ruler, but on the peaceful settlement of Muscovite colonists. Some Muscovites were fleeing the civil war that made life in the neighborhood of Moscow unbearable, and others were simply seeking opportunity in the fur country beyond the Volga. The Muscovites came as settlers, hunting and trapping but also clearing away the forest and tilling the soil. Novgorod, which claimed the district, sent into it only a few traders and fur-gathering expeditions, and soon its hold was broken by the colonists from Moscow who came to build homes. Novgorod protested and tried to get Vasily to agree to a division of the territory along boundaries that both would respect, but no settlement was possible, for the settlers from Moscow continued spilling over any line that could be drawn.

The reign of Vasily the Dark was an important one in the development of the Russian Orthodox church. In 1438, the Byzantine emperor at Constantinople, hard pressed by the Ottoman Turks who were driving against his borders, suggested to the pope at Rome a union of the Eastern and Western churches to heal the schism that had divided them since 1054. The emperor hoped that religious union might pave the way for cooperation of East and West in a great crusade to save his empire. A Church Council met at Florence in 1439, and to it went a great concourse of Eastern patriarchs, bishops, and metropolitans, including Isidore, the metropolitan of Moscow. The Western clergy offered to leave the Orthodox followers free to pursue their different ritualistic practice but insisted upon recognition of the pope's authority over all Christendom. Although the Eastern clergy refused to unite with the West on such grounds, the metropolitan of Moscow accepted them. Vasily the Dark and the bishops of the Russian church, however, would have nothing to do with the settlement, and the metropolitan was driven from Moscow.

When Constantinople fell to the Turks a few years later, in 1453, in part because the failure of religious union prevented political cooperation between East and West, the Russian church severed all connection with the patriarch of Constantinople. A council of Russian bishops elected its own metropolitan to rule over the Russian church as an independent body. After the fall of Constantinople, the Orthodox faithful all over Eastern Europe came to look upon the metropolitan of Moscow as the head of the Eastern church and upon Moscow as their religious capital.

Anxious that his son should not have to endure his own tragic experience of civil war, Vasily the Dark took Ivan, the heir apparent, into the administration long before his death and accustomed his subjects to regard the son as ruler in Moscow. Ivan's practical experience thus paved the way for an easy transition to the new reign after the death of his blind father. In 1462 Ivan succeeded to the grand principality without incident and to a territory far larger than that of any other prince in northern Russia. Only Novgorod controlled more territory, but the internal disturbances to which it was chronically subjected intimated its early demise.

Suggested Reading

ALMEDINGEN, E. M., *The Land of Muscovy: The History of Early Russia* (New York, 1972).

The Chronicle of Novgorod, 1016–1471 (Hattiesburg, MS, 1970).

BILLINGTON, J. H., *The Icon and the Axe: An Interpretive History of Russian Culture* (New York, 1966).

FEDOTOV, G., *The Russian Religious Mind: The Middle Ages: The Thirteenth to the Fifteenth Centuries* (Cambridge, 1966).

FENNELL, J., *The Emergence of Moscow, 1304–1359* (Berkeley, 1968).

HALPERIN, C. J., *Russia and the Golden Horde: The Mongol Impact on Medieval Russian History* (Bloomington, IN, 1985).

HOWES, R. C. (comp.), *The Testaments of the Grand Princes of Moscow* (Ithaca, NY, 1967).

KAISER, D. H., *The Growth of the Law in Medieval Russia* (Princeton, 1980).

KARGER, M., *Novgorod The Great: Architectural Guidebook* (Moscow, 1973).

MILIUKOV, P. N., C. SEIGNOBOS, and L. EISENMANN, *History of Russia*, vol. 1 (New York, 1968).

PASZKIEWICZ, H., *The Making of the Russian Nation* (Chicago, 1963).

_____, *The Rise of Moscow's Power* (New York, 1983).

PRESNIAKOV, A. E., *The Formation of the Great Russian State: Study of Russian History in the 13th to 15th Centuries* (Chicago, 1970).

THOMPSON, W. W. *Novgorod the Great: Excavations of the Medieval City* (New York, 1967).

VERNADSKY, G., *Russia at the Dawn of the Modern Age* (New Haven, 1959).

VERNADSKY, G., and M. KARPOVICH, *The Mongols and Russia* (New Haven, 1953).

VOYCE, A., *The Art and Architecture of Medieval Russia* (Norman, OK, 1967).

WALSH, W. B., *Readings in Russian History*, vol. I (Syracuse, 1963).

ZENKOVSKY, S. A. (ed.), *Medieval Russia's Epics, Chronicles, and Tales* (New York, 1963).

_____, *The Nikonian Chronicle*, 5 vols. (Princeton, 1984–1989).

CHAPTER 5

The Emergence of the Moscow State

The principality of Moscow constituted an almost solid block of territory straddling the upper Volga and the Oka, stretching away to the Northern Dvina in the northeast, nearly to Lake Onega in the northwest, almost to Kazan in the east, and into the Don basin in the south. The Lithuanian border was less than a hundred miles to the west of the city of Moscow, and Tver was even closer on the northwest. Moscow had just about reached the limit of possible expansion without encroaching on the possessions of the large states that surrounded it. Its princes had developed a habit of adding territory to their heritage and welcomed the title "collectors of the Russian soil." The Russian people wherever they might be living had come to look upon the Moscow princes as national leaders, as champions of the cause of national independence, as harbingers of national unity. The Russian church had supported and encouraged the princes of Moscow in their gathering of the Russian land. Now the new grand prince would continue along the course marked out by his predecessors.

Ivan III, The Great (1462–1505)

Ivan III at twenty-two was no stranger to the problems of governing his principality. For fifteen years he had been associated with his father in administration. Loyally devoted to the church as an institution but somewhat troubled by its principles, Ivan did not hesitate to imprison his brother and nephews when they conspired against him, although he wept copious tears at their deaths. For traitors—boyars, princes, or clergy—he calmly ordered the brutal tortures that all rulers of his time employed. He was not lacking in courage, although his enemies charged him with cowardice. He avoided war whenever possible or sent lieutenants to lead his troops into battle. Ivan inherited from his forebears a mastery of diplomacy, trickery, and double-dealing by which he often accomplished his purpose without the expense of a costly campaign. Like Ivan Kalita, he kept careful watch over the treasury and opened his purse only when there was a promise of good return.

Ten years after his accession Ivan, a widower, married Zoe, or Sophia, Paleologue, the orphaned niece of the last Byzantine emperor; she had lived for years in Rome as ward of the pope. Papal hopes that the marriage might generate the union of Orthodoxy and Catholicism under the pope were unfulfilled, however, probably as a result of stubborn resistance by the metropolitan of Moscow. That a prince who was still a vassal of a Mongol khan should be accepted by a bride of such noble connections suggests that Ivan of Moscow had won recognition far beyond the borders of his principality. The grand prince appropriated to his own use the dignity and recognition that his second marriage brought him. He added the Byzantine double-headed eagle to his crest and seal, adopted the court formality long practiced in the West, and, at least in correspondence with other rulers, referred to himself as Tsar, or Caesar. Later he announced himself to be Autocrat, a title which at the time only identified him as independent.

The Fall of Novgorod

The expansion of Lithuania under Olgerd and Vitovt had freed the Dnieper water road from the Tatars, and by 1450 Lithuania controlled the river from Smolensk to its mouth on the Black Sea. This tempted Novgorod to offer itself to the grand prince of Lithuania, for only by so doing could its merchants obtain the right to trade up and down the Dnieper. Kiev would once again lie open to Novgorod merchants, and from it Russian furs could pass by overland route into Galicia, Hungary, Austria, Bohemia, and south Germany. For centuries the Hansa had sold the furs of Novgorod in Western Europe. Now once more, if the great republic were to join Lithuania, Novgorodians themselves might control that profitable trade.

To break away from Moscow would mean excommunication from Orthodoxy, but there was a remedy for that. Kiev now had its own metropolitan—a heretic, it was true, who recognized the authority of the pope, but nevertheless a metropolitan—who could invest the archbishop of Novgorod if the metropolitan of Moscow should refuse to do so. Indeed, the commercial attraction of the Dnieper and Kiev as a gateway to Central Europe was so strong that a number of wealthy Novgorodians hailed the metropolitan of Kiev as the only bona fide church leader in the Russian land, and denounced the metropolitan of Moscow for serving a grand prince who was vassal to the infidel khan of the Golden Horde.

Finally, there was sound political reason for Novgorod's interest in becoming part of Lithuania. After Vitovt's death in 1430, the power of Lithuania and the vigor of its rulers waned, whereas Moscow was becoming more and more formidable and threatening. Novgorod's fur empire to the northeast was suffering encroachment by Muscovite settlers. The eventual inundation of its territory and the loss of its freedom seemed inevitable if Novgorod were to continue its tie with northern Russia. After all, there were many Russians, people and princes, who were part of Lithuania. Why should Novgorod not join them? It would not be as if it were completely deserting the Russian land. Perhaps, if its own declining power were added to the waning force of Lithuania, the union might prevent the absorption of all Russia by the insatiable prince of Moscow. By such reasoning some Novgorodians may have justified their hope to join Lithuania. That the

Ivan III, the Great

prince and metropolitan of Moscow would accuse them of treason to the land and the church they could have no doubt.

The Novgorodian leaders must have been fully aware that desertion to Lithuania and the metropolitan of Kiev would precipitate rebellion among the faithful Orthodox lower classes of the republic. However, the religious factor was not the only one impelling Novgorodian commoners to oppose their leaders. Politically, they opposed the boyar class in the city, for the "freedom of Novgorod" meant little to the lower classes. Economically, the wealth of Novgorod went chiefly to the boyars and the commercial magnates; the mass of urban and rural laborers faced increasing poverty. The lower classes tended to support Moscow because they hoped that Moscow would curb the power of the Novgorodian merchants.

Vasily the Dark had severely punished Novgorod for its pro-Lithuanian leanings, and exacted a promise not to shelter any prince who opposed his suzerainty over the city. Nevertheless, hardly had Vasily turned his back than the leading citizens brought in a Lithuanian to become the city's prince. He stayed only a short time, and another brought in later also left soon after arrival. As it turned out, for the Novgorodian leaders there could be no drawing back once they had named Lithuanians to the princely office. The city had broken its agreement with Moscow and revenge was sure to follow. Vasily was preparing to lead an army against Novgorod in 1462 when he died. In 1470 the city's leaders went the whole way, recognizing the king of Poland as their sovereign and promising him as much in taxes as they had been paying in Tatar tribute to Moscow. In return, they received his guarantee to safeguard the "ancient liberties" of Novgorod and not to restrict Orthodoxy. Moscow's answer to this precipitate step followed immediately.

Ivan III considered Novgorod to be part of his "patrimony," for the grand princes of Moscow had long insisted upon the right to name the princes of Novgorod. The khan of the Horde, Moscow's overlord, recognized that right. So, in 1471, Ivan led an army against Novgorod to put the rebellious republic in its place. Until then he had been amazingly patient and forebearing of the city's duplicity. In 1470, Ivan had warned Novgorod: "Mend your ways towards me, my patrimony, and recognize us; keep my name of Grand Prince in strictness and in honor as of old; and send to me representatives to do homage and to make settlement. I desire to keep you, my patrimony, in good favor, on the old conditions." The Moscow party in the city, led by the archbishop of Novgorod, demanded reconciliation with Ivan, but the Lithuanian party had won out. "We are free, we are no patrimony," some had shouted in the vieche, and the arrangement with the king of Poland passed the assembly. Thereupon, says the chronicler, Ivan "informed his patrimony that his power of endurance was exhausted, and that he would not suffer their misbehavior and contumacy any longer." The metropolitan of Moscow also had written repeatedly to Novgorod, urging the citizens not to give in to Latin blandishments and calling upon them to stand firm in the true faith. His pleas probably never reached the vieche and made no impression upon the wealthy boyars who favored the union with

Lithuania. Novgorod severed its connections with Moscow and braced itself against Ivan's wrath.

The campaign against Novgorod in 1471 was carefully planned. At the last minute Ivan sent another warning, "but the wicked people minded him not, and clung to the intention of abandoning Orthodoxy and giving themselves over to the King [of Poland]." Ivan at the head of a large army seized Torzhok and cut off the supply of grain on which Novgorod depended to feed its populace. The lower classes, starved when the city's access to grain was cut off by the seizure of Torzhok, rose against the officials and opened the city's gates.

Ivan's justice against those responsible for Novgorod's defection was stern but not vindictive. Only a few leaders of the pro-Lithuanian party were beheaded "for their conspiracy and crime in seeking to take to Latinism." Ivan transplanted to towns near Moscow many who had held high office; the rest of the citizens, led by the clergy, begged Ivan's forgiveness and received it. Novgorod had to pay an indemnity, admit Ivan's authority over its courts, and promise to have nothing to do with Poland-Lithuania.

The Lithuanian party in Novgorod did not completely disappear after the campaign of 1471. Only its leaders had been put to death, imprisoned, or exiled to other Russian cities. Other leaders rose to take their places, for as long as this border town retained control over its own actions, there was sure to be a group who honestly believed that the city's salvation lay in playing off one strong neighbor against the other. Ivan III returned to Novgorod in 1475 in his capacity as supreme judge in the city, put a number of the pro-Lithuanian party to trial on charges of treasonable intent and sympathy for Poland and Roman Catholicism, and packed them off to Moscow as prisoners.

Ivan demanded of Novgorod complete submission to his will and an end to pro-Lithuanian activity. When the warning went unheeded he sent an army against the city and put an end to its independence. This time the penalty was more severe. Again the leaders went to their deaths or to the torture chambers to confess or to incriminate others. Scores of leading families were scattered among other towns, their estates confiscated and turned over to families from Moscow who were moved to Novgorodian territory in large numbers. The aristocracy of Novgorod disappeared, and the peasants, freed from the oppression of the boyars, were organized into taxpaying peasant communes as in Moscow. On the whole, the peasants had no cause to regret the passing of the old order. In 1478, the republic officially died and it became part of the territory of the grand principality of Moscow. The great bell that had called its citizens to assembly was moved to Moscow to symbolize the end of the freedom of Novgorod.

Absorption of the Appanage Principalities

During the reign of Ivan III the power of the appanages of central Russia declined more and more until their rulers could not avoid incorporation with Moscow. Some found their territory surrounded by that of the grand prince. Others fell hopelessly into debt to Ivan for the Tatar tribute and could settle it only by willing their debts and their lands to Moscow. Some thought to take service with the grand prince of Lithuania, but any prince who tried to do so knew that he risked Muscovite wrath. Princes who entertained such thoughts found it safer and wiser to seek service with the prince of Moscow and to leave their estates to him. Where earlier appanage law had allowed the prince to settle his heritage on whomever he chose, now Ivan commanded that the lands of an appanage prince who died without heirs must pass to the grand prince. If these measures did not provide for every contingency there were still other ways to deal with an appanage prince.

The princes of Rostov and Yaroslavl offered their lands to Ivan III and took service at his court. Others with smaller estates—the princes of Viazma, Odoiev, Bielev, Mtsensk, Novosil, Vorotin,* and others followed suit. The addition of their domains to Moscow gave Ivan the entire right bank of the Desna to its mouth just above Kiev; it pushed the Lithuanian frontier far to the west, for some of these princes had been vassal to the grand prince of Lithuania since Vitovt's time. The last two princes of Riazan were Ivan's nephews, who were completely amenable to his will. One of them died without heirs, leaving half of the territory to Ivan, and the rest of it fell similarly to Moscow in the next reign.

The prince of Tver, who loyally supported Ivan against Novgorod, later sought an alliance with Lithuania in an effort to recover his freedom of action. In the meantime many of the Tveran boyars deserted their prince to join Ivan, won over by bribes or simply by the advantages of serving the wealthiest and most powerful among the Russian princes. Ivan accused the prince of treason and sent an army against him. The rest of the Tveran boyars deserted en masse, the prince fled to Lithuania, and in 1485 Moscow absorbed the principality, which struck no blow in its own defense. Viatka, an independent republic in the rich fur country to the northeast, which had joined Moscow during the campaign against Novgorod, was absorbed without opposition. At the time of his death in 1505 Ivan passed on to his son a territory three times as extensive as that which his own father had bequeathed to him forty-three years earlier.

The End of the Tatar Yoke

Vasily the Dark had appointed a Tatar friend to govern the region of the lower Oka, and his small, subject khanate of Kasimov provided a shield against raids into Muscovite territory from the east. Now Ivan III proposed to use his vassal, the khan of Kasimov, against the hostile khan of Kazan on the middle Volga. A rebellious party in Kazan, possibly motivated by Muscovite bribes, plotted to overthrow their ruler and replace him with the khan of Kasimov, whom they called to take over the throne. Ivan sent an army from Moscow in 1467 to help his vassal, but the attack failed. Two years later the grand prince sent a formidable army to the outskirts of Kazan, whose khan begged for peace and agreed never

---

* Many family surnames originated with the appanage principalities—Odoievsky, Novosiltsev, Bielsky, Vorotinsky, or with nicknames—Dolgoruky, from Yuri "Dolgoruky," or "Long Arm."

again to raid Muscovite territory. Ivan accomplished his purpose of weakening Kazan to free his hand for action elsewhere, and the khanate on the middle Volga was left to be added to Moscow later by his grandson.

Ivan's support of the Tatar khanate of Kasimov and his reduction of the power of the khanate of Kazan were part of an elaborate scheme that aimed at nothing less than the destruction of the Golden Horde, or at least the elimination of its titular control over the grand principality of Moscow. Although the Golden Horde was rapidly approaching collapse from internal weakness and external pressure, and by itself was no real menace to Moscow, the grand prince moved against it in his usual cautious way. Less than two years after his accession, Ivan began to weave a diplomatic net designed to encircle and isolate the Golden Horde. In 1464 a delegation from Moscow visited Herat. Two years later Ivan received envoys from the ruler of Baku beyond the Caucasus and sent an embassy to repay the call the same year. Only the year before, the khan of the Golden Horde had prepared a raid against Moscow, but an attack by the Crimean Tatars thwarted him.

For some years Ivan's hope to encircle the Golden Horde lay in abeyance while the grand prince faced the more immediate task of dealing with Novgorod. The cautious Ivan was not so rash as to embroil himself simultaneously with the Horde, with Novgorod, and possibly with Lithuania. Moscow was not yet powerful enough to deal with more than one enemy at a time. When Ivan returned to his capital in 1472, after the campaign against Novgorod, he took up once more his earlier plan to isolate and destroy the Golden Horde. In 1476, the khan ordered Ivan to resume the payment of tribute immediately and to present himself at Sarai, for the grand prince was still the khan's vassal, but Ivan sent back a scornful answer. Sooner or later, when the opportunity came, the ruler of the Horde would have to punish such insolence or admit that the grand prince of Russia was no longer his subject.

The king of Poland arranged with the khan of the Golden Horde for a combined attack on Moscow in 1480. Both had recent grievances to settle with the grand prince of Russia. Ivan had recently added to his domain the republic of Novgorod, whose officials had sworn allegiance to the king of Poland, and the khan's envoys had suffered humiliating insults in Moscow. In Moscow the coming war with Poland and the Horde aroused immense popular enthusiasm for a crusade against foreign heretic and foreign infidel.

In the autumn of 1480 the khan led his troops north against Moscow. Finding the Oka river well defended the horde turned west, hoping to join forces with the king of Poland, but the Polish army never appeared, for at that moment the Crimean Tatars attacked in the south, and the king could not spare troops for the war with Moscow. The khan pitched camp on the banks of the Ugra, the border between Muscovite and Lithuanian territory, to wait for his western allies. Ivan posted an army on the opposite bank, ordered Moscow to look to its defenses, and sent his wife north to safety should the Tatars assault the city. Then Ivan joined the army on the Ugra, his confidence strengthened by the metropolitan's blessing and assurance of victory. Always cautious, he refused to order the attack, but he spurned the khan's offer of peace and pardon if he would send one of his men to kiss the khan's stirrup. There was no battle but the assemblage of troops served to make Ivan's point. Whereas for years the grand princes had paid only token tribute, and that only occasionally, nothing so dramatic occurred as "the lifting of the Tatar yoke." The yoke had fallen away years earlier. Although 1480 is the date traditionally assigned to the end of Mongol or Tatar rule, it has little significance. The Golden Horde was in the last stage of disintegration. It collapsed of its own weakness, not from the pressure Ivan brought against it on the Ugra.

The following year, the Crimean Tatars attacked the Horde, and the khan who had fled from the Ugra river line was killed by one of his own men. By the end of the century, the Golden Horde had completely broken up. For nearly three centuries more, Russia was to know little peace from raids by Crimean and Nogai Tatars, but as devastating and exhausting as these raids were, the Tatars made no attempt to dominate Russia politically.

Some years after the "victory" on the Ugra, a son of the late khan of the Golden Horde attempted to halt the Horde's drift toward oblivion by winning control of Kazan. He won the support of a party within Kazan that aimed at fighting off the imminent control of Moscow by allying with the Horde, for some of its people feared Kazan might go the way of Novgorod. Civil war broke out in Kazan between those who favored uniting with the Golden Horde against Moscow and those who sensed the decline of the Horde and hoped, by coming to terms with Moscow now, to avert annihilation later.

Ivan sent a powerful army against Kazan in 1487; the city fell before the Russian assault, and the candidate of the Moscow party became khan of Kazan, taking an oath of loyalty as vassal to Ivan. Ivan was content with Kazan's subordination to Moscow and made no effort to absorb it. There was every reason to believe that in good time the khanate would fall to Moscow, as had Novgorod. When Ivan IV later brought to an end the separate existence of Kazan and added its territory to Russia, as the grand principality of Moscow must now be called, the task was easy because of Ivan III's earlier reduction of the khanate almost to impotence.

After bringing Kazan more firmly under his control, Ivan III turned against the Golden Horde. With an army of Russians and troops from his vassal khanates of Kasimov and Kazan, and allied with the khan of Crimea, Ivan almost completely crushed the Horde in 1491. The Crimean Tatars administered the final blow in 1502 and the Golden Horde collapsed. A small remnant of its once mighty power managed to survive as the khanate of Astrakhan at the mouth of the Volga, but this too became Russian territory under Ivan III's grandson.

The Western Frontier

With the absorption of Novgorod and the declaration of independence from the Golden Horde, Moscow, now Russia, became a nation-state. Henry VII in

England, Louis XI and Charles VIII in France, and Ferdinand and Isabella in Spain were contemporaries of Ivan III of Russia. After 1480, this nation-state of Russia had to concern itself with foreign affairs, to take notice of its relations with other sovereign states, not simply as a matter of national pride, but as a vital matter of national survival. There had been no problem of foreign relations when Russia was vassal to the Horde, nor could there have been until it had won its independence. Indeed, not until the power and wealth of Novgorod came under the control of the grand prince did the state have the strength to win the respect of other nations, even if it had been independent before then. The dual task of uniting all of north and central Russia under one leadership and of winning independence from foreign rule occupied the grand princes fully until its fulfillment in 1480.

Ivan III applied the same tactics to Poland-Lithuania after 1480 that he had used earlier with such success against the Golden Horde. He sought to neutralize Poland diplomatically by surrounding it with states friendly to Moscow. In 1482 a diplomatic mission from Hungary visited Moscow, and Ivan sent his chief diplomat to return the visit. At the same time he married his oldest son to the daughter of the prince of Moldavia. By these moves, he flanked Poland on the south and Lithuania on the southwest with Russia's allies. Southeast of Lithuania lay the khanate of Crimea, long friendly to Moscow. To strengthen the reliability of that friendship Ivan opened negotiations with the Ottoman sultan, to whom the khan of the Crimean Tatars owed allegiance. The Jews in Lithuania, suffering under government persecution, were given hope that their religion might expect more tolerance from Orthodox Russia than from Roman Catholic Poland-Lithuania; they too became active supporters of Moscow. Finally, when the German emperor sent an embassy to Moscow to offer Ivan the title of king, Ivan refused, saying that his title needed no confirmation from anyone else. However, Ivan gladly accepted the German emperor's offer to support Russia in the event of a war with Poland, in return for a similar promise of assistance. By this agreement in 1490, Ivan completed the encirclement of Poland. To discourage Sweden from going to Poland's assistance in case of war, Ivan arranged a treaty of friendship and support with Denmark. One provision of the treaty, by which Ivan agreed to expel the Hanseatic merchants from Novgorod, profited both Russia and Denmark. Henceforth Russian merchants would do their own trading with Western Europe.

With the death of the king of Poland in 1492, the union between Poland and Lithuania came temporarily to an end. The Lithuanians insisted that a younger son of the late king rule them separately, while the Poles chose the older son to succeed the father. Ivan III took the end of the dynastic union between the two countries as his cue to attack Lithuania. At the same time his ally, the khan of Crimea, raided through southern Lithuania and into Poland with such force that the new king of Poland was unable to help his brother in Lithuania against Moscow. Russian victory came easily in 1494, and the grand duke of Lithuania surrendered all claim to Novgorod, Pskov, and Tver, but the treaty was only a truce. Lithuanian persecution of Greek Orthodoxy drove some of the border princes in the valley of the lower Desna to desert Lithuania and carry their loyalty and their lands to Moscow; this gave Ivan III an excuse for going to the relief of his co-religionists. Again his armies were victorious, but his success drove Poland and Lithuania to restore their union and to call in the Teutonic knights to assist them against Moscow. The Russians were stopped, but the border principalities remained with Moscow when Ivan III's last war came to an end.

Ivan's aggressive policy in the west added territory to the state and contributed to the decline of his enemy Poland-Lithuania. Although the Polish gentry were encroaching on the power of their king and adding to their political as well as economic rights over their own estates, Ivan III gave the Russian Orthodox peoples living beyond his borders the comfort that they could look to Moscow for deliverance from religious persecution. Irredentism henceforth would embarrass Poland-Lithuania and serve the hope of Russia's rulers that the ''Russian land'' might be brought once more under Moscow. Indeed, Ivan III insisted that until ''all the Russian land which now doth appertain unto Lithuania'' became part of Moscow, there could be between the two countries no more than an armistice ''for the gathering of fresh strength and the drawing of fresh breath.''

Internal Developments

Ivan III's achievements in conquest and diplomacy were spectacular, and without a doubt, the accomplishments in the field of foreign relations brought about a considerable degree of internal change.

Ivan showed an interest in contact with the West that was prophetic of Peter the Great, and it seems in both cases to have grown out of an awareness of Russia's backwardness and how much the nation might gain by that contact. In Sophia's train in 1472 came both Greeks and Italians, who brought to Russia skills only found abroad. Some of them became Ivan's counselors in matters of government, such as the need to establish a regular diplomatic service. Others, like the Italian Marco Ruffo and the Greek Demetrios Ralo, served him as ambassadors to foreign courts. Aristotle Fioraventi became his military engineer and master of artillery. Pietro Antonio designed and built the new imperial palace and the Uspenskii Cathedral. Italian artists redecorated Moscow churches, Italian architects built new ones, and Italian engineers surrounded the Kremlin with a stone wall. The Italian metal-founder Paul Bossio and the gunsmiths who came with him taught the Russians improved methods of arms manufacture and made them less dependent on foreign producers for war equipment. Italian die-makers improved the minting of coins, and the effect of this, together with Ivan's order forbidding the appanage princes to coin money in their own principalities, was the establishment of one currency for the nation. Ivan, always interested in the work of these foreign artisans, time and again sent emissaries to the West to bring more of them to Moscow. German doctors served the court and a few German artisans joined the Italians from Venice and Rome, although Ivan seems to have had the greatest confidence in his Venetians.

The absorption of the appanage principalities brought into the service of Moscow a number of petty princes who theretofore had exercised certain local governmental authority, particularly in matters of coinage, foreign affairs, and justice. When they came to the court of the grand prince, their control over such matters fell to Moscow. Taking over the powers of coinage and dealing in foreign relations raised no problems for the central government; in fact, it eliminated them. However, wiping out the judicial authority of the petty princes raised the question of what to put in its place. The definition of crime, punishment for various crimes, and court procedures varied from one principality to another, and all differed from practice in Moscow.

To establish judicial uniformity over the land Ivan III published the Sudebnik, or code of law, drawn up in 1497 by Russian and Greek legal experts. This was the first important codification of Russian law since the old Russkaia Pravda of Kievan times, and its appearance was striking evidence of the fact that Russia had become a nation-state. Government representatives sat in provincial courts, and in each court a scribe took down the evidence and proceedings. There were safeguards against bribery of judicial officers, for the people of the newly acquired territories looked to Moscow for justice and protection. By the provision that peasants might move from one landowner's estate to another only during the two weeks around St. George's Day, November 26, Russia took the first step toward serfdom. Poland had first moved in that direction some forty years earlier.

There was a serious effort at the end of the fifteenth century to increase the ruler's revenue, for the new responsibilities of statehood, relations with other nations, the increase in court expenses, the new building in the capital, and the modernization of army equipment laid a heavy burden on the treasury. Assessors roamed the land to determine the taxpaying ability of the people, and each landowner's name and worth were entered in a great book. Revenue from levies on trade, which had always brought good income to Moscow, increased not so much by raising rates as by the fact that new markets with their fees and new commercial avenues with their tolls came under Muscovite control in the great expansion of the state territory. By far the richest addition to Ivan's revenue came from the absorption of the fur-bearing reserve of northeast Russia, for every trapper and trader had to forfeit the best pelts to the state. To meet the crying need for still more revenue, Ivan gave serious thought to the secularization of church lands, in which he had the support of sectarians who frowned on the growing wealth of the Russian church and urged a return to apostolic poverty and purity. However, a council of church leaders protested, and secularization was postponed for three centuries.

The state's need for men to serve in the military and in government service was much greater in Ivan's time than it had ever been before. At the same time, there was not the wherewithal to pay them in cash, even if Ivan had not found so many other uses for his money or had been less penurious than his predecessors. His father had hit on the scheme of paying those who served him in land rather than in money, and Ivan enthusiastically continued it. The practice, used consistently by Ivan and his successors, was known as *pomiestie*, by which land was provided in return for military or some other kind of state service. Such a landholder, called a *pomieshchik*, received no hereditary title to the land, but held it only during such service. Upon the pomieshchik's death the land reverted to the sovereign, unless there was an heir who could take up the service responsibility that was attached to the land. When the territory of Novgorod fell to Moscow, an enormous expanse of land, only part of which was habitable or arable, became available for pomiestie grants. In fact, the Muscovite families who were transplanted to Novgorod after the city's reduction moved to their new home on that basis, and the evicted Novgorodian boyars settled nearer Moscow as pomieshchiks. Boyars who deserted their appanage princes to serve with Ivan joined him on the same footing; they became landholders who had no better claim to their estates than the grand prince's revokable grant in return for faithful service.

In providing the state with civil and military servants the system was extremely efficient. The tenuous titles to their estates assured the pomieshchiks' loyalty and devotion to duty, for they could lose everything at the whim of the ruler. As Russia in later years moved south into the sparsely settled steppe, the pomiestie system of granting land followed the advance of the frontier. Although there were many in Ivan's time who held land by hereditary right, the percentage shrank from then on as such landowners died without heirs and their estates reverted to the crown, and as new grants of land were made only on condition of service— on terms of pomiestie. Ivan IV later erased all distinction between the two types and placed all landholders on a pomiestie basis. Not until the late seventeenth century did pomieshchiks receive the right to sell their estates, and then only if the purchaser was physically able to shoulder the burden of state service.

The adoption of Byzantine ideas of government, stimulated by Ivan's marriage to Sophia, enormously enhanced the autocratic nature of Muscovite rule. At the same time a strange check upon the autocracy developed. As each successive prince surrendered his lands to Moscow and moved to court, or as each boyar deserted his prince to join Ivan, he received a rank in state service and court functions commensurate with the date of his removal to Moscow or with his hereditary seniority. If two princes descended from Igor entered Moscow service, the one descended through the senior line took precedence over the one descended from the junior. The boyar whose ancestor had come early to Moscow enjoyed preferment over one whose forefather had come later, and the boyar whose family had served the prince of Moscow since the beginning of the principality took precedence over all other boyars.

This system of seniority, the *miestnichestvo* system or schedule of rank, required that all state offices be assigned in order of importance to members of the nobility in corresponding order of their genealogical position. If a prince descended in a junior line received an appointment to command an army, no prince genealogically his senior could be forced to accept a post under him. If a boyar were asked to serve under someone junior to him in the miestnichestvo system, he could refuse with impunity. The grand prince had no recourse, for the system enjoyed full legal sanction.

The ruler thus had little freedom of choice in appointments made from the ranks of the nobility. The only alternative open to the ruler was to give an important post to a foreigner or commoner who had, of course, no position in the miestnichestvo system. Indeed, Ivan III named many of the middle class and foreigners to office, and his grandson, Ivan IV, carried the practice much further.

Down to the time of Ivan III, central and western Europe had looked on Moscow as just another insignificant principality, an attitude that the facts fully justified. In 1486, the Holy Roman Emperor Frederick III sent an embassy to Moscow with a request for one of Ivan's daughters to marry his nephew and an offer to raise the prince to the rank of king. Ivan, who had recently won his independence from the Golden Horde, haughtily answered: "Touching what thou hast said unto us concerning the kingship, we, by grace of God, have been Emperors of our land from the beginning, and from our earliest forefathers, and do hold our commission of God himself. Therefore we pray God that He may grant unto us and unto our children to be Emperors of our land forever, even as we are now, and that we may never have need to be commissioned unto the same, even as we have not now." Of the inaccuracies in the statement, the German emperor would not be aware, but there could be no doubting Ivan's disdain for a delegation of authority from anyone less than God.

Once rid of the Tatar yoke, Ivan became the sole independent ruler in the Orthodox world. Heir to the political position of Byzantium, Moscow also claimed succession to the religious leadership of the East. According to the third Rome doctrine, which became popular after the death of Ivan III, the metropolitan of Moscow was the rightful ruler over true, or Orthodox, Christians. Moscow, according to the church scholars who interpreted history to fit the city's new aspirations, became the "third Rome." Western Rome had succumbed to heresy and papal domination. Constantinople, the second Rome, had fallen into heresy when its patriarch had accepted union with the West at the Council of Florence, and soon thereafter the city had lost its political independence as well. Now Moscow, the third Rome, was the capital of the true church, and politically and religiously it would survive forever. There would never be a fourth Rome. During the reign of Ivan the Terrible, when this religious dogma became popular, the image of "Holy Russia" grew steadily across the Russian land.

The Greatness of Ivan III

If Ivan had any claim to the title "the Great" that history has added to his name, it lay in his ability to make the most of his opportunities. Certainly, there was nothing grand or noble about his character or his manner. Russia accomplished great things during his reign, usually as a result of his foresight and understanding and frequently in spite of or perhaps because of his caution. The lifting of the Mongol-Tatar yoke came about because he had previously undermined the power of the Tatars by his diplomatic encirclement. He freed

Russia from the khan without striking a blow. In fact, Ivan showed no feeling of shame about his caution. He could look back upon some princely heroes—Vladimir Monomakh and Alexander Nevsky, among others—whose caution was a prime virtue, and upon others—Sviastoslav of Kiev and Vitovt of Lithuania, for example—whose rashness had cost them dearly. At Ivan's accession, Moscow was only a dependent principality, but by the time of his death, it had become a sovereign nation-state.

By destroying Novgorod, Ivan eliminated the last East Slav state capable of checking the unification of Russian territory. When Novgorod and the appanage principalities, with a few minor exceptions, were swallowed up, there was one Russia, not many, as there had been at the time of his father's death. Foreign powers still controlled much of the Russian land, it is true, and it remained to his successors to move against alien, non-East Slav states. Division among the East Slavs had disappeared, and a united nation could take up the struggle against those foreigners who still occupied the Russian land and held Russian people in subjection. When the Russian border had enclosed the last of Ivan's acquisitions, the state territory was four times the size it had been when he had moved to the first conquest.

When Ivan the Great moved diplomatically and militarily against the Golden Horde, his decision evidenced much more than a simple desire to be rid of foreign rule. The days of the Horde were numbered even without Russian pressure, for centrifugal forces were exploding it into a number of small independent khanates, and Russian interference simply hurried the process. Even more important than the lifting of foreign rule, Ivan's advance against the Tatars signaled the opening of the drive to return to the steppe. Although Ivan the Great did not accomplish much in this respect, every one of his successors, with the exception of Elizabeth, advanced the frontier farther to the south until near the end of the eighteenth century the border rested on the Black Sea.

The attack against the Tatars was significant too in that it opened the drive against foreign powers. Until then, with unimportant exceptions, Moscow's advance had been against other Russian principalities. From that day forward Russian territorial advance meant Russian encroachment upon land ruled by a non-Russian state.

Ivan was great also because his reign showed his successors many of the lines along which Russia must develop. When his successors showed an interest in winning access to the Baltic, they could recall that Ivan the Great was the first of the princes of Moscow to reach that sea. When Russian pioneers first looked out over the Pacific in 1638, they may have remembered that Ivan first crossed the Urals. When Ivan IV and Alexis and Nicholas I recodified Russian law, they could look back upon the Sudebnik of 1497. Many more such lines project from the fifteenth into later centuries, but above all, every Russian ruler from that day to this who has felt keenly Russia's need to maintain contact with the West and to learn from it could remember that it was Ivan the Great who first sensed the need and took steps to meet it.

Vasily III (1505–1533)

Vasily III, the son of Ivan and Sophia, was much more like his mother than his father. From her he inherited a preference for autocracy rather than compromise. He rarely consulted his Boyar Duma, the descendant of the druzhina of Kievan times, which once had had a right to give advice to the prince. Individual boyars who questioned his actions were quickly silenced; some went to prison and one went to the block for daring to complain because Vasily settled all matters alone. The German ambassador reported that the Muscovite ruler enjoyed more power over his people than did any other sovereign in the world. "He uses his authority as much over ecclesiastics as laymen, and holds unlimited control over the lives and property of all his subjects." The court became more brilliant than ever, and the sovereign lived in unprecedented luxury. Where dozens attended Ivan III, hundreds waited upon Vasily III. Westerners continued to come to Moscow, many of them fresh from studies with leaders of the Renaissance. Russian embassies appeared at a number of European courts. Vasily corresponded with popes and German emperors, Moslem sultans and Indian princes, and called the Holy Roman Emperor, Charles V, his brother.

The gathering of the Russian soil continued under Vasily, and the growing state absorbed the last of the appanages. In Pskov there developed the same schism between upper and lower classes that had cost Novgorod its independence, and in the same way, the Pskovian nobility and great merchants leaned toward Lithuania and Poland. Vasily summoned Pskov's leading citizens to Moscow

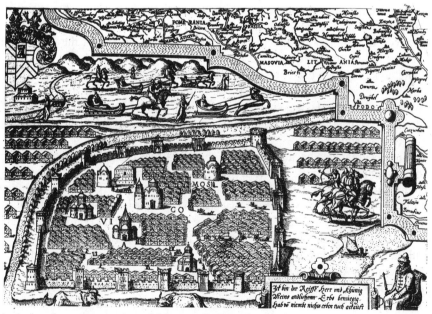

A sixteenth century print of Moscow's Kremlin and environs

and imprisoned them. Deprived of leadership the anti-Moscow party was unable to sway the vieche, and Pskov surrendered without lifting a hand in its own defense. Leading families were transported to the vicinity of Moscow, and Muscovite settlers came in to replace them. The last prince of Riazan conspired with the khan of the Crimean Tatars, and when he fled to Lithuania his principality fell to Moscow. Now there remained only one appanage principality, that of Staritsk. One day a monk with a broom paraded through the streets of Moscow, saying, "The Empire is not yet wholly cleansed. The time hath come to sweep up the last of the dust." The reference, of course, was to this last of the appanages. Soon afterward its prince was accused of seeking an alliance with Poland, and Moscow gathered up "the last of the dust."

With occasional interruptions, the war with Lithuania continued, as Ivan III had predicted it must. Upon the death of one Lithuanian prince, Vasily put forward his candidacy to the throne, but the Lithuanian nobles chose the king of Poland, and again the two united. The war that followed Vasily's failure to gain the Lithuanian crown ended in the declaration of a "perpetual peace," which lasted three years, and in the next campaign, Vasily seized Smolensk, whose citizens opened the city's gates to him. This strange war found the khan of Astrakhan, the king of Denmark, the Teutonic knights, the Ottoman sultan, and the prince of Wallachia fighting with Russia, whereas Poland-Lithuania enjoyed the support of the Crimean Tatars, the Dnieper Cossacks, and Sweden. Pope Leo X urged Vasily to come to terms with Lithuania and to turn his strength toward recovering his mother's inheritance, Constantinople. When the war ended, through the mediation of the pope and Charles V, Russia kept Smolensk.

Ivan the Great had considerable success in dealing with the various Tatar powers, but his son lost much of the gain. The Crimean Tatars, who had always been friendly to Ivan III, now supported Poland and at one time mounted a devastating raid through Vasily's territory up to the very walls of Moscow, carrying away thousands of Russians to be sold in the slave markets on the Black Sea. The next year Vasily led an army into the steppe to punish the khan, but the Tatars refused to fight and disappeared in the limitless sea of grass. Vasily dared not leave Moscow too long, for earlier the khanate of Kazan, which Ivan the Great had kept in subjection, had thrown out its ruler who had been sympathetic to Moscow. Attempts to force Kazan back into allegiance to Vasily had been unsuccessful, and the khanate on the middle Volga retained its independence until the following reign.

Vasily divorced his first wife for bearing him no sons and married Elena Glinsky, daughter of a Russian prince who had deserted the service of Lithuania to join Moscow. His second wife had grown up in a home where the influence of Western Europe was very strong, and Vasily even shaved his beard and wore Western clothes to please her. In 1530 Elena bore a son, Ivan. Three years later Vasily died, and the child became ruler of Russia as Ivan IV.

Between 1462 and 1533, in the reigns of Ivan the Great and his son, Russia changed from a land divided against itself to a powerful state. The years had brought great achievements, but still great problems remained. The grand princes had done well at gathering in the Russian soil and bringing all the Great Russian people under one rule, but their attitude had been not so much that of heads of state as that of landowners seeking to add acres to their estates and tenants to their rent rolls. A wide expanse had been swallowed but not digested, for there was little thought of organizing a state administration. To knit that wide expanse into a political as well as a territorial and ethnic unit was the problem facing Russia when a three-year-old boy came to the throne in 1533.

Suggested Reading

ALEXANDROV, V., *The Kremlin: Nerve Center of Russian History* (London, 1963).
BACKUS, O., *Motives of West Russian Nobles in Deserting Lithuania for Moscow, 1377–1514* (Lawrence, KS, 1957).
BILLINGTON, J. H., *The Icon and the Axe: An Interpretive History of Russian Culture* (New York, 1966).
CRUMMEY, R. O., *The Formation of Moscow, 1304–1613* (London, 1987).
FENNELL, J. L. I., *Ivan the Great of Moscow* (New York, 1962).
GREY, I., *Ivan III and the Unification of Russia* (New York, 1964).
HAMILTON, G. H., *The Art and Architecture of Russia* (New York, 1983).
HELLIE, R., *Enserfment and Military Change in Moscow* (Chicago, 1971).
HOWES, R. C., *The Testaments of the Grand Princes of Moscow* (Ithaca, NY, 1967).
KLIUCHEVSKY, V. O., *A History of Russia*, vol. II (London, 1912).
KONCEVICIUS, J. B., *Russia's Attitudes Towards Union with Rome, 9th to 16th Centuries* (Washington, D.C., 1927).
MEDLIN, W., *Moscow and East Rome: A Political Study of the Relations of Church and State in Muscovite Russia* (Geneva, 1952).
MILIUKOV, P. N., C. SEIGNOBOS, and L. EISENMANN, *History of Russia*, vol. 1 (New York, 1968).
NOWAK, F., *Medieval Slavdom and the Rise of Russia* (Westport, CT, 1957).
OVSIANKOV, Y., *Invitation to Russia* (New York, 1990).
RICE, T. T., *A Concise History of Russian Art* (New York, 1963).
VERNADSKY, G., *Russia at the Dawn of the Modern Age* (New Haven, 1959).
VON STADEN, H., *The Land and Government of Muscovy: A Sixteenth Century Account* (Stanford, 1967).
VOYCE, A., *The Art and Architecture of Medieval Russia* (Norman, OK, 1967).
_____, *Moscow and the Roots of Russian Culture* (Norman, OK, 1964).
ZENOVSKY, S. A., *The Nikonian Chronicle*, 5 vols. (Princeton, 1984–1989).
ZERNOV, N., *Moscow, the Third Rome* (New York, 1938).

CHAPTER 6

Ivan the Terrible

Russian history, at least down to the seventeenth century, seems often to be so little affected by happenings beyond Russia's borders that it is easy to overlook developments in the rest of Europe, or to dismiss them as of no consequence to Russia. One needs occasionally to call the roll of rulers contemporary with Ivan the Terrible: Henry VIII, Edward VI, Mary I, and Elizabeth I of England; Francis I, Henry II and his sons in France; Mary Queen of Scots; Charles V of the Holy Roman Empire; Philip II of Spain; William the Silent of Holland; Pope Paul III, who called the Council of Trent. Of men who were shaping Western civilization far more than many of the political leaders the list is nearly endless, but includes Luther, Calvin, Knox, Erasmus, More, Rabelais, Holbein, Michelangelo, Titian, Copernicus, and Galileo.

Both Russophobes and Slavophiles—in their insistence on the one hand that Russia's cultural birthplace lies in Asia or on the other that its cultural heritage is basically Slavic or Byzantine and Orthodox rather than Latin and Western— have scorned any suggestion that Russian society developed along lines similar to those of "European" society. They deny that Russia's rulers had to address problems similar to those faced by European rulers. Such myopia is not uncommon; of course, Britons, French, Germans, Poles, Chinese, Americans, and others have been at least as myopic in viewing their own past.

In his determination to build Russia into a strong centralized state, Ivan IV faced problems vaguely similar to those that plagued the contemporary rulers of England, France, Poland, Sweden, Spain, and Germany. The boyars of Russia fought, as did the nobles of Central and Western Europe, to recover some of the power and influence they had wielded a century earlier or to retain what power they still possessed but which the advance of strong monarchy was threatening everywhere. In Germany, Poland, and Sweden the nobles were ultimately victorious. In England, Spain, France, and Russia they were not, and although in every case the circumstances differed, control of the state church became a central issue in the struggle between those who supported a strong central government and those who fought it.

Ivan IV apparently lost the battle for strong monarchy, because after his death the Russian state faced collapse in a near fatal civil war. Toward the end of the following century, however, Peter the Great settled the question, for better or worse, in favor of strong central government. By that time, England, France, and Spain had long since reached the same decision. Poland and Germany had taken the road toward political chaos and bankruptcy.

Childhood and Character

The death of Vasily III in 1533 left the grand principality of Moscow under the titular headship of a three-year-old child in whose name his mother, Elena Glinsky, ruled the land. The people hated her for her Western tastes. Her chief advisers were her lover, Prince Ivan Obolensky, and her uncle, Prince Michael Glinsky. In the first five years of the reign these three managed by their capricious actions to stir jealousy and intrigue among the boyars, to drive some into conspiracy with Lithuania, and to provoke others to plot the assassination of the ruling clique and even of the young prince. The imprisonment of Ivan's uncles did not halt the plotting, and his mother died mysteriously in 1538. Those who had supported her were quickly dispatched. The child ruler escaped the purge and managed to survive.

For another five years the princely families Belsky and Shuisky alternately controlled the regency council. The defeat of one party would herald the imprisonment, torture, execution, or banishment of its members, but after a few short months the victors would suffer the same treatment. The bloody brawls in the Kremlin even reached the palace. Late one night boyars crowded into Ivan's bedroom in search of the metropolitan who opposed them. He never forgot the sight of drunken boyars lurching through the palace and of Prince Andrew Shuisky sprawling on the bed of Ivan's dead father, apparently a sign of taking power (or seeking to assume power). On state occasions those who ruled in his name prostrated themselves before the ermine-robed child. The ceremony over, Ivan was ignored and neglected to the point of suffering for want of food and clothing. He found solace in his books, reading the Old Testament, Byzantine history, the Russian chronicles, and patristical writings. Here he learned and memorized the stories of powerful rulers and of wise men who championed the cause of

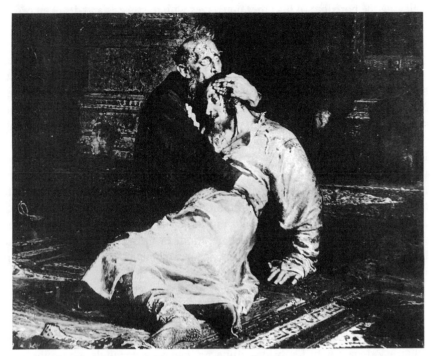

Ivan IV, the Terrible, and his dying son by Ilya Repin

good against evil, and stored up these examples against the day when he would rule and stamp out the sin that plagued the nation, and from which he suffered most of all.

These years of insult, fright, and neglect, emotionally scarred the young prince. Deprived of his father and abandoned by his wanton mother, he always felt himself alone and isolated. He wanted desperately to be loved and gave his own affection to his first wife and a few intimate advisers. In his later years, he was alone again, surrounded by enemies. He was moody and morbid, inclined to anger. In a towering rage, later in life, he killed his own son with the walking stick he always carried, and for days wandered aimlessly about the palace alternately moaning and crying out in the madness of his grief. When his coffin was opened in 1963, the body lay with arm raised as though to shield his head. Ivan may have died cowering in a fit of madness. A Soviet autopsy in 1969 showed the body to contain arsenic.

Always distrustful of others, Ivan looked suspiciously upon those who fawned over him and sought his favor. He was viciously cruel in an age renowned for its brutality—these were the times of St. Bartholomew's Day and the Spanish Inquisition. Ivan's fondness for drinking bouts, coarse entertainments, and cruel sports brought him popularity, for the tsar's peasant tastes made him seem one of the people.

After the death of his first wife, Ivan IV lived a life of the grossest immorality, relieving the boredom of his other marriages with mistresses and drunken orgies that lasted for days. Yet he was intensely religious, and sought to atone for his debauchery with hours of prostration before the altar.

Through the impressionable years of his youth and early manhood, Ivan suffered a succession of emotional shocks. There were the deaths of his father and mother, the plague that carried away thousands in the city of Novgorod, a fire that leveled Moscow, his near-fatal illness, the death of his infant son and then that of his beloved first wife, and the apostasy of his friend Kurbsky. In all of these events except the last, he saw the vengeance of God for his own sin and weakness. He resolved to turn away God's wrath by killing infidels or by striking down those who opposed the government God had put in his keeping. He earned the title "the Dread," or "the Terrible," as much by striking dread or terror into the hearts of his enemies as by committing shocking acts of cruelty. Indeed, a widely traveled Englishman held him to be the most feared and best loved ruler in Christendom, surely an exaggeration. Peter the Great considered him brave and wise, insisting that only one who knew nothing of Russia or the dangers it faced could call Ivan a tyrant.

Ivan showed himself to be most intelligent. His letters mark him as a man of considerable literary ability and in his debates with ecclesiastics, Orthodox or Lutheran, he often confounded his opponents. He had only scorn for illiterate priests who knew the liturgy only half as well as he. Ivan took keen delight in a literary debate with Kurbsky, filling his two long rebuttals with quotations from Scripture.

From his reading of the lives of strong rulers and his resentment at the insults of the boyars in his childhood, Ivan developed a sympathy for strong monarchy. He regarded himself as responsible only to God, as head of the church as well as of the state. In his handling of affairs he would allow no interference by any person or group, lay person or clergy, bishop or boyar. He regarded his officials and court functionaries as slaves of whose lives and fortunes he could dispose as he pleased. He looked on the ambition of the boyars as a threat to good government, as the example of the Polish nobles on his western frontier indeed proved it to be. Like the Tudors in contemporary England, he sought, but with less success than they, to undermine the power of the aristocracy and to assure its subservience to the throne.

Coronation and Marriage

Thrown early on his own resources, Ivan matured rapidly. At thirteen he had asserted his authority by ordering the keeper of his hounds to dispose of Andrew Shuisky, the leading boyar at court who had fouled his father's bed. The Glinskys, relatives of Ivan's mother, replaced the Shuisky party in control of the regency council, but they were imprisoned or murdered four years later soon after Ivan's coronation.

In 1547, Ivan was crowned "Tsar of All the Russias," the first ruler to assume the title at the time of his coronation. With a scholar's care, he examined the historical precedents for the ceremony and, with less concern for accuracy, claimed descent from the brother of Caesar Augustus, whose title he appropriated. It fit well with the preposterous "Third Rome" doctrine that the clergy concocted during his father's reign and to which Ivan IV subscribed.

There were profound religious and political implications to the title of tsar, and surely Ivan well understood them. In the Orthodox Church after the schism in 1054, the supreme power in ecclesiastical matters rested not with the patriarch of Constantinople but with the Byzantine emperor. The idea of state domination over the church and the claim of Orthodoxy as the only true faith had been transplanted to Russia from Constantinople and embraced by Russians from the time of the conversion. As long as there was an emperor in Constantinople, however, Moscow princes had resisted imperial interference in Russian church affairs. The grandfather of Ivan IV had insisted that "we have a Church, but we have no tsar or emperor, and do not want one," unless, of course, the tsar were Russian. The patriarch of Constantinople himself maintained that "it is impossible for Christians to have a church and not to have a tsar, for it is impossible to separate one from the other." In fact, he went on, the nature of things demanded that there be only one "tsar of the universe," just as there was only one true church.

Ivan IV, then, in assuming the title of tsar was not simply proclaiming an independent national church, as England, Scotland, the Netherlands, the Scandinavian countries, Prussia, and others in the West were doing. He was adorning the Russian monarchy with the title that announced his claim to the leadership of all true Christians and at the same time to political headship of "the universe." In addition, the divine origin of the secular power, which Ivan did not question, sanctioned absolutism and placed in the hands of the tsar the awful weapon of excommunication. There could be no room in any person's heart or mind for the divided loyalty—religious loyalty to the church and political loyalty to the lay ruler—which medieval Western society tolerated. Ivan's contemporary, Henry VIII of England, held much the same view. The Russian tsars were the absolute spiritual and political rulers over their subjects.

Soon after his coronation, the tsar announced that he would marry. Couriers rode to every corner of the land in search of candidates, and scores of beauties of noble birth from all over Russia paraded before the tsar. He chose Anastasia Romanov. The poor of Moscow loved her family but the great boyar families hated and envied it. Ivan's choice may have sprung from his bitterness toward the older families, and now their resentment must have given him keen satisfaction. He loved Anastasia deeply, and she was the only one who was ever able to restrain his savage cruelty toward others. Time and again he gave in to her pleas for the commutation of a severe sentence. He always attributed her mysterious death to some boyar's poison, and for it he took frightful vengeance. Toward the end of his life, he insisted that he would not have slaughtered so many boyars "had they not taken from me my little heifer."

Early Reforms

Soon after the tsar's coronation and marriage, a succession of fires swept through Moscow, a city so densely populated that an English contemporary insisted it was greater than London. The fire raged out of control, for the wooden houses of the common people kindled like firewood and thousands lost their lives. The citizens blamed the fires on sorcerers and, at the incitement of the Shuiskys and Romanovs, demanded punishment of the Glinskys, the boyar family then most influential at court. A mob lynched some of the Glinskys, imprisoned others, and drove the rest from the Kremlin.

For several years after the purge of the Glinskys, Ivan ruled with the advice of a "Chosen Council," some of whom were members of the middle class. Alexis Adashev became head of a new Office of Petitions that received appeals from the people to correct abuses of local officials. The new court chaplain, the priest Sylvester, suggested to Ivan a program of church reform. The old metropolitan Macarius tried to soften the tsar's passion for cruel punishments, urged him to crusade against the infidel Tatars, and argued against war with Christian Poland. These men could disagree with Ivan without exciting his suspicion, and for a while he sought their advice. They urged the tsar to undertake administrative reforms to improve the efficiency of local government and assure justice for all, to reduce boyar influence and concentrate power in the central government, and to foster the serving gentry as a responsible class loyal to the tsar and to national interests. There was no surer way to win the hearts of his people. Much of Ivan's tremendous popularity with the masses was the result of his appeal to their loyalty and his charge that the boyars were treasonous.

During the years that Ivan was under the wholesome influence of the Chosen Council, there were several governmental improvements. In 1549 the tsar announced a reform program. He promised a new legal code and a reorganization of financial, judicial, administrative, and military services. His aim was to strengthen and centralize the administration, to put an end to corruption, extortion, inefficiency and miscarriage of justice, and to give the land a government that was strong, just, efficient, and merciless to those enemies, foreign and domestic, who threatened Russia's well-being.

In keeping with his promise, Ivan promulgated a new law code, the Sudebnik of 1550. It sought to improve the administration of justice by eliminating antiquated court procedure and making local governors answerable for the misdeeds of their subordinates. The hope was to end corruption in local government. Previously provincial governors, appointed from the boyar class, had headed local administration, dispensed justice, and gathered taxes, keeping a part of what they collected for themselves. This practice, called "feeding," understandably encouraged abuses. Now Ivan assigned the police and judicial duties formerly handled by the governors to elected local officials chosen from among the serving gentry and freemen of the locality. Collection of taxes was taken out of the hands of the governors and assigned to locally elected elders.

Indeed, the transfer of these functions from the governor to elected district officials was not an unmixed blessing. Ivan made the district answerable for the proper conduct of the elected officials and made each locality collectively accountable for the maintenance of order and the payment of taxes.

The tsar encroached on the rights of hereditary landowners by making them subject to the same obligations as those who held their land by service tenure, thereby extending the practice of pomiestie followed by his father. Henceforth all landowners, regardless of the nature of their title to the land, would retain their holdings only so long as they rendered military service. A son might inherit an estate, but along with it he assumed the service obligation that attached to the land. He began his military career at the age of fifteen and continued it as long as he was physically able to do so. Daughters might inherit the estate if they married someone able to fulfill the service obligation. If a landholder had more sons than the size of his estate would warrant enrolling in service, the extra sons received their own holdings from the public lands. No son could escape his obligation to defend the nation.

In 1551 the tsar assembled a council of leading ecclesiastics and challenged it to put an end to the ignorance, sloth, and licentious living of the clergy. Obediently the council ordered the founding of schools for the education of priests, condemned the immorality of which many clergy were guilty, promised a scholarly examination of the holy books to eliminate errors that had crept in through centuries of bad copying and translating, and considered minor alterations in church ritual. However, it did no more than discuss the acquisition of land by the church and the possibility of forcing it to surrender the estates it had already acquired. Nor were any of the reforms ordered by the church council carried out. A century later, the problem of church reform had to be undertaken from the beginning, as though there had been no pious pronouncements in 1551.

Ivan's early reforms—his reliance for advice on commoners, his transfer of authority in local affairs from the governor to elected officials, his imposition of the service obligation on all landholders—were a deliberate attempt to reduce the power of the old boyars who held their land by hereditary right and not by service tenure. He suspected the boyars of wanting to bring down the authority of the crown to a position of impotence. Further, when many of the nobles escaped to Poland, where the influence of their class was waning, in Ivan's eyes they committed the worst of all treasons—forsaking Orthodox Russia and joining its Catholic enemy.

Ivan fell dangerously ill in 1553. Many expected that he would not recover, and he received the last rites of the church. The tsar demanded that the boyars swear to support his son Dmitry. Many demurred, preferring Ivan's cousin Prince Vladimir to an infant whose accession would mean the continued influence of the Romanovs. Even the commoners Adashev and Sylvester opposed Dmitry. When Ivan ordered the boyars to swear allegiance to his son they did so grudgingly, expecting to order affairs to their own liking after the tsar's death. Surprisingly, Ivan recovered, and he never forgave those who, within earshot of his sickbed, mumbled their plans to dispose of the succession in their own selfish interest.

With the tsar's recovery from the near-fatal illness, some of the boyars who had opposed swearing allegiance to the child Dmitry fled to Poland and Lithuania to escape Ivan's insane wrath. Among those who left the court were Sylvester and Adashev, whose counsel Ivan had sought for a dozen years, but whose increasing pressure to control affairs Ivan would not tolerate. Those who remained tried to undermine the influence of the Romanovs. When Anastasia died in 1560 Ivan suspected that she had been poisoned by plotters aided by Sylvester and Adashev. He imprisoned the latter and drove the priest into a monastery. Tension between the tsar and those allowed near him mounted steadily. In 1564 one of his army commanders, Prince Andrew Kurbsky, whose advice Ivan had long respected, deserted to Lithuania in the midst of a war with that duchy.

During the next fifteen years, while stirring Poland and Lithuania and the Crimean Tatars to attack Moscow, Kurbsky addressed several long, bitter letters to his former sovereign. He compared Ivan to the Old Testament tyrant Rehoboam and charged him with fiendish cruelty from which it was only right to escape. He warned that God would avenge those who had suffered inhuman tortures, particularly those who had been pursued into the churches and struck down in sanctuary. He protested that monasteries were becoming no better than dungeons where men and women whom the tsar disliked were forcibly tonsured. He reasoned that Ivan had committed heresy by presuming himself to be above the law of God and called the tsar antichrist. In his four letters to Ivan and in his published *History of the Great Muscovite Prince*, Kurbsky accused the tsar of all sorts of gross crimes and cruelties. He was expressing the general and widespread resentment of the gentry at the usurpation of local autonomy by the autocratic central authority. He spoke essentially for his class.

Ivan could not let such charges go unchallenged. In long answers filled with biblical references the tsar insisted that his power came from God alone and that no man could question his use of that power. He flung back the charge of treason and the sterner charge that Kurbsky had committed apostasy in fleeing the service of God's anointed ruler on earth. He warned that the prince had condemned himself and all his family to eternal damnation for violating his oath of fealty, sworn upon a relic made of the wood from the cross of Christ, and so had committed an unforgivable "crime against the cross." He protested that he had only done God's work in sweeping away those who had plotted against the power that God had given him. He had invoked God's blessing on all his actions and had even paid the clergy to pray for the repose of the souls of those he had executed. He argued that in attacking the boyars he was only defending the throne God had placed in his keeping and pointed to the fall of Constantinople as an example of what happened to those who did not guard their inheritance. In all this, Ivan was looking forward to a strong centralized nation-state. Kurbsky was looking backward to the days when princes ruled their petty appanages free of Moscow control and Russia was a divided land.

Ivan made unmistakably clear to all who challenged it his own extreme attitude toward the monarchy. This view was commonly held by other European monarchs regarding their own rules. In order to overcome the medieval divisions of his native land and to bring it the benefits of centralized administration, he must be ruthless. The tsardom of Muscovy is one and indivisible, and God has made it an unlimited autocracy. The tsar is responsible to God alone for his actions, as he is responsible to God alone for his sins and, indeed, for the sins of his people. Only his subjects are Christians; Catholics, Protestants, Moslems, and all the rest are "ungodly." He is the head of the only true Christian state, in fact of Christendom. His enemies are the enemies not only of Russia but of Orthodoxy, of Christianity. Because God has charged him to maintain the safety, the well-being, and the virtue of his Orthodox people, anyone who resists him is guilty not only of treason but of heresy. He does not punish his enemies for his own pleasure, but because evil must reward evil as good must reward good. He must save the souls as well as the bodies of his subjects, over whom by God's grace he must rule without respect of persons and free from accountability to any man, lay or cleric. The tsar alone has the power to decide what is fidelity and what is treason, what is piety and what is sacrilege, what is good and what is evil. Only God can judge the tsar.

The government of holy Russia encompasses all aspects of life on earth and beyond the grave for all Russians, and God meant no priest nor bishop to meddle with government. The tsar has a religious as well as a political mandate, for which he is answerable both for himself and for his people to God. He must use terror if necessary to punish traitors, and all are traitors who oppose his will. If he shrinks from the most ruthless methods, then tsardom will not be safe; it will know no internal peace and will fall to its internal or external enemies, as had the earlier "Romes." The tsar's authority is God's authority. It is absolute. Autocracy is an indivisible religious and political whole; the slightest opposition to it is an equally indivisible heretical and treasonous whole. No monarch ever made a more uncompromising claim to rule by divine right than did Ivan the Terrible.

Ivan Peresvetov, who spoke the point of view of the serving gentry, or pomieshchiks, fully supported Ivan's position on the merits of autocracy. To Peresvetov, the rule of the old hereditary landowning boyars spelled chaos, division, greed and evil. Good government could come only from the completely merciless exercise by the tsar of his divinely delegated power. Peresvetov laid his extreme views before the tsar, but it is doubtful that Ivan IV needed any prodding. He owed his power and his awareness of it to no one.

The Oprichnina

In 1565, after Kurbsky's desertion, Ivan packed his family, clothing, treasure and icons into a train of sleighs and drove out of Moscow, telling no one where he was going. The capital and the nation were without a governing head. From his summer home in the village of Alexandrovsk, where he came to rest fifty miles away, he sent two letters to the metropolitan bishop of Moscow. One charged the boyars and the clergy with treason, graft, and corruption and announced the tsar's decision to rule no longer in a land of traitors. The other, addressed to the people of Moscow, assured them that they were in no way the cause of his dissatisfaction and swore that he was their friend and protector. When the people in Red Square heard the message, they protested their loyalty to the tsar, clamored to support him in ridding the nation of its enemies, and sent a delegation to Ivan with a plea to return and govern as he pleased.

Ivan consented to return to Moscow only on certain conditions. He wanted complete freedom to deal with traitors as he deemed necessary and he proposed to establish, in part of the realm at least, a new administration responsible only to himself. The terms were granted without demur and Ivan came back, marking his return with the execution of several boyars.

Blocks of estates north, east, and west of Moscow and sections of the capital itself now became Ivan's own personal domain, the *oprichnina*—a word meaning reservation, or that portion of an inheritance set aside for a widow. The oprichnina, which grew to enclose a third of the land, eventually included much of Moscow and the richest commercial and industrial districts in the realm. The rest of the land, the poorest regions, made up the *zemshchina*—literally the old land, to be governed in the old way by the boyars. In the oprichnina the tsar would head a new well-ordered administration staffed by officials sworn to serve him without question. In the first year alone of the grotesque experiment, some twelve thousand landowners and their families were driven off their estates, which then went to the *oprichniks*—the citizens and administrators of the oprichina. A new administration, backed by a special army of oprichniks six thousand strong, governed in the land the tsar set apart. His object perhaps was to hold up to ridicule the zemshchina with its ancient, inefficient, and corrupt administration and contrast it with the new, efficient, loyal administration of the oprichnina which, by implication, would bring order, prosperity, and strength. The oprichnik army, robed in black and riding black horses, each rider with a dog's head fixed to his saddle and carrying a broom symbolic of the tsar's determination to hound traitors and sweep corruption from the land, rode at night through the countryside terrorizing the families of the old boyars. However, not all boyars suffered Ivan's fury, for some like Prince Vasily Shuisky were oprichniks. This was class war with a vengeance, pitting pomieshchiks and peasants against hereditary great landowners. Yet it was much more than class war. It reflected Ivan's determination to bend all citizens to his will, to force all subjects to accept the infallibility of his judgment, to admit that the only good government was that which the tsar decided and directed.

To dramatize his desire to be rid of the burdens and responsibilities of a government to which the old boyars were disloyal, as he reckoned loyalty, Ivan staged a mock retirement from the throne. He arranged the formal coronation of a new tsar, naming to the post a baptized Tatar, Prince Semeon Bekbulatovich. Ivan, calling himself Ivan Moskovsky, lived privately in Petrovka Street in

Moscow as an ordinary boyar. After two years he tired of this play acting, resumed the throne, and drove the Tatar into exile. Meanwhile, of course, Ivan had dictated every governmental order signed by "Semeon, Grand Prince of All Russia."

The oprichniks constituted a security police whose relentless aim was to purge the land of treacherous elements. Ivan's victims suffered heartless torture. Many were drowned, strangled, impaled, or flogged to death. The entire city of Novgorod was put to torture on the charge that its archbishop was planning to turn over the city to the Lithuanians. Sixty thousand of its citizens were butchered in a week-long orgy; members of the clergy, boyars, and merchants whom Ivan suspected of treason were not the only ones to suffer.

The name oprichnina disappeared seven years after its adoption, and the expanding territory under the new administration took on the name of "court land" or "domain land." It became a state within the state, complete with its own regularly constituted organization and functioned under time-honored administrative forms but under completely new, unquestionably loyal officials who owed their position, their land, and their very lives to the service they rendered the tsar.

Here in his "domain," where the tsar ruled without let or hindrance, Ivan executed, tonsured, or banished most of the old hereditary landowners and confiscated their estates. He transplanted thousands of leading families from one district to another in an obvious effort to destroy their influence, for he saw their power as a threat to good government and even to national survival. A few old boyar families voluntarily surrendered their lands and sought service in the new order, but in each case they received in exchange for their ancestral holdings distant new estates that they retained only under service tenure. The new relationship made the gentry in the domain land completely subservient to the tsar.

The overall picture of Russia was one of hopeless confusion. The oprichnina, or domain, affected only certain localities, some of them sprinkled about over the land and surrounded by the old boyar estates that made up the zemshchina. Two of Novgorod's five districts were domain (court) land, the other three were part of the zemshchina. Some of the streets of Moscow were in the oprichnina, the rest outside it. In general, the boyaral estates on the Lithuanian frontier and those lying to the east and south near Tatar territory remained as buffer zones outside the new domain administration. Such territories suffered their own confusion and turmoil from the wars with Lithuania and the annual Tatar raids.

The consequences of the oprichnina were revolutionary. Although Ivan did not destroy the aristocratic element in Russia—enough of it survived to launch a civil war after his death—he so weakened and altered it that the aristocracy was never again the same. In dispossessing the old boyars who had held their land by hereditary right, even when he merely transplanted them to some distant new estate that they held by service tenure, he uprooted them, destroyed their old connections, deprived them of their old adherents, and took away their local position of respect that generations on the old estates had brought their families. No longer was there any material or social basis for the haughty independence they had once known. From that time forward they were "service gentry," whose position and well-being depended on their service to the state. Ivan, however, left the task half-finished to Peter the Great a century later.

The old hereditary boyars were not the only ones to experience the rooting out of old ties. When the new pomieshchiks took over estates confiscated from defiant landowners, they received with it the peasants who had worked the fields for centuries. Whatever rights the peasants had maintained under their old masters melted away under the new, for the government tightened the curbs on the peasants' right to move in order to bind them firmly in the service of the pomieshchiks, who required maintenance and support if they in turn were to render their service obligation to the state. The system that the oprichnina created was a two-storied house of service, or in fact slavery, with the pomieshchiks occupying the upper story and the peasants, rapidly becoming serfs, occupying the lower.

Ivan and the Church

Ivan had strong convictions about the church as an institution and the men who staffed it. He believed, as did many clergy, that the church should give up its vast holdings. Although he never took the step of confiscating all church property, he often laid the church under heavy fine and taxation. At the tsar's order, the church council of 1551 forbade monasteries to accept further gifts of land, although the growth of church estates went on surreptitiously. Convinced as he was of the divine right of monarchy, he felt that the state should be supreme over the church. The metropolitan, Macarius, felt similarly and managed to lose neither the tsar's friendship nor his own position for twenty years. After his death, a succession of men served only short terms as metropolitan, for if they did not please him, Ivan dismissed them. One, Philip, braver than the rest, dared to warn Ivan of punishment for his sins. The tsar ordered Philip returned to his monastery and later strangled.

Ivan felt only contempt for most of the clergy for their greed, their sinful living, their sloth, and especially for their ignorance. Although most of his own officials could barely read and write, he had little patience with an illiterate priest. His delight in pushing aside celebrants in parish churches and conducting the service himself expressed his contempt for most priests. Ivan, who assumed that his every public act enjoyed divine approval, did not hesitate to work the same cruel punishment on wayward clergy that he imposed on the people. Priests were dragged from their altars to be flogged, flayed, or broken on the rack with no regard for the sanctity of their position. During the sack of Novgorod in 1570, the city's archbishop was trussed up in a bearskin and fed to the hounds. Yet Ivan, knowing no peace of mind after he killed his own son, followed custom in abdicating and becoming a monk a few moments before his death.

Eastward Expansion

During Ivan's reign, the frontier of Muscovy moved far to the east to incorporate the middle and lower Volga and western Siberia. Before the middle of the following century, the Moscow state had brought its boundary to the Pacific.

At the bend of the Volga lay the khanate of Kazan, a Tatar state that had seceded from the Golden Horde. Its government was often in turmoil from interference by Moscow or by the Tatar khanates to the south. Its nearness to Moscow and its accessibility by way of the upper Volga made Kazan a natural prey as soon as the Russian state could muster the strength to attack it.

Taking advantage of a dispute over the succession, Ivan led a huge force against Kazan in 1552. Prince Andrew Kurbsky, the tsar's best general, led the final assault. The fall of Kazan gave Moscow command of the middle Volga and the easy pathway up the Kama and through the Urals into western Siberia.

Three years later Ivan sent an army down the Volga to attack the khanate of Astrakhan, and in 1556 that Tatar stronghold fell to Moscow. Now Ivan ruled over the entire course of the Volga; now the Caspian Sea, and across it the Middle East, invited the attention of Russian merchants, as well as English and Dutch traders who sought permission to cross Russia to enter the markets of Persia.

The southern frontier of Muscovy was not yet secure from Tatar raids. The khanate of Crimea, which had come under Turkish rule eighty years earlier, annually sent raiding hordes north out of the peninsula to pillage and take slaves. To defend the land against these terrifying incursions, Ivan strung a line of fortifications and observation posts along the northern steppe from Voronezh to Kiev, but the raiders often slipped through the line, as they did in 1571, when they reached Moscow, burned the city, and dragged off thousands into slavery.

In 1583, just a year before his death, Ivan received all western Siberia to the Ob and the Irtysh and north to the Arctic as a gift from the Cossack Yermak. Yermak was employed by the Stroganov family, which held rich salt and mining interests in the Urals, to defend its holdings and explore the territory east of the mountains. The Cossack band drove eastward to the Irtysh, captured Sibir, the capital of the khanate, and forced the Tatars throughout the Ob basin to recognize Russian rule. Now the tsar added the new territory to his dominion; Ivan's acquisitions in the east had doubled the size of his territory.

Relations with the West

Soon after the capture of Astrakhan, Ivan's attention shifted to the northwest and the Baltic. He may have wanted a victory for Orthodoxy over its enemies, the Livonian Order, Sweden, and Poland. His adviser Sylvester warned Ivan that fighting other Christians would not meet with divine favor. Adashev, too, opposed war in the west, but both of these former friends of the tsar soon thereafter left Moscow. Ivan turned to the Baltic in the hope of improving communications with England, whose military goods and technical skills the tsar was anxious to acquire and to whose merchants he had recently extended a cordial welcome to trade in Russia.

In 1558, Ivan IV advanced into Livonia—modern Estonia and Latvia—and subjected the land to frightful pillage and the inhabitants to torture. Narva and Dorpat fell, the former giving the Russian ruler an outlet on the Baltic for the first time since the days of Kiev. A Russian army advanced south and west into Courland, forcing Poland to defend this land it had recently acquired. For several years Ivan's drive was successful, and the grand duke of Lithuania offered to surrender the territory the Russians had overrun if he might keep the rest. In 1566, the tsar called a Zemskii Sobor, literally "assembly of the land," to consider whether to accept the Polish peace offer. He had already decided on a course of action, and the advice the assembly gave him simply coincided with his decision to continue the war until he had recovered "all the Russian land." It was this continuation of Russian pressure that brought Lithuania and Poland to agree, in the Union of Lublin in 1569, to join under a common sovereign chosen by an assembly of the Polish and Lithuanian gentry.

To this first Zemskii Sobor came members of the Boyar Council, leading clergy, citizens from various districts, army officers, and a number of the pomieshchiks, or service gentry. The delegates were not in any formal way elected representatives, for they were appointed by the tsar. Still, the assembly was far more representative of the Russian people than was the Boyar Council alone, for there gathered that day in Moscow's Red Square elements of all classes of society except the peasantry. The Zemskii Sobor met rarely, certainly not enough to establish itself as an English Parliament, nor could Ivan have meant that it should do so. His clear intention was to enlist widespread support and to suggest with little subtlety that he had no confidence in the boyar element and would not rely upon its counsel.

Three years after the Union of Lublin, the hereditary line of Polish rulers died out, and an election followed to choose a successor. Ivan IV put forward his candidacy, but the Polish assembly elected Henry of Valois, brother of the French king. Henry abdicated a year later to succeed his brother as king of France, relieved to be rid of a throne whose prerogatives had fallen away before the privileges of the Polish nobles. Again Ivan was a candidate, but the election went to Stephen Batory, a Transylvanian prince renowned for his military skill. There was never any possibility that the Polish gentry would choose Ivan. His autocratic treatment of his own nobles made him wholly unacceptable to the nobles of Poland, who were already winning the struggle against royal power and in doing so destroying their nation's strength.

Ivan's effort to seize the east Baltic coast involved him in a war that dragged on intermittently until 1582. Russia's drive to the open sea provoked the bitter opposition of Poland-Lithuania, Sweden, and Denmark. The superior military equipment of the West and the fine leadership of the Polish king, Stephen Batory, decided the contest. Ivan lost all he had won—his gains in Livonia went to Poland, and he surrendered to Sweden all of Estonia, the south coast of the Gulf of Finland,

and the Karelian Isthmus. Russia's enemies in the Baltic had succeeded, at least temporarily, in their determination to prevent it from establishing contact with the West and equipping itself with the Western knowledge and technique that would make it a formidable military power. In addition, they had whetted that appetite for Russian land that they would seek to satisfy in the days of Russia's weakness after the old tsar's death.

During the reign of Ivan the Terrible, England established friendly relations with Russia, the first Western nation to do so. In 1553 the explorer Richard Chancellor sailed from England in search of a northeast passage to the Orient. In a "great ship" of 160 tons he sailed into the White Sea and landed near Arkhangel. Four months later, Chancellor and the London merchants who had come with him arrived in Moscow where the tsar warmly welcomed them. When they returned home early the following year, they carried with them Ivan's offer to Queen Mary to allow English merchants complete freedom to trade in all goods anywhere in the tsar's dominions.

Chancellor arrived back in Moscow in 1555 with full power to negotiate a commercial treaty. Over the objections of Russian merchants, Ivan agreed that the merchants of the Muscovy Company of London might carry on trade in Russia free of the dues and duties that even Russian merchants had to pay. The tsar proposed an alliance between the two governments and showed pique that Chancellor had the power to arrange only commercial relations. Ivan sent an ambassador to London, where Queen Mary granted Russian merchants reciprocal privileges to trade in England, privileges of which they had no opportunity to avail themselves. The Russian ambassador returned to Moscow with a number of artisans, doctors, and engineers, thus continuing Ivan III's policy of importing Western technical knowledge that Russian rulers would continue to pursue well into the twentieth century. Two years later, another group of English merchants led by Jenkinson traveled across Russia to Bokhara, and a series of expeditions to Persia followed, the merchants trading extensively in Russia en route.

When the Polish-Lithuanian union in 1569 threatened the security of Russia's western frontier, Ivan sent Queen Elizabeth a proposal for an offensive and defensive alliance. An English fleet in the eastern Baltic might have assured the tsar success in his Livonian war. He urged Elizabeth not to allow English merchants to trade with Poland and asked her to send him experts in shipbuilding and the manufacture of artillery. The Polish king then petitioned the English queen not to honor the tsar's request, admitting frankly that Russia could be beaten only if denied Western knowledge and skills. Elizabeth received similar protests from the Danish and Swedish kings and the German emperor. However, she did honor Ivan's request and sent artisans and other specialists to Russia.

The Legacy of Ivan the Terrible

Two years before his own death in 1584, Ivan quarreled with his oldest son and in the heat of argument clubbed him to death with a heavy rod staff. He never overcame the grief this vicious outburst of temper had brought him. The murder doomed the dynasty to extinction, for Ivan's sole remaining heir, his younger son Fedor, was a simpleton whose marriage was barren.

The end of the dynasty would bring turmoil. The chaos in which Ivan left the administration, the bitter resentment of the boyars who had survived his purges, the sense of insecurity and fright felt by men of every class, the foreign enemies who hated Ivan's campaigns of pillage, torture, and desolation—all compounded to leave the land weak and divided. For many years there would be serious question as to whether the nation could survive.

Fedor, The Bell-Ringer

The old tsar realized too late the tragedy he had brought upon his house, for he showed only contempt for Fedor (1584–1598) and observed that he was better fitted to enter a monastery than to occupy the throne. Fedor's only interest was the church, not in a spiritual way but in the observance of its ritual. He especially enjoyed tolling church bells and wandered the streets of Moscow entering churches to pull at the bell ropes. The common people loved him, for the Orthodox Church had long taught that God particularly loved and protected a saintly fool.

Before his death, Ivan IV had appointed a regency council to guide Fedor. Prince Ivan Shuisky, Prince Ivan Mstislavsky, the boyar Bogdan Belsky, and Nikita Romanov, an uncle of the young tsar, were members of the council. The fifth was Boris Godunov, son of a minor boyar of Tatar descent but Tsar Fedor's brother-in-law and Ivan the Terrible's last favorite companion. Cunning and intelligent, although nearly illiterate, ingratiating and ambitious, Boris played off the other four one against another until they all had been forced into exile. Within three years of the accession, Boris had taken into his own hands the power of governing Russia in the name of the witless tsar.

During the last fifteen years of the reign of Ivan IV, Boris had intimately associated with the tsar and had married the daughter of one of the chief torturers in the oprichnina. Yet he had taken no part in the brutality and had obtained freedom from prison and exile for thousands of victims soon after Fedor's accession. He had won considerable popularity among the people through his reputation for gentleness. However, the great boyar families hated him for the favoritism bestowed on him by the tsars, father and son, and for the dominating influence he quickly achieved over Tsar Fedor through the latter's wife, Godunov's sister.

Boris made no effort to mask either his power or his ambition. He grew immensely wealthy through the gifts the tsar showered on him. He held a lavish court and dispensed favors as though he were the real ruler of Russia, as in practice he was. Foreign ambassadors sought to win his support, seeing that Fedor was but a shadow of a tsar. During Fedor's fourteen-year reign, several important developments influenced the nation's future. Since the tsar had little reason or will and no interest in matters of state, Boris made government policy.

Ivan IV had left a third son, a child by his seventh wife. However, the Russian church, which would bless a third marriage but not more and would not recognize either the union or the child as legitimate. This infant, Dmitry, and his mother were driven into exile by the regency council before Fedor's coronation. Seven years later he died, some said at the orders of the ambitious Boris, although the government told the story that he had stabbed himself during an epileptic seizure. The incident was forgotten until the death of Fedor, when Dmitry's illegitimacy was overlooked and his death deplored and then denied.

In 1589 the patriarch of Constantinople, then in Moscow appealing for funds, was urged not to return to his home in a land ruled by infidels but to take up his residence in the Russian capital. He refused but consented to endorse the creation of a Russian patriarchate. The tsar chose the candidate, who was a close friend of Boris Godunov, and the other patriarchs of the Eastern church grudgingly recognized the new patriarch, Job of Moscow.

In the last year of Fedor's reign, the practice of serfdom drew closer when the government extended to five years the length of time in which runaway peasants—those who had moved without settling their debts to the land-owners—could be forcibly returned. Perhaps Godunov's intention was to protect small landholders against the loss of their peasants to the owners of large estates, the great boyars, of whose irritation at his growing power Boris could have had no doubt. The regent allowed the church to continue to acquire land and escape paying taxes in violation of Ivan IV's orders against such practices. The crafty Boris hoped to win clerical support of his own candidacy for the throne should Fedor die without heirs.

The Russian advance into Siberia continued after the Cossack chief Yermak's victory in the year of Ivan's death. The regency established several fortified posts along the Ob and Irtysh rivers, among them the fort later named Tobolsk. Russian influence also pushed down the west coast of the Caspian Sea around and beyond the Caucasus Mountains, where pockets of Christian peoples asked the tsar's protection against the Moslems.

Stephen Batory, the troublesome king of Poland, died in 1586. Boris put forward Tsar Fedor to succeed him. However, the Polish gentry chose Sigismund III, heir to the throne of Sweden. When he succeeded to that throne, Russia's enemies in the west—Poland, Lithuania, and Sweden—had one ruler. Fortunately for Russia, the Lutheran Swedes soon forced Catholic Sigismund to leave the country, and the union of the three Baltic powers most hostile to Russian interests came to an end. Boris then obtained a promise of Polish neutrality and attacked Sweden in the hope of recovering the foothold on the Baltic that Ivan IV had secured and lost. He did win back some of the towns Ivan had been forced to surrender and so edged closer to the Baltic, but Sweden retained the ports, and Russia's window to the West remained closed for another century.

Tsar Boris

Fedor's death without heirs in 1598 left the nation in a state of bewilderment that might have produced a panic. For nearly three centuries the descendants of Daniel had ruled in Moscow. When Fedor's wife refused the crown the nation faced a crisis.

Boris Godunov (1598–1605) was now offered the crown by his creature, Patriarch Job. No other man could have accepted the charge and eased the transition to a new dynasty with so little prospect of turmoil as could Boris. He had served closely with the last two tsars for nearly thirty years. He had been the real ruler of Russia for the past fourteen years, during which time he had handled matters ably and fairly and had healed the wounds left by Ivan the Terrible. Now Boris refused to accept the crown from the patriarch and called for a meeting of the Zemskii Sobor to elect a successor. There were several aspirants, the most serious of whom was Fedor Romanov, nephew of Ivan IV's first wife, Anastasia, but the Zemskii Sobor, made up of government officials many of whom owed their position to Boris and of those boyars who had avoided imprisonment or exile in Fedor's time, unanimously chose the man who for fourteen years had possessed all but the name of ruler. The mob in Moscow's Red Square shouted approval, and Boris's agents mingled in the crowd to prod the lukewarm into joining the chorus. A few days later, Fedor Romanov was driven into a monastery to become the monk Filaret. His wife was forced to become a nun, and his son Michael and the rest of the family went into exile.

Boris's concern from the moment he became tsar was to entrench himself as ruler and secure the succession of his house. He knew that many boyars resented his election, although few had dared to fight it openly. He hoped that by lopping off the tallest heads he might reduce the rest to submission. So the Belskys and the Romanovs were exiled or imprisoned. Others, like the craven Prince Vasily Shuisky, whose kinsman, Ivan, had been murdered by Godunov's henchmen, accepted employment under the new tsar.

Simeon Godunov, a relative of Boris, headed a network of spies whose job it was to report to the tsar any whispering of discontent. These spies shadowed every official, particularly men like Vasily Shuisky, whose name and rank among the boyars might win him a following. Informers reported suspicions and rumors; slaves were encouraged to testify against their masters, peasants against their landlords.

Boris gambled on the support of the middle and lower classes to remain in power. He freed the slaves of the boyars whose lands he confiscated. He ordered that peasant tenants on great estates might move on St. George's Day to the estates of small landowners but forbade any transfer of tenancy from small to great holdings. In so doing he risked the hostility of the wealthy boyars in exchange for the support of the lesser gentry. When famine swept the land in 1601 and continued for three years, Boris offered relief to starved-out peasants by distributing grain and putting men to work on public projects. Unfortunately, the drought and famine were too severe for the government to meet; hordes of starving peasants roamed the land in search of food, and many died.

Godunov soon lost the reputation for mildness that he had won in the time of Ivan the Terrible and maintained through Fedor's reign. Men suspected of disaffection were brought to the torture chambers, and once again victims were flogged, flayed, and impaled. When Ivan IV practiced such cruelty no one dared oppose him, but Boris's position—the fact that he had won the throne by election and not by hereditary right—made him vulnerable to criticism. Discontent mounted rapidly; men awaited only the call of a leader to rise against the new tyranny.

These closing years of the sixteenth century witnessed in the Ukraine a defection to Rome of some Orthodox bishops. By the Treaty of Brest in 1596, the pope sanctioned the creation of a Uniat Church, whose clergy and communicants would continue the ritual of Orthodoxy and the use of Slavonic in its services. However, these Uniats, sometimes called Russian Catholics, thenceforth accepted the headship of the pope.

Tsar Boris died suddenly in 1605, a suicide, it was widely believed. Patriarch Job, reluctant to call a Zemskii Sobor when the land was in ferment, proclaimed Boris's sixteen-year-old son as Tsar Fedor II. Ten weeks later this pretense of a reign ended when the so-called False Dmitry—the presumably dead son of Ivan IV—led his army through the gates of Moscow. A mob broke into the Kremlin and strangled Fedor Godunov and his mother. Their deaths opened a disastrous civil war that Russians call the Time of Troubles.

Suggested Reading

ALEXANDROV, V., *The Kremlin: Nerve Center of Russian History* (London, 1963).
ANDERSON, M. S., *Britain's Discovery of Russia, 1553–1815* (New York, 1958).
BERRY, L., and R. CRUMMEY (eds.), *Rude and Barbarous Kingdom* (Madison, WI, 1950).
BILLINGTON, J. H., *The Icon and the Axe: An Interpretive History of Russian Culture* (New York, 1966).
ECKHARDT, H. von, *Ivan the Terrible* (New York, 1949).
FENNELL, J. F., *The Correspondence Between Prince A. M. Kurbsky and Tsar Ivan IV of Russia, 1564–1579* (Cambridge, 1955).
FISHER, R. H., *The Russian Fur Trade, 1550–1700* (Berkeley, 1943).
GRAHAM, S., *Boris Godunof* (London, 1933).
GREY, I., *Boris Godunov: The Tragic Tsar* (New York, 1973).
_____, *Ivan the Terrible* (London, 1964).
HELLIE, R., *Enserfment and Military Change in Muscovy* (Chicago, 1971).
HOWES, R. C., *The Testaments of the Grand Princes of Moscow* (Ithaca, NY, 1967).
KLIUCHEVSKY, V. O., *A History of Russia*, vol. 3 (London, 1913).
KOSLOW, J., *Ivan the Terrible* (New York, 1962).
MILIUKOV, P. N., C. SEIGNOBOS, and L. EISENMANN, *History of Russia*, vol. 1 (New York, 1968).
PAYNE, R., and N. ROMANOFF, *Ivan the Terrible* (New York, 1975).
PELENSKI, J., *Russia and Kazan: Conquest and Imperial Ideology, 1438–1560's* (The Hague, 1974).
PUSHKAREV, S, G., *A Source Book for Russian History from Early Times to 1917*, vol. 1 (New Haven, 1972).

REDDAWAY, W. F. (ed.), *The Cambridge History of Poland* (Cambridge, 1950).
SKRYNNIKOV, R. G., *Boris Godunov* (Gulf Breeze, FL, 1982).
_____, *Ivan the Terrible* (Gulf Breeze, FL, 1981).
SOLOVIEV, A. V., *Holy Russia: The History of a Religious-Social Idea* (New York, 1959).
TROYAT, H., *Ivan the Terrible* (New York, 1984).
VERNADSKY, G., *Tsardom of Muscovy, 1549–1682*, 2 vols. (New Haven, 1969).
VON HERBERSTEIN, S., *Description of Moscow and Muscovy* (London, 1969).
VOYCE, A., *Moscow and the Roots of Russian Culture* (Norman, OK, 1964).
WILLAN, T. S., *The Early History of the Muscovy Company, 1553–1603* (Manchester, 1956).
WILSON, F. M., *Muscovy: Russia through Foreign Eyes, 1553–1900* (New York, 1971).
YANKOV, A., *The Origins of Autocracy: Ivan the Terrible in Russian History* (Berkeley, 1981).

CHAPTER 7

The Time of Troubles

Boris Godunov had occupied the throne only a year before men began to whisper that Ivan IV's son Dmitry was still alive. Rumor had it that a priest's son had died at Godunov's command back in 1591, not Dmitry, who had escaped.

The False Dmitry

In 1603, a Russian of obscure origin appeared at the home of a Polish landlord and announced himself as Dmitry, son of Ivan IV. He secured an introduction to the Polish king, Sigismund III, who accepted the claim of the Russian, whoever he was, in order to use him to further Polish and Catholic interests in Russia. When word of the adventure reached Moscow, Boris ridiculed the claimant as a former monk, once a serf belonging to the Romanov family. Patriarch Job anathematized this unfrocked monk, and Prince Vasily Shuisky, who at Boris's orders in 1591 had investigated the circumstances of Dmitry's death, repeated that the true Dmitry was dead, but Dmitry's mother insisted that her son had escaped. Boris forced her into a convent, where she became Sister Martha. After accepting baptism as a Catholic and promising to work for the conversion of Russia, Dmitry, known as the Pretender, received support in an attempt to seize his "rightful inheritance" from Sigismund III, a few Polish nobles, his Jesuit advisers, and especially from Russian boyars hoping to unseat Boris.

111

In the autumn of 1604, Dmitry led a small army of Polish adventurers and Russian refugees across the frontier and started for Moscow. The Zaporozhian Cossacks transferred their support to the invader, and later the Don and Volga Cossacks forsook their loyalty to Moscow. Runaway peasants welcomed Dmitry as a deliverer, as did small landholders impoverished by drought and loss of their peasants. Exiled boyars came into the Pretender's camp; others slipped away from Moscow to join the motley army. The movement had become a Russian uprising—a rebellion against oppression and a revolt against the approach of serfdom.

Dmitry (1605–1606), who was intelligent and well read, soon lost his enthusiasm for the Polish cause. He seems honestly to have deplored the plight of the Russian people and to have wanted to institute reform, but he was given little time. The household slaves expected immediate liberation; the peasants demanded freedom to move from one estate to another; the lesser gentry hoped for assurance that their peasants would not recover their right to move; the boyars insisted that Russia be governed by the Boyar Duma in the way that the gentry ruled in Poland; the Jesuits urged him to establish Catholicism immediately as the official religion and were resentful when he consented only to proclaim toleration; the Russian clergy were furious at losing their monopoly and outraged when Dmitry married Marina, daughter of a Polish Catholic noble; and the Poles at court resented the Russian boyars who were released from prison and restored to favor.

The Pretender refused to accept the crown of Russia until his presumed mother, the nun Martha, recognized him as her son. This she did in a staged emotional spectacle. The treatment she had received from the Godunovs was enough to win her support for their overthrow. The few Romanovs who had survived imprisonment returned. Thus Dmitry, representing new hope and national leadership, took power in Moscow.

Prince Vasily Shuisky, who had sought to gain favor by denying his earlier testimony and proclaiming that the child Dmitry had really not been murdered in 1591, sulked over the preferment shown the Romanovs and resented the fact that Polish advisers surrounded the new tsar. Now he reverted to his earlier stand, announcing that Dmitry had indeed died in 1591. He organized a plot among the boyars to overthrow Dmitry, and in the spring of 1606, a mob incited by Prince Shuisky stormed the palace in Moscow and killed the tsar. Dmitry had been crowned, married, and murdered in eleven short months.

Vasily Shuisky

The void left by Dmitry's assassination made easy Prince Vasily Shuisky's assumption of the crown. He claimed it not by election, which he spurned, but by right of birth, for he was a descendant of Igor through a junior line. To destroy the popularity of the False Dmitry, the body sworn to be that of the true Dmitry was disinterred and brought to Moscow for a pompous burial alongside the tombs of the tsars. The church obliged by proclaiming the child a saint. The nun Martha now declared that her son Dmitry had not been assassinated in 1606 and that he would return to claim the throne.

The four-year reign of Vasily (1606–1610) marked the flood tide of boyar influence and the ebb of royal authority. Vasily made certain commitments for the backing of the boyars who had helped him to the throne. He promised not to punish boyars arbitrarily, not to confiscate the property of those found guilty of less than capital crimes, and not to punish relatives of a guilty boyar unless they too were guilty. He swore to consult the Boyar Duma on important matters. In an obvious appeal for gentry support he increased restrictions on the freedom of peasants to move from one estate to another and extended from five to fifteen years the time allowable to hunt down a runaway peasant. To the mass of the people it soon became clear that Vasily would rule in the interest of the landowners and that serfdom would be the fate of the farming population.

The False Dmitry had driven Patriarch Job back to his monastery and named another to the high office. Now Filaret, the former Fedor Romanov, was elected metropolitan. However, Vasily insisted on the election of the eighty-year-old metropolitan, Hermogen, bishop of Kazan. Filaret, always ambitious for himself and his family, never forgave the slight.

Half of Muscovy refused to accept the rule of Vasily. The Volga from its bend to its mouth withheld recognition, as did the Cossack lands of the south, and the appearance of each pretender amounted to a call to join the standard of revolt. Vasily had worn the crown only a few months when an army dedicated to the restoration of Dmitry, who still lived according to some, advanced out of south Russia toward Moscow. Its leader was Ivan Bolotnikov, a former household slave who had spent years in Turkish captivity. Bolotnikov preached violent social revolution, urging the slaves and serfs to kill their masters and seize the landowners' land, goods, and women. Many of the impoverished gentry sided with him until the class hatred that the movement engendered drove them to desert to Moscow. There remained an army made up of runaway peasants and of Cossacks from all the river valleys of south Russia, determined to halt the approach of bondage and restore freedom to the land.

The threat to their privileges united the gentry firmly to Vasily Shuisky. A Moscow army marched into south Russia to wreak vengeance upon the rebels. Bolotnikov was taken and executed but the gospel he preached long continued to stir the blood of the peasants. The government sought to stifle opposition by fastening every peasant to the landowner—lord, state, or church.

Vasily had little time for elation at his triumph over Bolotnikov. Another pretender calling himself Dmitry, the "second False Dmitry," won the backing of the Polish king Sigismund. No one who knew him was fooled about his identity, but to maintain the pretense among the gullible, the nun Martha embraced him as her son, as she had done with the first False Dmitry, and Marina even accepted him as her husband. This pretender advanced into Russia with Polish troops; the Cossacks supported him and again the discontented of south Russia flocked to his banner, for the name of Dmitry promised relief from oppression.

The rebel army laid siege to Moscow, and Dmitry established his own capital at Tushino a few miles away. Filaret joined him there and was named patriarch of Moscow. Now the suffering land of Russia had two patriarchs, two tsars, two capitals, two administrations seeking to govern the nation. South, central, and west Russia recognized Dmitry, whereas Moscow and the provinces north of it remained loyal to Vasily. There was also a vertical division of loyalty. Most peasants tended to idolize the name of Dmitry; the landholders supported Vasily against social upheaval.

The second False Dmitry, known as "the thief of Tushino," lost all chance to unite the land behind him when his lawless supporters ravaged the central and northern provinces. The people organized an army of their own to defend their homes. Once they had rid their own districts of the Pretender's brigands they marched south to assist Moscow. Meanwhile, Vasily Shuisky had convinced Sigismund of the danger of trafficking with revolutionaries, and the Polish king called home the contingents serving under Dmitry. In return for a strip of Russian frontier in Livonia, Sweden promised to help Vasily's cause. A relief army of Swedes approached Moscow and broke up the siege. Forsaken by his Polish allies and deserted by lawless elements interested only in plunder, Dmitry abandoned his capital at Tushino and withdrew with his Cossacks.

Filaret and a few dissident boyars now prevailed upon King Sigismund of Poland to place his son Wladyslaw on the Russian throne. Filaret soothed his conscience with a Polish promise that Orthodoxy would continue as the state religion. The boyars with him received the assurance that there would be no relaxation of the restrictions on the Russian peasants and by the promise that the Pole would rule with the advice of the Boyar Duma. A Polish army marched on Moscow, while the Swedes held Novgorod and Dmitry and his Cossacks returned to the attack. In 1610 Vasily Shuisky was forced to abdicate by the Moscow mob. He entered a monastery, and Russia was rid of his disgraceful rule. Now there was no tsar. The Boyar Duma governed Moscow.

The Poles in Moscow

In midsummer 1610 two armies, each with its own candidate for the Russian throne, camped under the walls of Moscow. One was the Polish army which, if invited in, could be expected to defend the interests of the gentry against social revolution. The other, led by the second False Dmitry, consisted chiefly of Cossacks who would insist upon a generally egalitarian social order that would defend the rights of the peasants against the landlords. For the boyars and other conservative people in Moscow the choice was clear. Wladyslaw, the fifteen-year-old son of the Polish king, was elected by a hastily gathered assembly that passed for a Zemskii Sobor. Dmitry was driven off and later murdered, and the Polish army entered Moscow.

With Polish troops in the Russian capital, King Sigismund now withdrew his son's candidacy for the Muscovite throne and insisted upon his own election. Even the Moscow nobles, selfish as they were, took alarm at this turn of events. Although they were confident they could control the youthful Wladyslaw, there was little likelihood that they could manage his willful father. The prospect that Sigismund would surround himself with Poles and Jesuits suggested that Russians would receive little hearing. The clergy had most to lose, for Sigismund would favor Russia's entry into the Roman church.

The patriarch of Moscow, Hermogen, led a movement to awaken a national revival in the land, sending out letters to Russian cities calling upon the faithful to resist the Polish invaders. The Poles imprisoned the old man and starved him to death, but he had accomplished his purpose. An army of Cossacks and gentry stormed into Moscow and drove the Polish garrison back into the fortress of the Kremlin.

Kuzma Minin, a wealthy wholesale butcher of Nizhni Novgorod, assembled an army of all classes to save the nation from foreign rule. A Polish army was driven off, and the Poles in the capital surrendered. By the end of 1612, Moscow was again under Russian control. Three months later, a broadly representative Zemskii Sobor elected a new tsar. He was Michael Romanov, son of Patriarch Filaret, who was the nephew of Ivan IV's beloved Anastasia.

The Government of the Tsardom of Muscovy

Although Ivan IV left the government of Russia in chaos, the framework of the central administration remained essentially the same as it had been under Ivan III. The grand prince, now called tsar after the coronation of Ivan the Terrible, was customarily the oldest surviving son of the late ruler. The same dynasty succeeded in unbroken descent from the time of Daniel, the youngest son of Alexander Nevsky. Although Ivan IV claimed to rule by divine right and fought every check upon his authority, custom required the prince or tsar to seek the advice of the Boyar Duma, which met frequently with the tsar presiding. The Sudebnik, the law code that Ivan IV issued in 1550, even required the Duma's approval of important decisions. There can be no doubt of Ivan's ability to cow any who might oppose his will in the Duma. Yet it was to free himself from even this mild restraint that the tsar convoked the Zemskii Sobor to still the voice of the boyars in a chorus of commoners' votes and then organized the oprichnina, in part, to avoid meeting with the Duma altogether.

As the small principality of Moscow grew into the Russian state and acquired enormous territory, the household officials who had served the prince when his patrimony was hardly larger than a great landowner's estate could not handle the multiplicity of problems facing the nation-state. New government bureaus called *prikazes* were set up, each headed by an appointee of the grand prince and staffed with a corps of clerks. Some of these bureaus dealt with particular governmental functions, whereas others administered new lands added by conquest. One prikaz handled receipts and disbursements like any treasury department in the West; another supervised embassies like any foreign ministry in Western Europe; still another dealt with military matters like any Western war office. Alongside these bureaus created on functional lines were other bureaus whose responsibility it was to deal with all types of administrative matters in a given territory, particularly in one recently acquired. A prikaz for Novgorod governed that wide area after its absorption by Ivan III. The conquest of Kazan added another to the growing list, and late in the sixteenth century a prikaz, or bureau or colonial office, came into existence to govern Siberia. There was little logic in the way these bureaus proliferated. A new function added or a new conquered district seemed to dictate the creation of another prikaz. By the end of the sixteenth century there were thirty such departments; by the time of Peter the Great, a century later, the number had doubled. Often their functions overlapped; several of them gathered and spent revenue.

The government's income came from a variety of sources. There were customs dues, taxes on internal trade, fines, confiscations, occasional impositions on communities or groups, and produce from crown estates. Conquered areas provided what amounted to a treasure in the form of land with which the tsars paid obligations to those who had rendered them service. Continuing from the time of Ivan III, there was a rapid growth in the number of pomieshchiks, who obtained land in return for service and who retained it only so long as they and their heirs rendered the obligatory service.

Every year the tsars gathered a huge army, most often to fight off incursions of the Tatars from the Crimea. Frequently, they hired mercenaries from enemies with whom Moscow at the moment was not at war—Swedes, Poles, and even Tatars—and these had to be paid in coin. A picked corps of Russian sharpshooters, the *streltsy*, had the privilege of living in their own quarter of Moscow and carrying on trade free of the taxes that merchants had to pay. Ivan IV organized the streltsy, beginning with three thousand men; a century later there were twenty thousand. Stationed in the capital and constituting the most effective unit in the army, the streltsy became an important political force and dared in the seventeenth century to influence the succession.

Muscovite Society

No class had escaped the violence that had swept over the land in the last twenty-five years of the reign of Ivan IV. It was against the nobility, the boyars, however, that the tsar had concentrated most of his fury. The old princely families, descendants of appanage princes who had entered the service of Moscow, mostly during the period of the Mongol domination, had not all been slaughtered, but many of them had lost their estates and suffered banishment. This had reduced but not destroyed their political influence. Although the princely families had not dared to challenge the capricious doings of Ivan IV, those who survived the terror nursed grievances against the monarchy so bitter that it was a certainty they would seek vengeance if ever the opportunity came.

The second rank of the nobility, the boyars proper (those who had grown up as attendants or boyars in the service of the early Moscow princes and those who had moved to Moscow from boyar service under other appanage princes), had fared little better. Some, like the Romanovs and the Godunovs, had retained the tsar's favor, but many had suffered banishment. Many had been impoverished by heavy taxes and the crushing burden of service or by having their peasants flee to the southeastern frontier and so losing the labor force without which their land was worthless. The gentry, the pomieshchiks, who held their land by service tenure, often held too little land or land too thinly populated to provide a decent living. Some had only one peasant family living on their estates and had to till their acres themselves when they were not on campaign. Others had their peasants stolen from them by great landlords whose power they were too weak to challenge. The nobility and the gentry, sometimes poles apart economically, had one thing in common—their service obligation to the state.

The merchants as a class felt the oppressive burden of taxation imposed by Ivan the Terrible to finance the endless war against the Tatars and the fruitless effort to push through to the Baltic. The middle class was beginning to show the same cleavage that separated the rich from the poor gentry. Wealthy merchants, appointed to collect the government's taxes, enjoyed special trade privileges and exemption from paying taxes themselves. This increased the burden on the lesser merchants, many of whom fled the cities and the economic strangulation that threatened them. The state sought to halt the depopulation and the decline of the cities by binding members of the middle class to their occupations and forbidding them to move.

The church suffered least in the tumultuous reign of Ivan IV. Although individual members of the clergy suffered cruelly, the church as an institution grew increasingly wealthy. It avoided taxation even after a church council in 1580 at the tsar's order expressly forbade churches and abbeys to shirk their tax responsibility. It continued to receive land even after the council forbade such acquisitions. By the end of the sixteenth century, the great abbeys held thousands of acres and even maintained their own markets to dispose of surplus produce. More important, church estates prospered as peasants, anxious to escape the unsettled conditions they experienced serving the landholding gentry, flocked to the relative quiet of monastery holdings. An occasional member of the clergy spoke out against the church's mounting wealth and the profligate living it encouraged, but most in the church defended ecclesiastical holdings, and one even argued that sons of the well born would not enter the clergy if the church were poor.

The Approach of Serfdom

Many areas of Russia were being drained of their peasant population in the sixteenth century. The wars of Ivan IV took a heavy toll, for the armies he gathered every year melted away because of desertion, the taking of prisoners, and the frightful slaughter. There was a still greater leakage to the Tatars who raided Muscovy every spring to carry off children and young women. Finally, Muscovy lost thousands of peasants who ran away to the frontier to escape enserfment.

The mass of Russian peasants consisted of small farmers who rented from the landholding gentry, from the church, or from the state. These tenants rented the soil and buildings and borrowed from the landlord for seed, equipment, and livestock at high interest rates, normally 20 percent. Those who could not pay the interest had to work it off in compulsory labor, or *barshchina*, in the proprietor's fields. The peasants had an ancient right to terminate their tenancy at any time and settle under another landlord. Many did so in the fifteenth and sixteenth centuries, sometimes attracted to a new estate by promises of lower rent under a landholder who had just received a grant and needed peasants to cultivate it. Ivan III had moved to protect landlords whose tenants moved to another estate without settling their debts and arrears in rent, and the law code of 1497 had limited the peasants' right to move to the week before and the week after St. George's Day, November 26, when the harvest was in. As the service obligation of the gentry increased, there was all the more reason for preventing a landlord's sudden loss of his peasants. Furthermore, the landholder gathered the state taxes from the peasants on the estate, and the government forbade any peasant whose taxes were in arrears to move.

On state-owned lands the peasant villages were communally responsible for taxes and for the money or produce that went to the government in return for the use of the land. This joint accountability made possible the early development of local self-government among the state peasants, a privilege which later made their lot far more endurable than that of peasants on private estates. Thus, the joint responsibility for taxes and rent made the state, and indeed the peasant communities themselves, resist the movement of individual peasants or families away from crown estates. As each village paid a fixed sum in taxes and rent, the removal of one family left its share of the burden to the families left behind. Restrictions mounted on the freedom of state peasants to leave the village, and those who left without permission were pursued and brought back.

In the seventeenth century, rising taxes and the burden of debt made it increasingly impossible for peasants to leave the estates of private landholders legally. However, small proprietors, who constituted a majority of the pomieshchiks, lost their workers to great landowners who enticed the peasants with promises of easier conditions or who simply stole them away. Landholders often fought for possession of peasants, for there were not enough to cultivate every estate.

Landholders whose peasants had run away leaving debts or unpaid interest had the legal right to track down the fugitives and return them. Threatened with ruin, the owners of small estates—those having only a village or two—pressed the government to tighten the restrictions upon the peasants' freedom of movement and to lengthen the legal period for forcibly returning a runaway. In 1597, Fedor I extended to five years a landholder's right to track down any peasant who had left the estate illegally, and a few years later, Tsar Vasily inreased the period to fifteen years. Moscow later dropped this limitation and peasants lost their former right to move from one estate to another, on St. George's Day or at any other time. From then on peasants were no longer free but serfs, bound at first to the estate where they were born but later only to the estate-owners whose chattels they became. By the middle of the seventeenth century, the law recognized no peasant rights whatsoever. To assure itself of collection of taxes from the peasants and their conscription into the army, the government forced the agricultural population into bondage to the landholder, who might be a member of the gentry, a monastery, or the state itself.

The Cossacks

Beyond the line of fortifications and outposts that Moscow constructed along the southern rim of its populated lands in an attempt to halt Tatar raids, in the buffer zone between the tsar's dominions and the Crimea, there sprang up in the sixteenth century several free communities of adventurers and fugitives known as Cossacks. The most famous of the bands were the Zaporozhian Cossacks—staunchly Orthodox Russians, for the most part, who had fled from the exactions and impositions of the tsar of Muscovy and the king of Poland. With the approach of serfdom, with the increasing restrictions upon freedom to till the soil and move about, strong young men ran away to the frontier and banded together in a loosely knit, jealously free, and fiercely democratic association to live by fishing, hunting, trading, and plundering occasionally from Moscow, often from Poland, and incessantly from the Crimean Tatars.

The Zaporozhian Cossacks kept their camp on one of the many islands in the Dnieper at the cataracts, moving to a new island from time to time to escape detection. In the circle around the campfire where all important matters were decided by vote, all men were equals, loyal to each other and to the community. Every year they elected a new chief, or *hetman*, who led them to war and who had dictatorial authority over the band when on campaign. At the end of his year of leadership, the hetman returned to the circle, giving way to a newly elected hetman. When a Cossack married, he left the circle, for no women were allowed in the fortified camp. He and his family settled on the Dnieper bank to till the soil under the protection of the band or "Host" of warriors who lived a spartan life in the island camp.

The favorite target of the raids of the Dnieper or Zaporozhian Cossacks was the Tatar nest in the Crimea, but they also ranged over the Black Sea in their longboats and dared to raid the land of the sultan. Then Turkey would complain to Moscow, only to be told that these were not subjects of the tsar. However, the tsars provided the Cossacks with arms and at times hired them as mercenaries. Also, at times, the Cossacks hired out to fight for the Polish king; and often they fought against him. So bothersome did they become that the Polish king tried to limit the size of the Cossack band in the Dnieper, whose right bank he claimed as part of the grand duchy of Lithuania. In 1570 only a few hundred Zaporozhian Cossacks were "registered," or enrolled on the approved lists maintained by the Polish government. As serfdom crept over Russia and Poland, many fled to the frontier to join the Host, and by 1625 there were six thousand registered Cossacks beyond the Dnieper rapids. Thousands more lived with their families on the river banks north of the rapids, part of the Cossack community although not officially "registered."

In the sixteenth and seventeenth centuries, other bands of Cossacks appeared in the valleys of the Don, the Volga, and the Yaik or Ural rivers. As the Russian frontier moved south and east, still others sprang up in the valley of the Kuban and in Siberia. All but the Zaporozhian Cossacks professed loyalty to the tsar of Russia—all the while successfully maintaining their freedom from tsarist control, at least until the eighteenth century. Even the band in the Dnieper finally chose the protection of Orthodox Moscow in preference to domination by Catholic Poland. The Cossacks were reputed to be the world's finest horsemen, and the cavalry regiments that they later supplied to the Russian army were feared wherever they rode. Cossack units even reappeared in the Russian army in 1992.

The Significance of the Time of Troubles

Through the centuries, from Kievan times to the present, the course of Russian history has been set by its strong rulers. The story of the nation's past often seems to be simply the history of the state. The history of the Russian people is elusive. For decades on end they go unnoticed, serving the needs of the state anonymously, working and dying without identity. Occasionally, however, the people rise up and dominate events, pushing the state into the background. Momentarily the observer's attention focuses on the Russian masses and on the leaders who arose from their midst to lead them. Such moments would come with the rising of Stenka Razin in the seventeenth century and Pugachev in the eighteenth. The overthrow of the monarchy in early 1917 is another good example of the power of the masses, but no comparable Razin or Pugachev led the revolt that successfully toppled the government. Lenin's seizure of power in the fall of 1917 showed the power of a brilliant leader, but the Bolsheviks won as a relatively small conspiratorial effort rather than mobilizing the Russian masses to its side.

In the final collapse of the Soviet Union at the end of the twentieth century as an organized nation-state, very little violence was in evidence across the land. The fall of the government and the Communist system in 1991 occurred comparatively easily, with a slow ebbing of national unity and political leadership over several years. The collapse generally lacked charismatic leadership, although Boris Yeltsin did serve as a rallying point for the anti-Gorbachev discontent.

The Time of Troubles indeed was a moment of great national crisis. It brought about disunity within Russia and weakness with its neighbors. The deep-seated social unrest that followed Fedor's death in 1598 had been mounting throughout the reign of his father, Ivan the Terrible. The increasing burden of state service brought the patience of the people to the breaking point. They had borne the burdens and suffering to the limit of human endurance because the grand prince or the tsar, as God's anointed, had asked it. Thus, with the end of the dynasty, every class rebelled against the tyranny that had gone on so long. People fought against autocracy, against the approach of serfdom, against the bondage that was creeping over all classes. They fought against oppression—the oppression of peasants by landholders, of lesser gentry by great boyars, of boyars by the ruler, of church by the state, and finally, of Russians by foreigners.

The Time of Troubles was a period of national tragedy. Not only was the land scourged by the civil war, but the tragedy lay in the fact that the suffering accomplished nothing. Serfdom did come to the land, perhaps even sooner than it might have come had there been no Time of Troubles. Bondage spread over all classes and it would take centuries to cast off its yoke. Autocracy settled again over the nation, an autocracy more nearly complete and more demanding than anything Ivan IV had tried to impose. Yet the period of foreign rule was far shorter than the Mongol conquest and occupation lasting from the thirteenth to fifteenth centuries.

Suggested Reading

ALEXANDROV, V., *The Kremlin: Nerve Center of Russian History* (London, 1963).

BARBOUR, P., *Dmitry Called the Pretender, 1605–1606* (Boston, 1966).

CROSS, A. (ed.), *Russia under Western Eyes, 1517–1825* (London, 1971)

FLETCHER, G., *Of the Russe Commonwealth* (Cambridge, 1966).

GRAHAM, S., *Boris Godunof* (London, 1933).

GREY, I., *Boris Godunov: The Tragic Tsar* (New York, 1973).

HOWE, S. E., *The False Dmitri* (London, 1916).

MILIUKOV, P. N., *History of Russia*, vol. 1 (New York, 1968).

PLATONOV, S. F., *The Time of Troubles: A Historical Study of the Internal Crisis and Social Struggle in Sixteenth and Seventeenth Century Muscovy* (Lawrence, KS, 1970).

SKRYNNIKOV, R. G., *Boris Godunov* (Gulf Breeze, FL 1982)

_____, *The Time of Troubles: Russia in Crisis, 1604–1618* (Gulf Breeze, FL, 1988).

VERNADSKY, G., *The Tsardom of Muscovy* (New Haven, 1969).

CHAPTER 8

The First Romanovs

Order and peace returned slowly to the land that had known little of either for nearly a half century. The quiet and prosperity that Muscovites had enjoyed from the fourteenth century to the middle of the sixteenth would return more slowly still. The chaotic years of the Time of Troubles had produced some gains, however. The church profited enormously, both in the extent of its holdings and in the number of peasants who moved into the shelter of its mild proprietorship. Poland in its constitutional anarchy was growing steadily weaker, although the debility was not immediately apparent.

Tsar Michael

The Zemskii Sobor of 1613 elected a thoroughly colorless youth of sixteen, weak in body and in spirit, who was under the complete domination at first of his strong-willed mother, the nun Martha, and later of his ambitious and power-greedy father, Filaret. Relatives and favorites contested for influence at court during the first five years of the reign. Then Filaret joined Michael as co-tsar, a situation that recognized the helplessness of the young man to manage affairs alone.

Michael (1613–1645) was too young to have taken sides in the recent violence; he had spent much of the Time of Troubles with his mother. He had no education, lacked a will of his own, and was content to let others handle matters for him. His weakness probably made him attractive as a candidate for the throne. His chief recommendation came from the glory of the name Romanov and from the fact that Michael's great-aunt had been the first wife of Ivan IV. The Zemskii Sobor clung to a thread of hereditary descent when it chose the young man whose family had married into the old dynasty.

The Nation Exhausted

Russia had just passed through the most trying ordeal in its history. The land had suffered ravage by contesting native armies, plundering Cossacks, and pillaging foreigners ever since 1604, and the fighting would go on sporadically for years after Michael's election. Whole districts had lost all population as families fled or were driven away. Crops had been destroyed year after year, until farmers had given up planting and countless estates had passed out of cultivation. Towns had been deserted or destroyed. Markets had closed down; trade disappeared. There was no money in the treasury, for taxes had not been collected. How many men, women, and children had died horrible deaths no one would ever know. To put the nation back on its feet would require years of peace and rebuilding.

The Time of Troubles, following the violence and chaos that Ivan IV and Boris had provoked, helped to hold Russia several generations behind Western Europe, technically and intellectually. While the Renaissance spread from Italy over northern Europe, while the Reformation forced a soul-searching upon the Western church, while the nations on the Atlantic explored the seas and developed commerce, while the West made enormous technological strides, Russia stood still and then slipped below the level it had reached earlier. If in the early sixteenth century Russia was not far behind the West, from then on it rapidly lost ground while Europe moved ahead.

This loss of ground continued after 1613, for the settlement of the succession did not bring peace to the desolate land. The Swedes had pushed in from the Baltic shores and were occupying the Livonian towns that they had recently lost to Russia. Novgorod, still an important trade center, was in Swedish hands. The Poles were in Smolensk, and Wladyslaw, the son of their king, announced his determination to press his claim to the Muscovite throne. The Cossack chieftain, Ivan Zarutsky, who had supported the False Dmitry and even lived with Dmitry's widow, Marina, proposed to establish a kingdom on the Volga. Bands of Cossacks and deserted soldiers of several nations swarmed, looting, burning, and slaughtering over the countryside.

The Return to Peace

The Zemskii Sobor that elected Michael sat continuously for the first nine years of the reign, deciding state policy and giving direction to the mild-mannered tsar and the relatives who advised him. Along with the Zemskii Sobor, the Boyar

Duma, numbering perhaps fifty members, met in daily sessions to draft proposals for referral to the larger body and to answer the tsar's questions on matters of detail. Neither the Zemskii Sobor nor the Boyar Duma enjoyed any right to initiate legislation. They simply discussed propositions the tsar put forward and, when he asked for it, gave him advice. When something like order returned to the land and Michael's father wanted no such consultations, the Zemskii Sobor met infrequently. If this assembly of the land behaved only remotely like a Western parliament, it was the closest Russia was to get to such an institution until the twentieth century. The Zemskii Sobor met occasionally during the reign of Michael's son Alexis and again, for the last time, in 1682 to settle the succession.

The government's first concern was to put down the marauding bands that infested the nation, to restore the order without which trade could not revive nor agriculture recover. As there was no money in the treasury with which to finance the effort, the state sent groups of agents, guarded by soldiers, into the countryside to gather "voluntary" contributions.

The Cossack Zarutsky led an army north from his "capital" Astrakhan and captured Kazan. From there he turned against Moscow but was defeated, brought as a prisoner to the capital, and there impaled. The danger from the southeast declined, although pillaging bands kept the valley of the Volga in turmoil for years to come.

In the years after 1603, when Poland first used the False Dmitry to try to dominate Russia, Sweden joined Moscow to protect its own interests, which would surely suffer if the two great Slav countries united under the leadership of Catholic Poland. Vasily Shuisky encouraged the Swedes to seek to dominate northwest Russia, as their presence there would hold back the Poles. So the Swedes built a fortress on the Neva, advanced south and east of the Gulf of Finland, and seized Novgorod. The citizens of Novgorod, much preferring the rule of the Lutheran Swedes to that of the Catholic Poles if there was to be no other choice, listened sympathetically to the proposition that north Russia from the Baltic to the White Sea should become a Swedish duchy. With Michael's accession Gustavus Adolphus demanded the outright cession of north Russia to Sweden. Gustavus even considered moving his capital from Stockholm to Narva to be nearer the center of his growing empire.

Negotiations for a settlement dragged on for years until the Peace of Stolbovo in 1617. Sweden recognized Michael as the rightful tsar of Russia, received an indemnity, won the Karelian isthmus and the west shore of Lake Ladoga, and recovered the lands near the Baltic that Ivan IV and later Boris Godunov had won temporarily. Russia's exclusion from the Baltic thus continued, although at the time the weakened Moscow was happy to recover Novgorod.

With the Swedish problem settled, the Moscow government turned to face a renewal of the war with Poland. Wladyslaw had not dropped his claim to the Russian throne, and as soon as he could gather the money and men to try to recover it he set out from his base at Smolensk to storm Moscow. Twenty thousand Zaporozhian Cossacks joined him in the assault, but Moscow withstood the attack. Wladyslaw's army melted away after the failure to capture Moscow, and in 1619 he accepted the Truce of Deulino. The Poles acknowledged Michael as tsar. Poland received Smolensk, Chernigov, and Seversk, marking the farthest eastward advance in Polish history. With the conclusion of the armistice with Poland, which was satisfactory to neither signatory but which promised no hostilities for fourteen years, Russia obtained peace for the first time in a generation.

The Dyarchy

Filaret, the tsar's father, had served the second False Dmitry who had named him patriarch, but he had returned to Moscow after Vasily Shuisky's abdication. He had gone as an envoy to the Polish court to implore King Sigismund to consent to the conversion of his son Wladyslaw to Orthodoxy as a condition of election to the Russian throne. He had conducted himself with dignity, spurning any compromise on the religious issue; for his obstinacy, the Poles held him prisoner until the Truce of Deulino eight years later.

From the time of his return to Moscow in 1619, Patriarch Filaret ruled jointly with his son as co-tsar in a dyarchy. The two, sitting side by side, received foreign envoys and accepted separate gifts from each ambassador. Both signed important documents, but in his weakness, Michael left many matters to his father, and until his death in 1633, Filaret determined the course of government policy.

Filaret first set about to see that each citizen paid the proper amount of taxes. Theretofore government tax collectors had dealt softly with those who could bribe them, shifting the burden to those too poor to buy gentler treatment. Now the government compiled new tax lists and allowed tax groups to choose their own assessors. Russian merchants paid heavy fees to operate taverns and even laundries. The salt tax grew until the tax was several times more than the price of the salt. The greatest revenue came from the direct taxes that all free classes paid, but of which the peasants paid by far the most because they made up 95 percent of the population. People were forbidden to sell themselves into slavery, for slaves paid no taxes. Peasants suffered dire punishment for running away, for, unless the state could bind its population to a definite location where subjects could be found when needed for tax payments or army service, the nation's income and the nation's defenses would suffer.

The campaigns during the Time of Troubles were fought with irregular levies and mercenaries. The army, except for a few units, proved itself of little worth, particularly in action against better-equipped, better-led, better-organized Western armies. It often performed miserably even against the Tatars. Some of the infantry carried antiquated muskets that had been obsolete in western Europe for a century; other units carried spears and axes. The cavalry was poorly mounted and much of it armed with bows and arrows. Desertion from such militia units was common, and the troops panicked and fled at the first contact with the enemy.

The streltsy, privileged musketeers, now twenty thousand strong, received a regular wage and clothing allowance, living with their families in special quarters near designated towns where they tilled the soil and traded free of duty to the annoyance of the local merchants. When not on campaign, the soldiers served as local police and firemen. Some streltsy regiments were stationed near Moscow to serve as guards for the tsar. The officers were nobles, the men in the ranks city-dwellers. The streltsy constituted a chief element in the standing army. Only in time of serious threat were commoners drafted. The gentry owed military service to the state, but peasants and townspeople were more valuable to the government following their civilian pursuits of farming and trading and paying taxes.

With the restoration of peace in 1619, Filaret undertook to raise the efficiency of the armed forces. He hired foreigners to serve as officers and to teach native troops something of Western methods. Four hundred foreigners entered Russia—Poles, Germans, Irish, Swedes, Scots, English, Greeks, and Serbs. They received very high wages, some in money, others in land on which they settled to rear their families in Russia. Nevertheless, the task of modernizing the army was too formidable and too costly to be accomplished in a short time by a still weak government. The gentry shirked their service responsibility and hurried back to their estates as soon as a campaign ended.

To model the army after those in the West, Russia had to import Western arms and equipment or learn to make such things. Because buying them abroad was out of the question—access to Russia through hostile countries anxious to keep Russia backward was often impossible and always expensive—Filaret hired Westerners to open armaments and equipment factories in Russia. The first weapons factory was built in Tula in 1632 by Andrew Vinnius, the Russian-born son of a Dutch immigrant. Filaret died the next year, but he had laid the foundation of a war industry.

Westerners who could erect munitions plants were not the only ones who found welcome in Moscow. Filaret hoped that Russians might learn many skills and establish industries that would stimulate the economy and so produce revenue for the treasury. Swedes, Germans, and Dutch came from the West to tutor Russians in goldsmithing, bellmaking, leathertanning, masonry, clockmaking, and the manufacture of glass. Before Michael's death, a thousand foreign families were living in Moscow.

Although he was a layman with no religious education, Filaret appreciated the need for better training of the clergy. He ordered every archbishop to open a seminary for the education of priests, and he expanded the printing of church books, some of which he himself revised. He established a clerical institute to train Latin and Greek scholars, borrowing teachers from the recently founded seminary for Orthodox clergymen in Kiev. He brought learned Greeks to Moscow to inspire the ignorant clergymen of the Russian Church with an interest in the Greek language from which their own sacred books had been badly translated. In much that he did, Filaret prepared the way for the reforms of the next reign.

The Second Polish War

The loss of territory that Russia conceded in the Truce of Deulino in 1619 made certain that war with Poland would flare up again at the first opportunity.

That opportunity came in 1621, when both Sweden and Turkey proposed an alliance with Russia to destroy Poland. The Zemskii Sobor urged the co-tsars to take up the offer, and preparations for war began. Yet, before Russian troops could take the field, the Poles convincingly defeated the Turkish army, and Russian ardor subsided.

Eleven years later old Sigismund III died, and Moscow determined to take advantage of Poland's weakness during the confusion over the succession. Alexander Leslie, a Scot in the service of Moscow, hurried off to Stockholm to employ mercenaries and to bring back smiths, wheelwrights, carpenters, and munitions makers to stimulate Russia's production of war equipment, while an enthusiastic Zemskii Sobor encouraged prompt action and liberally appropriated funds to finance it.

The Russian army invested the Polish stronghold of Smolensk, but retired before a relief force of Poles and Zaporozhian Cossacks, led by the new king, Wladyslaw, Sigismund's son and claimant to the Russian crown. With the fighting over, the two governments pledged "eternal peace." Poland surrendered no territory and received a large indemnity, in return for which Wladyslaw gave up all claim to the Russian throne. The Poles remained in Smolensk.

The chief consequence of the Second Polish War was to destroy Michael's confidence in his army. He beheaded the commander and exiled the subordinates to Siberia, but never again risked humiliation. Whenever the sultan upbraided Moscow for the raids of the Don Cossacks—they were once at the outskirts of Constantinople—Michael's government humbly apologized. The Don Host seized Azov in 1637 and held it for five years. Then, when a Turkish army threatened to recover it, the Cossacks offered Azov to the tsar, but Michael succumbed to Turkish threats and ordered the Cossacks to surrender the Black Sea port. They did so after leveling it to the ground.

The First Autocrat

At the ceremony of his coronation Michael assumed the title of "Autocrat," the first of the tsars to do so at a coronation. In their personal conduct of affairs, however, there was nothing of the autocrat in either Michael, his son Alexis, or grandson Fedor. If the title meant anything in the seventeenth century, it did so because of the strengthening of the royal authority by those men, of whom Filaret was the first of several, who exercised power in the tsar's name. The term came to have meaning for the mass of the Russian people, every person of which was bound in service to the ruler by the middle of the century. Long before the century was out few would question the fact that the power of the tsar was that of an autocrat. Victims went to the block, to prison, or into exile at the autocrat's order, regardless of the social class from which they came. Indeed, it was rare for members of the lower classes to be favored with such punishment. Most often the victims were the gentry who took their service obligations lightly or who failed in tasks they had been ordered to shoulder.

After the death of his father, the patriarch, Michael again fell under the influence of courtiers. He died in 1645 at the age of forty-eight, leaving the throne to his sixteen-year-old son with an admonition to the child's tutor, the boyar Boris Morozov, to guide and protect him.

Alexis

Michael's successor was as harmless and gentle as his father. His kindness and generosity made him an easy prey to the relatives, favorites, and hangers-on with whom the court abounded. A host of beggars, dwarfs, buffoons, and simpletons lived off the tsar's bounty and entertained the court.

Unlike his father, Alexis (1645–1676) had received some education. Although his own schooling ended at the age of ten, Alexis determined that his children, or at least those by his first wife, should do better. He shocked conservative circles by abolishing the *terem*, the isolation of women at court, and by encouraging the education of his daughter Sophia. He was able and intelligent, yet he was intensely pious and devoted much time to practicing the formalities of his religion.

The Zemskii Sobor assembled to applaud, not to question, the succession of Alexis; then the tsar dissolved it. For the next three years Alexis was content to let Morozov handle affairs. The favorite, who married the tsar's sister-in-law, was as sympathetic to Western ideas as was Alexis. After three years, he was dismissed at the demand of a riotous mob but slipped back to the Kremlin and secretly lived out his life there as one of the tsar's advisers. His place of influence over Alexis went to Patriarch Nikon, who fell from favor ten years later because of his pompous and domineering manner, as well as leading the church's efforts to place itself over the secular rulers of the state. Then came the statesman Athanasy Ordyn-Nashchokin. Throughout his life the tsar was content to reign and to leave the ruling to others. He amused himself with his dwarfs and fools, watched ballet or dramatic productions or orchestral performances, all of which he introduced to the Russian court, or rode about in the luxurious European carriages that were a gift of his last favorite, Artamon Matveev.

Unrest

The first serious problem that Morozov had to face was the dissatisfaction of Russian merchants. English traders enjoyed such favored treatment in the capital that their activity threatened to bankrupt the Moscow merchants. In other towns the burghers felt the pinch of competition from streltsy, the clergy, and even members of the gentry, none of whom had to pay the trading fees levied on members of the mercantile class. Morozov answered the pleas of the merchants for relief by trying to force all who sold at retail to pay the traders' fees. He withdrew the privileges from the London merchants, and expelled them. Later they received permission to ship goods to Arkhangel but not to land.

Morozov sought to ease the burden on the treasury by reducing court expenses, strictly enforcing the salt tax and cutting salaries. His sale of grain to Germans and Swedes at a time when many were suffering from want stirred the resentment of Russians who accused him of a sympathy for foreigners. People blamed him for peculation by tax collectors and accused him of harboring fortune-hunters at court. Petitions against misconduct of public officials seemed never to reach the tsar. At least they went unanswered.

Riots broke out in Moscow in 1648, the leaders demanding Morozov's banishment. The participation of the streltsy in the disturbances was ominous. Morozov was dismissed, but the disturbances continued and spread to many cities. The most formidable riots occurred in the commercial cities of Pskov and Novgorod, where the mob held out for four months against a punitive force from Moscow. When the rioters surrendered on the promise that they would go unpunished, Russians must have been amazed that the tsar did not go back on his word and wreak a grim vengeance as Ivan IV surely would have done.

Bondage

The burden of military service and the growing need for revenue, both of which increased enormously in the seventeenth century as Russia fought the powers on its western frontier and expanded its commitments in the Black Sea region, bore down heavily on a population impoverished by the Time of Troubles. As the peasants in growing numbers fled to the frontier, the state faced the twin dangers of losing taxpayers and witnessing the impoverishment of those who stayed behind. The peasants who could not flee had to shoulder the added responsibility of paying the share of those who had deserted. Some chose to surrender their freedom, to become household slaves, in preference to growing insecurity and the threat of starvation. Soon the tax levy on those who could not run away, but who refused to volunteer themselves into slavery, became impossible to meet.

The gentry, whose land was valuable only so long as there was adequate labor to till it, faced ruin when their peasants slipped away. Yet they could neither avoid nor reduce their obligation of military service to the state lest they lose their claim to the land. Occasionally, even members of the gentry accepted slavery as an easy way out of the obligations they could not meet with their shrinking labor force. Threatened with bankruptcy stemming from the freedom to trade granted only to foreigners and privileged Russians, townspeople too sought the same escape that the peasants found attractive. They fled to the frontier or volunteered to become slaves.

The serious loss of revenue and the alarming possibility that there would not be enough human resources to meet military requirements forced the state to bind every class of society to its appointed task and its allotted location. A Zemskii

A meeting of the Zemskii Sobor in 1649

Sobor in 1649, most of whose members were of the gentry, appealed to the government for relief from the problems brought about by the vanishing population. The tsar must protect landowners—nobles, the church, and the state itself—from the flight of tenants delinquent in payment of rent or interest or taxes. So the government drafted a new law code, the Ulozhenie of 1649, which would be the last for nearly two centuries, legalizing bondage in Russia.

The Ulozhenie removed the time limitation upon the right of landholders to track down and return their peasants to their estates and assured the gentry that the police power of the state would assist them in doing so. The law provided harsh penalties for anyone found guilty of sheltering runaways. Peasants, thereafter serfs, were bound to the soil they tilled, but for a century they had the right to till it. Under Peter III in 1762, they lost even that right and became simply chattel—disposable at the landlord's whim. This deprivation of the right to move was fastened upon the former peasants for all coming generations, for serfdom became hereditary.

There was more than economic pressure to impel the nation toward curbing the freedom of its masses. Throughout the sixteenth century and most of the seventeenth, Sweden, Poland, and Turkey threatened to wipe out Russia's independence. Had the state been unable to locate the recruit and the taxpayer, it could not have survived. Because only men and boys were actual or potential recruits and taxpayers, no matter what their ages, the census rolls included only the names of males.

The government required landowners to collect and transmit the taxes that their serfs continued to pay even though they had lost their status as free peasants. Landholders also had to make serfs available to serve in the army in time of need. Consequently, they had to treat their serfs at least well enough so that they would not run away, look after their health and well-being, and feed them in time of famine. By the latter half of the eighteenth century, however, the gentry were ignoring these obligations to their serfs with impunity.

The 1649 code also imposed bondage upon the Russian urban population. All had to remain in the town where they were living in 1649 and accept restrictions on their movement from one district to another. Townsmen could not become slaves. They could not even marry women from another town. Sons must follow their father's occupation and remain in the town where they were born. On the other hand, the government sought to ease the plight of merchants by giving them the exclusive right to trade at retail.

The Ulozhenie froze the gentry in their status, just as it imposed bondage upon the rest of the population. No member of the class might henceforth become a slave. None might avoid the obligation to render military service. The class became hereditary, because all were born into the class and, with unimportant exceptions, none might enter it except by birth. Only the gentry could own serfs and no other could own land tilled by serf labor. All preferment in the army and in government was an exclusive privilege of the gentry. From 1649, all distinction between boyars and princely families and gentry tended to break down, for all bore the common duty to serve in the army. Similarly, distinctions between those who held their land by service tenure and those who held it by hereditary right tended to disappear. All came to hold their land by hereditary right and were obligated to render military service.

The Ulozhenie of 1649 produced little that was new. It codified, and therefore clarified, conditions that had been developing for years and that had tended to crystallize during Michael's reign. Bondage now had full legal recognition. The Ulozhenie would continue for over a century for the upper classes and for well over two centuries for the serfs.

Church Reform and Schism

The tsar's favorite churchman was a Moscow priest named Nikon, a man of matchless eloquence and some learning. The boundless ambition of this son of a peasant carried him to the highest church office before he was fifty. In 1652 the tsar ordered Nikon's election as patriarch of Moscow.

Nikon's elevation heralded decisive action on a program of church reform that had long been under consideration. Learned clergy of the church, particularly Greek and Latin scholars, had been protesting for generations that errors had persisted in church practice since Kievan times, through faulty translation of liturgical books. Through such errors, which had received official sanction in the church council of 1551, Russian priests followed the practice of using two fingers instead of three in the benediction and even justified it as symbolizing the divine and the human nature of Christ. The litany provided two Hallelujahs, not the three heard in Western churches. Faulty translation from the Greek had produced a misspelling of the name Jesus, and the Russian clergy persisted in perpetuating the mistake. Attention to the form rather than the substance of Christianity, which had long characterized Russian Orthodoxy, brought stubborn support for the strange practices even though they were demonstrably without scholarly foundation.

Ivan IV had called the church council of 1551 to undertake the reform of ritual as well as morals, but its caution in approaching questions of ritual had been disappointing. Filaret had begun a systematic correction of the liturgical books, and the work had gone forward through the reign of the first Romanov. Alexis, a pious man himself, for years had heard the view of leading ecclesiastics that there was need for further reform.

Soon after his election to the patriarchate, Nikon took up once more the correction of the ritual to conform with the best translations from Greek to Russian of the Byzantine liturgical books on which Orthodoxy rested. There can be no question that Nikon was right in undertaking the elimination of stupid errors, but, showing neither patience nor tact nor prudence, the patriarch overrode all opposition in the most highhanded way. He drove protesting clergy from the pulpit, torturing some and exiling others. Squads of Nikon's lackeys broke into homes to remove icons or holy images painted in a way that the patriarch considered heretical.

Nikon was not content to order reform of church practice. He presumed to dictate to the tsar in matters having nothing to do with religion and even claimed the title of sovereign, insisting upon signing state documents as Filaret had done in the previous reign. Alexis finally lost all patience with the patriarch's presumptuous manner and called Nikon to trial by a church council in 1666 that deposed him and banished him to a monastery. The charge against him was that he had presumed to put himself above the tsar. Many of the reforms that he had pushed through went undisturbed, however.

The state church continued ever after to follow the ritual as corrected by Nikon, but many Russians refused to accept the reforms. The fiery archpriest Avvakum wrote a defiant protest against the reforms, and his defiance brought him death at the stake. Avvakum and the other protesters were not ignorant men; in fact, they were some of the best educated of the Russian clergy. Indeed, they were intensely nationalistic, proud of Russian practice and of Moscow as the Third Rome, and resentful of Greek or foreign and implicitly subversive customs.

The Old Believers—or Schismatics, or Old Ritualists, or *Raskolniki*—clung to the old erroneous services and looked upon Nikon and the tsars who upheld his way of doing things as devils incarnate. Although their religious position could hardly maintain itself against that of intelligent people, the sect in later years attracted followers who resisted tsardom on political grounds as the Old Believers themselves resisted tsardom on religious grounds. Whatever the depth of their religious convictions, the Schismatics opposed the uncompromising surge toward autocracy. Millions embraced the faith that bordered on treason, and nineteenth-century emperors viciously persecuted them.

Correction of church practice was of far less importance in itself than was the extension of state control over the church that Nikon's reforms manifested. A century earlier, Henry VIII had done the same thing in England. The steady drive toward strong monarchy, so unmistakable in Western Europe in the sixteenth and seventeenth centuries, had appeared in Russia as far back as the reign of Ivan III. The extension of state control over matters spiritual as well as temporal went along with the emergence of the nation-state. The rulers of England, France, Spain, Prussia, and the Scandinavian countries all championed the cause of centralism against the medieval pattern of localism and weak national authority.

The Ulozhenie of 1649 codified this extension of state power, not only over social classes by freezing people in their professions and to the localities of their birth, but also by forbidding the church to acquire any more land. It established the Prikaz of Monasteries, which thenceforth controlled monastic jurisdiction, and it stipulated that parish priests, formerly elected by their parishioners, be appointed by the bishops. Because only monks could become bishops, because monasteries now were under state control, and because bishops now would name parish priests, the entire edifice of priestly jurisdiction came under the authority of the state, in effect, the tsar. Indeed, Nikon and Alexis showed less concern for the religious aspects of the controversy that followed than for the authority over matters spiritual and secular that they sought to impose.

Poland, the Cossacks, and Sweden

A sustained effort by the Polish government to bring the unruly Zaporozhian Cossacks under control culminated in 1638 in termination of the autonomy that Warsaw had allowed the Host. The Polish government named its own officials to replace the traditionally elected hetman and his officers.

By this time Warsaw had awarded much of the fertile steppe to Polish nobles who had brought their serfs with them and who now attempted to impose serfdom upon the Cossack families they found farming the land. Catholic missionaries had attempted forcibly to convert the Cossacks away from Orthodoxy and, meeting resistance, had won the pope's consent to make Uniats out of the Cossacks. A Uniat practiced religion according to Orthodox rites but accepted the authority of the pope. Some Cossacks became Uniats, but many became more staunchly Orthodox against this subtle effort to undermine their faith. To the mounting political and economic pressure from Warsaw, the addition of the religious issue was enough to provoke rebellion.

In 1649 the Zaporozhian Cossacks chose as their hetman Bogdan Khmelnitsky, whose family had suffered cruelly at the hands of Polish noblemen, to lead them in a fight to recover their autonomy. The entire Ukraine rose in revolt against Polish domination. Peasants, fearing the approach of serfdom, and even Tatars from Crimea joined the hetman and his Zaporozhian Host. Khmelnitsky was successful, at least for a while, in obtaining the restoration of Cossack autonomy and raising the number of Cossacks that Warsaw consented to register to forty thousand.

Because the Cossacks could not hope to maintain their independence of the Poles for long, Khmelnitsky offered the Ukraine to Alexis as a protectorate of Russia. However, with the Polish frontier no farther away than Smolensk, Moscow hesitated to receive the gift for fear of inviting attack from the west. Khmelnitsky prodded Alexis to action by threatening to offer his allegiance to the Turkish sultan and even talked of joining the Poles in a war against Russia should Moscow spurn his offer. A Zemskii Sobor urged Alexis to receive the Ukraine and, in 1654, Khmelnitsky and the tsar came to terms. Moscow granted autonomy to the Host, recognized sixty thousand registered Cossacks, and received the oath of allegiance. The hetman promised not to deal with Poland or Turkey except through Moscow.

The Zemskii Sobor that urged the incorporation of the Ukraine did so in full knowledge that the challenge to Poland would bring war. With enthusiastic national backing and with the help of the Cossacks, the Russian armies were everywhere victorious. Vilna, the Lithuanian capital, surrendered to the Russians as did Kovno, Grodno, and Lublin. Smolensk fell. While Muscovite armies ravaged central Poland, Khmelnitsky and his Cossacks overran Galicia. King Charles X of Sweden joined the war, seized Warsaw, and claimed the Polish crown. Threatened with annihilation, the Poles asked Alexis for terms. A truce signed at Andrusovo in 1667 provided that Poland cede Smolensk and the east bank of the Dnieper to Russia in exchange for the return of other Polish territory that Moscow had captured. Russia was to occupy Kiev, on the west bank of the Dnieper, for two years. Russia never gave it up. Again the hetman of the Zaporozhian Cossacks swore allegiance to Moscow, an oath that his successors repeated or refused as it suited their purpose. The wars between Poland and Russia, in which the Crimean Tatars occasionally joined with or fought against the Dnieper Cossacks, left the Ukraine prostrate.

No sooner had Moscow won "eternal peace," as the terms of every settlement with Poland declared it to be, than the government faced an uprising of the Don Cossacks. One of their leaders, Stenka Razin, raised the standard of class war, and peasants all along the southeast frontier joined him and the many Cossacks who followed him. Many of the Don Host were Old Believers, which made the rising an expression of religious as well as social discontent. Razin seized Astrakhan in 1669 and made it his capital. From there he extended his control over the Volga and Don basins and even into the Oka toward Moscow. The villagers rose to greet him, and peasants butchered the neighboring landowners to celebrate their freedom.

For three years Russian armies fought against the risings that Razin's class hatred inspired. At last, the provinces that had joined him were "pacified" after the slaughter of a hundred thousand peasants. Razin was captured and quartered alive in 1671, but neither the landowners whom it had threatened nor the masses whom it had stirred soon forgot the social upheaval that he had led.

The Growth of Western Influence

Without exception the chief advisers to Tsar Alexis were men who appreciated Western technical and cultural superiority over Russia. The number of Westerners brought into Russia to ply their crafts and teach the natives their skills grew rapidly during the middle years of the seventeenth century. The tsar even gave foreigners in Moscow their own area in which to live—the so-called "German," or foreign, quarter—where they could have their own homes, churches, and shops.

One contact with the West lay through Poland by way of Kiev, where the theological academy produced the Greek and Latin scholars who helped correct the liturgical books for Patriarch Nikon. Trade with Sweden provided another important contact with the Western world. By 1665, business relations with the Netherlands had become so important that the government hired an English agent to handle Russian commercial interests there. Dutch shipwrights, carpenters, and sea captains entered the Russian service to instruct, build, and direct the work of Russians assigned to learn Western skills.

The foreign quarter of Moscow set before those who visited it a way of living that attracted some and horrified others. Western men went clean-shaven or wore only mustaches. Their knee breeches, silk stockings, and shoes contrasted with the long, bulky robes and boots that burdened Russians. Their homes were neat and attractively decorated. Their conduct was less coarse and crude than that of Russians. Their women appeared in public gatherings with men. They rode about in fine light carriages and lived in brick houses adorned with flower gardens. There dwelt the families of many Dutch, English, Danish, and German traders, doctors, artisans, and school masters. Many French Protestant refugees lived there along with three thousand Scots—Gordons, Grahams, Hamiltons, Drummonds, Dalziels, Crawfords—who had fled England when Charles I lost his war with Parliament.

A few Muscovites dared to imitate the living they had come to know in the foreign quarter. Not many shaved their beards, used cosmetics and tobacco, or set aside their Russian garb, for to do so would have made them conspicuous and perhaps have invited bodily harm, but some redecorated their homes in the Western style, and a daring few bought Western carriages. In such homes, the seclusion of women came to an end with the abolition of the terem, the oriental custom of keeping women in well-born families from the sight of men until their marriage.

The tsar himself sympathized with Western customs. He shocked old Muscovites by introducing his second wife and his daughters to society. He hired a German orchestra. He rode through the streets in a Western carriage. Indeed, the most ominous conduct of all to those who regarded Western manners with suspicion was his association and counsel with men who believed Russia had much to learn from Western Europe. His chief advisers were men of such conviction. Their choice was no accident. Alexis wanted their counsel and leadership.

Of those near the tsar who symbolized this fascination with things Western, the most outspoken was Athanasy Ordyn-Nashchokin. As head of the Office of Foreign Affairs, he arranged peace with Sweden and Poland but left the service rather than condone the retention of Kiev beyond the two years agreed upon in the Truce of Andrusovo. As governor of his native Pskov, he sought to remove the advantages that German traders enjoyed in the area and encouraged Russian merchants to develop trade with Sweden. He keenly felt Russia's need to gain an outlet on the Baltic through which it could establish direct contact with the West. He urged the union of Poland and Russia under a single crown and proposed that Alexis's oldest son become Polish king. (On the death of his father he would also, of course, become tsar of Russia.) He sought to develop trade relations with Persia over the Caspian and directed the construction of the ship that Stenka Razin later destroyed at Astrakhan. He organized postal communication with Poland.

The old Muscovites, who called him "the foreigner," hated Ordyn-Nashchokin for his respect for Western customs and for his endless criticism of inefficient Russian ways of doing things. He insisted that Russians might learn improved techniques even from their enemies. He deplored the Russian's reliance on superior officials and urged subordinates to develop initiative of their own. He learned German, Latin, and Polish to better deal with foreigners. In his unselfish and conscientious devotion to the state in war and peace and as an administrator who sought to bring order to governmental processes, Ordyn-Nashchokin was an outstanding servant to the crown. In his awareness of Russia's backwardness and inefficiency, in his conviction that there need be nothing shameful in "borrowing what is good" even from the heretical West, in his belief that Russia must win an outlet on the Baltic, he was a forerunner of Peter the Great.

Fedor III

Upon the death of Alexis in 1676, his fourteen-year-old invalid son Fedor (1676–1682) succeeded to the throne. The dead ruler's chief adviser, Matveev, proposed that the succession pass over the helpless youth and also his idiot brother Ivan in favor of vigorous young Peter, four-year-old son of Alexis by his second wife. The Boyar Duma suspected the proposal as a way of assuring Matveev's continued influence, and thus insisted on the coronation of Fedor. The new tsar exemplified the growing interest in Western culture, for he had learned Polish and even Latin. Prince Vasily Golitsyn, who managed affairs for the bedridden ruler, knew German, Latin, and Greek.

While leading troops against the Turks and Tatars, Golitsyn became convinced that the ineffectiveness of Russian armies was attributable to the miestnichestvo, the practice that assigned military and civil rank in the Moscow state to boyar families according to their seniority in the service of the tsar. Fedor agreed and publicly burned the official book of ranks. Henceforth the tsar's will would determine all official assignments.

GROWTH OF **RUSSIA**,1462-1676

Fedor surrounded himself with men of Western sympathies, and his wife even urged courtiers to shave and dress in Western style. Such heresies were still suspect among most Russians, and many whispered that Fedor was antichrist for defending such actions, just as they had called his father and Nikon antichrist for permitting the rewriting of the sacred books by men suspected of knowing Latin.

The reign of Fedor lasted only six years. His death in 1682 again raised the question of the succession. Ivan, the last surviving son of Alexis by his first wife, was nearly blind, had difficulty in speaking, and was subject to epileptic seizures. There was also Peter, by this time ten years old, and there was a court party to support each of the remaining sons.

Suggested Reading

ALLEN, W. E. D., *The Ukraine: A History* (New York, 1941).

ALMEDINGEN, M. E., *The Romanovs: Three Centuries of an Ill-Fated Dynasty* (New York, 1966).

AVRICH, P., *Russian Rebels, 1600-1800* (New York, 1972).

AVVAKUM, S., *The Life of the Archpriest Avvakum by Himself* (London, 1968).

BAIN, R. N., *The First Romanovs, 1613-1725: A History of Muscovite Civilization and the Rise of Modern Russia under Peter the Great and His Forerunners* (New York, 1967).

BARON, S. H. (ed.), *The Travels of Olearius in Seventeenth Century Russia* (Stanford, 1967).

BLUM, J., *Lord and Peasant in Russia: From the Ninth to the Nineteenth Century* (Princeton, 1961).

BOLSHAKOFF, S., *Russian Nonconformity* (Philadelphia, 1950).

CHERNIAVSKY, M., *Tsar and People* (New Haven, 1961).

CONYBEARE, F. C., *Russian Dissenters* (New York, 1962).

COWLES, V., *The Romanovs* (New York, 1971)

CRUMMEY, R. O., *The Old Believers and the World of Anti-Christ* (Madison, WI, 1970).

FUHRMANN, J., *Tsar Alexis, His Reign and His Russia* (Gulf Breeze, FL, 1981).

GOLDER, F. A., *Russian Expansion on the Pacific, 1641-1850* (New York, 1971).

GREY, I., *The Romanovs. The Rise and Fall of a Dynasty* (Garden City, NY, 1970).

HELLIE, R., *Enserfment and Military Change in Muscovy* (Chicago, 1971).

HINDUS, M., *The Cossacks: The Story of A Warrior People* (Garden City, NY, 1945).

HRUSHEVSKY, M., *A History of Ukraine* (New Haven, 1941).

ISWOLSKY, H., *Christ in Russia: The History, Tradition and Life of the Russian Church* (Milwaukee, 1960).

KLIUCHEVSKY, V. O., *The Rise of the Romanovs* (New York, 1970).

LANTZEFF, G. V., *Siberia in the Seventeenth Century* (Berkeley, 1943).

LINCOLN, W. B., *The Romanovs: Autocrats of All the Russias* (New York, 1981).

LONGWORTH, P., *The Cossacks: Five Centuries of Turbulent Life on the Russian Steppe* (New York, 1970).

————, *Alexis: Tsar of All the Russias* (New York, 1984).

MEDLIN, W. K., *Renaissance Influences and Religious Reforms in Russia* (Geneva, 1971).

MILIUKOV, P. N., *Outlines of Russian Culture*, vol. 1 (Philadelphia, 1975).

O'BRIEN, C. B., *Muscovy and the Ukraine: From the Pereiaslavl Agreement to the Truce of Androsovo, 1654–1667* (Berkeley, 1963).

PALMER, W., *The Patriarch and the Tsar*, 6 vols. (London, 1905).

SHCHAKOVSKOY, Z., *Precursors of Peter the Great* (London, 1964).

VERNADSKY, G., *Bogdan, Hetman of the Ukraine* (New Haven, 1941).

CHAPTER 9

Peter the Great

No prince or tsar or emperor before or after his time ever made such an impact on the Russian land and its people as did Peter I (1682–1725). Not until the period of communist rule in the twentieth century would there be a regime of significance as great for Russia and for Europe as that of Peter the Great. Indeed, anyone who tries will find many similarities between the Petrine revolution of the early eighteenth century and the Bolshevik revolution of the early twentieth.

The sociopolitical storm that broke with such violence over the Russian people in Peter's reign, and the diplomatic storm that swept with similar force over Europe at the same time, may well have produced a greater shock both inside Russia and abroad than the one loosed by Lenin two centuries later. Inside Russia, Lenin's revolution may have added, but only added, to the turmoil and chaos to which Russians had grown accustomed through years of war. Outside Russia, the communist seizure of power met, after a futile attempt to undo it, with a mixture of indifference, contempt, and hostility.

Peter came to the throne at the age of ten, but left the main tasks of government to others for the first thirteen years of his reign. He assumed power at the age of twenty-three, and for the next thirty years he drove his people relentlessly forward and out of their medieval backwardness toward modern European civilization. His success was not complete, for Russia to the end of the monarchy was never able to keep up with Western strides. Nor did he begin the process himself, for his predecessors had been prodding Russia gently for two centuries toward Western culture. But Peter's reign was decisive for his nation and for Europe. This restless giant dedicated his enormous vitality and great ability, not to his own aggrandizement, nor even to that of the monarchy, but, as he himself insisted, "to the interests of the state."

Russia's emergence as a modern nation carried with it profound implications for the rest of Europe. From Peter's time forward European rulers and diplomats had to reckon with the potential impact of Russia's involvement beyond its borders. At the same time, its foreign entanglements frequently provoked a violent reaction upon its domestic affairs. There would scarcely be a year and never a decade following Peter's death in 1725 when Europe could afford to turn its back on Russia and indulge itself in the family quarrels that were endemic to European nationalism. Conversely, Russian society as Peter had refashioned it was forever sensitive, in one way or another, to outside stimulation.

The Regency

Fedor left behind a brother Ivan, a sickly idiot subject to fits and nearly blind, and six healthy sisters, all children of Alexis by his first wife, Maria Miloslavsky. There was also Peter, Alexis's son by his second wife, Natalia Naryshkin. In the absence of any law covering the succession, the patriarch Joachim asked the crowd gathered in Red Square which of the sons should become tsar, and the people, prompted by pressure from Naryshkin supporters, named Peter. His mother and other relatives and the patriarch embarked on a rule by favorites similar to the situation that had become so familiar under the early Romanovs.

A few days later, streltsy regiments massed outside the Kremlin to demand the punishment of their officers for withholding their pay. The government meekly gave in. The Miloslavsky clan, led by Alexis's daughter Sophia, saw an opportunity to drive the Naryshkins from the palace. Sophia promised the streltsy pay increases and whispered that the rightful tsar, her brother Ivan, was in danger of being murdered. The streltsy stormed the Kremlin, ignored the fact that Ivan was obviously safe, hacked to pieces their unpopular officers, and cut down many of Peter's supporters, including most of the Naryshkin family, while Peter and his mother huddled in fear for their lives. The soldiers roamed the streets of Moscow killing boyars and urging the masses to rise against bondage. At the insistence of the streltsy, a Zemskii Sobor was called to reorder the succession. It was the last time the assembly of the land would ever meet. Ivan and Peter became co-tsars by acclamation. Sophia consented to serve as regent.

Throughout the seven-year regency of Sophia, the streltsy were a constant threat to stable government. As a hereditary military force recruited among city dwellers, they enjoyed special trade and craft privileges living apart in their own quarters and feeding upon pride, arrogance, superstition, and political reaction. They served as standing army, police force, and palace guard, but showed less interest in military operations than in fostering discontent and defying authority. They encouraged unrest among the Cossacks. They called for an end to the

Tsarevna Sophia

reforms of Nikon, for many of them were Old Believers. They threatened the extermination of the boyars as a class and demanded an end to serfdom. They fought pitched battles with other regiments led by officers loyal to the government. They threatened to drive Sophia into a convent and raise to the throne their own favorite commander. They seized the Kremlin and forced the regent and her brother Ivan to seek refuge in the Trinity Monastery north of Moscow. Finally, loyal troops subdued the streltsy and they went free as though the government did not dare to put them in their place.

Aside from her unattractive personality, Sophia was a remarkable woman. Her father, Alexis, had allowed tutors to enter the terem to teach his daughter Polish, French, and Latin. Her chief adviser, Prince Vasily Golitsyn, proposed an end to serfdom and a wide extension of education and enthusiastically embraced Western learning. People suspected the two of wanting to return Russia to the Roman church. Sophia assumed the title of sovereign along with her brothers, and contemplated the removal of Ivan and Peter to leave herself alone on the throne.

In 1683 the Polish king, Jan Sobieski, joined with Austria to stop the Turkish drive into Europe at the very gates of Vienna. Determined to organize a Christian crusade against the Moslems, Sobieski brought Venice and the pope into the alliance. Russia joined the league in 1686 in return for another "perpetual peace" with Poland. Moscow promised to attack Turkey and received clear title to Kiev, which it had taken temporarily at the Truce of Andrusovo a generation earlier.

Golitsyn, who had arranged the alliance with Poland, led a hundred thousand Russians against the outpost of Turkish power in the Crimea. Then he withdrew without accomplishing anything more than warning the Tatars and Turks by his appearance there that they must some day lose control of the steppe.

This year of 1689 brought another defeat to the regent's government. By the Treaty of Nerchinsk, Moscow surrendered the basin of the Amur, to whose banks its troops and pioneers had driven only to be turned back by the Chinese. However, the treaty with China, which would last for a century and a half, provided for trade relations across the frontier. Tea, the chief import after 1689, became the Russian national drink. The treaty also had the effect of turning Russian interest in East Asia toward the northeast corner of the continent, toward the Bering Strait, and eventually across it to Alaska.

Peter's Youth and Character

While Sophia ruled, Peter and his mother—unwelcome at court—lived just outside Moscow on a royal estate in the village of Preobrazhenskoe, where the boy roamed the neighborhood free of all restraint. His mother could not control him, and Sophia was indifferent to his welfare and conduct.

Peter gathered about him a band of boys his own age, some from noble families and others from servant or middle-class homes. These playmates Peter led on pranks and escapades that terrorized the neighborhood. When Peter was eleven he organized his friends into play regiments, which he drilled and later led on maneuvers. The boys built a wooden fort they named Pressburg, complete with bastions and ditches. As the regiments grew older, the play became more serious, and the assaults on the "fortress of Pressburg" often produced casualties. "Bombardier Peter," as the young tsar called himself, enjoyed setting off fireworks and later firing cannons. From a Dutch citizen, Franz Timmerman, Peter learned the fundamentals of geometry, military engineering, and artillery. He became an enthusiastic drummer and to the end of his life liked to march in parades beating on his drum while others rode in state.

When Peter was fourteen, he and his companions found an old English sailboat in storage. Timmerman explained its operation, and Peter launched the craft in the river that flowed through Preobrazhenskoe. Later he moved the new toy to a lake nearby and there, under the direction of a Dutch shipmaster, built other boats, toiling at the work alongside Dutch carpenters from the foreign quarter of Moscow.

Such radical and dangerous pastimes alarmed Peter's mother, who thought to turn her son to a settled life by having him marry at the age of sixteen. But the match with Eudoxia Lopukhin distracted Peter only momentarily, and within weeks he returned to his boats. Five years later, the young tsar stood at Arkhangel and looked out fascinated upon the sea. He went on board foreign ships in the harbor, talked and drank with Dutch sailors, and labored on a ship of his own, which he launched in 1694. He learned some Dutch, wore the dress of a Dutch sailor, affected the walk and manner of a sailor the rest of his life, and traveled by sea whenever there was a choice.

From Preobrazhenskoe Peter often visited in the foreign quarter of Moscow. Here he became fascinated with Western manners and Western life. Of the many close attachments he made there, one was with the Scottish adventurer Patrick Gordon, who had served the tsars since the time of Alexis as diplomat and military adviser. Another of Peter's intimate friends was the Swiss Francis Lefort, twenty years older than Peter, a man notorious for his drinking prowess in an age renowned for drunkenness.

Peter chose his friends from all nationalities and all classes. Some of his Russian companions—men like Fedor Romodanovsky, Boris Sheremetiev, and the Dolgorukys—were from princely families who had served Moscow for centuries. Others were from humble homes. Alexander Menshikov, who became one of the wealthiest and most powerful men of his time, had once sold pies on the streets of Moscow. Paul Yaguzhinsky, procurator of the Senate, had been a swineherd. Vice-Chancellor Peter Shafirov had been a clerk in a small store. Alexis Kurbatov, once a noble's house serf, became vice-governor of Arkhangel. Most of these men served the tsar, drank with him, and took his violent abuse until their death, for Peter did not often demote or destroy those around him as Ivan IV had done.

Peter's appearance and manner were impressive. Nearly seven feet tall, broad-shouldered and powerful, taking long strides as he walked, he was a picture of contrast to the dwarfs and misshapen ones he kept about him for amusement. A nervous tic marred his features when angry. He was crude and vulgar, subject to fits of violent rage, and capable of heartless cruelty. Yet he was quick to admit a weakness, to correct an error. A man of tireless energy, he was surely the most hard-working man in Russia. He spent little time in the historic capital city of Moscow or in his newly created capital city of St. Petersburg, carved out of the northern marshes, but moved restlessly over the land investigating, inspecting, changing, correcting, leading his people even to the point of dragging or driving them into improved, particularly Western, ways of doing things. He literally set his people an example in the sacrifices he called on them to make. He was proud of his gnarled hands, marked with the calluses of a woodsman. He started at the bottom in both army and navy, learning the skills that common soldiers must learn and promoting himself rank by rank as his prowess grew— to general after Poltava (a major Russian victory over Sweden in 1709), to admiral after the war with Sweden.

Peter mastered many crafts and professions: he was a carpenter, shipwright, navigator, military engineer, joiner, woodsman, and dentist. His fascination with education prompted him to give Russia its first nonclerical schools. He studied military strategy and tactics and mastered both. He was a competent naval commander. Peter had little formal schooling, but he learned to read and write in Russian, and in Dutch, which he preferred. If he was not an intellectual, he was highly intelligent. To that he added the spices of curiosity and impatience to try out some new technique or art—for example, dentistry and surgery.

From the days of his childhood Peter looked on the West as a source of strength from which Russia must draw. To him the West meant progress, productivity, and efficiency; Muscovite Russia meant backwardness and inefficiency. Unless Russia could catch up with the West, it would not long endure. He read the lesson of the Time of Troubles with more perception than any other man.

The Turkish War

With the backing of the streltsy regiments in Moscow, Sophia made a move in 1689 to set aside Ivan and Peter and seat herself on the throne. Peter escaped to the Trinity Monastery and called his "play regiments" to his side. The plan collapsed when Golitsyn, the patriarch Joachim, and even some of the streltsy deserted the regent. Sophia was packed off to a convent and the nation continued under the two tsars.

For a while Peter's mother Natalia and her Naryshkin relatives directed the government while Peter, seventeen years old, returned to his war games and his ships. Natalia died five years later, and Peter had to leave his play to take over the direction of affairs in Moscow. The play regiments went with him to become the first of the Guards, the Preobrazhensky and Semenovsky regiments, named for the villages where they had fought their sham battles.

Immediately Peter decided again to challenge Turkish power on the Black Sea. In the spring of 1695 he opened his drive against Azov. Attempts to storm the fortress failed, however, and in the autumn the tsar abandoned the siege; he returned to Moscow to prepare for another campaign, sending off to Austria and Prussia for engineers, miners, and sappers. He ordered a warship from Holland and proposed to build others like it for a combined land-sea assault on Azov. He sent the Guards regiments, along with all the workers he could muster, to Voronezh to fell trees and build ships. The tsar moved into a two-room hut nearby to supervise the project, working hard alongside the men.

The fleet, with Peter commanding a squadron, slipped down the Don into the Sea of Azov and blocked off the port from any possible Turkish relief. Azov surrendered after a two-months' siege. Peter's new army and navy had won a notable victory. Then he ordered construction of a naval base near Azov, naming it Taganrog, and he swore to launch a great fleet on the Black Sea to station at the new base. This would mean long bitter war with the Turks. Young Russians would need to go to the West to learn about shipbuilding and fortification and gunnery. Peter ordered fifty sons of good families to set off at once, but the nation also needed allies. An embassy would need to visit Western courts to urge a European alliance against the Turks. It was decided that Peter himself would go.

Only days before Peter left for the West his agents uncovered a plot against his life. Several officers of the streltsy, most of them Old Believers who abhorred Peter's consorting with foreigners and his decision to leave the country, schemed to assassinate the tsar. They planned to restore Sophia as regent for Peter's son Alexis, because the witless Ivan had died. Six of the ringleaders confessed to the plot and were beheaded.

The Western Journey

A great embassy of two hundred well-born Russians, servants, guards, clowns, and dwarfs crossed the frontier in March 1697 and headed for the Swedish port of Riga. Lefort officially led the embassy; the tsar went along incognito as "Peter Mikhailov," who wanted to learn shipbuilding. At Libau, in Courland, Peter first looked out on the Baltic.

The embassy moved on to Köenigsberg, the tsar traveling by sea while the rest moved overland. There a Prussian colonel gave the tsar lessons in gunnery and awarded a certificate of proficiency to his royal pupil. He lingered in Köenigsberg waiting for news of the election of a new king of Poland and wrote to Romodanovsky to move troops to the Polish border if Augustus, the Russian candidate, should lose the election. When the Polish election turned out to Peter's liking, the tsar moved on to Berlin where he took another short course in military tactics.

Now Peter was impatient to visit Holland, the home of many artisans in Russian service. In Hamburg he boarded a ship for Zaandam. For a few days, "Master Peter, carpenter of Zaandam" worked in the shipyards and drank Dutch beer at the local tavern.

After a week in Zaandam Peter went to Amsterdam for four months and studied mathematics, architecture, astronomy, navigation, and fortification. He learned a little of engraving and printing. He visited hospitals and attended the anatomy lectures of a famous surgeon. He watched a dentist at work and supplied himself with instruments with which he later practiced on his own subjects. He filled notebooks with information on ship construction, sailed small boats on the inland sea, and worked as ship's carpenter on a galley for himself. He met the English King William III, who invited him to London to learn more of shipbuilding.

Peter crossed the Channel to England in January 1698, and stayed there another four months. He attended the opening of Parliament, received the Doctor of Laws degree from Oxford University, visited the Mint, the Greenwich Observatory, and the Tower of London. He bought a coffin to send home for the edification of Russian coffinmakers. He sat for his portrait by Kneller, studied clockmaking, discussed theology with Anglican bishops, visited the arsenal at Woolwich, and roamed the shipyards at Deptford.

From London Peter traveled to Vienna and expected to go on to Venice to learn still more about shipbuilding and also to urge the government to hold fast to the alliance against Turkey, but word came to him in Vienna that the streltsy were again in revolt. Romodanovsky had the uprising under control, but Peter hurried home to punish the leaders. He had been gone from Russia eighteen months.

In the capitals of the West, Peter found no one to listen to his appeal for a Christian crusade against the Turks. William III and his allies were between wars in their determination to thwart the ambition of Louis XIV. London even hoped that Vienna would come to terms with the sultan and join the alliance against France. The powers were willing to encourage Peter to continue his war with Turkey, for then the sultan would not be able to help his friend, the French king, but they would give Russia no aid.

As an educational venture for the tsar himself, the Western journey was a great success. Peter returned to Russia determined to impose on his people the techniques and even the manners of the West. He would rid his land of the ignorance that kept it weak, of the backwardness resulting from Russia's isolation from the West during those critical years from 1400 to 1700. He left scores of his companions in England and Holland to continue their schooling, and he hired hundreds of Scottish, English, Dutch, and German carpenters, shipwrights, sailors, doctors, teachers, cooks, musicians, and gardeners to return to Russia with him.

In August 1698, Peter was back in Moscow. He had been the first Russian ruler to travel abroad in six centuries. He would again visit the West, which symbolized to him the skills and the learning in which he knew his own land to be so backward.

Suppression of the Streltsy

The streltsy decided in the spring of 1698 to take advantage of the tsar's absence to restore the relatively gentle government of the regency. Where these privileged regiments had grown accustomed to a life of ease and indolence through long periods between occasional short campaigns, Peter kept them away from their families always busy at something. When not fighting the Crimean Tatars, the streltsy had to build ships at Voronezh or throw up fortifications on the Sea of Azov or march to the western frontier to interfere in Polish politics. They saw their influence at court slipping away as Peter favored the new Guards regiments. The crowning insult came when the tsar moved the streltsy regiments from Moscow to new posts around the Sea of Azov.

Leaders of the plot read a letter purporting to come from Sophia to the streltsy regiments in south Russia asking them to join her in reviving the regency. The men set off for Moscow determined to raze the German quarter and to kill the government leaders.

Patrick Gordon met the streltsy south of Moscow with a well-armed force of loyal troops and captured the rebels without losing a man of his own. He tortured scores to death on the spot and strung others on gibbets along the highways as a warning to any who would challenge the regime. The rest he threw into dungeons to await the tsar's return.

Preobrazhenskoe, where the trials took place, became a scene of unspeakable horror during the autumn of 1698. Peter set up fourteen torture chambers to deal with the rebels and even with their families. For days on end men and women were flogged or garroted or buried alive. Hundreds were beheaded, Peter often wielding the axe himself. Then there would be days of feasting and drinking, after which the tsar would return to the torture chambers and the scaffolds. For five months a thousand bodies lay where they had been cut down from the gibbets or kicked aside from the executioner's block. Early in 1699 in south Russia, Peter settled in the same vicious way with the mutinous streltsy who had stayed behind at Azov while the others had marched on Moscow. Hundreds more died before Peter satisfied his rage.

The tsar disbanded sixteen streltsy regiments involved in the mutiny, and denied their men and officers alike the right to enlist in any branch of the service. Families of the executed men, driven from their homes, went wandering over the land. A few of the regiments survived a while longer until 1705, but the political power of the streltsy never reappeared.

The Petrine Reforms

Peter was so impatient to pattern the ways of his land after those of the West that he began shaving beards even before he settled with the streltsy. He reckoned the beard to be the foremost symbol of Russia's backwardness and superstition. The day after his return he gathered the men at court about him, and with a large pair of shears cut away their beards. Peter realized that he could not shear every man and keep him shorn. So he decreed that men of the gentry who chose to keep a beard must pay a tax of a hundred rubles and wear a badge showing that they had paid it, and that every peasant who entered the gates of a town must pay a kopek or surrender his beard. The beard quickly lost its popularity among the upper classes; it became the mark of a peasant until the nineteenth century.

The wearing of Western-style clothing became obligatory for government workers and members of the gentry and their wives. Peter himself, with his preference for the garb of a Dutch sailor, also occasionally appeared at receptions wearing buckled shoes, breeches, and the Western short coat. Within a year or so this ''German manner'' of dress was popular in the capital and among the upper classes generally. To the end of tsardom, the peasant continued to dress as he had done for centuries in a long belted shirt and baggy trousers stuffed into high boots.

On January 1, 1700, Peter ordered the celebration of New Year's Day and proclaimed the Julian calendar. Theretofore Russians had observed the first of September as New Year's and had dated time from the supposed creation of the world. The year 7208 according to the ancient Russian calendar became the year 1700 by the Julian calendar. By 1700, the Julian calendar was already incorrect by eleven days, but from then on Russians at least had the year right. The nation clung to the Julian reckoning until after the 1917 Revolution, by which time the error had increased to thirteen days.

Soon after his return from the West, Peter ordered several books to be printed in Russian from a Dutch publisher, for the printing house opened in Moscow by Ivan IV rendered poor service. The difficulties of setting type in Slavonic characters discouraged the Dutch publisher, and Peter reorganized and modernized his government printing office. At the same time he simplified the alphabet by eliminating useless letters, and ordered the new characters used in all lay books. From that time on, only religious publications appeared in the old style, which came to be known as Church Slavonic. It was typical of Peter's practical interests that the first book to appear in the new orthography was a geometry text. In 1703, the first Russian newspaper began to acquaint the people with the new alphabet.

To the time of his death Peter was busy changing Russian ways of doing things. Some of the reforms were far-reaching, others trivial. Some failed or were abandoned by Peter himself; others lasted to the end of tsardom and beyond. Some were only mildly successful, others completely so. Many were ordered with little thought of their effect, for Peter often acted on impulse. Many of the reforms came during the long war with Sweden in an effort simply to win that war. With few exceptions, the reforms aimed at a practical result.

Reforms in the central and local administration appeared over many years and make sense only when arranged in a pattern. Peter spent more time than any other Russian ruler moving about the country and traveling abroad. His absence from the capital often left the administration in chaos, because the center of authority was wherever the tsar happened to be, and allowed officials to settle back into their usual sloth. The Zemskii Sobor never met again after 1682. The Boyar Duma, for which Peter felt only contempt, ceased to meet and simply faded out of existence. He temporarily replaced it with an "intimate council" of favorites that gave him advice when he asked for it. Peter saw the need for a permanent body to head the administration in the capital when he was away on campaign.

When Peter left for the Turkish campaign in 1711, he created the Senate of nine appointees whose task it was to head the administration during his absence. The Senate was also to act in a judicial capacity, serving as a sort of supreme court. Its chief concern, however, was to centralize the gathering of taxes and the levy of troops. He ordered the Senate to receive an accounting from the "chief fiscal," the head of a body of five hundred men who served as combination revenue agents, secret police, and spies, whose main function was to wring every last bit of taxes from the people. Finally, the Senate was to direct and supervise the governments of the eight provinces into which Peter divided Russia in the hope of improving the collection of taxes and the levy of troops. However, the power of some provincial governors who happened to be the tsar's favorites— Menshikov was governor of St. Petersburg province and Romodanovsky of Moscow—was greater than that of the Senate, which was unable to check Menshikov's peculation or Romodanovsky's capricious cruelty. The inability of the Senate to cope with the many tasks assigned to it led Peter to refashion the entire structure of the central government.

Peter swept away the old administrative offices, the prikazes that had multiplied in such profusion while Moscow was growing from a small domain to a national state with a sprawling territory. In their place he created modern government departments, called colleges, to deal with the various functions of administration. Each college was staffed at first with a Russian president and a non-Russian vice-president and clerks—Western Europeans imported for the purpose, Baltic Germans conscripted in districts conquered by the army, and even Swedish prisoners of war. As fast as Russians learned the work from these foreign experts, the foreigners received an assignment elsewhere. Each college was under a board of several men, usually eleven, rather than one man as had been the case with the prikaz. Peter supposed that many heads would be wiser than one and that there would be less dishonesty when all checked on each other. There were nine colleges at first, three to handle financial matters, and one each for industry, justice, commerce, foreign affairs, war, and the admiralty. Others followed later. Although the collegial principle was popular in Denmark, Prussia, and England, Peter borrowed it from Sweden and closely followed the Swedish regulations in setting up his own offices. That he was at war with Sweden at the time did not in the least deter him from appropriating his enemy's customs when he found them best suited to his own needs.

With the reorganization of administrative departments, the Senate assumed a new character. One of its functions was to coordinate the work of the colleges and to supervise their operation. Another was to serve as a supreme court to hear cases appealed from the College of Justice. A third task was the drafting of legislation, for the orders that rolled off Peter's tongue in an endless stream were often no more than ideas that had to be thought out in detail before their application.

To insure that the senators would not shirk their responsibilities, Peter stationed guards in the council chamber to warn the senators when they grew lax. Later the tsar created the office of Procurator of the Senate, a sort of viceroy who presided over Senate meetings, kept things moving along, and signed every decree. The procurator had an assistant responsible only to himself assigned to each college to check on its operation. This viceroy also controlled the "fiscals," or secret police, whose immediate concern was to run down deserters and tax evaders, but whose broader responsibility was to apprehend subversives. Paul Yaguzhinsky, the first procurator, came to wield more power than any other man except the tsar whose authority he represented.

The collegial principle later was applied to the administration of the church.

Although Patriarch Joachim had engineered Peter's accession, both Joachim and his successor, Adrian, opposed the tsar's actions. Both had reviled the foreign quarter and all it stood for. Adrian had disapproved of Peter's consorting with foreigners and his trip abroad, and had spoken out against the sacrilege of shaving. When Adrian died in 1700, Peter chose not to appoint a successor but named Stephen Yavorsky, who had attended Jesuit schools in Poland and who had strayed from Orthodoxy to Catholicism and back again, to be "administrator of the patriarchal see."

The government took other steps to curb the independence of the church. Ecclesiastical lands were seized, but not confiscated outright, and administered by a "monastery bureau." A fraction of the income from church estates went to the church to meet its expenses and the rest to the army. The Senate received the right to veto the election of any bishop.

Yavorsky owed his appointment as "administrator of the patriarchal see" to his known sympathy for things Western and his approval of Peter's reforms. However, he was impatient to be named patriarch. When it became apparent that Peter was content with the settlement he had made of church leadership, Yavorsky became bitter against the tsar. He condemned the "fiscals," the spies or secret police, and disapproved of Peter's sinful life with his mistresses. He sided with Alexis when Peter brought his son to trial on charges of plotting to sweep away the reforms after Peter's death.

The headship of the church was settled finally in 1721 when Peter approved the creation of the Holy Synod. The patriarchate was abolished, frankly, in the words of the ukaz, because simple people looked on a single head of the church as God's vicar on earth and this popular confidence gave him the power to encourage revolt. From then on, the church would be administered by the Holy Synod, a college, or board, of bishops and monks named by the tsar and presided over by the procurator of the Holy Synod, an appointed member of the laity. From the moment of its creation, the Holy Synod became a tool of the government, and so Peter meant it to be. Its procurator became a powerful official, often more influential than the procurator of the Senate. The church itself became an agency of the government. Peter forced Russians to attend church, and it was there that the priests read out proclamations the government wanted all to hear. The patriarchate reappeared only after the fall of the monarchy, and the Bolsheviks abolished it soon after.

Peter himself was not a religious man in the mold of Ivan IV. He attended service regularly and enjoyed singing in the choir, but he had little respect for members of the clergy, particularly for narrow and superstitious ones, and hated the monasteries, which he looked on as dens of sloth and wickedness. He favored Lutheranism and was tolerant of all sects who did not oppose his reforms. Those who did he punished, and he even ordered the Old Believers to wear distinctive dress. Otherwise, particularly if the sectarians were hard-working, he was willing to "let them believe what they like." He toyed with the idea of reuniting Orthodoxy and Catholicism, but would never have accepted the pope's terms or condoned his interference in lay matters. The scheming Jesuits he banished from the land. He also persecuted the Jews.

In local as in central government, Peter's initial reforms had to undergo modification when foreign ideas and institutions proved disappointing or unworkable in the Russian setting. In 1707 the tsar divided the nation into eight huge provinces—Siberia was one province, Kazan and the entire middle Volga another, Azov and south Russia a third. Each governor appointed by the tsar had to reside in his provincial capital. Peter hoped that this decentralization would reduce the inefficiency of tax collection and the drafting of men for the army that characterized the administration of everything from Moscow. Later there would be fifty provinces divided into counties and districts, each subdivision administered by an official responsible to the provincial governor for the collection of men and taxes, the maintenance of order, and the administration of justice in his county or district.

Peter's concern to improve tax collection lay behind his plan to alter municipal government. In 1699, the tsar offered cities, in return for paying twice as much in taxes, the privilege of electing their own officials, enabling them to escape the jurisdiction of the old governors, or "feeders," whose voracity Ivan IV had tried to curb. Cities that chose to double their taxes could elect burgomasters with power to levy taxes and to dispense civil justice. Local indifference proved too great to overcome. Plans for municipal and even district and provincial organization produced few results until long after Peter's death.

The new capital, St. Petersburg, received a model city "council" in 1720, and the College of Municipal Affairs extended the model to other Russian cities. Each town's inhabitants consisted of three groups—a "first guild" of wealthy merchants and professional men, a "second guild" of small traders and craftsmen, and the remainder of the inhabitants lumped together as commoners. Only citizens of the first and second guilds elected a city council of members of the first guild. The common people, who made up over half the population of Russian towns, had no right to vote. The city council was responsible for the collection of whatever taxes the central government imposed, administered justice, maintained order, and promoted industry and trade. It was accountable to the appropriate colleges and ultimately to the Senate for fulfilling its various functions—police, financial, commercial, and judicial.

Peter's concern in reorganizing central and local administration was to improve the state's war potential. His hopes for increased revenue were disappointed by corruption, and Peter carried an oaken cane with him and brought it down mercilessly upon the backs of those he heard were robbing the treasury. A governor of Siberia was hanged and the head of the secret police broken on the wheel for amassing fortunes at the state's expense. Only thirty rubles out of a hundred collected in taxes ever reached the treasury. The procurator told Peter that he could never wipe out corruption: "In the end you will have no subjects, for we all steal."

Attempts to build up the nation's military effectiveness would have been quite fruitless without a fundamental reorganization of the military establishment itself. Peter's campaign against the Crimea in 1695 failed largely because of the inefficiency of the old-fashioned militia and the streltsy. The success of his attack on Azov the following year was in part a naval achievement and in part the work of his "play regiments" and foreign leaders. Nevertheless, the rout of his army at Narva in the opening campaign of the Swedish war indicated that there was much to be done if Russian troops were to stand up against Western Europeans.

The Guards regiments expanded until they contained nearly four thousand men, most of them sons of the gentry enrolled for life. They constituted a small but thoroughly dependable core for the new army the tsar proposed to build. For the bulk of the new force, Peter conscripted recruits from among the peasants. Approximately every twenty households, later every seventy-five, had to provide one soldier and replace him if he died or deserted. Before assignment to units the recruits received training under Russian veterans or foreigners hired for the purpose. The soldier served for life. All landowners had to serve in the army. Improved artillery and flintlocks with bayonets were imported from England. Cavalry units received better training and learned to be more aggressive than in the old army.

Once the new army was brought together and adequately trained, Peter never let it go. The troops, never demobilized, occupied garrisons on the frontier or quarters in the provinces. By 1725, Russia had a well-drilled and well-equipped standing army of two hundred thousand soldiers, the largest in Europe, plus a hundred thousand registered Cossacks and a host of Asiatic soldiers on horseback, chiefly Bashkirs and Kalmyks, whose fearlessness and cruelty made them the most dreaded cavalry in the world.

Peter was the founder of the Russian Navy and he remained sentimentally solicitous of it to the end of his days. With his seizure of the mouth of the Nava from the Swedes in 1703, Peter concentrated his attention on building a Baltic fleet. He constructed the naval base of Kronstadt at the mouth of the river and established shipyards in St. Petersburg almost before there were houses for the workers. There were eight hundred ships in his Baltic fleet by 1725, a number of them built in England and Holland, and nearly thirty thousand men. But Peter's successors let the fleet rot rapidly away. Within a decade of his death only a few ships were serviceable and there were no officers to man them.

Peter sought to staff his military and civil service, and at the same time destroy the political threat of the nobility as a class, by opening the ranks of the nobility to anyone whose merit could carry him to a certain level in government service. He drew up a Table of Ranks in 1722 that listed all officer ranks in the army and navy and paralleled the list with a similar ranking of all civil offices. The table arrayed fourteen civil and military classes side by side, and the government ordered that every official must begin at the bottom and work his way up the scale as Peter himself had done in the army and navy. Every civil and military official who reached the ninth rank—army captain—no matter how humble his birth, acquired the status of hereditary noble. The four highest levels in both civil and military service carried with them the title of general, and the men who filled them came to be called "the generality." The Table of Ranks, which Peter borrowed from Prussia, continued to function until the end of the monarchy.

His successors, however, ignored Peter's intention to reward merit and to force his subjects to begin at the bottom of the ladder.

Although Peter had no scruples against raising men of any class to noble rank, he expected that the government's military and civil officials would come primarily from families of the gentry. To assure that sons of the gentry would seek government service and to guard against the impoverishment of noble families, Peter forbade the division of landed estates among several heirs at the death of their owner. A noble might settle an inheritance on only one son. The rest of the sons, in most cases, would have to enter government service in order to live. Peter thus forced the service obligation on the landowners in a way that none of his predecessors had dared attempt. Although the restriction on inheritance was abandoned soon after Peter's death, the near monopoly by the gentry of officer rank in the army and, to a lesser extent, of high civil office continued beyond the middle of the nineteenth century.

The Russian aristocracy, nobility, or gentry, as it is variously called, reached precise definition in Peter's reign. It occupied a position far different from that of other European aristocracies of the time, for it rested on obligatory service not to an overlord as in feudal Europe but to the state. Its lands were hereditary, but so was its service obligation. In clarifying its position, Peter intended to create an aristocratic class that was also a bureaucracy and at the same time a military officer class, maintained by possession of lands and serfs over which it would exercise justice and serve as police and tax collector, yet set apart from the rest of the population by tax exemption. State service must begin at the age of fifteen. Only one-third of a noble family might enter civil office; the rest must go into the military. Peter introduced borrowed German titles—count, baron—although they meant nothing in the way of rank. Menshikov was the first Russian, aside from descendants of Lithuanian, Tatar or appanage princes, to receive the title of prince.

The newly fashioned aristocrat found himself alien to Russians of other classes in law, dress, habits, point of view, and even language, for German first and French later became the preferred language at court. After Peter's death, the luxury of Russian court life exceeded even that of the French, and the nobles aped the monarch in conspicuous consumption. Many wealthy nobles invested their riches; some spent their fortunes on personal comfort and luxury.

The aristocracy, which became almost a closed class after Peter's time, never developed any political consciousness. It was one only in assuming that the state owed it a living—through its near monopoly of civil and military rank and its exclusive right to own land and serfs. It revealed constant division for one reason or another—division centering around certain old families or new favorites, separation of the nobility in the capitals from the provincial nobility, and a widening gulf between the wealthy aristocrat and the poor one. Peter's daughter Anne quickly rescinded his order forbidding nobles to divide up their estates, and the impoverishment of many quickly ensued. By 1777, a third of the nobles owned fewer than ten serfs, a fourth owned between ten and twenty, another fourth between twenty and a hundred, and only a sixth owned over a hundred.

Some landowners, in fact, owned no serfs and had to work their own estates.

Peter's new army and navy were costly. Native men and officers had to serve at a fraction of the wage foreigners earned, and even civil servants must take part of their pay in grain, furs, and goods produced in government-owned factories. Instructors and equipment imported from Western Europe were expensive and required specie. Government revenue, less than a million and a half rubles in 1680, doubled in the next twenty years and then trebled again in the next quarter century. The army and navy consumed four fifths of the income. The government strained at every possible source of revenue and still could not avoid deficits. Peter debased the coinage repeatedly and imposed taxes on stamps, hats, leather, shoes, harness, scythes, fuel, chimneys, troughs, baths, leases, boats, melons, cucumbers, nuts, meat, inns, mills, loans, beehives, beards, marriages, births, and the religious beliefs of dissenters. The government profited from the monopolies on the sale of salt, tar, fats, caviar, and tobacco. It even bought oak coffins and forcibly sold them to monasteries at four times their cost.

A direct tax on every peasant household brought in considerable revenue, but still not enough. Because the census on which its collection rested was thirty years old, the government decided in 1710 to take another census to bring in the new taxpayers that the increased population should have produced. The census-takers were shocked to find that the number of households had fallen by a fifth in the previous thirty years. Some of the shrinkage resulted from conscription of laborers to work on canals and in shipyards and on the new capital. Some households disappeared as peasants fled to the frontier and Siberia and even Poland to escape taxes and military service. The greatest shrinkage resulted from the practice whereby two or three families moved into a single house to reduce their tax burden by one half or two thirds.

To halt the revenue loss occasioned by the shrinkage in the number of households, the Senate in 1719 adopted a new basis of direct taxation. Thenceforth every male "soul" or serf or peasant, "from the old men down to the last infant," must bear an equal share of the cost of maintaining the army. During the early years, each serf paid eighty kopeks, four fifths of a ruble, the tax to be collected in cash by the estate owner, who was also the serf owner. The gentry, the merchants, and the clergy escaped this poll tax, the payment of which was the exclusive privilege of the peasants. The results were gratifying to the treasury. Receipts were over twice as great as from the former household tax. To be sure that no one escaped the burden there was a new census in 1719, at which time all remaining distinctions between serfs and slaves disappeared. From that time on all were serfs or peasants who paid the head tax or poll or soul tax that their owners were responsible for collecting. By the edict of 1722, the serf lost the right to leave the landowner's estate without the owner's written consent. This inaugurated the passport system that continued into the twentieth century. Peter had fastened bondage firmly upon the peasant masses for whom he professed so much sympathy. He did, however, forbid the sale of individual serfs away from their families, a prohibition that did not survive him.

The census of 1719, made necessary to discover the names of the new individual taxpayers, met stern resistance; army units had to march into the countryside to force registration and to threaten with death those who tried to conceal themselves. Thereafter, a "revision" of the census became necessary every generation or so to bring the lists up to date. Between revisions, the landowner simply collected from his peasant village the amount owed by those whose names were on the last census list, regardless of who had died meanwhile or how many were born.

Peter bent every effort toward reducing the nation's dependence on outside sources of military matériel. Except for the narrow entry through Arkhangel, Russia was still landlocked, and the barrier of hostile states across its western frontier made importation of Western goods difficult and at times impossible. Even with easy access to the factories of Western Europe, the cost of buying goods abroad would have been prohibitive. His predecessors had laid the foundations for an industrial plant to serve the nation's needs. Now Peter carried on from where his timid predecessors had left off.

During his Western journey in 1697 Peter had employed Western craftsmen of all sorts to develop Russian industry and teach their skills to Russians. Throughout his reign, he ordered young Russians abroad to study in the shipyards and the foundries of the West. He welcomed all foreigners except Jews, for Peter was bitterly anti-Semitic. By a proclamation issued in 1702, he invited Western military men and craftsmen to join the Russian service, offering to pay transportation and promising high wages, religious toleration, and extraterritoriality.

The government organized new plants to make arms, uniforms, and other military equipment, sometimes continuing to operate them itself for generations, sometimes turning them over to private companies after the enterprises had become going concerns. To encourage individual merchants to go into manufacturing, the government exempted them from taxation and military service, lent them state serfs as a labor force, allowed them to buy machinery and materials abroad without payment of duty, and granted them a monopoly of the home market or sufficient tariff protection to exclude foreign competition.

At first, Peter concerned himself with developing plants to turn out the military equipment that his new modern army needed. He had bought expensive flintlocks in England in 1698, and their price convinced him that Russia should produce its own. He immediately erected plants for their manufacture, and by 1701 Russia was turning out six thousand muskets and bayonets a year. Production rose to forty thousand annually in 1711, only ten years after the birth of the industry. During those same years new iron foundries appeared, especially in the Urals, where the Demidov family rose quickly to a prominence it did not relinquish until the Bolsheviks took over its plants. Native ordnance plants began to turn out excellent field artillery, which the nation had previously had to import and had not yet learned to use effectively. Textile mills were soon turning out sufficient uniforms to dress the new army respectably. New sail works provided the cloth for the navy.

Once heavy industry had moved ahead and war plants had started to equip the army, Peter turned to the promotion of industries to produce consumer goods and even luxury goods. Brickyards opened and stone quarries developed to make possible the building of fireproof dwellings in St. Petersburg. Factories started to produce china, glassware, linen goods, velvet, brocade, lace, ribbons, and stockings, and a high tariff protected the owners from foreign competition. Peter tried to provide a native source of raw materials for such firms by encouraging the raising of hemp and flax and by experimenting to improve the breed of sheep and the grade of wool.

The state serfs who were torn from their villages were given to the factory owners to "possess" and use, but not to own. The census bureau called such serfs "possessional" peasants. The government also assigned criminals, beggars, and orphans to private factories, for Peter could not bear to see anyone idle. A decade after Peter's death, the government imposed permanent bondage upon such factory workers, who then became a hereditary class of industrial slaves.

Peter stimulated domestic commerce by permitting anyone to trade who would pay the same taxes that the merchant class had to pay. On the other hand, he allowed some merchant firms a monopoly of wholesale and retail trade in certain commodities. The tsar was not interested in protecting anyone's rights or privileges. If he could obtain more tax revenue by encouraging competition he would do so, but when monopoly promised a greater return to the treasury, he willingly allowed it.

Peter's most dramatic achievement in the field of foreign trade lay in his forced shifting of ocean-borne traffic from Arkhangel to the new Baltic port of St. Petersburg on the Neva River. Merchants who had used the White Sea port for generations had little choice when the tsar demanded that they move to St. Petersburg and erect new houses for themselves or else lose the privilege to trade. Peter charged lower rates for ships loading and unloading in his new port than for trafficking through Arkhangel. To promote the use of the new port he proposed to grid the town itself with a system of canals on the order of his beloved Amsterdam. He began construction of a canal, finished after his death, which joined the Neva with the headwaters of the Volga and thus linked the Baltic with the Caspian. By 1725 nearly two hundred ships a year were calling at St. Petersburg, while Arkhangel quickly declined in significance. Russia's foreign trade increased four times over during Peter's reign, and by the year of his death most of it was passing through his "earthly paradise," the new port on the Baltic. He established permanent Russian embassies abroad to promote commercial transactions.

Peter was never able to ignore for a moment the perennial plight of his treasury, and many of his reforms aimed at reducing the pressure on the budget. Similarly, he expected his creation of an educational system to relieve the treasury of the burden of hiring foreigners and sending Russians abroad to school, although many of the gentry had to finance the educational tours of their own sons.

The nation's first school not operating under church auspices opened in Moscow in 1701 to teach mathematics and navigation to sons of the gentry who wanted to become naval officers. Some years later the Russian Naval Academy opened in St. Petersburg. By the end of the reign its enrollment ran to four hundred, most of them sons of the gentry. Two smaller schools soon were offering courses in gunnery and engineering for prospective army officers; eighty students enrolled in small medical schools in the capital and Moscow.

An elementary school system emerged in 1714 when the tsar ordered the opening of two "cipher" schools in every province. The students, ten to fifteen years of age, conscripted from merchant families, were to learn arithmetic, geometry, and trigonometry. Fourteen hundred students enrolled in these schools during the first ten years of their existence, but less than a hundred graduated. As punishment, the tsar forbade the marriage of any student who failed to graduate. A generation after Peter's death, the cipher schools became "garrison" schools staffed with army officers, and their curriculum aimed at training men for the army.

The Holy Synod set up a system of parochial schools, which by 1725 was catering to nearly three thousand students, most of them children of the clergy training for the priesthood. In later years, graduates of these elementary parochial schools went on to advanced study in both clerical and lay schools. Just before his death Peter arranged for the creation of the Russian Academy of Science to promote the study of science and to offer advanced courses in humanistic studies approximately on the university level.

Perhaps the most typical of all the Petrine reforms was the abandonment of the old capital and the building of the new. Peter always hated Moscow as a symbol of the old backward Russia. The very word Muscovite, applied by Western Europeans to all Russians before 1700, implied non-European and even oriental. Peter regarded Moscow as a center of superstition and as a bulwark of resistance to the reforms that were necessary to bring the nation out of its torpor. Moscow was an inland town shut off from the sea over which all that was modern and enlightened and efficient might come to Russia.

Peter laid the foundations in 1703 for his new capital, St. Petersburg, at the head of the Gulf of Finland deep in Swedish territory eighteen years before a peace treaty gave him legal title to the land. The site was hardly an attractive one aside from its nearness to the sea. The land was all swamp, and every building had to be set upon piles driven deep into the ground. The city took a decade to build and then was almost impossible to reach over the marshes that surrounded it. State peasants and landowners' serfs were conscripted from all over Russia to work at the brutal task of raising the new capital. Thousands died of disease and exhaustion.

In 1714 Peter ordered the Senate to move to St. Petersburg. Soon other government offices and foreign embassies followed. Peter then commanded nobles and merchants to move to the new capital and build themselves expensive houses. Determined that the city should not be subject to the fires that had so often ravaged Moscow, he ordered that houses must be of stone. The Admiralty, the Hall of the Twelve Colleges, the Fortress of St. Peter and St. Paul, the Orthodox and Lutheran churches, the mansions of the nobles, the shops of the merchants, the busy wharves, and the wide boulevards, or "prospects," made the city seem to a foreign observer in 1714 one of the wonders of the world. It is still a striking architectural city today especially since many structures from Peter's era still can be seen.

St. Petersburg became and remained to the end of the monarchy a city foreign to the Russian land, more Western than Russian. French and Italian architects worked on its design and on its buildings. Western gardeners laid out its flower beds and orangeries. Western sculptors carved the statues and fountains that dotted its parks. Peter meant his capital to be "a window on Europe." Through that window Russia would breathe Western air.

The Northern War

On his first journey to the West in 1697, Peter discussed with the elector of Brandenburg the possible gains from a war against Sweden, whose new king was only sixteen years old. On his way home, the tsar stopped off in Poland and listened to the proposal of the ambitious King Augustus II to dislodge Sweden from the south shore of the Baltic. A year later Poland, Denmark, and Russia agreed formally to attack Sweden, although Peter committed himself to march only after a settlement of the Turkish war.

The time seemed promising. Western Europe's attention focused on the coming crisis over succession to the Spanish throne. Brandenburg, which had won out earlier over Sweden, would be at least sympathetic to an attack against the power that threatened its own interests in the Baltic. After all, Sweden's king was a seventeen-year-old spendthrift whom no one expected to take his new responsibilities seriously.

In the spring of 1700, Poland and Denmark opened the campaign, but the Swedish King Charles XII soon knocked Denmark out of the war in the first of his brilliant victories. At that moment, the war with Turkey ended, and a Russian army immediately advanced into Swedish Livonia, besieging the fortress of Narva on the Gulf of Finland. The forty thousand Russians were getting nowhere with the siege when Charles XII attacked them with an army of only eight thousand men. Peter was not with the army, but his generals, his artillery, and most of his troops were captured. Narva was one of the most ignominious defeats ever suffered by a Russian army, and Peter, who had surprised Europe with his recent victory over the Turks, became the object of general derision. Now he determined to assemble a better army, launch a fleet, and obtain new cannons.

After Narva, Charles XII concentrated on Poland and drove Augustus II from the Polish throne, leaving Russia to fight on alone. Meanwhile, Peter, with a new force, invaded Ingria and Livonia without much opposition and, in 1703, presumptuously marked out the site of St. Petersburg. The tsar now had a Baltic port, which was really all he wanted, and offered peace to Charles XII. But when the Swedish king demanded the return of the districts occupied by the Russians, including St. Petersburg, the negotiations fell through.

Charles led a fine army into Russia in the fall of 1707, driving straight for

Moscow where, he announced, he would dictate terms. Meanwhile, he sent another army under General Löwenhaupt to recover the Baltic provinces and gather up supplies for an assault on the Russian capital. Charles advanced toward Smolensk on the road to Moscow, but the Russians stopped him. In the summer of 1708, the Swedish king decided to turn south and join hands with the rebellious Cossacks. A few months later, a Russian army met Löwenhaupt on equal terms and annihilated his force. When he joined Charles on the lower Dnieper he had only a few men and neither artillery nor supplies.

Mazeppa, the hetman of the Zaporozhian Cossacks, offered for a price to join the Swedish king. Charles turned hopefully to join Mazeppa, expecting the welcome of a deliverer from Russian rule. Only a small force of Cossacks followed Mazeppa when he joined the Swedish king. Peter's troops stormed the Zaporozhian fastness in the Dnieper and subdued the rest, who elected a new hetman loyal to Russia. From that time on, the Cossacks accepted the joint rule of their hetman and an official sent out from Moscow, and later Peter even appointed Russian colonels to command the Cossack regiments.

By the spring of 1709, Charles's once-splendid army was suffering seriously from a lack of supplies and a severe winter. Mazeppa's two thousand Cossacks and Löwenhaupt's stragglers added little strength when they came into camp. Opposed to Charles's pitifully small force Peter had a large, well-trained, and well-equipped army. At the battle of Poltava in June 1709, the Russians completely destroyed the Swedish army. Charles XII escaped across the Dnieper into Turkish territory with a few attendants. That night, Peter dined with the captured Swedish generals and offered a toast "to my teachers in the art of war."

In the following year Peter's troops, now meeting with little Swedish opposition in the absence of Charles XII, occupied Viborg, Tallinn, and Riga on the Baltic. Meanwhile the Swedish king was urging his Turkish hosts to assert themselves in the Black Sea, and the sultan answered Peter's demand to surrender Charles XII by declaring war against Russia. Peter led an army to the Pruth River, but he ran out of supplies, and there was no rising of Balkan Christians as he had expected. A much larger Turkish force surrounded the Russians, and Peter had no choice in 1711 but to accept the sultan's terms. Turkey recovered Azov, and Peter allowed Charles XII safe passage back to Sweden.

For the next several years, Russian armies and the new fleet won a succession of victories. One army overran Finland and another occupied the Aaland Islands after the Baltic fleet had won a resounding victory over the Swedish fleet at Hangö. Other Russian forces crossed north Germany and occupied the Swedish-owned ports of Lübeck and Hamburg.

Beyond all question, Russia had become the dominant power in northern Europe. Poland's power was rapidly waning, and both the king of Prussia and the Holy Roman Emperor were urging a partition of Poland. Sweden had sunk so low that Russian troops could advance to the gates of Stockholm with impunity. Prussia was under the rule of a cautious king who wanted territory but was unwilling to risk anything to gain it. Denmark certainly was too weak to challenge Russian dominion.

Peter now sought to strengthen his international position by establishing for the first time regular diplomatic embassies in various European capitals and by arranging marriage alliances that might bring him influence and recognition. Until the eighteenth century, the royalty of Central and Western Europe had spurned Russian marriages. Now Peter seemed to consider it part of the courtesy due him that his relatives should find welcome into the families of Western rulers. From the time of his victory at Poltava to the day of his death Peter was busy arranging marriages for his children and nieces. His son Alexis married Princess Charlotte Wolfenbüttel, whose sister was the wife of Emperor Charles VI. Anne, the daughter of Peter's half brother Ivan, wed the duke of Courland, and her sister Catherine became the wife of the duke of Mecklenburg. The tsar's own daughter Anne was betrothed to the duke of Holstein-Gottorp, an heir to the throne of Sweden. When Alexis's wife died, Peter proposed to the French court that his son should marry the daughter of the duke of Orleans. His most ambitious hope was that his daughter Elizabeth should marry Louis XV of France, but nothing came of it in spite of Peter's journey to Paris to urge the suit.

No good came of the Russian marriage alliances with the petty courts of north Germany. In subsequent years St. Petersburg often could not escape embroilment in minor German squabbles that it would have done well to avoid. These involvements only encouraged the suspicion that Russia was trying to interfere in German affairs to its own advantage, a suspicion rarely justified. The involvements usually were more costly than they were profitable.

Meanwhile, Russia and its allies—Poland, Saxony, Prussia, Denmark, and Hanover, whose elector was King George of England—took over Sweden's possessions in north Germany. Russian troops landed at will in southern Sweden to burn the coastal villages, and at one time Cossacks galloped to within two miles of Stockholm. After Charles XII fell in battle in 1718, Russia's allies one after another came to terms with the Swedish government. Peter had been anxious for peace ever since the battle of Poltava, and now the Swedes were willing to grant acceptable terms. By the Peace of Nystadt signed in August 1721, Peter received Ingria, Livonia—modern Estonia and Latvia—and the Karelian Isthmus including Viborg. He returned Finland to Sweden. Russia had its outlet on the Baltic.

Peter's addition of the Baltic provinces brought a new dimension to Russian expansion. Theretofore Russia's acquisitions of territory had produced the absorption of backward peoples, usually non-European. Now Russia acquired land inhabited by Lutheran Westerners who were more advanced than were Russians themselves. Peter took account of this by not imposing the Russian administrative system on the provinces, but leaving them in possession of their own firmly established local institutions. The German aristocracy that ruled over the Lettish and Estonian peasantry retained its position, and Russian nobles who hoped to obtain landholdings in the conquered territory gained nothing. From that time forward the Balts—the German gentry in the Baltic provinces—won preferment in the Russian civil and military service, bringing with them a sense of efficiency and order that Russians so sadly lacked.

When the tsar returned to St. Petersburg, there was a victory celebration with great festivities and the usual heroic drinking bouts. An ingratiating bishop acclaimed him Peter the Great and the Senate conferred on him the title of emperor.

Opposition to the Petrine Reforms

Many of the reforms of Peter the Great were part of an attempt to further the nation's war effort against Sweden. As the war dragged on for over twenty years the people became increasingly weary and resentful of the tsar who drove them relentlessly on to greater sacrifice. The burden of taxes and conscription for the army and of laborers fell chiefly on the peasants. The nation literally had to be driven with the knout to work and to war. Perhaps the people objected less to the actual reforms than to the bewildering speed with which one succeeded another.

Resistance to the rule of the tsar and his reforms appeared in every class and took many forms. Occasionally, church leaders spoke out against Western dress and Western manners and invited punishment for their insolence. Priests whispered that Peter was not really the son of Alexis but one of Lefort's illegitimate offspring. Old Believers swore that he was antichrist. Peasants hid from the recruiting officer or deserted from the ranks if they could not avoid enlistment. Others ran away

Peter the Great and his son Alexis, by Nikolai Ge

in a steady stream to the frontier to take up new land beyond the reach of the tsar's officials. The gentry, who resented the opening of their ranks to commoners, constantly shirked their responsibilities. The streltsy never gave up trying to recover their former influence until the last of them went to the block. The Cossacks of the Don and the Dnieper were in revolt on more than one occasion. Even those in whom the tsar placed his greatest trust stole from the treasury. Peter must often have felt that everyone in the land was against him.

After Poltava, the opposition clustered around the person of Tsarevich Alexis, the tsar's oldest son. Peter had shown little interest in the son by his first wife, Eudoxia. Alexis was raised by his disgruntled mother and weaned on her bitterness. After the streltsy revolt, the tsar forced Eudoxia into a convent. Alexis went to live with his aunt, Peter's sister Natalia, whom he thoroughly disliked. German tutors taught him French and German, and his father dropped in occasionally to set the boy problems in navigation. Peter made no effort to conceal his disappointment that the child had little aptitude for such subjects as gunnery, fortification, and shipbuilding. That the sensitive Alexis revealed an interest in religion only disgusted the tsar. The boy was a heavy drinker and, when under the influence of alcohol, let others know of his resentment toward his father.

At the age of nineteen Alexis went abroad at his father's orders to further his education. Again at his father's orders, he married Charlotte Wolfenbüttel. The son had Peter's weaknesses without his strength, and an interest in mistresses and a fondness for liquor made his son's marriage an unhappy one. Alexis was not long burdened with Charlotte, however, for she died at the birth of a son, Peter, who later became Emperor Peter II.

In 1715, the tsar wrote a stern warning to Alexis that he must show some interest in preparing himself for the succession or resign himself to entering a monastery. Alexis had neither the strength nor the taste for following the army or learning the chores of monarchy and wrote back confessing himself "your useless son," renouncing his rights to the throne and asking to be allowed to retire to a country estate. A year later, Peter wrote from Denmark that Alexis must come to army headquarters immediately or prepare to enter a monastery. Alexis consulted a friend and may have smiled when told that the monk's cowl would not be nailed to his head. He admitted to his confessor that he wished his father were dead and the confessor answered, "We all do."

A year later, when Peter wrote from Holland demanding an immediate decision, Alexis fled to Vienna and asked his brother-in-law, Emperor Charles VI, for sanctuary. Charles hid the tsarevich in one retreat after another, but Peter's agents finally tracked Alexis to Naples and promised his father's forgiveness if he would return home.

Back in St. Petersburg in 1718 the tsar forced Alexis to renounce the succession. Peter insisted on knowing who had helped the son escape and who was party to the suspected plot to repeal the reforms and turn Russia back to the old ways after his own death. Nuns were flogged in an attempt to force them to testify that their sister, the mother of Alexis, was one of the plotters. A bishop was broken on the wheel for knowing too much. Many suffered torture or execution or banishment as the evidence of treacherous thoughts and words mounted. Alexis was tortured repeatedly and finally condemned to death for allegedly having schemed to overthrow the tsar. Then he was tortured again to reveal still more names, but Alexis could endure no more, and the next day the government announced that the tsarevich was dead.

The extent of the tsarevich's complicity in the plot to overthrow the tsar is debatable, as is whether there was in fact a plot. There can be no doubt, however, that many Russians desperately wanted an end to Peter's violent rule. Nor can there be any doubt that such men looked to Alexis, renowned for his mildness and conservatism and known to detest most of the reforms, to restore the easy ways of old Moscow. So great was Peter's determination that Russia must continue along the road he had marked out for it that he would let nothing, not even his own son, stand in the way. Barbarous indeed were Peter's methods of fighting the barbarism that kept his country backward.

The End of the Reign

There is no evidence that Peter felt any such sense of remorse at the death of Alexis as Ivan the Terrible had known after the death of his son Ivan. That Russia should triumph in the war with Sweden seemed more important to him than the nation's loss of one of several heirs. And new reforms continued to flow from Peter's increasing restlessness and determination to finish the job.

Not for long did Nystadt bring peace to the Russian people. Within a year Peter had opened a campaign in Persia aimed at quieting the area for Russian traders and preventing the western shore of the Caspian Sea from falling to Turkey. With Catherine along, he led a hundred thousand men down the Volga to Astrakhan. There the force parted, most of it continuing by land while Peter went by sea. The Russians took Derbent and Baku with little trouble. The peace settlement in 1723 gave Russia the entire west and south coast of the Caspian Sea. Ten years later, however, Russia restored the land to Persia in return for its support in another Russo-Turkish war.

There was no limit to Peter's territorial imagination. Soon after the Caspian venture, two Russian ships left the Baltic with instructions to take the island of Madagascar and then to sail on to India. The fantastic expedition accomplished nothing, however, for the ships were leaky and had to return home. The next year the emperor ordered Captain Bering to discover whether Asia and America were parts of one continent. Semeon Dezhnev had proved in 1648 that a strait separated the two, but no one remembered the earlier expedition. Four years later, after Peter's death, Bering located the straits that bear his name.

Peter the Great had formed many casual attachments in the riotous life of the German quarter; the most enduring was with a peasant girl, Catherine Skavronsky. An orphan, Catherine was reared by a German pastor and put to earn her own living at an early age. As laundress and mistress she passed through many homes until she settled down with the tsar's favorite, Menshikov. Peter appropriated her to himself, and she bore him twelve children, at least three before they were married in 1712. Ugly, buxom, coarse, common, and lighthearted, she accompanied the tsar on campaigns, patched his clothes, laundered his linen, and stroked his brow to soothe him when violent fits of rage overcame him. She succeeded him as Catherine I (1725–1727).

In 1722, Peter announced a law giving the sovereign the right to name his own successor, but he never made use of the law himself. His health failed rapidly after the Persian campaign, and in 1724 his weakness increased with a cold he caught when he dashed into the Baltic to rescue some soldiers whose boat had overturned. Late in January 1725, he sat down to write out his final instructions but he was unable to complete them. He called his daughter Anne to finish the testament orally, but he could say no more than, "Leave all to _____." His death left the succession unsettled. A few months earlier, however, Peter had ordered his wife's coronation as empress, which seemed to indicate that he intended the illiterate Lithuanian peasant girl to succeed him. Certainly, he knew too much of Russia's history to leave the throne to a child, for Alexis's son, who later became Peter II, was only ten.

The Significance of the Reign

Of all Peter's remarkable accomplishments surely the most enduring was the opening of his "window to the West." While the spectacular beauty of St. Petersburg became a lasting monument to his determination, it was less the new capital itself than the winning of a foothold on the Baltic that proved to be most significant. Russia became a Baltic power, politically, militarily, and commercially. No maritime state could ignore the Russian warships stationed at Kronstadt. The cargo ships, many of them built in the new shipyards along the Neva, made the nation the foremost commercial power in the eastern Baltic.

Russia became not only a Baltic power, but a European power of tremendous importance. Its interference in European affairs from Peter's time onward was not always wholesome or welcome. Never again, however, could the continental nations afford to ignore Russia's interest in and concern about the Western nations and their squabbles. Few Russian rulers would be so indifferent as to turn away from Europe for some mystical civilizing mission in Asia, as the last German emperor urged the last tsar to do.

Peter the Great made Russia Western in many ways. Aside from the social changes that altered the face of Russia, the differences from the old Russia were perhaps most striking in government. Few Westerners would have recognized or understood the central administration of Russia before 1700. However, by the time of the emperor's death twenty-five years later, any perceptive person from Britain, France, Sweden, Prussia, or even Spain would have recognized the administrative pattern in Russia as being essentially the one employed at home. The conciliar, or collegial, pattern of organization was widespread. A state church,

Restored palace of Peter the Great. The original two-storied palace was erected between 1714 and 1728, the builder unknown. From 1747 to 1752 the palace was rebuilt by Rastrelli in the more elaborate style characteristic of the Russian baroque, but retained some features from Peter the Great's time.

or at least a controlled one, was common; nowhere did the church, Catholic or Protestant, operate free of restraint. Someone from England or Sweden might have disapproved of the absence of any parliament, but none of the others would have objected. In nearly all of continental Europe there was no popular check upon the ruler. Peter did not borrow autocracy from Byzantium or Asia; there was no need to do so. Indeed, his fascination with absolutism may have grown out of his abiding interest in Western culture, and in his awareness that autocracy was fashionable all over the continent.

Much of the Western veneer that Peter adopted—dress, manners, taste, technology, cultural values, and social attitudes—made a permanent impression on the gentry and the bureaucracy and almost no impression on the masses. In consequence, there developed a chasm between upper and lower classes that made the two extremes alien to each other to the point of seeming more like two nationalities than two classes. A rigidity of class emerged, a nearly total lack of mobility. There had been far more class mobility, upward and downward, in the centuries before Peter than there would be again until the closing decades of the empire.

The violence and the speed, the sternness and the ruthlessness with which Peter changed so much of Russian life provoked bitter resentment and opposition while he lived and long after his death. In forcing Western ways of doing things on his reluctant and defiant people, he incurred the criticism of Russians living in future times, although less in what he tried to do than in the manner of doing it. The great historian Kliuchevsky called attention to the fact that Peter's reforms often were contradictory, and noted "his errors, his hesitations, his obstinacy, his lack of judgment in civil affairs, his uncontrollable cruelty." Finding less to condemn than to praise, however, Kliuchevsky applauded Peter's "wholehearted love of his country, his stubborn devotion to his work, the broad, enlightened outlook he brought to bear on it, his daring plans conceived with creative genius and concluded with incomparable energy, and finally the success he achieved by the incredible sacrifices of his people and himself."

The impact of Peter the Great on Russia was cataclysmic. The effect of his reign was no less than to divide ancient Russia from modern Russia. Russian society remained for two and a half centuries essentially in the form in which Peter had molded it. To the end of the monarchy, the governmental structure of the state remained fundamentally what Peter had made it. He brought Russia out of oriental barbarism into contact with Western civilization. The fact that the transformation was not complete left the nation half Eastern and half Western, half medieval and half modern, half superstitious and half enlightened. From the reign of Peter I on, Russia as a nation and the Russians as a people seemed to Westerners full of contradictions and paradoxes.

Suggested Reading

BLACKWELL, W. L. (ed.), *Russian Economic Development from Peter the Great to Stalin* (New York, 1974).

BROMLEY, J. S. (ed.), *The Rise of Great Britain and Russia, 1688-1715/25 (The New Cambridge Modern History)*, (Cambridge, 1971).

CRACRAFT, J., *The Church Reform of Peter the Great* (Stanford, 1971).

_____, *The Petrine Revolution in Russian Architecture* (Chicago, 1988).

DE GRUNWALD, C., *Peter the Great* (New York, 1956).

DE JONGE, A., *Fire and Water: A Life of Peter the Great* (New York, 1979).

DMYTRYSHYN, B. (ed.), *Modernization of Russia under Peter I and Catherine II* (New York, 1974).

GASIOROWSKA, X., *The Image of Peter the Great in Russian Fiction* (Madison, WI, 1979).

GREY, I. *Peter the Great* (Philadelphia, 1960).

JACKSON, W. G., *Seven Roads to Moscow* (London, 1957).

KELLER, W., *East Minus West = Zero: Russia's Debt to the Western World, 862-1962* (New York, 1962).

KIRCHNER, W., *Commercial Relations between Russia and Europe, 1400-1800* (Bloomington, IN, 1966).

KLIUCHEVSKY, V., *Peter the Great* (New York, 1958).

LANTZEFF, G. V., and R. A. PIERCE, *Eastward to Empire* (London, 1973).

LINCOLN, W. B., *The Romanovs: Autocrats of All the Russias* (New York, 1981).

MASSIE, R. K., *Peter the Great* (New York, 1980).

MITCHELL, M., *The Maritime History of Russia, 848-1948* (London, 1949).

MULLER, A., *The Spiritual Regulation* (Seattle, 1972).

NICHOLS, R. L., and T. C. STAVROU, *Russian Orthodoxy under the Old Regime* (Minneapolis, 1978).

O'BRIEN, C. B., *Russia Under Two Tsars, 1682–1689* (Berkeley, 1952).

OLIVA, L. J., *Peter the Great* (Englewood Cliffs, NJ, 1970).

_____, *Russia in the Era of Peter the Great* (Englewood Cliffs, NJ, 1969).

PUTNAM, P. B., *Peter, the Revolutionary Tsar* (New York, 1973).

RAEFF, M., *Imperial Russia, 1682–1825* (New York, 1971).

_____, *Peter the Great: Reformer or Revolutionary* (Boston, 1965).

RIASANOVSKY, N. V., *The Image of Peter the Great in Russian History and Thought* (New York, 1985).

SUMNER, B. H., *Peter the Great and the Emergence of Russia* (New York, 1951).

_____, *Peter the Great and the Ottoman Empire* (Hamden, CT, 1965).

TOMPKINS, S. R., *The Russian Mind: From Peter the Great to the Enlightenment* (Norman, OK, 1957).

WILSON, F. M., *Muscovy: Russia through Foreign Eyes, 1553–1900* (London, 1971).

CHAPTER 10

The Age of Favorites

The inhabitants of the land Peter the Great inherited in 1682 numbered perhaps eight million, probably about the same as a century earlier. When he died there were thirteen million, in spite of the wars that took a frightful toll through all but a year of his reign. The next thirty-seven years of political turmoil and social turbulence still added six million more. The steady growth reflects in part a technological advance going on in Western Europe from which Russia profited, in large measure because of Peter's perception and leadership. It suggests that not even the dreary succession of rulers who followed him could divert the nation from the progressive course he had charted.

Two distinct periods with contrasting characteristics emerged. The first period, from the death of Peter the Great to the accession of his daughter Elizabeth, has been called the German period. The court swarmed with petty German princes and their lackeys, with German nobles from the Baltic provinces recently taken from Sweden, and with Germans whose forebears had lived in Russia for generations or whom Peter the Great had imported. This was a period of intrigue when the land was governed or misgoverned by those who jostled each other for the favors of rulers who cared nothing for the country's misery. During this first period many of the reforms of Peter the Great lapsed or changed, particularly those affecting the central administration.

The second period, the reign of Elizabeth (1741–1762), was Russian. The empress named Russians to the offices that for seventeen years foreigners had occupied. She restored the prestige of the Russian army by victories over the great Frederick II which were as impressive as those her father had won over Charles XII.

Through both periods the masses settled more firmly into bondage and the serfs lost most of whatever freedom Peter the Great had left them. Toward the end of the second period they began to show their resentment in the only way left to them—revolt. The church lost what little freedom Peter had not taken away, and became completely dependent on the state, even for the salaries of its officials. One class, the gentry, began to escape its service responsibility.

Catherine I and Peter II

Prince Alexander Menshikov had good reason for wanting to see Peter succeeded by his wife. Catherine, the illiterate peasant girl, had always defended the man whose origins were as humble as her own. Menshikov had acquired a fortune and an impressive list of titles. Peter had threatened him time and again for robbing the treasury, but the prince had gone free with no more than a few blows of Peter's cane; he had even managed to retain the tsar's favor. He owed his immunity to Catherine's frequent intercessions on his behalf, and he knew that his continued good fortune depended on her succession.

Peter's law on the succession and his failure to avail himself of it left the decision to intrigue and influence, for there were many claimants with some shred of right to the throne. While Peter the Great lay dying, Menshikov, Yaguzhinsky, and other favorites, some senators and leaders of the Russian military, gathered to decide the succession. While the drums of the Guards regiments rolled threateningly in the square below, the Senate went through the pretense of electing the former laundress to be Empress Catherine I. The pattern would reappear.

The Senate lost all dignity and influence during the empress's short reign (1725–1727), while a new body, the Supreme Privy Council—six favorites presided over by Catherine and dominated by Menshikov—directed the administration. There was an ominous appearance of Baltic Germans and petty German princelings near the throne, not in the capacity of consultants and teachers, as Peter had used them, but as favorites and intriguers. Baltic nobles jostled each other for Catherine's favors. Baron Andrew Ostermann, a born schemer who had ably served Peter on diplomatic missions, became vice-chancellor and sought to undermine Menshikov's influence. Anne, Catherine's oldest daughter, married Duke Charles Frederick of Holstein-Gottorp, who was heir presumptive to the Swedish throne. Then Catherine brought him to court to scheme his succession to the throne. Catherine died after reigning only two years. Anticipating her death, Menshikov hoped to insure his continuance in power by betrothing his sixteen-year-old daughter to Peter the Great's eleven-year-old grandson Peter II, who was the obvious successor. The Supreme Privy Council, the Holy Synod, and the Senate dutifully elected the young Peter, as the Guards, prompted by Menshikov, shouted their approval.

As the new tsar's future father-in-law, Menshikov felt himself secure. However, everyone soon tired of his haughty and domineering manner, and he went into exile. Anne and her husband had returned to their duchy of Holstein, where Anne bore a son, the future Tsar Peter III.

Now Prince Alexis Dolgoruky dominated the youthful Peter II (1727–1730). The tsar promised to marry the prince's daughter as the dreary play of intrigue went on with new actors. It was the Dolgoruky family, whose members represented the old boyar point of view, who persuaded Peter to transfer the capital back to Moscow. In 1730, the fourteen-year-old emperor died of smallpox—the last male of the dynasty—and there was the question of the succession to decide all over again.

Empress Anne and Ivan VI

The Supreme Privy Council, made up chiefly of Golitsyns and Dolgorukys, gathered to consider the various candidates for the throne. The most appealing of the candidates, because she was a widow without children, which meant that the council would be able to decide the succession again at her death, was Anne, duchess of Courland, second daughter of Peter the Great's simple half brother Ivan V. Anne could have the throne but only on condition that she accept restrictions that would make the Russian monarchy elective as was the Polish.

The conditions offered Anne seemed on the surface to aim at providing Russia with something like a constitutional government. In reality, they were intended only to perpetuate the influence of the Supreme Privy Council and of the princely families who dominated it. Anne must promise to retain the council as then constituted and not to marry again or to name her successor without the council's approval. She would not be able to make war or peace, levy any new taxes, create any new nobles, raise any civil or military officer to general rank, or make any court appointments without the consent of the council. She must agree not to spend more to maintain the court than the council allowed her. She must not condemn any member of the gentry without trial. She must not attempt to control the Guards, which were to be responsible only to the council. Anne accepted the conditions without question, although probably without any intention of fulfilling them, and left Courland for Moscow.

The conditions did not express the wishes of most of the gentry; they favored a return to autocracy rather than the rule of a self-perpetuating oligarchy, the Supreme Privy Council, which they looked upon as "ten tsars instead of one." Anne understood that the gentry were suspicious of the great families and the great families suspicious of each other.

Anne entered Moscow, listened to a discussion of the various proposals by the Supreme Privy Council, and heard the Guards demonstrating in the courtyard below in favor of a revival of the autocracy. When a delegation of officers broke in and petitioned Anne to renounce the conditions she had accepted, sweep away the council, and restore the autocratic power, the empress gave way to what she chose to regard as the popular will and tore up the conditions while the disappointed councilors looked on. The Supreme Privy Council was disbanded and its members imprisoned or exiled. To symbolize the restoration of autocracy, the empress moved the capital back to St. Petersburg.

The next decade makes for one of the darkest chapters of Russian history. Anne (1730–1740) was a boorish, fat woman of sour disposition, as unattractive in her manners as in her appearance. Always pinched for money while duchess of Courland, she wallowed in the luxury that the imperial revenue could provide her. During her reign, the court expenses rose to five times their total under Peter the Great.

The empress brought with her from Courland a train of favorites and lovers who, with Anne's approval, dipped into the public treasury and quickly acquired fortunes. The most influential of these was Ernst Biren, who became a count and then, at Russian dictation, received the duchy of Courland, which was a fief of the Polish crown. As Anne's chief favorite, Biren effectively controlled the administration. Under him, two other Germans who had long served tsardom, Ostermann and Count Münnich, directed civil and military affairs. The empress flaunted her contempt for Russians by making court fools of sons of famous old noble families.

To take the place of the Supreme Privy Council, Biren set up a cabinet made up of Ostermann and two Russians whom he dominated. Its chief function was to keep revenue flowing to the imperial treasury. The Senate, always a stronghold of conservatism, but also a symbol of Russian nationalism declined to insignificance. Taxes were wrung mercilessly from the serfs. Regular military expeditions marched through the countryside trying to force taxes from the people and imposing tortures, floggings, and deportations to Siberia upon those who could not pay. The Secret Chancery, the new name for the security police, tortured those who complained. Biren's name became a synonym for the system of spying, informing, banishing, and slaughter that he condoned. Many members of the old princely families, notably the Dolgorukys and the Golitsyns, suffered death or Siberian exile. The situation became so unbearable that even Ostermann and Field Marshal Münnich complained. The empress herself finally objected. Russians, commoners as well as princes, never overcame the hatred for things German brought on by the brutality of Anne's officials.

Through the years after the death of Peter the Great, the government lost sight of Peter's insistence that every last Russian must render service to the state. Neither Catherine I nor Peter II nor Anne cared whether the gentry fulfilled their service obligations; they were content as long as the peasants paid taxes. Even before Anne's accession, two-thirds of the gentry were on permanent leave from their regiments, Biren relaxed the military obligation of the gentry, cutting the period of service to twenty-five years and excusing second sons, who, however, still must obtain enough education to allow them to render civil service. Gentry sons could obtain officer commissions at the age of eight and report years later having met part of their service obligation. They need no longer serve in the ranks. Commoners were denied the privilege Peter had extended them of earning hereditary noble rank.

During Anne's reign, Baron Ostermann directed Russia's foreign relations. He concluded an alliance with Austria logical arrangement for Russia because both countries were natural enemies of the Ottoman Empire and because France, Austria's foe for centuries, steadily resisted Russian policy toward Poland, Sweden, and Turkey.

France and Russia had been at odds during the reign of Peter the Great over who should occupy the Polish throne, and the Russian candidate, Augustus II, had won with Russian support. In 1733 Augustus died, and as St. Petersburg promoted the candidacy of Augustus's son to be Augustus III, France supported the perennial anti-Russian candidate, Stanislas Leszczynski, the father-in-law of Louis XV. When the Polish gentry elected Stanislas, a Russian army marched into Poland to redress what St. Petersburg chose to regard as a threat to Russian interests. Stanislas ran away when Russian troops approached Warsaw, and the Polish gentry meekly held another election to raise Augustus III to the Polish throne. In this War of the Polish Succession, Russian troops assisted an Austrian army threatened by the French. The Russians even marched toward the Rhine and threatened to invade France.

Turkish objections to Russian interference in the Polish election, added to Ostermann's determination to put a stop to Tatar raids, provided sufficient excuse for another Russo-Turkish war in 1735. St. Petersburg believed the Turkish Empire to be on the point of collapse and expected the appearance of Russian troops across the Pruth to spark a rising of Balkan Christians. Constantinople remembered the ease with which the sultan's troops had halted Peter the Great in 1711 and continued to hold Russian troops in contempt. In 1735 Russia, Austria, and Persia—the latter bribed by a return of the Caspian shore which Peter I had won—declared war on Turkey.

The Russians were everywhere successful. Marshal Münnich overran the Crimea, the Tatar stronghold that so long had proved impregnable. Another Russian force captured Azov, while a third defeated the Turks on the lower Dnieper. In 1739 Münnich crossed the Pruth into Moldavia and received an offer of the gentry to make the Russian empress the ruler of the principality. There were setbacks mingled with the impressive victories, however. Russia's ally, Austria, fared poorly in the field and had to withdraw from the war. Although the men in the ranks fought commendably, Russia's armies were poorly supplied, as usual, and its generals argued over strategy. The gains from the costly war were modest enough. The Peace of Belgrade in 1739 allowed Anne to keep Azov and the land around it, but Russia had to promise not to launch a fleet on the Black Sea.

Anne's dissolute life undermined her health, and she died in 1740 after naming an infant (her grandnephew) as her successor and appointing Biren, now the duke of Courland, as regent. There was still no end in sight to the rule of German favorites.

The farcical parade of successors to Peter I now brought to the Russian throne

Ivan VI (1740–1741), two-month-old great-grandson of Peter the Great's half-witted half brother Ivan V. Biren's contemptuous and domineering manner provoked the hatred and jealousy of the influential Ostermann and Münnich, who had their own following: When the regent considered disbanding the Guards regiments, Münnich led a company of the Preobrazhensky Guards to take him prisoner, and Biren was overthrown and banished to Siberia just three weeks after the opening of the new reign. The infant emperor's mother, Princess Anne of Brunswick, assumed the regency.

The regent spent her time quarreling with her husband and gossiping with her German lover and her German lady in waiting. Münnich, who had become a sort of chief minister after Biren's exile, gave way in disgust to Ostermann, who encouraged the regent's worthless husband to seize control of the government.

Russians finally lost all patience with the German comedy that had dragged on for sixteen years. Their mounting hatred of Germans and Balts, and their disgust at the spectacle of foreigners quarreling over who should rule the land, led them to center their hopes for an end to German domination on a coup d'état by Peter the Great's younger daughter, Elizabeth. The initiative, however, came not from Russians but from the Swedish government. Stockholm announced magnanimously that Russia must be rid of foreign rulers. The French ambassador in St. Petersburg encouraged Elizabeth and rewarded officers of the Guards who promised to support her. A Swedish army entered Russia on the pretense of restoring the government to the Russians but with every hope of winning back some of the territory conquered by Peter I.

A delegation of officers pleaded with Elizabeth to throw out the Germans and mount the throne. On a November night in 1741 Elizabeth, cross in hand, appeared before the cheering Preobrazhensky regiment. At the head of a company of Guards she entered the regent's bedchamber and announced, "Time to get up, sister." Ivan VI, now fifteen months old, was sent to a dungeon, where he grew to manhood only to be murdered before a plot could restore him. His mother and father also went to prison and Ostermann and Münnich to exile in Siberia.

Elizabeth

A woman of striking beauty, Elizabeth (1741–1762) was thirty-two years old at the time of her accession. She had never married, although her father had tried to affiance her to the French king and later to the Lutheran bishop of Lübeck, who died before they could wed. Thoroughly Russian, she enjoyed the company of peasant women and common soldiers. Charming, friendly, and carefree, Elizabeth showed little interest in official papers and reports. Important documents might wait months for her signature while the empress dallied with her favorites. Her conviction that reading endangered health did little to reduce her colossal ignorance.

Elizabeth immediately announced that she would rule in the spirit of her father.

Although she did not emulate Peter in his attention to the details of government, she did revive the administrative machinery her father had created. She restored the Senate, whose sessions she occasionally attended, to its role of coordinating the work of the colleges and reactivated the office of procurator of the Senate, which had gone unfilled for nearly a generation. She dissolved the Cabinet that Anne had established and replaced it with "Her Majesty's Chancery" to manage and finance court functions. After Russia's entry into the Seven Years' War, she regularly met with the new "Ministerial Conference" to hear the advice of chief government officials on foreign affairs. The most welcome move to many of her subjects was the reappearance of Russian names—Razumovsky, Trubetskoy, Bestuzhev, Cherkasov, Vorontsov, Shuvalov—among those close to the throne.

There was a modest rise of French influence at the Russian court, in part the result of French support for Elizabeth's accession and in part a sympathy for French culture and French learning as a reaction to the German stuffiness of recent years. Russian interest in Western civilization now focused not on the techniques and skills that had fascinated Peter the Great but on literature, art, and thought. The founding of the University of Moscow in 1755 reflected the new cultural interest in Western Europe.

Elizabeth's reign witnessed the development of modern Russian literature, which borrowed unashamedly from the West in technique and in form—in poetry, drama, and the novel. The first Russian dramatist, Alexander Sumarokov, produced tragedies and comedies in some volume. He even staged his own plays and became first director of a native Russian theater. An Italian opera company had performed before Anne, and Elizabeth's court watched many operatic and ballet performances.

One of the founders of the University of Moscow was Michael Lomonosov, Russia's first great poet, who imitated French forms as he dealt with Russian subject matter. He prepared the first Russian grammar and the first multivolume dictionary, which contributed much to the development of the language. He pioneered in physics and chemistry, and taught the first course in physical chemistry anywhere in the world. His nation's leading geographer, geologist, metallurgist, mineralogist, and astronomer, Lomonosov made outstanding discoveries in heat theory, electricity, optics, and the preservation of energy and matter, which his contemporaries could not appreciate and all of which had to be accomplished again later.

During Elizabeth's reign the increase in war and court costs combined with a steady shrinkage of revenue to enlarge the government deficits that had been commonplace since the death of Peter I. Occasionally, government officials and the church were asked for a contribution to relieve the pressure, and in one year officials received their pay in commodities manufactured in government plants because there was no money in the treasury. The empress's Paris milliner even denied her further credit.

Elizabeth's security police chief, Count Peter Shuvalov, warned her that the tax burden upon the peasants was intolerable, and there was a reduction of the soul tax during the latter half of her reign. To make up for the loss of revenue, Shuvalov debased the coinage and raised the prices of salt and vodka, both sold through state monopoly. The government attempted without success to float a foreign loan, and Elizabeth even considered selling some of her gowns and pawning her jewels. As Anne had done, she settled upon her favorites many government estates whose villagers thereby became serfs. The peasants ran away by the thousands to the Caucasus and beyond the Urals and even sought sanctuary on the estates of Polish nobles. To relieve the depression among the gentry, the government established a Nobles' Bank that lent money to needy landowners at low interest rates.

The administration tightened the hold of the gentry over their serfs, who lost most of the rights they had had after the legalization of bondage. No serf could marry anyone from another estate without the owner's permission. The law regarded the serf as chattel, the property of the owner. Serfs were neither required nor permitted to swear allegiance to the ruler. Because the peasants could not enter the army without their owners' approval, the masses had no legal escape from bondage. There was always the illegal way, flight or revolt. The reign of Elizabeth was never free of peasant uprisings and mass flights to the frontier. She put an end to capital punishment, although the most heartless tortures left her unmoved.

The Swedish attack on Russia in 1741 opened the way for Russian victories that only demonstrated the decline of Sweden as a military power. Russian armies overran Finland, meeting with little opposition; Helsinki and Åbo both fell. By the Peace of Åbo in 1743, the Russian frontier edged farther to the west along the north shore of the Gulf of Finland, and Viborg became a Russian city.

The Swedish war made it momentarily impossible for Russia to assist its ally Austria in the War of the Austrian Succession. French support for the coup that enthroned Elizabeth, aimed at bringing her into it on the side of France and Prussia. St. Petersburg managed to stay out of the war, but during its course, Russia swayed between French intrigue and the Prussian inclinations of Elizabeth's nephew and heir presumptive on the one hand and English pressure and the pro-Austrian sympathies of the chancellor, Alexis Bestuzhev, on the other. Finally, the French sympathizers were driven from court, not so much from Russian affection for Austria as from a growing concern over the rising strength of Prussia.

In 1756, Russia sided with Sweden, Saxony, France, and Austria in the Seven Years' War against Prussia and England. A Russian army overran and devastated East Prussia, which the Prussian King Frederick II lost for the duration of the war. In the summer of 1758, the Russians met Frederick in person at the bloody battle of Zorndorf, which ended in a draw—something of an achievement against such a military genius as the Prussian king. A year later the Russians soundly whipped Frederick at Künersdorf and scattered his army in disorder. Frederick despaired of his country's ability to survive. But Künersdorf was a tribute to the fighting quality of the men in the ranks rather than to any intelligence among the Russian commanders. Time and again they threw away the fruits of victory by failing to follow up a tactical gain with vigorous pursuit. Costly as the war was to Prussia, Frederick was permitted time after time to escape. Only in the last year or two of the war did young, aggressive, talented generals—Peter Rumiantsev and Zakhary Chernyshev—provide Russian troops the leadership they deserved.

In the fall of 1760, a Russian cavalry squadron occupied Berlin, ransacked the shops, and laid the city under tribute. Had the occupation been carried out effectively and resolutely, Prussia might have had to sue for peace. Instead Frederick II bribed the Russian commander to withdraw and the advantage was lost. The Prussian king, years later, admitted that he still had nightmares at the thought of the Cossacks in Berlin.

Empress Elizabeth was determined that the Prussian king should be demoted in rank to elector and his territory so reduced in size as to make him impotent. She expected to retain East Prussia, which had been in Russian hands since the second year of the war. Had she lived, no one could have prevented it. With the later absorption of Courland, the entire south coast of the Baltic would have come under Russian control and Russia's western frontier would have rested on the Oder.

The sudden death of Elizabeth on the day of the Russian Christmas, December 1761 (January 1762 by the Georgian calendar)—saved Frederick II and Prussia. Peter III, the nephew whom the empress had considered ruling out of the succession, was so enamored of things Prussian that he often kissed the bust of Frederick II and wore a ring containing Frederick's portrait. He immediately ordered an armistice and invited the Prussian king to draft his own peace terms. Russia gave up everything she had won. Then Peter ordered the Russian army to switch to the other side and join Prussia against Austria. France had already settled its differences with England and the war soon came to an end. Except for the gain of considerable military prestige, Russia might as well not have entered the war that had cost so many Russian lives and so much treasure.

Peter III

Soon after her accession, Empress Elizabeth had called to St. Petersburg her nephew Peter, the thirteen-year-old son of the duke and duchess of Holstein, whose parents had died years earlier. Grandson of Peter the Great, he was also grand-nephew of Charles XII of Sweden. He was mentally defective, brutal, and vulgar, and he drank too much. Born a Lutheran, he became Orthodox, although it was no secret that he thoroughly hated the Russian church. Elizabeth made him a Russian grand duke and proclaimed him heir to the throne. In 1745, at the empress's orders and on the suggestion of Frederick II of Prussia, the youth married Princess Sophia Augusta of Anhalt-Zerbst, who took the name Catherine and the rank of grand duchess. She, too, accepted baptism into the Russian Orthodox church and embraced it fervently.

Relations between the bride and groom were cool from the very beginning. Peter much preferred the company of his mistresses and encouraged Catherine to find lovers of her own. Nine years after her marriage, Catherine bore a son, the Grand Duke Paul, whose father Catherine candidly admitted was not Peter but a courtier whom the empress allowed her to choose. There is no reason to question her testimony. Peter III, then, was the last of the Romanovs. Whatever the child's parentage, Paul was taken from his mother at birth and raised by Elizabeth, who wanted to direct his education as a possible heir. She quickly became disgusted with the child and admitted that he was not fit for the throne.

Peter, in the prejudiced view of his wife, was a scoundrel of no character whose intellectual growth stopped at a childish level. He enjoyed playing with toy wax or wooden soldiers at which, dressed in Prussian uniform, he shouted military commands. A rat that devoured two of his doll sentries was caught, court-martialed, and hanged from the ceiling. As a child, the military fascinated him, and his father commissioned him a second lieutenant in the Holstein army at the age of nine. He idolized Frederick II, whom he called "the king, my master," and knelt before his portrait. Peter made no secret of his detestation of things Russian and his fondness for his native Holstein and for Prussia. He detested Orthodoxy and attended church only to ridicule the services, pace up and down talking at the top of his voice, stick out his tongue at the priest or burst out in insane laughter when the congregation knelt in prayer, and then run cackling from the building. He issued orders for the removal of the holy icons from the churches and for priests to shave and dress like Lutheran pastors.

Peter III occupied the throne a bare six months in 1762, but in that short time his policy was in some ways constructive and mild. He abolished the Secret Chancery (the security police force that Anne had created), put an end to the system of informing that had sent many innocent men into exile, and refused to try men for their political sympathies. He freed those of his predecessors' victims who were still alive.

The gentry profited most from the so-called reforms of Peter III. He freed them from the responsibility of state service and allowed them to travel abroad. Thenceforth the nobles would serve in the army only as officers, leaving to the peasants the rank and file of the Guards regiments that had previously consisted almost exclusively of nobles in all ranks. He so favored the gentry that serfs lost all traditional right to the land they tilled. Landowners might transfer serfs from one of their estates to another, or turn some of them into household servants. This "new serfdom" bound the peasant to the proprietor, where the "old serfdom" of the 1649 code had bound the peasant to the land. Thenceforth, landholders could sell serfs off the land, give them away, or lose them at the gaming table, but they could neither free the serfs nor turn them into slaves. Proprietors alone administered justice among the serfs; they even owned the personal effects the serfs used, for legally they could not own property. The greatest of serf-owners, the state and the church, allowed a degree of self-government to their serf villages, but no serf, no matter who the owner, henceforth would enjoy any rights whatsoever. Serfs lived outside the law, beyond the protection of the courts that existed solely for the benefit of the proprietary classes. Peter's emancipation of the gentry from the burden of state service, however, led the serfs to anticipate their own early emancipation.

Peter III secularized the estates of the church and placed them under the control of an Economic College. In effect he put the clergy on salaries, and the revenue from church lands went to the state. Peter "reformed" the army by adopting the uniform and the "ballet dance" drill of the Prussian Army. He threatened to reduce the Guards to line regiments and replace them with his new Holstein Guards, whose officers, according to a spiteful critic, were "sons of German cobblers." He humiliated gouty old retired officers by ordering them into uniform and personally drilling them for long hours like common soldiers, immensely enjoying their discomfiture. When he involved Russia in a war with Denmark so that his native Holstein might recover Schleswig, a war that would have taken the Guards out of the capital and forced them to march to the Elbe, his wife's supporters decided they had had enough of Peter III. His threat to send Catherine to a convent and marry his mistress, Elizabeth Vorontsov, together with his alienation of the Guards who had decided so many successions since 1725, brought his downfall.

Catherine admitted in her memoirs that from the moment of her marriage, the ambition grew in her to become empress of Russia. She cultivated the friendship of Empress Elizabeth and made a great display of her respect for her newly donned Orthodox faith. She sought out the friendship of leading officials who resented Peter's insults. She won over officers of the Guards, one of whom, Gregory Orlov, was her lover.

On a midsummer night in 1762 while Peter was busy drilling his Holsteiners, Orlov and his four brothers led Catherine to the quarters of the Izmailovsky and Semenovsky Guards, who escorted her to the Winter Palace to announce that Peter III was no longer tsar. The Senate and the Holy Synod, carefully assembled beforehand, enthusiastically acclaimed Catherine as empress, thus ignoring the claims of her son Paul and the forgotten Ivan VI. Then, in the uniform of the Preobrazhensky Guards, Catherine led the joyous troops to Peter's residence in the suburbs to inform her husband that he no longer ruled. A week later he was killed at his country estate by a band of courtiers led by one of the Orlov brothers. The woman who had no blood right whatsoever to the throne now ruled as Catherine II.

Suggested Reading

BAIN, R. N., *The Daughter of Peter the Great* (New York, 1900).
_____, *Peter III, Emperor of Russia* (London, 1902).
BRENNAN, J. F., *Enlightened Despotism in Russia: The Reign of Elizabeth, 1741–1762* (New York, 1987).
CARMICHAEL, J., *A Cultural History of Russia* (London, 1968).
COUGHLAN, R., *Elizabeth and Catherine: Empresses of All the Russias* (New York, 1974).
COWLES, V., *The Romanovs* (New York, 1971).

CROSS, A. G. (ed.), *Russia under Western Eyes, 1517–1825* (London, 1971).

EGOROV, I. A., *The Architectural Planning of St. Petersburg: Its Development in the 18th and 19th Centuries* (Athens, OH, 1969).

HAMILTON, G. H., *The Art and Architecture of Russia* (New York, 1983).

KAPLAN, H. H., *Russia and the Outbreak of the Seven Years' War* (Berkeley, 1968).

KENNETT, A. and V. KENNETT, *The Palaces of Leningrad* (New York, 1973).

LINCOLN, W. B., *The Romanovs: Autocrats of All the Russias* (New York, 1981).

LONGWORTH, P., *The Three Empresses: Catherine I, Anne, and Elizabeth of Russia* (New York, 1973).

MANSTEIN, C. H. von, *Contemporary Memoirs of Russia, 1727–1744* (New York, 1968).

MENSHUTKIN, B. N., *Russia's Lomonsov: Chemist, Courtier, Physicist, Poet* (Princeton, 1952).

RAEFF, M., *Imperial Russia, 1682–1825: The Coming of Age of Modern Russia* (New York, 1971).

_____. *Plans for Political Reform in Imperial Russia, 1730–1905* (Englewood Cliffs, NJ, 1966).

RAFFEL, B., *Russian Poetry under the Tsars: An Anthology* (Albany, 1971).

CHAPTER 11

Catherine the Great

Catherine II (1762–1796), the Great, considered herself the heir and executor of the reforms of Peter the Great. Unlike Peter, however, whose reforms were thoroughly practical if not always thought through, Catherine was doctrinaire in the reforms that she conceived. They breathed the spirit of enlightened despotism of which Catherine was a devotee and a classic example.

Youth and Character

Catherine grew up in the atmosphere of the remote little German principality of Anhalt-Zerbst. Her father, a general in the Prussian army, was thrifty and sober, her mother a woman of extravagant taste. Catherine received a modest education but acquired a good knowledge of French from her Huguenot tutor. Her native intelligence, her acquaintance with writers of the day, her bearing, and her vivacity made her attractive, but her awareness that she was not beautiful stimulated her vanity, and she surrounded herself with young and handsome men. The older she grew, the younger were her favorites: Mamonov was twenty-six when the empress was fifty-seven, and the last of them was twenty-two when Catherine was over sixty. Her disappointing marriage led her unashamedly to welcome liaisons. In her galaxy of lovers the most influential were Gregory Orlov, who was her "personal adjutant general" for eleven years and the one-eyed Gregory Potemkin, who may secretly have married her. She richly rewarded each lover, when he dropped from favor, with a gift of crown peasants, thus condemning nearly a million of them to serfdom.

Catherine did not abandon herself to sensuality as had some of her immediate predecessors. She worked conscientiously at the job of governing Russia, while relying frequently for counsel on such favorites as Orlov and Potemkin. Like Peter the Great, who considered himself the first servant of the state, Catherine labored as diligently as anyone in the government.

The extent of her knowledge and her appetite for reading made her one of the best-read women in Europe and the most unusual and outstanding woman in Elizabethan Russia. For that reason she much preferred the companionship of men and prided herself on her ability to converse and correspond, as an equal in many cases, with the best minds of her day. Voltaire was one of her most uncritical admirers. Diderot visited Russia to become a keen admirer of her remarkable gifts both as a woman and as an intellectual. She corresponded at great length with such fellow rulers as Frederick II, Joseph II, Gustavus II, and with D'Alembert, Falconet, Grimm, and others of the Encyclopedists. She read Plato, Tacitus, Blackstone, Buffon, Montesquieu, Rousseau, Bayle, and Beccaria, as well as the *Encyclopédie*, which fascinated her. She was an author of perseverance if not of great merit, turning out comedies, tragedies, and essays in French and Russian, and even a history of Russia in addition to a great volume of letters.

Catherine was extremely ambitious. Even at the time of her marriage, she looked forward to becoming the ruler of Russia. With her husband out of the way she was still ambitious—to add to the glory of her reign, to acquire territory, to win recognition abroad for herself and her empire, and even to insure that her policies would continue after her death.

The Nakaz and the Legislative Commission

Steeped in Western liberal thought, determined not to dilute her autocratic power but to use it for the benefit of her subjects, Catherine conceived an ambitious plan to provide the nation with a new law code that would reflect Western humanitarian principles. There had been no revision of the Russian code since 1649. There were at least ten thousand laws on the books, many of them contradictory or obscure or hopelessly out of date. The chaotic state of the law made it impossible for officials or subjects to interpret and administer or even to know the law. Peter the Great had been fully aware of the need for a revision, but the press of day-to-day problems left him no time to deal with something that could be put off. The spate of legislation for which he was responsible made the situation still more hopelessly confusing. Both Anne and Elizabeth had called assemblies of elected nobles and merchants to draft a new law code, but nothing had come of their labors. In the last year of her reign, Elizabeth had complained of the inefficiency of her administration and noted

Catherine II, the Great

that the laws were neither observed nor enforced. Now Catherine hoped to correct a situation that her predecessors had done nothing to relieve.

The empress decided to convoke a great national commission of elected delegates to work out the principles on which to base a new law code. She knew nothing of Russian law and no more of the principles on which it rested. Of the enlightened principles on which she sought to rest the new law code, she was comfortably knowledgeable. To give direction to the deliberations of the delegates, the empress herself worked for two years on a Nakaz, or set of instructions. Finally, the remarkable volume appeared, not only in Russia to guide those who would sit on the commission, but abroad as well, where its daring acceptance of liberal thought delighted reformers and shocked conservatives. Louis XV forbade its distribution in France, but Frederick II expressed his approval by making the empress a member of the Berlin Academy. Voltaire compared her to Solon.

Catherine's Nakaz, written with her own hand but considerably modified by her advisers, contained over five hundred paragraphs suggesting principles to which the enlightened state should adhere in politics, economics, social welfare, culture, and religion. Some of the statements came straight out of Montesquieu's *Spirit of the Laws* or Beccaria's *On Crimes and Punishments*; the empress quickly admitted as much. Yet there was something of Catherine in it too—of her ignorance of Russian society, of her naïve assumption that principles worked out tortuously over centuries in other countries could be transplanted, of her supreme confidence in absolutism. The final draft, at the prompting of serf-owning advisers, avoided suggestions to improve the lot of Russian serfs. Catherine gave way before the insistence of court nobles that there be no hint of emancipation. She remembered, perhaps, that she had no right to the throne, that she owed her accession to the support of the nobles who might easily unseat her by withdrawing that support.

Even with all the editing that Catherine accepted, the instructions retained much Western liberal thought that was far in advance of the practice of the time. The Nakaz spoke of citizens, but this excluded the vast majority, the unprivileged, who were the chattels either of the gentry or of the state. It declared that all citizens should be equal before the law; all should obey the law; the state should aim less at the punishment than at the prevention of crime; capital punishment is rarely justifiable; serfdom is excusable only if it serves the state, but to sweep away bondage at a stroke would be rash and dangerous; all people should be free to do whatever the law does not specifically proscribe; religious dissent is not a threat to domestic peace; the right even of serfs to own land encourages agriculture; autocracy's aim is "not to deprive people of their natural freedom, but to guide their actions so as to attain the natural good." No nation in Europe accepted the validity of all these ideas, and few on the continent practiced any of them.

The empress unquestionably believed the propositions put forward in the Nakaz. Still Catherine was a true benevolent despot. There was no hint that these high-minded principles should operate through a representative assembly. Rather, they should guide the sovereign, who would retain in his or her own hands the full power of absolute monarchy, the only sensible type of government for a land as sprawling as Russia. It is better to be subject to the rule of law under one ruler than to be subservient to many. The ruler is the source of all civil and political power, but that power must be used wisely and justly with the welfare of the people in view. The principle that the people exist not for the ruler but the ruler and the people for the security and prosperity of the state was one that Peter I would have applauded.

The empress sent the instructions all over Russia, and six months later she called for the election of delegates to a legislative commission whose assignment was to draw up a new law code. In the summer of 1767, over five hundred elected representatives gathered in the Kremlin in Moscow. There was a delegate from each of two hundred towns, eighty chosen by the crown peasants, fifty from the Cossacks, twenty-eight high officials, a hundred and sixty from the gentry, and thirty-four to represent "foreign" peoples in the empire—including Bashkirs, Kalmyks, and Samoyeds. The very mention of the unfamiliar names made disbelieving Europeans laugh at such an "ethnographic exhibition." There were no representatives from the landowners' serfs who made up more than half of all peasants and nearly half the nation's population. No one spoke for the clergy as a class, for they voted with merchants in the election of town delegates. Delegates came with statements of grievances or recommendations drawn up by those who had chosen them. The statements some of the delegates brought with them contained only petty, carping criticisms. Others expressed dismay over high taxes or called for a clear definition of the rights and obligations of each social class; state peasants sought an end to bondage or at least a clarification of serf rights and gentry obligations. The Nakaz had proposed that the commission interest itself in such lofty ideals as the rights of all living individuals. The concerns of most of the delegates ran to more immediate needs.

Meetings and committee sessions went on to the end of the year, when the sittings moved to St. Petersburg to go on for another year. In December 1768, just after the opening of the first of Catherine's wars with Turkey, the plenary sessions adjourned and most of the delegates went home. However, committees continued to meet for another six years.

The Legislative Commission held over two hundred sessions and innumerable committee meetings. Many of the speeches were less constructive than complaining. Some of the nobles from old families resented the intrusion into their class of those who became gentry through Peter's Table of Ranks. The merchants resented the loss of their trade monopoly and the growing threat of competition from factories, worked by serfs, on landowners' estates. Commoners resented the gentry's monopoly of the right to own serfs, and merchants and Cossacks appealed for the same right.

There were a few constructive suggestions along with the selfish demands. There was a plea for a legislative assembly and constitutional restrictions on the autocratic power. Several enlightened nobles appealed for a reduction of the landowners' authority over serfs or at least for a definition of serf rights so that abuses might not go unpunished. The accomplishments were disappointing. There was no new code. The debates, however, were a source of information to the empress. Some of the things she learned from them helped her in defining some of the later reforms.

The Reforms of Catherine II

From the moment of her accession, Catherine felt a responsibility to carry on the reforming work of Peter the Great. Within a month of Peter III's death she was busy annulling his edict secularizing church estates. Early in 1764, however, she changed her mind and again confiscated the lands of the church, putting their administration and the supervision of two million church-owned serfs under the Economic College as her predecessor had done. The clergy and the few monasteries that were not closed received their income from the state.

There were minor alterations in the machinery of the central government. During her first Turkish war, Catherine created an Imperial Council to advise her on war policy and foreign affairs. The council continued to function to the end of the century. She abolished most of the colleges and turned their functions over to new local agencies responsible to the Senate. The Admiralty, the Army, and the Department of Foreign Affairs were the only colleges to survive. The procurator, who was removed earlier from his contact with the Senate and made a separate and powerful official, assumed the responsibilities of colleges that had dealt with the collection of revenue and the administration of justice. This abolition of some offices and transfer of duties from one agency to another was so confusing that when Alexander I later asked the senators what their duties were, they were not sure of the answer.

Catherine's reforms in the area of local government were more impressive. Peter the Great had despaired of developing much governmental initiative on the local level when he found there were not enough capable and intelligent candidates to staff local administrative offices. That such was the case was primarily owing to the obligation of every member of the gentry to serve in the armed forces, leaving no one in the provinces to accept civil assignment. The situation altered quickly after Peter's death, however, when most of the gentry shirked their service responsibilities with impunity and returned to their estates. Then Peter III freed the gentry entirely from their obligations.

By a succession of orders between 1764 and 1785, Catherine refined the system of local government that Peter the Great had begun. Each province—there were now fifty—would contain three hundred thousand inhabitants; each was divided into districts of thirty thousand inhabitants. A governor named by the crown was responsible to the Senate for the administration of each province. However, certain functions—finance, police, and social welfare—were assigned to provincial boards that answered not to the governor but to the procurator's office in St. Petersburg. Civil and criminal courts in the provinces were also accountable to the procurator. All these provincial officials were appointed, the governor typically from a well-to-do and influential noble family, the others from the lesser and poorer gentry. The effect of this reorganization of local government was not to promote self-government but to improve the machinery for carrying out the sovereign's will.

The gentry of each district and each province had received the privilege of electing delegates to a district assembly or to a provincial assembly that met every three years. The assemblies, within certain limits, voted assessments for local needs, and each elected a "marshal of the nobility." The provincial or district marshal had to be a person of some influence, to plead the needs of the nobles before the provincial governor or the appropriate official in St. Petersburg.

The provincial and district plan of local organization extended eventually into the Baltic provinces, Russian Finland, and the Ukraine. Serfdom spread to the border areas where it had not already appeared, and the peasants had to pay the Russian soul tax. The Cossacks lost the little independence left to them—the office of hetman was abolished, the circle or assembly broken up, and the Cossack lands divided among the three provinces carved out of the Ukraine.

The gentry, who made up 1 percent of the population, received complete freedom from irritating restraints and from all obligations to the state in Catherine's Charter of the Nobility, proclaimed in 1785. The charter considerably increased the rights granted by Peter III's emancipation of the gentry. It relieved the nobles of all responsibility to enter the service of the state. They were to be free from corporal punishment and from payment of direct taxes. No nobles were to lose their lives, estates, or titles except by the verdict of their peers. If, by court sentence, they were to lose their estates, those estates must go to one of their heirs and not to the state. None but the gentry could own serf-populated lands, and none but they were free to travel abroad. They could sell their estates or maintain factories on them and sell the products, thus sharing the trade rights of the merchants without having to pay the merchants' fees.

When the gentry won legal emancipation, it began to take on some of the coloration of Westerners of the same class. Some nobles, the less wealthy ones, lived in their own country houses and directed the field work or the manufacturing labor of their serfs. Wealthy nobles frequently owned town houses in St. Petersburg and Moscow, attended plays, operas, ballets, and court functions. They might never see their estates, but leave the operation to bailiffs. Their tables were set with fine silver and with Sèvres or Dresden china. Men and women dressed in the finest cloth—silk, satin, and brocade—and in blue fox and sable furs. With their oriental perfumes they even smelled different from the unwashed masses who made up the vast majority of Russians.

By the terms of laws issued at various times during the century and by unwritten privileges tacitly admitted by the sovereign, the gentry won almost unlimited control over their serfs. They could sell or give away their slaves singly or in families, with or without land. They could move serfs out of the village and off the land into their manor houses at will. They could send any serf to the army for the twenty-five-year enlistment period, or exile a serf to Siberia, which one out of four never reached because so many died along the way. Landowners could subject their serfs to unlimited floggings; while they could not condemn their serfs to death, they could order as many strokes of the lash as they pleased. Peter the Great had held the gentry accountable—even to the loss of their estates—for abusing their serfs, but this restraint lapsed after his death. In Peter I's time, serfs might petition the tsar against mistreatment by their owners, but such complaints Catherine forbade.

The serf had no enforceable rights whatsoever. The gentry-owned serfs, who made up over half the nation's population, could not own property, real or even personal. The very rags they wore and the miserable huts in which they lived were legally the property of the noble who owned them. Their labor and their earnings were at the disposal of the estate owner. There were few differences beyond that of color between the Russian serf and the black slave in the United States.

As chattels, the market value of serfs depended on their skills. Although a good borzoi puppy might bring three thousand rubles, a young serf girl might sell for from three to thirty rubles, and a child for ten kopeks, a tenth of a ruble. Yet the cost of a good musician or cook might run high, and a twenty-serf orchestra sold for ten thousand rubles. Wealthy serf-owners might advertise in St. Petersburg or Moscow newspapers the sale of "a girl of sixteen and a used carriage" or "a barber and four beds" or "tablecloths and two trained girls." Only one-sixth of the gentry owned a hundred serfs or more, however, and a third owned fewer than ten. Prince P. B. Sheremetiev owned sixty thousand "souls" or male serfs, Count K. G. Razumovsky forty-five thousand, Count A. S. Stroganov twenty-three thousand.

Serfs might live in miserable one-room huts clustered in a village near their owner's roomy, sometimes palatial, mansion. Villagers on an estate under cultivation customarily owed the landholder three days of work each week (the *barshchina*) on that part of the arable land that the estate owner cultivated for personal use. Ideally, the landowner assigned half of the arable land to the serfs. In these fields, the village elders allotted strips on which a serf family could raise its own food. However, landowners, particularly in the rich black soil area, often forced serfs to work in the fields five or six days a week and added villagers' fields to their own, doling out whatever food was necessary to keep the workers alive. In the gray soil area of central Russia, a proprietor might take the fields out of cultivation and put the serfs to work in factories on the estate. On the other hand, the landowner might let bondsmen till the land on their own in return for their paying an annual *obrok*, a money payment in lieu of labor, or the landowner might let them work in a nearby town and pay the obrok out of whatever wages they received. Where the barshchina serfs worked under the lash in the proprietors' fields and suffered constant interference in their daily lives from the bailiffs of the estates, the obrok-payers were comparatively free to govern themselves and to use their time as they chose as long as the village elders saw that each serf paid the obrok.

Although Catherine did nothing to help landowners' serfs, she certainly improved the lot of state-owned serfs by making them all obrok-payers instead of barshchina serfs. Left to govern themselves in their own village assemblies, and enjoying generous land allotments, they were much better off than privately owned serfs and were commonly known as peasants rather than serfs. Whatever rights they enjoyed, however, they possessed only by sufferance of the state, which was a milder, or perhaps merely less efficient and less grasping, landlord than were many nobles. Some state peasants suffered during Catherine's reign, however, for the empress gave away hundreds of thousands of them to her favorites for "service to the fatherland." The reign saw the lot of the peasants reach its lowest point, for the government refined the control of the landowners over their serfs and legally swept away whatever rights the privately owned serfs had previously retained. In addition millions more peasants were depressed into serfdom as bondage spread to the Baltic provinces, the Ukraine, and to that part of the Polish-Lithuanian lands that Catherine acquired where serfdom did not already exist.

Midway in her reign, the government took a census, the third since Peter's first. Of the thirteen million males—the census-taker counted only males until the middle of the nineteenth century—nearly seven million were gentry-owned serfs; another 4.5 million were the property of the state itself. The figures do not include the inhabitants of areas incorporated during Catherine's reign. By the time of Catherine's death the population of Russia was approximately thirty-six million and the percentages of the unfree elements were approximately the same as those reflected in the previous census.

Peter's efforts to establish a municipal government had met with little success outside the capital. In a 1785 Charter to the Towns, Catherine announced a new basis for self-government in the nation's cities, placing the control over local government machinery in the hands of the wealthy merchants. For most Russian cities, however, Catherine's proposed municipal self-government never went beyond the paper stage. A confusion of appointed officials maintained order and collected taxes until the last half of the nineteenth century. Town inhabitants were exempt from payment of the soul tax, which became the exclusive privilege of the "souls" living on state-owned or private estates.

The urban population reached 1.5 million by the end of the eighteenth century, five times its size when Peter the Great died. The increase resulted in part from an imperial invitation to foreign merchants and manufacturers to enter Russia and enjoy subsidies and tax exemptions. A sixth of the inhabitants of St. Petersburg's 220,000 were foreign born or descendants of immigrants who had come in generations or even centuries earlier. Names like Cameron, Patrick, Gordon, Falk, Panin, Rinaldo, Rastrelli, Bush, and Tooke were common.

Some new towns came into existence during Catherine's reign. The government claimed to have built a hundred of them, scattering the breadth of the land from the Baltic to the Black Sea. In 1787, accompanied by a following of Western ambassadors and by the Austrian Emperor Joseph II, Catherine moved grandly down the Dnieper and into the Crimea to view the accomplishments of her government in the land so recently under Turkish rule. Prince Gregory Potemkin, now governor of the area, carefully planned the itinerary to visit a number of new or recently acquired cities along the way—Nikolaev, Sevastopol, Odessa, Kherson, and Ekaterinoslav.

Catherine encouraged foreigners to settle in the thinly populated lands of the empire, allowing them tax exemptions and freedom to practice their religion in the hope that they would set Russians an example of industry and improved farming methods. Over a hundred colonies of Germans settled in the lower Volga and the Ukraine, jealously clinging to their language and customs into the middle of the twentieth century, by which time they numbered six hundred thousand.

There was a modest approach to laissez-faire principles in economic policies under Catherine. The empress put an end to the monopolies that Peter the Great had granted to encourage Russia's infant industries. Tariffs were scaled down to encourage competition. Foreigners entered to establish factories under preferred conditions, with the privilege of buying serfs to work in their plants, a right that Russians no longer enjoyed. The elimination of the monopoly of Russian merchants, however, was a blessing primarily to the gentry, who obtained the right to build factories on their estates.

In spite of the rise in prices brought about by large issues of paper rubles, Russia's foreign trade increased markedly during the reign. The government arranged treaties with Western nations, stimulated imports by moderate tariffs, and expanded seaports through which the goods could flow. The empress had visions of a thriving Black Sea trade through the Bosporus, which she hoped Russia might some day control.

Catherine made a beginning on a system of lay schools. She ordered two-year elementary schools for every district in every province, although many never opened and a few closed for want of teachers, students, or funds. Four-year secondary schools were operating in the important cities by the end of her reign. The government established a teachers' college to produce the teachers with which to staff its new schools. By 1790 there were sixteen thousand students in lay and church schools out of a population of thirty-six million—pitifully small percentage, but still a beginning. Most of the students came from middle-class families, for serfs as chattels were ignored, and the gentry employed private tutors. There were still no schools of any kind in the villages, which meant that most of the nation's population had no educational facilities.

The empress founded a school for orphans in St. Petersburg and another in Moscow, and she opened the Smolny Institute in the capital as a finishing school for daughters of the gentry. Most sons of the gentry obtained their education either at the officers' schools founded by Peter or from French tutors. They learned to read the works of the French radicals of the time whose writings were popular at court. Many aristocrats enrolled their sons in Western schools when Catherine ended the proscription on foreign travel. The son of Princess Dashkov, a friend of the empress, attended the famous Westminster School in London and later studied economics in Edinburgh with Adam Smith. Young Russians were studying in Leipzig, Göttingen, Strasbourg, Paris, London, Oxford, Glasgow, and Edinburgh at a time when only two students were attending classes at the Academy of Science.

Catherine organized a college of medicine at the University of Moscow. It had graduated only one student by the end of the century, for most Russian medical students sought their education abroad. She set her people an example of confidence in new medical practices by being the first to accept vaccination against smallpox, the scourge of the villages. She encouraged the health authorities to use quarantine and to forbid the kissing of icons when the plague swept over south Russia during the Turkish war. She organized the Free Economic Society to stimulate interest in Russian agricultural development. In its first year, the society offered a prize to the citizen of any country who should submit the best essay on the problem of serfdom. The winner, a resident of Aix-la-Chapelle, suggested abolition of serfdom. He received the prize, but the society, most of whose members were nobles, refused to publish his essay. They were willing to discuss social theories among themselves, but refused to broadcast this concrete proposal for the alteration of the social order from which they drew so much profit.

Catherine did much to add to the beauty of Peter's new capital on the Neva. She completed some of the buildings Elizabeth had ordered and added many of her own. She finished the fifteen-hundred-room Winter Palace, one wing of which became famous as the Hermitage. Here in this private and intimate section she entertained Western men of letters when they visited St. Petersburg. She added to the Hermitage a wing to house one of the world's outstanding collections of paintings. The works of the Western masters hung there in profusion alongside those of Russia's best. She also added a theater where she could watch the performance of her own plays and translations of Shakespeare or see opera and ballet performed by foreign troupes and occasional Russians. Opera and ballet written in Russian and performed by Russians appeared for the first time. There was even an orchestra consisting entirely of Russians.

The Catherinian reforms differed from those of Peter the Great in one fundamental way. Peter did not pretend that his reforms were carefully thought out or based on any philosophical precepts. Almost invariably Peter's reforms were of the practical sort, unadorned with philosophical folderol to lend them dignity. On the other hand, Catherine's reforms, which with few exceptions were much less substantial and much less enduring than Peter's, were conceived in the spirit of enlightenment that was the fad of the age. The empress was proud, if not vain, of her correspondence with other enlightened despots and philosophers and was most anxious to be known abroad as one of such people. She did her best to cultivate among Westerners the belief that Russia was a Western state, a European nation and, beyond that, that Russia was particularly prosperous and contented under Catherine's rule. Catherine always felt concern over what people thought of her and Russia. Peter cared little about what others thought as long as he could whip the nation to a level of achievement that would satisfy Russia's own needs. However, it was Catherine, and not Peter, who set the intellectual tone of modern Russia. If Russian merchants and industrialists looked westward in Peter's time, it was the Russian intellectual who looked westward from Catherine's time onward.

Pugachev's Rising

Catherine's reign witnessed perennial outbursts of popular resentment against the bondage system, which reached its worst condition in the last half of the eighteenth century. In keeping with a long tradition of pretenders to the throne, there was a succession of peasant leaders claiming to be Peter III or Ivan VI, whom Catherine had ordered slain. Each such claimant won a following among the masses, who had sufficient cause to welcome a change of rulers. At other times, when there was no leader of glamorous name to follow, the peasants fled the settled districts in an endless stream toward the frontier—to the lower Volga and beyond into Central Asia, to the southern steppes, and frequently to Poland to seek the supposedly gentler treatment of a Polish landholder.

The government had long since grown used to such discontent and had even come to take armed risings with a certain unconcern. In 1773, however, a wave of revolt swept over south Russia that frightened the government and the privileged classes out of all complacency. The leader was a Don Cossack, Emelian Pugachev, who had served in the army but who had suffered severe punishment several times for desertion and had just escaped from prison. Pugachev claimed to be Peter III, the sixth or seventh rebel in a decade to do so.

In the spring of 1773, Pugachev gathered about him a motley band of followers. There were Cossacks from the valley of the Yaik or Ural river, and others from the Don and the Volga. There were Old Believers who cheered the leader's promise to restore the old faith. There were four thousand criminals released from the prisons of Kazan. There were swarms of peasants, bitter at the exactions of the tax gatherers and the recruiting of their sons, who resented Peter III's emancipation of the gentry from service and hoped to force their own. There were Bashkirs, who had risen under Peter I, and Tatars and Kirghiz and Chuvash and Votiaks who resented the Russian seizure of their lands.

The rebellion met with alarming success through the autumn of 1773 and the following spring. There were only handfuls of soldiers in the sparsely populated lands between the Volga and the Urals, and local authorities enjoyed little respect. The government was busy with the Turkish war, and for the moment there were no troops to spare. Pugachev's thirty thousand pillaging followers swarmed over the countryside. Lacking discipline and having no leaders with command experience, the rebels behaved less like an army than a horde. Still, they took Saratov and Kazan, looting, burning manor houses of the gentry, and torturing officials and Orthodox priests. Pugachev swore to rid Russia of landowning gentry and abolish the laws against beards. After taking Kazan he threatened to march on Moscow, and the governor of the old capital prepared to defend his province.

For some time Catherine persisted in believing that this was just another Cossack disturbance that would quickly subside. Finally, she admitted the seriousness of the challenge and sent her best commanders against the outlaw. With the end of the Turkish war, troops were available to turn against the rebellion. After two years of leading a class war that swept aside all government authority, Pugachev was captured and taken in a cage to Moscow to be executed. The Yaik Cossacks were reorganized and renamed the Ural Cossacks, and the Yaik river became the Ural in an attempt to efface the name of Pugachev's most loyal supporters.

Pugachev's rising was the last widespread outbreak against the institution of serfdom. From that time on, resentment smoldered in the countryside and occasional revolts brought destruction and death to scattered estates. One of her generals told Catherine, "It is not Pugachev that matters, but the general indignation." The name Pugachev went down in the language as a synonym for peasant fury against the landowner as a symbol of oppression. The gentry never quite got over their fear of another Pugachevshchina, or wave of Pugachevism. From that time on, the government stationed garrisons among its own people to move sternly against any threat of revolt.

Catherine's Wars with Turkey

In maintaining pressure on Turkey and the sultan's vassals, the Crimean Tatars, Catherine was following the lead of Peter the Great and Anne. Her patience was exhausted at the perennial Tatar raids into her territory, and the empress attacked their overlord, Turkey, in 1768. Russian troops under Count Peter Rumiantsev advanced into the Balkans, captured Bucharest, and pushed the Turks across the Danube. A coordinated drive to the Don and into the Crimea under Prince Vasily Dolgoruky was successful, and a Tatar khan sympathetic to Russia replaced the sultan's vassal in the peninsula.

In the following spring, the Russian Baltic fleet, under Alexis Orlov, arrived in the eastern Mediterranean. However, its landings in Greece were feebly manned, and the general rising of Christians in the Balkans did not materialize. Then in July 1770, Orlov and his English squadron commanders completely destroyed the Turkish fleet at Chesme in the Aegean, winning the most convincing victory in the annals of the Russian Navy.

Now other Christian capitals began to feel alarm lest too much Turkish territory fall to Russia. Western Europe's fear of a great Slav state that would bring the Balkan Christians under Russian rule, a fear that plagued Russia's relations with the West through the nineteenth and twentieth centuries, emerged during Catherine's first war with the Ottoman Empire. Now Frederick II of Prussia thought to appease Russia's appetite for Slavic lands by suggesting that he and Catherine partition Poland.

Peace talks with the sultan in 1772 accomplished nothing, and the following summer the greatest of all Russian generals, Alexander Suvorov, crossed the Danube and threatened Constantinople. Now the Turks had had enough, and at Kuchuk Kainardji in 1774 they accepted the Russian peace terms. The Pugachev rising made Catherine as willing as the sultan to see an end to the war.

Catherine's gains by the Treaty of Kuchuk Kainardji were modest enough. Turkey recovered Bessarabia, Moldavia, Wallachia, and the Aegean islands that Russia had overrun. Except for the tip of the Kerch Peninsula, which went to Russia, the Crimea became independent. The land between the Bug and the Dnieper rivers also went to Russia, thus returning it to the coast of the Black Sea for the first time since the days of Kiev. The mouth of the Kuban went to Russia, whose territory now completely surrounded the Crimea, which soon would be ripe for plucking. Russian merchant vessels were to enjoy free use of the Black Sea and entry and exit through the straits. In return for Russia's evacuation of the Turkish provinces on the Danube, the sultan promised to allow the Balkan Christians the free practice of their faith. The Russian government won a vaguely worded right to protect Christians in the Ottoman Empire. Nineteenth-century tsars interpreted this clause as recognizing Russia's right to intervene in Turkish affairs on behalf of all Christians living under Ottoman rule.

Catherine could not long be satisfied with the Treaty of Kuchuk Kainardji, for she planned nothing less than the complete expulsion of Turkey from Europe, as Peter had done. To make this possible, Russia needed the support of Austria, not so much for the military as for the diplomatic value of that support. England, France, Sweden, and Prussia, whose king was wholly unreliable from Catherine's standpoint, were sure to oppose further aggrandizement by Russia at the expense of Turkey, but Austria might, for a price, welcome the partition of the Ottoman Empire that had cost her so much blood. So Catherine dropped the alliance with Prussia that had lasted for the first eighteen years of her reign and shifted her favor to Austria.

At Catherine's invitation the Austrian Emperor Joseph II visited Russia in 1790; the two discussed the partition of the European portion of the Turkish Empire, but nothing definite came of the meeting. Basic to Catherine's solution was her famous "Greek project," which aimed at the revival of the Byzantine Empire, for which Catherine wanted to provide an emperor in the person of her infant grandson, whom she significantly named Constantine. Moldavia and Wallachia were to become independent under an Orthodox ruler; the empress had Potemkin in mind for the post. The Russian frontier was to advance from the Bug river to the Dniester.

Catherine proceeded to nibble away at the Ottoman Empire. In 1783 the Russian-appointed khan of the Crimea resigned and turned over his principality to Catherine. South of the Caucasus Georgia became a Russian protectorate in the same year. Four years later the Russian and Austrian rulers paraded down the Dnieper and into the Crimea, stopping at Sevastapol to review Catherine's new Black Sea fleet. The English, French, and Prussian ambassadors in Constantinople bolstered the sultan's courage to protest this obvious threat to Turkey by imprisoning the Russian ambassador. In the Second Turkish War that followed, Austria and Russia fought as allies.

Catherine's second war with the Ottoman Empire opened in 1787. Russian troops crossed the Dniester but found it was hard going against a Turkish army newly reorganized and noticeably stiffened. Suvorov covered himself with glory, but Rumiantsev and Potemkin accomplished little. Catherine lost her ally when Joseph II died in 1790 and his successor withdrew from the war.

Meanwhile, Sweden, encouraged by England and Prussia, attacked Russia in the hope of recovering some of the territory lost to Peter the Great. Without support from those who had pushed it into the war, Sweden had to withdraw before it gained or lost anything.

Catherine persisted in her determination to weaken Turkey further, and Russian victories in 1791 forced the sultan to sue for peace. By the Treaty of Jassy in 1792, Turkey surrendered to Russia the land between the Bug and the Dniester and admitted Catherine's absorption of the Crimea. The end of her Second Turkish War brought Catherine far less than she had hoped, but the empress had not yet finished with the sultan. Early in 1795 she arranged a treaty with the new Austrian emperor, Francis II, who agreed to press once more for the expulsion of the Turks from the continent. Europe's growing involvement in the French Revolution and Catherine's death in 1796 put a temporary end to Russia's ambitious drive toward the Dardanelles. Her grandson would return to the attack after the turn of the century.

The Partitions of Poland

Of all Catherine's triumphs in diplomacy the most shady and unscrupulous, in the minds of Western moralists, was her participation in the destruction of the Polish kingdom. The heinous crime of the Polish partition has continued through the centuries to shock those who persist in ignoring the setting in which it took place. Catherine has borne the odium of the partition almost alone, although the idea was not hers and the partition was certainly not in Russia's interest. Had Russia swallowed all of Poland, as Catherine would have preferred, the outcry would not have been so loud as it was over the division of Poland among its three neighbors. By some obscure reasoning, this seemed to be a more monstrous crime.

Suggestions to partition some country or other were popular in the seventeenth and eighteenth centuries. At various times since the closing years of the sixteenth century, there had been proposals, sometimes lengthy discussions, and frequently overt attempts to partition Spain, Sweden, Prussia, Poland, Turkey, Austria, and Russia. At the accession of Maria Theresa, the Prussian King Frederick II had led the powers to a vulture's feast on the Austrian woman's inheritance. Catherine discussed with Joseph II the partition of the Ottoman Empire, and Voltaire encouraged her. Presumably, to carve up the dominions of the Turks would have been not a crime but a commendable deed worthy of the praise of all Christian rulers. Prussian kings for generations had been suggesting the partition of Poland, and Frederick II urged it again in 1771 as a way of saving Turkey, whose support Frederick might some day need against Austria and Russia.

Poland's weakness was attributable to many factors—its vulnerable geographic position without defendable frontiers, the voracity of its powerful neighbors, the adventuresome character of some of its kings, and the running sores of religious strife, class hatred, and rivalries of noble families among its own people. The most obvious factor contributing to Poland's decline was the selfishness of the gentry and their willingness to sacrifice the nation's strength to further their own interests. Successive kings, elected by the assembly of nobles, or Diet, had so bargained away their authority in return for their election that they retained no power whatsoever over the nation whose throne they occupied. If they went to war, they did so at their own expense and had to provide their own armies. They could not recruit soldiers or levy taxes upon their Polish subjects. The *liberum veto*, the right of any member by a single vote to block legislation and force dissolution of the Diet, made the enactment and execution of national laws impossible. There was no order in the land. Civil war was a normal state of affairs as powerful families, around whom the lesser gentry clustered, contested for power; they did not hesitate to call in Swedes, Russians, Cossacks, and Turks

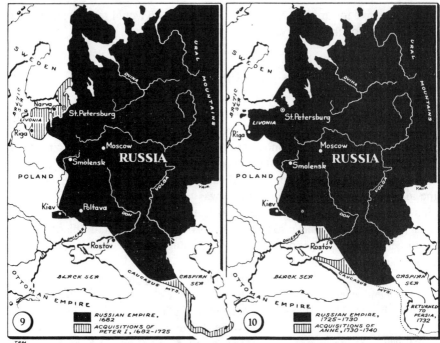

GROWTH OF **RUSSIA**, 1682-1796

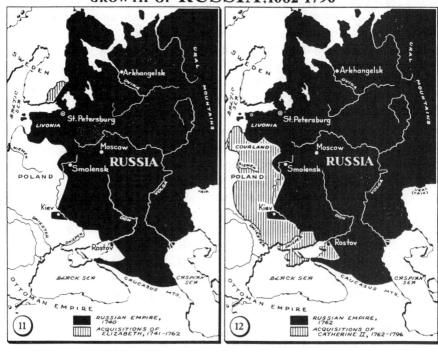

to help them. The mass of the people were serfs, as badly used as were those in Russia. A sizable minority of Protestants in western Poland and another of Greek Orthodox in eastern Poland constantly suffered persecution from Catholic landowners.

The death of Augustus III in 1763 prompted the usual scramble among Polish factions. Powerful neighbors, along with France, whose dabbling in Polish affairs aimed to keep Warsaw hostile to France's Habsburg enemy, began to influence the succession. The Russian candidate for the Polish throne was Stanislas Poniatowski, a native Pole and one of Catherine's discarded lovers. Catherine and Frederick II of Prussia agreed to back his candidacy, with troops if need be, to fight together if the intercession brought war with Austria or France, to force the Poles to grant toleration to Orthodox and Protestants, and to "defend" the Polish constitution by preventing any revival or strengthening of the power of the Polish government. The noble faction led by the Czartoryski family supported the Russian candidate, and Russian troops in Warsaw helped the Diet to make up its mind in favor of Poniatowski as the new king of Poland.

Once elected, Poniatowski set to work to make his kingship hereditary and to recover something of royal power. This brought a Russian army into the country, ostensibly to defend the Orthodox minority from persecution. A confederation of Polish nobles dedicated to resist Russian domination had little success against Suvorov, who distinguished himself against a Polish opposition that could not agree on the question of abolishing the monarchy. When Russian troops overran the country and drove the Polish patriots to the Turkish border in 1768, the sultan declared war.

The succession of Russian victories over the Turks prompted Frederick the Great to intercede with Russia, posing as Catherine's friend. He warned her of Austrian resentment if Russia were to seize Moldavia and Wallachia, and suggested that Catherine take Polish rather than Turkish territory. Austrian resistance could also be bought off with some Polish land, and, of course, Frederick himself should receive a reward for thinking up the happy solution. Catherine went along with the plan, even suggesting that Frederick was an old hand at finding such legal loopholes in the property titles of other rulers. Certainly, Catherine had some claim on historic and ethnic grounds to the land she proposed to take.

Austria, Russia, and Prussia agreed in a series of treaties in 1772 on the First Partition of Poland. The Austrian Empress Maria Theresa professed to abhor the partition, but Frederick II observed that "the more she wept the more she took." Catherine suffered a diplomatic defeat in sharing Poland with the others, but with the Turkish war, the Pugachev rising, a terrible plague in Moscow, Austrian indignation, and Prussian pressure, there was little else she could do.

A year after the signing of the treaties the Polish Diet was bribed and cowed into approving the partition. The kingdom lost over a fourth of its territory and almost a third of its inhabitants. Catherine's share was 35,000 square miles of territory—the Russian and White Russian lands around Polotsk, Vitebsk, and Mogilev—and 1,300,000 people who were predominantly Russian and overwhelmingly Orthodox in religion. Austria took nearly as large a bite in Galicia, with twice as many inhabitants, and Frederick II received the smaller but richer basin of the lower Vistula.

Russian troops stayed on in Poland after the partition, presumably to prevent the overthrow of the king who had accepted the loss of his territory. Cautiously, the king, with the support of some of the gentry who discovered a belated sense of loyalty to the nation, recovered some of the royal power that his predecessors had bargained away over the centuries. There was growing resentment against the presence of the Russian army in the land and the contemptuous treatment of Poles by the Russian ambassador.

In the midst of Catherine's second war with Turkey, the Polish government concluded an alliance with Prussia aimed against Russia. Supposing the Prussians to be trustworthy, the Polish king and the noble faction that supported him won over the Diet to a new constitution that made the kingship hereditary, swept away the liberum veto, created a bicameral legislature with middle-class representation, and strengthened the powers of the king. Under threat of war with Prussia and Poland the Russian troops went home, and Catherine temporarily surrendered her position as guarantor of the old Polish constitution.

When her wars with Sweden and Turkey came to an end, Catherine sent an army to the Vistula to punish the Poles for their arrogant behavior. Russia received the support of a faction of Polish nobles embittered at the loss of their influence. Prussia's new king, Frederick William II, went back on his pledge to help the Poles, and the Russians overran the country with little opposition. The Polish king had no alternative but to scrap the constitution that the Diet had adopted and to consent to the restoration of "Polish liberties"—the elective kingship and the liberum veto. Fearful that Russia might confiscate all of Poland, the Prussian king demanded compensation for his consent that Catherine should pare away another slice of Poland.

By the terms of the Second Partition of 1793, Poland lost half of its remaining territory and population. Prussia received the port of Danzig and the rich districts of Poznan and Torun with a million inhabitants. Catherine took three million people and ninety thousand square miles of territory, including most of Lithuania and the western Ukraine. Again the presence of Russian troops in Warsaw prompted the Diet to approve the seizure. Austria did not share in the second partition.

A national revival and a war in 1794 to rid the land of Russians came too late to save Poland. Guerrilla bands slaughtered many Russian soldiers and a revolutionary government sprang up in Warsaw, but the cause was hopeless. A Prussian army advanced against the Poles and Catherine sent Suvorov to retake Warsaw. The fighting was all over in six months. By the terms of the Third Partition of Poland, Russia received the rest of Lithuania and the Ukraine and took formal title to the duchy of Courland, which she had controlled for over thirty years as a protectorate. Austria received the Cracow region, and Prussia obtained the remainder of Poland, including the city of Warsaw. The kingdom of Poland disappeared from the map of Europe.

The territory that Russia gained in the partitions of Poland brought with it some complications. A large Jewish minority became part of the population of the Russian Empire for the first time, as most of the Jews who in medieval times fled from Western Europe had settled in the eastern Polish provinces that Russia now acquired. The Uniats—members of the Orthodox faith who accepted the jurisdiction of the pope—also became Russian subjects. Both Jews and Uniats suffered persecution under Russian rule. The fact that now Russia had a common frontier with two powerful potential enemies altered Russia's diplomatic position. A weak Poland had provided something like a cushion protecting Russia from Central Europe. On the other hand, the three partners in the crime against Poland were drawn together to some extent by their suppression of Polish nationalism. The submerged hostile peoples came to feel a greater loyalty to their language, their customs, and their cultural heritage than they had ever felt before the death of the Polish state.

Catherine and the French Revolution

Catherine's correspondence with French men of letters and her sympathy for the ideas of the Enlightenment did not prevent her from turning violently against the French Revolution. The excesses of the Paris mob sickened her. She condemned equality as a "monster" and called for the extermination of "the very name of France." She ordered home the sons of Russian nobles who had been living in France and exiled to their estates those who had caught the infection of radicalism, which she denounced as the "French madness." She looked upon the Polish patriot Thaddeus Kosciuszko and his followers as "eastern Jacobins" for their promise to emancipate the Polish serfs in 1794.

Catherine moved sternly against her own "Jacobins." In 1790 Alexander Radishchev, son of a nobleman who owned two thousand serfs, published his *Journey from St. Petersburg to Moscow*, which bitterly condemned autocracy and serfdom as institutions, not a specific autocrat or serf-owner, and attacked the corrupt and brutal rule of Russian officials. In tender and sympathetic sketches Radishchev drew attention to the bestiality and degradation of village life—the traffic in human flesh, the forced marriages, the back-breaking toil, the breakup of families. The empress flew into a rage when she read it, and ordered the court that tried him to bring in a death sentence. Authorities collected and burned copies of the controversial book.

The brilliant satirist, Nicholas Novikov, who took up Freemasonry because of its concern for orphans and the poor, edited several journals in which he mounted an attack on autocracy, bondage, police cruelty, and other institutional blights under which the nation languished. His enormous influence, particularly among young reform-minded nobles, made the empress decide against a trial; she simply ordered a fifteen-year prison term.

As long as the revolutionary government in France kept its attention upon

Western Europe, Catherine was content to fulminate against it. However, when General Bonaparte defeated the Austrians in north Italy and threatened to move on to Vienna, Catherine could no longer afford to ignore the French danger. France under the Bourbons had long opposed Russian interests in Poland, Sweden, and Turkey. Russia could not allow a more aggressive republican France to dominate Austria as well. In the autumn of 1796, Catherine made plans to march Suvorov, now a marshal, with sixty thousand men to the relief of the Austrians in north Italy, but before Suvorov could leave Russia, the old empress died, and her son Paul canceled the expedition. Without the help of Russian troops, Austria could only accept the costly Peace of Campo Formio.

The Significance of Catherine's Reign

In many ways Russia seemed to be a part of European civilization for the first time in Catherine's reign. Educated Russian nobles could travel abroad and show themselves to be perfectly at home in the salons of Paris. They spoke the languages of Western Europe, particularly French, and some even disdained to speak Russian because it was the language of the unwashed masses. They steeped themselves in the thought, particularly the liberal thought, of the West, and some few of them felt a sense of shame for their own Russian society. This fascination for things Western was a result of the example set by the court, for Catherine deliberately patterned court society after Versailles.

Polite society became "civilized" in Catherine's reign, in contrast to the "barbarous" time of Peter I. All Russian nobles now wore Western dress and were quite indistinguishable from Western Europeans. Peter had been ashamed of his Russian companions in the salons he visited in 1697. The coarseness of manners in Peter's time—the filthy language, the crude jokes, the lewd dances, the drinking bouts, the fights and brawls—gave way to a gentility in Catherine's time that put the two reigns ages apart. Yet, when Catherine saw her position threatened, as it was by the Yaik Cossacks and Pugachev, the sentences she handed down were as savage and brutal as any in Peter's time. Of even greater importance, insofar as it affected all society, was the fact that the fear and resentment the empress felt against Pugachev and her hysterical reaction to the French Revolution turned her sternly against the concern for reform that she had so piously proclaimed early in her reign.

By the end of the eighteenth century Russia had won respect and even fear as a great power. Its armies, when well led, were the equal of any in Europe. Its naval power was formidable. Its diplomats were well received and its sovereign treated with the same flattery shown any Western ruler. Other nations sought alliances with Russia, and Frederick II acclaimed Catherine as the arbiter of German affairs.

If, by Catherine's time, the nation had taken on a veneer of Western manners and had developed an outward strength that commanded respect, internally Russia was not sound. The condition of the serfs was worse than ever before. The gentry completely dominated Russian society. The central government was in a state of chaos. What there was of local government was managed by and in the interest of the serf-owning landholders. Pugachev's followers gave awful warning that there was a limit to the patience of the masses. Catherine's successors would not long be able to ignore the demand for correction of the worst abuses.

Catherine earned her reputation as a benevolent despot. Like most of the others, she donned the mantle of benevolence, but did little in any substantial way to merit the admiration she sought. Peter the Great had had no such illusions or fancies. Autocracy was the fashion of the eighteenth century and Peter accepted that; indeed, above all he perfected the autocracy in Russia. At the very least he was honest. When Catherine sought to veil the autocracy behind a screen of benevolence, she perpetrated a fraud upon her people for the sake of the plaudits of Voltaire and others in the West whose praise she sought.

Emperor Paul

Catherine II had seriously considered passing over her son, as she had every right to do under Peter the Great's succession law, and settling the throne upon her grandson Alexander. She was well aware of Paul's serious limitations—of his pettiness, his vicious temper, his strange quirks, his resentment, and particularly his hatred of everything she had sought to accomplish. So she had carefully prepared Alexander for the succession and directed his education in the philosophy of the Enlightenment. Everyone knew of the empress's intention, but Alexander insisted, when the time came, on letting his father have his turn as emperor. Paul I, the senior claimant after the death of Peter III, had stood aside for thirty-four years for his ambitious mother, who had had no legal title to the throne whatsoever.

Paul I (1796–1801)—Catherine's son probably by a lover Empress Elizabeth forced upon her to produce an heir—was reared by his great-aunt Elizabeth and saw little of his mother during his childhood. Through the long years of waiting to succeed Catherine he developed an insane hatred for her. As soon as Catherine died the new emperor lashed out at his mother's memory, spitefully repealing much of her legislation and seeking to undo everything his mother had done. He took grim delight in exhuming the body of Peter III, which Catherine had refused to bury among former sovereigns, and laying it alongside the wife who had been privy to her husband's murder.

At the time of his accession Paul seemed sane enough, although he was subject to violent fits of rage. He was extremely eccentric, however, and many of his subsequent actions were those of a man not quite sane. Perhaps it was only to demonstrate his power that he forced everyone along the highway to kneel at the approach of the royal carriage and to remain kneeling until the tsar had passed. There was a rigid formality to court ritual, and neglect or violation of it brought stern punishment.

During Catherine's reign Paul and his second wife—the first had died in childbirth—had lived on the estate of Gatchina near St. Petersburg. The "little court" was the center of intrigue, occasionally involving foreign ambassadors. Catherine's impatience with the meddling and the scheming is hardly surprising. She thought to keep her strange son amused by assigning to Gatchina a battalion of troops for him to command, but Paul took the assignment seriously and spent long hours every day parading, drilling, and inspecting his soldiers. Enamored of the Prussian dress and drill, he ordered his troops into the stiff, uncomfortable Prussian uniform and forced them to wear pigtails and to lard and powder their hair with flour or brickdust. He adopted the ballet-type marching and posturing so typical of the Prussian parade ground, and gave the orders himself for the endless drills. He most enjoyed inspections, when he took a martinet's delight in finding a button missing or a uniform soiled and ordering the culprit to be knouted. After his accession he "reformed" the army by extending to all units the discipline and stupid formality of the Gatchina battalion. The Guards regiments were threatened with removal from the capital and the Gatchina battalion became their equal.

There was little design or intelligent thought behind Paul's governmental alterations other than his peevish determination to change his mother's pattern of doing things. Where Catherine had attempted to decentralize the administration, Paul sought to centralize it. He attempted to bring back into his own hands powers that his mother had encouraged subordinates to accept. He restored some of the colleges that Catherine had abolished but gave them no power. He revived the office of procurator but every few months dismissed the man appointed to fill it, as though he feared that long tenure might increase the appointee's influence. He abolished many elective posts in provincial or district government or made them appointive. He annulled Catherine's Charter to the Towns and filled town offices with his own nominees. Paul's political philosophy was simple and clear. "The only man in Russia who is important is the one to whom I happen to be speaking," he once said, "and he is important only while I am speaking to him."

The reign began and continued on a note of reduced privileges for the gentry. Paul ordered the serfs as well as other classes to take the oath of allegiance to him, thus implying that the serf owed loyalty first to the tsar and only second to the landowner. Merchants again received the right to own serfs as factory laborers, thus ending the monopoly of the gentry and encouraging the competition of the merchant class against the estate industries of the landowners. In effect, he repealed the Charter to the Nobles. He levied direct taxes on the gentry and forced the nobles back into military service. Those found guilty of a crime might be flogged, a humiliating disregard for one of the fundamental exemptions of the gentry since Catherine's time. The tsar discontinued the provincial assemblies and appointed the marshals of the nobility, and the gentry lost their right to petition the throne. Paul's insulting treatment of the nobles, his abrogation of their privileges, his capricious dismissal of nobles from office, and his imprisonment of many of them made them sympathetic to his assassination.

The serfs fared no better at Paul's hands than did the gentry. The tsar's announcement that the serfs must take the oath of allegiance led them to suppose that they were now free. Many of them refused to go back to their work. Widespread rebellion at the time of the coronation had to be put down by regular military expeditions. During the four years of his reign, Paul gave away a half million state-owned peasants to favorites, whereas his mother had given away only eight hundred thousand in thirty-four years. He forbade the gentry to work their serfs on Sundays but made no effort to enforce the rule. He ordered landowners to exact no more than three days' barshchina from their serfs—Radishchev had seen some serfs working six days a week for their proprietor, leaving only evenings and Sunday to till their own small plots—but provided no system of inspection to insure their obedience. The effect of the order was to increase by half the amount of barshchina for the serfs in Little Russia—the Ukraine—where the peasants customarily had worked only two days in the landowners' fields.

Autocrat that he was determined to be, Paul had only the most intense hatred for the French Revolution. He forbade Russians to travel abroad but he welcomed French émigrés and provided the future Louis XVIII with a pension and an estate in Courland. He banned the wearing of revolutionary dress—top boots, frock coats, and round hats—and personally stripped such clothes off anyone he found wearing them. He proscribed the importation of Western books, and even music, lest they spread revolutionary ideas.

Paul followed a foreign policy as erratic as that in domestic affairs. He opened his reign with a pledge to remain at peace and criticized his mother for keeping the nation at war for forty years. He canceled Catherine's order to Suvorov to assist Austrian troops in north Italy. However, his loathing for the French Revolution soon made Paul forget his promise of peace.

Catherine had tried to enlist the support of the Knights of Malta in her wars with Turkey, and individual knights had served in the Russian armed forces. In 1797, a delegation from Malta prevailed upon Paul to accept the title of Protector and later that of Grand Master of the order. Napoleon's seizure of the island, on his way to Egypt in 1798, Paul took as a personal insult. Consequently, Russia joined England, Austria, and Turkey in a war against France.

The Russian Black Sea fleet cooperated with a Turkish squadron to recover the Ionian Islands from the French. The Baltic fleet joined British warships in landing Russian and allied troops in Holland. The most brilliant, if fruitless, action of the war was Suvorov's campaign in Italy and Switzerland in 1798. Paul had driven the old marshal into retirement, but the allies requested the tsar to allow the Russians, with other troops, to serve under the supreme command of Suvorov. He time and again defeated one French general after another in the summer of 1798, and the marshal announced his intention to drive on to Paris. His troops' march over the St. Gothard pass in a driving blizzard to relieve the allied force in Switzerland and their victories over the French after their arrival made an epic story of heroism in spite of privation and poor equipment.

In 1800 Paul deserted the coalition and shifted to the French side. He resented the Austrians for their lukewarm support of Suvorov; he blamed the British for the defeat and capture of the Russian force in Holland; and he lost his temper completely when the British recovered Malta from the French but refused to turn it over to the Russian fleet. First he joined Denmark, Sweden, and Prussia in the "League of Armed Neutrality" to maintain the freedom of the seas against the British. He closed Russian ports to British shipping and even imprisoned English sailors stranded in Russia.

Napoleon carefully cultivated Paul's friendship. He freed Russian prisoners of war and offered to turn Malta over to Russia, knowing full well that he could not do so as long as the British controlled it. He let Paul believe that the two should divide up the Turkish Empire. As a result, the tsar annexed Georgia and dreamed of acquiring Constantinople and the entire eastern half of the Balkan Peninsula. To help his ally Napoleon undermine British strength, Paul early in 1801 dispatched an army of twenty thousand Cossacks to conquer India.

Paul's Assassination

There had been talk of Paul's assassination within two years of his accession. Several nobles close to the emperor worked out the plot which enlisted the support of Guards officers under the leadership of Count Peter Pahlen, then military governor of St. Petersburg. Paul's oldest son, Alexander, was privy to the plot, although he may not have given his consent to his father's murder. Apparently, Alexander, naïvely to be sure, thought it would be possible simply to remove the emperor and put the government in the hands of a regency.

One night in March 1801, the conspirators broke into Paul's bedroom and strangled him. Alexander nearly collapsed at the news of his father's death and had to be carried to the balcony overlooking the courtyard where troops had already assembled to cheer his accession.

Paul's most constructive act was the repeal of the law of succession to the throne, which had permitted such chaos since the death of Peter I. Paul's new law settled the succession in the Romanov family, a pointed insult to his mother, and ordered the throne to pass from father to oldest living son. Fortunately for Russia, the reign of Paul did not last long enough to leave any permanent scars. The trend of developments after the accession of Peter the Great, and particularly after the accession of Catherine II, suffered only momentary interruption. Alexander quickly reverted to the policies of his grandmother.

Suggested Reading

ALEXANDER, J. T., *Autocratic Politics in a National Crisis: The Imperial Government and Pugachov's Revolt, 1773–1775* (Bloomington, IN, 1969).

_____, *Bubonic Plague in Early Modern Russia: Public Health and Urban Disaster* (Baltimore, 1980).

ALEXANDER, J. T., *Emperor of the Cossacks: Pugachov and the Frontier Jacqueries of 1773-1775* (Lawrence, KS, 1973).
_____, *Catherine the Great: Life and Legend* (New York, 1989).
ALMEDINGEN, E. M., *So Dark a Stream: A Study of the Emperor Paul I of Russia, 1754-1801* (London, 1959).
ANTHONY, K., *Catherine the Great* (Garden City, NY, 1925).
BLEASE, W. L., *Suvorof* (London, 1920).
COUGHLIN, R., *Elizabeth and Catherine: Empresses of All the Russias* (New York, 1974).
DESCARGUES, P., *The Hermitage Museum: Leningrad* (New York, 1961).
DMYTRYSHYN, B., *Imperial Russia, A Source Book, 1700-1917* (New York, 1974).
DUKES, P., *Catherine the Great and the Russian Nobility: A Study Based on the Materials of the Legislative Commission of 1767* (London, 1967).
_____, *The Making of Russian Absolutism, 1613-1801* (New York, 1990).
DUKES, P. (ed.), *Russia Under Catherine the Great*, 2 vols. (Newtonville, MA, 1977, 1978).
EGOROV, I. A., *The Architectural Planning of St. Petersburg: Its Development in the 18th and 19th Centuries* (Athens, OH, 1969).
FISHER, A. W., *The Crimean Tatars* (Stanford, 1978).
_____, *The Russian Annexation of the Crimea, 1772-1783* (Cambridge, 1970).
FREEZE, G. L., *From Supplication to Revolution: A Documentary Social History of Imperial Russia* (New York, 1988).
GREY, I., *Catherine the Great* (Philadelphia, 1962).
HAMILTON, G. H., *The Art and Architecture of Russia* (New York, 1983).
JONES, R. E., *The Emancipation of the Russian Nobility, 1762-85* (Princeton, 1973).
_____, *Provincial Development in Russia: Catherine II and Jakob Sievers* (New Brunswick, NJ, 1984).
KAPLAN, H., *The First Partition of Poland* (New York, 1962).
KENNETT, A. and V. KENNETT, *The Palaces of Leningrad* (New York, 1973).
LANG, D., *The First Russian Radical: Alexander Radishchev* (London, 1959).
LOBANOV-ROSTOVSKY, A. A., *Russia and Europe, 1789-1825* (Durham, NC, 1947).
LONGWORTH, P., *The Art of Victory: The Life of Suvorov* (New York, 1966).
LORD, R. H., *The Second Partition of Poland* (Cambridge, 1915).
McCONNELL, A., *A Russian Philosophe: Alexander Radishchev, 1749-1802* (The Hague, 1964).
McGREW, R. E., *Paul I of Russia, 1754-1801* (New York, 1992)
MAROGER, D. (ed.), *The Memoirs of Catherine the Great* (New York, 1955).
MASSIE, S., *Land of the Firebird: The Beauty of Old Russia* (New York, 1980).
OLDENBURG, Z., *Catherine the Great* (New York, 1965).
OLIVA, L. J., *Catherine the Great* (Englewood Cliffs, NJ, 1971).
RADISHCHEV, A., *A Journey from St. Petersburg to Moscow* (Cambridge, 1958).
RAEFF, M., *Catherine the Great: A Profile* (New York, 1972).
_____, *Origins of the Russian Intelligentsia: The Eighteenth Century Nobility* (New York, 1966).
RAGSDALE, H., *Tsar Paul and the Question of Madness: An Essay in History and Psychology* (Westport, CT, 1988).
RANSEL, D. L., *The Politics of Catherinian Russia* (New Haven, 1975).
REDDAWAY, W. F. (ed.), *The Documents of Catherine the Great* (New York, 1931).
SAUL, N., *Russia and the Mediterranean, 1797-1807* (Chicago, 1970).

SOLOVEYTCHIK, G., *Potemkin* (New York, 1947).

THOMPKINS, S. R., *The Russian Mind: From Peter the Great through the Enlightenment* (Norman, OK, 1953).

THOMPSON, G. S., *Catherine the Great and the Expansion of Russia* (London, 1947).

TROYAT, H., *Catherine the Great: A Biography* (New York, 1980).

VUCINICH, A. S., *Science in Russian Culture: A History to 1860* (Stanford, 1963).

CHAPTER 12

The Enigmatic Tsar

Paul's assassination set upon the Russian throne one of the most baffling personalities ever to rule in any land. His contemporaries puzzled over the mystifying character of Alexander I (1801–1825) as historians have ever since. The violent disagreement over his nature and motives has never subsided. If the word of his grandmother is credible, that his father Paul was not the son of Peter III, then Alexander was not even a Romanov, and his heredity is obscure. Surely few historical personalities offer a greater challenge than does "the sphinx" or "the enigmatic tsar."

Alexander's Character

The Empress Catherine took Alexander from his mother soon after his birth and carefully directed his life from then until his marriage. The grandmother named the child, designed his clothes, played with him, taught him the alphabet, and wrote a book of maxims for him.

At the age of seven, the boy's formal education began under a staff of carefully selected tutors. The most formative of the influences to which Alexander was subject for the next seven years was that of the Swiss Frederic de La Harpe, a liberal, at least in his youth. The youthful grand duke studied Demosthenes, Plato, Tacitus, Montesquieu, Locke, and Gibbon, and the teacher added his own strong views on the evils of tyranny, the ugliness of serfdom, and the merits of liberty, equality, and justice. By drawing vividly on the lives of Genghis Khan, the Borgias, and Philip II, La Harpe inspired in his pupil a hatred of despotism and a fondness for liberty. At sixteen Alexander's formal education ended, and soon after he married a princess of Baden who took the name Elizabeth. Their only child died in infancy.

Alexander and his brother Constantine spent weekends at Gatchina, in his father's court a few miles away from the capital. Paul forced his sons to join the maneuvers of the troops he endlessly drilled. The heir apparent developed an intense passion for armies and parades despite having to witness Paul's disgusting fits of temper and the brutal punishments he imposed for deviation from the strict Prussian drill. Perhaps Alexander's later reputation for diplomacy and charm owed much to the necessity for adapting as he shuttled between the profligate court at St. Petersburg and the harsh discipline of Gatchina.

Alexander I

In a land where all power rests with the ruler, the sovereign's character may strongly influence national development. Throughout the nineteenth century Russia's progress toward reform or the country's descent into reaction often depended upon the tsar's moods. Although bureaucrats often formulated policies and administered them intelligently or punitively, such officials were responsible only to the emperor or empress, appointed and dismissed at his or her will.

The character of Alexander I was extremely puzzling to his contemporaries. "Of great loftiness of character," Napoleon admitted, "he possesses both intellect and charm and is highly accomplished; easily led astray, one cannot trust his ingratiating manners; he is . . . a true Byzantine." Later he mused, "It would be difficult to have more intelligence than the Emperor Alexander, but I find . . . something lacking in him, and I have never [discovered] what it is." The Frenchman named him "the Talma of the North" after the most accomplished actor in the Paris theater at the time. "Alexander's character," remarked Metternich, "represents a strange blending of the qualities of a man and the weaknesses of a woman." One of his tutors analyzed the tsar as vain, cunning, stubborn, and "brilliantly gifted" but lazy. He always turned away from difficult or unpleasant matters. To his intimate friend, Prince Adam Czartoryski, the tsar was no puzzle. The prince found him "lacking in profound and definite convictions." Even his doting grandmother considered Alexander "a bundle of contradictions."

The grand duke's education in the lofty principles of democracy and justice left him with a theoretical approach to government that was to prove completely unrealistic when he ascended the throne. He often showed little understanding of the practicalities of government and particularly of the need to temper his ideals with reason. Frequently, his actions seemed to mock the ideals he proclaimed. "I shall always be a republican," he insisted, but at the same time he drew back from creating a representative assembly to share his legislative power. He professed to hate despotism, but resented every challenge to his own authority.

That the planning of his father's assassination had gone forward with his tacit consent left Alexander with a growing sense of guilt. "His grief and the remorse . . . he was continually reviving in his heart were inexpressibly deep and touching," wrote his friend Czartoryski. "He continually saw in his imagination the mutilated body of his father, and his mental tortures never ceased." His efforts to escape from this feeling of guilt in the closing years of the reign drove him to feverish journeys from one end of the country to the other, leading his critics to grumble that "Russia was being governed from the seat of a carriage." It may have been an effort to avoid being left with his own thoughts that made him seek the love that his wife was unable or unwilling to provide him. Women fell easily under his charm, and the cynics insist that his life was a parade of conquests.

Alexander's idealism may have been sincere, but it rested on a shallow theoretical base, for he was never a serious student and accepted the views of his tutors without question. His professed interest in enlightened policies of reform was superficial and easily misunderstood. By the standards of his time, some of his promises if implemented would have meant improvement in the lives of his subjects, but this potential existed in his younger years of adulthood, on the eve of his assumption of power and in the earlier years of his reign. For the last fifteen years of his life, the more conservative and traditional outlook tended to dominate his personality and leadership. Later interpreters often assert the elements of Alexander's liberalism, but the cold facts seem to provide little concrete basis for such *ex post facto* optimism. Yet he was not a double-dealing man, nor a weak one easily influenced by others. He stubbornly maintained positions that found little favor with his family or advisers, although he often backed away from the frontal attack and made his point by going around the opposition. On occasion he could turn away naïvely from unpleasant realities; he even talked of abdicating and giving up the responsibilities he had inherited.

The emperor's fondness for the military nearly reached that of his father, although not perhaps in such senseless and brutal ways. The details of army administration, uniform design, drills, and parades fascinated him. He spent long hours drilling the Guards regiments and frequently devoted time to military details to the neglect of important assignments.

The liberty that Alexander hailed as every person's birthright was not the liberty of people to govern themselves through representative institutions but the right, without regard to class, to equal and just treatment under a benevolent autocrat. He was so suspicious of any attempt by the aristocracy to curb his power that he had the secret police spy on court officials and even members of his own family. He talked to the end of his reign about granting his people a constitution, but to him a constitutional regime meant an autocracy, not a tyranny nor a despotism, dedicated to justice and the orderly rule of law with all subjects enjoying fundamental rights, not the least of which was the right to own property. His ambition was to create a clear and well-defined hierarchical arrangement of government agencies that would rid the administration of chaos, contradiction, and caprice. Yet he had neither the patience nor perseverance to apply himself to the tedious work necessary to see his hopes through to completion.

The Early Years of Reform

Paul's death brought Russians a sense of welcome relief. The new emperor walked unguarded through the streets seeking the confidence of his people by appearing to be one of them. To Europe, his accession seemed to herald a new Russian policy of opposition to tyranny and oppression. Reformers remembered the liberal education to which Catherine had subjected her grandson. They forgot her abhorrence of revolution, which Alexander undoubtedly shared.

Alexander promised to rule in the spirit of his grandmother. After the nightmarish cruelties of Paul's reign, men only dimly remembered Catherine's shortcomings, and looked back upon her rule as progressive. Although Alexander was never the liberal he professed to be, he probably was sincere in his determination to follow Catherine's lead in bringing much-needed reform to the nation.

On the very night of his father's murder, Alexander recalled the Cossack force that Paul had sent to conquer India. He released twelve thousand political prisoners whom Paul had locked up. He announced the abolition of the secret police "forever," along with the tribunal that tried political prisoners; he forbade torture, and promised to try the accused and to punish the convicted according to the law. He restored to their jobs thousands of officials whom Paul had dismissed for trifling offenses. He lifted the proscription on foreign books and allowed private publishing houses to reopen. He permitted Russians once more to travel abroad. He reissued Catherine's charters of freedom to the gentry and townspeople, which Paul had repealed. He forbade advertisements in capital newspapers for the sale of serfs without land. These orders, issued in the first week of the new reign, simply removed the most odious offenses of the mad Paul. Later the emperor appointed a commission to codify the law, but nothing came of it. There could be no fundamental reform before devoting months of study to the needs of the state.

To discuss national problems—especially autocracy and serfdom—and to help him reorganize the administration and consider other reforms, Alexander selected a committee of four intimate friends who began to meet with the tsar three months after his accession. The "four young friends" were Nicholas Novosiltsev, Prince Adam Czartoryski, Count Victor Kochubey, and Count Paul Stroganov, one of the wealthiest men in the empire. All were moderate liberals whose education was similar to that of the tsar. All were under forty.

The committee first set itself the task of discovering what conditions actually existed in Russian government and society, because some of the committee members, especially the tsar, possessed only a superficial knowledge of Russia. The committee hoped then to move on to a reorganization of the governmental machinery and possibly some reform of society; to assure that such reorganization and reform would continue, they planned to draft a constitution or "fundamental laws." Finally, Alexander wanted to cap the new edifice with a formal declaration of human rights. He discussed the American constitution with Ambassador John Quincy Adams and corresponded with Thomas Jefferson, who sent him commentaries on the document.

Alexander's own view of a constitution was not the Anglo-American nor the French, but rather the Austrian and Prussian view. He had in mind less a document providing representative institutions to curb the royal power than one that, although guaranteeing certain civil rights to the subjects of the nation, created an efficient and orderly administration resting upon a clear definition of the law but left the autocratic power intact. He had no patience with despotism, but he had little more with democracy. Autocracy, which left full legislative authority undisturbed in the hands of the ruler, was to Alexander a constructive and progressive institution, not the capricious and irresponsible administration of a tyrant. This was the conviction of the typical eighteenth-century enlightened autocrat—that an orderly, well-organized, and efficient bureaucracy could best maintain the conditions that would assure the well-being and happiness of his people. For the most part, the Russian gentry supported this eighteenth-century view, preferring to take its chances with an absolute monarch who would tend to respect the institutions born under various predecessors as opposed to popular sovereignty devoted to radical social innovation.

When the problem of what to do about serfdom came before the committee, the members revealed their caution and their concern because they did not want to be tarred as radicals by their fellow nobles. Some witnesses appeared before the committee to warn it not to meddle with private property that included serfs; others were willing to free their serfs only for generous compensation. Novosiltsev questioned the advisability of forcing freedom on irresponsible wretches probably incapable of supporting themselves. He was most insistent on the need to avoid irritating the gentry. Kochubey cautioned against freeing some of the serfs and so making the others restless. Stroganov reminded the tsar that the serfs had withdrawn their loyalty from the ruler in Catherine's time and might do so again if their hopes for emancipation were shattered. La Harpe, whom the committee questioned, expressed a fear of abolishing serfdom until the masses were educated but noted the danger of educating the people before they were free. The committee agreed that serfdom was an evil institution, but it did no more than express the pious hope that some day it might disappear.

At the suggestion of the committee, Alexander abolished the colleges that headed the administrative branches of the government and replaced them with ministries each headed by a single appointee responsible to the tsar. Ministries of foreign affairs, war, navy, interior, finance, education, justice, and commerce were established, the ministers to submit annual reports to the Senate. The emperor, however, retained the final legislative, executive, and judicial authority unshackled by any restriction.

Perhaps the greatest accomplishment of the Unofficial Committee was to provide Alexander with some knowledge of the conditions in Russia and of the workings of the machinery of government. The committee's deliberations may also have made clear to Alexander the practical difficulties of providing theoretical solutions to the problems that he had expected to solve simply. Unquestionably, the reorganization of the executive agencies that the committee recommended was an important achievement. Thereafter there was less disorder in the administration and more responsibility for executive action. The chaos that had characterized the collegial system lessened considerably.

From his consultations with the Unofficial Committee, Alexander became convinced that the nation's most critical need was a well-run and well-financed school system. In this opening period of the reign, he provided more for education than did any earlier ruler of Russia. He ordered the creation of three universities, the establishment of a gymnasium, or secondary school, in every provincial capital, and the maintenance of primary schools in all counties. Attendance at the schools was to be free to all classes of society. By the end of the reign, nearly fifty secondary schools were serving an average of over a hundred students each, and more than three hundred primary schools could boast nearly the same average attendance. An institution to train teachers opened in St. Petersburg, and six universities were in operation by the end of the reign. This flurry of interest in education brought university enrollment to perhaps two thousand and secondary school enrollment to fifty-five hundred by 1825, surely a modest achievement in a national population of fifty million.

A number of liberal magazines, some of them subsidized by the state, began publication in the early years of the century. Articles critical of serfdom and arguing for constitutional government passed the official censor who had orders to be lenient. Books on economics, politics, and philosophy appeared in volume, among them translations of liberal writings from Western Europe. The government paid for the translation of Adam Smith's *Wealth of Nations*, the whole tenor of which was an indictment of nonfree elements in the economy.

Although the Unofficial Committee drew back from any proposal to abolish serfdom as an institution, Alexander himself ordered several measures that constituted a modest first step in the direction of emancipation. His early prohibition of notices for the sale of serfs in capital newspapers met derision in St. Petersburg, but it had the effect of serving notice that serfdom did not enjoy unqualified royal approval.

An edict in the first year of Alexander's reign granted to any free person the right to own land. Although it did not affect landowners' serfs, the order did put an end to the monopoly of land ownership by the gentry. Another law granted the gentry permission to free whole serf villages, but only with land, or individual serf families without land, provided the financial arrangement met with government approval. Well over a hundred thousand serfs, called "free farmers," purchased their freedom from nearly four hundred landowners during the sixty years the law was in effect.

In 1804, the government liberalized conditions among the serfs of the Baltic provinces, strictly limiting the dues collectible by the landowners, forbidding the sale of serfs without land, and granting the peasants the right of self-government. In 1816, however, the serfs in these same provinces were freed without land, and as a consequence became tenants or hired laborers completely at the economic mercy of the landowning gentry.

War with Napoleon

As Alexander's ardor for reform cooled after 1803 and the meetings of the Unofficial Committee adjourned, the emperor's interest turned to foreign affairs. When the truce between Great Britain and France ended, the British prime minister put together an alliance—the Third Coalition—to defy Napoleon once more. Austria and Sweden joined the alliance, and the tsar, who earlier had halted Paul's support of France, began to realize that Russian interests coincided with those of Great Britain, Russia's best trade customer. By 1804, Alexander came around to the view of William Pitt, the British prime minister, that unless the nations of Europe stood together against the insatiable ambition of Napoleon, they would go down one by one. The disturbance of the power balance in Europe posed a deadly threat to every state. By the end of the year, Napoleon took upon himself the title Emperor of the French, an affront in itself to the crowned heads of Europe.

Alexander's awakening to the threat of Napoleonic imperialism began when, early in 1804, Napoleon spurned the tsar's naïve proposal that France satisfy itself with its natural boundaries and withdraw from all territory beyond the Rhine and the Alps. The tsar then sent his friend Novosiltsev to England to explore the possibility of a European crusade against France. Novosiltsev's instructions were to propose a coalition to restore peace in Europe and a legitimate government in France. With the return to peace, disputes among nations or threats to legitimate governments should be settled by mediation. The British prime minister had little sympathy for Alexander's lofty ideals, but he was willing to subsidize a Russian army against Napoleon.

Napoleon's most brilliant victory came at Austerlitz in December 1805, over Austrian and Russian troops. An armistice gave Alexander time to put together another army, and this one managed a draw with Napoleon at Eylau in February 1807. A few months later Alexander was forced to ask for peace when Napoleon decisively defeated the Russians at Friedland. Meanwhile, the Poles had welcomed the French emperor to Warsaw, for the tsar had foolishly ignored Czartoryski's advice to liberate Poland, and would suffer now and later for his shortsightedness. Finally, Alexander was impatient that British subsidies were slow in coming, for he could not carry the financial burden alone.

The two emperors signed the Peace of Tilsit in 1807, by which the tsar accepted the realignment of territories in Germany and Italy that Napoleon had engineered prior to the war. He held out successfully against French plans for destroying Prussia, but had to swallow his indignation at the partial revival of Poland—the newly created Duchy of Warsaw under the rule of the king of Saxony—as a French puppet and military outpost on the shores of the Vistula. Russian ports were not to admit British shipping, as Napoleon's new ally joined his Continental System. Yet Alexander might have congratulated himself upon dealing so successfully with a victor who had never granted a soft peace. The loss of the war had won Alexander some territory and the assurance of much more to come.

The Peace of Tilsit left control of continental Europe divided between two giants suspicious of each other. The lesser powers and Great Britain were still in the field, however, and they would carry on the struggle until Russia could sufficiently recover its breath for another test of strength.

Alexander hurried home after Tilsit to quiet the popular grumbling at the loss of a war that seemed to most Russians to concern only Western Europe. Now the alliance with Napoleon brought new expressions of dissatisfaction. The emperor's mother was particularly bitter, and those who gathered around her even hinted at a conspiracy to overthrow the tsar. Alexander resented the criticism implicit in the manner of those near him, but he had to bear it. Disillusioned, he never fully recovered his motivation for improving conditions in Russia, and when he returned to consideration of domestic reform, he did so halfheartedly.

Meanwhile, Russia would add significantly to its national territory. At relatively little cost, Alexander took Georgia and Daghestan on the southern slope of the Caucasus from Persia. A six-year war with Turkey, in which General Michael Kutuzov distinguished himself, added Bessarabia to the southwest Russian border. The richest gain resulted from a war with Sweden that gave Finland to the tsar as its grand duke.

Return to Reform

When the Peace of Tilsit relieved Russia of the strain of war with France, Alexander determined to take up once more the internal needs of his country. Although the conflicts with Sweden, Turkey, and Persia mildly sapped Russian strength and distracted the tsar, they did not require the concentration of nation and ruler as had the war with Napoleon.

The man who now became the emperor's confidant, although he had held important administrative posts for years and had drafted most of Alexander's legislation, was Michael Speransky. A commoner, son of a village priest, Speransky began his career as professor of mathematics and physics at the St. Petersburg Seminary. As state councilor in Paul's reign, at the age of twenty-five he reached the eighth rank of the civil service, an achievement that made him a hereditary noble. He rose rapidly because of his integrity, his tact, his rare perspicacity, his fondness for hard work, and his unusual talent in written composition.

Alexander and his new adviser took up once again the discussion of administrative reorganization and social reform that the dissolution of the Unofficial Committee had interrupted. The two talked vaguely of a constitution, the shibboleth of liberals everywhere at the time. The emperor did not have in mind, however, any such limitation of the autocratic power as the British had imposed on their monarchy but rather the orderly arrangement of executive responsibility and the legal guarantee of civil rights to all Russians. Fascinated as he was with enlightened absolutism, he had no thought of sharing his legislative power with any elected body. His views were those of his grandmother and of the Enlightenment generally. Most of the gentry were sympathetic to the emperor's view, although some of them wanted the Senate to become the overseer of the bureaucracy and to have a consultative voice in legislation. They also wanted a constitution or "fundamental laws" to keep inviolable their personal and property rights. Speransky, like the emperor, hoped to provide the nation with a code of precise and succinct fundamental laws that no bureaucratic agency could ignore or violate. As a bureaucrat of long experience, he realized that only such a code could insure against the chaotic and arbitrary administrative system that so frequently turned the autocracy into a despotism.

A year after Tilsit, Speransky completed for the tsar's consideration the draft of a constitution, the most ambitious of several reform proposals that he worked out during Alexander's reign. The document examined the weaknesses of the political and social structure of Russia and detailed the corrective measures that Speransky considered necessary. He had told Alexander earlier that Russian society consisted not of various classes of free and unfree peoples but only of two estates—the gentry, who were slaves of the sovereign, and the serfs, who were slaves of the landowners.

The plan envisaged a society of free people, all of whom would enjoy constitutionally guaranteed civil rights: the right to own and dispose of property, real and personal; freedom from obligatory service or dues—barshchina or obrok; and freedom from punishment without trial. Reform must begin, then, with the emancipation of the privately owned serfs. Speransky, whose father was born into serfdom and like all serfs until Catherine's time possessed no family name, realized more intimately and personally than any hereditary nobleman the need to end bondage. Yet he did not suggest breaking up the great estates of the gentry to give the peasants land, and so would have made them landless proletariats working for wages or renting or purchasing their own plots as they found the means.

The plan provided for an elected Duma, or assembly, to meet every three years in every township, district, and province to levy taxes to meet local needs and manage local affairs. An Imperial Duma would meet annually in St. Petersburg, petition the sovereign for action to meet national needs and correct official abuses, and give the ruler advice when requested to do so. At the pinnacle of the government edifice there would be a Council of State and an Imperial Chancery, headed by an imperial secretary to serve the Council of State as reference bureau and secretariat.

The proposal for a narrowly representative hierarchy of Dumas would have provided a contact between the sovereign and the people through which they could have dealt with local problems and advised the ruler on domestic matters of national concern. Later generations of Russian intellectuals chose to see in Speransky's plan a blueprint for a genuine constitutional system of the American or French variety. Neither the emperor nor his adviser ever considered or intended such a thing. Indeed, Alexander was so adamant in opposing any limits upon his authority that he regarded as subversive anyone who suggested it.

The emperor pondered and discussed the plan with Speransky but, reluctant to move too rapidly to alter the machinery of the state and so invite chaos, decided to adopt it piecemeal. He inaugurated the consultative Council of State and honored the plan's author by naming Speransky imperial secretary. He never went beyond this timid step.

The Council of State continued into the twentieth century to function essentially as Speransky recommended. For nearly a century the council controlled the ministry, appointed officials and held them accountable, planned state finances, distributed favors, and drafted laws and decrees—always, to be sure, at the will of the tsar. It gave Russia a central coordinating agency whose job it was to oversee the ministers and all other state officials. Never had there been such order in affairs of state. From then on there was at least a right and a wrong way of conducting government business.

As imperial secretary and the tsar's chief adviser, Speransky carried through a number of reforms designed to improve the administration. He insisted that officials pass educational tests before promotion. Those holding titles of nobility had to perform some government service or lose their privileges as nobles. The internal administration of the ministries became more efficient through subdivision into orderly, intelligible departments. Prophetic of later stern measures was the creation of a ministry of police—successor to similar agencies dating back into the sixteenth century—to tighten internal security.

To improve the financial plight of the government, Speransky inaugurated a number of economic and fiscal reforms. He halted the issue of paper money, funded the amount in circulation as a public debt, and assured a gradual retirement of the almost worthless paper. Government expenses were drastically curtailed. To correct Russia's unfavorable trade situation, Speransky halted the importation of luxuries, a measure that struck particularly at French goods.

Speransky's plans stirred up so much bitter opposition that Alexander had to dismiss him. His proposal to abolish serfdom found little favor among the gentry. His suggestion that only university graduates hold high office struck at the class privileges of the nobles. His tax program played no favorites, and his restrictions on foreign trade irritated the wealthy. Speransky's opponents finally invented the charge that he was dealing with France. Seeing the need for unity as the nation faced another war, Alexander sent his faithful minister into exile just three months before Napoleon invaded Russia.

The French Invasion, 1812

The discontent in court circles that had greeted Alexander on his return from Tilsit in 1807 continued unabated through the five years of truce that followed. The hatred for the alliance mounted, for Russia's partnership in the Continental System threw the nation into a depression: landowners lost the foreign market for their grain, hemp, timber, and flax when the nation's ports closed to British shipping; wheat exports fell to a sixth of their volume before Tilsit; internal trade suffered from the decline in foreign commerce. Speransky reminded the emperor that the system was supposed to harm England but was destroying Russia. When in 1810, Alexander, on Speransky's advice, opened Russian ports to British vessels flying neutral flags and to American ships carrying British goods, levied a tax on French wines, and forbade the importation of luxury goods from France, Napoleon received the news as though it announced a declaration of war. Russia's foreign commerce quickly revived, and agriculture and internal trade responded to the stimulus.

From the French point of view, war became inevitable the moment Alexander curtailed trade with France and abrogated the Tilsit agreement by deserting the Continental System, the only weapon Napoleon could effectively use against Great Britain. From the Russian point of view war became certain when the French emperor restored the Polish state. The war fever against France that never waned in Russian court circles only strengthened the tsar's hand. Probably from the moment of Tilsit, Alexander considered himself destined to deliver Europe from the scourge of Napoleon.

By 1810, two years before the French invasion, Alexander was busily seeking allies against the enemy he knew he would soon have to fight. He offered to compensate Sweden for the loss of Finland by supporting its acquisition of Norway from Denmark, a staunch friend of Bonaparte. The Swedes accepted the offer, but promised support only in a war outside Russian territory. In 1811, special Russian envoys sought to win over Austria, even promising Moldavia and Wallachia in exchange for an alliance. However, the Russophobe minister, Metternich, managed to hold his sovereign to the French alliance. In the same year Prussia offered to join with a hundred thousand men against Napoleon, provided the Russian armies crossed the Vistula to fight the war in Central Europe. Alexander, however, chose to fight a defensive war, and Prussia later had no alternative but to join Napoleon against Russia. At the same time, the Poles spurned the tsar's offer to restore Poland to its borders before partition and to revive it as an independent nation. They persisted to the very end in their confidence that their best assurance of revival lay with Napoleon.

Russia entered the war with all Europe arrayed against it except Turkey, Sweden, and Portugal. The French emperor endeavored to buy Turkish support by promising the sultan the Crimea and the north coast of the Black Sea, but Turkey had had enough of war with Russia. That war, which Turkey had begun at French prodding, came to an end less than a month before the French invasion. Russia satisfied itself with the acquisition of Bessarabia and returned the Danubian Principalities to Turkey in order that the army on that front might hurry north to defend the homeland.

Alexander succeeded diplomatically, then, in putting himself in the best possible posture to face the French attack. By neutralizing Turkey and Sweden, he avoided attacks on both flanks that might have proved disastrous. Prussian support of Napoleon was unavoidable, but it was certain to be given grudgingly.

In the spring of 1812, Napoleon offered Alexander peace in exchange for Russian compliance with the Continental System and a favorable trade treaty with France. The tsar countered with the proposal that France evacuate Prussian territory, but he warned that Russia would not again close its ports to English shipping. The French emperor realized that he could not completely dominate Europe until he had conquered Russia, and he must conquer Russia in order to destroy British commerce. The conquest would accomplish the elimination of the last remaining power that blocked his scheme of world domination.

Nearly six hundred thousand men made up Napoleon's Grand Army. Even after dropping strong detachments to defend communications with his base at Danzig, Napoleon crossed the Nieman on June 24 with upward of half a million

Kutuzov at a council of war, 1812

troops. Almost half were French, but Italians, Dutch, Belgians, Swiss, Germans, Danes, Austrians, Magyars, Spaniards, Poles, and Illyrian Slavs marched with them. Napoleon hoped for an early decisive battle that would destroy the Russian army and force the tsar to sue for peace, but the tsar had sworn that if Russia were invaded he would retreat to the Pacific rather than do so.

The three armies that gathered to meet the French numbered only 180,000 soldiers. The main army of about a hundred thousand assembled at Vilna under the war minister, Barclay de Tolly, a Scot whose forebears had emigrated to Russia. Barclay, cautious but realistic, understood that any but defensive tactics were out of the question. The second, or southern, army gathered east of Bialystok under Bagration. Suspicious of Barclay and impetuous by nature, Bagration favored an advance westward across the frontier to attack Napoleon's supply line.

Four days after ferrying the Niemen, the French occupied Vilna, but Napoleon ignored entreaties to revive Poland-Lithuania as an independent state. A sizable French force marched south to destroy Bagration's army, or at least to prevent it from joining Barclay. For three precious weeks Napoleon stayed in Vilna, awaiting word of Bagration's defeat. However, the Russian army successfully fell back to the northeast, and Barclay withdrew to the east to join Bagration, a meeting that Napoleon had hoped to prevent. Barclay fought a bloody battle at Smolensk and then withdrew still deeper into the Russian interior.

When Barclay pulled out of Smolensk, Alexander gave in to the clamor of the people and the army for a new leader. Kutuzov, fresh from the successful

Turkish war, became supreme commander. He was popular in the army as well as with the gentry, who hoped that he would stop the French advance and so the threat that Napoleon might free the serfs. Then sixty-seven years old, and so fat that he had to be lifted into the saddle, he showed a personal bravery that had long since won him the respect of the men in the ranks. Napoleon called him "the old fox of the North." Confident of his ability to conquer the great man, by guile if not by battle, Kutuzov knew that all Russia insisted he fight one great battle in defense of Moscow. He chose his position at Borodino, seventy miles west of the city.

The six hundred miles that the Grand Army had marched since entering Russian territory had cost the French sorely. The summer heat was intense, and thousands had dropped exhausted along the way. Dysentery and typhus had taken a heavy toll. The sick or wounded would return to their regiments, but many had deserted or died; discipline was poor and there was much straggling. The horses, short of grain, were too weak to draw the wagons and artillery, so that many guns had to be abandoned.

The Russian armies lived off the country. The peasants willingly turned over their food and grain to the troops and then burned what they could not carry away. The Cossacks stripped the farmland clean for miles on both sides of the road of retreat, and the scorched earth offered nothing to the invading horde. The peasants picked off French foraging parties and then fled to the woods to creep out noiselessly at night for hit-and-run raids. The foreigners grew desperate as they plodded on into the unknown, hostile, deserted land, the horizon aflame in every direction from burning cottages and haystacks. The French, aroused to ferocity by the desolation around them, were fiendishly cruel to the few peasants they captured. In turn, their cruelty prompted a surge of anger among the peasants, who dealt all the more savagely with the enemy.

The opposing armies at Borodino were nearly equal in strength. Napoleon had 130,000 men, Kutuzov slightly fewer. The slaughter was frightful on both sides, and Napoleon considered it the most terrible of all his battles. Forty generals, including Bagration, fell on the field. The Russians lost a third and the French nearly half of those engaged.

After Borodino, Kutuzov once more took up the withdrawal and chose to retire beyond Moscow, taking with him most of the residents. The city was ominously still—no welcoming delegation of citizens, no one on the streets, the shutters drawn and shopfronts locked—as Napoleon's troops entered. No other European capital had prepared such a reception. The French emperor took up residence in the Kremlin. Fires broke out and raged unchecked because the mayor had withdrawn all fire-fighting equipment during the evacuation. For six days the holocaust continued, consuming more than three-fourths of the city.

The invaders ransacked Moscow for provisions to satisfy the hunger of troops who had been living on horseflesh since before Borodino. Their fury mounted as they saw themselves cheated of the food and luxury they had toiled so far to enjoy. Looting and savage destruction were widespread. Knowledge of such depredation only stung the Russians to greater wrath when the opportunity came for revenge.

For five weeks Napoleon paced restlessly in his Kremlin palace waiting for an answer to his peace proposals. When none came by mid-October, he ordered the evacuation of Moscow. The army of 110,000 filed out of the city accompanied by thousands of foreigners—men, women, and children who feared the vengeance of returning Muscovites—and encumbered by a huge baggage train containing the furs, art treasures, furniture, and other spoil the looters had accumulated. Kutuzov, his army rested and re-equipped, forced Napoleon to return over the same scorched earth by which he had come.

In the retreat from Moscow, the French army suffered incessant pressure from Russian regulars, Cossacks, and guerrilla and partisan bands; Napoleon was fighting not an army but a nation. The partisans took no prisoners and were shot without trial when captured. The French dragged on, eating only horses and dogs. The weather favored the retreating army, for the winter came late and October was pleasantly mild. In November, however, the nights turned cold, and late that month the temperature dropped to fifteen degrees below zero. Napoleon approached the Berezina river under heavy Cossack pressure, and artillery bombardment turned the rush for the crossing into a panic. Ten thousand civilians drowned at the crossing. After the most dependable troops had crossed, the French burned the bridges, leaving behind half their army. Of the six hundred thousand who invaded Russia, perhaps thirty thousand crossed the Niemen in December.

Kutuzov's army, well supplied, operating in friendly territory, might conceivably have cut off the retreat, captured Napoleon, and thus spared Europe and Russia another thirty months of war. However, the old general refused to risk a pitched battle and confessed his willingness simply to usher Napoleon out of Russia. His indifference to all considerations except defense of his homeland allowed the French emperor to escape.

The campaign cost Russia two hundred thousand casualties, of whom perhaps half were killed. Yet, it cost Napoleon nearly five hundred thousand men, fully half of whom had died in Russia. Of the remainder, over one hundred thousand were taken prisoner and the rest deserted or returned to France badly wounded. The French emperor left the army soon after the disastrous river crossing, blaming defeat on the early Russian winter. The Grand Army, however, was wiped out by starvation, savage battle action, and Cossack and partisan raids. Except for Borodino, the invader had been destroyed without a battle, or perhaps there was one continuous battle from the time the Grand Army entered Russia until a miserable remnant fled back across the Niemen.

The Downfall of Napoleon and the Congress of Vienna

Many Russians considered the war at an end when the last foreigner had fallen back across the frontier, and Kutuzov bitterly opposed any further fighting. Still,

Alexander felt himself destined to free Europe from oppression. After losing a three-day battle at Leipzig and winning several sterile victories in France, Napoleon was forced to abdicate and retire to the island of Elba, where he would remain in exile until his return to Europe in 1815 in the Hundred Days. Meanwhile, on March 31, 1814, flanked by an Austrian general and the Prussian king, Alexander rode into the French capital at the head of his troops. He returned to Russia momentarily, but left in September for the Austrian capital where the major powers gathered to redraw the map of Europe.

An assembly of emperors, kings, minor princes, and diplomats met in Vienna to restore peace. Alexander took with him a corps of advisers that included the Germans Stein and Nesselrode, the Swiss La Harpe, the Greek Capo d'Istria, the Corsican Pozzo di Borgo, and the Pole Czartoryski. Austria retained the Polish territories it still held in 1815. Prussia recovered most of the land it had gained in the three partitions in addition to receiving about two-fifths of Saxony. The remainder of Poland, thus partitioned for the fourth time, became a kingdom with the tsar of Russia as king. Had Alexander had his way, as in effect he ultimately did, Russian influence would have been overwhelming in Central Europe and would have threatened even Western Europe. France and Britain were represented at the Congress of Vienna by Talleyrand and Castlereagh who were quick to recognize Alexander's intentions. It would, in a sense, have posed for Europe the very threat that the allied powers had warded off in Napoleon.

Bonaparte's escape from Elba and his Hundred Days ended at Waterloo before Russian armies could participate in his defeat. Napoleon went into exile on St. Helena and the French border returned to that of 1789 in the Second Treaty of Paris in 1815. The allies organized a Quadruple Alliance to maintain the peace settlement, and agreed to meet again to review matters of common interest and to assure continued peace.

While the negotiations for the Second Treaty of Paris were under way, the rulers of Austria, Prussia, and Russia signed a pronouncement called the Holy Alliance, by which they declared themselves to be ''delegates of Providence'' and ''members of one great Christian nation'' and swore to act thenceforth toward each other as brothers and toward their subjects as fathers of families. Letters to other princes invited them to join this union founded upon ''the precepts of justice, charity, and peace.'' The pope and the sultan of Turkey did not join the alliance, but the other European rulers, with the exception of the prince regent of England who pleaded lack of authority, subscribed to the pious document.

That Alexander should have conceived the idea of the Holy Alliance is not really surprising. Although his education had inclined him toward agnosticism, the burning of Moscow seems to have stirred in him a profound sense of religious values. His fascination was not so much with the teachings of any particular sect as with the basic precepts of Christianity. He took to studying the Bible daily and to discussing meaningful passages with friends. Many of those close to the tsar were devotees of the various brands of mysticism and pietism so popular in Europe at the time. In his journey from Vienna to Paris in 1815, he granted long audiences with various mystics with which battle-torn Germany abounded.

During his stay in the French capital he often met with the Baroness Juliana de Krudener, widow of a Russian diplomat, who had forsaken a sinful life for one of pietistic evangelism and prophecy. The baroness convinced Alexander, who probably needed little convincing, that he had been divinely appointed to bring peace to Europe and to lead mankind back along the paths of virtue. When in England, the tsar met with Quaker leaders and assured them of his love of peace. That he honestly felt an abiding horror of war is beyond question.

The Holy Alliance grew out of something more than the "sublime mysticism and nonsense" that Castlereagh scorned. Behind it lay the tsar's sincere conviction that only an acceptance of Christian principles could bring an end to war and all its misery. "If men lived as Christians, there could be no wars," he told a Quaker leader. "High-sounding nothing," the Austrian statesman Metternich termed it, and agreed to it only to please the tsar.

With peace apparently assured, Alexander returned to St. Petersburg ready to take up once more the problems of internal reform that he had laid aside three years earlier. Those who had traveled with him in Western Europe had come to know a civilization far in advance of that in Russia and had observed and discussed institutions and ideas quite foreign to the Russian experience. That such men would be impatient for reform of their homeland no one knew better than the tsar. Alexander left Paris with the avowed intention to free Russian society from its feudal bondage. "With God's help," he swore, "serfdom will be abolished before my reign ends." On the way home, he stopped in Warsaw and proclaimed an extremely liberal constitution for Poland, in spite of the fact that the Poles had fought to the end alongside Napoleon. Three years later, he spoke to the elected Polish Diet of his intention to extend the constitutional experiment to Russia "at an appropriate time." In fact, however, these declarations and promises meant little or nothing.

Reform Efforts

The awful desolation that the war of 1812 had wrought in Russia took years to remove. Peasants had lost their huts, carts, tools, animals, and poultry, and seed for the spring planting was very scarce. A hundred thousand corpses lay still unburied west of Smolensk in the spring of 1813, and the consequent epidemics carried away many who had survived the war.

The nation set about to repair the war damage. Moscow and the other burned cities quickly rose again. Farm areas came back more slowly, for decimated herds needed years to build up. Factories had been ruined or forced to evacuate to other locations, but industry in general had grown rapidly under the protection of the Continental System and suffered relatively little from the war. The cost of living remained insufferably high for years.

The government took several steps to ease conditions brought on by the invasion. It forgave unpaid taxes, halted further issue of paper money, reduced the government debt in an effort to revive public confidence, and restored and improved roads to provide relief from crop failures. It liberalized the tariff by removing prohibitions on foreign trade and by drastically cutting duties on raw material imports in an effort to encourage rapid industrial recovery.

The emperor's acceptance of the Polish constitution raised the hope of liberals that a similar step would soon follow in Russia. At Alexander's order, Novosiltsev drafted a Constitutional Charter of the Empire, which envisaged a federal system vaguely similar to that of the United States. Novosiltsev, like Speransky, proposed a hierarchy of indirectly elected, narrowly representative dumas with advisory power, the emperor to retain all legislative and administrative authority. The plan partially began during the last years of the reign when the tsar named a governor-general to administer each Russian province with an executive council to advise him. With the institutional variation typical of the western border areas, Novosiltsev's suggestion of federation was sensible, but Alexander's death terminated all consideration of reform. His successor proved even more intransigent toward democratic change.

When Alexander formally opened the first session of the Polish Diet in 1818, he urged the Poles to show the world that free institutions could work. However, conditions in Russia were not like those in Poland. After all, the Poles had long enjoyed a constitutional regime before the partitions. Alexander went to the heart of the matter when he told the Diet:

> The former existence of this constitutional order in your country has enabled me to grant you at once that which has not ceased to be the object of my cares, and the beneficial influence of this free institution I hope to expand to all countries entrusted to my care. Thus you have given me a means to demonstrate to my own country that which I have long been preparing for it, and which it will enjoy as soon as the foundations for such an important matter reach the necessary ripeness.

The constitution Alexander had in mind for Russia was not the sort of document that would impose any check on his autocratic power. Any sort of plan to improve efficiency, the emperor felt with honest conviction and with considerable justification, could not successfully emerge in Russia at one stroke. Too many obstacles had first to be cleared away. Bondage must come to an end. There must be a reduction of illiteracy. There was a shortage of honest and efficient public servants. Soon after his return from Vienna, Alexander undertook to fill the thousands of official positions over the nation with reliable and qualified personnel. The task seemed hopeless. "I know that the majority of the administrative officials should be dismissed," he admitted, "and that the evil comes both from the higher officials and from the poor selection of lower officials. But where can you get them? I am unable to find fifty governors, and I need thousands of other officials. The army, the civil administration, everything is not as I would have it, but what can you do? You cannot do everything at once."

The problem of serfdom was perhaps less difficult of solution than was that of inaugurating a constitutional regime in Russia. Yet the tsar was not entirely a free agent who might move without fear of interruption to put an end to bondage. Palace revolutions had plagued the monarchy since the last quarter of the seventeenth century, and assassins had struck down Alexander's father. The Romanovs stayed on the throne by tolerance of the gentry, and with few exceptions, the rulers chose to tread softly in dealing with it. Catherine II, a much more imperious ruler than Alexander, chose not to abolish the serfdom that she recognized as evil for fear of antagonizing the nobles to whom she owed her throne. Alexander's desire to abdicate, which was common knowledge after Vienna, may have grown in part from a feeling that he was helpless to provide Russia with decent institutions. He talked of retiring to some forest retreat in America or to a cottage on the Rhine. He felt resentment at the frustrations he could not escape. In addition, he found no solace in the knowledge that the United States also found that the problem of bondage was not easy to solve.

There was some indication in Alexander's Russia that serfdom might gradually disappear because it was uneconomical. Some who testified before the Unofficial Committee in 1802 had expressed the belief that serfdom could not last. In 1816 the nobles of Esthonia successfully appealed to the tsar for permission to free their serfs without land. The industry of the province, which the gentry controlled, was far ahead of that in Great Russia, and the owners realized that free labor was less costly than serf labor. The following year, the serfs of Courland obtained their freedom in the same way, and in 1819 bondage ended in Livonia. The result of emancipation was to stimulate industry in the Baltic provinces by providing a free landless labor force. Some of the gentry of Great Russia urged the tsar to extend emancipation without land to the rest of his dominions, but the vast majority of nobles opposed it.

In 1818, Alexander ordered his chief adviser, Arakcheyev, to draft a plan for the emancipation of the Great Russian peasants with land, but he cautioned that the gentry's interest must be protected if the plan were to be acceptable. Arakcheyev faithfully proposed that the government spend five million rubles a year to purchase the serfs of landowners willing to sell, along with five acres of land for each peasant. The laudable suggestion was doomed partly by the fact that there was no room in the state budget for any such expenditure, but chiefly by the unwillingness of most of the gentry to surrender their serfs without government pressure.

One special religious and social group hoping for reform in Alexander's reign also discovered that it would not be forthcoming, despite the tsar's assurances of fairness and justice for his people. Jews long had faced the ravages of anti-semitism, both in Russia and its Eastern European neighbors. Such bigotry reached as far as England. Restrictions on Jewish religious practices and doctrines, life styles, education, occupations and residence reveal a long and constant pattern of prejudice and oppression. Earlier Russian monarchs, Peter I and Catherine II among them, did not reduce the official and public harassment of the Jewish population.

One particular form of discrimination can be seen in what came to be known as the ''Jewish Pale'' or ''Pale of Settlement.'' This refers to a large region in parts of former Poland and reaching substantially into Ukrainian territory. In the time of Catherine, Paul, and Alexander I, Jews were required to move into what became a very large super-sized ghetto area. This facilitated official observation and control. One effect was to increase substantially the proportion of Jews in the general population living in the "Pale," and Alexander I expanded this policy during his rule. The liberal reformer fell far short of his public image.

Military Colonies

After Vienna, the emperor believed that Russia needed an army equal to those of Austria and Prussia combined. The cost of the recent war, however, made a reduction in government expenditures imperative, and the burden of enlistments imposed a severe drain on manpower in the villages at a time when every person was needed to restore the land.

In a sincere effort to ease the hardship of military service by permitting the soldiers to train at home and in a grim determination to establish model communities and so Westernize rural Russia, Alexander, in 1810, created the first so-called military colony in an area near Novgorod where land and serfs were the property of the crown. All male peasants between eighteen and forty-five became soldiers in the new regiment which was staffed and instructed by a cadre brought in from the regular army. Every peasant family lived in a new cottage, furnished at government expense, and each village had its hospital, library, school, and church.

Male children from the age of seven dressed in uniform and drilled in preparation to take their places in the ranks at the age of eighteen. Except at harvest time, all adult males spent half of every week at drill and maneuvers. Marriages were permissible only with the consent of the military authorities who thoroughly regimented the lives of the colonists. Discipline was extremely harsh; the inhabitants were flogged for minor infractions. Any colonist charged with a crime, however, received a trial before a jury that contained three peers elected by the colonists at large.

Although the idea to create the military colonies was his own, Alexander received the inspiration from a visit to the estates of Count Alexis Arakcheyev. The count's serf villages were immaculate, with identical well-built cottages laid out symmetrically along well-maintained roads. He administered his estates as brutally as he had commanded his army unit at Gatchina in Paul's time; still his villages were the best managed in all Russia. So impressive were they that Alexander proposed to use them as a model for the reform of estates belonging to the crown. By releasing the land to these peasant soldiers, providing them with livestock and equipment, and erecting new neatly ordered cottages for them, he would turn the crown serfs into prosperous farmers and rid the nation, at least on crown lands, of the poverty and squalor that distinguished rural Russia from its Western European counterpart. He even planned that ultimately the manpower of the armed forces should come from the military colonies, thus eliminating the need for the hated draft.

After returning home from Vienna, Alexander appointed Arakcheyev supervisor of the colonies, and the count managed them to the end of the reign. His brutality earned him the undying hatred of the colonists, and "Arakcheyevism" became a synonym for the discipline and cruelty that characterized the count's administration. The emperor may not have known of the bestial punishments that his faithful subordinate visited upon his charges, but knowing would not have dampened Alexander's ardor for what he regarded as a constructive measure. He would never have understood the colonists who pleaded to return to their former status, saying they preferred to have a son taken from every household as in earlier times to having the entire family drafted. They resented the discipline more than the punishments, which were no more cruel than on many private estates.

By the end of the reign, the military colonies provided a third of the Russian army. Had Alexander lived to see the fulfillment of his plan to reform the countryside, the colonies would have provided all the troops the country needed and would have embraced four-fifths of the crown peasants, or nearly a third of the nation's entire male population.

The Last Decade

Alexander seemed unable, after 1815, to recover the apparent enthusiasm for reform that had marked his early years. His mysticism and religious groping may have turned him away from worldly interests. He spent so much time traveling about Russia and attending international conferences that he had little left for internal problems.

After returning home from the Congress of Vienna, the tsar seemed willing to leave the administration to others. His reliance on Arakcheyev may be attributable to the fact that this "corporal of Gatchina" was honest, faithful, and had no other ambition than to please his master. So fully did the tsar trust his loyal slave that all business passed through his hands, and Arakcheyev intercepted complaints addressed to the throne. If Arakcheyev needed any prompting, he had it from his confessor, Photius Spassky, a fanatical monk who spent his nights wrestling with the devil.

The reaction that Arakcheyev led and that Photius inspired first appeared in the field of education. Prince Alexander Golitsyn, former liberal and intimate of the tsar, added the ministry of education to his position as procurator of the Holy Synod. Alexander himself contributed to the drift toward church domination of education with the pronouncement in the spirit of the Holy Alliance that "Christian piety should always be the foundation of all true education." Golitsyn investigated the University of Kazan for the dissemination of "dangerous" ideas. Several professors were dismissed and the rest warned that henceforth their teaching, whether in science, social science, or humanities, must conform to Biblical principles. In geometry the triangle should represent the Trinity. Copernicus and Newton must not be mentioned in physics classes, for their laws were contrary to the Bible. There must be no dissection by medical students, for it was disrespectful to the dead. Economics professors must uphold serfdom. The director of the university learned that the purpose in educating students was "the bringing up of true sons of the Orthodox Church, loyal subjects of the state, and good and useful citizens of the fatherland." Other universities underwent the same sort of purge. Foreign professors lost their positions, and Russians who had studied in foreign universities failed to win appointments. Again, as in Paul's time, Russian students lost the freedom to study abroad. Even Golitsyn was too liberal for Photius and had to resign as minister of education. His place went to Admiral Shishkov, who believed that increasing literacy might prove disastrous. He warned that "to teach rhetoric to the son of a peasant would make him a bad and useless subject, if not a really dangerous one."

Alexander had accepted the Finnish constitution when he conquered the duchy in 1809, and had guaranteed complete autonomy except in foreign affairs. In the closing years of his reign, however, he deliberately violated the Finnish laws that he had sworn to uphold. The Diet did not convene, and the finances of the duchy were managed arbitrarily from St. Petersburg.

The guarantees provided in the Polish constitution fared similarly after the honeymoon of the first few years. Press censorship operated in the kingdom in violation of the constitutional sanction of freedom of the press. The Diet of 1820 protested breaches of the constitution, but it met from Alexander—now fearful of the revolutions breaking out all over Europe—only the stern warning that Poland's continued survival depended on a docile Diet. For five years the Diet did not meet, although the constitution provided for biennial sessions. The Russian government interfered in the elections for the Polish Diet in 1825, and troops surrounded the palace where the Diet held its meetings. The Poles took the hint and restrained themselves so well during the session that Alexander seemed well satisfied.

In 1820, while Alexander was abroad attending an international congress, he received word of a mutiny in the Semenovsky Regiment of the Guards, the tsar's favorite. Earlier in the year the regiment had received a new commanding officer, the martinet Colonel Schwarz. In his zeal to bring the troops back to "discipline" and good order, by which he meant Prussian formalism, he flogged several soldiers who were expressly exempt from corporal punishment. The troops complained in a body, whereupon Schwarz imprisoned an entire battalion. The affair was hardly a mutiny, and certainly the men had been unduly provoked. The commander of the Guards corps assured the emperor that the affair was unimportant, but Alexander refused to believe it and ordered an investigation of the secret societies whose activities the police had already reported to him. The news convinced the tsar that revolution threatened his empire. He never had any patience with revolution, which to him meant chaos and war. Liberal institutions were desirable, he felt, but must be the gift of a benevolent monarch.

He always looked upon any popular pressure for reform as evidence of ingratitude and an infringement on his authority.

The Tsar Abroad

The great powers agreed at Vienna to convene periodically to take notice of any threat to peace. In 1818, the tsar was off to the first meeting at Aix-la-Chapelle. At his initiative, France, whose government seemed stable enough, joined in what now became the Quintuple Alliance. A plot to assassinate the members of the British cabinet, the murder of the French king's nephew, and the outbreak of revolutions in Spain and in Naples in 1820 indicated the need for another conference. The meeting at Troppau dealt only with the Neapolitan uprising. It was there that Alexander received word of the Semenovsky mutiny in St. Petersburg. Convinced that this was but a phase in an international conspiracy, the tsar assured Metternich of his opposition to popular uprisings. Now Austria, Prussia, and Russia formally agreed to suppress revolution by joint action wherever it appeared. Then the powers adjourned to Laibach near the Adriatic to hear testimony from the king of Naples on the uprising in his dominions.

At Laibach, Austria received Russian and Prussian approval to march into south Italy to suppress the revolution in Naples. The powers could not agree on intervention in Spain. In the meantime, the conferees learned of rebellion in Greece against Turkish rule, but decided to postpone action until a later meeting.

By the time the powers convened at Verona in 1822, the sultan seemed to have the Greek situation momentarily in hand, but the Spanish revolutionists had imprisoned their king and established a government of their own. The tsar offered an army to restore order, but the assignment went to France. Restoration of Spanish rule in the Americas, where Spain's colonies were declaring their independence, proved unattractive; President Monroe, assured of British backing, announced that European intervention in the Western Hemisphere would not be tolerated.

The Turkish problem was of more immediate concern to Russia than to any other power. The sultan had not carried out the terms of the Treaty of Bucharest which, in 1812, had ended the last of the Russo-Turkish wars. He had violated the autonomy promised Serbia and the Danubian Principalities, for which Russia stood guarantor, and had subjected Russian commerce through the Straits to unpredictable levies and downright interruption. All points at issue, however, were settled soon after Alexander's death, but the settlement lasted less than two years.

The Greek revolt, then, was only an irritant to relations between Russia and Turkey that had long been under strain. Aside from the fact that he could not, with good grace, have supported revolution in Greece while opposing it elsewhere, Alexander seems to have proceeded with a high-minded determination to keep the peace at almost any cost. His restraint in dealing with the sultan won high praise from British Foreign Minister Canning, who admitted that "Russia can conquer Turkey and Greece when she pleases."

The Decembrists

Within months of the end of the Napoleonic wars, a small group of young army officers in St. Petersburg organized a society called the Union of Salvation to discuss the need for reform. All were nobles whose service in Western Europe had stirred in them shame at Russia's backwardness. The respect for the individual, which the orderly rule of law and an efficient bureaucracy seemed to assure, had impressed them, and they had seen Prussian and German peasants more prosperous than the poorer sort of Russian nobles. Several members of the Union of Salvation were on the emperor's own staff. All were well read, steeped in the philosophy of the Enlightenment. Although the members differed in aims and methods, all agreed on the need to abolish serfdom and win constitutional government. They had lost confidence in Alexander, who had won constitutions for Spaniards, Poles, Neapolitans, and French, but who seemed to them to have lost his ardor for reform at home.

Others joined the group, among them the ambitious Colonel Paul Pestel, whose father was governor-general of Siberia. Although some members were inclined to caution and urged a policy of cooperation with the government, Pestel insisted that the society must be secret, like the Masonic bodies of which many Decembrists were members. From the very beginning, he assumed that the aim of the society was revolution to establish a constitutional regime. A change of name to Union of Welfare accompanied the enlistment of other sons of nobles and wealthy merchants, and a constitution called upon the members to treat their serfs humanely, build schools, support hospitals and orphanages, agitate for prison reform, oppose bribery of officials, and work for economic development.

The St. Petersburg group lost its vigorous leadership when the army transferred Colonel Pestel to Tulchin in Podolia province where he established another branch that, from the beginning, reflected his own radical views. On a visit to the capital in 1819, Pestel succeeded in revitalizing the society in the north and even won the members over to his conviction that Russia should become a republic.

Many of the officers of the Semenovsky Regiment were members of the Union of Welfare. After the mutiny, the regiment was broken up and its officers scattered among other units. Not all the members of the society, however, had been officers in the Semenovsky Regiment. Enough remained in the capital to carry on the work. Soon after the mutiny, Alexander forbade secret societies and created a corps of secret police to watch subversives. The organization decided to disband. In its place there arose two groups, the Northern Society, with headquarters in the capital, and the Southern Society, located at Tulchin.

The leader of the Northern Society, the twenty-six-year-old Nikita Muravev, who had six cousins in the society, drew up a constitutional blueprint for the new Russia he envisaged. It proposed to abolish serfdom and to guarantee freedom of speech, press, religion, and trial by jury. It would divide Russia into thirteen states with limited autonomy, suggestive of the American system. A bicameral legislature, consisting of a Supreme Council representing the states and a House of Representatives chosen in electoral districts, would ratify treaties, confirm appointments, impeach officials, and share in passing laws. The lower house would control tax measures and initiate all bills. The executive was to be the hereditary emperor, with powers comparable to those of the American president. The right to vote would reside only with property owners on such a restrictive basis as to exclude all but the gentry and merchants. The former serfs, who were to receive five acres at the time of emancipation, would have no political status. It was to this provision, which "legalized a terrible aristocracy of wealth," that Pestel most objected.

The detailed plan of the Southern Society—Russkaia Pravda, or Russian Justice, was its title—was the work of Pestel. Russia was to become a republic by the assassination of all members of the imperial family to eliminate claimants to the throne. With regard to Muravev's federal principle, Pestel opposed a highly centralized state with Great Russian the only language and Russian Orthodoxy the official religion. The church would function as a branch of government, as indeed it already did, with the clergy as state employees. There would be toleration for Islam, but the Jews were all to be packed off to Asia. Local institutions and customs were to continue only among the Poles, to whom Pestel conceded a measure of autonomy in order to win support of Polish revolutionaries. Russia must conquer all border territories—Mongolia for example—that Pestel deemed vital to national security. He was proposing a supernational state in which there was no room for the identity of Finns, Ukrainians, Georgians, or even Great Russians.

The society that Pestel proposed was a strange mixture of capitalism and socialism. Class would disappear with the abolition of serfdom and the elimination of all social distinctions and privileges. Great landowners would be dispossessed and their land divided, part to remain with the state to provide revenue, the rest to go to the peasants, each family to have a plot sufficient for its support. Pestel would promote industry by encouraging individual enterprise and by freeing trade and production from restrictive tariffs, taxes, and regulation.

Pestel proposed a dictatorship to govern the country during a ten-year period of evolution to a new order. During the transition period all Russians would enjoy freedom of speech, press, and assembly and the right to vote. There would be no societies, open or secret, and a secret police force would ferret out all discontent. After the passing of the period of tutelage the nation would be governed in much the same way as Speransky had proposed earlier, with a hierarchy of elected dumas and administrative boards to handle local problems, and a national duma. A "Directory" would serve as a national executive. Pestel left the details of governmental powers to be worked out later, for his greatest concern was the overthrow of the monarchy and the abolition of serfdom.

The programs of the Northern and Southern Societies reflected the two extremes that liberal thought in Russia was to pursue to the end of the monarchy: evolution, constitutional monarchy, federalism, and tolerance versus revolution, republicanism, centralism, and intolerance. Some regard Pestel as the first socialist, others as the first communist, long before there were either socialists or communists. Muravev, the founder of Russian liberalism, represents the position taken by moderate reformers in the early twentieth century.

Although the Northern and Southern Societies were at odds on aims and methods, they were completely in accord in insisting that the new Russia must emerge under the leadership of a few. All members feared mass uprising; consequently, there was no effort to enlist widespread support. Membership in the two societies never exceeded a few hundred. This lack of faith in the masses was typical of Russian revolutionary movements at least until the end of the nineteenth century.

Alexander knew not only of the existence of the secret societies but of their programs and membership, for the secret police kept careful watch over their activities, and one of the Decembrists was a government spy. He refused, however, to punish them for liberal views that he himself had done so much to encourage, thus handicapping the security officials, who were ineffective at best. Shortly before his death when he learned that they were plotting his assassination, the emperor decided to act, but died before issuing any orders. Plans for the "first Russian Revolution" went forward without interruption from the throne it aimed to overturn.

The End of the Reign

The cynicism that greeted Alexander's efforts to keep peace among the nations on a high moral plane and the ingratitude that many Russians showed for his well-meaning, but admittedly, ineffective attempts to improve domestic conditions, indicated to the tired reformer that his life had been a failure. He came to regard such catastrophic events as the terrible St. Petersburg flood of 1824 and the death of his natural daughter, of whom he was sentimentally fond, as divine punishment for his sins.

As early as 1822, Alexander informed his brother Nicholas of his intention to abdicate and retire. Because Alexander had no sons, his next older brother Constantine would, by Paul's succession law, succeed to the throne. However, Constantine had disqualified himself by divorcing his wife, marrying a commoner, and formally renouncing the throne. Thereupon Alexander declared Nicholas the successor and in 1823 drew up a statement to that effect, which for some reason he kept secret, giving copies to the State Council, the Senate, and the Holy Synod. Only a few were privy to the act—the tsar's mother, Constantine, the metropolitan, and Golitsyn, then procurator of the Holy Synod. The secrecy that surrounded the matter would lead to awkwardness and nearly to disaster at the opening of the new reign.

In the autumn of 1825 Alexander left St. Petersburg for Taganrog on the Sea of Azov. A short time later the emperor fell ill. He died at Taganrog in December 1825. He refused to take medicine, as though he were impatient to have done with a life that had lost interest for him. The suddenness of his death gave rise to a rumor that he did not die until 1864, that he lived on as Fedor Kuzmich, a saintly recluse who had settled in Siberia in about 1825. Even members of the royal family in the nineteenth century credited the tale, and in 1966 Soviet historians gave it a degree of credibility.

Liberal and moderate writers generally have been critical of Alexander, in part because they have misread his attitude toward a constitution and in part because he did not abolish serfdom. It is only fair, however, to recall that feudalism in Western Europe disappeared only with the French Revolution and Napoleon. That the problem should prove more formidable in Russia, backward and almost completely agricultural as it was, was only reasonable to expect. Indeed, not all medieval trappings disappeared from Russian society until the twentieth century and then only at a bloody cost. Alexander's reign gave more promise, particularly in its early years, of ending autocracy and bringing about an end to serfdom, than any other reign between Peter the Great and the end of the monarchy.

One week after Alexander's death, when the news reached St. Petersburg, royal officials swore allegiance to Constantine, and all the troops in the capital took the oath without demur, along with Nicholas, who knew nothing of his brother's will. Pictures of "Constantine, Emperor and Autocrat of All the Russias" appeared in the streets. When Constantine heard of it in Warsaw, he repeated his disavowal of any interest in the succession and vowed allegiance to Nicholas. There followed weeks of correspondence, Nicholas pressing Constantine to renounce the throne if he did not want it, Constantine repeating that he had surrendered his rights and threatening to flee abroad. Those who accepted his decision swore allegiance to two emperors in a single week.

Meanwhile, the Northern Society, meeting daily at the home of the poet Ryleyev, learned of the confusion in court circles and decided to refuse the oath of allegiance to Nicholas. The members spread word that this was a trick to exclude Constantine from the succession. Although Constantine was notorious in the army for his brutality and paranoid behavior, some of the members of the Northern Society seem to have credited him with liberal tendencies. The very reverse was true. Metternich preferred Constantine, an unbending reactionary, to Nicholas as the new emperor.

Troops in the capital were paraded on the morning of December 14 to take the oath of allegiance. Nicholas had learned of the activities of the secret societies only after hearing of his brother's death. Forewarned of their plan to exploit the occasion, he personally arranged the troops in Senate Square—now Decembrist Square—so that he could call upon those of unquestioned loyalty, should the need arise. When the soldiers were ordered to take the oath, many, however, shouted "We don't want Nicholas! We want Constantine!" They were supporting not the overthrow of the monarchy but the "rightful" ruler, Constantine, from whom they suspected Nicholas of usurping the throne. When told that there was no other way to clear the square, Nicholas ordered up artillery. The canister tore gaps in the ranks of the mutinous regiments, and many civilian bystanders died as well. The Decembrist uprising had failed. The throne was secure.

In the south, Pestel was arrested by the police the day before the uprising in the capital, but the rest of the Southern Society went ahead with its own revolution. Several companies of troops marched hither and yon in the neighborhood of Kiev. After four days of campaigning, the rebels lost a bloody battle with loyal troops, and the leaders were carted off to St. Petersburg to stand trial.

The government moved quickly to round up not only the known leaders but everyone suspected or accused of any association with members of the secret societies. The emperor presided over a committee that interrogated every suspect and decided whether each prisoner in turn was to be jailed, chained, dismissed under surveillance, or freed. Priests visited the cells as though administering to condemned men, and the confessions they heard immediately went to the tsar. Many who held firm under the foul conditions of the jails broke under grueling night-long interrogations. Speransky and the poet Pushkin were suspected of complicity, but there was little more to implicate them than the desperate testimony of witnesses broken by mental torture.

After five months of gathering evidence, the investigating committee submitted its findings and recommendations to a special tribunal that found 121 prisoners to be most culpable. The five leaders, including Pestel and Ryleyev, were hanged; thirty-one condemned to hard labor for life in Siberia; and the rest given various terms in Siberian mines. The executioner bungled his job and three of the five sentenced to death had to be hanged twice. One lamented, "Poor Russia! She cannot even hang decently."

Suggested Reading

ALMEDINGEN, E. M., *The Emperor Alexander I* (London, 1964).

ALSTON, P., *Education and the State in Tsarist Russia* (Stanford, 1969).

BARRATT, G., *Voices in Exile: The Decembrist Memoirs* (Montreal, 1974).

BLACK, J., *Nicholas Karamzin and Russian Society* (Toronto, 1975).

BLINOFF, M., *Life and Thought in Old Russia, 1466–1881* (University Park, PA, 1961).

CAULAINCOURT, A., *With Napoleon in Russia* (New York, 1935).

CROSS, A. G., *N. M. Karamzin: A Study of His Literary Career* (Carbondale, IL, 1971).

CZARTORYSKI, A., *Memoirs of Prince Adam Czartoryski and His Correspondence with Alexander I* (Gulf Breeze, FL, 1968).

DUFFY, C., *Borodino and the War of 1812* (New York, 1973).

GRIMSTEAD, P., *The Foreign Ministers of Alexander I: Political Attitudes and the Conduct of Russian Diplomacy, 1801–1825.* (Berkeley, 1969).

JELAVICH, B., *A Century of Russian Foreign Policy, 1812–1914* (New York, 1964).

JENKINS, M., *Arakcheev: Grand Vizier of the Russian Empire* (New York, 1969).

JOHNSON, W. H. E., *Russia's Educational Heritage* (Pittsburgh, 1950).
KORNILOV, A., *Modern Russian History*, 2 vols. (New York, 1970).
LOBANOV-ROSTOVSKY, A. A., *Russia and Europe, 1789–1825* (Durham, NC, 1947).
McCONNELL, A., *Tsar Alexander I: Paternalistic Reformer* (New York, 1970).
MAZOUR, A. G., *The First Russian Revolution, 1825: The Decembrist Movement, Its Origins, Development and Significance* (Stanford, 1961).
OLIVIER, D., *The Burning of Moscow, 1812* (London, 1966).
O'MEARA, P., *K. F. Ryleev: A Political Biography of the Decembrist Poet* (Princeton, 1984).
PALEOLOGUE, M., *The Enigmatic Tsar: The Life of Alexander I of Russia* (New York, 1969).
PALMER, A., *Alexander I: Tsar of War and Peace* (New York, 1974).
PARKINSON, R., *The Fox of the North: The Life of Kutuzov, General of War and Peace* (New York, 1976).
PIPES, R., *Karamzin's Memoir on Ancient and Modern Russia* (Cambridge, 1959).
RAEFF, M., *The Decembrist Movement* (Englewood Cliffs, NJ, 1966).
_____, *Michael Speransky, Statesman of Imperial Russia* (The Hague, 1969).
SAUL, N. E., *Russia and the Mediterranean, 1797–1807* (Chicago, 1970).
STRAKHOVSKY, L. I., *Alexander I of Russia* (New York, 1947).
TARLE, E., *Napoleon's Invasion of Russia, 1812* (New York, 1971).
THADEN, B. C., *Russia Since 1801: The Making of a New Society* (New York, 1971).
TROYAT, H., *Alexander of Russia: Napoleon's Conqueror* (New York, 1982).
WREN, M. C., *The Western Impact upon Tsarist Russia* (Chicago, 1971).
YARMOLINSKY, A., *Road to Revolution: A Century of Russian Radicalism* (New York, 1959).
ZETLIN, M., *The Decembrists* (New York, 1958).

CHAPTER 13

The Policeman
of Russia and Europe

The death of Alexander produced temporary confusion over the succession, but there was no interruption of the reactionary policy to which the dead emperor had resigned himself in the closing years of the reign. Nicholas I (1825–1855) greatly admired his older brother, whose views on autocracy he shared, and saw no need to alter policies which he strongly supported. If for whatever reason those policies had not been aggressively carried out, Nicholas proposed now that they should be. The trial of the Decembrists set the tone for the new reign. The tsar never relented in his bitter hatred of those who had dared to defy authority. A year after his death and thirty years after the trial, his successor pardoned the twenty exiles who were still alive.

The Tsar's Youth and Character

Born in the year of Catherine's death and nineteen years younger than Alexander, Nicholas spent a childhood very different from that of his oldest brother. His mother, the domineering Empress Marie, directed his education along very conservative lines. As a child he was arrogant and rude, and thrashings by his tutor did not break him of pugnacity, stubbornness, and outbursts of temper. He was always a poor pupil, and at fifteen his formal education ended. He accompanied Alexander to Paris in 1814, where he enjoyed watching the endless parades. He took a whirlwind journey through Russia and Western Europe soon after the war. When he returned home at the age of twenty, he won a promotion to the rank of general of a brigade of Guards, and soon found his forte in restoring the discipline that had slipped with the end of war.

Nicholas, who surrounded himself with soldiers, always slept on a hard camp bed. Although he was suspicious of intelligence, he was conscientious and did his modest best to give Russia good government as he understood it. If he was rigidly doctrinaire, he was consistent. He saw the problems that faced him in simple terms, and regarded those who opposed him as either treacherous or insane. He never shied away from a problem, as had Alexander, but he almost invariably underestimated its complexity. His penchant for order gave him a simple confidence in regimentation. In speaking of his regard for the army he said, "Here is order, a strict unconditional legality. All things flow logically one from the other. Everything has its purpose." Indeed, he was fond of drilling troops, designing uniforms, and beating a drum. He preferred military men as his advisers and chief administrators. Even the procurator of the Holy Synod, Count Nicholas Protasov, was a cavalry commander. Nicholas had a passion for things German, especially Prussian, and fondly admired the Prussian court and army. His wife was Princess Charlotte of Prussia, with whose father and brothers Nicholas maintained a close family relationship.

The emperor's appearance and bearing made him the very picture of an autocrat. He stood six feet three inches in height, carried himself erect and his head high, and his facial features made him handsome. He knew what he wanted and what was best for Russia—he idolized Peter the Great—and he took a hand personally even in the minutiae of administration. His was a platoon commander's view of his executive position. He simply gave orders to carry out his will. He did not hesitate to ask others for a report on facts, but he set policy and expected subordinates to execute it, as any good soldier must obey his commanding officer.

With a temper difficult to control, the emperor could be fiendishly cruel. One man whose death sentence had been commuted had the number of his grave entered in the official register, and his wife was forced to wear mourning. Subjecting suspects to the torture of a death sentence and, when the men were ready to die, commuting the sentence to exile in Siberia was perhaps his most notorious act of cruelty. Yet he was kind to his wife and his mistresses, if stern and exacting with his children.

Nicholas received no practical experience in administration before his succession, for Alexander never invited him to attend council sessions or introduced him to the work of any governmental agency. Few expected him to succeed to the position of tsar, as he was not the next in line to follow Alexander. His training and experience were totally in the military. He knew little of conditions in Russia until he heard the testimony of Pestel and others. He was the most consistent of autocrats, as his predecessor was surely one of the most inconsistent.

Administrative Alterations

As he questioned the Decembrists, Nicholas felt less fear than disbelief that anyone should presume to question the autocracy. He moved at once to correct the slackness in his brother's administration that had made the uprising possible. The new tsar's abiding faith in authority never wavered; especially after the uprising, he had full confidence that what was necessary was a strengthening of the autocracy, not a relaxation of it.

Within a year after the Decembrist rising, the new emperor appointed a special committee—always his favorite method of procedure—to sift through the testimony of the Decembrists for their specific criticisms of the regime. As Nicholas read the report he found there the tale of disillusion with Alexander after the promising early years of his reign and of resentment against the social and political quagmire of Russia after breathing the free air of Western Europe. He read of the Decembrists' awakening to Russia's need for clear laws fairly administered, for a reorganization of the bribe-ridden court system, for improving the economy and reducing the grinding poverty of the masses, for relieving the peasants of the sort of taxes and labor dues that the French Revolution had swept away in France, for abolishing the military colonies, and for representative government of some kind. Nicholas attempted to meet some of those criticisms. That he met with such little success is hardly surprising, and he soon cooled to the effort.

Before his accession, the agency known as the Imperial Chancery had dealt primarily under the tsar's personal direction with matters affecting the royal household. Nicholas added to its duties, organizing new sections or departments to deal with specific tasks. The First Section retained the functions of the former chancery. The Second Section, under Speransky, received orders to publish a new law code. The infamous Third Section directed the political police force whose responsibility it was to discover unrest and track down subversives. The Fourth Section handled royal charities. The Fifth Section managed the state-owned serfs, and the Sixth worked on a plan to administer Transcaucasia.

Nicholas would have preferred to run every government department himself, but he kept in personal touch with important bureaus by making their heads accountable personally to him. He showed little confidence in the old time-serving bureaucracy, repeatedly bypassing it and relying upon unofficial committees and new agencies, each headed almost invariably by a general. The emperor left the Council of State and Senate with little to do, for he was impatient of any limitations on his arbitrary will. He personally inspected troops, prisons, government offices, and schools, traveling over eighty thousand miles by carriage.

Impressed with the Decembrists' animosity toward influential officials in the closing days of Alexander's reign, Nicholas dismissed those who had been running the government. Arakcheyev went into retirement and Photius returned to his monastery. The emperor chose advisers who were conservative but not reactionary. Speransky, the best legal mind in the nation, had returned to the

Nicholas I

capital in 1822, and Kochubey won the tsar's confidence but had forsaken his liberal views of 1801 and now firmly believed that Russia could only be governed by autocracy. Kankrin and Kiselev, both sympathetic to mild peasant reforms, remained from the previous reign. No matter who occupied government posts, however, the emperor never lost firm control of the administration, unlike Alexander in the waning years of his reign.

Nicholas hoped that Russia's ills might disappear under a disciplined, militarylike bureaucracy; he considered himself the nation's commander-in-chief. The peace and quiet of the countryside he held to be the responsibility of the serf-owning gentry, whom he looked upon as a corps of unpaid police. However, Nicholas really trusted no one. The government became a quagmire of regulations, reports, investigations, and orders. No official could take any action without filling out a mass of documents. Halfway through the reign, the Ministry of Justice reported a backlog of over three million cases pending in its courts; all the other ministries were equally far behind. The primary concern of government agencies came to be not the conduct of business but ''the evacuation of paper.'' As Nicholas's reign drew to a close, it became apparent to all that the officialdom had so bogged down in bureaucratic gridlock that it was unable to govern the nation.

Reform Measures

Nicholas set himself resolutely to resist political progress, and he never wavered from that course. He was willing, however, to consider any measure that would make autocracy more efficient. It is from that point of view that his interest in what he termed "just reform" is understandable. "I shall always distinguish," he pronounced, "those who desire just reforms and expect them to emanate from the legal authority from those who want to undertake them by themselves, employing God knows what means." At his coronation the tsar warned that faults in government might be corrected, "not by impertinent, destructive dreams," but only by act of the sovereign.

Under the leadership of Speransky, the Second Section of the Imperial Chancery gathered together in an orderly collection all the laws issued since the publication of the Ulozhenie in the time of Alexis. The nation had sorely needed the codification for generations. Speransky had already done much to prepare himself for the assignment. Alexander had asked him to prepare a recodification as early as 1801 and had returned him to the task after 1807.

Before 1833, when the new code appeared, judges and lawyers had no way of knowing what the law was. Justice had been haphazard if not impossible. The codification that made the law understandable now revealed many abuses that had crept into relations between serfs and their owners. People discovered how serfdom had developed—that it had once seemed excusable as a way of making possible the gentry's service contribution to the state. Now that the upper classes no longer owed that obligation, the institution of serfdom obviously was without justification.

When the last of the Decembrists had been dragged off to Siberia, Nicholas appointed the first of his "secret committees" to consider the nation's problems. Headed by Kochubey, the committee included Speransky, Golitsyn, and three generals. The group received orders to learn what plans for reform Alexander had been considering, what problems existed, and what should be done about them. Nicholas became concerned about conditions among the serfs, for the first of over seven hundred peasant revolts during his reign flared in 1826. Indeed, the emperor voiced his intention to end serfdom, although he refused to risk stirring gentry opposition, inviting violence and disorder in the countryside. With the resurgence of revolution in 1848, however, Nicholas abandoned all thought of freeing the serfs and cast his lot with the gentry in their determination to resist all social change.

Nine other committees sat during Nicholas's reign to consider reform needs, particularly the problem of serfdom. However, because the emperor chose not to reorganize Russian society administratively as well as socially, there was only tinkering with the system. The ownership of serfs made landowners the local administrators. They were responsible for the collection of taxes, which only the serfs paid, and yet they owned the land that made the payment possible. The landowners also were responsible for drafting people into the army, and if the serfs were freed to roam at will, recruiting would be difficult. Yet to free the serfs with land, without compensating the owner, would punish the very class that most consistently supported the autocracy. Only autocracy, Nicholas insisted, was appropriate for Russia, and serfdom was the cement that bound the nobility to the crown. The emperor recognized the evil of serfdom, however, and feared an organized widespread uprising that might topple the monarchy. He reminded a meeting of nobles that Alexander had considered emancipation early in his reign and then decided against it.

A few corrective measures appeared during the reign, but their effect was pitifully negligible. A number of gentry found guilty of abusing their serfs had their land and chattels seized by the government. General Kiselev, Nicholas's "Chief of Staff for Peasant Affairs," permitted owners to free their serfs and give them land to use but not to possess, in return for which the freed slaves must pay in labor or produce for a specified period. In the thirteen years the law operated, only three landowners worked out such agreements with their peasants. The emperor forbade serf owners to sell peasants apart from their families, but the order proved unenforceable. Another order forbade the gentry to transfer ownership of their serfs in payment of debt without first giving the serfs opportunity to buy their freedom. Such peasants had only thirty days to raise the money, and there were no financial institutions from which they could borrow. Serf owners could not sell land unless their estates were large enough to provide eleven acres for each peasant, but the published revision of the law code unaccountably omitted this enactment. What the Imperial Chancery gave

Doré's biting illustration of serf-owners using their serfs as gambling chips

to the peasants, government underlings or serf owners took away. As a result, revolts became increasingly common and severe.

Industrial development during the thirties and forties did much to condemn serfdom to an early end. The number of factory workers, most of them serfs, grew from slightly over two hundred thousand at Alexander's death to a half million before the Crimean War. Some factories had been erected by the government and sold to middle-class entrepreneurs, who were often foreigners exempted from taxes as an inducement to bring their skills into Russia. Such plants were staffed with state serfs assigned to the manufacturer, with free peasants, or with obrok serfs whose owners approved their working for wages in order to exact from them higher dues. Other factories were the property of landowners who utilized their own barshchina serfs. Those workers, however, often performed inefficiently, and a few nobles preferred to free their peasants and hire them for wages. Also, those who worked in estate factories in the winter and returned to village agriculture in the summer took with them a knowledge of the skills they learned in the factories. They set up looms in their cottages, and the sale of the cloth they wove there added appreciably to their income. The gentry did not object to this, for it permitted them to charge a higher obrok or sell freedom to the serfs at a high price.

Conditions in possessional factories—those leased or sold by the government to professional manufacturers—were even worse than in Western Europe and America. The sixteen-hour day was typical. Punishments ranged from flogging to exile to Siberia or enrollment in the army. Serfs received half the wage of the free people with whom they worked. Poor food, filthy quarters, and hazardous machinery made the life of the factory serf more intolerable than life in the village. Strikes, although illegal, were frequent and costly. Kankrin, the finance minister responsible for regulation of the possessional factories, drew up Russia's first factory act in 1835. Its requirement that employers keep accurate account of wages paid meant nothing because there was no government inspection. Another act a decade later forbidding night work by those under twelve was not enforced.

The rapid growth of cottage industry—in 1850 there were eighteen thousand looms in manufacturing plants in the province of Vladimir and eighty thousand in the villages—prompted manufacturers to protest to the government, but the administration would not interfere with a trend that improved the finances of the gentry by permitting them to reap higher obrok. Manufacturers quite naturally supported emancipation of the serfs, without land, in order to tap the country's great potential labor supply.

Kankrin encouraged industrial growth by maintaining a protective tariff, but kept the duties low to force entrepreneurs to keep abreast of technical improvements abroad under the threat of competition. Spinning and weaving machines entered tariff-free, and the production of cotton, linen, and wool cloth rapidly expanded. The government's financial plight eased noticeably under Kankrin's leadership. The paper money that had flowed from government printing presses since Elizabeth's time fluctuated widely in value and so hampered trade. Now the government retired the almost worthless paper rubles and replaced them with paper money redeemable in silver. This long-needed reform restored public confidence and did much to stimulate commerce. The St. Petersburg Bourse, or commodities-and-securities exchange, flourished under Kankrin, who also promoted interest in economic progress by organizing Russia's first industrial exhibits. He founded the forestry and mining institutions that soon won worldwide respect. Although Kankrin was skeptical of railroads, Russia's first lines, from St. Petersburg to the imperial village of Tsarskoe Selo and from St. Petersburg to Moscow, were completed during his long term (1823–1844) as finance minister.

Economic progress in the first half of the nineteenth century was impressive when one considers only the raw figures of increase in number of looms, factories, industrial output, or imports and exports. The record is far less impressive, however, when held up to comparison with Western Europe. Great Britain, France, and Belgium were in the midst of the Industrial Revolution, while Russia was hardly on the threshold of industrialization. England had passed a stage that Russia would not reach for fifty years. Russia did cut a less impressive figure in world industry in 1800 than it did at the death of Nicholas I, but if the percentage of townspeople in the population had doubled between 1800 and 1850, it still came to less than 8 percent. If the bourgeoisie in Great Britain and France had become a formidable political force by mid-century, such was not the case in Russia, where the anemic middle class posed no threat to the autocracy and the political power of the aristocracy.

The End of the Polish Kingdom

Nicholas chafed under the restrictions that the Polish constitution imposed upon him. Poles involved in the Decembrist uprising had to be tried in Polish courts, which handed down insultingly mild sentences. The Diet flaunted its independence by refusing to pass measures sponsored by the Russian viceroy. The Poles kept up their clamor for the return of the provinces of former Lithuania as well as those of western Russia, which, although not inhabited by Poles, had been under Polish rule before the first partition. Nicholas quickly dashed all hope of such a return by refusing to consider the transfer of lands populated by Russians.

The year 1830 was one of many revolutions in Europe, and the fever spread to Poland. In November a band of students and army officers broke into the vice-regal palace in Warsaw and killed a number of the guards. The Diet, seeking to gain independence from Russia, terminated allegiance to Nicholas, established a provisional government, and took over command of the Polish national army. The revolutionaries issued a call for Lithuania and Volhynia to join them, but met with cool indifference. Many Polish army officers refused to support the revolt, the peasants in general were suspicious of the upper class movement, and the leaders quarreled among themselves over how radical the change should be. General Paskievich, at the head of a hundred and fifty thousand Russian troops, brushed aside the Polish army and advanced to the suburbs of Warsaw.

The rebels had no choice but to surrender.

The Polish constitution was rescinded, the Diet and the separate army were abolished, and Poland was made an internal part of the Russian Empire. Poland thenceforth was ruled from St. Petersburg. Over the ensuing years, and particularly following the later Polish revolt of 1863, the Poles suffered relentless persecution. Russian became the official language and the only one taught in the schools. The universities of Warsaw and Vilna were closed and Poles were forbidden to go abroad. Many of them managed to escape to Western Europe, where they kept up a hatred against Russia from that day forward. Russian censorship prohibited the writings of Polish scholars and the study of Polish history. The Roman Catholic Church in Poland lost its estates and had its clergy put on state salaries. The tsar imposed a policy of Russification in an effort to break Polish nationalism, but the greater the pressure applied, the more stubbornly did the Poles cling to their national spirit and aspirations.

Censorship and Repression

Nicholas I could never recall the Decembrist revolt without shuddering at the thought. Subversive ideas, he believed, were unnatural and foreign to Russia and must not be allowed to enter the country. When the specter of revolution reappeared in Western Europe in 1848, the emperor attempted to seal the frontier. Students might not study abroad, for that would be to risk infection. No Russian must cross the border except on official business.

The pillar of the autocracy as Nicholas perfected it was the Third Section of His Majesty's Chancery. A secret police agency of sorts had operated since the sixteenth century, and Paul's dreaded agents had merited the hatred they received. Alexander's distaste for his father's method led him to abolish the political police, and, when he revived the force in 1810 at Speransky's suggestion, he withheld from it the power it needed to be effective. He set aside, apparently without reading them, the reports and recommendations of the agency's director. His misplaced idealism may have disposed him against a secret police system as being somehow reactionary. It was revolutionary France, however, that created the first modern internal security agency in order to protect the revolution from those who would overturn it. Austria established a similar system before the end of the eighteenth century, a system that Alexander observed during the Congress of Vienna. Nicholas regarded his predecessor's failure to maintain effective internal security as the fundamental weakness of his government.

The emperor now assigned to General Benckendorf, its first director, the task of creating a system of secret or "higher police." He brought the new force into his own chancery, the better to maintain his own personal influence over it. The Third Section assumed control over a wide range of affairs that various ministries had previously controlled, to gather information and to report to the tsar on all events, "without exception" and whatever their nature, that took place anywhere in the land. The agency was omnipotent. As the tsar's own agency responsible to him alone, the Third Section extended and tightened autocratic rule throughout Russia. Through its eyes, Nicholas observed everything that went on. Nicholas's expressed intention that his new police force should "redress the wrongs which are unknown to the public and punish such crimes as the law cannot reach" made clear his conviction that he and those who carried out his will stood above the law. Yet his uncomplicated mind probably regarded the Third Section as simply an agency charged to enforce strict observance of the law. Its assignment was not only to procure information and report it to the tsar; it must take such action as it knew the tsar would condone. It must prevent even the threat of destructive action. The files of the political police carried the name of the radical Alexander Herzen because he was "not dangerous, but could be dangerous." Even in procuring information, the "higher police" might resort to any sort of force or pressure, physical or psychological.

The principles to which the emperor clung in the discharge of his divinely appointed responsibility as ruler of Russia were those of "Orthodoxy, Autocracy, and Nationality." Lumped together as the doctrine of "Official Nationality," they were the program of Count Sergei Uvarov, minister of education from 1833 to 1848. Although each of this triad had been present in Russia for many centuries, going back to Ivan the Great and even earlier, Uvarov's new emphasis created a powerful influence on Russian society. Orthodoxy, the only true Christian doctrine, became a tool deliberately used to preach meekness and obedience to the tsar, the military officer, the government official, and the landholder. Autocracy proclaimed the absolute power of the emperor, a power that God has transmitted to his anointed viceroy, the tsar. This link of Autocracy to Orthodoxy, the only authentic Christianity, made revolution not only treason but sacrilege. Nationality, the third element in this official trinity, glorified the Russian language and Great Russian element in the nation's history and culture, and denigrated not only the non-Slav elements but even the Ukrainians, Belo-Russians, and the Poles, whom Nicholas intensely hated. The exceptions were the Baltic Germans, descendants of the Teutonic knights, who occupied many important posts in the army, the bureaucracy, and the court. This doctrine of Nationality lay at the heart of the government's Russification policy, designed to snuff out cultural autonomy of the subject peoples throughout the empire. Indeed, Nationality in the form of Russian language, history, and culture was to be the unifying force, joined with Autocracy and Orthodoxy, which bound the disparate peoples of the empire together and set the nation apart from the hated West, breeding ground of revolution. It encouraged Pan-Slavism—the union of all Slavs, presumably in an expanded Russian Empire—fostered resentment at the treatment of Slav minorities in Austria and Turkey. Nationality promoted a national Russian mission of liberating brother Slavs and fellow Orthodox Christians from oppressive foreign rule.

Nicholas took a keen interest in education as a means of inculcating loyalty and obedience. Count Uvarov declared "Orthodoxy, Autocracy, and Nationality" to be the principles upon which education must rest. Schools once more catered to particular classes, as they had before Alexander's reforms. Children of state peasants attended the village schools, offspring of merchants the district schools, and nobles the gymnasia and universities. Teaching of the nonprivileged classes aimed at making the people content with their lot and providing them with skills that would be of service to the state. Uvarov admitted that he would die happy only if he could "retard the [intellectual] development of the country by fifty years," and looked upon the schools as the agency by which he might accomplish this end. The University of Moscow, which the tsar termed "the wolf's den," lost its chair of philosophy. The teaching of higher mathematics, which might encourage speculation, was banned in all universities. Only theologians might teach logic. Courses in comparative law and constitutional history were ended. History professors must glorify Russian history and could not mention such topics as the Reformation. As for the humanities, Uvarov expressed the hope that Russian literature might cease to exist. Indeed, even Uvarov seemed dangerous to Nicholas when he used the word "progress" in an official report. "Progress? What progress?" Nicholas wrote in the margin. "This word must be deleted from official terminology."

Censorship tightened early in the reign in an attempt to gag Russia intellectually. Texts on physiology could not contain anything that might "offend the instinct of decency." Musical scores could not enter Russia from Germany, for the notes might constitute inflammatory messages in code. Newspapers were suppressed for mentioning the names of seditious writers. No book or newspaper might mention any secret society or even assume that any secret society had ever existed anywhere. So many agencies operated the censorship that the tsar appointed a supervisory censorship committee, but even it was censored by another committee. Soon there were more censors than books. One observer referred to the supervision of the pitifully frail Russian press by the enormous censorship structure as "a cannon aimed at a flea."

Nicholas had no patience with sectarianism, for conformity to the state religion was a distinguishing mark of loyalty. The police drove the Dukhobors, or "Spirit Worshippers," from their villages into Siberian exile for their refusal to render military service and dealt similarly with the Molokane, who showed their opposition by drinking milk during Lent, which Orthodoxy forbade. Both sects had enjoyed protection under Alexander I. The Raskolniks, or "Old Believers," who refused to accept the church reforms of the seventeenth century, were particularly suspect because their religious dissent masked political unrest. A government commission set out to ascertain the number of sectarians, presumed to be less than a million, and discovered that there were probably eight million of them. Since the church in Russia was simply a branch of government after Peter's time, the dissenters were guilty of treason, and most of them proudly flaunted it by omitting the sovereign's name from their prayers. The number of trials and persecutions of dissidents mounted as the reign dragged on, but the sects continued to prosper until the end of the monarchy.

The Intelligentsia

The origins of the intelligentsia lay back in the eighteenth century. By the mid-nineteenth it consisted of those young men and women of all classes whose social conscience led them to dedicate their lives to rousing their land from its cultural stupor. One of them reported that what united these young Russians was "a profound feeling of alienation from official Russia." Some came out of the universities; some had studied in the West or under Western tutors living in Russia. They embraced the new romanticism and idealism and deplored the skepticism and materialism of the Enlightenment that had brought on the excesses of the revolutionary age. They read the works of the Romantics, particularly Schiller, and became disciples of Kant, Fichte, and most especially Hegel. The French writers Fourier, Saint-Simon, Proudhon, and Blanc fascinated them. They discussed Western thought in each other's homes in Moscow and St. Petersburg.

In 1836, Peter Chaadayev, whose Moscow home was a gathering place where young Russians discussed the nation's cultural lag, published a *Philosophical Letter*, the appearance of which had "the effect of a pistol shot in the night." He argued plausibly that the nation's institutions had been imposed from outside, from Byzantium primarily, and that the consequent cultural pollution had poisoned Russia's relations with the West of which it should be a part. Russia must turn away from the Byzantine-Orthodox path that had led it into stagnation and embrace the modern progressive West. When the emperor learned of this "libel against the fatherland, the faith, and the government," he ordered Chaadayev to be declared insane and placed under house arrest. The punishment, more than his *Philosophical Letter*, won the writer immortality. In his *Apology of a Madman* he tried to soften official censure.

The Chaadayev incident came on the eve of that "marvelous decade" that preceded the revolutionary conflagrations of 1848. Those years witnessed a mounting defiance of Official Nationality by the early giants of literary and social criticism.

Even before 1848 there were modest beginnings of protest against the repression. Groups or "circles" of young progressives gathered in private homes to comment on works of Russian writers and to discuss political and social problems. Such meetings were common in provincial capitals, but perhaps the most famous was the one that met in the St. Petersburg home of Michael Petrashevsky, a young noble. Some of the group were moderately socialist in their thinking, but there were no such brave plans for uprising as the Decembrists had laid a generation earlier. When Nicholas learned of the meetings, Petrashevsky and a score of his fellows were seized and sentenced to die, among them Dostoevsky. The emperor spared their lives, however, and sent the men off in fetters to Siberia. He insisted upon regarding the Petrashevsky circle as a serious threat to the throne, even though the Third Section regarded it as a "handful of depraved youths" who dreamed and talked idly of socialism. Yet the secret police, never half so effective as the Austrian and French security agencies, proved incapable of stilling discontent or even of discovering much of it.

The great debate that raged among young Russians in the thirties and forties was that between Westernizers and Slavophiles. The Westernizers sought less to force Western intellectual garb upon Russia than to lift it from the slough of its Slavic past to the cultural level of Western Europe. For the nation to resist the progress and modernization that becoming Western would bring was to work against Russia's best interest. Although they shared no common program, they generally urged constitutional government, freedom of expression, and the rule of law, while opposing autocracy, bondage, and the chasm that separated the illiterate and depressed masses from the favored few.

One influential Westernizer was that "potentially dangerous" Alexander Herzen, illegitimate son of a wealthy noble. Having been expelled from the University of Moscow for radical activities, he joined the discussion circles that met in aristocratic homes. He settled philosophically among the non-Marxist socialists.

The works of Washington Irving, James Fenimore Cooper, and Harriet Beecher Stowe made Herzen sentimentally fond of the United States. He was aware of American weaknesses; black slavery and lynchings appalled him, but he admired the federal system, the strength of local self-government, and the absence of a stifling bureaucracy. He even urged those who sought escape from the Russian quagmire to emigrate to "some place in Wisconsin or Kansas."

This "father of Russian populism," as younger men would later call him, left Russia for Paris and later London. In England, Herzen published a Russian language newspaper, *Kolokol*, or *The Bell*, in which he called first for emancipation and eventually for social revolution.

Another influential Westernizer, Russia's greatest literary critic, was Vissarion Belinsky, son of a poor physician. He won expulsion from the University of Moscow by criticizing bondage. Belinsky eked out a poor living as an editor and critic and died at thirty-seven of disease at the very moment when the secret police were on their way to arrest him.

Belinsky's immortal letter to the writer Nicholas Gogol heaped such criticism upon tsardom that censors refused to allow its publication until 1905. Manuscript copies circulated freely, however, and many young idealists committed it to memory. Gogol, whose *Dead Souls* and *Inspector General* had so deliciously ridiculed bondage and the bureaucracy, put together a collection of hortatory essays, *Select Passages from Correspondence with Friends*, in which he appeared to support the autocracy and even serfdom. Belinsky's devastating reply reviewed the burdens the Russian people had to suffer: corrupt officialdom, religious bankruptcy, a system of justice that condoned the flogging of the innocent and the guilty alike, the absence of human dignity, the traffic in people "without even having the excuse of American plantation owners who claim the Negro is not a man." Belinsky's long letter had tremendous influence on later writers; very few ever read the work that had inspired it.

There was little room for moderates among the intelligentsia, but not all were leftists. If the conservatives were less numerous than the liberals, they were hardly less vocal. Nicholas suspected Slavophiles and Westernizers alike, for both criticized the government, although for different reasons. Members of both groups aired their views in the same circles in each other's homes, and this alone made them suspect.

Such Slavophiles as Ivan and Constantine Aksakov, Ivan and Peter Kireyevsky, and Alexis Khomiakov all agreed that Western influence had seriously damaged the nation. They all shuddered at the possibility of constitutional government, although the Aksakov brothers would accept a consultative assembly—the Zemskii Sobor of earlier centuries. Slavophiles regarded democratic government as alien to Russian nature and therefore subversive. They approved the harmonious and serene development of the nation down to Peter's time, and insisted that the importation of ideas and institutions from the decadent West had caused social unrest. The only true Christianity was Orthodoxy; the Poles, Czechs, Croats, Slovenes, and others who had deserted to Catholicism were apostates. Only Khomiakov, who visited Lutheran and Catholic friends on his western travels, wanted a universal Christian brotherhood, but not a universal church.

The Slavophiles opposed serfdom, state domination of the church, the bureaucratic suffocation, and Prussian militarism. In later years their attitude toward autocracy softened, and many officials and members of the imperial family became ardent Slavophiles. The support of such elements brought to respectable conservatism a reactionary taint that some of the scholars of the "marvellous decade" would have found distasteful.

The Golden Age of Russian Literature

Modern Russian literature matured in the reign of Nicholas, in spite of the heavy hand of censorship that officialdom pressed down upon it. Owing much to the heritage from the revolutionary age in the West, and yet intensely nationalistic as a result of the French invasion in 1812, Russian writers won acclaim rapidly at home and slowly abroad.

Sometimes the works of these literary giants appealed to the pride of the Russian people, or at least to that of the educated and literate few, in the nation's history. Alexander Pushkin, Russia's greatest poetic genius but a master of prose as well, wrote of Pugachev in *A Captain's Daughter*, of Peter the Great in *Poltava and The Bronze Horseman*, and of the tragedy of a child tsarevich in *Boris Godunov*. Nicholas Gogol's *Taras Bulba* told of a carefree Cossack and his sons who opposed the king of Poland.

Not infrequently writers used whatever medium—poetry, prose, drama, the essay—in comedy or satire or thinly veiled polemic to challenge the social, political, and moral corruption that tsardom epitomized. Nicholas suspected Pushkin of sympathy for the Decembrists, and indeed the author dedicated a poem to them that was published posthumously. The poet Ryleyev was a leader of the Decembrists. Griboyedev's caustic drama *Woe from Wit* or *The Misfortune of Being Clever* was a derisive attack on Russian society for its slavish imitation of Western customs and manners and the preference of both Alexander and Nicholas for foreign advisers. Gogol's *Dead Souls* and *The Inspector General* were indictments of serfdom and the bureaucracy, although the author was by inclination conservative and had no intention of affronting the autocrat. Others, not least of all Belinsky, read into the works much that the author may not have intended. Gogol's introspective short story *The Overcoat* had a much greater impact on Russian literature than did either of the works so often cited. Dostoevsky recognized his debt to Gogol in the grateful tribute, "We all came out of *The Overcoat.*"

Censorship often kept the work of Russian writers from print, but many circulated in manuscript. Sometimes works found foreign publishers or came off presses hidden from the Third Section. Only rarely did authors give up the struggle against oppression and succumb to the threats or to the rewards of officialdom. Such men risked condemnation to obscurity, for when they stopped crusading they lost their following. Some suffered cruelly from the Third Section. Dostoevsky, for example, was condemned to death and reprieved at the last moment to serve ten years in Siberia. His novel *The House of the Dead* grew out of his Siberian experience.

The importance of the literary richness and productivity of the reign lies not in the success with which it overcame the obstacle of censorship, but rather in the fact that the writers of the time set the course of Russian literature for a century to come. Thenceforth all Russian writers worth their salt took a stand on the social issues of his day.

The Failure of Nicholas's System

The year 1848 had hardly opened before a mounting wave of revolutions broke out all over Europe. Only the Romanov throne escaped the threat that year, for revolutionary movements in Russia were without leadership for a generation after the Decembrist mutiny. Lest there be any misunderstanding of his implacable opposition to "impertinent, destructive dreams," Nicholas issued a manifesto warning Western rebels against trying to import their subversive ideas into Holy Russia.

Although the emperor had no need to fear for his throne in 1848, he understood that his repressive measures had produced only modest success. In spite of the gagging censorship, writers managed to get into print their ridicule of the regime and some, like Bakunin and Herzen, wrote freely in exile. Uvarov's trinity—Orthodoxy, Autocracy, Nationality—had failed. Persecution of the sects only multiplied their numbers. The longer serfdom continued, the more numerous became the peasant revolts against it. Russification only provoked Poles to cling to their language and culture with greater determination, and the Westernizers argued convincingly against the policy of nationalism.

The Crimean War rudely shook the tsar's faith in his system. The Russian land again suffered invasion, but this time there was no patriotic surge to repel the attack. Official corruption hamstrung the prosecution of the war. Peasants showed enthusiasm for the war only because they expected emancipation when they enlisted, and they revolted when informed that there had been no such order. Army equipment had not kept pace with improvements since the Napoleonic war, and the leaders with few exceptions were stupid and unimaginative.

Nicholas died as much of disappointment at the failure of the system in which he so confidently believed as of the cold he contracted in the spring of 1855. Rumors persisted that he committed suicide. Russians could not believe that the head of this "despotism tempered by assassination" could die any but a violent death. On his deathbed he admitted to his son, "I am not turning over the command to you in good order." He warned his successor that unless he abolished serfdom from above, it would abolish itself from below by a revolution that might overturn the monarchy. It is improbable that Nicholas seriously considered or could have faced up to carrying through the reforms that could no longer be postponed. Hated as he was, he could not have counted on popular cooperation. One contemporary maintained that "the main failing of the reign of Nicholas consisted of the fact that it was all a mistake."

Nicholas, Europe, and the Near East

Nicholas I showed himself just as determined as his brother to play a leading role among the powers of the world. Where Alexander I was inclined to finesse and patience, however, Nicholas was frank, direct, and brusque. Throughout his reign Nicholas accepted a personal responsibility to defend the monarchs of Europe against the threat of revolution. He supported reaction abroad as well as at home in the conviction that a threat to legitimate government anywhere was a challenge to his own throne.

War with Turkey

Alexander I bequeathed to Nicholas an urgent need for settling the problems that had irritated relations between Russia and Turkey since the Treaty of Bucharest in 1812. The Turks never could be held to their commitments without force, and Alexander had hesitated to use it. The Greek war for independence that had been dragging on since 1821 only complicated an already difficult problem. Unable to put down the uprising himself, the sultan called upon his vassal Mehemet Ali, the pasha of Egypt, to send an expedition to Greece. The pasha's son with a well-trained army quickly overran the Peloponnesus in 1825 and alarmed all Christendom with the threat of merciless punishment of the Greeks. Just before his death, Alexander called for a conference of the powers to consider steps to ease the pressure on the Greeks.

Soon after the new reign opened, England and Russia agreed to push for Turkish recognition of Greek autonomy. France joined the other two in an ultimatum to Turkey calling for an end of hostilities, but the sultan ignored the request. Thereupon naval squadrons of the three allies moved into Navarino Bay to tie up the sultan's fleet and prevent the landing of additional forces in the Greek peninsula. In the battle that followed, in 1827, the Turko-Egyptian fleet was blown out of the water. The sultan was so furious at the allied action that he stepped up his pressure on the Greeks. When all Christians were driven from Constantinople, Russia, acting as protector of Christians in the Turkish Empire, declared war.

In the summer of 1828 Russian armies drove the Turks out of Moldavia and Wallachia, which the sultan had occupied earlier, and passed the Danube. A year later they crossed the Balkan Mountains, seized Adrianople, and threatened the Turkish capital. The Russian Black Sea fleet entered the Bosporus and sailed to within sight of the sultan's palace. Meanwhile, a Russian force crossed the Caucasus, drove deep into eastern Turkey, and carried the forts of Kars and Erzurum. England and France moved their fleets to the Dardanelles, ostensibly to protect foreigners in the Turkish capital from mob violence but in reality to prevent Russian seizure of the Straits. The capitals of Europe accepted the collapse of the Turkish Empire as almost a certainty. The Egyptian pasha was bargaining for French assistance to conquer Syria. The Barbary States were threatening secession. Greece was lost. The Danubian Principalities and Serbia already enjoyed Russian protection. Bosnia and Bulgaria hoped for independence. One Russian army was well inside Asiatic Turkey, and another was in bivouac within a day's march of Constantinople.

The great powers toyed with various schemes for the partition of Turkey, and particularly with the notion of setting up a new Christian state to control the Straits. Nicholas I, however, was not sympathetic to the appearance of a state that almost surely would come under Western domination. Nor did he relish the thought of partitioning Turkey even though he might receive the Straits, for Russia's position there would be difficult to defend against an alliance of hostile powers. Nicholas preferred that Turkey survive and come under Russian protection. He agreed with his advisers that "the advantages of the maintenance of the Ottoman Empire are superior to the inconveniences which they present; its fall therefore would be contrary to the true interests of Russia." Consequently, the terms he offered the sultan were surprisingly mild. By the Treaty of Adrianople in 1829 Russia took no territory. The sultan confirmed the autonomy of Serbia and the Danubian Principalities, conceded Greek independence, guaranteed freedom of commerce through the Straits to all nations, and promised to abide by his earlier treaties with Russia.

The guarantee of commercial access to the Straits assured the prosperity of Russian Black Sea ports and particularly of the landowners who shipped their wheat either in Russian or British vessels. The economic potential of south Russia could not develop without free use of the Straits. Within fifteen years, more than twice as much grain was cleared from Black Sea points as from all other Russian ports combined, and Odessa by 1843 was handling a tenth of all Russian commerce.

The Sick Man of Europe

Russia did not publicly announce the decision to maintain Turkish integrity, but all the powers recognized that the sultan continued to rule only by Russian sufferance. The new Russian policy was soon tested. Within two years of the tsar's decision, Mehemet Ali, the sultan's troublesome governor of Egypt, invaded Syria and marched toward Constantinople. The sultan called for Russian help, and a Russian fleet sailed to the Bosporus. Soon afterward Mehemet Ali and the sultan came to terms.

Two years after the settlement of the Egyptian crisis, Nicholas signed a mutual defense pact with Turkey. By this treaty of Unkiar Skelessi of 1833, the two nations promised to join forces in case of attack upon either. Russia agreed, however, that in case of war, Turkey could fulfill its obligation simply by closing the Dardanelles to the warships of all other nations. With the signing of the eight-year agreement Russia satisfied its need for closing the breach in its southern defense; at that moment it enjoyed the strongest position at the Straits ever won by any Russian government.

When Mehemet Ali with French support rebelled against the sultan in 1839 and again threatened Constantinople, Nicholas decided that Turkey could only survive through common action among the powers. Austria, Russia, Prussia, and England agreed to defend the Turkish capital against Mehemet Ali, whose ardor cooled with the offer of control of Syria for the rest of his life. The sultan agreed to close the Dardanelles and Bosporus to warships of all nations when Turkey was at peace, a simple restatement of ancient Turkish policy. Russia's adherence to this "Pacification of the Levant" in 1840 constituted a resignation of its position as sole protector of the Ottoman Empire won at Unkiar Skelessi. The tsar's willingness to back down was the result of his determination to uphold Turkish independence and of his eagerness to dispel British suspicions and reduce the possibility of a Franco-British alliance against Russia at the Straits. France avoided permanent isolation by joining with the other powers the following year in the Straits Convention by which the signatories agreed to respect the practice of closing the Dardanelles to foreign warships except when Turkey itself was at war.

Nicholas was certain by this time that Turkey, "the sick man of Europe," was dying and that plans should be made for disposing of the remains. He considered the possibility of creating a Christian state under international guarantee to control the Straits. In 1844 he visited Queen Victoria in London and suggested that Austrian and Russian armies and a British fleet assemble at the Straits to preside over the demise of the Ottoman Empire. The Liberal ministry that governed England at the time accepted an agreement with Nicholas whereby the two powers promised to defend Turkish integrity and come to an understanding on partition if Turkey could no longer be kept alive. When Anglo-Russian relations cooled nine years later, however, the friendly Liberals were no longer in power. The Crimean War was the result.

The Policeman of Europe

In 1830, a revolution in Paris drove the French king into retirement. The duke of Orleans, of the younger branch of the Bourbons, became "King of the French People" and accepted a liberalization of the constitution. Nicholas was furious at this violation of the principle of legitimacy that had guided the settlement at Vienna in 1815. Louis Philippe, the new French ruler, was a dangerous character in the eyes of Nicholas, for he had expressed sympathy for republican ideas and for the American constitution.

The Paris outbreak was the signal for risings all over Europe. The Belgians rose against their Dutch rulers and declared their independence. Several German states won constitutions from their rulers. Italians rose against their princes but were overborne by Austrian intervention. Revolutions broke out in Portugal and Spain. Riots developed all over England against the refusal of the government to reform the House of Commons. The spirit carried even to the Vistula, but the Polish rising failed miserably before the threat of Russian guns. Nicholas took the initiative in bringing together the governments of Austria, Prussia, and Russia in a reaffirmation of the Holy Alliance. The three invited any sovereign threatened by revolt to call upon them for assistance in suppressing it. In 1846, the three acted together to wipe out the Republic of Cracow, set up by the Congress of Vienna, which had become a haven for Polish exiles from the eastern monarchies.

The revolutions in Central Europe in 1830 were doomed to failure by France's inability to support them in the face of warnings from Austria, Russia, and Prussia, but the movements did not die out. "Young Italy," an organization that aimed to unite Italy under a republic, numbered thousands in its membership. German liberal thought continued to thrive in spite of persecution. Slav and Magyar minorities dreamed of independence from the Habsburgs. Nationalistic fervor continued to mount in the Balkans.

Early in 1848, the monarchy in France gave way to a republic, and again the epidemic spread over Europe. Bohemia demanded autonomy, and Hungary set up a liberal government. All Italy was in revolt, and the Sardinian king had to grant a constitution. Liberals from all the German states gathered at Frankfurt to work for a united Germany, and rioters in Berlin frightened the king of Prussia into accepting a constitution. Thousands marched in London to point up the need for further reform of Parliament.

Nicholas accepted these disturbances as a personal challenge. Although he rejoiced at the ill fortune of Louis Philippe, he insisted on sending an army to the Rhine to contain the radicalism in France. When informed that the treasury would not stand such a campaign, Nicholas contented himself by broadcasting a warning to all revolutionaries. "Take heed, ye peoples, and submit, for God is with us."

On the Austrian front Nicholas could take a hand against the forces of revolution without marching his troops so far and at such expense. The Austrian emperor called for Russian assistance to put down a Hungarian revolt that had declared the end of Habsburg rule. A Russian army crossed the Carpathians and forced the surrender of the rebel forces. This broke the back of revolutionary movements elsewhere in Austrian dominions, and the youthful Emperor Francis Joseph quickly recovered control of his inheritance.

The failure of the revolutionary movement in Central Europe in 1848 was in no small measure the result of support rendered by Nicholas to the conservative cause. The tsar firmly backed Austria in its policy of dominating Germany and dousing every spark of liberalism as soon as it appeared. He patched up disagreements between Austria and Prussia over leadership of the German Confederation. It was primarily through his efforts that the three monarchs of the east stood squarely against the tide of liberalism that threatened to engulf all Europe. Not until his death could Europe feel free from the shadow of the gloomy East.

The Crimean War

The French Republic established in 1848 was short-lived. Four years after its birth the president, Louis Napoleon, tore up the constitution and proclaimed himself emperor. A drab character, this Napoleon III contrived to catch the fancy of the French people by embarking upon a bold foreign policy. To gain Catholic support in France he insisted that the sultan grant members of the Catholic clergy the right to maintain the holy places in Palestine. As defender of Greek Orthodox Christians in the Turkish Empire, Nicholas protested and marched his armies into Moldavia, which was Turkish territory under Russian protection. With the British ambassador's assurance of support, the sultan declared war against Russia in 1853. When the tsar rejected an ultimatum to evacuate the Danubian Principalities, England and France joined Turkey against Russia.

The Crimean War was not fought over control of Christian sanctuaries in Palestine. England was not willing to allow Russian domination of Turkish domestic policy, which seemed to be the aim of Nicholas's impatience with the sultan's surrender to French demands. On the other hand, Nicholas accepted the sultan's concession to France as an indication that the time had come to partition Turkey. Its government merited no trust and lacked the strength to maintain itself effectively. Nicholas conferred with the Austrian emperor on putting an end to the "filthy housekeeping on the Bosporus" and to the oppression of impoverished Christians by the "Turkish dogs." But Francis Joseph had little sympathy for the tsar's suggestion that the Balkans become a joint Austro-Russian protectorate and Constantinople a free city under international guarantee.

British statesmen believed that Nicholas might seize Constantinople, thus precipitating the demise of the Ottoman Empire. England could not afford to see that happen, for it profited much more from trade with the sprawling Turkish domain than it could expect to do if the territory broke up into free states or came under the sway of protectionist Austria or Russia. Nicholas, convinced that the Turkish Empire was breaking up, was as determined to prevent England from gaining control of the Straits as were the British to keep Russia from seizing them. Austria, too, preferred to keep "the sick man" alive, for it might suffer commercial strangulation if the mouth of the Danube came permanently under Russian control. France seems to have bludgeoned England into supporting its strong stand at the Straits by threatening to attack Belgium. Indeed, England's attitude toward Russia was much more cautious than that of Napoleon III, who hurried his fleet to Turkish waters in an obvious attempt to goad the sultan into rejecting Russia's offer to negotiate the quarrel over the holy places. In the diplomatic seesaw preceding the war, the British seemed convinced of the tsar's decision to preside over the partition of the Ottoman Empire. They were determined to prevent the partition that French diplomats warned would be the signal for France to seek territorial compensation in Western Europe—that is, in Belgium.

Hardly had the war begun when Austria joined the Western powers in diplomatic pressure aimed at restoring peace. In fact, Austria threatened to attack Russia unless the tsar accepted the terms, which prompted Nicholas to deprecate the duplicity of the nation to whom he "had given a tribute of blood" in 1849. As soon as the diplomatic wrangling began, British war aims became clear—Russia must not maintain a naval base on the Black Sea and must limit its warships there to four. Austria refused to go to war and veered toward supporting Russia against British intransigence, while French public opinion eventually cooled toward a war that produced no brilliant victories.

The war touched scattered points from one end of the Russian Empire to the other. British naval forces attacked Russian outposts in the Baltic, the White Sea, and Kamchatka, and bombarded Odessa. The naval raid on eastern Siberia convinced the Russian government that Alaska was indefensible, and soon after the war it sold the territory to the United States. Russian troops entered Moldavia but withdrew at Habsburg insistence, and Austria occupied the principalities as a precaution against a Russian drive to the Danube. This act of "malevolent neutrality" may have cost Russia the victory. Western Europe had believed for a generation that Russia could take Constantinople by land whenever it wanted and bottle up any warships caught in the Straits or the Black Sea. Considering the weak and backward state of the Russian army at the time, however, this was conjecture. The only Russian success came in Asia Minor, where Kars surrendered in the closing days of the war.

The allies threw their main effort against the Crimea, where they could use both their modern steam-driven warships and their armies. In the fall of 1854 the British, French, and Turks landed sixty thousand troops in the peninsula and attacked the naval base at Sevastopol, after quarreling long enough over policy to allow the Russian commander, Todtleben, to prepare a stout defense. The Russians sank their wooden Black Sea fleet in the neck of the harbor at Sevastopol to prevent close-in bombardment, and sallied out occasionally to attack the allied base at Balaklava. The British counterattack produced the gallant but futile "Charge of the Light Brigade." The troops on both sides suffered unspeakably from winter cold, shortage of provisions, cholera, and foul medical care. Florence Nightingale improved British hospital service during the campaign and succeeded in overcoming prejudice against the appearance of women as nurses with the army. Her Russian counterpart, Darya Sevastopolskaya, did what she could to relieve suffering among the defenders. With the approach of another winter, Todtleben decided to withdraw. After a year's siege the great base fell to the allies, and the war quickly ended. Nicholas had died six months earlier, and his successor expressed a willingness to meet honorable terms.

The conduct of the war did not redound to the credit of either side, but the Russians outdid their opponents in mismanagement. The campaign cost the allies a hundred thousand casualties, the Russians three times as many. Nicholas mobilized a million troops, but most of them saw no action. The Russian supply system broke down completely, and England serviced its troops less ineffectively from London than the tsar could do in his own land. The Russian army had not kept up with technical improvements and fought with the same weapons as at Borodino. The unbelievable corruption and stupidity that characterized the conduct of Russian officialdom destroyed even Nicholas's confidence in the bureaucratic system he had perfected. Popular disinterest in this invasion of Russian territory must have dispelled any illusions the tsar may have had about what his subjects thought of him.

Stunned at what he considered English perfidy in refusing to cooperate over the Turkish question, shocked at the betrayal of Austria, saddened at the poor showing of his troops, amazed at the corruption that sapped the nation's strength, and disturbed at the peasant resistance to recruiting, the tsar was unable to face the future. Rumor soon had it that Nicholas took poison.

The Treaty of Paris, 1856

His nation exhausted, his treasury empty, and faced with an overpowering alliance against him that now included Sardinia, Alexander II had no excuse to continue the war after the fall of Sevastopol. The Allies, too, were tiring of the conflict. Austria was supporting Russia diplomatically. France had lost interest. By the Treaty of Paris, both sides restored territory they had seized, Russia returning Kars to Turkey and the allies returning the Crimean forts to Russia. In order to safeguard shipping down the Danube, Russia surrendered the southern tip of Bessarabia to Moldavia, and the river came under international guarantee. All the powers undertook the protection of Christians in the Ottoman Empire, and all guaranteed the autonomy of Serbia and the Danubian Principalities. The Black Sea was neutralized; commercial vessels had free access to it, but the treaty closed it once more to the warships of all powers when Turkey was not at war. This simply meant that any future enemy of Russia must drag Turkey into a war in order to use the Straits. England, France, and Austria bound themselves in a separate agreement to defend the independence and integrity of the sultan's empire against any aggressor, but they ignored the contingency that the empire might explode from internal pressure. All the powers swore to abolish privateering and to respect ships flying neutral flags in time of war unless carrying contraband and agreed that blockades to be binding must be effective.

Alexander II was not happy with the terms of the treaty, but he was in no position to refuse them. All the diplomats were skeptical about how long the settlement could last. Great Britain's prime minister, Palmerston, hoped that the Russians would suffer the restrictions for ten years and openly warned the Turks that Russia would be at war with them again within a decade. Actually, the limitations on Russian use of the Black Sea lasted fifteen years, and the Russo-Turkish truce for twenty.

The Crimean War was the first conflict among the great powers since the Napoleonic period. Its outbreak signaled an end to the Concert of Europe by which the powers had managed for forty years to settle differences by negotiation. For Russia, the war was decisive in that it made imperative a radical overhaul of society. Nicholas had sought to maintain internal pacification and external security. This "most consistent of autocrats" believed that the two went hand in hand. When the one dissolved, the other collapsed, and the new ruler faced the dual problem of domestic and diplomatic readjustment.

Suggested Reading

ANNENKOV, P. V., *Extraordinary Decade: Literary Memoirs* (Ann Arbor, 1968).

BARKER, J. F., *The War against Russia, 1854–1856* (New York, 1971).

BLACKWELL, W. L., *The Beginnings of Russian Industrialization, 1800–1860* (Princeton, 1968).

BOWMAN, H., *Vissarion Belinsky: A Study in the Origins of Social Criticism in Russia* (Cambridge, 1954).

BROWN, E. J., *Stankevich and His Moscow Circle, 1830–1840* (Cambridge, 1954).

CALDER, A., *Russia Discovered: Nineteenth Century Fiction from Pushkin to Chekhov* (New York, 1976).

CHMIELEWSKI, E., *Tribune of the Slavophiles: Konstantine Aksakov* (Gainesville, FL, 1962).

CURTISS, J. S., *The Russian Army under Nicholas I, 1825–1855* (Durham, NC, 1965).

CUSTINE, MARQUIS DE, *Empire of the Tsar: A Journey through Eternal Russia* (New York, 1989).

DE GRUNWALD, C. *Nicholas I* (New York, 1954).

EVANS, J. L., *The Petrashevsky Circle, 1846–1848* (The Hague, 1974).

FADNER, F., *Seventy Years of Pan-Slavism: Karamzin to Danilevsky, 1800–1870* (Washington, DC, 1962).

GLEASON, A., *European and Muscovite: Ivan Kireevsky and the Origins of Slavophilism* (Cambridge, 1976)

GOLOVINE, I., *Russia under the Autocrat, Nicholas the First* (New York, 1970).

HARE, R., *Pioneers of Russian Social Thought* (New York, 1951).

HERZEN, A., *My Past and Thoughts: The Memoirs of Alexander Herzen* (New York, 1973).

HINGLEY, R., *Russian Writers and Society, 1825–1904* (New York, 1967).

JELAVICH, B., *A Century of Russian Foreign Policy, 1814–1914* (Philadelphia, 1964).

KOHN, H., *The Mind of Modern Russia* (New Brunswick, NJ, 1955).

LENSEN, G. A., *The Russian Push toward Japan: Russo-Japanese Relations, 1697–1875* (Princeton, 1959).

LINCOLN, W. B., *Nicholas I, Emperor and Autocrat of All the Russias* (Bloomington, 1980).

LUKASHEVICH, S., *Ivan Aksakov, 1823–1866* (Cambridge, 1965).

McNALLY, R. T., *Chaadaev and His Friends* (Tallahassee, 1971).

MAGARSHAK, D., *Pushkin, A Biography* (New York, 1968).

MALIA, M., *Alexander Herzen and the Birth of Russian Socialism* (Cambridge, 1961).

_____, *The Major Works of Peter Chaadaev* (South Bend, IN, 1961).

MASSIE, S., *Land of the Firebird: The Beauty of Old Russia* (New York, 1980).

MONAS, S., *The Third Section: Police and Society in Russia under Nicholas I* (Cambridge, 1961).

MOSELY, P. E., *Russian Diplomacy and the Opening of the Eastern Question in 1838 and 1839* (Cambridge, 1934).

NICHOLS, R. L. and T. C. STAVROU, *Russian Orthodoxy under the Old Regime* (Minneapolis, 1978).

PAYNE, R., *The Fortress* (New York, 1967).

PINTNER, W. M., *Economic Policy under Nicholas I* (Cambridge, 1968).

PRESNIAKOV, A. E., *Emperor Nicholas I of Russia* (Gulf Breeze, FL, 1974).

PURYEAR, V. J., *England, Russia and the Straits Question, 1844–1856* (Berkeley, 1931).

RAEFF, M., *Russian Intellectual History: An Anthology* (New York, 1966).

RIASANOVSKY, N. V., *Nicholas I and Official Nationality* (Berkeley, 1959).

_____, *Russia and the West in the Teachings of the Slavophiles* (Cambridge, 1952).

SEATON, A., *The Crimean War: A Russian Chronicle* (New York, 1978).

SIMMONS, E. J., *Introduction to Russian Realism: Pushkin, Gogol, Dostoevsky, Tolstoy, Chekhov, Sholokhov* (Bloomington, 1965).

SQUIRE, P. S., *The Third Department* (Cambridge, 1973).

TAYLOR, A. J. P., *The Struggle for Mastery in Europe, 1848–1918* (Oxford, 1954).

THADEN, E. C., *Conservative Nationalism in Nineteenth Century Russia* (Seattle, 1964).

TROYAT, H., *Divided Soul: The Life of Gogol* (New York, 1973).

_____, *Pushkin: A Biography* (New York, 1950).

VICKERY, W., *Alexander Pushkin* (New York, 1970).

WALICKl, A., *The Slavophile Controversy: A History of a Conservative Utopia in Nineteenth Century Russian Thought* (Oxford, 1975).

WHITTAKER, C. H., *The Origins of Modern Russian Education: An Intellectual Biography of Count Sergei Uvarov, 1786–1855* (DeKalb, IL, 1984).

ZIMMERMAN, J. E., *Midpassage: Alexander Herzen and European Revolution, 1847–1852* (Pittsburgh, 1989).

CHAPTER 14

Reform and Reaction

Russia's defeat in the Crimean War indicated to all classes and even to the emperor that fundamental political and social reform could wait no longer. Alexander I had held out the promise, although those who worked for reform mistook what he had in mind, that profound political and social change was forthcoming. Nicholas I had sought to still the demand for reform by providing the nation with the sort of state machinery that would give his people a fair and just government as he judged fairness and justice. Neither had succeeded in his good intentions. Now the nation would wait no longer.

The Tsar Liberator

There was much in the new sovereign's background to encourage the view that the "gentry era" would continue. Alexander II's (1855–1881) youth had passed under the stern direction of his father; the court poet Zhukovsky had done his plodding best to inspire the heir with a love of letters, but his pupil had shown more interest in the parade ground than in his books. Speransky had taught Alexander something of law, and other officials had added a smattering of finance, diplomacy, and military tactics. Nicholas had appointed him to the State Council, to a succession of military commands, and to the Council of Ministers. Although such contacts had exposed the heir only to conservative influences, at least they gave him more of an introduction to affairs of state than his father had had.

By temperament as well as by training the new tsar seemed disposed to resist reform. Alexander had little patience with those who disobeyed orders. Irritable and short of temper, he was often callous and cruel. Haughty and indifferent, he had none of the warmth and charm of his uncle, the first Alexander. Inclined to take the easy way, he was not a leader. He must have seemed flabby and colorless to those who compared him with his predecessors. Alexander II placed his trust in the autocracy and in the exercise of the autocratic power by the bureaucracy, in whose hands he felt the empire safe. The conservative nobles soon discovered that it was not from the gentry but from the bureaucrats that the tsar would take his cues.

The Law of February 19

The rural outbreaks of violence that greeted the new emperor—the flames of burning manor houses and the pitchfork murders of landowners—brought regular military expeditions into the countryside. The smell of smoke awakened Alexander to the realization that fundamental reform must come now. "Better to abolish bondage from above than to wait for it to abolish itself from below," he told the nobles of Moscow province.

Early in 1857 Alexander named a committee to consider ways of abolishing serfdom. To spur the effort, he appointed his liberal brother Constantine to the chairmanship. Provincial governors and marshals of the nobility received the tsar's approval should the nobles set up committees of their own. When their recommendations appeared it was apparent that the gentry had resigned themselves to the fact that bondage must go, but had determined to exact the highest possible price for the liberation of their serfs. Nobles from the rich but overpopulated black-soil provinces were not unwilling to free their serfs, but demurred at giving up much land. Those from the poor, gray-soil, central provinces were generous about giving land to the peasants, but pressed for substantial reimbursement for the obrok they would lose. The committee prepared a tentative draft of the emancipation manifesto, the tsar gave his approval, and on February 19/March 3, 1861, bondage came to an end for twenty-two million gentry-owned serfs. Ninety-nine years earlier the nobles had received their own freedom from the service obligation.

A general act freed all serfs from personal bondage; special acts dealt with house serfs, serfs working in factories, and serfs in provinces where local conditions dictated exceptional treatment. A special act set up machinery for redemption of land by the peasants, and another provided that appointed nobles called "village arbitrators" supervise the conversion and settle land disputes between landowners and peasants.

All twenty-two million landowners' serfs were immediately relieved of personal bondage to their former owners and could now own property, marry at will, and sue and be sued at law. No longer were they subject to sale as chattels,

Alexander II

or liable to transfer from field work to stable duty or house service at the master's whim, or be "sent for a soldier" or packed off to Siberia for insolence or insubordination. Now at last they were human beings in a legal sense, and this was the most important aspect of the emancipation.

Those who drafted the law of February 19 decided that the serfs must be freed with land and so provided the wherewithal to maintain themselves. To have freed twenty-two million people without land in a nation so overwhelmingly agricultural and so lacking in industry to absorb them would have caused chaos and misery. By the terms of the law, the peasants might work out with the landlord an agreement to purchase the amount of arable land contained in the allotments or plots they had cultivated for their own use under bondage. Because the area of land available to the former serfs for their sustenance may have been in dispute or deemed inadequate, the government required that the allotments be at least of a certain size, varying from district to district according to fertility of the soil.

When the peasants and former landowner agreed, under the eye of the arbitrator, on the amount, kind, and location of the land to be transferred, the government advanced four-fifths of the price to the estate owner. The peasants were to pay the other fifth, but the owner frequently had to forego that fifth because of the poverty of the people. The landholder received not cash but government bonds, the price of which soon fell to three-fourths of par as the nobles flooded the market with the securities. The peasants must pay to the government over a forty-nine-year period the amount, plus interest, that the government had advanced to the former slave owner. Before paying the noble the amount due, however, the government subtracted whatever the noble had borrowed; the gentry had mortgaged two thirds of all serfs for government loans. The land went not to the individual peasant in most cases but to the village community, which in its corporate capacity held the land in trust and collected money from the villagers to meet payment of the annual redemption dues to the government. Only when the state had received the last of the forty-nine payments was the land finally redeemed, at which time the individual peasant might claim a share of the village land to own and maintain, or to sell.

Peasants had the privilege of accepting only a quarter of the allotment that they otherwise would have received, and gaining exemption from the schedule of redemption payments that other villagers must pay. Because the amount of land in these "beggarly allotments" was nowhere near enough to provide for individual peasants and their families, the peasant who chose this settlement usually left it to the village and went to the city to find work. The house serfs—those who had been torn from the village to serve as domestics in the manor house— were freed without land. A few returned to their families in the village, some stayed on with the estate owner as hired hands, and others moved into the cities.

Not until the village had worked out a redemption agreement with the landowner was the peasant rid of the money payment—obrok—or labor service— barshchina—that was owed under bondage. Many villagers refused to believe that the law required the continuation of the hated services, and had to be whipped back to work under "temporary obligation"—that is, until a redemption agreement could be worked out with the estate owner. Indeed, the full statement of the emancipation law was heard in an air of skepticism as the landholder read the provisions to the village assembly. In the days of bondage the serfs had come to believe that the land belonged to those who tilled it. "We are yours but the land is ours," they had maintained to the gentry. How could it be that the tsar now ordered them to have only their allotments, roughly half the arable land on the estate? Furthermore, who could believe that they would actually have to pay for what was rightly theirs? The common reaction was to dismiss the law's provisions as a trick of the nobility. When it became clear that the enactment of February 19 had been correctly explained to them, the peasants commonly looked forward to a second act of emancipation that would turn over to them all the land and call an end to the payments and services that the first had required.

In some districts the villagers were slow to seek redemption agreements with the gentry. Some held back in the conviction that a second act of emancipation was forthcoming and that it would be better to wait for more favorable terms. Many put off a settlement with the landowner, however, because the burden of redemption payments, taxes, and contributions for village services was a greater burden than they had borne under serfdom. In 1881 the government ordered the completion of redemption agreements for all former serfs, of whom a sixth still had not accepted a settlement.

The annual payments to the government were so high, based on an inflated valuation of the land, that the peasant communities frequently defaulted.

Arrearages mounted until they had to be canceled, only to have the villages fall again into arrears. In 1896 the government announced a new schedule of payments to stretch the installments beyond 1950. During the revolution of 1905, however, all further payments were forgiven.

The amount and character of land transferred to the village community varied widely over Russia. In general, the grants tended to be parsimonious in the black soil areas of the south and liberal in the central and northeast districts of the country. Roughly half of the plow land on the former estate went to the landowner; the remainder went to the village, which commonly received a disproportionately small share of the woods, pasture, and meadow land. Because the peasants received at best only that amount of land that they had tilled for their own use under bondage, a task that had required their attention only three days a week, the land assigned them under the redemption program was sufficient only to occupy half their time. What was more important, the grant was not generous enough to provide them sustenance and a surplus with which to meet taxes, make redemption payments, and purchase necessary equipment. In many cases, individual peasants rented land from their former overseer; in others, the village community rented a block of land to work as a corporate enterprise. In the black soil provinces, where allotments were grossly inadequate, competitive bidding for the additional acres so necessary to permit the peasants to make ends meet drove rentals sharply upward; the land hunger in south Russia never ended.

For generations past, the gentry had farmed their portion of the estate as a production unit of two or more large fields. On the other hand, that part of the estate assigned the villager often had been scattered in small fields over the estate, some of them miles distant from the village. In each village field the land had been divided into a crazy quilt pattern of strips, typically a few yards wide, with several of such strips in each field assigned to each peasant household. In some villages the serf held the strips in heredity. In others, the village assembly periodically voted to reassign strips among heads of families, thus permitting equitable treatment by providing that all must share the good and the poor land in every field and making possible adjustments to allow for changes in size of families. Each village field, cut into ribbons of individual holdings, necessarily was tilled as a unit—the same crop planted at the same time and harvested at the same time so that the village cattle could be turned in to gather what the gleaners had missed. Until long after emancipation, one-third of the arable land lay fallow to recover its fertility, for there was a chronic shortage of animal fertilizer and frequent redistributions discouraged the peasant from investing commercial fertilizer in plots that might not be his to work next year.

If peasants achieved the dignity of human beings in a strictly legal sense by the law of February 19, in an economic sense they were hardly more free than before. They had exchanged the landowner for a new overseer, the mir, or village assembly, a master perhaps less cruel but often more exacting. The village assembly reassigned plots in the open fields, assessed and collected taxes levied by the national, provincial, or district government, and dispensed justice among its members as it had always done. After emancipation, the community was responsible for the police functions that the gentry had fulfilled under the old regime. Because the corporate village had to account to the government for the annual redemption payment, it was understandably merciless in wringing the appropriate share of the burden from each family head. Default was punishable by flogging, forced labor, seizure of property, or assignment to military service, and the peasants who managed to scrape together their share of the payment did not deal softly with one who tried to escape this obligation. It was almost impossible to withdraw from the community; travel beyond the village was illegal without a passport endorsed by the village elder. Emancipation had little meaning for the average *muzhik*, or peasant, at least in an economic sense.

In 1863, two million peasants living on crown lands and those belonging to the imperial family were freed. By 1866, the twenty-six million state-owned serfs or peasants won their freedom under conditions substantially better than those applying to landowners' serfs. Land allotments were more generous and redemption dues were lower, though for the most part the state peasants lived in north, central, and east Russia, where the quality of land was far below that in southern Russia, in which most of the privately owned barshchina serfs lived. The terms of the settlement for the state peasants were carried out through the agency of the mir, as was true with the landowners' serfs. The emancipations had freed the last 85 percent of the Russian people.

Reform of Local Government

The termination of bondage, and the collapse of the administrative authority of the estate owners over their "souls," forced a revision of local government machinery. The reforms that followed seemed designed to bring a measure of local self-government to Russia, but in practice the new institutions ultimately suffered near paralysis from bureaucratic interference. The Emancipation Act transferred to the village many administrative functions formerly performed by the gentry. From then on landowners were strangers in the midst of the peasants, living among them with all the sentimental memory of their past authority. The act combined several villages into a township. Heads of families, acting as an assembly, chose a township elder, an executive council, and a court to deal with minor civil and criminal offenses. The assembly rarely met, and its elder, together with the elders of the villages that made up the township, managed peasant affairs and passed sentence upon wrongdoers. Because the elders were required to report to officials appointed by the central government to control each district, there was little real self-government in the villages.

Early in 1864 the second great act of reform, the Zemstvo Law, put into operation the local government suggestions offered by Speransky in 1809. There were to be agencies of local self-government, called *zemstvos*, in each county and province. Each county was to elect an assembly—presided over by the marshal of the county nobility—chosen by three classes of electors: private landowners, village communities, and townspeople in the county. Each three thousand land allotments in the villages sent one delegate, and one or a group of landowners owning approximately the same amount of land also chose one delegate. There was similar representation for an equivalent amount of town property, the right of townsmen to vote being limited to those owning real estate or operating a business. The delegates selected from among their number an executive board of five or more members. The assembly itself might number as few as fourteen or as many as a hundred, depending on the amount of property and number of allotments in the county. The county assembly elected delegates to the provincial assembly, which chose its own zemstvo board.

The county zemstvo assembly met annually to vote the county budget, levy taxes, and approve projects to be carried out by the zemstvo board. Maintenance of county roads and bridges; construction and support of hospitals, asylums, prisons, and schools; the extension of medical and veterinary services; stimulation of industry and trade; instruction in improved farming methods; poor relief; public health needs—to such problems did the zemstvo devote its attention, the county zemstvo on the county level and the provincial zemstvo on the provincial level. However, so haltingly did the government put its own law into operation that fifty years after its promulgation, seven of the fifty provinces of European Russia had no zemstvo.

The new institutions of self-government suffered from the beginning from financial embarrassment. Part of what monies the zemstvos did take in went at government order for expenses from which the county or province drew no benefit—meeting the costs of drafts for military service and providing subsistence for various government officials. The zemstvo organization came increasingly under bureaucratic suspicion and restraint. Even so, the zemstvos did yeoman service for rural Russia in relieving suffering, reducing ignorance, and improving generally the miserable conditions that blighted agricultural life. The deliberations of the zemstvo assemblies provided political schooling for many men who later became leaders in national affairs. Those who participated in zemstvo politics were almost without exception citizens of honor and conscience, whose enthusiasm for the welfare of the lower classes made them suspect in official circles.

In 1870, Alexander ordered the cities to establish governmental machinery similar to the rural zemstvos. Each city was to have a legislative duma and an executive board headed by a mayor. The right to vote for delegates to the duma went only to taxpayers of three classes: those few who paid one-third of city taxes chose one-third of the delegates; those who paid the second third of taxes elected another third of the delegates; and the many small taxpayers also chose one-third. Control of the city council, then, rested with the relatively few large taxpayers, a fact deliberately intended to make the dumas conservative. As in the zemstvos, the duma chose its executive board and mayor. The city councils were to concern themselves with the same sort of problems with which the zemstvos might deal; their tax resources suffered similar limitations, and they came under the same suspicion and restriction that their country cousins endured as the government grew increasingly reactionary.

Judicial Reform

Pre-reform Russia had known only imperfect and limited justice, for an equitable court system catering to the needs of all classes without discrimination did not exist before 1864. Judges were notorious for their immorality, ignorance, and downright illiteracy; for the cruel sentences they imposed; for their readiness to wink at the law for a bribe; for their tenderness with the well-born; and their heartlessness with those who came before them empty-handed. However, the faults lay not entirely with the judges. Normally years and sometimes decades passed before cases were adjudicated. The secret police employed torture on witnesses and principals in inquisitorial sessions before the trial. Court sessions were secret; defendants were not allowed counsel; decisions were handed down without argument or cross-examination.

One committee after another had managed to postpone court reform. The end of bondage created a judicial void, however, that would permit no further delay. In 1864, the emperor signed the Judiciary Act, which applied various elements borrowed from Western Europe. Justice was to be available to all without discrimination. The judiciary was to be rid of bureaucratic meddling, and judges were subject to removal only for malfeasance. Trial by jury applied to all criminal and some civil cases. The judicial process was simplified and speeded up, and all trials were to be open to the public. Preliminary investigation was removed from the "unclean hands" of the police, and the accused was to enjoy representation by counsel and the right to appeal the judgment to a higher court. Cruel punishments, such as flogging and branding, were forbidden. Regulation of costs and fees aimed to prevent the corruption that had made a mockery of justice in the old courts.

A justice of the peace, chosen by the county zemstvo, heard minor cases on the local level, but a litigant might appeal the judgment to a monthly session of all the county justices of the peace sitting in the county capital. More serious cases went to the district court, final appeal lying with the Imperial Senate acting as supreme court. The imperial minister of justice chose the district court judges from a list of qualified candidates drawn up by the bar association.

The government established the court system slowly and piecemeal, not extending it to Kiev, for instance, until 1881. Neither jury trial nor justice of the peace ever reached the Polish and Lithuanian provinces. Only those owning 270 acres of land or other property worth 5,000 rubles were eligible for jury service. Many types of cases did not come within the purview of the new courts—church courts retained control over the clergy and over divorce cases among the laity; administrative tribunals punished wayward officials; courts-martial dealt with crimes against public safety; violations of publishing laws were tried in special courts; the police still handled disturbances of the peace; and crimes against the state could be decided without reference to any court.

Although the law suffered from limitations and further mutilation under the later reaction, the reform of the judiciary was in principle the most radical of all the great reforms. European liberals generally hailed it as qualifying Russia for admission to the family of civilized nations. The law profession thenceforth attracted persons of high purpose and integrity who fought stubbornly for the principle that legal justice should not be made subject to the whims of an arbitrary bureaucracy. To the dying days of the monarchy, those trained in the law marched in the vanguard of those who battled against tyranny and oppression.

Reform of the Army

The military establishment, particularly, stood indicted by the humiliating defeat in the Crimean War. The army had marshaled over two million troops, less than a fourth of whom had seen front-line service. Bungling mismanagement of supply, training, recruitment, and troop movement kept the rest lying idle in camps when they might better have remained in the villages to do the spring sowing. With the return to peace, the war minister, Dmitry Miliutin, moved to reform the many abuses from which the army suffered.

Since Peter the Great, Russia had maintained an enormous standing army in which the enlisted ranks served a term of twenty-five years. Landowners annually received a draft call for so many recruits, based on army needs at the time and on the number of male serfs they owned. Some of the gentry left the choice of recruits to the villages, whereas others sent up the names of insolent or lazy peasants. Condemnation to military service was a common form of punishment, and those who had their lives ruined by being sent away for twenty-five years looked upon the sentence as no better than penal servitude. Alexander I had established military colonies in part to lighten the burden of army service. Once in the army, the individual led a miserable life. Army contractors made fortunes from providing poor food, shoddy clothing, and drafty quarters. Flogging and running the gauntlet between files of men armed with birch rods or rifle butts were common punishments. In combat, troops learned to carry enemy positions with the bayonet rather than to rely upon their firearms, which were poor in comparison to those of Western armies. Worst of all, the burden of conscription fell chiefly on the villages. Nobles were exempt from military service, and those subject to the draft could evade it by hiring substitutes.

Reforms in the army spread over two decades. The hated military colonies, symbols of abject slavery against which there were perennial revolts, were abolished in 1857. Miliutin equipped the infantry with rifles to replace the smooth-bores in use during the Crimean War, reorganized the medical and supply services along Western lines, and prohibited the humiliating punishments characteristic of the old army. Court-martial procedure became less harsh and an accused soldier might have defense counsel. Schools for officers were modernized and the curriculum liberalized. Enlisted men were to learn to read and write, and the army became a significant adjunct to the nation's educational system.

In 1874 a new draft law reduced the term of active service from twenty-five years to six, after which discharged soldiers spent nine years in the reserve, when they engaged only in summer maneuvers. Finally, they spent five years in the militia, called up only in time of national emergency. Every male, regardless of class and without substitution, was liable for military service, and the one drafted out of four or five eligible was chosen by lot. Breadwinners and only sons were exempt, university students had to serve for only six months, high-school graduates for two years, those who had finished primary school for four years, and all students might volunteer and cut their required service by half.

Of all the great reforms, only those in the army continued unchanged in later years, for Miliutin stayed on as minister of war to the end of Alexander II's reign. The democratizing effect of subjecting all classes to service, of teaching the peasant soldier to read and write, and of abolishing the bestial treatment of the soldiers, created in the minds of conservatives a fear that the army might prove unreliable when called upon to defend the state. Liberals, however, welcomed this end of military bondage with the claim that now the soldier could look upon each person's service as fair and honorable.

Reforms in Education and Censorship

All levels of education had suffered from the crippling policy of Nicholas I, but it was the universities that endured the sternest regulations. To make it easy for police to spot them in a crowd, students had to dress in uniform and wear their hair in a peculiar trim. A government official, the inspector of morals, kept strict check on student conduct in and out of school. The minister of education approved texts for every course. Professors had to submit advance copies of their lectures to the Ministry of Education and deliver their lectures precisely as they had written them. Only theologians might teach philosophy or psychology, and logic and metaphysics were not in the curriculum. Nicholas reduced the number of students allowed to enroll in every Russian university and sharply increased the fees in an effort to ensure that only sons of the safely conservative wealthy would attend. There were fewer than four thousand students in the six Russian universities in 1855, of whom over two-thirds were sons of nobles, officials, or the clergy; half the rest came from the merchant class, and the remainder were sons of artisans or state peasants.

Students at all Russian universities grew restless after the accession of Alexander II and demanded educational reforms. Soon after the emancipation, the tsar appointed as minister of education the unbending Count E. V. Putiatin, who issued a new code of university regulations outlawing all student organizations and forbidding students to assemble for any purpose without the consent of university officials. The new code precipitated further demonstrations which ended in street fights between students and police or soldiers. Three hundred students at the University of St. Petersburg were arrested and many expelled. The more the Cossack whips danced on their backs, the more determined the students became to put an end to their own bondage until the tsar finally realized that repression would accomplish nothing and replaced Putiatin with A. V. Golovnin, who was well known for his liberal views.

In 1863, Golovnin issued a new code of regulations granting autonomy to Russian universities. Each faculty received the right to elect university officials. Responsibility for disciplinary action was assigned to a court of three professors. A faculty council was to control instruction, requirements for graduation, and approval of university publications. Courses proscribed in the preceding reign returned to the curriculum. The code abolished limitation on enrollment and reduced fees, waiving them for those too poor to pay. The universities were still not open to women, who customarily went abroad for their education; nor did the students recover the privilege of organizing their own associations.

A new regulatory code issued in 1864 reorganized the secondary-school system, providing for two types of high schools. The curriculum of the "classical school," emphasizing the Greek and Latin languages and the humanities, was designed for the student who would enter the university. The other category omitted the classics and concentrated on the sciences, to prepare the graduate for study in technical or professional institutions or for immediate entry into commerce or industry. The graduate of the second type was not eligible for admission into the university. Neither type of high school admitted girls, although a number of private schools catered to daughters of the gentry. The class character of the school system, which directed sons of nobles and wealthy merchants into the universities and those of the middle and lower classes into trade schools, was clearly intentional. The secondary schools were completely controlled by the minister of education, whose temperament and outlook determined the curriculum, course content, point of view, and personnel for every secondary school in the land. Women still might not attend the old universities, but women's colleges opened in Kiev and Kazan.

The weakest link in the educational chain was primary education. Official records in the last year of the reign of Nicholas claimed 7,500 primary schools with an enrollment of 216,000 in a population of over 70,000,000. Official estimates were notoriously inaccurate, however, and many schools existed only on paper. Of the schools in operation, the Holy Synod maintained approximately half, and the Ministry of State Domains maintained the other half in communities of state-owned peasants. With the rare exception of an occasional school operated by an enlightened noble for the local peasants, the serfs of the gentry enjoyed no education facilities whatsoever.

In 1864, the emperor approved a system of primary education. Schools were built and maintained by the communities they served, and attendance was open to all who could afford the tuition set by local authorities. In each county a board made up of zemstvo members, a cleric, an inspector, and the chief of the district police supervised the primary schools and employed the teachers. In practice, the inspector controlled the system under the supervision of the Ministry of Education. The law proclaimed it to be the duty of primary teachers to inculcate religious and moral principles and disseminate "useful elementary knowledge." Because zemstvo budgets were pitifully small and had to meet many local needs, primary school facilities came only slowly into existence. By 1914, however, the zemstvos were spending nearly a third of their budgets on primary education, and illiteracy was declining.

Reactionary ministers of education—for example, Golovnin's successor, Count Dmitry Tolstoy, who stayed on for fourteen years—attempted in later years to cripple the educational system created in the 1860s. Teachers were constantly under suspicion and subject to discharge without hearing. Textbooks and lectures were censored, curricula dictated, the views of teachers and students secretly scrutinized, and their personal associations reported. As it turned out, the more rigid the censorship became, the more determined was the fight against it and against the bureaucracy that decreed it. Many students reacted to the flogging, expulsion, or exile that constantly threatened them by joining a secret organization whose avowed aim was to put an end to the despotism under which all society languished.

The closing years of the reign of Nicholas had witnessed a respectable increase in the number of newspapers and periodicals, although the law, requiring all copy to be submitted to official censors before publication, effectively gagged the press. With the accession of Alexander II, the government vacillated between relaxing the censorship laws and forbidding discussion of social problems.

A new censorship law, referred to as "temporary regulations" appeared in 1865 and remained in operation for forty years. Books of more than ten pages were freed from preliminary censorship, a provision aimed to keep pamphlet literature and political broadsides under control. The government, of course, could confiscate all copies of a book discovered after publication to be subversive. The minister of interior received power to decide the degree of censorship under which newspapers and journals might publish; a publication might be warned, fined, or forced to suspend publication if it criticized the government or discussed forbidden matters. The list of punishable offenses lengthened after 1865, and soon the press slipped back into the mire of bureaucratic oppression from which it had escaped momentarily in the first decade of the reign. One vigorously liberal periodical, *The Bell*, published in London by Alexander Herzen, managed to escape the official controls, as copies were regularly smuggled in from London.

Economic and Financial Reform

All the so-called great reforms would cost money, and this made the minister of finance an important administrative figure. The nation's poverty and backwardness did not disappear immediately when the emperor signed whatever reform was before him. Russia's illiteracy rate was scandalous. Only schools in great number could reduce that rate of illiteracy, and schools cost money. Public health and welfare—sanitation, hospitals, crime, and the relief of poverty—all demanded attention if the nation were to appear civilized. An improved transportation system was imperative from a political, a military, and a social point of view. Tax arrears would continue to mount unless those who tilled the soil could get their produce to market. Rural distress would go unrelieved unless the means for relief could reach the villages. Russia's limitless supply of personnel would go unused in time of war unless that supply could reach the training centers and the front. All these problems ended up on the desk of the minister of finance.

The need to modernize the nation's finances became apparent to the new emperor. The first step was to send someone to Western Europe to learn modern budget procedures and replace the confused array that Alexander II inherited from his father. The man who spent some time in Prussia and in the United States and who became the first finance minister after the budget reform of 1861 was Michael Reutern. He held this position until 1878.

Reutern was keenly aware of the nation's need to reform the currency. He was equally aware that in the absence of a significant program of railroad building, the economy would languish, with consequent disastrous effects on the nation's prosperity and its ability to tap the "paying powers of the population." His first step was to seek more revenue by increasing taxes—he nearly doubled the soul taxes over their pre-emancipation level. Yet, the poverty of the countryside placed an absolute limit on this source of income. His next step was to borrow heavily abroad, but this only made the problem more difficult for his successors, for a default in interest payments would surely dry up foreign sources of credit. During the Russo-Turkish war of 1877–78, the payment of interest on foreign loans cost over a third of the government's budget.

Reutern's most constructive step toward solving the government's woes was to stimulate the building of railroads. The effect would be to encourage both industry and agriculture by bringing markets closer to their sources of production. The idea was sound, but the shortage of native capital committed Russia to an overreliance on foreign borrowing, and the willingness of the government to leave railroad construction to private enterprise invited abuses in capitalization and in construction.

Furthermore, the nation's poverty and its effect on tax revenue, the political unrest from which Russia was never free, and the vicious anti-Semitism of officialdom made foreign bankers reluctant to invest heavily in any Russian enterprise. The German chancellor, Bismarck, was confident of his ability to bend Russian policy to German liking simply by drying up his government's loans to St. Petersburg. When French sources became available in the last decade of the century as a consequence of the Franco-Russian Alliance, Russian foreign policy became more subservient to the will of the French Foreign Office. Foreign policy, in fact, made a mockery of Reutern's best efforts to build the economy and to put government finances on a sound basis. The Russo-Turkish war that broke out in 1877 was so costly that soon treasury receipts and expenditures had returned to their earlier chaos. The government's choice was not a happy one. Either it must leave Balkan Slavs to Turkish control or it must postpone economic and financial progress. It chose to rescue the Balkan Slavs.

With all the problems facing the finance minister, the years immediately following the accession of Alexander II were years of economic growth. Talk of emancipation of the serfs inspired the business community to dream of a free labor market and a consequent fall in production costs. The government legalized the limited liability of corporations, and the sum of private capital invested in corporate organizations jumped four times between 1856 and 1859. By 1879, nearly six hundred limited-liability enterprises were in operation, with a capital of three quarters of a billion rubles, most of it subscribed by Russians. The individual state-owned banks functioning before 1860 closed down after the government had destroyed public confidence in them by heavy borrowing during the Crimean War; they were replaced by a central state bank designed to stimulate commerce and stabilize the currency. Count Reutern was most anxious, however, that private interests rather than the government should lead the way in developing the economy. Private banks, savings and loan associations, and mortgage companies appeared for the first time in the 1860s, and their numbers and volume of business rose steadily through Alexander's reign.

By the death of Alexander II, Russia possessed fifteen thousand miles of railway, constructed in part by foreign syndicates but chiefly by Russian companies with money borrowed by the government from foreign bankers. Fifty thousand miles of state-owned telegraph lines appeared during Alexander's reign. Foreign trade more than doubled between 1860 and 1880, although Russia's share of expanding world commerce remained the same.

Although private capital and management undoubtedly profited from the post-emancipation boom, the lot of the workers failed to improve. Unsanitary and unsafe working conditions, overcrowded housing, and a working day twelve to eighteen hours long typified industry as the coming of the Industrial Revolution brought to Russia the same hardships Western Europe and the United States had endured earlier. Management ordinarily paid wages quarterly or semiannually, and fines for absenteeism or damaging equipment ran as high as one-fourth of the annual wage. The substitution of machine- for hand-methods of production and the flow of population from rural to urban areas in an attempt to escape the growing poverty of the village produced an expanded labor force and a competition for employment that drove real wages down approximately a fourth in the generation after 1860.

The dawn of industrial capitalism broke slowly in Russia for various reasons. Certainly, the politico-economic climate was less favorable there than in the West, where a government policy of laissez faire had freed business growth from interference. A shortage of investment capital at home, and the reluctance of foreign capital to enter a nation so frequently threatened by rebellion, hampered economic progress. The return of many factory workers to the village during the slack season of production slowed the appearance of an industrial labor force skilled in modern manufacturing techniques. The encouragement given to immigration of foreign organizers and technicians suggests a shortage of management skills so necessary to industrial development. Perhaps the lag in cultural tradition and the lack of civilized habits among the mass of the people accounted in part for the halting pace at which the nation approached industrial maturity.

The Significance of the Great Reforms

The full consequences of the great reforms were not immediately apparent; nor in some cases could they become so for another half-century. In general, they constituted a beginning rather than an end, and in some cases even the beginning was more apparent than real. The emancipation of the serfs, for example, did little to change life in the villages. In the countryside life went on, indeed well into the twentieth century, pretty much as it had gone on for centuries. The primitive methods of working the soil, the slavish toil of farm work, the brutish nature of personal relationships, the simple religious faith and yet the contempt for the village priest, the ancient legends and folk songs, the crude diet, dress, and dwelling, the respect for the person of the tsar and yet the burning hatred of his officials and all they represented—such things the emancipation did little to alter. For the mass of peasants, now technically free, the future held out small hope of a better life. Rural Russia remained sullen, hostile, resentful of being cheated by emancipation, ready at the least provocation to lash out against authority.

Once the government promulgated the reforms, it seemed reluctant to carry them forward, as though it had no confidence in its own handiwork or as though it resented the pressures that had forced its hand. Yet no matter how slowly society moved forward into Western civilization, the great reforms set the nation upon a course from which there could be no turning back.

The "Tsar Liberator" and his successors may have done their best to weaken the reforms, but there could be no return to the old feudal society. Bondage once swept away could not be reimposed. The voice of local governmental institutions might be hushed, but it could never be stilled. The Western system of justice might be perverted, but its ideal could never be effaced. Economic reform made Russia a member of the capitalistic system of the West, and even the cataclysmic upheaval of 1917 could not relieve the nation of the economic interdependence of modern states on one another.

Russian society accepted the changes of the sixties and called for still further reform. The repression that followed those changes could not for long be successful and had rather the reverse effect of calling into existence a succession of popular movements whose aim was to speed up national progress toward the new social milieu envisaged by the great reforms.

The Polish Rising

The oppressive reign of Nicholas I was no more successful among Poles than among Russians in halting the rumblings of discontent. An émigré center established in Paris under Prince Adam Czartoryski clamored for an independent nation under the liberal constitution of 1791. Another agency, the Polish Democratic Society in London, demanded not only an end to Russian rule but a radical political and land reform program. Both groups maintained contact with Poles at home, and both hoped to enlist the support of Western European states in the struggle for independence.

The accession of Alexander II brought hope that the new tsar would lift the pall of oppression that had settled over Poland after the 1830 rising. Indeed, there were several moves toward moderation. Prince Michael Gorchakov, the new viceroy, listened patiently to Polish pleas for reform. An amnesty freed those who had languished in Siberian prison camps and pardoned others who had fled abroad. St. Petersburg permitted the opening of a medical college in the Polish capital and hinted at the revival of the University of Warsaw. With the tsar's approval, the Poles organized an agricultural society whose members soon passed beyond a consideration of land reform to a discussion of the restoration of Polish liberty. In 1861 Alexander named a Council of State to receive petitions from Poles and charged a newly appointed committee on education and religion to restore the use of the Polish language in the schools. The tsar established councils of self-government for towns, districts, and provinces, and in some respects emancipated the Jews. A Polish committee was allowed to grant modest land reforms, which, however, left the peasants with even less land than their Russian counterparts received at the same time. Grand Duke Constantine, credited with liberal views, replaced Gorchakov as viceroy in a further attempt to calm Polish opposition to Russian rule.

Nothing less than independence would satisfy the Poles, and the few who had cooperated in carrying through the reforms faced ridicule as traitors to the cause of Polish nationalism. Attempted assassinations of Grand Duke Constantine and of Poles who had collaborated with him miscarried, and in retaliation, an order went out for widespread drafting of Polish young men into the Russian army. This produced the creation of a left-wing revolutionary committee in Warsaw which called for a national rising and proclaimed Polish independence. A conservative committee of landowners appeared at the same time in an attempt to prevent the movement from becoming a radical social revolution, and the two groups working at cross purposes caused the peasantry to become suspicious of the revolt. A pitifully small Polish army scattered at the appearance of a Russian force many times its size, but guerrillas carried on sporadic fighting for more than a year. The revolution in Russia that Polish nationalists hoped would catch fire from the spark in their own country did not materialize, and the nations of Western Europe limited their intervention to feeble protests that St. Petersburg met with firm rejection. Prussia's Bismarck supported Russia throughout the crisis, partly in fear that a revived Poland would demand a return of the territory annexed by Prussia during the partitions, and partly in the hope of winning Russia's benevolent neutrality in the coming Austro-Prussian conflict.

The rising of 1863 had been gentry-inspired and gentry-led. For the most part, the peasantry had stood aloof. After the rebellion collapsed, the Russian government sought, by introducing certain reforms, to make permanent the split between the upper and lower classes and so reduce the likelihood of united Polish action in the future. It divided the great estates and assigned the peasants allotments considerably more generous than those provided by the earlier emancipation act in Russia. The Polish peasants paid no redemption dues but contributed through taxes, as did all landowners, noble and non-noble, to the fund from which the gentry received reimbursement for loss of their land. By a reform of local government, township assemblies included gentry and peasants on equal terms, a provision that tended to submerge gentry influence under a sea of peasant votes.

By a policy of stern repression and Russification St. Petersburg sought to stamp out every vestige of Polish nationalism after 1864. Russians replaced Poles in official positions. The University of Warsaw became a Russian university. Use of the Russian language was required, first in administrative circles, then in secondary and primary schools. The Roman Catholic Church, whose priests generally had sided with the insurgents, suffered increasing restrictions, and Uniats were forced back into the Russian Orthodox Church. The Poles suffered stern punishment for their failure to appreciate the earlier mild measures of their Russian superior.

Revolutionary and Reform Thought and Action

News of Nicholas's death in 1855 brought a sense of relief to many Russians. Those who had defied the late emperor wanted to believe the best of his successor. The imperial announcement that the Crimean War had ended closed with an expression of hope that the ''internal organization'' of the nation might improve and that ''equal justice to all'' might come about. Those who had detested the father now applauded the son without pondering the vague terms in which Alexander II had couched his hopes. Their resentment was all the keener when the great reforms proved to be, as many liberals viewed them, puny and halfhearted. The resistance they mounted appeared in a variety of programs. Individuals offered some, organizations others; some were moderate and reformist, others were strident and called for violent action; some appeared inside Russia, others in some western sanctuary. The battle against the regime went on with rising fury and ended only with the emperor's assassination.

Herzen greeted Alexander's vague promise in 1856 of better things to come with the words, ''Thou hast triumphed, O Galilean.'' His words turned to gall, however, when the terms of the emancipation became clear. An editorial in his fortnightly newspaper, *The Bell*, asked ''What do the people need?'' The answer was ''land and freedom,'' words that rallied opponents of autocracy for generations. Herzen criticized the terms of the emancipation as fraudulent, insisting upon a more generous land settlement immediately without any increase in peasant dues, and he demanded a national parliament chosen by universal suffrage. Herzen was not so naïve as to suppose that the government would meekly surrender. Thus he urged the appearance of an underground press and secret societies to raise the peasants, ever the element in society that he most admired. He called for a Polish uprising, although the one that came later in 1863 certainly needed no prompting from Herzen. When in 1861 the government closed the universities to put an end to student riots, Herzen urged them to ''go to the people'' in protest against oppression. The ''going-to-the-people'' movement, the Russian populist movement, was the answer to Herzen's admonition. His death in 1870 silenced the voice of a leading advocate for reform.

Nicholas Chernyshevsky, whose articles in the periodical *The Contemporary* had praised Alexander for his promise to free the serfs, bitterly resented the terms of the emancipation when they appeared. His persistent call for revolutionary socialism—hardly a liberal stance—cost him his own freedom. He lay two years in a dungeon in the capital before being sentenced to twenty years in Siberia. While in prison, he wrote the tendentious novel *What is To Be Done?* It achieved such popularity among young radicals that it set the style for political novels, less for any literary merit it revealed than for its socialist preaching. Chernyshevsky was Belinsky's heir as a literary critic, and his essays in *The Contemporary* encouraged Turgenev, Dostoevsky, and Leo Tolstoy.

Michael Bakunin, son of a wealthy nobleman, roamed over Europe and America from 1843 on, preaching not liberalism but revolution wherever he went and taking part personally in as many uprisings as possible. Herzen called him "the wanderer." He joined Karl Marx in founding the First International in 1864, but quarreled with the German over the role of the state in revolution and suffered expulsion from the organization. Bakunin traced all social ills, especially crime and corruption, to the state. He preached the abolition of the state, marriage, the family, religion, and private property. Defiance of such social conventions as marriage and the family was part of the creed of many Western social rebels as well as of Russia's "romantic exiles" who settled in France, Italy, and Switzerland. While he received the title of "father of anarchism," he deserved it less than Proudhon and others whose works he found time to read. He owed much to Marx, whose attitude toward religion and property he shared.

Herzen was one of those "men of the forties" who inherited the ideas of the Decembrists and their dream of political reform. The novelist Ivan Turgenev, author of the popular *Fathers and Sons*, was another. He spent much of his life in Germany and France and lost touch with the younger generation whose impatience with moderation he deplored. As one of the "fathers" of the older generation, he believed that Russia should wait for economic growth and popular education to bring ultimate reform.

The "men of the sixties," the "sons" of the Turgenev novel, had no confidence that the political reform and parliamentarianism that satisfied Herzen would bring social justice; such superficial change would only impose the rule of a landed or commercial aristocracy. The sons would have none of the fathers' liberalism; only socialism of some sort, in which political formality was unimportant, appealed to these young adults of the sixties. Nor could they abide the patience of the old; the gradualism that Herzen had seemed willing to accept, at least before the Act of February 19, must give way to violent action.

They placed their confidence in the Narod—the people, the masses of Russia. Narod, however, meant the rural masses, for there was no urban industrial base of any strength in this land so overwhelmingly agricultural. Of vital importance was the mir, or village assembly, where heads of peasant families gathered in a setting of social equality unknown outside Russia. The peasant village symbolized a socialism of sorts, a welcome kind of socialism that knew nothing of the slum evils of the industrial West.

Among the readers of Turgenev's novel were young men and women of all classes of society, a few from noble families but many who came from families of merchants, priests, officials, doctors, and teachers—the *raznochintsy*. Many were university students. They rejected the humanistic interests of an earlier time and focused their attention on material values. Technical knowledge would bring industrial progress, and therein lay the hope for justice. They earned the name "nihilist," a term that Turgenev used disparagingly in *Fathers and Sons*, by their insistence upon accepting nothing—hence the term nihilism—that contradicted the principles of science.

Dmitry Pisarev, a landowner's son who welcomed the title of nihilist, called upon the individual to reject the past and advance into the future along the path indicated by reason, science, and "thinking realism." Old values in art and literature must be cast aside unless they served social needs. The Third Section arrested him for disseminating revolutionary materials and incarcerated him in prison where he was free to continue his writing. He died in 1868 at the age of twenty-eight.

An early call for violence came from P. G. Zaichnevsky, a landowner's son who studied the French socialists and later was attracted by the youth movements of Central Europe. In imitation of the declarations of Mazzini's secret society, Young Italy, Zaichnevsky published a revolutionary manifesto, *Young Russia*, while in prison. In it he proposed an immediate violent revolution to establish a new democratic socialist society free of such impedimenta as marriage, the family, and property. The village assembly would issue parcels of land to anyone who needed it, but for use only. "Social factories" under elected managers would manufacture goods to be sold in publicly owned shops. Regional and national assemblies chosen by universal suffrage would provide the necessary legislation. The emancipation of women, a free education for all, and the elimination of class would bring the end of privilege, ignorance, discrimination, and tyranny. He died in Siberian exile in 1896.

Another who preached violence was Serge Nechaev—the "Jacobin" his friends called him—a student at the University of St. Petersburg. He drafted, perhaps in cooperation with Bakunin whom he visited in Switzerland, a detailed plan for his secret terrorist society and added to it a catechism that directed his followers to kill, steal, and spy on anyone upon whom Nechaev's disfavor might fall. When he became suspicious of the loyalty of one disciple, he ordered him killed. Dostoevsky immortalized the murder in his novel *The Possessed*. Nechaev spent the end of his life in a dungeon in St. Petersburg, dying in 1882.

Peter Tkachev was first arrested for revolutionary activity in 1861 at the age of seventeen, but later escaped and fled abroad. In Geneva he published a journal, *Nabat*—tocsin—in which he insisted that true reform could not succeed without a tightly knit, highly disciplined elite to seize power. Tsardom must be overturned quickly, for a prolonged period of peaceful propagandizing would permit the landed aristocracy and the bourgeoisie to gather the strength to survive. Lenin later acknowledged his debt to Tkachev, who was not, however, a Marxist;

Tkachev's focus was not the proletariat but the peasantry. He spent his last years in Paris, dying there in 1886.

Peter Lavrov, a colonel of artillery, came before a court-martial for showing "disrespect" for the emperor and an intention to publish "pernicious ideas." He was exiled to a lonely spot in the country, a common sentence for a crime not sufficiently serious to warrant imprisonment. Many of Lavrov's essays were published abroad under the title *Historical Letters*. The author indicted the regime for permitting the economic enslavement of peasants and urban workers to benefit the few. He reasoned with those few to nourish an "inner sense of justice" and to take up the moral responsibility of striving to create a society in which all would share equally. When university students demonstrated in the streets in 1869 against the repression of the authorities, Lavrov urged them to pay their debt to the masses, whose toil made their education possible—to teach socialism and democracy to the people in factories and villages, and to prepare them to fight for those principles. Only the people could win their own freedom, but the students, turned Populist missionaries, could show the masses the need to rise against their oppressors.

Lavrov's disciples in the 1870s formed circles whose members went into schools, factories, and villages as their mentor had called them to do. They took with them socialist tracts and taught and preached to whatever gatherings would listen. These were the true Narodniks—those who went to the people as Herzen had urged. Nicholas Tchaikovsky formed one of these circles in St. Petersburg. Years later Tchaikovsky and some of his friends sailed to America to set up a communist farm community in Kansas. When the colony collapsed, its members returned to Russia.

Mark Natanson and his wife Olga joined the Tchaikovsky Circle. So, too, did Sophia Perovsky, daughter of the governor-general of St. Petersburg. Another member of the circle was Prince Peter Kropotkin, whose *Memoirs of a Revolutionist* recalled the tendency of young idealists to join several socialist "circles of self-development" at once, the louder to proclaim their detestation of the regime.

Hundreds of young Narodniks, or Populists, men and women, went into the villages in the early 1870s to share the lives of the peasants and to take upon their own shoulders some of the drudgery of life in the poverty-ridden countryside. They served as midwives, teachers, veterinarians, social workers, and laborers. They talked untiringly to the peasants, a few of whom listened perhaps with some cynicism toward these young people who showed none of the gnarled hands, rough language, and coarse manners of the typical muzhik. The very peasants whom the Populists sought to help often turned them over to the police; hundreds were brought into open court where judges permitted them to air their views to the applause of the many who filled the room. Some welcomed arrest in order to lecture the court to the accompaniment of the cheers of the crowd.

The police rounded up hundreds of Narodniks, members of various circles. Many were sons and daughters of wealthy and noble families. Of the nine hundred who were sentenced to prison or to Siberian exile, a third were children of nobles, a hundred were from families of officials, and two hundred were sons or daughters of Orthodox priests. Police pressure dampened the ardor of the Populists; many became disgusted with the stolid peasants who would not bestir themselves even in their own behalf. The young radicals came round to the view that they should not wait for popular support but must themselves attack the regime in the interest of society.

Disillusioned by the indifference and hostility of rural Russia, Mark Natanson joined others in 1876 to form a secret organization named Land and Freedom, the title of a society briefly active in the early sixties, which derived from Herzen's identification of land and freedom as the primary needs of all Russians but of peasants most of all. The new society would solicit the support and the skills of all who opposed the autocracy and everything it represented. Thus far, young radicals had wasted their energy by letting themselves be led off in several directions by Lavrov, Bakunin, Nechaev, and others. This splintering was a fatal weakness that Land and Freedom sought to avoid. It offered an array of choices to those who would fight the government. One who joined the administrative section could forge passports and other papers that would facilitate travel inside and outside Russia; another could work among students to recruit new members and to promote student unrest; a third might mingle with factory workers to incite strikes and riots; a fourth could seek peasant support in another going-to-the-people movement whose hopes, incidentally, proved as forlorn as those of the earlier Populists. If one joined the "disorganizing" section, the person might kill members of the police or other public officials in revenge for the brutality with which Narodnik prisoners were treated; a disorganizer might rescue Populists from jails or seek out traitors and police spies who always bedeviled such popular movements. The work of this last category met with the most success. It brought down many officials, and members seemed confident that the assassination of a sufficient number of officials, or of the tsar himself, might destroy the government.

In 1878, a noble's thirty-year-old daughter, Vera Zasulich, who at nineteen had been imprisoned for revolutionary activity, shot and wounded the chief of police of St. Petersburg. In a jury trial, the judge handed down a verdict of not guilty and was wildly cheered for it. An attempt to rearrest her failed, and she fled abroad. Mild and gentle people in the Land and Freedom movement felt an increasing sense of revulsion at such bloodletting. The squeamish ones left the organization to found the Land Partition or Black Partition, which would work openly for a new land settlement, the most persistent problem plaguing rural Russia. The people of violence created their own secret society, the People's Will, whose aim was to assassinate public officials. In 1881, several members killed the emperor with a bomb thrown on a signal given by Sophia Perovsky. She and several others died on the gallows for their efforts.

The reform and revolutionary movements in the reign of Alexander II continued to reflect the two extremes that had appeared among the Decembrists in the time of the first Alexander. One segment of Russian thought and action sought by peaceful propaganda to win popular support for continued reform and hoped to convert the government to such a policy. These advocates tended to place their confidence in the peasants and to concentrate on the problem of land reform to the exclusion of all others. Opposed to these moderates were the radicals, who despaired both of government sincerity in carrying through fundamental reforms and of peasant support for the revolution that alone could rid the nation of its wretchedness and oppression. Some men and women believed that only among the working class in the cities could they find appreciation of the need for thoroughgoing social revolution. Many others, reasoning that agriculture was Russia's primary concern, sought peasant support for agricultural reform—the breaking up of great estates, an end to redemption dues, and indeed peasant uprisings. These radicals were naïvely confident that terror and assassination could sweep away the old regime.

The Artists' Defiance

Pisarev, the harbinger of nihilism, had urged individuals—he was talking to the artists and the intellectuals—to become unchained from the peculiar sort of bondage that held them in thralldom. However, even before Pisarev undertook his serious writing in prison after 1862, Russian musicians were declaring their own independence. In the early sixties several brilliant composers defied the conservatism of the Russian Music Society and the St. Petersburg Conservatory and set up the Free School of Music in the capital in 1862. Of "The Five," or "The Invincible Band"—César Cui, Mili Balakirev, Modest Moussorgsky, Alexander Borodin, and Nicholas Rimsky-Korsakov—only Balakirev was a professional musician; Cui was a military engineer, Moussorgsky an army officer, Borodin a chemistry professor, and Rimsky-Korsakov a naval officer. They resented the popularity of Wagner and of Italian opera and embraced realism with the same enthusiasm as did their contemporaries, the men of the sixties, in political and social thought. They composed symphonies, concertos, sonatas, ballet music, and operas, using heroic national themes and lacing folk melodies into their compositions. The glorification of the peasant appealed as much to Russian composers as it did to Herzen, Lavrov, Nicholas Tchaikovsky, and the Narodniks. In a commentary on his Fourth Symphony, Peter Tchaikovsky sought to make clear to a layperson what his musical language proclaimed: "If you can find no happiness in yourself, *go to the people*." The feeling ran strong among musicians, painters, and writers that "truth and justice," indispensable ingredients of happiness, were to be found only in the Narod. Appropriately, the Fourth Symphony carries scenes in a peasant village as well as the harsh and ominous blare of a military band.

Painters, too, staged their own revolt against the classical tradition of the Academy of Art, the humanistic approach in the way that Pisarev scorned. His emphasis on realism and social concerns received expression in the paintings of Vasily Vereshchagin, whose work condemned the idiocy of war less in a

Volga Boatmen *by Ilya Repin*

philosophical way than in a starkly social way; his *Apotheosis of War* shows a pyramid of skulls to be a monument to the "brave generals" who were its architects. Ilya Repin's *Volga Boatmen* pictures the brutish life of the peasants who pulled river boats up the Volga by ropes that bow them down and cut sores into their shoulders; only a blond youth holds up his head in defiance of those who would break his spirit.

The sixties and seventies produced their literary giants, inheritors of Pushkin, Gogol, Lermontov, and Belinsky not so much in a philosophical manner as in their brilliant craftsmanship. The Golden Age of Russian literature that had begun near the end of the reign of Alexander I continued without interruption to 1880. Whereas the earlier writers reflected the romanticism and the philosophical idealism of their time, their successors in the reign of Alexander II turned to the very realism that other artists and the political activists were adopting.

Ivan Turgenev, who studied at Russian universities and then in Berlin, spent most of his life in France and Germany. The son of an impoverished noble, Turgenev knew rural Russia and wrote about the gentry and the peasants with equal facility. *A Sportsman's Sketches* appeared in 1852 and, with its tender stories of the human emotions that even serfs could feel, made emancipation more acceptable than it might otherwise have been. His novels dealt with the Russia of his time and won acceptance immediately. *A Nest of Gentle Folk*, *On the Eve, Fathers and Sons*, and *Smoke* found an enthusiastic audience in England and America. By the end of the century, when the works of Tolstoy and Dostoevsky as well as those of Turgenev had long since been available in English, the British critic Arnold Bennett argued that the twelve best novels in literature were all Russian and six of them were by Turgenev.

Count Leo Tolstoy, whose father owned two thousand serfs, found so little challenge at the University of Kazan that he did not bother to graduate. After

Leo Tolstoy telling his grandchildren "A Tale About the Cucumber"

some years in the army—he served in the Crimean War and published his *Tales of Sevastopol* serially while an artillery officer in the Caucasus—he spent the rest of his long life writing some of the greatest novels and short stories in any language and turning in his mature years to anarchism, nihilism, pacifism, apostolic Christianity, and progressive education. He was constantly at war with the authorities; he fought the stifling censorship, the obscurantist Orthodox Church, the social conventions of his day and his class, the bureaucracy, and the secret police. His estate, Yasnaya Polyana, became a mecca for admirers from all over the world.

Tolstoy's masterpieces include, among many others, *War and Peace*, the epic novel that carried the story of Russia before, during, and after the Napoleonic invasion of 1812; *Anna Karenina*, telling of war within a family; and *Resurrection*, the story of a man at war within himself. His novels revealed his defiance of social conventions—he affected the dress of a peasant and even worked in the fields with them—and his contempt for the pomp and artificiality that he saw in Western society. He scorned property, put his holdings in his wife's name, and pleaded poverty while keeping his servants about him.

The life of Fedor Dostoevsky (1821–1881), a doctor's son, parallels the period of the Golden Age. His first novel, *Poor Folk*, was published when he was twenty-five. *Crime and Punishment*, *The Idiot*, *The Possessed*, and *The Brothers Karamazov* reveal the unique ability of this "tortured genius" to "plumb all the depth of the human soul," as he said of his own efforts. His life was as sordid and troubled as that of many of his characters. He was an epileptic, a gambler always in debt, a distraught lover of a woman so evil that he called her "infernal." Politically, Dostoevsky toyed with socialism and joined the Petrashevsky Circle, but turned against his youthful moderation to become a Slavophile and a champion of Orthodoxy. He was anti-Semitic, anti-Catholic, anti-German, anti-Western, in essence an apologist for the obscurantism and reaction that had driven him into Siberian exile.

Another novelist of some talent writing at mid-century was Alexander Goncharov whose only work of note was *Oblomov*. This is the story of a sleepy noble who suffers from an intellectual paralysis that makes him indifferent to the life he passively endures. Michael Saltykov, who used the pen name Shchedrin, left among other pieces a hilariously comical short story entitled "How a Muzhik [Peasant] Fed Two Officials." The censors who passed it were too stupid to recognize themselves as the two officials.

Artists, whatever their medium, found in the stifling censorship under Nicholas and during much of the reign of Alexander II a challenge that quieter times might not have provided. In the sixty years of the Golden Age, Russian art triumphed over the adversity it was forced to endure.

Russia in Asia

The Treaty of Nerchinsk in 1689 had fixed the boundary between Russia and China along the Stanovoi Mountains, from north of the Amur River to the Sea of Okhotsk. Further Russian pressure in Eastern Asia had concentrated on the northeast corner of the continent. The Kamchatka peninsula was soon occupied and the port of Petropavlovsk opened near its tip. By the middle of the following century Russian merchants had landed in the Alaska region in search of the rich furs that the area offered. The Russian-American Company, chartered in 1798, obtained a monopoly of trade in Alaska, and an ambitious director extended the company's influence as far south as California, building a trading post forty miles north of San Francisco.

Russia made no attempt to encroach upon Chinese territory until 1847 when Nicholas Muravev became governor-general of eastern Siberia. Accepting his appointment as a challenge to expand Russian influence, he sent parties into the forbidden Amur Valley and others to land on Sakhalin and the Kuriles. Three years after landing in eastern Siberia he established the port town of Nikolaievsk

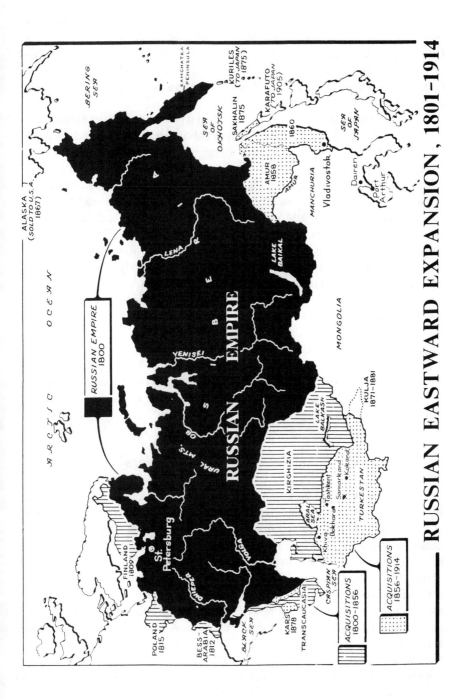

RUSSIAN EASTWARD EXPANSION, 1801–1914

at the mouth of the Amur. In 1858 he wrung from the Chinese the Treaty of Aigun, which gave to Russia all the land north of the Amur. Two years later China surrendered the east bank of the Ussuri River, and at the southern edge of the new province Russia built the naval base of Vladivostok. A threat of war over Sakhalin was averted in 1875 when Russia won control of the island by ceding the Kuriles to Japan.

In the reign of Nicholas, Russia had pushed its Siberian frontier farther south by conquering the Kazakh tribes that roamed the steppe between the Caspian Sea and Lake Balkash. This first step stimulated Russian conquests in Central Asia, which continued beyond the reign of Alexander II. The wild tribes of the eastern Caucasus were subdued as the Russian boundary moved down the west coast of the Caspian Sea to meet the Persian border. East of that sea, the Russian frontier lay up against the Moslem khanates of Khiva, Bokhara, and Kokand, from which raiders were wont to seize Russian traders. The foreign minister, Prince Michael Gorchakov, insisted that Russia could win security on its middle Asian border only by subduing the khanates that constantly pressed against it; he reminded the powers that their own colonial histories had followed a similar course. Only, he argued, when Russia established common boundaries with other civilized states in the area—Persia, Afghanistan, and China—could the nation feel secure.

The Russian government named General Michael Cherniaev to attack the khanate of Kokand. Tashkent fell to his assault in 1865. Three years later the ancient city of Samarkand surrendered and the conquest of Kokand was complete. Bokhara fell in the same year, and Khiva in 1873. Later revolts in the area were ruthlessly suppressed.

Russia and the Great Powers

The Crimean War and the humiliating peace that terminated it forced Alexander II to reconsider Russia's relations with the European powers. Prince Gorchakov, charged with the conduct of foreign policy after 1856, worked hard to bring about cordial relations with Russia's recent foes. France and Russia agreed on the union of Moldavia and Wallachia as the principality of Romania, a move opposed by Great Britain and Austria for fear the new principality might become a Russian satellite. A palace revolution in Serbia that brought a pro-Russian dynasty to the throne received French blessing. When France went to war against Austria in support of Sardinia's bid to unite Italy, Alexander posted a threatening force on the Austro-Russian frontier. The tsar was never really happy with the friendship of France, however. Napoleon III was almost too much for the legitimist Alexander II to accept with good grace. Any illusion that Franco-Russian understanding could last long faded when Napoleon tried to arrange an international conference to intercede for Poland in the uprising of 1863. The tsar would brook no interference in what he considered a domestic problem.

Prussia's relations with Russia, consistently cordial throughout the reign of Nicholas I, improved steadily after the Crimean War. Otto von Bismarck, Prussian ambassador in St. Petersburg from 1859 to 1862, did his best to steer Russia away from a close tie with France and to capitalize on the good will that existed between the tsar and his uncle, William I of Prussia. When nearly every state in Europe joined France in pleading the Polish cause in 1863, Bismarck, as Prussian chancellor, offered to permit the passage of Russian troops through Prussia if necessary to put down the Polish rebellion. That Prussia could hardly condone an uprising that might spread to its own Polish provinces did not lessen the tsar's gratitude for his uncle's support. When Prussia and Austria seized the Danish duchies of Schleswig and Holstein in 1864, Russia raised no objection. Prussia and Austria fought over the division of the spoils, and the Prussian victory won both duchies for William I. Again St. Petersburg did not protest. When in 1870 Bismarck was planning a war with France to complete the unification of Germany, Alexander II gave his word of neutrality.

In the midst of the Franco-German War, Russia notified the other great powers that the Black Sea clauses of the Treaty of Paris of 1856 would no longer be honored. Since Germany backed Russia in the abrogation, there was nothing the other powers could do but acquiesce. Henceforth Russia was free to station war vessels on the Black Sea and to provide the naval establishments necessary to maintain them.

Bismarck had worked persistently to prevent Russia's alignment with either France or Austria. The latter possibility was remote, considering the display of Habsburg ingratitude during the Crimean War, and a Franco-Russian alliance was much less likely than the German chancellor feared. After the defeat of France in 1871, however, and the French clamor for revenge that followed, Bismarck sought to insure Germany's gains at the Peace of Frankfurt by diplomatically isolating France. In 1873, the emperors of Russia, Austria, and Germany drew together in an entente, the Three Emperors' League or Dreikaiserbund. The agreement of the three emperors called for consultation and cooperation in their respective spheres of influence, especially in Eastern Europe. However, the effort to find solutions of common problems soon came to be tested.

Pan-Slavism

Ever since the Treaty of Kuchuk Kainardji in 1774, Russian rulers had assumed the right to protect Christians in the Ottoman Empire. Turkey and the Western powers, however, insisted that the right extended only over the Serbs and the Romanians. Nicholas I had held to the broader view and had gone to the assistance of the Greeks in part because of their Orthodoxy.

After the Crimean War, many Slavophiles began to think of compensating for the Russian defeat by extending Russian influence over all other Slavic peoples, of freeing those peoples from subservience to Turkey and the Western powers. To such Pan-Slavs, the incorporation of all Slavs into the Russian Empire was necessary to Holy Russia's defense against the West, in a political, military and cultural sense. Narrower Pan-Slavs, like Ivan Aksakov, clung to the Slavophile tenet that Orthodoxy was the only true Christianity and that Russia should spread its mantle only over Orthodox Slavs. Another problem that divided the Pan-Slavs was whether the Slavic nationalities should band together in a federation allowing local autonomy or be welded into a single strong power under Russian domination. To those who held the latter view, Pan-Slavism was simply Russian imperialism in the Near East. Tsardom must extend its boundaries to the Straits, the Aegean, and the Adriatic.

Pan-Slavs of all persuasions were extremely sensitive to disturbances in the Balkans. Some would rush to the assistance of oppressed peoples in the peninsula simply to relieve their co-religionists or support their cousin Slavs. Others would use any unrest in the area as an excuse to push Russian influence nearer the strategically important seas. Pan-Slavs of one stripe or another were influential at court, in the army, and in the press from the mid-nineteenth century to the end of the monarchy. The tsar's occasional opposition to their ideas did not prevent such individuals from stirring up incidents that embarrassed the administration.

Another Russo-Turkish War

Uprisings in Bosnia and Herzegovina in 1875 threatened to spread among all the Balkan Christians languishing under the sultan's misrule. Because the powers signatory to the Treaty of Paris a generation earlier had guaranteed the integrity of Turkey, the revolt called forth prompt action. The Russian, Austrian, and German governments, with French and Italian support, called upon the sultan to ease the tax burden of the rebels, to assure equal treatment of Christians and Moslems before the law, to clean up the rotten police administration in the area, and to provide representation of both groups in local government The sultan, certain of British support against the other powers, spurned the advice, whereupon Serbia and Montenegro declared war on Turkey. The Bulgars joined their fellow Christians and mounted a pitifully weak attack, only to be butchered with a savagery that stirred the world to protest.

When the Serbs were defeated and the small nation threatened with annihilation, the Russian government stepped in and forced an armistice. During the lull in the fighting, the great powers—Russia, Austria, Germany, Great Britain, France, and Italy—called upon Turkey to grant autonomy to Bulgaria and Bosnia and Herzegovina under Christian governors. Confident that Britain, suspicious of Russia, would support him in a showdown, the sultan rejected the proposal. Russia obtained Romanian consent for the passage of troops through its neighbor's territory in return for a promise to respect Romanian integrity, and in June 1877, the Russian armies crossed the Danube. Austria had earlier consented to the

Russian attack on Turkey on condition that no large independent Slavic state be created in the peninsula. Romania, Serbia, and Montenegro soon joined in the holy war against the forces of Islam.

The Russian General Gurko crossed the Bulgarian plain, seized a vital pass in the Balkan Mountains, and threatened Constantinople. Then the Russian advance collapsed in the face of pressure on its flank from the fortress of Plevna. Repeated efforts to storm the stronghold failed, but Plevna was finally starved into submission. The Russians crossed the Balkan Mountains in January 1878 and pressed on to the shores of the Sea of Marmara. The British fleet, standing off the Dardanelles since the early days of the war, threatened to steam to the Bosporus if the defense of the Turkish capital collapsed. The combatants agreed to an armistice, and a month later, in March 1878, they signed the short-lived Treaty of San Stefano.

By the terms of the treaty, Turkey recognized the complete independence of Serbia, Romania, and Montenegro; ceded sizable blocks of territory to Serbia and Montenegro; surrendered to Russia—in addition to the Asian towns of Ardahan, Kars, and Batum—the Dobrudja south of the Danube, which Russia arranged to exchange with Romania for southern Bessarabia; promised reforms in the government of Bosnia and Herzegovina; and agreed to pay Russia a cash indemnity. Most alarming to the great powers was the creation of an autonomous Bulgaria with an elected Christian prince who would vaguely acknowledge Turkish suzerainty, the new state to extend from the Danube River south to the Aegean, east to the Black Sea, and west to the Serbian and Albanian frontiers. Fifty thousand Russian troops would occupy Bulgaria for two years, ostensibly to help the new state to its feet.

The Congress of Berlin, 1878

Although the borders of the new principality approximated Bulgarian ethnic limits, the other powers, particularly Great Britain and Austria-Hungary, refused to accept the creation of this extensive Slav state that might become a Russian satellite. British troops hurried from India to Malta, and the Austrian army prepared to march to prevent the execution of the Russo-Turkish treaty. Bismarck, insisting that Germany was impartial and disinterested in the threatening tension, offered his services as ''an honest broker'' and invited the powers to Berlin to consider revision of the treaty.

At Berlin, the powers forced the Russians to scrap the Treaty of San Stefano and replaced it with a document both punitive and humiliating to Russia. Great Britain and Austria insisted on carving up the greater Bulgaria sketched out at San Stefano. The principality was trimmed to one-third its former size; another third, now called Eastern Rumelia, received autonomy under a Christian prince responsible to the sultan; the final third returned to Turkey. Bosnia and Herzegovina were to be occupied and administered ''temporarily'' by Austria,

Russia, Austria, and the Balkans, 1856–1914

although theoretically they still belonged to Turkey. Thirty years later, the temporary occupation came to an end and Austria annexed these two Serbian districts outright. Southern Bessarabia, inhabited largely by Romanians, went to Russia. Romania received compensation with the Dobrudja south and east of the Danube. Romania, Serbia, and Montenegro became independent. Prime Minister Disraeli pocketed Cyprus for England.

The Russians had gone to Berlin fully confident that, in return for their support of Prussia in 1871, they could count on Germany's support. However, Bismarck and Gorchakov were bitter personal enemies, and the German chancellor threw his influence behind England and Austria at every turn. The Russians left the congress feeling cheated and blamed Bismarck and Germany for their diplomatic defeat. Slavophiles at home spoke out bitterly against the tsar for accepting such terms, for San Stefano had been hailed as a victory of Greek Orthodoxy over the infidel and of Slavdom over the hated Turk.

Soon after the Congress of Berlin the aging Gorchakov retired, and the direction of foreign affairs fell to his assistant, Nicholas Giers. Whereas Gorchakov's personal feeling always colored his handling of foreign relations, Giers handled the Foreign Office with a cold detachment that served Russian interests better than had his predecessor. The new minister understood that Russia's real enemy was not Germany but Great Britain, who stood unswervingly athwart Russian advances in the Balkans, in Turkey, and in the Middle East. Giers won the tsar's consent to press for a Russo-German alliance. Because Germany had recently signed a defensive agreement with Austria, Bismarck suggested a league of the emperors of Austria, Germany, and Russia, and Alexander II agreed.

Assassination of the Tsar

Alexander II had carried the nation into war against Turkey with the enthusiastic support of his people, but once victorious war had ended in ignominious peace, he quickly lost that support. In addition, although the Bulgars received a constitution at the hands of their liberator, the Russian tsar, there was no letup in the police-state rule imposed by that same tsar on his own people.

The revolutionary movement flared anew. The People's Will, under its brilliant organizer Alexander Mikhailov, returned to the attack on the government. The chief of the infamous Third Section was shot in broad daylight, as was his successor. The governor of Kharkov province died similarly, and Vera Zasulich wounded the military governor of St. Petersburg. One high official after another fell under an assassin's bullets, and the government's ruthless persecutions only evoked new acts of violence.

During the last two years of the reign, the revolutionaries concentrated their efforts on the emperor, and blatantly published his death sentence for all to see. After several attempts failed, members of the People's Will mortally wounded the tsar in March 1881.

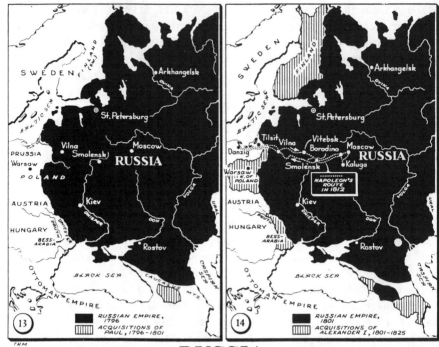

GROWTH OF RUSSIA, 1796-1881

The government rounded up the leaders of The People's Will, and six of them, including Sophia Perovsky, died on the gallows. A few dozen brave and ruthless people had defied the largest police force in the world and slain the world's most powerful and best-guarded autocrat.

Loris-Melikov's Plan

The extremists were not alone in opposing the benighted reaction of the government. Although the dedicated assassins in The People's Will looked to the tsar's murder as the spark that would ignite a general rising, less violent people hoped that reform might come about through an urgent appeal to the ruler. When the government called upon the people to have done with lawlessness, several zemstvo assemblies in effect answered that the government had been as guilty of lawlessness as had the revolutionaries. Conference after conference of zemstvo representatives asked the tsar to revive the reforms of the sixties, to replace the courts-martial with civil courts, and to grant freedom of speech and press and assembly. The answer to the revolutionaries was not further repression, they reasoned, but an extension to the people of the means by which they might freely and in full legality plead the cause of reform. However, the government paid no heed to these sincere liberals. The arrests, the floggings, and the executions went on.

After the bombing of the imperial palace in February 1880, Alexander had established a Supreme Commission under the chairmanship of General Loris-Melikov to deal with the mounting danger of revolution. With one hand, the general tightened police controls, but with the other he offered some concessions to zemstvo opinion. He abolished the brutal Third Section and internal security became the responsibility of the minister of the interior. The reactionary minister of education, Dmitry Tolstoy, retired and there was some relaxation in press censorship. These modest gestures pleased neither the conservatives, who considered them dangerously liberal, nor the radicals, who aimed at a thorough revamping of society. The Supreme Commission sat only a few months, but its chairman stayed on as minister of interior.

More constructive than the mild measures initiated by the Supreme Commission was the plan Loris-Melikov proposed for bringing elected representatives of the people into consultation with government to suggest ways of completing and clarifying the great reforms. He suggested that zemstvos and town councils choose delegates to sit with appointed officials in a national commission to advise the Council of State on administrative and financial reform. The step would have been a significant one. That elected representatives of the Russian people should have even a consultative, advisory voice in national matters would have been a radical departure from current government practice.

A few hours before his assassination, Alexander II signed his approval of Loris-Melikov's plan. Whether his wish would prevail would depend on the will of the new tsar.

Suggested Reading

ADAMS, A. E., *Imperial Russia after 1861: Peaceful Modernization or Revolution?* (Boston, 1965).

ALSTON, P. C., *Education and the State in Tsarist Russia* (Stanford, 1969).

BERGMAN, J., *Vera Zasulich: A Biography* (Stanford, 1983).

BILLINGTON, J., *Mikhailovsky and Russian Populism* (New York, 1958).

BLACK, C., *Aspects of Social Change since 1861: The Transformation of Russian Society* (Cambridge, 1960).

BROIDO, V., *Apostles into Terrorists: Women and the Revolutionary Movement in the Russia of Alexander II* (New York, 1977).

BROWER, D. R., *Training the Nihilists: Education and Radicalism in Tsarist Russia* (Ithaca, NY, 1975).

CALDER, A., *Russia Discovered: Nineteenth Century Fiction from Pushkin to Chekhov* (New York, 1976).

CARR, E. H., *Michael Bakunin* (New York, 1937).

_____, *The Romantic Exiles: Herzen and Other Russian Exiles of the Nineteenth Century* (Boston, 1961).

COSTLOW, J. T., *World within Worlds: The Novels of Ivan Turgenev* (Princeton, 1990).

CRANKSHAW, E., *The Shadow of the Winter Palace: Russia's Drift to Revolution, 1825-1917* (New York, 1976).

_____, *Tolstoy, The Making of a Novelist* (New York, 1974).

DALLIN, D. J., *The Rise of Russia in Asia* (New Haven, 1949).

ENGEL, B. A., *Five Sisters: Women against the Tsar* (New York, 1975).

_____, *Mothers and Daughters: Women of the Intelligentsia in Nineteenth-Century Russia* (Cambridge, Eng., 1983).

FIGNER, V., *Memoirs of a Revolutionist* (Westport, CT, 1968).

FISCHER, G., *Russian Liberalism from Gentry to Intelligentsia* (Cambridge, 1958).

FOOTMAN, D., *Red Prelude* (New Haven, 1944).

FRANK, J., *Dostoevsky: The Stir to Liberation, 1860-1865* (Princeton, 1986).

FREEBORN, R., *The Russian Revolutionary Novel: Turgenev to Pasternak* (Cambridge, Eng., 1982).

FURNEAUX, R., *The Breakfast War: The 143 Day Siege of Plevna in 1877* (New York, 1958).

GRAHAM, S., *Tsar of Freedom: The Life and Reign of Alexander II* (Hamden, CT, 1968).

HARDY, D., *Land and Freedom: The Origins of Russian Terrorism, 1876-1879* (Westport, CT, 1987).

HARE, R., *Portraits of Russian Personalities Between Reform and Revolution* (New York, 1959).

HINGLEY, R., *Russian Writers and Society, 1825-1904* (New York, 1967).

JELAVICH, C., *Tsarist Russia and Balkan Nationalism* (Berkeley, 1958).

KOHN, H., *Pan Slavism* (South Bend, IN, 1953).

KROPOTKIN, P. A., *Memoirs of a Revolutionist* (New York, 1968).

KUCHEROV, S., *Courts, Lawyers and Trials Under the Last Three Tsars* (New York, 1953).

LAMPERT, E., *Sons Against Fathers* (London, 1965).

LANGER, W. L., *European Alliances and Alignments, 1871-1890* (New York, 1950).

LAVROV, P., *Historical Letters* (Berkeley, 1967).

LEONARD, R., *History of Russian Music* (London, 1956).

LESLIE, R. F., *Reform and Insurrection in Russian Poland 1856–1865* (London, 1963).

LINCOLN, W. B., *In the Vanguard of Reform: Russia's Enlightened Bureaucrats, 1825–1861* (DeKalb, IL, 1982).

LOBANOV-ROSTOVSKY, A. A., *Russia and Asia* (Ann Arbor, 1951).

LOSSKY, N. O., *History of Russian Philosophy* (New York, 1951).

MacKENZIE, D., *The Serbs and Russian Pan-Slavism, 1875–1878* (Ithaca, NY, 1967).

MAYNARD, J., *Russia in Flux* (New York, 1948).

_____, *The Russian Peasant and Other Studies* (London, 1942).

MILLER, F., *Dmitri Miliutin and the Reform Era* (Nashville, 1968).

MIRSKY, D. S., *History of Russian Literature* (New York, 1927).

MOCHULSKY, K., *Dostoevsky: His Life and Work* (Princeton, 1967).

MOSSE, W. E., *Alexander II and the Modernization of Russia* (New York, 1958).

OFFORD, D., *The Russian Revolutionary Movement in the 1880s* (Cambridge, Eng., 1986).

PAYNE, R., *Dostoyevsky: A Human Portrait* (New York, 1971).

PETROVICH, M. B., *The Emergence of Russian Panslavism* (New York, 1966).

PIPES, R., *The Russian Intelligentsia* (New York, 1961).

POMPER, P., *Petrashevsky and the Russian Revolutionary Movement* (New York, 1970).

PRAWDIN, M., *The Unmentionable Nechaev* (New York, 1961).

RAFFEL, B., *Russian Poetry under the Tsars: An Anthology* (Albany, NY, 1971).

RANDALL, F. N., *N. G. Chernyshevsky* (New York, 1967).

ROBINSON, G. T., *Rural Russia Under the Old Regime* (New York, 1949).

SETON-WATSON, H., *The Decline of Imperial Russia, 1855–1914* (New York, 1952).

SIMMONS, E. J., *Leo Tolstoy* (New York, 1960).

SINEL, A., *The Classroom and the Chancellery: State Education Reform in Russia under Count Dmitrii Tolstoy* (Cambridge, 1973).

STARR, S. F., *Decentralization and Self-Government in Russia 1830–1870* (Princeton, 1972).

STAVROU, T. G., *Art and Culture in Nineteenth Century Russia* (Bloomington, 1983).

SUMNER, B. H., *Russia and the Balkans, 1870–1880* (New York, 1937).

TOMPKINS, S. R., *The Russian Intelligentsia* (Norman, OK, 1957).

ULAM, A. B., *In the Name of the People: Prophets and Conspirators in Prerevolutionary Russia* (New York, 1977).

VENTURI, F., *Roots of Revolution: A History of the Populist and Socialist Movements in Nineteenth Century Russia* (New York, 1960).

VOLIN, L., *A Century of Russian Agriculture: From Alexander II to Khrushchev* (Cambridge, 1970).

VUCINICH, W. S., *The Peasant in Nineteenth Century Russia* (Stanford, 1968).

WALKIN, J., *The Rise of Democracy in Pre-Revolutionary Russia* (New York, 1962).

WALLACE, D. M., *Russia* (New York, 1970).

_____, *Russia on the Eve of War and Revolution* (New York, 1961).

WOERHLIN, W. F., *Chernyshevskii: The Man and the Journalist* (Cambridge, 1971).

WORTMAN, R., *The Crisis of Russian Populism* (London, 1967).

YANEY, G. L., *The Systematization of Russian Government: Social Evolution in the Domestic Administration of Imperial Russia, 1711–1905* (Urbana, IL, 1973).

YARMOLINSKY, A., *Road to Revolution: A Century of Russian Radicalism* (New York, 1959).

ZAIONCHKOVSKY, P. A., *The Abolition of Serfdom in Russia* (Gulf Breeze, FL, 1978).
_____, *The Russian Autocracy in Crisis, 1878–1882* (Gulf Breeze, FL, 1979).
ZELNIK, R. E., *Labor and Society in Tsarist Russia: The Factory Workers of St. Petersburg, 1855–1870* (Stanford, 1971).

CHAPTER 15

The Age of Counterreforms

There seemed some justification for believing in 1881 that there might be some relaxation in the autocracy, and that Alexander II might bring elected representatives into consultation on important government affairs. Loris-Melikov's proposal envisaged just such consultation. With the assassination of Alexander II, however, all hope for such reform rapidly faded away. The Tsar Liberator's son quickly concluded that any relaxation of the autocratic power would seem to be a sign of weakness. There must be no compromise with evil forces. Neither Alexander III nor his successor, Nicholas II, showed any willingness to surrender the slightest bit of the unlimited authority that both inherited. The monarchy seemed condemned to stagnation or to extinction because of the unbending will of the last two Romanovs.

The Pan-Slav Autocrat

Alexander III (1881–1894), his father's' second son, was thirty-six years old at the time of his accession. A man of giant stature and powerful physique, he was proud of his ability to straighten horseshoes with his bare hands. His obstinacy and violent temper, coupled with his fabulous strength, made him a dangerous man to those near him when he flew into a rage. Awkward, shy, and reticent, he was uncomfortable in court society and preferred the informal intimacy of his family circle. He was honest and industrious to the point of insisting on reading every document he signed. To his tutors he must have seemed as impervious to education as his grandfather, Nicholas I, whom he resembled in many ways. A man of no imagination and extremely modest intellect, he lacked the mind to deal with the problems that faced the nation. At least he recognized his limitations and left many decisions to his ministers.

Alexander's chief tutor, Constantine Pobiedonostsev, sometime professor of law at the University of Moscow, had helped to draft the judicial reforms of 1864. Since then he had lost all sympathy for reform and had grown steadily more conservative. As procurator of the Holy Synod from 1880 to 1905, he became the symbol throughout this reign and into the succeeding one of stubborn, blind reaction. As chief adviser, he dominated the mind and the actions of Alexander III. An uncompromising foe of Western liberalism, he held up to derisive scorn freedom of press and religion and jury trial and referred to parliamentary government as "the great lie of our time." Russia's salvation, he swore, lay in clinging to its native Slavic institutions, to be safeguarded by Autocracy, Orthodoxy, and Nationality.

Alexander III took his cues from Pobiedonostsev and his friend Michael Katkov—the rabid Slavophile editor of the *Moscow Gazette*—who years earlier had been a Westernizer and a liberal. Suspicious of liberalism of any sort, Alexander III had fought the softer touch of Loris-Melikov and looked upon the assassination as proof of the fallacy of such a policy. An enthusiastic communicant in the Russian Orthodox church, he would not ameliorate the persecution of the sects. Anti-Austrian, anti-British, anti-French, anti-German— his Danish wife was the first non-German consort of a Russian ruler since Peter the Great—the tsar was by his own inclination an ardent nationalist. He was sympathetic toward Pan-Slavism, the extension of Slavophilism into the field of foreign affairs, although it contained some tenets to which he could not subscribe. He would look with favor upon the freeing of south and west Slav peoples from German, Hungarian, or Turkish rule, but he frowned upon the democratic tendencies of some of the Balkan Slavs. He was suspicious of all non-Orthodox Slavs. Pan-Slavism to him, as to Pobiedonostsev and Katkov and Count Nicholas Ignatiev, who had dictated the Treaty of San Stefano, meant that all Slav states should follow the Russian lead in Autocracy, Orthodoxy, and Nationality.

Counterreform Measures

One week after his father's murder, Alexander III called together his ministers and Pobiedonostsev to decide the fate of Loris-Melikov's proposal to invite representatives to advise the government on reform. Loris-Melikov and Miliutin, the liberal war minister, urged the proposal's adoption but had to defend it as in no way introducing a constitutional regime. Pobiedonostsev attacked the scheme as a subtle way of bringing on limitation of the autocracy; he thundered that this would mean the end of Russia. As usual, the tutor had his way with his royal pupil, and Alexander decided against accepting the proposal that his father had signed. The liberal ministers immediately resigned to give way to individuals nominated by Pobiedonostsev.

The procurator of the Holy Synod then received the assignment to draft the imperial manifesto that would announce the course that the new emperor would follow. In it, Alexander avowed his "complete faith in the strength and truth of the autocracy" and swore that, "for the good of the people," he would "maintain and defend the autocratic power against attack."

The new minister of interior, Count Ignatiev, opened his brief term of office by cracking down on the liberal press and preparing a law allowing the government to declare a state of emergency—in effect, martial law—to deal with local unrest in any designated district. Administrators of any locality assigned emergency status had the authority arbitrarily to fine, imprison, seize property, remove officials, close schools, curtail publications, or transfer cases from civil to military courts. Announced as a temporary measure, the vicious law remained in operation until 1917.

Ignatiev next appointed a committee to submit recommendations on the reorganization of local government, reform of the police system, and reduction of peasant dues. Several zemstvo assemblies protested that the committee should include elected representatives of the people, but the protest went unheeded.

Like many Slavophiles, Ignatiev had little confidence in the bureaucracy that seemed to constitute a barrier between the emperor and his people. He and his Slavophile friend, Ivan Aksakov, conceived the idea of reviving the Zemskii Sobor of the sixteenth century. It would have no right to pass upon legislation but would gather at odd times to hear lectures by the tsar or his ministers. It would bypass the bureaucracy (a product of Western influence introduced by Peter the Great) and restore the contact between the ruler and his faithful subjects. The growing clamor for representation in government would be stilled and the danger avoided that the parliamentarianism of the radical West might creep into Holy Russia.

The scheme of the Slavophiles Ignatiev and Aksakov ran into the bitter opposition of the Slavophiles Katkov and Pobiedonostsev. The latter warned the emperor that this was but another attempt to lead the nation into a constitutional regime. On Pobiedonostsev's advice, Alexander dismissed Ignatiev and replaced him with the conservative Dmitry Tolstoy, minister of education in the preceding reign. As minister of interior, Tolstoy followed a policy of uncompromising reaction until his death in 1889, and his successor, Durnovo, followed the same policy.

Tolstoy and Durnovo reorganized local government, seeking to undo or to cripple the reforms of the sixties. An 1889 act abolished the justice of the peace and placed the peasant township under a new official, the zemstvo chief, or land captain, who served as both judge and administrator of the township. He had to be a member of the landowning nobility, chosen by the minister of interior from a list drawn up by the provincial governor and marshals of the nobility.

Township elders, formerly elected by the township assembly, were now appointed by the land captain, who could discharge peasant officials at will, fine and arrest peasants without trial, and abrogate enactments of the township assembly. The act maintained a sham self-government, yet it preserved for peasant Russia the rule of petty officials recruited from the landed nobility and controlled by the minister of the interior.

The Zemstvo Act of 1890 amended the Act of 1864 by arranging those entitled to vote for members of county zemstvo assemblies into three classes: nobles, peasants, and all others. Township meetings nominated candidates from which the provincial governor selected men to represent the peasants in the county assembly. The right to vote in nonpeasant categories was limited to real-estate owners. Jews had no vote whatsoever. Fifty-seven percent of the seats in county and provincial assemblies went to the nobility, less than a third to the peasants, and the remainder to "the others." The provincial governor could veto, suspend, or amend enactments of the zemstvo assembly at will and approved all officials, even teachers and doctors, whom the zemstvo named.

The Municipal Act of 1892 retained the machinery of the Act of 1870, but tightened property qualifications and so reduced the electorate in most cases to a third or less of its size under the earlier act. Jews outside the Pale—the area in eastern Poland to which most were restricted—were disfranchised; inside it, they chose only a tenth of the membership of the municipal council. City officials were responsible to the minister of interior, and matters handled by city governments were sternly curtailed. Those few citizens who could share in city government showed an increasing lack of interest in civic improvement. At the opening of the twentieth century there were many municipalities in Russia with a population running into tens of thousands that had no hospital or primary school financed from city funds.

During the decade of the eighties, the court system inaugurated under the act of 1864 came under a number of restrictions. Ignatiev's law of 1881, permitting the creation of emergency districts to deal with unrest or sedition, placed such a district completely outside the court system during the period of the emergency and left the administration of justice under the arbitrary control of the local administrator. Jews could be admitted to the bar only with the explicit consent of the minister of justice; only one gained admission during the first decade when the restriction was applied. The right of trial by jury was withdrawn from those who attempted to assassinate public officials, such cases coming under the jurisdiction of special courts. Justice for the peasants after 1889 came under the control of the land captain, always a member of the local gentry. Curiously enough, Alexander did not abolish the jury system when urged to do so by the Slavophiles. Perhaps he felt that the care used to appoint only safe deputy judges, who by law enjoyed no judicial tenure, would assure that the court system would not become a threat to the autocracy.

Minister of Interior Tolstoy steadily increased restrictions on the press. After three warnings that its policy was contrary to the government's interest, a newspaper or periodical had to submit all copy for official censorship before publication. A committee headed by the procurator of the Holy Synod could suspend or permanently close any publication.

The University Code of 1863 was repeatedly amended by bureaucratic action during Alexander III's reign. Under a revised code issued in 1884, university officials and professors owed their position to appointment by the minister of education rather than to election by their colleagues as under the earlier reform. The government proscribed student organizations. It blocked admission to the secondary schools of those who were not children of the gentry, government officials, or wealthy merchants, and it restricted the enrollment of Jews in secondary schools or universities to a tenth of the student body in schools in the Jewish Pale, to 5 percent outside the Pale, and to 3 percent in St. Petersburg and Moscow.

Even primary schools came under official scrutiny. Private schools operated by Roman Catholics or Protestants came under the Ministry of Education. In Poland and in the Baltic provinces, instruction in even the primary grades had to be conducted in Russian, even though the language at home in those areas might be Lithuanian, Yiddish, Polish, or German.

Religious persecution went hand in hand with the tightening of controls in other areas. Baltic Lutherans, Ukrainian Uniats, Polish Catholics, and even the Moslem tribes of Siberia were under constant pressure to give up their religion. The Dukhobors and Stundists, or Russian Baptists, particularly felt the wrath of the government because of their pacifism and resistance to military service. Regular military expeditions marched against their colonies, and their leaders were packed off to Siberia. Toward the end of the century, the Dukhobors emigrated to Canada.

A rabid anti-Semite, Alexander III allowed organized pogroms against the Jews—popular uprisings often led or instigated by police officials. "Temporary" regulations, announced by Ignatiev in 1882 and continuing to the end of the dynasty, forbade Jews to acquire rural property and closed their shops on Sunday. Jews could not hold government office and could elect only a tenth of the delegates to their own city dumas. Subject to military draft, they could not obtain commissions. A Jew could always get around the law by bribery, and petty officials levied regular tribute from the Jewish community in return for softening the regulations against them. Yet, the influential Pobiedonostsev expressed the hope that a third of them would become Christian, another third emigrate, and the rest be harried into destruction.

Under the leadership of the hated Pobiedonostsev the government followed a policy of widespread persecution of religious dissenters and Russification of ethnic minorities, who were officially classed as aliens. Even the Russian Orthodox Church, of which Pobiedonostsev was the leader, suffered from his punitive policies. Clergy who showed any disposition to criticize the government must have their sermons approved by a church censor before being allowed to deliver them. Parish priests must report to the police the names of parishioners whom they suspected of subversive conduct.

Government efforts to deal with unruly students, disobedient clergy, agitators for rights of minority ethnic groups, or real and alleged revolutionaries became highly organized and institutionalized during the rule of the Romanov monarchs. This was especially true during the reigns of Alexander II, Alexander III, and Nicholas II. These three generations utilized and expanded the system of numerous prisons and labor camps, many in remote regions of the Empire. Siberia became known, both in legend and in fact, as the dumping ground for those suspected of anti-state views.

Siberia's reputation as a vast prison for many ordinary Russians reached its highest level during the reign of Alexander III in the 1880s and 1890s. His character and leadership certainly fit the image of an autocratic ruler who would permit no opposition in the aftermath of the assassination of his father in 1881. While his suspicion of reform and change is understandable, the destructive impact of his anti-liberal ideas on Russian society showed how far the nation had to go to approach more balanced and moderate monarchies of Western Europe, such as Great Britain.

Stories about the camps and the treatment meted out to the inmates gradually reached the West. In several cases, hardy foreign visitors were allowed to travel to exile camps in Siberia to see for themselves what they were like. The most famous American to do this was George Kennan, who spent many months in Russia (and Siberia) in the late 1880s. On his return to the United States, he published a series of damning articles about the camps, followed in 1891 by a substantial two-volume work, *Siberia and the Exile System*. His accurate descriptions of the camps and their inmates, accompanied by his outrage at their treatment by the authorities, gripped Western audiences. His influence in the 1890s created a very negative impression of the Russian government and created sympathy for those incarcerated in that environment. A number of famous Russians survived their Siberian exile and played important roles in later reform movements and revolutionary events. Notable Siberian exile prisoners included Lenin (in the 1890s) and Stalin (before and during World War I). Their treatment at the hands of the tsarist state convinced them of the need for a forcible overthrow of the regime.

Agricultural Distress

The most pressing problem in rural Russia in the decades after emancipation was that of a shortage of arable land, a situation that grew progressively worse as the century wore on. The acreage of allotment land available for distribution by the village to its peasant families increased slowly, perhaps by a tenth by 1905. However, the peasant population of European Russia increased by more than half between 1860 and 1897. The average size of allotments per family diminished by a fifth between 1877 and 1905.

From their shrinking plots, peasants needed to feed and clothe their families, meet their annual redemption dues, contribute their share to village expenses, and pay taxes to the zemstvos and the national government. Added to this array was a heavy burden of indirect taxes on such items as vodka, sugar, tobacco, kerosene, and matches and tariffs on such imports as tea, cotton, and iron. Over nine-tenths of government revenue in the reign of Alexander III came from direct and indirect taxes that fell primarily upon the peasants. The burden became simply unbearable. Often there was no money to pay taxes. Tax collectors might go into the countryside and literally flog whole villages in an effort to wring collections from the penniless peasants. Something had to give way. The chief financial burden that the peasant could dodge or postpone was the redemption dues, and these fell steadily deeper into arrears. The government could not ignore the problem and, in 1881 and again three years later, reduced the redemption debt of former landowners' serfs. Bunge, the finance minister, abolished the soul tax in 1886. Such measures provided only temporary relief, however, and arrearages continued to mount. The only possible solution was a drastic reduction and finally the elimination of redemption payments, a step that the government eventually accepted under political pressure after 1905.

Certainly, the plight of the average peasant was bad enough, but land distribution in rural Russia was extremely uneven. Although the few most fortunate—one-fifth of one percent of the peasants—belonged to villages whose allotments averaged 275 acres, nearly 30 percent of peasant families were members of villages whose average allotment was thirteen acres, and 2 percent lived in communities where the allotment averaged only 2.5 acres.

The average allotment of all Russian peasants, thirty-five acres, was nearly four times the size of peasant holdings in Western Europe, but the peasant's yield per acre in no way compared with that of other grain farmers elsewhere. The Russian peasant's wheat crop produced about nine bushels to the acre, one-fourth as much as in England and only two-thirds as much as in the United States, where farmers were notoriously wasteful of their land. Shallow plowing and lack of fertilizer, both imposed by lack of capital, brought the Russian farmers little return for their labor. Even if they had possessed the money for fertilizer, they would have been discouraged from using it by the practice of periodic redistribution of the allotments; the plot which this year a farmer had enriched with fertilizer might pass next year to another farmer. Rotation of crops was impossible where one peasant's strips intermingled with those of many others in a huge field that must be sown and harvested at the same time. In central Russia, the land was cropped for years on end and then left fallow for several years to recover its fertility. In the black-soil provinces, where the three-field system was common practice, one-third of the arable land always lay fallow. Over much of Russia, allotment land did not provide enough grain and potatoes to feed the family and leave seed for the coming year.

Many found relief from this sorry plight by renting additional acres from the landowner, but this drove rents up sharply, leaving the tenant little profit from this enterprise. A few managed to buy land, and a Peasants' Land Bank was established by the government in 1883 to assist in such purchases. By 1905, the peasants had bought or were buying sixty-five million acres, about one-sixth the amount they were cultivating. Competitive buying drove land prices unreasonably high, and as they rose, the average peasants were squeezed out of the market for the land they needed so urgently. Many contracted to buy land for which they could not pay and so lost the partial payment they had managed to make. Grain prices, determined in a world market, fell off in the 1880s and remained low through the rest of the century, while the cost of the commodities the peasant needed to buy remained artificially high, for Russian manufacturers enjoyed the protection of high tariffs. Peasants found slight relief by selling wheat and buying rye, with which they made the coarse black bread that was their staple food. The declining number of draft animals reflected the growing poverty of the countryside; in the last year of the reign of Alexander III, a third of farm households had no horses, and nearly another third had only one. The peasant husband and wife became beasts of burden.

Some found relief from low income by hiring their services out to others, but wages were wretchedly low. Forty kopeks—twenty cents—a day was an average rate for work at harvest time, when wages were unusually high. Thirty rubles—about fifteen dollars at that time—a year plus subsistence, less than the American farm laborer received in a month, was normal for the worker who hired out for the year. Others trooped to the cities when work was slack in the villages, to bid against each other for jobs in industry and consequently to depress the wage rate not only for themselves but for the city workers as well. As industry mechanized and insisted upon year-round operation, transient workers had to make their choice either to take their chances in the city or return to the hungry village. Workers might move their families to the factory town or send money home to their families who continued to till the land.

One avenue of escape lay open to the sturdy peasant who could break away from the village community. Some obtained the consent of the elders to move eastward through the steppe and into Siberia. Many more left without permission. Construction of the Trans-Siberian Railway encouraged the movement, and the government even decided to lend money to those who moved to the eastern frontier. By the end of the reign of Alexander III, perhaps 80,000 peasants were moving into Siberia every year, a pitifully small number from a total population of 125,000,000, at least three-fourths of them peasants. The rural population of European Russia was increasing at a rate fourteen times the number who emigrated.

Those who could not escape from the village were never far from starvation. The terrible famine of 1891, followed by a severe cholera epidemic, affected thirty million peasants, killing thousands and emptying the villages. Yet the 1891 famine stands out only because it was more severe than those preceding and following it. Famine was endemic in the countryside.

In a puny effort to reduce the threat of peasant revolt, Alexander III adopted a number of relief measures. In 1881, the government ordered the completion of redemption agreements by those former serfs who had not yet worked out a solution with their landlords. Fifteen percent of the former landowners' serfs came under the command. In the same year, the government opened blocks of state-owned lands to be leased by village communities but not by individual peasants. In 1893 the redistribution of allotment land by the village came under the scrutiny of the land captain. However, such measures were of little avail in mitigating the agricultural distress that the nation suffered. When conditions passed human endurance, the peasants rose against the system that held them captive. In the first seven years of the reign of Alexander III, there were three hundred uprisings of sufficient magnitude to require military expeditions to suppress them. Local authorities put down countless others. Government officials comforted themselves with the conviction that disorders had reached a stable figure, that the average number would not go beyond fifty a year, and prayed that there would be no general rising, or Pugachevshchina.

Industrial Progress

Emancipation of the serfs produced a decline of industries operated with serf labor and a rapid growth of those that depended on free labor. Production in the home also fell off in favor of manufacture in factories. The most remarkable shift from hut to factory came in the field of cotton textiles. St. Petersburg, the Moscow area, and Lodz in Poland, the most important textile-manufacturing centers, grew rapidly in population. Villagers flocked to the cities to work seasonally in a desperate effort to eke out a living that the land could not provide. Ivanovo-Voznesensk, a textile suburb of Moscow, grew from a village of a thousand people to a city thirty times that size between emancipation and the end of the century. Expansion of cotton textile production during the time of Alexander III caused a tripling of raw cotton imports, most of which came from the United States, to a total of 300,000 tons, and there was a steady growth in the production of home-grown cotton in the Trans-Caspian area. Protected by a high tariff, the industry enjoyed a monopoly of the domestic market and managed to export some cotton prints to the Middle East.

Output of the mining industry rose sharply during the same period. Russia produced 1,300,000 tons of coal in 1880, about 5,000,000 in 1895, and more than doubled that figure again in the next five years. Its iron mines yielded nearly 1,000,000 tons of ore in 1880 and three times as much fifteen years later. Over half its output of coal and iron came from the Donets Basin in the south. By 1895, the nation was producing 1,000,000 tons of steel each year and over 6,000,000 barrels of oil, the latter from the Baku fields. Its oil wells, developed through French and British capital, outproduced those of any other nation before 1900.

The construction of railroads, begun so dramatically by Nicholas I with the Moscow-St. Petersburg line, went on apace during the last decades of the nineteenth century. At the death of Nicholas, the nation had boasted only 1,000 *versts*, or 670 miles of track. At the accession of Alexander III, the figure had risen to 14,000 miles, and during his reign another 8,000 were added. A fourth of the railway net was owned by the government, the rest by a host of small companies who fought each other for business with such cutthroat methods that the government had to step in to regulate rates, force consolidation, and buy out the weakest lines. By the turn of the century, two-thirds of Russia's 35,000 miles of railroad were government-owned. A most remarkable achievement was the construction of the Trans-Siberian line, over 4,000 miles in length, begun in 1891 and financed by French loans. With its completion by 1903, the vast Siberian frontier could receive a flood of immigrants from the overcrowded provinces of European Russia.

Industrial expansion brought to Russia, as to other countries, the growth of big business. By Alexander III's last year three-fourths of Russian textile workers labored in factories that employed over one hundred workers. The trend was observable as well in the paper, steel, chemical, metal-working, mining, and oil industries. Small operators continued, by and large, to run sugar and vodka plants, the food-processing industry, and the making of samovars, bast shoes, coarse linen, carts, and the like. Capitalistic techniques even crept into such industries as these, as craftspeople sold their products to merchants who wholesaled the goods to retailers. At the time of the great reforms, there was hardly a corporation in Russia; by the end of the century, there were over seventeen hundred.

Government Economic Policy

As the Industrial Revolution crept slowly into Russia, it brought with it the cycle of business fluctuations that the Western world had known for a long time. The early years of the reign of Alexander III were depression years. Many factories closed down or curtailed production, and the rate of business expansion, which had been steady since emancipation, fell off sharply.

The government nurtured the nation's infant industrial plant and sought to shield it from the effects of the business cycle in a number of ways. The extension of the railway net under government ownership or subsidy freed the coal and iron interests and steel manufacturers from the vagaries of the world market. Government purchases of iron and steel for railway construction at twice the market price drove the cost of railroad building beyond all reason but guaranteed good profits to the favored firms. The tariff of 1891, fixing import duties at the highest level in the nation's history, sought to preserve the domestic market of consumers' goods as well as raw materials for Russian producers. It forced the consumer to pay twice as much for poorly made domestic goods as Western Europeans had to pay for similar products. Taxes on the business community continued at such low levels as to produce only one-fifteenth of the national revenue, whereas the peasants and town laborers in contrast returned over four-fifths of the government's yearly income. The presence of members of the merchant class in official positions, and investment of members of the gentry class in business enterprise, guaranteed that government would deal softly with management.

By 1890, the industrial labor force numbered two million. Of these, one-fourth worked in textile mills, another fourth in metal-processing plants, and still another fourth on the railroads, leaving only a half million workers in all other types of industry. As the century drew to its close, the tie between urban worker and the agricultural village was dissolving. The labor force was rapidly becoming committed to city dwelling as its members gave up their allotments in the village and took their chances on industrial employment.

Conditions of work in Russian factories came under no legal standard but were left to the whim of the employer. Women and children worked along with men and slept with them in the same straw-carpeted barracks provided by the factory owner or on the floor of the shop where they worked. Hours of work, not yet fixed by law, ran normally to fourteen a day and frequently to sixteen or eighteen. The accident rate was high as exhausted workers fell into unguarded machines. Employers paid wages annually or at irregular intervals. In U.S. terms, men received seven dollars a month on the average, women five, and children three. Even this pittance was reduced by fines for breakage or nonappearance for work and by deductions for the worker's purchase of all provisions at the company store.

The end of the Russo-Turkish War in 1878 brought an end to government orders for cotton and woolen goods, and the mill owners cut wages sharply. In protest, the workers went on strike, the first important walkout in Russian history. Other strikes followed in the early 1880s, almost exclusively among textile workers asking for better pay, shorter hours, and better working conditions.

Alexander's finance minister, Nicholas Bunge, promulgated a number of factory reforms designed to meet the chief complaints of the workers. This succession of regulations forbade the employment of children under twelve; set an eight-hour maximum on the work of persons between twelve and fifteen; prohibited night work for women and youths; ordered that boys employed in factories be allowed time to attend school; defined legitimate causes for dismissal; required regular payment of wages; and made strikes illegal and encouragement to strike a grave crime. Factory inspectors responsible to the finance minister had the power to arbitrate disputes, limit fines, regulate housing of workers, inspect factories, and enforce the conditions imposed by the new regulations.

However radical Bunge's reforms may have seemed to the mill owners, they did not arise out of any humanitarian sympathy for the plight of the workers. Officialdom hoped, by meeting the workers halfway, to prevent them from moving in desperation from economic to political rebellion. Whatever the inspiration behind the factory legislation of the 1880s, an influential segment of the business community hounded Bunge from office in 1887, and his successor, Vyshnegradsky, allowed the new laws to become practically inoperative.

Bunge carried through a number of other reforms designed to improve Russian finances and to ease the nation's transition into modern capitalism. The Peasants' Land Bank founded in 1883 proposed to lend money, occasionally to individuals but ordinarily to village communities or cooperative groups, for the purchase of land. By 1905, the peasants had purchased nearly a third of the land retained by the gentry at the time of emancipation, most of it with the aid of the Land Bank, but the bank did nothing to relieve the land hunger of the poor peasant. Only the well-to-do peasant, the *kulak*, who already owned an extensive acreage for collateral or who could pay down a fifth of the purchase price, was likely to win approval for a loan. A Nobles' Land Bank was also established to advance loans to the gentry, one-third of whose lands by 1905 were mortgaged and the payments far in arrears.

While the nation was at peace, Bunge found it possible to curtail the issue of paper currency and even to begin the accumulation of a gold reserve that would some day permit Russia to go on the gold standard. Bunge juggled the state revenues by abolishing the soul tax and reducing the redemption dues, attempting to offset these losses by tightening the collection of revenue, raising the tariff, and levying a modest inheritance tax. He even considered, but did not adopt, an income tax. His successor made the sale of liquor a government monopoly, a move that brought the government one of its chief sources of income.

The economic policy of the government, like its social and political policies, deliberately aimed at favoring the merchants and the gentry, those classes from which it drew its chief support. Any favors to the lower classes came in an effort to deter the masses from political action.

The reign of Alexander III saw Russia move slowly away from the agrarian economy of serfdom toward modern industrial technology. Yet the nation would fail to come abreast of the industrial West for years to come. Indeed, to the end of tsardom and beyond it would lag far behind Western Europe, intermingling even in the twentieth century much that was medieval with much that was modern. Russia's greatest enterprise—agriculture—retained many archaic features long after emancipation. Its industry, born and nurtured under the stifling control of bureaucracy, would never rid itself of that paternalistic blight.

Foreign Relations

The renewal of the League of the Three Emperors in 1881, allying the empires of Germany, Austria, and Russia, had occurred before the death of Alexander II. By its terms, the powers agreed to remain neutral should one of them go to war with an outsider. They promised to agree among themselves before sanctioning any revision of Turkey's frontiers, and each swore to consult the others on peace terms before going to war with Turkey. The three vowed to maintain the principle of closure of the Straits, a provision that assured Russia there would not be another Crimean War. Austria might exercise its right to annex Bosnia and Herzegovina at a time of its own choosing. The three agreed not to oppose the union of Eastern Rumelia with Bulgaria if that should come about. Russia promised Germany neutrality in the event of a French attack and agreed not to disturb the status quo in the Balkans. The three-year agreement was renewed in 1884 but lapsed in 1887.

Substantial advantages accrued to Russia by its membership in the league. It escaped the isolation it had suffered immediately after the Russo-Turkish War, and it won Austro-German guarantees to maintain the closure of the Dardanelles. The improved relations with Germany, and particularly with Austria, however, did not please the Pan-Slavs, who charged that the government had surrendered its freedom of action in the Balkans.

The government of Bulgaria, whose autonomy the Treaty of Berlin recognized, was organized under Russian guidance. The Russian-drawn constitution established a national legislature, which elected Alexander II's favorite nephew, Alexander of Battenberg, to rule the new principality. The Battenberger received two Russian generals as intimate advisers; the principality's high civil administrators were all Russians; Russian officers staffed the new Bulgarian army; and Russian capital constructed the first railway. It seemed evident that Bulgaria must become a Russian satellite, a stepping-stone in Russia's projected march through the Balkans toward the Straits. However, Alexander of Battenberg was so piqued at the cavalier treatment he received at the hands of his Russian advisers that he sent them home. Now the tsar's enthusiasm for the union of Eastern Rumelia with Bulgaria waned, and when the two joined in spite of his protest, he called home the Russian officers in the Bulgarian army, leaving it stripped of all officer personnel. Serbia, encouraged by Austria to protest against the expansion of Bulgaria, threw an army across the Bulgarian frontier. The Bulgars surprised everyone by hurling back the Serbs and threatening an invasion of Serbia, but withdrew in the face of Austrian threats.

A Russian-inspired coup d'état overthrew Alexander, and the Bulgarians elected another German prince to succeed him, this time a Roman Catholic, whose election the tsar declared to be illegal. Not until 1896, when the new prince embraced Greek Orthodoxy, did the Russian government recognize him. Meanwhile, Russian influence in Bulgaria had rapidly disappeared and Russian prestige in the Balkans had suffered a serious setback. The Slavophile press heaped opprobrium upon Foreign Minister Giers for allowing the nation's influence in the Balkans to fade and, particularly, for his known friendliness to the German powers.

Soon after the Bulgarian fiasco, the alliance of the three emperors expired. Giers worked for its renewal, but the tsar overruled him. Austria's support of the Russophobe ruler of Serbia and Austria's role in the recent Serbo-Bulgar affair were not to be condoned. Giers did succeed, however, in winning the emperor's approval of a "Reinsurance Treaty" with Germany in 1887. By its terms, each promised neutrality if the other went to war, but this would not apply if Russia attacked Turkey or Germany attacked France. Germany admitted Russia's "historic rights" in the Balkans, and the two agreed that there should be no alterations in the Balkan map without their mutual consent. Bismarck had won the assurance of Russian neutrality in the event of a French attack upon Germany. Giers had won German recognition of Russia's preponderant influence in the eastern Balkans.

Assurances of German sympathy for Russia's interests in the Balkans, however, were of little value. Bismarck frankly told Giers that Germany was first and irrevocably allied with Austria, the implication being clear that if Russia and Austria should tangle anywhere, Germany must side with the latter. Even before the signing of the Reinsurance Treaty, England, Austria, and Italy had agreed to maintain the status quo in the Mediterranean, Adriatic, Aegean, and Black seas, thus serving notice on Russia that the powers would not countenance further pressure into the Balkan Peninsula. The Foreign Office admitted that the nation was checked in the area. Russian interest quickly shifted to the Far East, not to return actively to southeastern Europe for a generation.

The great accomplishment of the reign of Alexander III in the field of foreign affairs was the conclusion of a defensive alliance with France. The Reinsurance Treaty between Germany and Russia lapsed in 1890, partly because Bismarck, with his fear of a Franco-German war and his concern to propitiate Russia, had been driven into retirement by the German emperor. Once more Russia was isolated, and once more Giers moved to end the fearful isolation. Because relations with England over Russian pressure in the Middle East were anything but cordial, and because Italy joined with Austria and Germany in the Triple Alliance, France was the only possible alternative. A rapprochement between republican France, birthplace of revolution, and autocratic Russia, symbol of reaction, seemed fantastic; yet many French advocated such an alliance to permit a war of revenge against Germany for the ''wrong'' done in 1871, and the Slavophiles had long protested that the nation should ally itself against the Teuton, not with him. In 1892, the two parties signed an agreement that would last until 1917.

By the terms of the alliance, Russia would support France if the latter were attacked by Germany or by Italy and Germany together, and France would join Russia if the latter were attacked by Germany or by Austria and Germany together. Each swore not to accept peace without the other when and if war should come. Soon French loans poured into Russia, and French rifles supplied Russian troops. Thus, within two years of Bismarck's retirement, an alliance directed against Germany had emerged. Russia had been driven into opposition, and France had found a friend.

The reign of Alexander III stands out as an era of peace. Although there were border incidents and minor engagements in Central Asia as Russian expansion moved slowly southward, there had never in Russian history been such a span of years without a major war. Alexander III was the ''Tsar of Peace.''

Revolutionary and Counterrevolutionary Movements

The assassination of Alexander II in 1881 accomplished little. Indeed, it served only to alarm liberals and conservatives alike. Many liberals, shocked at the regicide, deserted reform movements that would go to such extremes. Conservatives organized a group calling itself the Holy Host, which swore to counter terror with terror against the revolutionaries. Led by a high palace official, its followers cooperated with the police, organized pogroms against the Jews, and attacked radicals wherever it found them. It soon withered away, finding its work amply carried out by officialdom.

The People's Will group offered to stop terrorism if the new ruler would pardon the regicides and call a representative national assembly, but the tsar would not bargain with his father's assassins. The party languished, ineffective, into the next reign and finally disappeared as its remaining members joined new movements. There was only one serious attempt to assassinate Alexander III, and that miscarried. For plotting it, five university students, among them Lenin's brother, Alexander Ulianov, went to the gallows. On one occasion, the imperial train was wrecked while trying to make too much speed on the faulty roadbed. The tsar's daughter clutched her father about the neck and sobbed, ''Oh! papa dear! Now they will come and murder us all!'' Even the tsar's children lived in constant fear of death.

The assassination of Alexander II and its consequences indicated to some leaders a need for reorganization and reorientation of the entire reform movement. The peasants, who would profit as much as anyone from the overthrow of the regime, took little notice of the tsar's murder. The countryside remained sullen and unmoved. Terror and assassination brought only brutal revenge.

Some of the less extreme reform leaders turned to the teaching of Karl Marx, foregoing for the time being any resort to terrorism and giving up all hope that the peasants would support any political movement. George Plekhanov, long active in the Land and Freedom movement of the seventies, fled to Switzerland and there in 1883, established the first Russian Marxist party, called the Emancipation of Labor. The new organization, expecting that Russia must first become capitalist before it could become socialist, placed its confidence in the city worker, not in the peasant as earlier movements had done. A few disciples gathered round Plekhanov in Geneva, and others more daring organized small Marxist groups among students and intellectuals in Russia. Such groups met to discuss the writings of Marx and Engels and took a very limited part in the labor disturbances that broke out during the eighties and early nineties. In the next reign, the Russian Social Democratic party and its tangential offshoots— the moderate Mensheviks and the more determined and relentless Bolsheviks— would emerge from Plekhanov's Emancipation of Labor.

Nicholas II

Alexander's death in 1894 left to his son an array of problems that a ruler of far greater ability than Nicholas II (1894–1917) would have found formidable. An autocrat only in name, the new emperor was the weakest of the nineteenth-century tsars. Dominated by his tutors and by his imperious wife, the decisions he made were as unfortunate as was the choice of advisers who influenced him.

Nicholas and Alexandra

Born in 1868, the twenty-six-year-old Nicholas had grown up in the way of many heirs to the throne, with only modest preparation for the office he would some day occupy. From the age of fourteen, his head tutor was the Slavophile Michael Katkov, who imbued his pupil with the principles of Nationalism and Autocracy; Pobiedonostsev, the "evil genius of Russia," assisted in the grand duke's education. Narrow-minded and weak-willed as an adult, disliking responsibility, lacking in self-confidence, Nicholas's opinion was usually that of the last person to whom he talked.

The tsar's political credo, from which he never graduated, was childishly simple. His unfailing confidence in the autocracy stemmed from the teachings of Pobiedonostsev and Katkov and the convictions of his father. Like many Slavophiles, Nicholas was skeptical of bureaucracy and hoped to establish a close communion between the ruler and the people. This would come about, however, not through representative institutions, of which the tsar was suspicious, but in some vague, mystical way or perhaps through the impotent Zemskii Sobor, whose revival Ignatiev had urged upon Alexander III. Russia's last emperor was an anachronism, a relic from the sixteenth century. He never honestly accepted the Duma that the Revolution of 1905 forced upon him; he looked upon that modest compromise of his authority as a personal affront and a violation of the sacred trust he bore.

Puny and nervous as a child, Nicholas sought relaxation in play and continued his enthusiasm for childish games and pranks far into adulthood. At the age of twenty-five, he enjoyed playing hide-and-seek with others his own age. Nicholas confided to paper the details of these frivolities and the childish satisfaction they gave him. In his remarkable diary, he entered notes about the weather, picnics, frolics with his dogs, visits with his relatives, games with his children, reviews of his troops, walking, riding, and hunting excursions, but seldom a word about the grave problems of state from which he was never free and the important decisions he must make.

A month after his father's death Nicholas married Princess Alice of Hesse-Darmstadt, granddaughter of Queen Victoria. The bride took the name Alexandra; friends called her Alix. She embraced Orthodoxy with all the fervor of the convert, accepting it not only as a comforting faith but as a bulwark of the autocracy that she and her husband revered. Her abiding and frequently hysterical hatred of democratic institutions and her concern that her husband should rule as a benevolent despot and hand down the autocratic power to his son undiluted grew in some measure from her borrowed religious convictions. Even Orthodoxy could not satisfy her religious craving completely, and she enthusiastically fell in with the fad of mysticism so popular in court circles at the turn of the century, attending séances and consorting with quacks and charlatans and wandering fanatics. Rasputin was only the last and most sinister of such influences.

The tsaritsa bore her husband four beautiful daughters, and as each came along the concern for the succession grew deeper. In 1904, however, she bore a male

Nicholas II and his family, 1913, on the occasion of the 300th anniversary of the Romanov dynasty

heir, who proved to be a victim of hemophilia, an incurable disease inherited by many of Queen Victoria's descendants. The slightest accident—a bump or a fall—might start the bleeding that the best physicians had difficulty halting. Every attack threatened to be fatal. The empress, despairing of saving the child by medical care, besought her God to send her a savior. The tragic answer to her prayer was Gregory Rasputin, a nearly illiterate Siberian peasant who was in the capital when the eighteen-month-old tsarevich was suffering an attack. Highly recommended by the grand duchesses and ladies-in-waiting no more stable than the tsaritsa, Rasputin was hurried to the palace and introduced to the royal family as a miracle worker. The bleeding boy recovered as he listened spellbound to the endless yarns about frontier Siberia spun by this "man of God." As Rasputin left the palace, he warned the parents that the destiny not only of the child but of the dynasty was irrevocably linked with his own life. The tsaritsa believed him, and for the next decade the influence of this "holy devil" over the empress, and her influence in turn over the tsar, determined high matters of state.

Gregory Rasputin, who had left his wife and family in Tobolsk in western Siberia, was one of those wandering holy men so familiar to imperial Russia. Straying aimlessly to and fro over the land, filthy and in rags, living off the bounty of simple peasants, healing, working miracles, and preying upon the

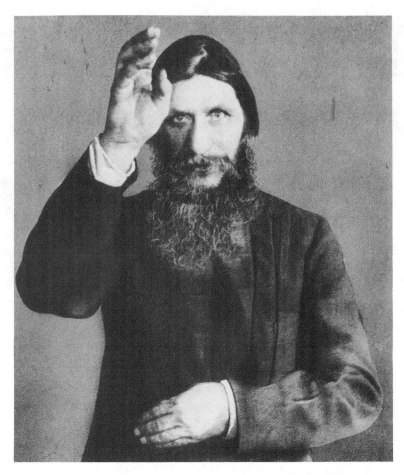

Gregory Rasputin

credulous, "men of God" or "Holy Fools" stirred the imagination of humble folk much more than could the clergy of the state church. From the practices of the strange sect of the Khlysty, whose meetings Rasputin attended, the "mad monk" came to believe and to preach that one was nearest to God when one felt a spirit of contrition and that the surest way to reach that contrition was to indulge one's appetite for sin. The sessions that he led ended in feverish dances and sexual orgies after which the communicants were presumably overwhelmed with a desire for forgiveness. Women at court joined his following, and many sought his favor as his power over the imperial family gave him authority to influence bureaucratic appointments and decisions.

Rasputin's influence at court led to questioning in the Imperial Duma. The empress never forgave the man who raised the question, and she told the tsar that democratic institutions always led to such meddling. During World War I, army commanders came and went at the nod of Rasputin, who had not the slightest knowledge of military matters. The tsaritsa influenced the tsar to dismiss officials of cabinet rank by telling him that "Our Friend" wanted this man or that relieved of office. Rasputin was poisoned, shot, and drowned in December 1916 by a group of patriots that included the tsar's nephew in a desperate, but belated, effort to save the nation.

The Early Years

The accession of Nicholas II seemed to signal an end to the militant conservatism of the late tsar. Many, particularly the liberal zemstvo leaders, hoped that there would be a return to the Loris-Melikov plan that Alexander II had signed on the morning of his assassination.

Among the delegations that came to the palace to congratulate Nicholas on his accession and marriage was one from the zemstvo assembly of the province of Tver, an assembly that consistently led liberal thinking in the closing years of the monarchy. Their address expressed gratitude for the tsar's earlier pronouncement that he would devote himself to the happiness and welfare of the nation and voiced confidence that the welfare of the people would advance under the new tsar's leadership. It went on, however, to express the hope that the law would henceforth be observed not only by the emperor's subjects but also by the bureaucrats, whose whimsical administration encouraged disrespect for the law. A plea for protection of the rights of individuals according to law accompanied a request that zemstvo delegations in the future might once again have the right to petition the throne.

Nicholas answered with a prepared speech: "It has come to my knowledge that . . . there have been heard in some zemstvos the voices of those who have indulged in senseless dreams that the zemstvos might participate in the direction of the internal affairs of the state. Let all know that I shall devote my energy to the service of the people, but that I shall maintain the principle of Autocracy as firmly . . . as did my father."

Thenceforth there could be no misunderstanding about how Nicholas looked upon "senseless dreams." Some considered the speech as the tsar's declaration of war on his people. No longer would those outside the law include only revolutionaries and assassins. Now they were joined by any zemstvo leader or moderate liberal who dared to protest vocally against a hated order of things.

Nicholas II initially kept around him the same advisers who had served his father—Durnovo as minister of interior, the vicious Delianov as minister of education, Witte as minister of finance, and Pobiedonostsev as procurator of the Holy Synod. Beyond these he chose his ministers with little thought or care and dismissed them whenever the whim struck him or whenever some backstairs influence-peddler whispered calumny in his ear. His apologists point to his kindness in informing an official of his dismissal by mail, perhaps only hours after a friendly conversation. Whereas Alexander III would tell an official bluntly of the tsar's decision to terminate his services, Nicholas preferred a less direct and unpleasant confrontation. Dismissals often were performed in more circuitous ways, indirectly through emissaries or in writing. The authority of the autocracy continued as a fact, but the personalities and temperament of the father and son did not create the same impression. The autocracy lacked a true autocrat of the old mold. However, dismissal by any means must often have come as a relief. No official, even of ministerial rank, knew when his directives would be countermanded by the tsar. The tsar might not work through the official but go behind his back.

During these early years the policy of the government continued to be that of Alexander III. Repression of educational freedom provoked university students to rebel, but student strikes were broken up by Cossacks, and the strikers were inducted into the army or imprisoned. Thirteen thousand Moscow and St. Petersburg students struck in 1899, and all were expelled or ordered into the army. One student who had twice suffered expulsion shot and killed the minister of education in 1901.

Persecution of ethnic and religious minorities went on uninterrupted. Finland, partially autonomous since its acquisition, saw its long-cherished rights willfully violated. In 1904, the theretofore docile Finns assassinated the governor-general. Georgia and Armenia underwent similar official harassment and similarly reacted by sprouting revolutionary movements.

Developments in Industry

The Russian economy, in agriculture and in industry, had suffered the doldrums through the eighties and early nineties, the depression reaching its depth in the famine and cholera epidemic of 1891–93. During the preceding decade, industry had progressed but at a much slower rate than had the economies of Western and Central Europe.

With the accession of Nicholas II, industry began to recover and expand at a steady pace. By 1897, the number of industrial enterprises had increased by nearly a third over the number a decade earlier, the labor force had grown by more than half, and the value of factory output had more than doubled. Forty thousand factories were employing over two million workers and producing nearly three billion rubles worth of goods. Furthermore, industrial production came increasingly to be characterized by large-scale enterprise. Indeed, the rate of concentration, stepped up by business casualties during the depression of the eighties, far exceeded that of Germany with all its cartels.

If Russia's rate of industrial growth fell below that of Western Europe in the eighties, it far surpassed that of the West in the nineties. During the nineties the smelting of iron grew in England by 18 percent, in the United States by 50, in Germany by 72, and in Russia by nearly 200 percent. By the turn of the century, Russia stood fourth in the world in iron smelting, in which it had ranked sixth a decade earlier. Coal and iron ore production and the number of spindles turning out cotton thread showed similar advances. The high percentage of increase was the result, of course, of the low initial level of production—Russia jumped into the middle of the Industrial Revolution. It did not have to plod through the slow and costly period of invention and experimentation in which England, particularly, had led the way.

Railroad building went on at a phenomenal rate in the closing years of the century. In 1895, thirty-two thousand miles of railroads were operating, but half as many more opened during the following decade. This included the dramatic achievements of completing the Trans-Siberian Railway connecting the Baltic with the Pacific over a stretch of six thousand miles and a Central Asian line connecting Tashkent with the European railway net. These were respectable accomplishments, certainly, but they gave Russia a mileage of less than one-fifth that of the United States, comparable in many ways but much smaller in area. Some of the capital for railway construction came from abroad, but a good deal of it came from Russian investors, particularly from the government which raised the money by borrowing from the savings banks, spending the income from the vodka monopoly and levying high excise taxes. Construction companies made huge profits, as was generally true in other countries.

The influx of foreign capital had reached sizable proportions by 1890. One-third of the corporation capital was foreign. The adoption of the gold standard in 1897 did much to encourage foreign investors to take their risks in Russian enterprise. By the turn of the century, 70 percent of the mining industry and 40 percent of metallurgy were foreign-owned. On the other hand, the manufacture of textiles and the processing of food were entirely native-owned. French, Belgian, and British capital dominated foreign investments in Russia, whereas Germany, which had provided most of the funds in the eighties, fell far behind.

The increase in production during the reign of Nicholas II was primarily an increase in raw-material production, and much of that went abroad. For example, the average Russian was consuming an eighth of a ton of coal a year, whereas the average Briton used over four tons and the American and German two and a half tons each. Per capita consumption of pig iron was only one-seventh that of the American or English figure and a fifth that of the German. Much of its wheat and sugar went abroad; its flax was exported as raw material and returned as finished cloth. Lenin would argue, in the clever way in which he was a master, that Russia's economic relations with the industrial giants to its west, both in regard to foreign investments and the nature of its foreign trade, were essentially those of a colonial area.

The Labor Force

Production in large-scale units tended to concentrate the labor force in relatively large bodies. By the early twentieth century half the factory workers in Russia were employed by only 4 percent of the firms. This concentration promoted the rapid growth of the economic and political consciousness of the Russian worker. It made the worker more receptive to agitation, more anxious to organize, more attentive to appeals for political reform. In addition, the Russian laborer was influenced by the example of the growing power of labor in foreign lands.

The factory worker in Russia was rapidly becoming a permanent, city-dwelling proletarian. Although there was a steady rise in the number who walked to town for seasonal employment and trudged back to the village as business fell off, there was also a rapid growth in the number of those who did not return to the village but dwelt in the city the year round and took their chances of finding sufficient work to keep themselves alive. By 1900, half the industrial labor force of Russia were sons and daughters whose parents before them had been factory workers. Practically all those employed in metal-processing plants were permanent, city-dwelling laborers, as were 90 percent of the workers in the St. Petersburg area, politically the most tender spot of the nation. Many peasants cast adrift from their villages could no longer accept whatever wages were tossed their way to add to their basic income from the land. Now peasants and their families must live, or try to, entirely on earnings from working in factories, for they had given up their rights in the villages and lost their allotment land. There were still many others, however, as late as the turn of the century who lived in town and sent home part of their wages to the family who stayed on in the village and who themselves returned to the village at the times of unemployment or old age.

Bunge's factory reforms of the eighties, aimed at reducing the worst abuses in the employment of women and children but doing little for adult males, fell largely into disuse during the last half of the reign of Alexander III. The normal workday ran to twelve hours, often stretching to sixteen with overtime. Wage rises came slowly and were more than offset by rising prices. The walkout of spinners and weavers in the St. Petersburg area in 1896 set off a wave of strikes that swept all over Russia and Poland. The government was prodded into announcing a new set of factory laws in 1897. The workday for adult male workers was limited to eleven and a half hours, and Sundays and holidays were set aside as rest days. Children under fifteen could not work more than nine hours, and those under seventeen, ten hours. The regulations applied only to shops hiring twenty or more workers, thus leaving conditions in small enterprises untouched. The inspection system was ineffective, and presumably the factory inspectors were no more above taking bribes than was the rest of officialdom.

The advances made by the Russian economy in the nineties were largely the work of the minister of finance, Sergei Witte. Rising from the position of railway worker to that of head of the southwestern group of railroads, he was minister of communications until appointed minister of finance, a position he occupied for eleven years. His energy was behind the rapid expansion of the railway net in the eighties and nineties, and the Trans-Siberian began under his direction. He put Russia on the gold standard, thus winning the confidence of foreign capital which theretofore had hesitated to enter Russia because of the unpredictability of currency values. Witte created the state monopoly on the sale of vodka, ostensibly to reduce liquor consumption, and it was his office that harvested the revenue as liquor sales mounted to alarming proportions. Strongly sympathetic to the business community and particularly to big business, Witte carried through only such modest factory reforms in 1897 as were necessary to quiet labor unrest. He used a high protective tariff more intelligently than it had ever been used before, practically excluding items that he felt Russia could and should produce and admitting at nominal rates such things as machinery and agricultural equipment that the nation did not manufacture. Under his leadership, private business was stimulated by stepped-up government enterprise in railroad construction, banking, and the development of state-owned mines and timber resources as well as by tariff protection and subsidy and favorable government contracts. The state budget doubled to two billion rubles during his ministry, and the national debt rose by 40 percent to nearly seven billion. Indirect taxes, of which the peasant paid the greatest share, brought in most of the revenue. Witte's influence showed itself in every phase of economic activity in which the government interested itself. Among ministers of finance, he stands pre-eminent.

Depression

National economies the world over reached a crisis at the close of the century, and Russia had become so intertwined with other nations economically that it tumbled into depression along with all the rest. The money panic abroad soon affected Russia, and both the foreign and the domestic demand dried up. Between 1900 and 1902, when the falling market stabilized, prices of the raw materials that were the nation's chief exports dropped by nearly half. Production declined markedly, and again, as in the eighties, thousands of weaker firms sold out to stronger ones or simply went out of business, leaving the shrunken market to those who were able to weather the storm.

As employers cut wages and laid off workers, the number of strikes mounted. Walkouts spread from St. Petersburg and Moscow to as far away as the Lena gold fields, the Baku oil wells, Tiflis, Novgorod, Kiev, Astrakhan, and Batum. The infection spread to rural Russia, particularly to the Volga and Ukraine. Land hunger, the chronic cause of discontent, and the grinding poverty that grew out of it drove the peasants in the black-soil provinces to desperation. Allotment land in some of the rebellious villages amounted to no more than an acre per male peasant, and many families were without a single cow. As usual, the risings witnessed the seizures of timber and grain, the burning of manor houses, and the callous murder of landowners. The cause of the widespread rural distress lay to some degree in the wholly unsatisfactory land settlement of the emancipation. Without some dedicated effort to reorder the agricultural situation, the mounting pressure in the villages would produce an explosion, and peasant and urban desperation did reach a climax in the Revolution of 1905.

In 1900, when labor unrest was at a peak, the government received a daring plan for counteraction from the head of the Moscow security police, Sergei Zubatov, a former revolutionary who now supported the government and sought to turn his earlier acquired skills to the service of the administration in the interest of peace and order. Under the plan, the government would encourage and indeed organize and participate in pseudo-labor unions, which would be encouraged to put forward economic demands but steer clear of political action. The "Society for the Mutual Help of Workers in the Engineering Industry" included not only the workers in Moscow metalworking factories but also plant supervisors and members of the police and clergy. The chief of police of Moscow took over as treasurer and named the members of the society's executive council. Subsequently, Minister of the Interior Plehve thought the movement potentially dangerous when the first meeting brought out fifty thousand workers, even though the session opened with solemn prayers before the monument to Alexander II. Professors from the University of Moscow, momentarily duped into thinking the movement bona fide, addressed the audience on the need for higher wages and improved working conditions, while police circulated through the crowd. On later occasions, officialdom supported strikes and even paid strike benefits.

This "police socialism," which the government was willing to promote in all industries to insure that the working-class movement would not adopt a political program, made little appeal to factory owners. The French ambassador protested when the Zubatov organization struck a French-owned plant; other foreigners showed similar resentment. Moscow textile manufacturers raised bitter objections to "Zubatovism." The movement collapsed in the Moscow area when Zubatov was driven from office, but it appeared later in St. Petersburg under the leadership of the Orthodox priest Father Gapon.

Social Democrats

The government failed to still the cry of protest against the nation's economic and political evils either by ruthlessly punishing its opponents or by trying to infiltrate their illegal organizations. This was largely so because a variety of groups and platforms were educating rural and urban Russia. Some were moderate, some extreme. Some urged political, some economic, pressure, and some urged a combination of both. Some sought their support among peasants, some among city workers, some among intellectuals.

George Plekhanov's Emancipation of Labor movement won many converts among the Russian intelligentsia after its founding in 1883. It aimed immediately at winning constitutional government and the basic freedoms of press, speech, and association by means of which the working class would learn ultimately to take political and economic action. From its office in Geneva, the organization fed a stream of Marxist writings to small discussion groups of Russian students and intellectuals. In spite of its title, the Emancipation of Labor never became a serious working-class movement. It had no contact with the strikes of the eighties and early nineties, which aimed not at political but at economic goals. At that time, the Emancipation of Labor groups were concerning themselves only with violent arguments over the meaning and application of Marx's theories.

George Plekhanov

In 1895, Vladimir Lenin and Julius Martov led a number of these discussion groups into a new organization, the Fighting Union for the Liberation of the Working Class. Branches appeared in Moscow and elsewhere. Lenin and Martov determined to carry their cause into the ranks of labor, which they hoped to inspire with Marxist sympathies and to organize for revolutionary as well as economic purposes. Printing presses working in hidden basements turned out a spate of Marxist pamphlets; other tracts were smuggled in from abroad. A magazine that managed to keep within the censorship laws carried subtle preachments by Lenin, Plekhanov, and other Marxists. Members of the organization took some part in stirring up the strikes of the mid-nineties.

The Fighting Union lasted only three years. In 1898 several delegates from its five branches and from the Jewish Social-Democratic Bund assembled in Minsk and organized the Russian Social Democratic Labor party. This congress chose a Central Executive Committee to direct party activity at home and abroad. From its very birth, the new party was torn with bitter disagreement over tactics and refinements of Marxist doctrine. The columns of its first newspaper, *The Workers' Gazette*, carried the arguments and recriminations of Lenin, Martov, Plekhanov, and Vera Zasulich, who in 1878 had shot the military governor of St. Petersburg and escaped.

Bolsheviks and Mensheviks

The second congress of the Russian Social Democratic party convened in Brussels in 1903 but moved on to London at the invitation of the Belgian police. Before the delegates split in disagreement over the election of leaders, they managed to agree on a maximum and a minimum platform. The long-term goals included a socialist revolution, the overthrow of capitalism, and the creation of a dictatorship of the proletariat. The minimal or short-term aims included the replacement of the autocracy with a republican government, an eight-hour day for city workers, and expropriation of the gentry's estates and their allocation to the peasants. A later amendment called for the socialization of land—the ownership and control of all agricultural land not by individuals but by local communities. These remained the party's aims down to 1918, although the members could not agree on how the program should be carried out or on who should lead them.

The contest to fill the chief offices—membership on the Central Executive Committee and the editorial board of *The Workers' Gazette*—produced such bitterness that the newborn party split into two sections. Those who followed Lenin won the elections and hence came to be called Bolsheviks, or men of the majority. Those who followed Martov—the Mensheviks, or men of the minority—refused representation on the governing boards because they could not control them. The wound never healed. In 1905, the Bolsheviks met again in London, the Mensheviks in Geneva; the two met in Prague and Vienna respectively six years later, by which time the Mensheviks found a new supporter, Leon Trotsky.

The divorce of Bolshevik from Menshevik was in some measure inevitable because of a clash of personalities. The suave, professorial Plekhanov considered himself the dean of Russian Marxists and resented the intrusions of the younger upstart Lenin. The latter had none of Plekhanov's mildness of manner or of aims. The rest of the party divided its loyalty between the two leaders, shifting from one side to the other as expediency or conscience dictated.

Underneath the rivalry of prima donnas lay a fundamental difference in approach to the socialist revolution to which both groups looked forward. After the overturn of the autocracy, the Mensheviks expected Russia to become a democratic republic and later in some vague, distant future a socialist state. Consequently, they would work with non-Marxist liberals in achieving the overthrow of the Romanovs and continue that cooperation as long as the republic survived. The Bolsheviks, however, would have nothing to do with this approach. They would replace the monarchy with a dictatorship of the proletariat that would immediately overthrow capitalism and develop a socialist state. Lenin played no favorites between monarchists and capitalists, but would sweep away both at once. As for party organization, Lenin demanded unquestioning obedience of a small party and wanted its program and tactics dictated by the party leadership. Among the democratic-minded Mensheviks, on the other hand, all would share in the drafting of policies and the approval of tactics.

Socialist Revolutionaries

The Socialist Revolutionary party, founded in Kharkov in 1900, brought under its banner the sort of revolutionary who had supported the People's Will party back in the seventies. One of its distinguishing marks was its confidence in terrorism and the assassination of public officials, a type of action that the Bolsheviks and Mensheviks ostensibly disapproved of in their own followers but applauded when carried out by the SRs, so-called to distinguish them from the SDs or Social Democrats. Along with their practice of terrorism, the Socialist Revolutionaries had a platform based in part on the principles of Herzen. They worked for the overthrow of tsarism, but expected it to be followed immediately by a socialistic society whose birth the weak Russian capitalism would be unable to prevent. Making their appeal primarily although not exclusively to the peasants, they would abolish private ownership of land and turn its control over to the peasant village. Among the leaders of the SRs were Catherine Breshkovskaya, "the little grandmother of the revolution," and the party's brilliant theoretician, Victor Chernov, who led the party through the 1917 revolutions. Chernov's goal was peaceful reform, and the party divided between those favoring violence and those seeing this approach as counterproductive.

An important section of the Socialist Revolutionary party was its Battle Organization, created a year after the party's birth. This element specialized in the murder of public officials and in armed robberies of banks and government agencies. Plans to assassinate the tsar miscarried, but an SR bomb-thrower managed to kill Minister of Interior Plehve in 1904.

The leader of the Battle Organization who ordered Plehve's murder was Evno Azev, who at the same time was an agent of the Okhrana or secret political police, the descendant of the Third Section of the Imperial Chancery of Nicholas I. Azev attained high office in the SRs and became their leading terrorist organizer. The government gave him freedom to instigate the murder of officials and then turn over to the police the names of those implicated in the crime. He organized the assassination of the Grand Duke Sergei, Minister of Interior Plehve, and a number of army colonels, provincial governors, and other officials, in addition to attempting others that did not succeed, including those of Grand Dukes Vladimir and Nicholas. By the terms of his arrangement with the Okhrana he promised not to touch the imperial family but, carried away with his work, organized three attempts on the life of the tsar. After each enterprise, Azev carried to the secret police the names of those who took part in the project and thus was responsible for sending hundreds of revolutionaries to their death. The later revelation that he was both a revolutionary leader and a police spy undermined the confidence of many SRs in their own movement.

The sensational acts carried out by the Socialist Revolutionaries gave them an importance far beyond the size of their membership. Even the Bolsheviks, hardly less numerous, boasted only eight thousand members by 1905. The strength of both movements, however, was not apparent from the number of card-carrying members nor even from the hundreds of thousands of pamphlets distributed each year. It lay, rather, in the widespread discontent and resentment that infected the entire countryside and that made the peasants attentive to revolutionary propaganda.

Liberals

Political liberalism in late nineteenth-century Russia traced its origin to the moderate wing of the Decembrist movement led by Muravev. In the forties it found comfort in the Petrashevsky circles, but it burgeoned in the sixties as a consequence of the creation of the zemstvos. Moderate liberals in the zemstvo assemblies called for continued reform, hoping to see a national Duma, with consultative if not with legislative power. The weakening of the reforms of the sixties caused many conscience-stricken nobles to become Narodniks of the Tchaikovsky type. When the Narodnik movement declined in popularity, these modest social reformers soon utilized their energy in promoting the erection of schools and hospitals to serve the rural communities and in financing the activities of veterinarians and agricultural agents to teach peasants improved methods of farming. During the awful famine of 1891, the zemstvo worked wonders in relieving widespread misery and in doing so gained a sense of importance and a realization of the need for more effective organization.

The Zemstvo Act of 1890 had aimed at curbing the liberal tendencies apparent in some provincial assemblies by drastically reducing the electorate. Nevertheless, liberal and even radical thought continued to grow in the zemstvos, to some extent in the assemblies but most considerably among the doctors, nurses, veterinarians, teachers, engineers, accountants, and clerks who served under the zemstvo boards. Many would become Socialist Revolutionaries; a few were Social Democrats; probably most were simply liberal in point of view.

One of the most substantial accomplishments of the zemstvo movement was the production of a number of leaders of liberal thought and action. Ivan Petrunkevich, of the province of Chernigov, had been sent to exile for daring to suggest to Alexander II that the only way to relieve revolutionary pressure was for the government to grant freedom of press and speech. Fedor Rodichev, a brilliant lawyer of Tver, had helped to draft the appeal to the throne at the time of Nicholas's accession. Dmitry Shipov, who would have been content with a national assembly having only consultative authority, found his reelection as president of the zemstvo board of Moscow province canceled by Plehve.

When the zemstvo leaders gathered in Moscow to attend the coronation of Nicholas II, they agreed thereafter to hold annual congresses. After the first meeting that same year, however, the government warned them that such congresses could not continue because they were "unconstitutional." Forbidden to organize among themselves, the zemstvos advocated and supported the organization of the professionals who served under them. There sprang up unions of doctors, lawyers, teachers, and engineers that soon became nationwide in scope. Ultimately, the Union of Unions embraced all the individual professional organizations—doctors, lawyers, engineers, professors, accountants, pharmacists, veterinarians, agronomists, and others, along with a union for the emancipation of women and another for the emancipation of Jews—and even some labor unions later joined. By this time, such outspoken opponents of the autocracy as the historian Paul Miliukov and the political economist Peter Struve, a former Marxist, had come into the liberal movement and were urging their students to leave school and join in the struggle against the regime. Students at the University of St. Petersburg went on strike and the movement spread to all universities and secondary schools, forcing them to close for want of attendants.

The liberals could no more agree on a program than could the Social Democrats, but where the latter split into two factions the former splintered into many. They were in general agreement that the autocracy must go, but they were at odds on what should replace it. Some preferred a constitutional monarchy like that of England, the bulk of governmental power to reside in a bicameral legislature. Some would place executive power in a responsible ministry. Others would leave to the emperor a modified executive authority, possibly making the ministers responsible to him. Still others would make the national assembly purely consultative. Most could agree on the guarantee of the civil rights of speech, assembly, press, and conscience. Many were suspicious of the masses, rural or urban or both, and would have preferred a limited suffrage.

By 1900 liberal leaders, representing the various professions and conservative labor unions, were meeting quietly to exchange views. Later they formed the Union of Liberation and agreed to press for a constitution. Meetings continued in hiding, for the government proscribed even this mild action. Their newspaper, *Liberation*, was printed in Germany and smuggled into Russia, where it was read as avidly as were the pamphlets of the revolutionaries.

Liberals probably much more than revolutionaries gave Russia a bad name abroad. During their frequent visits to the spas and resorts of Europe and in their tours as visiting professors at American universities, the Russian intellectuals of liberal persuasion constantly criticized their native land for its ignorance, its superstition, its poverty, and its autocracy. These travelers chose to ignore or play down the progress of recent decades. In their obvious love of things Western and in the ease with which they moved in polite society, they won friends not for Russia but for themselves. They, together with the Polish émigrés, may have contributed to the weakening of Russian credit abroad, and certainly they made all the more difficult the work of honest, sincere, hard-working diplomats and government officials.

Witte, who earlier had warned Nicholas that the zemstvos must be abolished unless he cared to face the prospect that they would grow into a national assembly, began to curry the favor of zemstvo men as part of the struggle for power between his Ministry of Finance and Plehve's Ministry of Interior. Some zemstvos had recently complained of the government's scorn of civil rights and the limitations that burdened their own activities. Some had called for the right to discuss all laws applicable to local problems before their enactment and even the right to help write such legislation. Witte now permitted the zemstvos to consider the needs of agriculture, but Plehve warned them against taking a stand. The great majority of such meetings came out strongly not only for agricultural reform but for correction of bureaucratic abuses, recognition of civil rights, and the convening of a national assembly. These requests pointed squarely at Plehve, who as minister of interior was responsible for vicious police action and suppression of civil rights. Plehve won the tsar's support over Witte, who was dismissed as finance minister. Plehve, now the tsar's chief minister, closed the zemstvo discussions and stepped up his program of repression. Witte warned him that such methods would lead to his assassination. Plehve answered that the approaching revolution could be prevented by "a little victorious war." The war, with Japan, was perhaps little but hardly victorious and succeeded only in precipitating the revolution that Plehve had hoped to avoid. Soon after the Japanese attack, Plehve fell before an assassin's bomb.

The Writers

The Golden Age of Russian literature faded in the dreary times of Alexander III. Dostoevsky died in 1881 and Turgenev soon after. Tolstoy would live on into the twentieth century but underwent a conversion away from the Orthodox Church into which he had been born. In his crusading zeal he left no room for organized religion of any creed; there remained for him the greater substance of apostolic Christianity. His dedication to pacifism won converts who came from all over the world to see him. Mohandas Gandhi was a disciple.

If the artists of the closing years of the century could not match the giants of the sixties and seventies in technical skill or panoramic vision, they could pursue with their more modest ability the realistic goals of their illustrious teachers. Anton Chekhov, son of a poor grocer, studied medicine at the University of Moscow but never practiced it. Even as a student, he was writing and publishing short stories, the genre in which his genius carried him to the peak of success. He took little part in the political debates of his time and supposed revolution in Russia to be unlikely. Yet his works showed deep concern for those who knew the harshness of village life or city slum. The popularity of his short stories, however, was less enduring than that of his plays—*The Three Sisters*, *The Cherry Orchard*, *The Seagull*, and *Uncle Vanya*.

Maxim Gorky, an orphan too poor to attend school, learned to read and write while working as a cook's helper on a Volga steamer. He knew the hardships of hunger and unemployment and wandered for years over south Russia, taking any job that came his way. He joined the Social Democrats and won official attention and arrest for revolutionary activity in 1905. His writings, often tendentious, depict the misery and frustrations of life among the vagabonds and unskilled workers with whom he consorted before his writings brought him wealth. His play, *The Lower Depths* (1902), is a good example of Gorky's ideas. The harshness of his realism was appropriate for his time and true to his own experience. He was the writer laureate of the Bolsheviks until his death in 1936.

The Silver Age of Russian literature between 1880 and 1914 covered the last three decades of tsardom with far less glitter than had the Golden Age. Gorky and Chekhov were its outstanding authors; there was only modest talent among the others. Ivan Bunin, son of a landed aristocrat, told in realistic measures of the decline of the gentry in *The Dry Valley*. Alexander Kuprin published a daring novel dealing with prostitution entitled *The Pit*. Leonid Andreyev vied with Dostoevsky in giving Russian literature a reputation for morbidity; he wrote of madness, despair, death, and horror. *The Seven That Were Hanged* was a tribute to the revolutionaries of the late nineteenth century. He held meetings of revolutionaries in his home and won the attention of tsarist officials by doing so. He later forsook his leftist views and during World War I edited a virulently reactionary newspaper. The foremost of the symbolist poets of the Silver Age was Alexander Blok who carried a red flag in a street demonstration in 1905 and welcomed the fall of the monarchy in 1917. He died a year later, a bitter foe of the Bolsheviks. *The Twelve*, his greatest poem, epitomizes all revolutions in their bloody yet fascinating turmoil and tragedy.

Had Nicholas II faced only the problems raised by his own Russian people, he would still have had to deal with an array of difficulties for which his feeble abilities ill prepared him. However, other problems, some of which he inherited and some of his own making, pressed in upon him. The Poles, both abroad and at home, never let up in their relentless attack on tsardom. The Finns, loyal for a century, rebelled at the Russification that they too now suffered. A strong nationalist movement urged separation and the creation of an independent Ukraine. Jews who could not leave for America joined revolutionary bands or subscribed funds for the restoration of the Jewish homeland in Palestine. Georgians and Armenians, proud of their own long history, chafed under the Russian yoke. Estonians and Latvians hated their Baltic masters who had so long enjoyed the favor of the Romanovs. German colonists brought into Russia by Catherine II still kept to their native customs and language, despising the Russians and their inefficient ways of doing things.

Witte once remarked that foreigners should not be surprised that Russia had a government far from perfect but rather that it had any government at all. Thoughtful Russians might well have asked themselves what held the empire together. The answer lay, at least in part, in a neutralizing balance of hatreds deliberately encouraged by the bureaucracy. Not only did the administration do nothing to soften the hatred of Pole for Russian, of Ukrainian for Pole, of Latvian for Balt, of Uniat and Catholic for Orthodox, of Moslem and Jew for Christian, but Pobiedonostsev deliberately stimulated such bitterness. Not only did the administration do nothing to soften the hatred of peasant for landowner and of both for the merchant, of worker for employer, of student for Cossack, of civilian for bureaucrat, but Plehve and others like him felt that such mutual animosities would protect the regime against a revolution.

Suggested Reading

BARON, S. H., *Plekhanov: The Father of Russian Marxism* (Stanford, 1963).

BECK, S. M., *Year of Crisis, Year of Hope: Russian Jewry and the Pogroms of 1881–1882* (Westport, CT, 1985).

BONNELL, V. E., *Roots of Rebellion: Workers' Policies and Organizations in St. Petersburg and Moscow, 1900–1914* (Berkeley, 1983).

————, *The Russian Worker: Life and Labor under the Tsarist Regime* (Berkeley, 1983).

BRESHKOVSKAYA, E., *Hidden Springs of the Russian Revolution* (Stanford, 1931).

BYRNES, R. F., *Pobedonostsev: His Life and Thought* (Bloomington, IN, 1969).

CALDER, A., *Russia Discovered: Nineteenth Century Fiction from Pushkin to Chekhov* (New York, 1976).

CHARQUES, R., *The Twilight of Imperial Russia* (New York, 1958).

DAN, F., *The Origins of Bolshevism* (New York, 1970).

FIELD, D., *Rebels in the Name of the Tsar* (Boston, 1976).

GALAI, S., *The Liberation Movement in Russia, 1900–1905* (Cambridge, Eng., 1973).

GATRELL, P., *The Tsarist Economy* (New York, 1986).

GETZLER, J., *Martov, A Political Biography of a Russian Social Democrat* (New York, 1967).

GLICKMAN, R. L., *Russian Factory Women: Workplace and Society, 1880–1914* (Berkeley, 1984).

GURKO, V. I., *Features and Figures of the Past: Government and Opinion in the Reign of Nicholas II* (New York, 1970).

HAIMSON, L., *The Russian Marxists and the Origins of Bolshevism* (Cambridge, 1955).

HAMBURG, G. M., *Politics of the Russian Nobility, 1881–1905* (New Brunswick, NJ, 1984).

HARDING, N. (ed.), *Marxism in Russia: Key Documents, 1879–1906* (Cambridge, Eng., 1983).

HINGLEY, R., *Nightingale Fever: Russian Poets in Revolution* (New York, 1981).

JUDGE, E. H., *Plehve: Repression and Reform in Imperial Russia, 1902–1904* (Syracuse, NY, 1983).

KEEP, J. L., *The Rise of Social Democracy in Russia* (Oxford, 1963).

KENNAN, G., *Siberia and the Exile System* (New York, 1970).

LANGER, W. L., *European Alliances and Alignments, 1871–1890* (New York, 1950).

————, *The Franco-Russian Alliance, 1890–1894* (New York, 1929).

LEVIN, D., *Stormy Petrel: The Life and Work of Maxim Gorky* (New York, 1965).

LINCOLN, W. B., *In War's Dark Shadow: The Russians before the Great War* (New York, 1983).

LOWE, C., *Alexander III of Russia* (London, 1895).

MAGARSHAK, D., *Stanislavsky: A Life* (Westport, CT, 1975).

MANNING, R. T., *The Crisis of the Old Order in Russia: Gentry and Government* (Princeton, 1982).

MASSIE, R. K., *Nicholas and Alexandra* (New York, 1967).

MAYNARD, J., *Russia in Flux* (New York, 1948).

McKAY, P., *Pioneers for Profit: Foreign Entrepreneurship and Russian Industrialization, 1885-1913* (Chicago, 1970).

MENDELL, A. P., *Dilemmas of Progress in Tsarist Russia: Legal Marxism and Legal Populism* (Cambridge, 1961).

MILIUKOV, P., *Russia and Its Crisis* (New York, 1962).

NAIMARK, N. M., *Terrorists and Social Democrats: The Russian Revolutionary Movements under Alexander III* (Cambridge, 1983).

OBERLANDER, E.; G. KATKOV; N. POPPE; and G. VON RAUCH, (eds.), *Russia Enters the Twentieth Century* (New York, 1971).

PARES, B., *Russia and Reform* (London, 1907).

PIPES, R., *Social Democracy and the St. Petersburg Labor Movement 1885-1897* (Bloomington, IN, 1972).

_____, *Struve: Liberal on the Left, 1870-1905* (Cambridge, 1970).

POBEDONOSTSEV, C., *Reflections of a Russian Statesman* (Ann Arbor, 1965).

RAFFEL, B., *Russian Poetry under the Tsars: An Anthology* (Albany, 1971).

ROBBINS, R. G., *Famine in Russia, 1981-1892: The Imperial Government Responds to a Crisis* (New York, 1975).

ROBINSON, G. T., *Rural Russia under the Old Regime: A History of the Landlord-Peasant World and a Prologue to the Peasant Revolution of 1917* (New York, 1961).

ROGGER, H., *Russia in the Age of Modernization and Revolution, 1881-1917* (London, 1983).

SCHNEIDERMAN, J., *Sergei Zubatov and Revolutionary Marxism: The Struggle for the Working Class in Tsarist Russia* (Ithaca, NY, 1976).

SERVICE, R., *Lenin: A Political Life* (Bloomington, IN, 1985).

SLONIM, M. *Russian Theater: From the Empire to the Soviets* (Cleveland, 1961).

SNOWMAN, A. K., *Karl Faberge: Goldsmith to the Imperial Court of Russia* (New York, 1983).

STAVROU, T. G., *Russia under the Last Tsar* (Minneapolis, 1969).

STITES, R., *The Women's Liberation Movement in Russia: Feminism, Nihilism and Bolshevism, 1860-1930* (Princeton, 1978).

TIMBERLAKE, C. (ed.), *Essays in Russian Liberalism* (Columbia, MO, 1972).

TROYAT, H., *Chekhov* (New York, 1986).

TUPPER, H., *To the Great Ocean: Siberia and the Trans-Siberian Railway* (Boston, 1965).

ULAM, A. B., *The Bolsheviks: The Intellectual, Personal and Political History of the Origins of Russian Communism* (New York, 1965).

VASSILYEV, A. T., *Ochrana: The Russian Secret Police* (Philadelphia, 1930).

VOLIN, L., *A Century of Russian Agriculture: From Alexander II to Khrushchev* (Cambridge, 1970).

VON LAUE, T. H., *Sergei Witte and the Industrialization of Russia* (New York, 1963).

_____, *Why Lenin? Why Stalin?* (New York, 1964).

WALKIN, J., *The Rise of Democracy in Pre-Revolutionary Russia* (New York, 1962).

WEEKS, A. L., *The First Bolshevik: A Political Biography of Peter Tkachev* (New York, 1968).

WHELAN, H. W., *Alexander III and the State Council: Bureaucracy and Counter-Reform in Late Imperial Russia* (New Brunswick, NJ, 1982).

WILDMAN, A., *The Making of a Workers' Revolution: Russian Social Democracy, 1891-1903* (Chicago, 1967).

WITTE, S. I., *The Memoirs of Count Witte* (New York, 1967).
WOLFE, B., *Three Who Made a Revolution* (New York, 1964).
ZAIONCHKOVSKY, P. A., *The Russian Autocracy under Alexander III* (Gulf Breeze, FL, 1976).

CHAPTER 16

Constitutional Monarchy

The monarchy would have one more opportunity to grant the political and economic reforms that might assure its own survival. It was not in the nature of the Romanovs, however, to surrender their autocratic power if it were possible to avoid doing so. Nicholas II (1894–1917) followed along in the time-honored way of his predecessors, ignoring the signs that were there for all to see—signs that his people were losing patience, that his dynasty could not for long survive another refusal to grant his subjects some voice in government. It would take a revolution to make him modify the autocracy, and the way in which he gave in to revolutionary pressure did not inspire any confidence that he did so in good faith.

The Russian Advance in Asia

The reign of Alexander III saw continuing pressure southward into Central Asia. In 1884, the district of Merv fell to the tsar, and now Russia shared frontiers with Persia and Afghanistan. The Trans-Caspian Railway pushed east to Bokhara and Samarkand and then on to Tashkent, bringing Russia close to the Indian border. In 1891, a Russian force moved into the Pamir mountain country, almost within sight of India.

The shift of Russian interest to Asia under Nicholas II grew out of many stimuli. Nicholas's journey through Asia while heir to the throne and his driving the first spike on the eastern terminus of the Trans-Siberian focused the ruler's attention on the area. The completion of the railway made easy the migration of thousands of peasants into Siberia, a movement encouraged by the new tsar. Russian influence at the court of China had been strong for centuries, and Russian trade with its eastern neighbor had flourished since medieval times. The advance of Western powers and Japan into East Asia encouraged Russia to join the struggle for position in an area in which it had long felt an interest. The tsar's cousin, Wilhelm II of Germany, constantly reminded Nicholas of Russia's destiny in the Far East and excited his fancy by calling him "Admiral of the Pacific." The Slavophile press never tired of calling upon the nation to have done with Europe and its dangerous radical philosophies. Witte championed peaceful penetration into the Far East over the Trans-Siberian Railway that he had built.

The Sino-Japanese War brought quick and decisive victory in 1895 to the new Japan over feudal China. The victor seized Formosa and the Liaotung Peninsula in southern Manchuria and forced the Chinese to recognize the independence of Korea. The provisions of the treaty threatened to block the ambition of Russian expansionists to obtain an ice-free port in south Manchuria. When Russia, France, and Germany warned Japan against demanding the Liaotung Peninsula, Japan agreed to an indemnity, which China paid with money borrowed from the Russian government, which in turn had borrowed it from French bankers.

The grateful Chinese government signed a mutual-defense pact with Russia against future Japanese aggression and allowed Russia the privilege of extending the Trans-Siberian Railway straight across Manchuria to Vladivostok, a short cut that reduced the length of the railway by six hundred miles. Over this Chinese Eastern Railway, Russia might move troops even in peacetime and was to control the right-of-way and telegraph lines.

The Japanese triumph broke the back of Chinese resistance to foreign encroachment upon its soil. Over the next few years, the great powers carved China into spheres of influence, forcing the dying empire to grant them concessions to build railways and generally exploit their spheres economically. Great Britain took Wei-Hai-Wei and the Yangtze Valley, France southwest China, Japan the mainland opposite Taiwan. The United States took the high-sounding "moral" position of the "Open Door," insisting that all powers should have free access without discrimination to all of China. Germany leased Kiaochow and won mining and railway rights in the neighboring province of Shantung.

Russia joined in the scramble for bits of China, securing a twenty-five-year lease on the tip of the Liaotung Peninsula and gaining the right to build a commercial port at Dairen and a naval base at nearby Port Arthur; both were ice-free the year round. That Russia should now seize Port Arthur, which it had forced Japan to surrender after the recent war, was an insult. Russia also won the right to connect these south Manchurian ports by rail with the Chinese Eastern, thus obtaining military as well as commercial access to all Manchuria and the freedom to develop China north of the Great Wall as an economic sphere of interest.

Witte opposed some of the pressure into northern China, but his influence in foreign affairs was dwindling. Nicholas came under the sway of adventurers who did not scruple to involve the nation in serious conflict to further their own pocket-lining schemes or wild imperialist ventures. Alexander Bezobrazov, whom Witte opposed and Plehve supported, led the group in urging the tsar to permit Russian political and economic pressure not only in Manchuria but in independent Korea as well. Admiral Alexeyev became viceroy of the Far Eastern provinces, responsible not to the foreign office but directly to his friend Bezobrazov and the tsar. Russian troops poured into Manchuria; Harbin, Port Arthur, and Dairen became thoroughly Russian cities. The province became a base of political and military operations and intrigue in Korea, the "independent" kingdom, where Japanese influence also was strong. The Bezobrazov clique organized a company to exploit the timber resources on the Yalu River in northern Korea.

An awakening nationalism in China produced the Boxer Rebellion which aimed to throw the foreign "devils" out of the empire. When the Boxers rose in Manchuria and destroyed a section of the Chinese Eastern Railway, a Russian force moved in to restore order. When the rebels attacked the foreign legations in Peking, Russian troops marched to the capital to save European lives. Upon this show of strength, the Chinese agreed to withdraw their troops from Manchuria and to surrender all military depots in the province. An appointee of the Russian Foreign Office settled in Mukden to supervise the administration of Manchuria, and to all intents the country became a Russian province.

After forcing China to recognize Korean independence at the close of the Sino-Japanese War, Japan moved quickly to extend political as well as economic domination over Korea. Aggressive Japanese agents provoked anti-Japanese feeling in Korea, whose king sought sanctuary in the Russian legation, and from his refuge announced a program of Russian-dictated reforms. Japan and Russia agreed to share in the development of Korea, but Russian advisers to the king and a military mission threatened to relegate the Japanese to second place. When the railroads under construction in Korea turned out to be the Russian broad gauge, and therefore simply a spur of the Trans-Siberian and the Chinese Eastern, the Japanese had reason for alarm. Korea under Russian control would become a "dagger poised at the heart of Japan."

By the Anglo-Japanese Alliance of 1902 the two nations promised neutrality if either's interests in Korea or China were threatened by an outside power, but each agreed to assist the other if the aggressor received aid from another. If its differences with Russia could not be settled, Japan could now face Russia without fear of intervention by a third power friendly to the tsar. When Bezobrazov's timber company moved into north Korea, bringing with it Russian soldiers disguised as laborers, Japan broke off the dragging negotiations for settlement and attacked Port Arthur. The diplomatic world could hardly believe that Japan, which had emerged from isolation only forty years earlier, should show the audacity to challenge the Russian colossus. Few realized the extent to which Russia's internal weakness had sapped its military strength.

The Russo-Japanese War

This "little victorious war," which some of the tsar's advisers welcomed as
a way of shifting the nation's attention away from its domestic grievances, of
"dispelling the revolutionary fumes," turned out to be fatal to the autocracy.
The war minister assured Nicholas that the Japanese were unprepared and that
they had not mastered the military techniques they had studied in Russian and
German academies. Russia, he argued, was completely ready and could throw
into Korea quickly three times as many troops as would be necessary to defeat
the contemptible Asiatics. The campaign, he promised, would be a simple military
parade. In fact, it turned out to be a parade of defeats, for the Russians won
not a single victory.

The Japanese attacked the Russian base at Port Arthur in February 1904.
Russian troops retreated north across the Yalu and fell back upon Mukden. When
the army under Kuropatkin, the Russian war minister, advanced to relieve Port
Arthur, it was soundly beaten and the great naval base had to surrender early
in 1905. An eight-day battle at Mukden in March 1905 between a half million
men ended in another Russian withdrawal. The Baltic fleet steamed half way
around the world to the Tsushima Strait; there in May 1905 it lost all but two
capital ships, which limped away to Vladivostok. The Japanese seized Sakhalin
Island and landed a force at the mouth of the Amur River to threaten the Russian
rear. The war was characterized on the Russian side by gross mismanagement,
contradictory orders, personal jealousies, and stupid judgments bordering on
treason. As usual the men in the ranks fought with futile bravery under army
commanders who were overly cautious, inexperienced, or downright incompetent
and who seemed determined to repeat the old maxim that "there were no bad
Russian soldiers, only bad officers." The government kept its best troops in
Europe, sending to Manchuria chiefly reservists, men near forty who had not
campaigned for years. Some of the troops carried new magazine rifles that they
did not know how to operate, and the artillery lacked adequate training with
the new rapid-fire field piece issued as the troops left for the front. The service
of supply was at its worst, although the nation faced an almost insuperable
logistical problem in having to depend solely on the partially completed single-
track Trans-Siberian Railway, a supply line over four thousand miles long.

By the summer of 1905, the Japanese, nearing military and financial exhaustion,
were ready to accept a peace offer. The Russian government, although growing
in military strength, was facing a crisis at home and also was anxious for peace.
The American President Theodore Roosevelt invited the two to send peace
delegations to Portsmouth, New Hampshire. Theretofore strongly pro-Japanese,
Roosevelt grew uneasy about continued Japanese successes that might lead to
a serious disturbance of the balance of power in the Far East.

By the terms of the September 1905 Treaty of Portsmouth, Russia recognized
Japan's special interests in Korea, surrendered the southern half of Sakhalin,
and turned over to the Japanese the lease on the Liaotung Peninsula. Both powers

agreed to withdraw from Manchuria, leaving it to Chinese rule. Witte, who led the Russian delegation, successfully parried Japan's demand for an indemnity. In gratitude, the tsar awarded him the title of Count.

Rural Unrest

The hope of Alexander III's advisers that serious peasant disturbances would level off at around fifty a year faded in the early years of the twentieth century. In 1902 the figure reached well over three hundred, and there were nearly half as many the following year. The uprisings were most severe in the rich black-soil provinces of Poltava and Kharkov, where the villagers broke into the landowners' barns to secure grain for themselves and their cattle. The peasants, frustrated and violent, destroyed some eighty mansions. In Kharkov, the authorities were unable to quell the outbreaks which ended only when the rioters tired of their looting and burning. On the other hand, in Poltava, the police responded with brutal vengeance. Innocent and guilty alike—the authorities did not trouble to sort them out—were flogged into insensibility. After two hundred lashes from the birch rod, some spent two months in the hospital; others were dragged off to prison instead.

To determine the cause of the outbreaks, government officials questioned village elders. One of them answered that his village had too little land, no grain, no hay, and no pasture. The village was perennially short of food, the crop each year carrying them only into December. When asked whether the propaganda pamphlets of the Socialist Revolutionaries had stirred up the people, he answered, "It is not the little books that are dangerous, but that there is nothing for us to eat." The poor peasant did not need to be told that he was hungry. Indifferent to such pleas, the authorities imprisoned eight hundred peasants and forced the villagers to pay the landowners a quarter million rubles in damages.

It is true that the Socialist Revolutionaries distributed thousands of leaflets in the villages of south Russia, that the Social Democrats were not idle in the countryside, and that teachers and doctors and veterinarians not only sympathized with the misery they could hardly relieve but urged the peasants on to revolt. However, what moved the peasant most of all was the sight day after day of the great, rich fields of some neighboring landowner lying just across the fence from the peasant's own stingy plot. Yet, the problem was even more complicated. The Bolsheviks were opposed in the Ukraine by the Ukrainian Social Democrats, who objected to Lenin's ruthless centralization of power. Only a few Russified Ukrainians supported the Bolsheviks in 1918.

Official half-measures to reduce tension in the villages began in 1903, when the government ended the mir's collective responsibility for payment of taxes and redemption dues in most of the provinces. It may have hoped that by breaking up the group it would promote individual selfishness and so set villager against villager, rich peasant against poor. The desired effect followed, but the vast majority grew still poorer and more desperate.

Urban Unrest

Witte observed in 1895 that Russia had no working class in the same sense as did the countries of the West. He congratulated himself that the nation consequently had no labor problem. A year later, the minister of interior was bemoaning the fact that not only had a working class appeared but that it was becoming revolutionary in outlook and impatient to organize. The event that had disturbed the official slumber was a determined but orderly strike of thirty thousand spinners and weavers in the St. Petersburg area.

In the autumn of 1902 workers walked out of the railway shops in Rostov in protest against long hours and low wages. Soon employees in the ironworks and other factories joined them. The Social Democrats moved in to organize daily meetings attended by thirty thousand people of all classes, haranguing the crowds with demands for higher wages and better conditions of work, denouncing capitalism and the autocracy. Police and Cossacks fired on the crowd and galloped away, leaving several dead and wounded, but the meetings went on for three weeks, after which the strikers gave in and returned to work. Although the strike failed to accomplish any of its aims, it was a huge success in the support it commanded.

During the summer of 1903, all south Russia was in ferment. There were meetings again in Rostov, a strike of the employees in the oil fields of Baku joined by every laborer in the city, and general strikes in Batum, Kiev, Kerch, and Odessa, the number of strikers running over two hundred thousand. All shops closed, transportation halted, streets were dark, and food shortages developed. Industrial life came to an end. Tension mounted as workers paraded, throngs gathered to hear speeches, and police and troops sullenly waited for someone to cast the first stone that would justify the swinging of whips and sabers. In every city the demands were the same—substantial pay raises, a minimum wage, an eight-hour day, an end to fines, the legalization of unions, recognition of the right to strike. All these were part of the program of the Social Democrats, but to these usual trade-union requests the SDs added a call for the freedoms of speech, press, conscience, and association, an end to arbitrary arrest, and the convening of a national assembly. By 1904 nearly two thousand strikes flared over south Russia.

The most significant development in labor circles in the early twentieth century was the growing political consciousness of the workers. The Social Democratic agitators and speakers contributed to the political education of the proletariat, interweaving economic with political goals. The two went hand in hand. Without civil rights, there could be no agitation for economic gains. Indeed, the strikers seemed to sense this, for they often lost sight of their trade union demands in their hatred of the government. This growing political consciousness brought the laborers into the streets to mingle there with other workers, students, and clerks to hear the harangues of the revolutionary firebrands. Their meetings were attacked by the police and Cossacks until the right to gather was vindicated by the simple process of meeting in such numbers that dispersal was impossible. The strikers and revolutionary leaders tore the initiative from the government and simply seized and exercised the rights of free speech, assembly, and press that they were denied in quiet times. Occasionally, barricades appeared in the streets, a sure indication of a growing determination to put an end to a regime no longer tolerable. The only solution to the mounting pressure that suggested itself to tsardom was Plehve's "little victorious war."

Resort to Violence

Through the years when peasant disturbances were increasing in fury and strikes were paralyzing the industries of south Russia, the Battle Organization of the Socialist Revolutionaries was scoring frequently against government officials. In February 1901, an expelled university student shot Bogolepov, the minister of education, and became the hero of student demonstrations in St. Petersburg and Moscow. An attempt on the life of Pobiedonostsev a month later barely missed its target. In 1902, a student killed Interior Minister Sipiagin, whom Plehve succeeded. The governor-general of Finland fell to an assassin's bullet. The Grand Duke Sergei, a relative and friend of the tsar, was murdered, as was the military governor of Moscow. Plehve himself died in 1904 by a bomb thrown on the orders of Azev, the police agent who was at the same time head of the terroristic organization of the SRs.

The liberals, too, grew bold in their distaste for autocracy. Forbidden to meet openly, zemstvo leaders held regular private conferences from 1901 onward and smuggled into Russia the periodical *Liberation*, published in Germany. The liberal movement created the Union of Liberation in 1904. Mild though its program was, it had to meet as clandestinely as the most uncompromising revolutionary societies. Plehve ordered the zemstvo of Tver disbanded because he thought it subversive, and refused to allow the re-election of the conservative Shipov as chairman of the zemstvo of Moscow. When the liberals called a halt to pressure on the government while the war with Japan was in progress, they established a society for war relief, but Plehve did his best to prevent this harmless enterprise from functioning. Even the liberals had no choice but to believe that the country's real enemy was not Japan but the government.

Plehve's assassination brought to the interior ministry Prince Sviatopolk Mirsky, a known liberal. During "the spring," as Mirsky's brief tenure is called, there was some relaxation in the severity of bureaucratic controls; a few political exiles obtained pardon; press censorship softened, and the cry for constitutional government went unpunished.

A convention of liberal and radical organizations met in Paris in the autumn of 1904 and agreed to work for constitutional government. A month later, the Union of Liberation announced its call to action: it urged zemstvos to demand a national constitution; it arranged a series of banquets, ostensibly to commemorate the anniversary of the court reforms of the sixties, which would propagandize for a constitution; it stimulated the organization of unions of professionals, all eventually joining a Union of Unions.

Prince Mirsky permitted a congress of zemstvos to gather in St. Petersburg in November 1904. Shipov, the president, was unable to curb the liberals when the assembly drafted a program. The famous "eleven points," which came to be the program for all liberal and many radical thinkers from that moment to the end of the monarchy, demanded freedom of speech, press, association, and conscience; freedom from arbitrary arrest; a broadened franchise for local elections; equality of all classes and nationalities before the law; an end to martial law in peacetime; amnesty for political prisoners; and the creation of a representative legislature. On the question of whether the assembly should possess legislative or only consultative power, the liberals overwhelmed Shipov and his conservative fellows three to one in favor of full legislative power.

In the succeeding months one zemstvo after another passed resolutions approving the eleven points. "Impertinent and tactless," the tsar called such resolutions. An imperial order repeated earlier vague assurances of reforms. Nicholas spurned Prince Mirsky's suggestion that the State Council should be enlarged by bringing in members elected by the zemstvos. Blaming the liberals for the popular unrest that was sweeping the nation, he ordered them to stop dabbling in matters that were none of their concern.

A Russian Orthodox priest, George Gapon, Zubatov's agent of the "police socialism" movement in the capital, organized in 1903 the "Assembly of Russian Factory and Mill Workers of St. Petersburg." The constitution of this police-sponsored organization announced its aims to be "the sober and rational passing of leisure time by the members" in search of "spiritual and moral" values and the stimulation of "prudent views upon the duties and rights of workers." Local units or "clubs" would meet weekly to join in religious singing or to debate religious and moral issues. Its most dangerous activity would be the accumulation of a fund to dole out sickness and unemployment benefits, but no payments were to go to men on strike. The first gathering in 1904 heard the reading of the constitution, approved by Plehve on the promise that the group would stick to nonpolitical subjects and broke up after joyfully singing "God Save the Tsar." Later, Sunday meetings provided tea, dancing, or lectures on Russian history, literature, geology, and economic problems. In less than a year the membership numbered nine thousand workers, but many thousands more were attending the weekly meetings.

The feeling was widespread among the workers of the time that Russia's sorry plight was not the work of the tsar but of the bureaucrats who surrounded him. If that bureaucratic curtain could be brushed aside, the tsar surely would receive a petition from the hands of his loyal subjects and would correct all the abuses of society. Over Gapon's objection, the central committee of the organization drafted a petition and proposed to march with it to the Winter Palace. The central theme of the petition was the blame the petitioners heaped on officialdom for their beastlike lives. Then came an enumeration of measures the group thought

"Bloody Sunday" in St. Petersburg, January 1905

indispensable to the nation's salvation, including the "eleven points," termination of the war, an end to redemption payments, substitution of an income tax for excise taxes, cheap credit, legalization of trade unions, and separation of church and state.

On the bitterly cold, snowy morning of Sunday, January 9/22, 1905, two hundred thousand workers marched on the Winter Palace. The emperor's uncle, Grand Duke Vladimir, commanded the city's security forces which fired into the crowds, killing over a hundred and wounding hundreds more. This was "Bloody Sunday," or "Vladimir's Day." Father Gapon fled abroad, whence he addressed an open letter to the tsar warning that he had invited a bloody revolution by his refusal to receive the petitioners. "Let all blood which has to be shed fall upon thee, hangman, and thy kindred." However, he returned to Russia and again joined the political police. The Battle Organization of the SRs, under Azev, ran him down in Finland and murdered him.

Bloody Sunday opened the Revolution of 1905. The reception given the marchers destroyed all popular faith in the tsar; henceforth, he and his bureaucrats were lumped together as responsible for the nation's ills. The demonstration revealed to the workers of the capital that they could muster in sizable and formidable numbers. Moscow and south Russia had learned the lesson years earlier, but few had thought it possible that such an assembly could gather and throw up barricades in St. Petersburg. Workers over the rest of Russia were quick to take heart from the bold action of their fellows in the capital. Four hundred thousand struck during the month of January 1905, more than the total number who went out on strike during the entire preceding decade. The government had reason to grow fearful.

Creating a Parliamentary-style Government

The lengthening list of assassinations and the growing restlessness of the masses, rural and urban, prompted Nicholas reluctantly to grant concessions. He agreed to "summon the worthiest men elected by the people to participate in the drafting and consideration of legislation" (clearly a consultative assembly or Duma only), restored the right to appeal to the throne, repealed the laws against dissenters, and extended religious toleration to all sects. How these orders would be carried out would depend, of course, on local police, against whose actions all complaints would be looked upon as subversive.

These halting steps came too late to satisfy even the moderates. The Union of Liberation demanded universal suffrage and a direct secret ballot to elect an assembly empowered to give Russia a constitution. The Zemstvo Congress drew up a constitutional proposal incorporating Western democratic practices and promised to work closely with "the broad masses of the people" in promoting political reform. The newly formed Peasant Union met in Moscow to press its demand for distribution of gentry land. The Union of Unions passed a resolution referring to the Romanovs and the bureaucracy as a "gang of robbers." Even the armed forces defied authority. A mutiny broke out aboard the newest battleship in the Black Sea fleet, the *Potemkin*, whose crew hoisted the red flag off the port of Odessa, and finally was interned in Romania when the ship docked.

In June 1905, a delegation of zemstvo men explained to the tsar the growing sullenness and frustration that was sweeping the country. Prodded into further action, the government announced the conditions under which the promised Duma would assemble. Delegates would be chosen by indirect election—voters would choose electors who in turn would select those who would sit in the Duma. The indirect election process did not provide equal representation of the entire population, although it did offer some rough balance within the Duma of most of the diverse constituencies of the Russian nation. But the rules excluded several major groups from voting: those under twenty-five years of age, students, women, military personnel, and some nationality or ethnic groups, among them. For those promised the franchise, voting eligibility depended primarily on economic criteria: income, ownership of property, or level of taxes paid. It was a start toward representative government, although the government's terms pleased neither extreme: reactionaries opposed any Duma at all, while many of the radical elements decided to boycott the elections.

In early fall the bakers and printers of Moscow walked out on strike, and workers in St. Petersburg struck in sympathy. Then the illegal but active railway union called a strike in Moscow. The movement quickly spread to the ends of the empire. The strikers demanded an eight-hour day and improved working conditions, a general amnesty, full civil rights, and a constitutional convention. Other workers joined in, closing down shops, food stores, schools, banks, public utilities, government offices, and even the ballet theater; the strike became a general strike. Crowds milled in the streets shouting revolutionary slogans and singing the "Marseillaise." Shortages of food and fuel threatened to become critical. The nation faced paralysis. Some cities lost all contact with the rest of the nation. Barricades went up in Kharkov and Odessa, and civilians fought back the troops with sticks and stones instead of running away.

In mid-October a new organization appeared in St. Petersburg—the Soviet, or Council, of Workers' Deputies, consisting of some forty representatives of various labor groups in the capital. Within a month it had grown to over five hundred delegates, two-thirds of whom came from metallurgical plants, others from textile factories and printing firms. Organized simply as a council of strike committees, the soviet assumed political functions, sending workers' demands to the city government and to the police. The St. Petersburg Soviet's executive committee consisted of twenty-two labor delegates and three each from the Bolshevik, Menshevik, and Socialist Revolutionary parties. The Mensheviks' George Khrustalev-Nosar and Leon Trotsky served as chairman and vice-chairman of the executive committee. The only printing press operating in the capital turned out the soviet's official newspaper, *Izvestia*. Soviets appeared in towns all over Russia.

The government seemed likely to collapse. The tsar sent Pobiedonostsev into retirement and called in Count Witte as his chief adviser, but political power lay for the moment in the hands of the St. Petersburg Soviet, to whom soviets in the provinces sent calls for aid and requests for orders. Witte dealt with Khrustalev as though he and not Witte was Russia's chief minister. Bewildered and frightened, and left with no alternative, the emperor signed a constitutional manifesto drafted by Witte.

The manifesto of October 17/30, 1905, granted freedom of speech, press, association, and conscience; accorded freedom from arbitrary arrest; promised almost universal adult male suffrage to elect Duma delegates; guaranteed that no enactment should become law without the consent of the State (national) Duma; and gave the Duma the power of controlling administration officials. Russia finally had its constitution. Whether the government that granted it would respect it was another matter.

Miliukov's recently organized Liberal party of Constitutional Democrats, or

Cadets for short, welcomed the October Manifesto as a victory for moderation over extremes of right and left. The soviet, spurred on by the show of strength of the working class, continued the general strike and demanded a constituent assembly, a democratic republic, and eventually a socialist state. However, the people had had enough of unemployment and shortages; the soviet was forced to call off the strike.

Reactionaries among bureaucrats, service officers, gentry, and priests organized a "Union of the Russian People" to counteract the forces of liberalism and radicalism. The grand dukes and even the tsar and his son became members. Other extreme counterrevolutionary groups, known to their enemies as Black Hundreds, operated with full knowledge of the police to stamp out left-wing action or sentiment wherever they saw or imagined it. They beat up students and professors and arranged hundreds of pogroms against the Jews beginning the very day after the issuance of the October Manifesto. Beatings, lootings, burnings, and mutilations were common sights all over the Jewish Pale. In Odessa, Black Hundred hooliganism went on for four days while the police stood quietly by or joined in the rampage. Thousands died or were injured. Reactionary hoodlums murdered two members of the first Duma and sought twice unsuccessfully to assassinate Witte.

At the very moment the tsar was signing the October Manifesto peasants all over south Russia were attacking the estates of the gentry. They burned or tore down over two thousand manor houses in a fortnight's time. Mutiny broke out among the sailors at the Baltic naval base at Kronstadt and later at Sevastopol and Vladivostok. Troops in Siberia and Manchuria became rebellious. Meetings across Poland demanded autonomy. A general strike in Finland aimed at restoring the duchy's ancient freedoms. The government gave in to the Finns but imposed martial law on Poland and broke the mutinies in the armed forces with loyal troops. Expeditionary forces marched into the provinces to quell the peasant revolts; then, to pacify the peasants, redemption payments were cut by half for 1906 and abolished for 1907 and after.

The spectacle of the government issuing the October Manifesto and then lashing out at the elements that had forced it prompted the St. Petersburg Soviet to thunder that Russia did not want "a Cossack whip wrapped up in a constitution." The soviet ordered a second general strike demanding an end to death sentences and to martial law. Witte appealed to the workers for patience and moderation. The city had had enough of work stoppages and shortages, and the soviet again had to call off the strike.

Prime Minister Witte now moved cautiously to recover control of the nation. Khrustalev, president of the St. Petersburg Soviet, was arrested, as were the members of the Executive Committee of the Peasant Union meeting in Moscow. The administration put the capital under martial law and outlawed strikes and public meetings.

The soviet issued a manifesto of its own, demanding the overthrow of tsardom and the calling of a constituent assembly; it urged the people to refuse to pay taxes, to withdraw all savings from the banks, and to hoard gold in an attempt to drive the government into bankruptcy. The government closed newspapers that published the manifesto, but the citizens of the capital responded by withdrawing a hundred million rubles from the banks. Witte ordered the entire soviet seized and thrown into prison. The members, including Trotsky, were tried later, and most were exiled to Siberia.

The Moscow Soviet issued a strike call in December, and for ten days the strikers fought off loyal troops brought in from St. Petersburg. The soldiers crushed the rebellion with savage cruelty as the commander ordered his men not to bother with prisoners. Government troops killed perhaps a thousand men, women, and children on the rebel side. The Revolution of 1905 burned itself out in the futile rising in Moscow where the Bolsheviks led the way, although unrest continued to smolder in the countryside for another year.

The peasants were no more content than were urban workers with the political concessions granted by the tsar in October. Nor did the cancellation of redemption payments satisfy them. An All-Russian Congress of Peasants met in Moscow in November to provide vocal leadership for the action the peasants were taking all over Russia. Some speakers condoned the expropriations that continued spontaneously, expressing doubt that the Duma, when it met, would sanction the work. Others urged the congress to follow the lead of the Socialist Revolutionaries, who encouraged the people to seize the land and to defend themselves against any who would take it back. Some argued for the convening of a constituent assembly, denouncing as traitors those who supported the elections to the Duma. Nevertheless, it was the land question that drew the most fire. There was general support for the socialization of agricultural land, its use to go only to those who worked it without the aid of hired labor.

It was not the All-Russian Congress of Peasants that provided leadership for the peasants, however, but rather the other way around. The peasants were already smoking out the landowners, turning them out into the road and warning them not to return, driving away livestock, tearing off iron roofing to patch their own leaky huts, carting off furniture and food and equipment, and burning what they could not carry away. Some villagers seized a neighboring estate, fenced it off in plots, and seeded it to their own crop. Others turned their cattle into the landowner's pasture. It was the worst rising since the days of Pugachev and much more widespread.

There was no decline in the extent or intensity of the rural unrest after the October Manifesto. The peasants went on seizing land while voting for their delegates to the Duma they hoped would approve the expropriations they had carried through on their own initiative. Many of the gentry took for granted that these seizures of land would be permanent, that the peasants would not give up what they had already taken. General Dmitry Trepov, the governor-general of St. Petersburg, whom the strikers soundly hated for his vicious use of troops against them, told Witte that he would gladly surrender half his estate without remuneration, for he feared that only by doing so might he keep the other half.

Troops marched into the countryside as though to war. Some peasants gave in at the sight of armed forces; others threw stones and so invited attack. Whole village populations were flogged, huts burned, and leaders summarily shot. Minister of Interior Peter Durnovo ordered the risings put down at all costs: "It is a useful thing to wipe the rebellious villages off the earth, and to exterminate the rebels themselves without mercy." The government could not forgive the nation for forcing it to make concessions and seemed to take satisfaction in torturing its own people. Government officials admitted to carrying out thirty-five hundred executions between 1906 and 1908. It did not bother to reckon the number killed and wounded in street fighting or in campaigns against the villages.

The Duma

Under rules laid down by Witte, the representatives were elected by a suffrage so broad that the royal family never forgave his "radicalism." All who paid real estate or business taxes had the right to vote, as did most urban renters. There were three classes of rural voters: great landowners, small landowners, and peasants, each group voting separately for electors who in turn chose the representatives to sit in the Duma. There were similarly two classes of city voters: those who paid high taxes and "the others," each group choosing electors who selected the Duma delegates. The government deliberately weighted the Duma elections heavily in favor of the rural segment of the population, in the confidence that landowners and peasants were more likely to be conservative than were city dwellers.

Meanwhile, the tsar had weakened the October Manifesto by creating a second legislative chamber with power equal to that of the Duma. The State Council became an upper house, half of its members appointed by the tsar, the other half elected by the clergy, provincial zemstvos, the nobility, business managers, and faculty from the universities and the Academy of Sciences.

Before the first Duma convened, the government issued "Fundamental Laws" that detailed the powers of the legislature. Bills to become law must pass both houses and be signed by the tsar, who had an absolute veto. Ministers were responsible to the emperor who appointed them, not to the Duma. Many budgetary items the Duma could not question; the finance minister controlled currency and loans; the army and navy, along with their budgets, were beyond the jurisdiction of the legislature; if the two houses approved different budget figures, the tsar could accept either; the Duma could not even discuss its own powers. The tsar's control over foreign affairs, appointments, censorship, police, armed forces, and even summoning and dismissing the Duma was complete. When the Duma was not in session, the emperor might govern by "decrees," to be submitted for confirmation within a month after the Duma reconvened. The government managed to get around this provision by simply ignoring it. The Fundamental Laws reaffirmed that "the supreme autocratic power belongs to the Emperor of All the Russias" and warned that obedience to the royal will was "ordained by God Himself."

With the publication of the Fundamental Laws in early 1906, Witte was no longer indispensable and was rudely dismissed. His place went to Ivan Goremykin, a confirmed reactionary who detested the idea of a Duma. The new finance minister, Vladimir Kokovtsev, was thoroughly competent in the long tradition of capable men in that ministry; the new minister of interior, Peter Stolypin, had been unusually successful as a provincial governor in handling the peasant revolts of 1905, with a minimum of bloodshed.

Before 1905, political parties in Russia had existed only outside the law. Now the October Manifesto legalized all parties, even the revolutionary groups that spurned the cloak of respectability. Two new parties now stepped forward to lead the parliamentary movement. The Cadets (Constitutional Democrats), led by the historian Paul Miliukov would have preferred the calling of a constituent assembly to replace the monarchy with a republic, but seeing no immediate prospect of this they were willing to support the Duma, which they hoped would draft a constitution turning the autocracy into a constitutional monarchy. They promised to work for full civil rights, for universal and equal suffrage, for distribution of land belonging to the state and the church, and, "when necessary," for payment to individual proprietors for giving up their land. The other new party, the Octobrists led by Alexander Guchkov, wanted to hold closely to the October Manifesto; it would support the government in resisting popular pressure; it would challenge the effort by Cadets and others to carry through extensive land reform. The Zemstvo Congress and the Union of Unions ceased to be political agencies as their members lined up with the new parties.

The Duma that convened on April 27, 1906, included an array of forty parties and national groups—for example, the thirty-member Polish Circle, whose primary interest was autonomy for Poland. By far the largest parties were the Cadets, who won 180 of the 520 seats, and the leftist but not socialist Laborites, who marshaled over a hundred. There were a dozen Octobrists, a hundred unattached peasant members who usually voted with the left, and a few Social Democrats, all Mensheviks, for the Bolsheviks had boycotted the elections until the last minute. There were few conservatives, at least none to the right of the Octobrists, for the conservatives, hostile to a full-blown parliament, had boycotted the elections.

After listening to a flabby and pointless speech by the tsar, the Duma unanimously passed an address to the throne demanding amnesty for the seventy-five thousand political prisoners who crowded the nation's jails, universal suffrage, an end to indirect elections, dissolution of the State Council as a legislative upper house, ministerial responsibility, and expropriation of large estates to be divided among the peasants. The government introduced its first bill—a measure to provide a laundry at the University of Dorpat. Then Goremykin arrived to tell the house that its demands were not admissible and that it was not even free to discuss such things as ministerial responsibility and the existence of the upper chamber.

The Duma managed to sit for another two months, during which time it clamored for land reform, demanded an end to capital punishment, insisted that civil rights be respected, and censured the government for allowing the pogroms to continue. The tsar, meanwhile, considered firing his ministers and replacing them with Cadets in an attempt to buy off the opposition; but he gave up the idea at Stolypin's urging and ordered the Duma dissolved. Troops surrounded the palace where it met, and Russia's first modern legislative session closed. Only one measure had passed both houses and received the tsar's signature—a bill providing famine relief for the lower Volga.

One week after the emperor closed the first Duma, a Russian garrison in Finland refused to obey orders, and the mutiny spread to Kronstadt, the location of the base of the Baltic fleet. The Battle Organization of the SRs stepped up its attack on officials, from generals to village police. The terrorists struck down sixteen hundred in 1906 and fifteen hundred more the following year before the government could bring the murders under control. A member of the SRs blew up Stolypin's summer home, killing thirty and wounding others, including the prime minister's children.

Two hundred deputies, most of them Cadets, crossed the border into Finland, where they drew up the famous "Viborg Manifesto." The members reviewed their labors on behalf of civil rights, responsible government, and land reform—the proclamation used the felicitous phrase "land and freedom"—and took the stand that the government had acted illegally in dissolving the Duma. They insisted that the government had no right to gather taxes and draft men for military service without the consent of the Duma, a claim that had, of course, no legal foundation. They called upon the people to refuse payment of taxes and military conscription and warned that the government could contract no loan legally without the consent of the Duma. All who signed the manifesto were placed on trial and given a three-month prison sentence, marking them as criminals and therefore ineligible for election to the next Duma, which the government promised to convene in seven months. The emperor's advisers supposed that they had stilled the voice of opposition.

Peter Stolypin, a marshal of the provincial nobility at the age of twenty-five and a provincial governor at forty, became prime minister at the age of forty-four, succeeding the doddering Goremykin. No doubt the emperor was impressed by the governor's ruthless suppression of peasant disturbances. At least he came with fresh ideas. He was convinced that the solution to rural poverty could only come about from the emancipation of the peasants from the stifling atmosphere of the village.

Stolypin took over as prime minister after the dissolution of the first Duma and set about to insure that the next one would be more amenable to royal will. Thousands lost the vote through legal technicalities; "undesirable" candidates were eliminated; Black Hundred gangs of hoodlums broke up assemblies of leftist groups; the priests urged their parishioners to vote for safe candidates. The arrest of their leaders after Viborg had effectively disposed of the Cadets as serious political force. Although the party did campaign in the new elections, the Bolsheviks attacked its program as ineffective, and police scattered its meetings which they considered to be dangerous to the public peace.

Stolypin's efforts to assure a conservative Duma brought disappointing results. Social Democrats and Socialist Revolutionaries together commanded a hundred votes, Laborites another hundred, and the Cadets a few less. This leftist block outnumbered government supporters more than three to one. Nearly half the members of the Duma had at one time or another been in prison or exile or suffered some indignity from the government.

The session accomplished nothing. Radicals sought without success to force the government to account for the brutal acts of the police against peasant uprisings, but Stolypin announced arrogantly that there would be "first pacification, then reform." Leftists and rightists hurled recriminations at each other, while the Cadets worked to save the Duma as a public platform and agency of political education. The government trumped up a charge that the Social Democratic party was plotting the murder of the tsar and mutiny in the army and demanded that the Duma hand over its SD members for trial. The Duma refused, and after the Duma sat for just a hundred days, the government dissolved it.

On the very day of dissolution, the emperor signed an *ukaz* declaring that the composition of the first two Dumas had not been satisfactory and ordering new electoral regulations. The ukaz reduced membership of the house by eighty; the nationalities of Central Asia, now held to be "foreigners," lost their franchise, and others—peoples of the Caucasus, Poland, and eastern Siberia—had their representation cut by two-thirds.

The harsh revision of the method of choosing members radically altered the complexion of the Duma. The law of 1905 provided that provincial assemblies—elected by landowners, peasants, and industrial workers—should name the Duma members. By this indirect method, landowners chose 1,200 electors, peasants 2,500, and industrial workers 200. The 1907 law gave landowners 2,644, peasants 1,168, and industrial workers 114. This juggling of numbers of electors produced the results the government sought. The landowning gentry, 200,000 in number, chose over half the Duma members. The peasants—of whose conservatism the government was no longer confident—chose one-fifth, property-owning townsmen one-fourth, and urban workers 2 percent. Two hundred and fifty peasants, or twice that number of city laborers, had the same voting power as a single landowner. As a consequence, the third Duma (1907–1912) contained a substantial majority of Octobrists and other rightists and a pitiful sprinkling of Cadets, Laborites, and Social Democrats. The third Duma seemed so satisfactory in composition that the government did not tinker with the law by which it was elected. The fourth and last Duma (1912–1917) showed the same complexion and about the same people as the third and yet later found occasion to voice opposition to the bungling conduct of World War I. Docile as the last two were, the administration occasionally ran up against an adverse vote. To overcome it, the emperor simply recessed the Duma for three days, issued the bill in question as an "emergency decree," and forced the Duma when it reconvened to acquiesce in the accomplished fact.

Although the nation was disillusioned by the collapse of the 1905 Revolution and the official policy of repression that followed, the Duma sought by patience and persistence to become a true parliament. The Cadets, steeped in the British tradition, generally acted with restraint in their role of opposition, whereas the Octobrists, at least initially, supported the government. Stolypin, considered far too liberal by the reactionaries at court, leaned upon the Duma and actively sought its backing. The Octobrist leader Alexander Guchkov much preferred to try to work with the prime minister than see him replaced by someone far more conservative. As a merchant, Guchkov sincerely believed in the emphasis Stolypin placed on individual enterprise, and so the Duma majority gave its support to Stolypin's land reforms. The Duma also won the government's consent to expand educational facilities, constructively criticized and gained some improvement in budget procedures, and debated military expenditures to make sure that the government got its money's worth.

With the election of the fourth Duma in 1912, observers debated whether the institution had come to stay. In its questioning of ministers, its promotion of such sound practices as scientific budgeting and use of statistical services, its being more liberal than the administration in assigning funds to the armed forces when it saw the need, its sharpening its own methods by careful attention to composition of committees, the determination of the Octobrists not to accept cabinet appointments until the tsar should grant ministerial responsibility—in all these things, the Duma worked conscientiously for improved government. The nation came to respect it. The Duma in turn served the nation as its only effective sounding board. With the coming of the First World War the members did not hesitate to protest against corruption and inefficiency. As the tsar and his advisers persisted in going their own way regardless of legislative counsel, the Duma increasingly became a body of opposition by 1916.

The Stolypin Regime

Stolypin began a carrot-and-stick policy of bludgeoning rebels into submission and at the same time offering concessions intended to reduce the opposition. He set up field courts-martial to deal with public disturbances. These military tribunals received orders to complete work on each case in three days: investigate a crime in one day, try the accused in secret the next day, and carry out the sentence—usually death by hanging ("Stolypin's neckties")—on the third. At the same time, peasants obtained the privilege of leaving the mir. The land captain could no longer sentence villagers to fines or imprisonment. Peasants could now win election to zemstvo assemblies and hold any government office. The Peasants' Bank received orders to step up its purchase of land from the gentry for resale to the peasants. The bank bought up more land in 1906 than in the preceding thirteen years, paying the nobles an exorbitant price for it, but the peasants were loath to buy the land, expecting that revolution would bring them the land without payment.

The most significant of the Stolypin reforms had to do with land tenure. The pressing need for land reform becomes manifest from a review of developments in rural Russia after 1861. Emancipation probably contributed in some degree to the population increase from 75,000,000 in 1861 to 125,000,000 in 1897 and 170,000,000 by 1917. That phenomenal rise was reflected in competitive bidding for arable land, which drove up land prices: they doubled between 1860 and 1905, and nearly doubled again by 1917. Peasant purchase of gentry land did not keep up, however, with population growth. More than a fourth of peasant families after emancipation could not support themselves on the allotments they received, and by 1900 over half of them could not do so. No matter that the average peasant family received an allotment—to use but not to own—comparable to peasant holdings in Central and Western Europe. The reassignment of strips in "repartitional" villages discouraged investment in fertilizer, and the technological state of Russian agriculture trailed far behind that in the West. The peasant paid in annual taxes and redemption dues an amount ten times per acre as much as the amount paid by the noble. Peasants managed to survive by renting a few acres from a neighboring landowner at a high price or by taking up seasonal work in a nearby city or on some estate.

By 1905, the state, the church, and other institutions possessed 40 percent of the land of European Russia, the overwhelming bulk of it in nonarable forest and tundra expanses in the north. Private landowners—nobles, townspeople, and others—held a fourth of the land. Peasant allotments constituted 35 percent of European Russia. The average allotment per peasant household in European Russia was thirty acres, but the average in the poorest province was ten acres, and the average in the twelve least prosperous provinces was only twenty. All these are averages. Desperately poor villages might occupy allotment land running to no more than three acres for the typical peasant family of husband and wife, children, grandparents, and unmarried aunts. The persistent clamor in the Duma for dividing state-owned land and for breaking up the great estates, with compensation to the gentry, carried tremendous appeal.

By the terms of the imperial decree of November 1906, the head of a peasant household received the right to claim a land allotment in freehold tenure and to apply for the consolidation so that the separate, small strips into which the allotment typically was divided could become one large piece of land. State-employed surveyors and local committees were to work out the details between the individual and the village, or commune. The law provided that the allotment would go completely and solely to the head of the family. Junior members of the household lost all claim to the allotment that both law and custom had long granted them the right to inherit. They continued, however, to share responsibility for taxes levied against the household. The government proposed three steps in carrying out the provisions of the law. First, the individual would apply for and must receive full title to the land segments and at the same time obtain legal freedom from the commune's authority. Second, application would be made to consolidate the numerous strips into a single plot. If no further steps were taken, the farmer would retain a hut and vegetable garden in the village. If the individual decided to proceed to the third stage, the hut and garden in the village would be exchanged for a new home site on the consolidated land. The farmer, land

and house would be completely separated from the mir or commune on a farmstead similar to that found in England and the United States. Of the thirteen million allotment holdings existing in forty of the sixty provinces of European Russia in 1916, nearly a fourth were privately owned or application for private ownership had been filed with the government; half of those had passed through Stolypin's second stage and become consolidated farms.

The plan to break up the village commune and promote individual proprietorship won the approval of the vast majority of the nobility and the vigorous support of Witte, although the conservative, liberal, and radical parties alike opposed it. The idea behind the scheme was to deflect the peasant's potential for massive expropriation of property, a view found in the programs of several of the radical political movements, by making the farmer a landowner. The authorities hoped that the rural population, interested in protecting their own property rights, would learn to respect those of others. Landowning peasants, officialdom reasoned, would be conservative peasants. Well-to-do farmers—kulaks—would oppose expropriation by which they might lose their lands to the poor peasants. The kulaks, in turn, must necessarily support the government that defended their property. Stolypin was candid about it when he reviewed the program for the Duma: "The government has placed its wager, not on the needy and the drunken," by which he meant the poor peasants, "but on the sturdy and the strong—on the sturdy individual proprietor who is called upon to play a part in the reconstruction of our tsardom on strong monarchical foundations."

The "sturdy and the strong" steadily added to their holdings once they had broken away from the commune. Individuals, most of them peasants who already owned a hundred acres or more, bought nearly twenty-five million acres of farm land through the Peasants' Bank by 1917. Individuals bought another twenty-five million acres of land directly from the gentry without going through the bank. Although some peasants were adding to their holdings, the nobility were rapidly losing theirs. In the forty years prior to World War I, the lands of the gentry shrank to about half the amount they had owned in 1877. Finally, some peasants sold their holdings in the village and trekked east to find free land in Siberia. The flow across the Urals counted seven hundred thousand colonists in 1908 and again in 1909, although 15 percent returned to European Russia disappointed. In the twenty years preceding the outbreak of World War I, over three million peasants moved into Siberia, but that same generation saw the rural population of Russia increase by nine times that number.

The government undertook a revolution of its own in inaugurating the land reform program, but the program barely got underway before the war of 1914 slowed it down, and the overturn of the monarchy in 1917 brought it to a halt. In breaking up the mir, it dissolved the last of the social ties that had bound rural society since the sixteenth century. In encouraging individual initiative in agriculture, it sought an end to the collectivism that had contributed to the retardation of farming for generations. Had the peasant's land hunger been satisfied at the time of emancipation in 1861, the nation might have avoided the travail it would suffer in 1917. There was not time in the few years after 1906 to stem the tide that would sweep over the unhappy land.

The Last Years of Peace

There were slow gains in agricultural production in the years immediately following the inauguration of the Stolypin program. The growth of the cooperative movement—in credit, production, consumption, and marketing—made possible an appreciable rise in peasant income. Well-to-do peasants showed an interest in improving breeds of livestock and careful selection of seed. Farm machinery, whose use was impossible in the days of the strips, became increasingly popular, although there were still only 160 tractors in all Russia in 1914.

Living conditions of the peasant masses continued to be desperately low by European and American standards. Three-fifths to three-fourths of the average family budget went for food alone and most of the rest for clothing, fuel, and repairs to the hut. In Tula province, a hundred miles south of Moscow, a committee appointed to look into the needs of agriculture described peasant life in 1902:

> the dwelling of a Tula peasant is usually a cottage of eighteen by twenty-one feet and seven feet high. Cottages having no chimneys are still very common, the smoke being let out through a hole in the roof. Almost all cottages have thatched roofs which often leak, and in the winter the walls are generally covered with dung to keep the place warm. Earth floors are the rule because in cold weather lambs, calves, pigs, and even cows are brought into the cottage. In localities that have no forests the peasants use straw for fuel, and in the years of poor harvest even dung, thus depriving their fields of much-needed manure. Bathhouses are practically nonexistent. The peasants almost never use soap. Meat, meal, lard and vegetable oil appear on the family table on rare occasions, perhaps two or three times a year. The normal fare consists of bread, kvass and often cabbage and onions. In brief, the poverty of the peasant establishment is astounding.

Industry prospered in the years after 1910, if not for the workers at least for its owners. Production figures rose sharply, although Russia continued to occupy about the same position relative to the production of other nations. Consolidation of production units into giant enterprises continued; by 1914 well over half the nation's workers worked in plants whose labor force exceeded five hundred in each facility. Foreign capital continued to flow into the country, chiefly from the Entente powers of France and England. France alone controlled three-fourths of Russia's iron and coal output.

The government recognized labor unions in 1906 but banned strikes. Denied their most effective weapon, union membership dwindled from the peak of a quarter million to practically nothing by 1914. There were numerous strikes, however, although not under trade union leadership. Seven hundred thousand were out on strike during 1912 and twice that many in the first six months of

1914. Strikes practically disappeared, however, after the outbreak of World War I. The standard of living of the workers continued to be far below that of Western workers: eleven dollars a month was the average industrial wage in 1913, a year of relatively high prices. Man-hour productivity of the Russian worker was less than a fifth that of the English worker, a reflection of much heavier capital investment in the British Isles.

Soon after its election, the third Duma drew up a program intended to require at least four years of free primary education for all Russian children. Over the next six years, the number of primary schools increased by half to one hundred-fifty thousand. The plan was to have every child of school age in school by 1922. In 1914, however, only half the eligible children could find or take advantage of the facilities. The nation still had a long way to go to overcome illiteracy.

The government sufficiently relaxed press censorship after the 1905 revolution to permit a phenomenal increase in the number of Russian periodicals and, curiously, a wide spread in their political views. Over two thousand journals were appearing in 1912, running the gamut from extreme reaction to the Bolshevik daily newspaper *Pravda*.

Stolypin, whose supposed liberalism made him suspect at court, was shot in 1911 by a police agent who was a Socialist Revolutionary. Many suspected that reactionaries at court plotted his assassination. His successor was Kokovtsev, whose feeling toward the Duma was clear from his remark, "Thank God, we still have no parliament." From then on there was no strong man to set the course, and the government was content to drift. Goremykin returned to the office of prime minister early in 1914 and headed the government through two years of war. By the end of his term, it made little difference who was prime minister. The nation was on the brink of revolution.

Foreign Affairs 1894–1914

Russian foreign policy after 1894 was focused on Russia's alliance with France. Although Western democracy and Eastern autocracy seemed poles apart politically, many in both countries approved the alliance, apart from the security it promised both against Germany. Russian liberals hoped that closer ties with France might promote parliamentary democracy at home. French liberals thought it more likely that Russia might become Westernized and democratic than that Hohenzollern Germany or Habsburg Austria might ever do so. Liberal and nationalist circles in Russia blamed the Japanese victory on Germany, whose kaiser had so encouraged the tsar to turn eastward into Asia.

The wounds of the Russo-Japanese War healed quickly. The two powers, in 1907, signed an agreement to respect each other's territory and to support the "Open Door" principle in Manchuria. Yet they manifested their contempt for this "open-door" policy by dividing Manchuria into Russian and Japanese spheres of influence. However, in a secret codicil, Russia agreed not to interfere in

Japanese action in Korea; Japan reciprocated by leaving Russia a free hand in Outer Mongolia. Three years later, Japan annexed Korea, and soon after Outer Mongolia declared its independence from China and then became a Russian protectorate. In 1912, the two recent enemies divided Inner Mongolia into spheres of influence. They also shared a common fear of penetration of East Asia by American capitalists—an American syndicate proposed to sink heavy investments in Manchuria and lend money to China in return for concessions in north China.

Having mended its fences in the Far East, Russia sought a settlement with Japan's ally, Great Britain, who had come to an understanding with France. Now that Russia had patched up its disagreement with Japan, and because Britain was now a friend of Russia's own friend France, a Russo-British agreement recommended itself, particularly in view of the waxing ambition of Germany and Austria-Hungary. By the terms of the Convention of 1907, Russia received northern Persia, including the capital, Teheran, as a sphere of influence. Southern Persia became a British sphere, the two separated by a neutral zone.

The Anglo-Russian Convention settled between the signatories the issues in the Middle East. Now Russia joined with Great Britain in an attempt to block German and Austrian encroachment in the Near and Middle East, areas where Russian and British interests were vital. The 1907 conventions would determine, in part, the alignment of the powers in the coming World War. The Triple Entente—Great Britain, France, and Russia—would stand against the Central Powers—Germany, Austria-Hungary, and Turkey.

When the Young Turk revolution of 1908 indicated a weakening of the Ottoman Empire, both Austrian Foreign Minister Aehrenthal and Russian Foreign Minister Izvolsky saw an opportunity to gain advantage. The two agreed that Austria should annex Bosnia and Herzegovina—the provinces that had been Austrian protectorates since the Congress of Berlin—and Russia should force the opening of the Bosporus to Russian warships. Izvolsky supposed that the two actions would occur simultaneously and only with the approval of the powers signatory to the Berlin treaty, but the announcement of the annexation of the provinces came while Izvolsky was on his way to Paris and first read of it in French newspapers. Pan-Slav circles in Russia were furious. Serbia challenged the annexation and prepared for war, fully expecting Russian support. Because the Russian army was not ready for war and because St. Petersburg received notice that Austria had Germany's backing, there was nothing for the Slav powers to do but to back down and accept a major diplomatic defeat. Serbia halted its preparations for war and agreed to the loss of the provinces. Bitter hatred for Austria and Germany characterized Russian opinion from the moment of the humiliation of the Bosnian crisis of 1908–1909.

Soon after the Bosnian crisis, Izvolsky left the Foreign Office to Stolypin's brother-in-law, Sergei Sazonov. Foreign Minister Sazonov was a relatively mild Pan-Slav who wanted to push Russia's interests at the Straits controlling Russia's access from the Black Sea to the Mediterranean. He also would support the Balkan powers in their encroachment on Turkish territory but who would stop short of war in pursuit of such policies. However, Russian diplomats less cautious than the foreign minister urged the Balkan powers to aggressive action toward Turkey and Austria. These diplomats promoted the birth of the Balkan League, in which Serbia, Greece, Montenegro, and Bulgaria banded together to attack Turkey at the moment of its weakness after losing a war with Italy.

In the First Balkan War, the allies were everywhere victorious over Turkish armies. By the Treaty of London in 1913, the sultan surrendered the island of Crete and all his European territory except a strip of land along the Straits. Then the allies fell to quarreling over the division of the spoils. When Austria refused to allow Serbia to take former Turkish territory on the Aegean, Serbia demanded compensation from Bulgaria, who refused to grant it. The Second Balkan War found Bulgaria fighting alone against its former allies and Romania and Turkey. The peace settlement deprived Bulgaria of much of its earlier gains and even regained for Turkey a bit of what it had lost; Greece, Romania, and Serbia won sizable additions. Bulgaria, embittered at its losses, would side with the Central Powers when global war broke out a year later.

After the poor showing of its troops in the Balkan Wars, Turkey brought in General Liman von Sanders with a staff of German officers to improve the Turkish army. The Liman von Sanders mission announced to the world that German influence in Constantinople was predominant. Turko-German solidarity would block Russia at the Straits and in the coming war would make Anglo-French-Russian cooperation through the Straits difficult, if not impossible. The German kaiser realized what had happened when he admitted, ''Russo-Prussian relations are dead once and for all! We have become enemies!''

In the early months of 1914, Sazonov put before the cabinet the seriousness of the situation at the Straits. The tsar decided to build up the Black Sea fleet and to push forward with army reform and reorganization. Such measures had hardly begun when the nation went to war. Russia's inability to command the entrance to the Black Sea would be a crippling handicap.

Those who prayed for peace among the great powers in this fateful year of 1914 could find much to comfort them. Although there had been many small fires there had been no great conflagration among the leading powers in nearly a century. Although there had been many points of friction in colonial areas, the tension had never brought conflict. A succession of crises in the Near East had reached an amicable settlement. Even the Balkan Wars had not embroiled the great powers.

However, there was little cause for optimism. Austria and Russia might easily come to blows in the Balkans and drag their allies with them into a major conflict. The primary cause for concern lay in the ambitions of the south Slavs, particularly those of Serbia and in the increasing restlessness of Slavic peoples within the Austro-Hungarian Empire. The very existence of the empire was at stake. If it gave in to Serbian demands it would face immediately the insufferable demands of Czechs, Slovaks, Ruthenians, Slovenes, Poles, Romanians, and Italians. On the other hand, no foreign office in Europe expected that Russia would stand idly by and see Serbia destroyed. The next crisis would show to what extent Germany would back its ally Austria and how far France would support its ally

Russia and whether the other nations, joined in the one camp or the other, would enter the struggle.

The Coming of the War

On June 28, 1914 in Sarajevo, Bosnia, a Pan-Serb Bosnian student assassinated the Austrian heir-apparent, the Archduke Francis Ferdinand. Convinced of the complicity of the Serbian government and determined to put an end to this perpetual menace to its own tranquility, Austria, with assurances of German support, delivered an ultimatum to Serbia. The Austrian foreign minister, who drew up the ultimatum, deliberately made its terms so severe that, in the words of an official in the Austrian Foreign Office, "no state possessing the smallest amount of national pride or dignity would accept them." Yet Belgrade agreed to everything except the stipulation that Austrian officials join in the Serbian search for the archduke's murderers and in the suppression of anti-Austrian propaganda. Even the German kaiser believed that the Serbian reply removed "every reason for war." Austria felt otherwise, however, and three days later declared war.

Meanwhile, Sazonov had urged Serbia to use "extreme moderation" in answering the Austrian ultimatum and to ask the great powers to mediate the dispute. Austria spurned the Serbian offer to put the case before the tribunal at The Hague. Sazonov proposed that the Austrian government reconsider the terms demanded of Serbia, but Austria put off answering Sazonov until after declaring war on Serbia, then pleading that it was too late. The Austrians took action in spite of German insistence that its ally negotiate with Russia. Great Britain, France, Italy, Germany, and Russia all exerted pressure on Austria and Serbia to prevent war, but to no avail.

From the moment of the Austrian declaration of war on Serbia the initiative rapidly slipped from the hands of the diplomats into those of the military leaders. Sazonov announced that the next day Russia would begin partial mobilization against Austria but not against Germany. However, the chief of the general staff protested that there were no plans for partial mobilization and that such a program was unworkable. The tsar gave in to the pressure of his generals and ordered full mobilization on July 30. Two days later, France and Germany mobilized, Russia refused a German demand that it halt mobilization, and on the first of August, Germany declared war on Russia. France, Great Britain, Belgium, and Japan soon joined Russia and Serbia, and Turkey lined up with the German powers. None believed that the conflict could last long because of the cost of modern war.

Like all combatants, Russia made no financial or industrial preparation for a long war. Although the nation might expect its industries to meet the army's needs for a short while, there was no plan to mobilize economically. There was a shortage of railroad equipment and a dangerous concentration of railway lines in the western districts whose seizure by the enemy would cripple the transportation system. For the most part, the lines ran perpendicular to the front rather than parallel to it, complicating the problem of shifting men and equipment from one section of the front to the other. With the closing of the Baltic and the Black Sea to allied shipping, the nation had to rely on the Trans-Siberian and a line running south from Arkhangel, whose narrow gauge would not handle most railway equipment. The warm-water port of Murmansk was of little use until the war was nearly over.

Army reforms since the Japanese war had aimed to improve training and the quality of equipment, but the reforms had been halfheartedly carried out. Training and equipment in the Russian army was more inadequate than in any other major army except the Austrian. The shortage of officers became quite alarming after the costliness of the early campaigns. The commander-in-chief, the Grand Duke Nicholas, knew his own shortcomings and wept at the news of his appointment. The situation grew worse in 1915, when the emperor took over as commander-in-chief. Medical service was pitifully inadequate as huge numbers of wounded overwhelmed its resources. The supply of equipment and munitions was inadequate from the outbreak of the war. Shortage of artillery and shells was responsible for higher casualties on the Russian front than on any other. Morale remarkably held up through the first year, but the troops had little understanding of why they were fighting. The peasant soldier did not know where Constantinople was, much less why it was worth such sacrifice. By 1916 the army began to break apart.

Military Operations

Russian war plans envisaged two offensives: one into East Prussia to relieve German pressure on France, the other against Austria to aid Serbia and prevent an invasion of Poland. Generals Rennenkampf and Samsonov, who were bitter personal enemies, advanced into East Prussia, the former from the east, the latter moving north from Warsaw. While Rennenkampf moved cautiously, Samsonov drove too rapidly through unfamiliar woods and swamps, neither knowing of the other's whereabouts, toward an undetermined rendezvous in the rear of the German defenders. The German commander, von Hindenburg, boldly attacked Samsonov at Tannenberg and killed or captured so much of his army that Samsonov shot himself. Then Hindenburg turned on Rennenkampf and drove him back out of Prussia. Russia lost 260,000 men and 600 guns. The disaster gave some comfort to the allies, however. The Russian advance into East Prussia brought German troops hurrying from the western front, thus helping to make possible the victory over Germany at the Marne River near Paris. The German plan to "lunch in Paris and dine in St. Petersburg" fell through.

Meanwhile, the Russians, enjoying better success against Austria, drove to the Carpathian Mountains, captured Lemberg, and besieged the fortress of

Przemysl. The campaign cost Austria more casualties than Russia had suffered in East Prussia. Russian leadership on the Austrian front was greatly superior to that against the Germans; the opposition was much inferior; and the Slav units in the Austro-Hungarian army were indifferent or hostile to the cause they served. The Russian advance faltered when Hindenburg shifted his attack to southwestern Poland, forcing the Russians to move armies to meet it and so relieving the pressure on the Austrians. German troops were within sight of Warsaw before the Russians regrouped and stabilized the front as winter set in.

The spring of 1915 opened favorably on the eastern front. British and French troops landed at the Dardanelles in an effort to pry open the Straits to allied shipping and so move supplies into the Black Sea. Italy joined the Entente powers and provided some relief for Russia by a back-door attack on Austria-Hungary. Russian armies took Przemysl and a hundred thousand men. When they threatened to cross the Carpathians into the Hungarian plain, the Dual Monarchy faced imminent destruction.

Hindenburg now massed troops and artillery for a drive to relieve the pressure on Austria. In May, the Germans drove the surprised Russians back in confusion; never had they seen such artillery preparation. Hindenburg stepped up the pressure all along the thousand-mile front from the Carpathians to the Baltic, so that the defenders could not shift forces from one sector to another. The Germans took 150,000 prisoners before the month was out. The Russians fell back beyond Przemysl and then beyond Lemberg, and by early July were retreating through Poland. Warsaw collapsed in early August, and the forts behind it gave up without a struggle. Most of Galicia, all of Poland, Courland, and Lithuania, and part of White Russia fell to the invader. As the Germans overran these western provinces Russia lost the most vital portion of its railway net. Thenceforth delivering adequate supplies to its retreating front became almost impossible.

At Tannenberg Russia had lost so many guns that every battery in the army had been cut from six guns to four. Neither home industry nor allied aid managed to make up the shortage. In addition, Russia had practically no heavy artillery. The Germans advanced eastward in the summer of 1915 confident that they would run into no heavy fire. The Third Russian Army, for example, had only four heavy guns to the two hundred the Germans used against it. Because of the shortage of ammunition, the Russian field pieces could fire fewer shells a day than the Germans were firing per minute. Waves of infantry went into battle without rifles, hoping to arm themselves with the weapons of comrades shot down in front of them. Machine guns and cartridges for them were in short supply. Food and clothing were scarce. Soldiers even went without bread for as much as five days at a stretch. Grand Duke Nicholas complained at one point that his troops could not advance because of the shortage of boots. Apparently they could retreat without them.

It should have surprised no one that the morale of the troops ebbed rapidly. They took the attitude that there was no use in fighting, because they always lost. Many played sick, thousands ran away to their homes, and thousands of others surrendered. During the summer of 1915, the killed and wounded alone

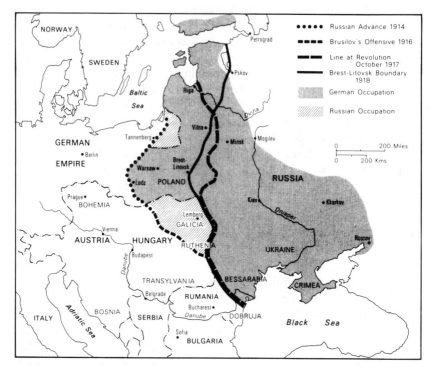

The First World War: The Eastern Front.

numbered nearly 1,500,000; the loss in prisoners ran to nearly a millon, over
three times the average on all fronts for the entire war. Those who deserted
communicated to the civilian population in the rear their sense of hopelessness
and their suspicion that treason in high circles was responsible for the shortages
of equipment and arms.

During the great retreat the civilians behind the front fled in panic. Refugees
moved east in a solid mass, trampling down the fields, destroying the meadows
and woods, leaving a desert behind them. What the refugees did not trample
the army high command ordered deliberately destroyed. Unfortunately, the
scorched-earth policy that had succeeded so well in 1812 was disastrous now.
Where Napoleon had advanced into Russia along a narrow road, Hindenburg
was driving forward along a front hundreds of miles wide. The entire Polish
and White Russian countryside suffered devastation; the villagers were forcibly
removed if they had not already fled. The Germans were saved the trouble of
caring for a conquered population and had no need to fear sabotage of their supply
lines by guerrillas.

In late summer, as the retreat dragged on, Grand Duke Nicholas was removed
to the Caucasian front and the emperor in September took command against the
Germans. The shift came as a final stunning blow. What little morale remained

in the army was owing to the popularity of the grand duke among the rank and file. Cabinet ministers begged the tsar not to take the step, and warned of grave consequences to Russia and to the dynasty. The emperor spurned the advice of all except Rasputin and the empress, who urged the move.

By the late autumn of 1915, the Germans had advanced as far into Russia as they cared, and the line stabilized just west of Riga, then southeast to the Romanian border. The new war minister, the able General Polivanov, worked frantically to heal the wounds of the great retreat. Production and importation of rifles, artillery, and ammunition increased; the training of recruits improved, and they received better equipment; units were brought up to full strength. The army was ready for another offensive, and the Russian government promised its allies to return to the attack in mid-1916.

Three months before Russia was pledged to open the 1916 campaign, the Western allies came forth with their perennial cry for help, this time to ease the pressure of the German assault on Verdun in the northwest corner of France. Soon the Italians made a frantic plea for a Russian drive into Galicia to draw Austrian troops away from their attacks on the Italian front. The Russian high command came to the rescue once more, and General Brusilov mounted a two-pronged attack around the Austrian flanks designed to knock the Dual Monarchy out of the war. Through the summer of 1916, Brusilov advanced into Galicia, overrunning 10,000 square miles of territory and capturing 400,000 prisoners and 600 guns. Meanwhile, Russian forces attacked the German lines south of Vilna, gaining no ground but running up long casualty lists. The pressure, however, pinned down German divisions that otherwise might have gone south against Brusilov. The summer's work cost the nation over 2,000,000 dead and 350,000 prisoners. It is little wonder that most Russians looked upon the war as senseless butchery.

In the early months of 1917, the generals of the Western allies gathered in Petrograd, as the capital had been renamed after the outbreak of the war, to plan the campaigns for the coming spring. The Russian staff once more committed itself to a share in the attack, but the government that made the pledge did not live to fulfill it. Hardly had the visiting staffs left Petrograd when revolution toppled the dynasty.

Russia in the Economic War

The government drafted 6,500,000 people into the armed forces by the end of 1914 and 5,000,000 more the following year. By March 1917, Russia had mobilized 15,000,000 for military service. Of working-age men 15 percent were thus withdrawn from civilian production in 1914, 25 percent by 1915, 36 percent by 1917. The effect on the economy was disastrous.

At the very moment when there was crucial need for a rapidly expanding labor force, industry lost enormous numbers, many of them key workers, to the army.

Prisoners of war, refugees, children, and women—by 1917 over half the industrial workers were women—could not compensate for the loss. Increasing the length of the working day could not make up for declining productivity; by 1917 man-day output of the average worker had fallen to two-thirds or less of the prewar output. The coal and iron mines and the sugar, textile, and machine plants of Poland and Lithuania were lost to the Russian economy as the front moved eastward. The manufacture of ironware and steel, agricultural equipment, textiles, and leather goods fell off sharply, and industrial output, what there was of it, went chiefly to the army. The industrial plant was simply incapable of satisfying both military and civilian needs.

Rail transport broke down early in the war. The great retreat cost the nation the provinces best served by the railway net. French investment in Russian railroads had aimed at gridding Poland and White Russia with a system that could quickly assemble Russian troops against the common enemy. Now that network was no longer in Russian hands. Even for the remainder of the nation, rail service declined sharply. Equipment not properly maintained fell rapidly into disrepair. By 1917 over half the prewar locomotives were standing idle for want of repairs, only a third of the freight cars were still in use, and rail output had fallen to barely a fourth the prewar figure. What remained, the army commandeered, and manufacturing output slowed down for want of raw materials.

Agricultural production declined sharply. The huge block of farm land, eight million acres, pared away by the German advance cut grain output but did not commensurately reduce the number of mouths to feed as the peasants fled eastward. The conscription of agricultural workers into the armed forces left owners of great estates, whose output went almost wholly to market, helpless to carry on production. The peasant communities as well felt the pinch of conscription. It was "getting empty in the villages," noted one who had lost three brothers and inherited the care of their families. The loss of horses drafted for the army affected the great landowners far more than peasant operators. Cereal acreage on the great estates fell during the war to less than a third of the 1913 acreage. In addition to Poland, all of whose farm land fell to the Germans, the arable land of Russia itself shrank by 10 percent during the war. The mounting food shortages grew rapidly more severe with the collapse of the transportation system. As industry turned out fewer goods for civilian consumption, peasants grew ever more reluctant to produce more than they could eat. Indeed, with the loss of the foreign market, the peasants fared better than they had in peacetime. The nation consumed more of its produce than ever before, although the sharing was far from equitable.

People in the cities, particularly the urban working class, suffered most when the army took the bulk of the marketed produce and the transportation system could not adequately distribute the rest. Bread, flour, vegetables, and dairy products flowed in a dwindling stream from the farms, and yet the urban demand for them rose because of the urban population growth. Wages doubled during the war, but the worker's living costs by 1917 had climbed to three or four times the 1913 level. The government came round slowly to ration food and fix prices, but a flourishing black market hampered the feeble efforts at control. There were food riots as early as 1915, and the revolution opened two years later to the shouts of angry mobs before the bakers' shops of Petrograd.

During the first six months of 1914, there were nearly twice as many strikes and strikers as during the entire preceding year. Then, with the coming of the war all political parties except the Bolsheviks urged a moratorium on political and economic demands for the duration. Strikes all but disappeared during the first few months of war, but with the military collapse and economic chaos that set in the following year, morale rapidly waned. The year 1915 saw over a half million workers marching in a thousand strikes. In 1916 there were half again as many strikes and twice as many strikers. During the last two months of the old regime, seven hundred thousand workers were in the streets. Most ominous was the fact that as the war progressed, the demands of the strikers became increasingly political. City workers were blaming the government for their deepening misery.

The rural population, too, became steadily more restless as the war dragged on. As prices of needed manufactured goods rose more rapidly than the prices peasants could claim for their produce, they did not bother to plant as many acres as formerly. When the government forbade the sale of liquor during wartime, peasants started to make their own from the grain they harvested, grain whose sale to the government at fixed prices would bring them little reward for their labor. There was mounting resistance to conscription, especially during the 1915 retreat. The authorities were unable to cope with the growing number of peasants who fled into the woods to escape the draft. Deserters and refugees brought back to every village a grim tale of shortages at the front as well as of military disaster and frightful casualties.

The war cost the Russian government nearly forty billion rubles. Over half of this was borrowed, eight billion from abroad; the rest was made up by printing additional currency. From a billion and a half rubles in mid-1914 the amount of money in circulation rose to nearly twenty billion by the fall of 1917. The effect of such an increase was to drive prices precipitately upward and to concentrate property in the hands of those who had the wherewithal to buy from those who in desperation had to sell. The government made no serious effort to finance the war by taxation. The nation as a whole, of course, paid for the war as it went along in the capital destroyed, in the civilian goods not produced, and in the seven million casualties, half of them killed and wounded. A fifth of the cost of the war was shifted to foreign governments, whose loans Russia never repaid.

The War and the Russian Government

Russia in 1914 was a curious blend of medievalism and Western democracy, and the war strengthened both of these contradictory forces. Nicholas II resented the limitation of autocracy imposed by the 1905 settlement. Now the war gave him an opportunity to recover personal command of the government. It also, for a brief period, elevated the public image of the monarch. This could be seen on the occasion when the tsar spoke from the balcony of the Winter Palace and assured his listeners below that Russia would fight until every enemy soldier had been vanquished. The crowds massed in the square below cheered their ruler, sang patriotic songs and religious hymns, and shared an emotional bonding between tsar and people.

As one sign of national patriotism, the capital was renamed Petrograd as the Russian equivalent of the Germanic-sounding St. Petersburg. This new designation of "Peter's City" continued throughout the war and beyond, until the authorities renamed it Leningrad in 1924 after Lenin's death. (That name continued until 1991, when the historic terminology of St. Petersburg was restored.)

One irony at this time of emotional and patriotic unity between Nicholas and his subjects in the late summer of 1914 is that their public and enthusiastic response in Petrograd occurred in Palace Square, adjacent to the Winter Palace. This was the same site where the "Bloody Sunday" massacre took place in January 1905, when Russian troops fired point-blank into the crowds in the square and nearby streets. As it turned out, events during the First World War all too soon shattered the sense of unity and common sacrifice for the motherland. Criticism, frustration and growing opposition in the face of huge casualties and other problems began to permeate society, with ominous implications for the future.

Another consequence of the wartime atmosphere could be seen in the national Duma. The war contributed to the dignity if not to the power of the Duma and opened the way for participation by zemstvos and municipalities, by representatives of business and labor, in the conduct of the war. As these autocratic and democratic tendencies gathered strength, the clash between them became inevitable. Thus did the war contribute to the rapid collapse of the old regime, a collapse toward which the nation had been drifting for generations.

One week after the nation went to war, the members of the Duma gathered for a one-day session to assure the government of their support. Laborites, Mensheviks, and the five Bolsheviks refused to vote war appropriations, but the rest joined in a "sacred union," agreeing to postpone political differences until the delivery of "Europe and Slavdom from German domination." Within the month the nation's municipalities formed a Union of Cities, and provincial and district zemstvos joined a Union of Zemstvos, to care for the wounded and establish military hospitals.

After the brief opening session, the Duma adjourned for six months. Many of its members remained in the capital, however, and met frequently to discuss the conduct of the war. When the new session opened in 1915, the aging Prime Minister Goremykin hardly bothered to veil his contempt for the Duma and his impatience to dismiss it, while the grossly corrupt and inefficient war minister, Sukhomlinov, gave his glib assurance that all was well at the front. Members pressed for a protracted session and demanded that the bungling and unpopular cabinet give way to those "enjoying the nation's confidence," by which they meant individuals the Duma could trust. After meeting for six weeks, members of the Duma were sent home on the tsar's orders.

In June 1915, when Russian armies were pulling back all along the front, the tsar called the nation to greater effort in prosecuting the war, summoned the Duma to meet again a month later, and dismissed several of the most objectionable ministers, including the contemptible Sukhomlinov. Goremykin, however, stayed on for another six months as prime minister in the face of near unanimous opposition from the Duma.

When the Duma met in mid-July 1915, its six leading parties, conservative as well as liberal, joined in a Progressive Bloc that adopted a program of modest reform. The members, disturbed at the handling of the war and alarmed at the enemy advance, hoped to stiffen the nation and encourage it to greater effort. The Bloc's platform called for a ministry of confidence, amnesty for political prisoners, religious toleration, the granting of civil rights to Jews, an end to persecution of ethnic minorities, restoration of autonomy to Finland and Poland, legalization of labor unions, and equality of all classes before the law. It sought to free wide areas behind the front from the dictatorship of military commanders by which civilians, hundreds of miles from the front, came under martial law.

Several cabinet members sympathized with the proposals of the Progressive Bloc, but Goremykin considered them a challenge to the crown and prorogued the Duma. The Union of Zemstvos, the Union of Cities, the Russian Red Cross, and other agencies took up the program of the Progressive Bloc; some called for the convocation of an assembly to draft a constitution. It was immediately after the dismissal of the Duma that the tsar assumed the position of commander-in-chief of the armies in the field.

From the moment the emperor left to assume command of the army, the government, or what passed for government, came under the direction of the empress, Alexandra. Nicholas encouraged her to pick up the reins of administration, writing from the front, "Wifey, dear, don't you think you should help hubby while he is away?" "Wifey" took up her new assignment with enthusiasm, firmly convinced that she must guide the nation safely through to victory.

One of the tasks the empress undertook was the strengthening of her husband's will against the advice of those she considered pernicious. She constantly urged Nicholas to be "more autocratic," "use the whip," "teach them to fear you for Baby's sake." She harped, as she had since their son's birth, on the need to pass on the autocratic power undiluted. "Be Peter the Great, Ivan the Terrible, the Emperor Paul; smash them all," she wrote when Duma leaders questioned the administration. She called the ministers "rotten" and asked if it were not possible to hang "that fat Rodzianko" and exile Duma leaders and the Grand Duke Nicholas to Siberia.

In her unofficial but defacto position as head of the civilian administration, Alexandra looked for direction to her "man of God," Rasputin. The influence of the "holy devil" on the empress had grown steadily since his first appearance at court in 1905. Until 1915, however, he had interfered in political matters only rarely. With the emperor's departure from the capital Rasputin came quickly to exercise near-dominant influence in the making of military as well as civilian policy. The empress who now decided so many matters turned constantly to "Our Friend," as she called Rasputin, for advice. Campaign plans were brought to the holy man to be blessed. He who had no military knowledge whatsoever called for an advance near Riga in the winter of 1915, giving as reason only that "it is necessary." Six months later he advised that "we should not yet strongly advance" in the same area.

When Nicholas left for the front, the cabinet consisted momentarily of exceptionally honest and, aside from Goremykin, liberal men. However, during the next few months Rasputin and the empress changed all that. Few would have mourned the passing of Goremykin except for the fact that the premiership went to the contemptible Boris Sturmer. Sturmer, believed to be sympathetic to Germany, also assumed the office of foreign minister in spite of pleas by allied governments that Sazonov might stay on. The highly respected Alexander Krivoshein, who commented bitterly that "the government is no longer a government," was driven from the Ministry of Agriculture. The capable minister of interior, Nicholas Shcherbatov, gave way to the craven and nearly insane Alexander Protopopov, who continued in office at the insistence of the empress when even the tsar had had enough of him. Nicholas faintly protested that so many dismissals and appointments "make my head go round." The reactionary Duma leader Vladimir Purishkevich referred to the comings and goings of shadowy cabinet members as "ministerial leapfrog" and later joined the plot to assassinate Rasputin.

During the nine-month premiership of Sturmer in 1916, the government simply let matters drift. Strikes increased ominously in Petrograd. Basic living became nearly impossible for many as prices quadrupled while wages only doubled. The food situation was approaching a crisis. The transportation system was breaking down. Financial scandals came to light implicating Sturmer and the petty, scheming toadies who surrounded him. With continued military reverses, a mood of defeatism spread over the capital. In November 1916, Professor Miliukov rose in the Duma to call attention to the "dark forces" at work in government circles and to charge the empress and Rasputin with leading the nation into chaos. He reviewed the story of ineptitude, bungling, and corruption in officialdom point by point, asking after each point, "Is this stupidity or is it treason?" Purishkevich, the most zealous monarchist in the lower house, repeated the reference to the "dark forces" that were ruling Russia. He bitterly assailed Sturmer, Protopopov, and the loathsome Rasputin and called for an end to this treacherous leadership.

Sturmer was forced from office by these biting attacks, leaving the management of affairs to the despicable Protopopov and to Rasputin and the empress who pulled the strings. The new prime minister, Alexander Trepov, offered Rasputin a bribe of two hundred thousand rubles if he would consent to the dismissal of Protopopov, but Rasputin spurned the offer. There seemed little other recourse but violence. In December 1916, Rasputin was poisoned and shot by Purishkevich,

Grand Duke Dmitry, and Prince Felix Yusupov, husband of the tsar's niece; the prince announced, "I have killed Rasputin, the enemy of Russia and the tsar."

On the eve of Rasputin's murder Nicholas prorogued the Duma for a month and replaced Trepov with the nonentity Prince Nicholas Golitsyn. Protopopov and the empress retained control. The tsar postponed the promised session of the Duma until late February 1917, thereby adding to the causes for popular resentment against this caricature of a government. There were many to prophesy where such a course would lead. The tsar's brother-in-law, the Grand Duke Alexander, warned, "Disaffection is spreading very fast. Strange as it may seem, it is the government which is preparing the revolution." General Krymov reported to Duma leaders that the army would welcome a coup d'état. Rodzianko, the Duma president, told Nicholas to his face that for twenty-two years the tsar had been pursuing a wrong course.

The Fall of the Monarchy

In late February 1917, the Duma convened at last, its members resolved not to accept another prorogation. Discontent was showing itself in every segment of Russian society. Aristocrats bent on saving the monarchy were considering the possibility of replacing Nicholas II with another Romanov. Business leaders, in spite of the enormous profits they were making, resented arbitrary government and interference by army leaders in the administration of areas as far from the front as Petrograd itself. Soldiers, interested only in an end to the war, were deserting in droves and infecting the communities to which they returned with the spirit of hopelessness that pervaded the front. Peasants, who had never supported the war and whose fathers and sons made up the long casualty lists, wanted peace; failing to get it, they vented their wrath against neighboring landowners, the symbols of the authority they hated. Strikes spread to every industrial center. The populace of the capital was growing surly over the severe hardships brought about by the shortage or maldistribution of food and fuel and the strangling effect of rising prices. All Russia was sick of war. Even those few who wanted to see it through to victory complained that the government was crippling the nation's war potential.

On February 23/March 8 bread riots broke out in Petrograd. Homemakers, clamoring for their lean ration at the meagerly stocked food shops joined thousands of workers who walked out in protest against their decreasing real wages. Banners reading "Down with autocracy" appeared, and there were clashes with the police. The giant Putilov plant locked its gates rather than give in to the demand of its well-organized metal workers for higher pay, and fifty other factories closed down.

The next day the number of strikers had swelled to two hundred thousand. The Petrograd garrison, called out to quell the rioting, showed little disposition to attack the crowds. Even Cossacks were seen to wink at the strikers as they moved gently against them. The action was significant. The Cossacks had always been the most reliable strikebreakers, and now they were going soft. Three days later most of the troops had joined the mob. Now the insurgents had rifles and machine guns, and soldiers and civilians joined in attacking public buildings, opening the jails, hunting down police, and breaking into the arsenal to arm those who came into the streets empty-handed.

The Duma received orders to disperse on February 27/March 12 but decided to remain in session. It chose a Provisional Committee, under the chairmanship of the Duma president, Rodzianko, to assume leadership in the growing chaos. Alexander Kerensky, leader of the radical but non-Marxist Labor party and the Menshevik, Nicholas Chkheidze, joined with Miliukov, Guchkov, and others of the Progressive Bloc to form the Provisional Committee. Rodzianko telegraphed the tsar at army headquarters pleading with him to save the situation by appointing a cabinet in whom the nation could feel confidence. There was no reply. A few days later the committee, supported by the army's leading generals, demanded that the tsar abdicate. He abdicated on March 2/15 in favor of his brother, Grand Duke Michael, who abdicated the next day and threw his support to the Provisional Committee. After three centuries of occupying it, the Romanovs gave up the throne almost without a protest.

Meanwhile on February 27/March 12, some 250 delegates elected from factories and army units in Petrograd gathered to organize the Soviet of Workers' and Soldiers' Deputies. The soviet, or council, developed as a revolutionary institution during the 1905 rising; many who sat in the Petrograd Soviet in 1917 had attended the sessions twelve years earlier. Remembering the 1905 disappointments and failures and swearing to avoid them now, the delegates determined to seize the initiative and hold it. Nonsocialist parties, branded as capitalist or "bourgeois," were denied seats in the Soviet. The Executive Committee of the Petrograd Soviet assumed various governmental functions. It created a commission to control the supply of food in Petrograd; established a militia of workers to succeed the police who had been shot or driven into hiding; allowed only left-wing newspapers to continue publication; and named the terms upon which it would cooperate with the Provisional Committee of the Duma.

A Provisional Government emerged out of this political and social turmoil. The president of the new government was Prince George Lvov, a moderate who had won respect as chairman of the Russian Red Cross and president of the Union of Zemstvos. The brilliant if obstinate Miliukov, the Cadet leader who would have preferred a constitutional monarchy on the British model to the republic he now served, became foreign minister. The Octobrist Guchkov, also a monarchist in sympathy, headed the War and Navy Ministry. The thirty-six-year-old lawyer Kerensky, an emotional and flamboyant orator and soon to emerge as the dynamic spirit of the new cabinet, became minister of justice. As vice-chairman of the Executive Committee of the Petrograd Soviet and member of the Provisional Government, Kerensky was the only link between the two groups that contended for power through the spring and summer of 1917. With the exception of Kerensky, the cabinet consisted of moderate liberals of such

Alexander Kerensky

renowned respectability as to win cordial approval abroad if not at home. The United States extended recognition to the new government within a week of the tsar's abdication, and Great Britain, France, and Italy soon followed suit.

The Provisional Government quickly announced its program. There was to be an immediate amnesty for all political prisoners, freedom of speech, press, and assembly, and labor was to enjoy the right to organize and to strike. Restrictions on individual freedom because of class, creed, or ethnic origin were removed. Soldiers, when not on duty, would enjoy the same privileges as civilians. Troops that had taken part in the overthrow of the monarchy were not to be disarmed or removed from Petrograd. The death penalty was abolished. Finally, the government would begin preparations for convening a national assembly chosen by secret and universal suffrage to draft a constitution. The Provisional Government also appointed one committee to draw up a program of land reform to submit to the Constituent Assembly and another to suggest a democratic reorganization of local government. The peasants undertook their own land reform, however, and local soviets appeared all over Russia to tear away the power from provincial governors and zemstvos.

The Petrograd Soviet rapidly gathered strength in both numbers and influence. Fifteen hundred delegates attended the second day's meeting, and there were twice that number a week later. Many who represented nobody just wandered in off the streets to hear and, especially, to speak. In an effort to bring about some order in representation, the soviet decreed that each delegate should be chosen by two thousand factory workers or soldiers dwelling or stationed in the capital. Soviets soon appeared in Moscow and other cities and also in army units at the front. By the end of summer there were six hundred soviets in towns and army posts all over the land.

Although most leaders of the Bolsheviks and Socialist Revolutionaries were abroad or in Siberian exile, the Petrograd Soviet was dominated by socialists and made its appeal to and was supported by the proletariat. On the other hand, the Duma and the Provisional Government largely consisted of business and professional men and reflected liberal, middle-class interests and attitudes. The March Revolution developed into a contest for power between the radical, socialist, proletarian-oriented Petrograd Soviet and the liberal, democratic, bourgeoisie-oriented Duma members who predominated in the Provisional Government. It was inevitable that the two groups should look upon each other with suspicion and distrust.

Although the soviet was overwhelmingly socialist in spirit, there was sharp disagreement over what role the organization should play at this stage of the revolution. On the far left, the Bolsheviks, who had not yet come round to the view that the soviets should put themselves forward as agencies of political power, initially wanted a revolutionary government to assume control only until the election of the Constituent Assembly. On the right, the conservative minority urged full cooperation between the Petrograd Soviet and the liberal bourgeoisie in the Provisional Government. Between these extremes lay the mass of delegates, who accepted the revolution as middle-class in character, with which it would not be seemly for socialists to associate, but who believed that the soviet itself should not overturn the Provisional Government. This was in keeping with the conviction of many Marxists, Mensheviks particularly, that Russia must become a mature capitalist society before it could evolve to socialism. The Bolsheviks, a small minority, were many times outnumbered by the Mensheviks and Socialist Revolutionaries who made up the great bulk of delegates to the soviet. Indeed, total Bolshevik strength in Russia was surprisingly small. The party may have had thirty thousand members at the time of the revolution and only forty thousand a month later.

At the insistence of the soviet, the imperial family was placed under house arrest at the palace of Tsarkoe Selo, twenty miles outside Petrograd. When Miliukov put out feelers to obtain asylum for the family in England, the soviet demanded imprisonment of the tsar. This proved unnecessary when the Provisional Government promised that "Citizen Romanov" and "Alexandra the German," as some revolutionaries delighted in calling them, might not leave Russia without the consent of the Executive Committee of the Petrograd Soviet. In midsummer, the family was moved to Tobolsk east of the Urals and in the following spring to Ekaterinburg. The Bolshevik government in the summer of 1918 announced that the imperial family had been executed. Several of the grand dukes and duchesses were shot as well.

The ease with which the dynasty fell must have come as a surprise to those who pondered the bloody vengeance wrought upon revolutionaries in the eighteenth and nineteenth centuries. Only two days before the fall of tsardom, Kerensky had declared the overthrow of the regime to be impossible at that moment. The revolution broke out spontaneously, with no planning and without leadership. Lenin was not even in Russia at the time. Those who joined the bread riots and strikes, won over the troops, agitated among the sailors at the Kronstadt naval base, or led the mobs to torch the public buildings, seize the arsenal and break open the prisons—they were all nameless. Only later did revolutionary leaders catch up with the movement and attempt to set its course.

The March Revolution cost surprisingly little in human life. The killed and wounded in Petrograd numbered only thirteen hundred. Many naval officers died at Kronstadt. Elsewhere the revolution was accomplished "by telegraph" as soldiers and officials deserted the old regime at the first command to surrender. Over the entire nation the change came about too easily and too generally to involve much bloodshed. Nevertheless, from the moment of its birth, the government that replaced tsardom lived a turbulent and precarious existence.

Suggested Reading

ASCHER, A., *The Revolution of 1905: Russia in Disarray* (Stanford, 1988).
BOCK, M. P., *Reminiscences of My Father, Peter A. Stolypin* (Metuchen, NJ, 1970).
BONNELL, V. E., *Roots of Rebellion: Workers' Politics and Organization in St. Petersburg and Moscow, 1900–1914* (Berkeley, 1983).
BRUSILOV, A. A., *A Soldier's Note-Book, 1914–1918* (Westport, CT, 1970).
BUCHANAN, G., *My Mission to Russia*, 2 vols. (Boston, 1923).
BUSHNELL, J., *Mutiny Amid Repression: Russian Soldiers in the Revolution of 1905–1906* (Bloomington, IN, 1985).
CHAMBERLAIN, W. H., *The Russian Revolution*, 2 vols. (New York, 1952).
CONROY, M. S., *Peter Arkad'evich Stolypin: Practical Politics in Late Tsarist Russia* (Boulder, 1976).
CURTISS, I. S., *Church and State in Russia: the Last Years of the Empire, 1900–1917* (New York, 1940).
DE JONGE, A., *The Life and Times of Grigori Rasputin* (New York, 1982).
DEUTSCHER, I., *The Prophet Armed: Trotsky, 1879–1921* (New York, 1954).
EDELMAN, R., *Gentry Politics on the Eve of the Russian Revolution: The Nationalist Party, 1907–1917* (New Brunswick, NJ, 1980).
EDMONDSON, L. H., *Feminism in Russia, 1900–1917* (Stanford, 1984).
FITZLYON, K., and T. BROWNING, *Before the Revolution: A View of Russia under the Last Tsar* (Woodstock, NY, 1978).

FLORINSKY, M. T., *The End of the Russian Empire* (New York, 1961).

FREEZE, G. L. (ed.), *From Supplication to Revolution: A Documentary Social History of Imperial Russia* (New York, 1988).

FUHRMANN, J. T., *Rasputin: A Life* (New York, 1990).

FÜLÖP-MILLER, R., *Rasputin, The Holy Devil* (Garden City, NY, 1928).

GOLDER, F. A., *Documents of Russian History, 1914–1917* (Gloucester, MA, 1964).

GOLOVINE, N. N., *The Russian Army in the World War* (New Haven, 1931).

GRONSKY, P. P., and N. J. ASTROV, *The War and the Russian Government* (New York, 1973).

HARCAVE, S., *First Blood: The Russian Revolution of 1905* (New York, 1964).

HARGREAVES, R., *Red Sun Rising: The Siege of Port Arthur* (Philadelphia, 1962).

HASEGAWA, T., *The February Revolution: Petrograd 1917* (Seattle, 1981).

HOSKING, G. A., *The Russian Constitutional Experiment: Government and Duma, 1907–1914* (Cambridge, Eng., 1973).

HOUGH, R., *The Fleet That Had to Die* (New York, 1958).

KATKOV, G., *Russia 1917: The February Revolution* (New York, 1967).

KNOX, A., *With the Russian Army, 1914–1917* (London, 1921).

KOHN, S., and A. F. MEYENDORFF, *The Cost of the War to Russia* (New York, 1973).

KOKOVTSEV, V. N., *Out of My Past* (Stanford, 1935).

LEVIN, A., *The Second Duma* (New Haven, 1940).

_____, *The Third Duma, Election and Profile* (Hamden, CT, 1973).

LIEVEN, D. C. B., *Russia and the Origins of the First World War* (London, 1983).

LINCOLN, W. B., *In War's Dark Shadow: The Russians before the Great War* (New York, 1983).

LOCKHART, R. H. B., *British Agent* (New York, 1933).

McCORMICK, R. R., *With the Russian Army, Being the Experiences of a National Guardsman* (New York, 1915).

McNEAL, R. H., *Russia in Transition, 1905–1914: Evolution or Revolution* (New York, 1970).

MAKLAKOV, M. A., *Memoirs of M. A. Maklakov: The First State Duma: Reminiscences* (Bloomington, IN, 1964).

MALOZEMOFF, A., *Russian Far Eastern Policy, 1881–1904* (Berkeley, 1958).

MEHLINGER, H. D., and J. M. THOMPSON, *Count Witte and the Tsarist Government in the 1905 Revolution* (Bloomington, IN, 1972).

MILIUKOV, P., *Political Memoirs, 1905–1917* (Ann Arbor, 1967).

MILLER, M. S., *The Economic Development of Russia, 1905–1914* (London, 1926).

The Nicky-Sunny Letters: Correspondence of the Tsar and Tsaritsa, 1914–1917 (Hattiesburg, MS, 1970).

NIKOLAEVSKII, B. I., *Azeff, the Spy* (New York, 1934).

NOLDE, B. E., *Russia in the Economic War* (New Haven, 1928).

OBERLÄNDER, E.; G. KATOV; N. POPPE; and G. VON RAUCH (eds.), *Russia Enters the Twentieth Century* (New York, 1971).

OWEN, L. A., *The Russian Peasant Movement, 1906–1917* (London, 1937).

PALEOLOGUE, M., *An Ambassador's Memoirs, 3 vols.* (London, 1931).

PARES, B., *The Fall of the Russian Monarchy* (New York, 1961).

_____, *My Russian Memoirs* (London, 1931).

_____, *Russia and Reform* (New York, 1962).

PAVLOVSKY, G., *Agricultural Russia on the Eve of the Revolution* (London, 1930).

PEARSON, R., *The Russian Moderates and the Crisis of Tsarism, 1914-1917*, (New York, 1977).

PIPES, R., *The Russian Revolution* (New York, 1990).

POLNER, T. J., *The Zemstvos and the All-Russian Union of Zemstvos* (New Haven, 1930).

RIHA, T., *A Russian European: Paul Miliukov in Russian Politics* (Notre Dame, 1969).

RODZIANKO, M. V., *The Reign of Rasputin: An Empire's Collapse: Memoirs of M. V. Rodzianko* (Gulf Breeze, FL, 1973).

ROGGER, H., *Russia in the Age of Modernization and Revolution, 1881-1917* (London, 1983)

ROMANOV, B. A., *Russia in Manchuria, 1892-1906* (New York, 1974).

RUTHERFORD, W., *The Russian Army in World War I* (London, 1975).

SABLINSKY, W., *The Road to Bloody Sunday: Father Gapon and the St. Petersburg Massacre of 1905* (Princeton, 1976).

SALISBURY, H. E., *Black Night, White Snow: Russia's Revolution, 1905-1917* (Garden City, NY, 1978).

SAZONOV, S., *Fateful Years, 1909-1916* (London, 1928).

SERGE, V., *Memoirs of a Revolutionary, 1901-1941* (London, 1963).

SERVICE, R., *Lenin: A Political Life* (Bloomington, IN, 1985).

_____, *The Russian Revolution, 1900-1927* (Atlantic Highlands, NJ, 1986).

STAVROU, T. G., *Russia under the Last Tsar* (Minneapolis, 1969).

TROTSKY, L., *History of the Russian Revolution, 3 vols.* (New York, 1936).

_____, *My Life* (New York, 1930).

_____, *1905* (New York, 1971).

ULAM, A. D. B., *The Bolsheviks: The Intellectual, Personal, and Political History of the Origins of Russian Communism* (New York, 1965).

VASSILYEV, A. T., *The Okhrana: The Russian Secret Police* (Philadelphia, 1930).

VERNER, A. M., *The Crisis of Russian Autocracy: Nicholas II and the 1905 Revolution* (Princeton, 1990).

WALDER, D. W., *The Short Victorious War: The Russo-Japanese Conflict, 1904-1905* (London, 1974).

WALLACE, D. M., *Russia on the Eve of War and Revolution* (New York, 1961).

WARNER, D. P., *The Tide at Sunrise: History of the Russo-Japanese War 1904-1905* (New York, 1974).

WEISSMAN, N. B., *Reform in Tsarist Russia: The State Bureaucracy and Local Government, 1900-1914* (New Brunswick, NJ, 1981).

WHITE, J. A., *The Diplomacy of the Russo-Japanese War* (Princeton, 1964).

WILSON, C., *Rasputin and the Fall of the Romanovs* (New York, 1964).

WILSON, E., *To the Finland Station* (New York, 1940).

WITTE, S. I., *The Memoirs of Count Witte* (New York, 1967).

ZENKOVSKY, A., *Stolypin: Russia's Last Great Reformer* (Princeton, 1985).

CHAPTER 17

Troubled Times

The monarchy had been drifting for several years toward a political vacuum. Its inertia had grown steadily more apparent. With the demise of the monarchy the political vacuum became complete. Not one formal agency but two stepped forward to fill the void, to speak for the people, and to lead the nation through the travail of a new political birth.

Contest for Power

No sooner had the tsar abdicated than it became apparent that those who cooperated to bring about the revolution had done so for contradictory reasons. The middle-class and professionals, liberal in outlook, had supported the revolution in the belief that a new administration would more energetically prosecute the war and in the real fear that Nicholas might even seek peace with the Central Powers, whom he regarded as sympathetic to the autocracy so dear to his heart. Most peasants and workers, on the other hand, tired of the war to the limit of their endurance, had supported the revolution in the determination that it must bring peace. The liberal element never had its roots among the people and failed utterly to understand their longing to end the war. The leaders of the Provisional Government aimed at establishing Western political liberalism, whereas most peasants and urban workers, when not confused, bewildered, or indifferent, wanted socialism. The socialists did not trust the Provisional Government and supported the system of soviets as a counterbalance and check on it. The liberals had little sympathy for social revolution. Some segments of the masses would insist upon it.

From the moment of its creation the Provisional Government enjoyed little power and saw its orders carried out only when approved by the Petrograd Soviet dominated by socialists. Whereas the Bolshevik members were few in number and not influential, the Mensheviks controlled the soviet; their leader, Chkheidze, presided as chairman of the executive committee. Chkheidze refused a cabinet post in the Provisional Government, but Kerensky, who deserted the Labor party for the Socialist Revolutionary, accepted the Ministry of Justice while retaining his position as vice-chairman of the Petrograd Soviet and member of its executive committee.

The first split between the Provisional Government and the Petrograd Soviet developed over control of the army. On the eve of the creation of the Provisional Government, Duma and soviet leaders had agreed that soldiers should have full civil rights and that the Petrograd garrison be neither disarmed nor sent outside the capital. However, before the announcement, the soviet newspaper *Izvestia* proclaimed the famous Army Order Number One, which called for the election of regimental delegates to the soviet; ordered the organization of company committees to maintain "discipline," punish "rudeness" of officers to men, arbitrate differences between them, and assume control of the issue of arms and prevent their falling into the hands of officers; abolished the salute; and forbade troops to carry out orders of the government unless they bore the approval of the soviet. Several days later the executive committee of the Petrograd Soviet announced that it had not intended enlisted men to elect their own officers, as some had been doing, and that it meant Order Number One to apply only to the Petrograd garrison. The harm had already been done, however. Discipline in the army—or what was left after earlier murders of officers, desertions, and mutinies—melted rapidly away. Army and navy committees or soviets, whose election the Provisional Government could do nothing to halt, looked to the Petrograd Soviet for direction. Troops debated and voted on every order to advance. When the government thus lost control of the armed forces, Minister of War Guchkov resigned in disgust. Kerensky succeeded him.

The Petrograd Soviet and the Provisional Government were soon at odds over foreign policy. Miliukov, the foreign minister and dominant figure in the cabinet, refused to understand the revolution as a protest against further participation in the war. He insisted that Russia must honor its commitments to the allies and that the war must go on to victory. Derisively he was named "Miliukov Dardanelsky" for his stubborn position that the nation must continue fighting to gain the spoils—Constantinople, and the Dardanelles, among others—promised by the allies in the secret Treaty of London in 1915. His defiance of Prime Minister Lvov, who was willing at least to discuss with the Western powers the possibility of peace without annexations, led to Miliukov's withdrawal from the cabinet just two months after joining it.

Soviet leaders were not of one mind on the question of war or peace. The right wings of the Menshevik and Socialist Revolutionary parties professed their opposition to offensive war but pledged themselves to defend the nation. The left wings of the two parties urged an early "peace without annexations or indemnities on the basis of the self-determination of peoples." Socialists of all parties agreed in supposing that the March Revolution in Russia would quickly spread to other countries. *Izvestia* called upon the peoples of the world to reject the war aims of their governments and to take upon themselves the power and the will to end hostilities.

With Guchkov and Miliukov gone, Prince Lvov reorganized the cabinet in an effort to strengthen the Provisional Government. Six of the fifteen portfolios went to socialists, including Kerensky as minister of war. From then on Kerensky was the outstanding figure in the government. Left out of the cabinet, Bolsheviks refused to support it and waited for the moment when they could turn out both liberals and moderate socialists whom they regarded as enemies of the revolution.

Return of the Exiles

On the morrow of its birth, the Provisional Government granted an amnesty to political leaders imprisoned or exiled under the old regime. Prince Kropotkin, Martov, the novelist Gorky, and Plekhanov came back from Western Europe. Nicholas Bukharin and Leon Trotsky, who for a year had published a socialist newspaper in New York, returned from America. The Polish revolutionary Felix Dzerzhinsky, soon to head the secret police, emerged from a Moscow prison. Kamenev and Stalin came out of Siberia. Zinoviev, Radek, and Lenin returned from exile in Switzerland, having obtained passage from a German government hopeful that their appearance in Petrograd would weaken the Russian war effort.

In mid-April Lenin stepped from the train at the Finland station in Petrograd to receive a magnificent welcome. The next day he presented his views in the "April Theses" to Bolsheviks assembled from all over Russia. He declared that the revolution was only in its first, or bourgeois, stage and branded the Provisional Government as capitalist in sympathy, imperialist in aim, and incapable of or unwilling to bring peace. The revolution soon must move into its second stage, where power would shift from the Provisional Government to the soviets, the truly revolutionary form of government. The Bolsheviks did not yet control the soviets, but Lenin expected that they would soon win control because of the party's superior discipline over that of the other two socialist parties, both torn by dissension. The second stage of the revolution would not yet introduce socialism but would pave the way for it: agricultural land would be nationalized and parceled out under soviet control to the peasants, and banks would be consolidated into one national institution under soviet management. Soviets, in other words, would direct and control production and distribution. The "bourgeois" army, police, and administration would disappear, their places taken by a people's militia and officials chosen by the soviets of elected delegates of the workers, soldiers, and peasants. The Bolsheviks, he urged, must assemble a party congress to adopt the new revolutionary program and work out the tactics for its enactment. Because the Second Socialist International had broken up over support of the war, a new Third International, which would admit only "real revolutionaries," must come to birth to turn the "imperialist" war into a civil war against capitalism in every country. To make clear the distinction between uncompromising revolutionary socialism and the moderate socialism of the Mensheviks, it was time for the Bolsheviks to drop the name "Social Democrats" and adopt the more proper name "Communists." Then the party must lead the revolution into its second stage by winning control of the soviets. Once that control was sure, the Bolsheviks would raise the cry "All power to the soviets" and advance to the overthrow of the Provisional Government.

Lenin's proposals seemed "delirium" and "the raving of a lunatic" to Menshevik leaders, and even the Bolshevik Kamenev wrote them off as unacceptable, but the rank and file of the party and, in growing numbers, the masses of the people caught up the cry for peace and land that Lenin had voiced in the "April Theses." The National Conference of Bolsheviks, which met in the capital in early May, adopted Lenin's program by an overwhelming majority. From that moment Lenin's leadership and command over the party, although frequently questioned, were never seriously challenged. His driving energy, his refusal to compromise, his sharp, biting sarcasm, his genius for cutting through theoretical verbiage to express in catch phrases the demands of the people made him tower above all others, with the possible exception of Trotsky, in popular appeal.

Lenin addressing street crowds

The Government Challenged

In mid-May 1917, an All-Russian Congress of Peasants' Deputies gathered in Petrograd. A majority of the delegates were Socialist Revolutionaries; most of the rest were not members of any party. The gathering voted to back the Provisional Government and to support the continuation of the war. It disapproved Lenin's demand for nationalization of land immediately, calling for socialization only with the sanction of the Constituent Assembly, whose meeting the government had scheduled for early fall.

The First All-Russian Congress of Soviets assembled in the capital in mid-June. Of the nine hundred delegates over half were SRs and Mensheviks; the Bolsheviks could muster a scant hundred. When the Bolsheviks announced that they were going to organize demonstrations against the war and the "capitalist ministers," the Congress of Soviets forbade the move and denounced Lenin for seeking to overthrow the government. The Congress of Soviets then announced its own demonstration in support of the Provisional Government, but the Bolsheviks joined the parade in overwhelming numbers, carrying banners denouncing the government and shouting out their demand for peace and land. The administration stood helplessly by while some of the marchers mildly cheered it and others boisterously jeered it.

The Provisional Government had promised the Western allies another offensive to ease German pressure in France. Kerensky, the war minister, attached to each army unit commissars whose task it was to mediate differences between the soldiers' committees and the officers and to try to restore morale among the troops. Kerensky visited the front, seeking by the power of his colorful oratory to inspire the men, but he won for himself only the derisive title "persuader-in-chief." On July 1, the Russians advanced in Galicia. The assault was momentarily successful against Austrian troops, but when German reinforcements appeared, the Russians fled in disorder. The awful attrition of three years of war, the effect of Order Number One, the success of Bolshevik peace propaganda among the troops, and the fraternization of the soldiers with the enemy had completely demoralized the army.

The troops in Petrograd, sympathetic to bolshevism, heard the rumor that they were to go to the front and called upon Bolshevik leaders to order a demonstration against the government. Lenin, believing the time not yet ripe, refused. However, the next day, July 17, the streets filled with workers, soldiers, and sailors proclaiming a new revolution and demanding the arrest of the ministers. Kerensky stood firm, but Chernov was rescued from a lynching by Trotsky, who had just joined the Bolsheviks. Some members of the party were for overturning the government. Lenin, however, counseled caution; the time had not yet arrived, he felt, for a Bolshevik seizure of power. While the party leaders argued over a course of action the ardor of the mob cooled. The next morning a government-inspired press story charged Lenin with being a German agent. Some of the troops accepted the lie and threw their support to the Provisional Government.

Police smashed the presses of the Bolshevik newspaper *Pravda* and rounded up Trotsky and other Bolshevik leaders. Lenin escaped by crossing into Finland. The government did not ban the party, however, and its members continued to serve in the soviets.

With the failure of the unplanned July uprising, the first period of the revolution, a period that produced "the deepening of the revolution," came to an end. The four months after the fall of tsardom witnessed the collapse of discipline in the army; the widespread seizure of land by the peasants; the clamor of the proletariat for higher wages and worker control over production and distribution; the growth of separatist movements in the borderlands; and the mounting insistence of the majority to an end to the war. A Bolshevik manifesto voiced these hopes of the masses in simple language: "The peasants want land, the workers want bread, and they both want peace." "Peace, land, and bread" became a rallying slogan that caught the fancy of the masses. Many parties, not the Bolsheviks alone, voiced their support for these aspirations.

Swing to the Right

The second period of the revolution, the two months following the suppression of the July rising, witnessed Kerensky's juggling efforts to balance the revolution between extremes of left and right. The "July Days," which Lenin viewed as "something more than a demonstration and less than a revolution," constituted a test of strength between the Bolsheviks and the government. Prince Lvov gave up the premiership to Kerensky, who vowed to save the nation from bolshevism. The Provisional Government had apparently won out when it locked up some of the Bolshevik leaders, drove others into hiding, and smashed the party press, but it had lost its own struggle for liberal government. Kerensky drifted into the position of dictator, forced to rely on the backing of the old officer class in the army, a backing that to many exemplified reaction and restoration of the monarchy.

In response to pressure from the generals, Kerensky named the war hero Kornilov commander-in-chief. The general accepted the nomination only if he could be free to name subordinates and restore discipline. Reputed to have "the heart of a lion and the brain of a lamb," Kornilov was politically illiterate and saw no difference between Bolsheviks and right-wing socialists who opposed Lenin as much as he. Rightists and moderates of every hue—conservative constitutionalists like Miliukov and Rodzianko, industrialists who feared the seizure of their plants by the workers, landowners who saw their estates being expropriated by land-hungry peasants, officers who deplored the waning strength of the army, Cossacks who dreaded the social revolution that might spread to their own lands, members of the clergy who regretted their loss of influence, monarchists who hoped to bring back the Romanovs—came to look upon Kornilov as a possible savior of the land from further turmoil and anarchy.

Even before Kornilov's appointment the general had proclaimed that the Petrograd Soviet must be swept aside and the Bolsheviks all hanged. In early September, he gave the orders for troops loyal to him to march on Petrograd, ostensibly to save the Provisional Government from the Bolsheviks and from German armies advancing toward the capital. Kerensky dismissed him, but Kornilov refused to step down. His contemplated coup quickly evaporated, however. Railway workers sided with the government and refused to move the trains loaded with his troops. Telegraph workers refused to dispatch orders to his subordinates. Soldiers loyal to the government mingled with Kornilov's Cossacks, urging them not to fire upon their brothers. Generals on other fronts could not support Kornilov, for their own men refused to move against the government.

Alarmed at the threat to the capital, many forgot their differences of July. Mensheviks and Socialist Revolutionaries asked the Bolsheviks to cooperate in defending Petrograd. Trotsky and the other Bolshevik leaders arrested in July were released. A Committee to Fight Counterrevolution, which included Bolshevik members, was organized and called for similar committees all over Russia. It legalized the so-called Red Guard, or Bolshevik militia, twenty-five thousand strong and well armed with rifles and machine guns, but the attack never came. Kornilov's troops deserted to the Provisional Government. He and the generals who had supported him were arrested. (After the November Revolution they all escaped to organize the resistance movement in south Russia.)

The Kornilov mutiny, which closed the second period of the revolution, proved the futility of attempting to restore the old regime. The fiasco had one important consequence—it freed the Bolsheviks and restored them to a position of influence, permitted the rearming of their fighting force, and paved the way for their eventual seizure of power.

On the Eve

In the final period after the March Revolution, through the eight weeks following the Kornilov rising, pressure on the government steadily increased. Having survived a threat from the left in July and another from the right in September, Kerensky now maneuvered desperately to avoid further crisis. He reshuffled the cabinet, retaining a few nonsocialists but relying chiefly on moderate socialists and keeping to himself the chief executive power. He declared Russia a republic, implying that the government was no longer "provisional," and by this mild step invoked the criticism of liberals generally, who accused him of appropriating authority that only a national body should possess. He canceled Kornilov's plan to restore the death penalty at the front. Then he announced that elections of delegations to the Constitutional Assembly would take place in November. Finally, to win broad support for his new coalition cabinet, he gathered about him in Petrograd the so-called Democratic Conference, consisting of fourteen hundred delegates of rural and city governments, soviets, and trade and professional unions, representing all shades of political opinion. Even the Bolsheviks took part, but the conference did nothing but establish the Council of the Republic—five hundred of the nation's keenest minds—to sit regularly as a consultative body until the Constitutional Assembly could gather in late autumn. Much to Lenin's disgust the Bolsheviks voted to elect delegates to the new body.

The council met and did nothing before Bolshevik bayonets scattered it in November. Trotsky rose in the first session of the council to accuse it and the government of treason to the revolution and of seeking to drag out the war. Then he and the other Bolsheviks dramatized their contempt for the council by walking out of the session. Three weeks later it passed unnoticed and unmourned into the limbo of pre-Bolshevik institutions.

Social Upheaval

In the eight months during which the Provisional Government managed uneasily to cling to power, Russia was undergoing a social revolution far more fundamental than the relatively mild political disturbances occurring in Petrograd. The real revolution swept into the countryside and the industrial centers and through the army. Leaders in the capital often could not keep up with the radical thoughts and demands of those they professed to represent. In their resolution to divide up the land, the peasants were far ahead of the Socialist Revolutionaries who spoke for them. In their impatience to seize control of industry, the workers of Petrograd and Moscow moved too rapidly even for Lenin. In their determination to end the war quickly, the soldiers were far out in front of most Bolshevik leaders.

At the beginning of 1917 there were nearly seven million Russians under arms. In the next eight months a millon of them "demobilized themselves" and went home. Those who remained—poorly armed, shabbily clothed, and miserably fed—had lost all stomach for the war. Troops at the front, their morale riddled by socialist propaganda, passed the time listening to speeches of revolutionaries from the capital, debating social and political questions, electing new officers and demoting old ones so that "cooks became colonels and colonels cooks,"— choosing standing committees to arbitrate disputes with officers and special committees to investigate the food situation, sending off delegations to Petrograd to ask "Comrade" Kerensky if he had really ordered an advance as their officers insisted, hounding the doctors to give them medical discharges, trading their arms to the Germans for tobacco, and querying every arriving batch of replacements as to whether conditions at home were as bad as rumor made them. Resistance to authority showed itself in refusal to obey commands, unwillingness to drill, beating and killing officers and even commissars sent out by the government or the Petrograd Soviet, restraining the artillery from firing at the enemy lest it bring reprisal, feigning sickness, and deserting. Peasant soldiers disappeared into the night in droves to hurry back to their villages to share in the expropriation of land. As Lenin put it, the "army voted for peace with its legs."

Defeat, war-weariness, poor equipment, propaganda, and the committee system stipulated in Order Number One, all contributed to such demoralization in the old army that when the November Revolution broke out, the Provisional Government could muster to its defense only military students, women, some companies of soldiers, and a few hundred Cossacks of the millions in uniform at the time. The Bolsheviks later had to organize an entirely new fighting force. The old army simply evaporated in the summer and autumn of 1917.

In some sections of the navy the situation was even worse than among the land forces. The garrison at Kronstadt was strongly Bolshevik in sympathy. The sailors of the Baltic fleet, although not all Bolshevik, were hostile to the Provisional Government from the very beginning. Admiral Kolchak kept the Black Sea fleet in line for a while, but by June 1917, the sailors were hurling their officers overboard and electing new ones. Kolchak resigned in disgust and later led the anti-Bolshevik movement in Siberia.

Over four-fifths of the population of Russia in 1917 were peasants. Never reconciled to the land settlement of the sixties, they persisted in the belief that the land should belong to those who tilled it. They begrudged the absentee landowner, the imperial family, the state, and the church their rich acres. Traditionally much of the land was cultivated communally, and "the sacred right of private property" held no meaning for the majority of Russian peasants.

Very few Russian peasants were as prosperous as were those of Germany and France. The great majority were miserably poor, and both their numbers and their plight were growing worse in the twentieth century. Although many districts of south Russia were heavily overpopulated, the problem was less one of land shortage than of backward methods. The peasants persisted, however, in attributing their sorry condition to the size of the small plots they tilled and the high rents they had to pay the neighboring gentry for leasing an additional acre or two. They had felt strongly for generations that the only way out of their misery lay in seizing as much of the landowners' fertile estates as their fellows would let them fence off. Government statisticians could show them that the percentage of arable land under peasant proprietorship was steadily rising, but the poor peasant or the "middle" peasant could draw little comfort from the fact that a few kulaks were renting or buying hundreds of acres from the nobles. Many could look beyond their own tiny plots upon the broad expanses of a neighboring aristocrat or rich peasant unable distinguish between the two.

The war demanded its heaviest sacrifice from the rural community. The army took nearly twelve million of the strongest peasants and two million horses. Much land went out of cultivation because of the manpower and animal shortage. Army purchases made up for the loss of foreign markets, but the government paid in paper money that fell in value as its volume increased. Peasants grew loath to sell their produce because the factories were turning out so few of the goods they needed and the rubles they received would buy so little. The Provisional

Government inaugurated a system of requisitions at fixed prices, but the peasants' response was simply to hide their grain.

The overthrow of the monarchy and the rapid disintegration of authority gave peasants the opportunity to order the land settlement to their own liking. Remembering the government's ferocious vengeance after the 1905 Revolution, however, they now moved cautiously. They sickled a few sacks of grain at night from the neighboring aristocrats' fields or raided their forests for firewood. Peasants pastured their cows in the nobles' meadows. Peasants and villagers demanded prohibitive wages for their labor and would not allow prisoners of war to work on the great estates. Gangs raided the barns and granaries of the gentry, carrying off grain and livestock. Growing bolder by the day, the villagers advanced on the manor houses with clubs, axes, and scythes. Manor houses went up in flames and with them deeds, leases, and mortgages. Great landowners, peasant and noble, all suffered the scourge; they poured into the capital demanding that the Provisional Government save them and their estates. Punitive expeditions marched again as in 1905 into the countryside. This time the troops refused to fire at the villagers and often joined them. There were nearly six thousand peasant "disturbances" in 1917, the number growing rapidly in the months just prior to the Bolshevik Revolution. Most of the attacks were against the gentry. The rich peasants, or kulaks, knowing the peasant mind, usually gave in to the demands of the villagers and went along with the movement to save their own lives.

In the mid-May Congress of Peasants' Deputies that convened in Petrograd, many delegates had orders to support a model land law that would forbid the private ownership of land, allowing only its use by any citizen and limiting the amount any individual might cultivate to what he or she could work with his or her own labor. Although the resolution became the basis for communist land policy, the Congress of Peasants' Deputies turned it down and condemned the expropriations. The congress expressed sympathy for the confiscation of church lands and great estates but insisted that the coming Constituent Assembly approve such confiscation. Such, too, was the policy of the Provisional Government, and so it remained until the November Revolution. The peasants, however, refused to allow the government to defer the land question until the meeting of the Constituent Assembly. They took the law into their own hands and divided up the great holdings, so that gentry estates disappeared and even peasant-owned farms of fifty acres were broken up. Before the Bolsheviks came to power the land question had already been settled.

Army mutiny and rural outbreaks would not of themselves have overturned the Provisional Government. The soldier and the peasant felt concern primarily over local or individual problems. Many a village, focusing its attention on its land shortage and the nearby means of correcting it, lost all interest in the war. The soldier, the peasant in uniform, wanted only to get back to the village and claim a personal share of the neighboring estate. Furthermore, those most anxious to upset the government, namely the Bolsheviks, had very little and only spotty support among soldiers or peasants. If the government were to be turned out it must be with the help of urban workers, the class upon which the Bolsheviks had long focused their efforts.

The urban working class constituted only a small percentage of society, but the middle class was smaller, relatively, than in Western Europe. Furthermore, as Lenin clearly foresaw, the urban proletariat could expect at least the tacit support of most peasants who, having little sense of private property, probably would not defend the existing regime. When the troops withdrew their support from a government bent on continuing the war, the proletariat became the most influential segment of society in determining the course of the revolution. Their poverty, insecurity, and brutish labor and living conditions gave the workers every incentive to destroy the society that gave them so little. That they would swing far to the left once the bands of restraint relaxed might easily have been predicted. Yet it is misleading to suggest that the proletariat or masses or merchants or wealthy held tightly to any creed. There were conservatives, moderates, liberals, non-Marxist socialists, Marxists, and anarchists in every class and segment of society.

The war had brought increased hardship to Russian workers whose prewar standard of living was far below that of Western labor. Per capita income just before World War I in Germany, was three times, in England four and a half times, in the United States, seven times that in Russia, where it stood at a hundred rubles or fifty dollars a year. Average factory wages in 1913 were twenty-two rubles, or eleven dollars per month. Although the ten-hour day was not unusual, the legal limit was eleven and a half and many workers exceeded this. Some lived in barracks where guards kept order with the lash. Money wages rose during the war, but prices climbed even faster and real wages fell by 40 percent between early 1916 and November 1917. The poor harvest of 1917 forced the bread ration from a meager pound a day to a half pound by late autumn. Urban population grew rapidly, bringing overcrowding and squalor. The progressive breakdown in transportation threatened the city workers with starvation in the spring of 1917. Strikes multiplied during that spring and summer. The strikers demanded higher wages, an eight-hour day, and worker control over employment and dismissal. Owners answered strikes with lockouts. In many instances the workers forcibly kept the plants open, in many others the factories closed down permanently, adding to the mounting unemployment. Often there was worse violence; brutal foremen and employers were beaten and occasionally killed, although in general city workers were much less bloodthirsty than the peasants and soldiers. By the fall of 1917, labor had gone beyond the usual trade union demands and was calling for socialization of industry and the surrender of political power to the soviets.

Elected factory and shop committees sprang up in the capital during the March Revolution to speak for the workers in negotiations with employers and in dealings with the government. Soon the committees all over the capital and in other industrial centers ware demanding that management of factories come under the control of workers' committees. Trade unions, legal since 1906 but harmless and almost nonexistent before the overthrow of the monarchy, expanded quickly thereafter. Membership exceeded 1,500,000 by June 1917, when Petrograd was host to an All-Russian Conference of Trade Unions. The unions tended to be moderate, whereas the factory committees were radical in outlook. The unions tended to limit their program to seeking improved wages, hours, and conditions of work. The factory committees added political and social to economic demands. Mensheviks and Socialist Revolutionaries predominated in the trade union leadership, whereas the Bolsheviks strove for and won the support of the factory committees. The trade union leaders supported the Provisional Government; the factory committees turned against it.

As the government seemed unwilling to satisfy the soldiers' hope for peace and the peasants' need for land, so it proved completely ineffective in meeting the workers' problems. Prices continued to rise, real wages to fall, food to grow scarce, factories to close down, unemployment to increase, and strikes to spread. The patience of the worker, like that of the soldier and the peasant, was nearing exhaustion.

The Bolshevik Surge

In early August 1917, the Sixth Congress of the Bolshevik party, the first in a decade, met secretly in Petrograd to appraise the July uprising and plan future action. Lenin, still hiding in Finland, did not attend but spoke through party leaders Stalin, Molotov, and Sverdlov. The party saw that power was slipping away from the Provisional Government into the hands of militarists and reactionaries, and declared that only a Bolshevik-led armed rising of workers and peasants could save the revolution. It assumed that the Bolshevik Revolution in Russia would touch off similar risings in Western Europe. Some party leaders insisted that a socialist experiment in Russia must inevitably fail unless capitalism collapsed in the West. The principle of ''democratic centralism'' was adopted, providing that differences of opinion were permissible only up to the point where the party ''line'' or policy became clear. Thereafter there must be no deviation; members must accept the policy without criticism and obey all orders without question. Lenin had insisted on such discipline from the moment of his entry into the socialist movement. Now he had his way. Finally, the party agreed to shelve the demand ''all power to the soviets,'' because there seemed no immediate prospect of driving the Mensheviks and SRs from control, particularly in the Petrograd Soviet. Party membership now numbered a quarter million, an eightfold increase since the abdication of Nicholas II.

The Kornilov mutiny removed from the Bolsheviks the stigma of official disapproval, for the government needed their help to survive. Now armed and respectable, their influence quickly grew. On the day of Kornilov's arrest, a Bolshevik resolution passed the Petrograd Soviet, which thereby deserted its Menshevik and SR leaders. Many members of the two parties, the one growing increasingly conservative and the other badly split between right and left wings, joined the Bolsheviks. Soon the latter took over control of the soviet, and Trotsky became its chairman. A week later, the Moscow Soviet also turned Bolshevik, and the drift in their favor was apparent in many of the provincial soviets. In the third week of October the Petrograd Soviet chose a Military Revolutionary Committee, with Trotsky as chairman, to organize troops in the capital for a defense against an expected German advance from Riga. The Bolsheviks now had an army, for the soldiers of the Petrograd garrison showed themselves more willing to take orders from the Military Revolutionary Committee than from the Provisional Government.

Through October Lenin poured forth a barrage of letters and pamphlets, trying to win over the other party leaders to his view that the time was at hand for the Bolsheviks to drive "Kerensky and Company" from power. Some urged that the party must wait for the meeting of the Second All-Russian Congress of Soviets, scheduled to assemble in Petrograd on November 7. However, Lenin, believing that the people had had enough of speeches and resolutions and that Bolshevik influence might decline if the coup were postponed, insisted that "to wait is a crime, a childish play at formality." To those who protested that the Bolsheviks were not sufficiently numerous to seize power and hold it, Lenin retorted, "After the Revolution of 1905, 130,000 landlords governed Russia. Cannot 240,000 members of the Bolshevik party govern Russia in the interests of the poor against the rich?"

On October 10/23 the Bolshevik Central Committee met secretly in the capital to argue the party's position. After ten hours of heated debate Lenin carried the others with him in concluding that the time for action had arrived; the crescendo of peasant disturbances, the growth of Bolshevik strength, and their victory in the soviets made this the moment when the party must make its bid for power. A resolution to this effect carried by ten votes to two, Kamenev and Zinoviev opposing. To act as the general staff of the revolution, the group chose from among its own membership a Political Bureau, or "Politburo," consisting of Lenin, Trotsky, Stalin, Zinoviev, and Kamenev. Zinoviev and Kamenev continued openly to oppose an early rising down to the very moment of the Bolshevik Revolution, a flagrant violation of the party discipline on which the Sixth Congress had insisted.

That the Bolsheviks were planning to overthrow the government was no secret, but Kerensky seemed to scorn the threat. The administration took no military measures, and perhaps none was possible. The Petrograd soldiers had grown so accustomed to loafing about the streets that no one could expect them to put up a vigorous fight for anything, and the troops at the front were hardly more reliable. The government seemed confident that a Bolshevik uprising would fail as surely as the July demonstration. Just four days before the November Revolution Kerensky voiced the hope that the Bolsheviks would attempt something and expressed confidence that he would crush them once and for all. While he was speaking, the workers of a munitions plant, on orders from the Military Revolutionary Committee, were turning over five thousand rifles to the Bolsheviks. Reports were coming in from as far away as the middle Volga and the Caucasus that popular meetings were calling for the overthrow of the Provisional Government. Delegates from nearly all the regiments in the Petrograd garrison promised the Military Revolutionary Committee full support in whatever action it should choose to take.

The Communist Victory

On October 22/November 4, the Bolshevik-dominated Military Revolutionary Committee issued a proclamation accusing the Provisional Government of serving counterrevolutionary interests and calling upon the Petrograd garrison to disregard all orders except those of the committee. At government headquarters the cabinet decided at last to take up the challenge. It agreed on the night of November 5 to close down the Bolshevik newspapers the next morning, arrest the party leaders, disband the Military Revolutionary Committee, and bring some supposedly loyal troops to the capital. After a few hours' delay, the Bolshevik newspapers appeared—the print shops were now guarded by soldiers called out by the Military Revolutionary Committee. Meanwhile Kerensky was addressing the sterile Council of the Republic, swearing to put down the uprising and asking for a vote of confidence. Not getting it, he threatened, but only threatened, to resign.

At the Smolny Institute—former convent and girls' school now headquarters of the Petrograd Soviet—the Bolshevik leaders met on November 6 to analyze the situation. Lenin took up residence in the Smolny, from which he directed the revolution. That night, soldiers under orders from the Military Revolutionary Committee seized railway stations, strategic bridges over the Neva, the state bank, and the telephone exchange, shutting off all communication between the ministry and the outside. Even the Cossack regiments refused to rescue Kerensky. To his hysterical calls for help, they answered repeatedly that they "were getting ready to saddle their horses."

On the morning of October 25/November 7 the Bolsheviks announced that the Provisional Government had fallen. There was no resistance. Most shops and theaters remained open, but government offices closed a few hours early. Kerensky escaped from the city in a car owned by the American Embassy. The capital fell to the Bolsheviks almost without the firing of a shot. The Winter Palace—where the rest of the cabinet was defended by the women's battalion, some cadets, and a few stray Cossacks—surrendered after a few artillery shots and a rush by the Red Guards. Six of the attackers were killed, but the defenders suffered no losses. The members of the cabinet were arrested. The "October Revolution" succeeded with far less bloodshed than the March Revolution, which itself had cost remarkably few lives. The Provisional Government could find fewer defenders than the monarchy it had replaced.

In Moscow the Bolsheviks ran into heavy opposition and managed to win control of the city only after a week of hard fighting. In the industrial centers of central and northern Russia the revolution encountered little resistance. In the Urals

The Bolshevik attack on the Provisional Government at the Winter Palace, November 1917

and western Siberia the Bolsheviks won easily. A hostile regime appeared in the Georgian capital of Tiflis, and in Kiev nationalist Ukrainians moved to set up an independent republic. The Don and Kuban Cossacks successfully resisted the Reds. Fighting went on in most of the provincial capitals, some of which did not surrender to the Bolsheviks until the following spring.

Back in Petrograd, the Second All-Russian Congress of Soviets of Workers', Soldiers', and Peasants' Deputies met on November 7 even before the firing had died down. Of the 650 delegates, most of them from northern and central European Russia, the Bolsheviks and the left-wing Socialist Revolutionaries who supported them numbered over 500. The Mensheviks and the right-wing Socialist Revolutionaries walked out of the very first session, ridiculed by Trotsky as "so much refuse that will be swept into the rubbish heap of history."

Lenin put before the Congress of Soviets a proclamation addressed to the peoples and governments of all belligerent powers demanding immediate peace without annexations or indemnities and announcing that Russia annulled and would immediately publish all the secret treaties. The proclamation asked British, French, and German workers to help force an end to the conflict. Put to the vote, the document won unanimous approval. In effect, the new government, only one day old, thereby announced Russia's withdrawal from the war.

Next, Lenin presented a decree outlining the government's land policy. It wiped out ownership of great estates without compensation, turning over such estates together with church- and state-owned lands to local land committees and peasant soviets for distribution among poor peasants. It forbade private ownership and the sale or rental of land. The Constituent Assembly would finally settle the land question. Meanwhile, anyone could use as much land as the individual and his or her family could work, but no one could hire labor. In the interest of fairness, the arable land would periodically be reallotted. The Bolsheviks had borrowed the principles of the decree on land from the Socialist Revolutionaries, who in turn had based their program on practices operative in the village communes for centuries.

The Congress of Soviets approved a new cabinet to be called the Council of People's Commissars. The slate consisted entirely of Bolsheviks, for the Left Socialist Revolutionaries refused to join a ministry that was not open to all socialists. Lenin became president of the Council, Trotsky commissar for foreign affairs, Rykov commissar for internal affairs, and Stalin commissar for nationalities. Finally, the Congress elected an All-Russian Central Executive Committee, two-thirds of which were Bolsheviks and the rest Left Socialist Revolutionaries, to serve in place of the Congress of Soviets until the latter should convene again. Then the Congress adjourned. It had organized the new administration and launched the new government.

For a few weeks the Bolsheviks tolerated an array of oppositional fragments, perhaps because they underestimated their own strength or overestimated that of their opponents. They had toppled the Kerensky regime with a ragtag army of Red Guards, civilians, sailors, and disorganized soldiers, perhaps twenty thousand strong, but there were millions of troops at the front who, for all the Bolshevik leaders could be sure, might turn against them.

A group of former members of the Petrograd municipal government called upon the populace not to obey Bolshevik orders. Congresses of non-Bolshevik members of trade unions and factory committees passed resolutions condemning the change of government. Mensheviks and Socialist Revolutionaries held meetings to debate what sort of government they would support. Cabinet members of the Provisional Government, freed from prison, declared themselves still in office and issued orders and gave out press releases until the Council of People's Commissars drove them from the capital. The Imperial Senate continued its sessions unnoticed until it handed down a decision that the new government was illegal, whereupon it was dissolved. Bureaucrats in government offices continued to function, refusing to recognize the new administration until they were driven from their desks or forced at pistol point to serve the new order.

There was discord too among the Bolsheviks themselves. Many party members urged freedom of the press when some Menshevik newspapers were closed. Others questioned Lenin's determination to end the war at all costs. Many—among others, Kamenev and Zinoviev—favored a coalition cabinet that would include other socialists, and several members of the Council of People's Commissars resigned because they believed that a government made up solely of Bolsheviks could maintain itself only by political terror. Some left-wing Socialist Revolutionaries then won seats on the Council, but they only added to the disagreement and resigned three months later. Lenin, like Lvov and Kerensky, had trouble with his early cabinets.

During the first several weeks of the Soviet regime there was a spate of legislation, much of it of far-reaching importance. By the decree on land that Lenin read to the Congress of Soviets, the peasants won the government's sanction of the steps they had already taken to redistribute the land. Now the proletariat received somewhat similar power over private industry by a decree giving workers a determining voice in management, production, and price setting. In addition, railroads, shipping, and all banks were nationalized, and foreign trade became a government monopoly. The eight-hour day became legal. The debts of earlier governments to foreigners were disallowed. Inheritance of private property was made illegal; all such property was to fall to the state when the owner died. Municipalities were to take over all private homes and apartments; local soviets might remove bourgeois families in favor of workers, the furniture of the former occupants to remain for the use of the new.

After proclaiming freedom of worship, the administration ordered complete separation of church and state, forbidding the church to own property but allowing the churches to be used for religious functions upon application to the government by organizations of the laity. Religious instruction was forbidden in the schools. The government assumed the recording of births and marriages, heretofore a church function. Only civil marriages were now legal. Divorce became possible by a simple declaration of both parties or by application by one of them to a court. The Gregorian calendar, never officially accepted in Orthodox Russia because a Roman pope had developed it, came into operation, thus ending the thirteen-day difference between the Western and Russian calendars. The complicated Russian alphabet, a plague to students, was rid of its superfluous characters.

A decree of the Council of People's Commissars swept away the old institutions of local government and installed in their place a hierarchy of soviets, elected as all soviets were by professional or occupational groups rather than by geographic areas. A system of "People's Courts" with judges elected by the people and juries chosen by the soviets replaced the old court system. The functions of the tsarist police system came under the control of local soviets. A security police agency, the infamous Cheka, was created to ferret out counterrevolutionaries and saboteurs. Its first chief, the Polish revolutionary Felix Dzerzhinsky, made it into the most efficient and the most dreaded secret police system the nation had ever known. A thoroughly unselfish and dedicated fanatic, he deserved full credit for creating a mystique of terror that marked the regime then and ever after.

Finally, the new government "democratized" the army. Rank, titles, decorations and epaulets disappeared, and all positions of command were filled by election. There was no attempt to keep the troops at the front, and the old army evaporated as the demobilized soldiers set out for home. Early in 1918 an entirely new force, the Red Army, came into being with the usual military discipline restored.

The effect of these early decrees was to wipe out many vestiges of capitalist society as Russia had come to know it. Much of the legislation continued in operation until recent time. Some of it, for example the partial democratization of the military and the easy laws on divorce and abortion, was modified during the Stalin years. Only more recently, from the Gorbachev era to the present, is a more sustained effort being made to alter or eliminate many of the legal codes, bureaucratic measures, and social mores created during the period of authoritarian communist rule.

Early in November 1917, there took place the elections to the Constituent Assembly that the Provisional Government had ordered. This was the only free election Russians had ever experienced up to that time and was further remarkable in that well-organized political parties with clearly defined programs and divergent goals campaigned for support. There was universal, equal, and direct suffrage and a secret ballot. Twenty-five splinter or local parties and five major parties— Bolsheviks, Mensheviks, Socialist Revolutionaries, Cadets, and a bloc of Ukrainian nationalist parties—entered the lists. The elections were handled by commissions named by the Provisional Government.

Of the forty-two million votes cast, 38 percent went to the Socialist Revolutionaries, twenty-four to the Bolsheviks, three to the Mensheviks, five to the Cadets, and twelve to the Ukrainian bloc. The Bolsheviks scored most heavily in Moscow and Petrograd, in the central and western provinces, and in the Baltic Sea fleet and the armies on the northwestern front. Of the seven hundred seats, the Bolsheviks and their allies won slightly over two hundred. Over two-thirds of the delegates were definitely anti-Bolshevik. Lenin did not forbid its meeting after he came to power, but he published a statement of his views on its position. Declaring that the soviet system was "a higher form of democratic organization" and referring to the Constituent Assembly as a "deceptive form of bourgeois-democratic parliamentarianism," he proposed that the assembly abdicate its power to the Congress of Soviets.

The assembly met for its first and only session on January 18, 1918. It rejected Lenin's proposal that it surrender its authority to the Congress of Soviets and spent the rest of the session in tedious and pointless debate. At five o'clock the next morning, the armed Bolshevik at the door ordered Chernov, the chairman, to adjourn the meeting because "the guards are getting tired." During its recess the government dissolved the assembly. Its passing under other circumstances would have been a tragedy. It had come too late to bring democracy to Russia. With its dissolution, a rare example of a freely elected, multi-party representative body in over a thousand years of Russian history came to an end. Only eight decades later in 1989, in the waning period of Communist rule in the Soviet Union, would a comparable parliamentary body based on democratic values with an independent voice reappear, as the Congress of Peoples' Deputies.

Breathing Space

One month after the November Revolution an armistice with the Central Powers was agreed to at Brest-Litovsk. In the peace talks that followed, the Germans insisted upon keeping all the territory behind their lines—all of Poland, most of the Baltic provinces, and part of White Russia. Trotsky, who accompanied the Russian delegation, refused to concede such a crippling loss and announced to the Germans that there would be "no war, no peace" on such terms. Back in the capital the Bolsheviks violently debated the German offer, with Lenin finally having his way after threatening to resign; he insisted that it was a matter of life and death for the nation to have a breathing space at any price if the revolution were to survive. Because the army had already gone home, there was really no choice. By a vote of seven to six the party Central Committee agreed to the enemy's terms, which by how were even harsher than those offered earlier.

By the Treaty of Brest-Litovsk, March 3, 1918, Russia recognized the independence of the Ukraine and Georgia and confirmed the independence of Finland. It surrendered Poland, Estonia, Latvia, and Lithuania to Germany and Austria-Hungary, and Kars, Ardahan, and Batum to Turkey.

The treaty cost Russia 1,250,000 square miles of land and 62,000,000 people. It lost a third of its farmland and population, a fourth of its railway mileage, nearly half of its industrial plants and equipment, four-fifths of its iron, and nine-tenths of its coal production. Russia was deprived of the territorial acquisitions of the last two centuries. The "obscene peace," Lenin named it.

The general peace settlement at Paris in 1919 ostensibly abrogated the Treaty of Brest-Litovsk. Nevertheless, in effect the harsh terms continued to stand. The allies recognized the independence of Finland, Poland, Estonia, Latvia, and Lithuania, as well as the cession of Bessarabia to Romania. Four-fifths of the Ukraine, however, was returned to Russia.

Brest-Litovsk had seemed to Lenin necessary if the Soviet regime were to endure, but the breathing space, cut short three months later by armed rebellion, provided no relief from the economic crisis that the war and the revolution had caused. The food situation in the cities had grown steadily worse through the summer of 1917 and the harvest that autumn was far short of normal. With the loss of the Ukraine and the Caucasus the situation became critical. The "bony hand of hunger" threatened to throttle the people of Petrograd in the spring of 1918. Bread riots broke out all over European Russia, and mobs beat Soviet officials to death because they had no food to distribute. The administration banned private trading in grain and ordered the sale to the government at fixed prices of all grain not needed to feed the peasants' families.

Bolsheviks created "Committees of the Poor" in the villages to force the rich peasants to turn over their surplus. Armed squads of city workers joined the poor peasants in smelling out hidden stores and seizing livestock before the rich peasants could eat it. The Committees of the Poor disbanded that autumn, but the village soviets, made up chiefly of poor peasants, continued the raids. This policy of confiscation did bring enough food into the cities to prevent widespread

RUSSIA AFTER THE TREATY OF **BREST-LITOVSK, 1918**

starvation, but only at the cost of stirring uprisings among the well-to-do peasants that only military force could put down. The only other solution to the food shortage in urban areas lay in producing enough industrial goods to encourage the peasants to trade their produce for the output of urban factories. This proved impossible, partly because of the collapse of labor discipline, partly because of the complete disruption of the transportation system, which was either worn out or in enemy hands, partly because of the loss of the Ukraine and with it nearly three-fourths of the nation's iron and steel output and nine-tenths of its sugar production.

Industrial production almost disappeared in the spring of 1918. War industries closed, their output no longer needed. Fuel and raw material dwindled away, forcing many firms out of business. Factories that managed to keep running saw their output curtailed by constant interference of workers' committees in management. Three fourths of the laboring population of Petrograd was out of work, many of whom returned to their villages to get something to eat.

The food crisis and industrial stagnation contributed to a growing anarchy in the spring of 1918. As unemployed workers deserted the cities in quest of food, the very class whose support had brought Lenin to power melted away. Socialist Revolutionaries and Mensheviks won control in many soviets, although in the chief cities the Bolsheviks managed to retain slim majorities. Anti-Bolshevik forces met covertly to plot the overthrow of the regime. Armed bands of anarchists and criminals roamed the streets, plundering and murdering almost at will. Red Guards often deserted and joined such parties. Many who had helped to turn Kerensky out of office now rebelled at the government's efforts to restore discipline in the factories and on the railroads. There were many uprisings, particularly along the middle and lower Volga, but they were put down one after another because there was as yet no effort to coordinate them. The Bolshevik secret police, the Cheka, had its hands full trying to restore order in that spring of 1918, and many Cheka agents lost their lives in the struggle.

The Borderlands

The Bolsheviks early proclaimed, in a "Declaration of the Rights of the People of Russia," the sovereignty of all the nationalities that made up the old empire and declared their right to secede and announce their independence. The government hoped, however, that the minorities would not claim the right and that they would take their place along with Russia as member states in a communist federation.

The concession of independence to Poland cost the Bolsheviks nothing, because the entire area was back of the German lines. In December the Finnish Diet proclaimed the duchy's independence, and the Council of People's Commissars approved. An attempt by Finnish socialists to seize control received support from Russian troops but Finnish nonsocialists with German support defeated the effort.

(Finland's independence was confirmed in 1921.) Bolshevik and anti-Bolshevik forces, abetted by Russian and German support, contested for power in Estonia, Latvia, and Lithuania.

Immediately after the abdication of the tsar, Ukrainian nationalists set up a parliament, or Rada, in Kiev. It named a cabinet, organized an army, proposed to administer the entire Ukraine, proclaimed the Ukraine a "people's republic," and announced elections for an Ukrainian Constituent Assembly. It arranged its own peace with Germany, exchanging foodstuffs for a promise of German support against the Bolsheviks. Ukrainian Bolsheviks fought the separatist movement and joined Russian troops in driving the nationalists out of Kiev in February 1918.

The Czech Odyssey and Allied Intervention

The government's battle to establish discipline and maintain control soon was complicated by open war with the famous Czech Legion. The Provisional Government had freed Czechoslovak prisoners and deserters from the Austrian army and had armed thirty-five thousand of them to fight against the Germans on the eastern front. After Russia's withdrawal from the war, the Czechs received permission to join the Western allies and started over the Trans-Siberian Railway toward Vladivostok on their journey round the world to the western front in France. To prevent the Czechs from supporting an anti-Bolshevik movement in Siberia, Trotsky ordered local soviets to disarm the legion. The Czechs, however, refused to surrender their arms to the feeble soviet forces sent against them, and town after town from one end of the railroad to the other fell under their authority. Local anti-Bolsheviks from stranded army officers to Socialist Revolutionary peasant leaders joined the legionnaires in driving the Bolsheviks from power throughout Siberia. The allies soon forgot their aim of moving the Czech corps to the western front as they saw an opportunity to overthrow the government that had deserted them in the war.

After Brest-Litovsk, the Western powers looked to anti-Bolshevik Russians to remove Lenin and restore the eastern front against Germany; the opponents of the new regime looked to the allies for support in their war against bolshevism. Many Western statesmen recommended that their governments aid resistance groups, but little came of it until the Czech corps offered a nucleus of strength. French, British, and American troops landed at Murmansk in the spring of 1918, ostensibly to prevent supplies stored there from falling into German hands. Other allied detachments landed at Vladivostok to join hands with the Czechs who were to maintain control of the Trans-Siberian and support anti-Bolshevik movements all over Siberia. The United States landed seven thousand men at Vladivostok, Japan ten times that number, and there were smaller British, French, and Italian contingents.

Outbreak of Civil War

The Czech defiance and the decision of the Western powers to intervene against Lenin's government encouraged the desertion of the left-wing Socialist Revolutionaries from their uneasy coalition with the Bolsheviks. The Fifth Congress of Soviets met in July 1918 in Moscow, which three months earlier had replaced Petrograd as the capital of Communist Russia. The SRs refused to accept the Peace of Brest-Litovsk and favored reopening the war against Germany. When their stand lost to the Bolshevik majority, the SRs resorted to armed resistance. Their attempt to seize Moscow was defeated by a whiff of grapeshot, but they embarrassed the government by assassinating the German ambassador in the hope that Germany would reopen the war and force Russia back into the alliance with the Entente powers. The Germans, however, were too busy on the western front to afford another war in the east. The government rounded up and shot some of the SR leaders while others escaped into hiding. Now the Bolsheviks remained alone to rule Russia. The dedication of all other parties—Socialist Revolutionaries, Mensheviks, Cadets, and monarchists—to the overthrow of bolshevism in effect outlawed them.

During that summer of 1918 the Whites—or counterrevolutionaries, to distinguish them from the revolutionary Reds—organized on various fronts and received support from foreign governments. A combined British and American force landed at Arkhangel and established a counterrevolutionary government with the aid of local anti-Bolsheviks and white forces commanded by General Evgeni Miller. At Samara, Chernov and other SR members of the Constituent Assembly announced the birth of a "democratic" government and organized their own "People's Army." They proposed to link up with the allied forces at Murmansk and Arkhangel and drive on to Moscow. General Krasnov, hetman of the Don Cossacks, organized the Don valley as a White fortress and hoped to join hands with the Czech Legion and the Samara government. General Denikin, sometime chief of staff under the Provisional Government, gathered a "Volunteer Army" of former officers and Kuban and Terek Cossacks, won control of the northern Caucasus, and captured the Black Sea port of Novorossisk, thus assuring himself of Western support and supplies. In the southwest General Skoropadsky commanded the army of the Ukrainian Republic, which enjoyed the backing of the Central Powers. The democratic-minded Samara government gave way to a dictatorship under the former commander of the imperial Black Sea fleet, Admiral Kolchak, who extended his authority over all the land from the Volga east to Lake Baikal. The Cossack leader Semenov, encouraged by the Japanese, ruled Siberia east of Lake Baikal. The tsarist general Horvath controlled the Chinese Eastern Railway and much of Manchuria. The so-called Northern Corps, commanded by General Yudenich, advanced toward Petrograd from the Baltic provinces.

Although Kolchak called himself "Supreme Ruler" and was so acknowledged by Denikin, Yudenich, and the Western allies, there was little cooperation among

Intervention and Civil War, 1918–1920

these several challenges to Soviet authority. They were similar in many ways, disparate in others. Some, like Semenov and Horvath, were no better than bandits; others, like Denikin, were men of high principle who tried desperately to curb the violence their motley armies wrought. Some were avowed monarchists, whereas others—notably Denikin and perhaps Kolchak—were liberal or conservative moderates. The moderate element among the Whites steadily lost ground, however, and the entire movement invited suspicion of wanting to restore the Romanovs and the great landowners. For this reason, the White armies never won the confidence of the peasants; they endured only so long as they retained the support of foreign governments and the Cossack hosts. All the White leaders received money and equipment from abroad—Horvath and Semenov from the

Japanese, the others from France, Britain, the United States, Italy, Serbia, Finland, Germany, Austria-Hungary, and Turkey. The population in all the pockets of White control suffered unspeakable atrocities. Pogroms against the Jews were worse than under the tsars, and peasants who resisted the restoration of the great estates were tortured and flogged without mercy. The White Terror was at least as cruel, and certainly more widespread, than the Red Terror of which foreigners heard so much.

The Revolution Defends Itself

Lenin recognized by midsummer of 1918 that there was serious question whether the new government could survive. The food crisis was at its worst just before the harvest; the people were literally at each other's throats in the fight for the few remaining scraps of nourishment. The White armies of Siberia were in the outskirts of Kazan, barely four hundred miles from Moscow. The Ukraine and the Caucasus were lost, and counterrevolutionary forces were converging on the capital from Arkhangel and from Estonia. The Russian state controlled a territory smaller than that of the principality of Moscow late in the fifteenth century. The government was without an effective administration, because many tsarist bureaucrats had deserted or been purged and those who remained were not always trustworthy. There was no army worthy of the name, for the old army had evaporated and the undisciplined Red Guards were unreliable. The disaffected Socialist Revolutionaries went underground and worked sabotage at every opportunity. A former army officer assassinated the chief of the Petrograd Cheka, Uritsky, and an SR, Fanny Kaplan, shot and seriously wounded Lenin on August 30, 1918.

These attacks on government leaders prompted the administration to take the most drastic steps to defend itself. The nation's economy was placed under thoroughgoing governmental control in what came to be known as War Communism. The Cheka inaugurated a reign of terror aimed at wiping out subversion. The administration organized a new Red Army to fight off the attacks of counterrevolutionary forces.

The Bolsheviks had nationalized banks, railroads, shipping, foreign trade, and the land on the morrow of their coming to power. Lenin had refused to go further than that, realizing the professional revolutionaries who had assumed leadership had no knowledge of the management skills required to run the nation's factories. During the so-called "breathing space" he had hoped that business leaders, if allowed to keep their factories, would go along with the revolution, as they had with the Provisional Government. However, with the outbreak of civil war, Lenin gave up all thought of cooperating with the industrialists, who were anti-Bolshevik. During the summer of 1918 the state confiscated one plant after another. The government put itself in the business of producing sugar, petroleum, textiles, minerals, pottery, cement, and many other commodities. The food commissar had full authority to seize all stocks of food, fuel, and clothing and even to dictate the use of large private dwellings. Private trading became illegal.

State control extended to every branch of production under a 1920 decree nationalizing all mechanized plants that employed more than five workers and all nonmechanized plants that employed more than ten. Labor was subject to conscription for critical work. Military units, when not needed on campaign, were to maintain roads and railroads. The entire economic life of the nation came under the authority of a Supreme Economic Council. At first committees managed individual plants, but because of low production, each enterprise received an individual manager—often an earlier owner or director of a plant. The commissar for agriculture sought to force the peasants, even at bayonet point, to turn over to the government an ever increasing supply of grain. The peasants reacted by planting less and less because they knew that they might not retain any surplus. All food was strictly rationed. Workers received two or three times the dole allowed to professionals and the unemployed. A year after the introduction of War Communism, the highest ration for Petrograd workers consisted of a half pound of bread a day and a pound of sugar, a pound of salt, half a pound of butter, and six pounds of fish a month. Peasants raised their own food and so did not feel the pinch of rationing. The government attempted slowly but steadily to abolish money as a medium of exchange, and what goods did change hands ordinarily did so by barter. Decrees at the end of 1920 ordered the distribution of all food through government stores without charge to holders of ration cards and announced an end to collection of taxes except in kind. The government paid wages in goods and services, and assigned rent-free dwellings. There was no charge for postal service or transportation. The last bank was closed in 1920—it was no longer necessary.

In an effort to insure production and avoid the slowdowns that might have occurred if industry were left in private hands, the government tried to become the sole producer and the sole distributor in the nation; in other words, it nationalized production and distribution. As an experiment in production, War Communism was a sorry failure because, with the removal of all incentive but force, individual production fell far below prewar standards. By 1921 the government admitted the failure and abandoned the experiment. The New Economic Policy adopted in that year was a retreat from the communistic practices of the previous three years. It was a compromise with private enterprise and individual initiative that seemed necessary to restore production to respectable levels.

The second step the administration took to defend the revolution was to liquidate its opponents inside the territory it ruled. Heretofore the Cheka had acted with surprising moderation in handling cases of defection and sabotage. Now the government began to regard itself as a beleaguered garrison in a hostile land. The political police dealt ruthlessly with enemies of the regime. They shot five hundred Petrograd citizens, including four former tsarist ministers, in retaliation for the murder of Uritsky and the attempt on Lenin's life. They took hostages from among known Socialist Revolutionaries and Cadets and shot a hundred and fifty of them to avenge the death of one Petrograd worker killed from ambush. Torture wrung confessions or revealed accomplices. Many well-to-do peasants received the death sentence for resisting grain requisitions. In the towns, the Cheka directed the terror primarily against tsarist officers and bureaucrats, professionals, the clergy, and the wealthy. All of the Romanovs who did not escape abroad were shot.

The number of victims of the Red Terror during the Civil War may have reached fifty thousand. The Cheka had the power to execute without trial. The leaders believed it better that ten innocent ones suffer than one guilty person escape. Numbering perhaps thirty thousand agents, the Cheka had branches in every province and its own network of spies. Rumor had it that many agents of the Okhrana, the secret police of tsarist times, found their way into the new organization.

The White Terror was as savage and ruthless as the Red Terror led by Felix Dzerzhinsky. Each White government maintained its counterespionage agency that vied with the Cheka in indiscriminate slaughter of those suspected of opposing it. Furthermore, in every White district thousands were killed and tortured by vicious soldiers whom their leaders seemed unable to control. Captured Bolshevik troops customarily were shot by White commanders. Territory that changed hands suffered vicious recrimination now by Whites and then by Reds. Kiev, for example, was taken and lost nineteen times during the course of the Civil War, and each time hundreds paid with their lives for the city's misfortune.

The new leaders took a third step to defend their revolution when they organized the Red Army early in 1918. At first they called for volunteers, but when this produced a scant hundred thousand, the government fell back on universal conscription. Within two years the Red Army numbered five million, although only a fraction ever saw front-line service. More important than the mere numbers swept into the ranks were the stern discipline and the reorganization imposed by War Commissar Trotsky. He abolished the election of officers and staffed the army, not only with officers it could trust, but with thousands of tsarist officers whose families were held hostage for the officers' good behavior. Political commissars joined every unit to propagandize among the men and to keep under surveillance the old officers whom the government had to use. As quickly as trustworthy men in the ranks gained military experience, they became officers to replace those whose service in the old army made them suspect. Politically reliable subalterns and noncommissioned officers in the tsarist army rose to high rank in the Red Army. A former lieutenant, Michael Tukhachevsky, eventually became a marshal, as did Sergei Budenny, a cavalry sergeant during the First World War, and Klement Voroshilov, a former noncommissioned officer. The man most responsible for whipping the new, green force into a respectable army was Trotsky. He dashed restlessly from one front to another in a special train to inspire the men to greater effort, to order traitors shot, and sometimes even to interfere with strategic plans. The contribution of this organizer of victory to the military success of the new government was undoubtedly greater than that of any other man.

Leon Trotsky

The End of Civil War

During the summer of 1918 the White armies advanced far into European Russia and threatened the communist regime with annihilation. The People's Army drove north from Samara to take Kazan at the bend of the Volga and threatened to join hands with the allies who were to press south from Murmansk. Denikin and his Volunteer Army consolidated the Caucasus; his ally Krasnov won control of the lower Don. If the two could capture Tsaritsyn, later renamed Stalingrad, they could link up with the Czechs and the People's Army and so control the entire lower Volga. Instead, the Reds, inspired by Trotsky's fiery exhortations, drove the Whites out of Kazan back into Siberia, and another army led by Voroshilov and spurred on by Stalin refused to surrender Tsaritsyn. The threat that the White armies in the north, south, and east might join forces was momentarily beaten off.

With the end of the World War, the allies no longer had the excuse to intervene in Russia to prevent military stores from falling into German hands. President Wilson of the United States and Prime Minister Lloyd George of Great Britain preferred that Russia work out its own destiny unfettered by foreign interference. However, French Premier Clemenceau and Winston Churchill, then in charge of the War Ministry in the British cabinet, pressed for vigorous intervention. The allies finally agreed on a degree of participation in the Russian Civil War too modest to be of much service to the Whites and yet sufficiently active to embitter East-West relations for decades afterward. The French landed a division in Odessa; the British moved troops to the oil-rich cities of Batum and Baku; both moved supply ships into the Black Sea, the Baltic, and the Arctic Ocean. The armies of Kolchak, Denikin, Yudenich, plus Miller at Arkhangel received British, French, Italian, and American weapons and supplies. Finland, under the leadership of Mannerheim, became a base for allied pressure in the Baltic provinces. Finland's effort was financed by a substantial American loan. The allies found no need to plead any greed for territory in the light of Lenin's dedication to the principle of world revolution and the elimination of capitalism.

In the spring of 1919, Admiral Kolchak, with a British staff and a river fleet of British gunboats, pushed his forces into the Volga valley and again threatened Kazan and Samara. Allied hopes that he could press on to Moscow dimmed quickly, however, for Red troops stopped him before he reached the river. He had lost the support of the Czechs, his troops were poorly disciplined and badly trained, and the peasants behind his lines had turned against him because he conscripted men and confiscated grain. Trained for the sea, he was thoroughly inept as a land commander. By early July he withdrew back across the Urals and retreated steadily into central Siberia. His motley army deserted, and finally he was handed over to the communists who tried and executed him.

While the Reds were dealing with Kolchak, General Denikin in the south had better success. During the summer of 1919 he drove west out of the Don basin to take Kharkov, Kiev, and finally Tsaritsyn, thus consolidating all of south Russia from the Dnieper to the Volga. Then he advanced north, pushing to within 250 miles of Moscow by early autumn. But the peasants behind his 700-mile front were bitterly hostile to him because of the savagery of his troops and because they had little to gain from the restoration of the old regime which he and most of his officers were suspected of favoring. The Ukrainian nationalist, Petlura, who had no love for any Russian, Red or White, preferred cooperating with the Poles to joining Denikin, whose triumph meant the revival of the old frontiers and the inclusion of border minorities within the new Russia.

Denikin reached Orel by October 1919, but that was as close to Moscow as he could get. From then on, his strength ebbed rapidly. Every engagement cost him casualties that he could not replace. His long front and lengthening communications became increasingly difficult to man. On the other hand, Red strength grew to twice that of Denikin's force, and the Red cavalry under Budenny surprisingly proved superior to the Cossacks of the Volunteer Army.

Before the year was out, Denikin was in retreat, the morale of his troops broken and his officers' confidence in their leader destroyed. The Reds swarmed over the Ukraine, and Denikin was left, in the words of Lloyd George, "occupying a little back yard near the Black Sea." In the spring of 1920 the tattered remnant of the White Army in south Russia escaped aboard British ships to the Crimea. Denikin turned over the command to Baron Peter Wrangel, an avowed monarchist, and went into exile.

In the autumn of 1919, General Yudenich with British, Finnish, and Baltic-German support was advancing on Petrograd from Estonia at the same time that Denikin was threatening Moscow from Orel. Unfortunately for the Whites, the Red Army had the great advantage of fighting on interior lines and being able to use what remained of the railway net of which Moscow was the hub. By late October Yudenich was within thirty miles of Petrograd. Although Lenin favored abandoning the city, Trotsky fired the city's workers to set up barricades in the streets, swearing to contest every house if necessary. Yudenich, with thirty thousand troops, had too small a force to attempt such a fight in a city still left with a million people. During the closing weeks of the year, while Denikin was being routed in the south, the Northwestern Army retired in good order to Estonia where it disbanded. With the withdrawal of Yudenich, there remained only Wrangel in the Crimea, but his troops needed rest and equipment. For the moment he was in no position to renew the attack.

The Polish War

By 1920 the Western powers had lost hope that the Bolsheviks could be overthrown. Mutinies among allied troops in Russia forced their recall, and Western workers even refused to load ships with supplies destined for the White armies. The allied governments stopped sending goods and money, particularly to the succession states on Russia's western frontier; they recommended that such states seek a peaceful settlement with the Bolsheviks. During the year, Russia signed treaties of peace with Estonia, Latvia, Lithuania, and Finland, recognizing the independence of each and delimiting boundaries. With Poland, however, such a settlement was to come only after another campaign.

The allies at the Paris Peace Conference of 1919 suggested a boundary between Poland and Russia, the so-called Curzon Line. Proposed by a British diplomat whose name stuck to the plan and based essentially on which groups controlled the territory at the time, it was reasonably accurate in setting off Poles to the west and non-Poles to the east of the line. However, the new Polish government, not interested in ethnic frontiers, demanded Poland's "historic" boundaries—those of 1772 before the First Partition—and called upon Russia to surrender all land west of the 1772 border. When Moscow refused, the Polish dictator, Marshal Pilsudski, launched an attack in the spring of 1920, confident that the Bolsheviks were now impotent from civil war. Poland had held back from joining the White forces earlier because the White leaders, particularly Kolchak and Denikin, had pledged to restore the boundaries of imperial Russia.

Polish troops moved into the Ukraine, reaching the Dnieper and capturing Kiev by early May 1920, but the Ukrainian separatist movement that they counted on for support fizzled out. Budenny's cavalry relieved Kiev and drove Pilsudski, whom Trotsky dubbed "a third-rate Bonaparte," back into southern Poland. Another Red force under Tukhachevsky advanced into northern Poland and threatened Warsaw. Then the Bolsheviks offered peace and a frontier more favorable to Poland than the Curzon Line; the Poles refused and the war went on.

Pilsudski, with newly arrived French equipment and the French general Weygand at his elbow, opened a counterattack that pushed the Russians back, deep into their own country. The Polish workers had had enough, however, and the Russians wanted a free hand to deal with Baron Wrangel in the Crimea. In October 1920, the two powers agreed to the terms of the Peace of Riga. The new frontier was well to the east of the Curzon Line but short of the 1772 boundary for which Pilsudski had hoped. It left 4,500,000 Belo-Russians and Ukrainians inside Poland, a humiliation that Soviet leaders were quick to wipe out in 1939.

Peace at Last

In the autumn of 1920 the Reds drove Wrangel's disorganized army and a horde of 150,000 civilian refugees through the Crimean Peninsula to the Black Sea shore. There they boarded French ships to Constantinople, whence they scattered to centers of Russian exile in Europe and America. With the collapse of White strength in south Russia and the withdrawal of allied support, the anti-Bolshevik governments in Georgia, Azerbaidzhan, and Armenia were helpless in the face of Russian pressure. The three surrendered their brief existence and became new Soviet states as socialist republics, ostensibly independent but in fact tributary to Moscow. The Central Asian provinces similarly returned to Russian rule soon after the defeat of Kolchak.

The area east of Lake Baikal proved more difficult for the Reds to recover. There the Cossack Semenov with Japanese backing sacked and pillaged the peasant communities while Japan seized the northern half of Sakhalin and ravaged coastal Siberia. To serve as a buffer against these foreign and bandit forces, Moscow encouraged the creation of the Far Eastern Republic under liberal local leadership. Its socialist, but not Communist, government provided for an elected parliament and guaranteed the usual democratic civil liberties along with the right to own land. A treaty with Moscow recognized the republic and delimited its boundaries. The new government rid the land of Semenov and his cutthroats and, with strong American support, prevailed upon the Japanese to depart. However, with peace and order established and the foreigner gone, the early demise of the Far Eastern Republic was a foregone conclusion. Too small to defend itself against powerful neighbors to east and west, the people could only choose between the two. Because they were bitterly anti-Japanese, there could be no question where the choice would lie. Late in 1922 the national assembly of the republic voted to become a part of the new Communist Russia.

The final victory was a credit to Lenin's leadership and Trotsky's driving energy in building the Red Army. Heroic as the struggle of the nation and its leaders was, there was help from the opposition and from the military situation as it developed. The governments of Great Britain, France, Japan, the United States, Italy, and a dozen others showed far less determination than they were credited with by Soviet writers ever after. There can be no question that those who intervened hated bolshevism and Marxism and socialism in every form. Although that hatred nourished men like Churchill and Weygand for a generation, the people of Britain, France, the United States, and others were tired of war, and their governments found it impossible to carry on a policy that found so little favor at home. Poland actually preferred the Bolsheviks to the White generals who wanted to restore the old imperial boundaries; when they had won back as much as they could of "pre-1772" territory, the Poles came to terms.

The White generals and their supporters among politicians, industrialists, merchants, gentry, Cossacks, and intellectuals mounted a gallant counterattack against the Reds, but their efforts never really had much promise of success. They advanced against the Communists from north, south, east, and west, but they could never join hands around the perimeter. The Bolsheviks took full advantage of their interior lines to shift men and supplies from one front to another along the spokes of the rail axis that fanned out from Moscow.

Communist rule won out, partly from popular indifference and finally because the Russian masses feared that a White victory would mean a restoration of the old order. Peasants would lose the land they had taken from the gentry. City workers dreamed of a better living than the merchants and factory owners had allowed them before the revolution. Most of the nation's youth, when the choice was theirs to make, preferred the vision of a new future to a retreat into a past that had offered so little hope.

After eight long years of war, foreign intervention, and civil strife peace came at last to the Russian land. By far, most of the fighting had taken place on Russian soil. Millions had died in battle, had suffered cruel death during the Red and White Terrors, or had succumbed to famine or the plagues that followed in the wake of drought. The battered land had been made unproductive for years to come. Much of Russian humanity had been uprooted as people deserted the cities for the countryside in search of food and others fled or were driven from home by the marching armies. The Russian land, certainly no stranger to invasion and fratricidal war, had never known such bitterness, hatred, torture, and suffering. Now the nation faced the staggering task of rebuilding.

Who Won and Who Lost

The battle for control of Russia ended less in Lenin's winning it than in his opponents' losing it. Prince Lvov, cautious and mild-mannered, offered a dismal lack of leadership. Miliukov stubbornly refused to see popular enthusiasm for the overthrow of the monarchy as anything but a demand for more vigorous prosecution of the war. These two and their followers doomed liberalism from the very dawn of the revolution. Kerensky and the moderate socialists whose support he enlisted learned nothing from Miliukov's sorry mistakes and added others of their own. They seemed unaware of the massive indifference to legality, constitutionality, and democratic formality; there was no tradition for such Westernisms and surely little longing for them. The agrarian revolution surged relentlessly forward in defiance of whomever was in power. Even with all of Kerensky's persuasive oratory, the army simply would fight no more. Soldiers flung away their arms and hurried back to their villages to share in the carving up of gentry estates. Had Kerensky accepted the inevitable—had he withdrawn from the war and urged the peasants to parcel out the land among themselves—he might have stemmed the tide and saved the nation from the tragedy to which his wrongheadedness condemned it. Of course, the allies and their intellectual friends in Russia would have fought any peace and any seizure of gentry land that was bolshevism! Such measures, however, might well have proved successful. Their rejection only assured Lenin and his followers of victory.

The ultimate Bolshevik triumph did not depend entirely on Lenin's genius. Whatever the effectiveness of party organization, the quality of its leadership, and the merit of Bolshevik doctrine, these factors do not account for the party's success. Marx's prediction of the collapse of capitalism and the inevitability of socialist revolution, with all Lenin's tortured reasoning to bring it up to date, simply did not fit the Russia of 1917. Even if the theory had seemed applicable, an illiterate and backward agricultural nation cared little about philosophical justification for its action. Indeed, Lenin won no large following immediately in the countryside and often had difficulty in holding his own party leadership together.

When all the demurrers and disclaimers are in, however, it remains inconceivable that anyone but Lenin could have led the party to victory in the battle to seize power and hold it. His unfaltering drive, his dedication, his unswerving sense of direction, his singleness of purpose, his political skill and acumen, his concentration on the goal and his refusal to be turned aside from it, his uncanny judgment of what was possible—all these elements contributed immeasurably to the final Bolshevik triumph. In addition to them all, Lenin was shrewd and ruthless in identifying opposition, to himself or to the party, as opposition to the revolution itself. Who could reasonably oppose the revolution— or its vanguard, the party, or that vanguard's leader—and not reveal his betrayal of the interests of the people? To be identified as "counterrevolutionary" was to be marked for punishment and probable death. The period became dominated by a struggle for sheer power, and Lenin's ruthlessness was succeeded in its intensity only by that of Stalin against his real or imagined enemies.

Suggested Reading

ABRAHAM, R., *Alexander Kerensky: The First Love of the Revolution* (New York, 1987).

ANWEILER, O., *The Soviets: The Russian Workers', Peasants', and Soldiers' Councils, 1905-1921* (New York, 1974).

ASCHER, A., *The Mensheviks in the Russian Revolution* (Ithaca, NY, 1976).

BOLL, M. M., *The Petrograd Armed Workers' Movement in the February Revolution (February-July, 1917): A Study in the Radicalization of the Petrograd Proletariat* (Washington, DC, 1979).

BRADLEY, J., *Civil War in Russia, 1917-1920* (New York, 1975).

BROWDER, R. P., and A. KERENSKY, *The Russian Provisional Government, 1917*, 3 vols. (Stanford, 1961).

BUNYAN, J., *Intervention, Civil War and Communism in Russia, April-December, 1918: Documents and Materials* (Baltimore, 1936).

_____, *The Origin of Forced Labor in the Soviet State, 1917-1921: Documents and Materials* (Baltimore, 1967).

BUNYAN, J., and H. H. FISHER, *The Bolshevik Revolution 1917-1918: Documents and Materials* (Stanford, 1934).

CARR, E. H., *The Bolshevik Revolution, 1917-1923* (New York, 1953).

CHERNOV, V., *The Great Russian Revolution* (New Haven, 1936).

CURTISS, J. S., *The Russian Revolutions of 1917* (Princeton, 1957).

DANIELS, R. V., *Red October. The Bolshevik Revolution of 1917* (London, 1968).

_____, *The Russian Revolution* (Englewood Cliffs, NJ, 1972).

DEBO, R. K., *Revolution and Survival: The Foreign Policy of Soviet Russia, 1917-1918* (Toronto, 1979).

FERRO, M., *The Russian Revolution of February, 1917* (Englewood Cliffs, NJ, 1972).

FISCHER, L., *The Life of Lenin* (New York, 1964).

FISHER, H. H., *The Famine in Soviet Russia, 1919-1923* (New York, 1927).

FITZPATRICK, S., *The Russian Revolution, 1917-1932* (New York, 1982).

FOOTMAN, D., *Civil War in Russia* (New York, 1962).

_____, *The Russian Revolution* (New York, 1962).

GANKIN, O. H., and H. H. FISHER, *The Bolsheviks and the World War: Documents* (Stanford, 1940).

GETZLER, I., *Kronstadt, 1917-1921: The Fate of a Soviet Democracy* (Cambridge, Eng., 1983).

GOLDER, F. A., *Documents of Russian History, 1914-1917* (Gloucester, MA, 1964).

HAIMSON, L. H., *The Mensheviks from the Revolution of 1917 to the Second World War* (Chicago, 1974).

HASEGAWA, T., *The February Revolution: Petrograd, 1917* (Seattle, 1981).

HINDUS, M., *The Russian Peasant and the Revolution* (New York, 1920).

KATKOV, G., *Russian, 1917: The February Revolution* (New York, 1967).

KENEZ, P., *Civil War in South Russia, 1918: The First Year of the Volunteer Army* (Berkeley, 1971).

KENNAN, G. F., *The Decision to Intervene* (Princeton, 1958).

_____, *Russia Leaves the War* (Princeton, 1956).

KERENSKY, A., *Russia and History's Turning Point* (New York, 1965).

KOENKER, D. P. and W. G. ROSENBERG, *Strikes and Revolution in Russia, 1917* (Princeton, 1989)

LEHOVICH, D. V., *White Against Red: The Life of General Anton Denikin* (New York, 1974).

LINCOLN, W. B., *Red Victory: A History of the Russian Civil War* (New York, 1989).

LUCKETT, R., *The White Generals: An Account of the White Movement and the Russian Civil War* (New York, 1971).

McCAULEY, M. (ed.), *The Russian Revolution and the Soviet State, 1917–1921: Documents* (New York, 1975).

MEDLIN, V., and S. PARSONS, *V. D. Nabokov and the Russian Provisional Government, 1917* (New Haven, 1976).

MEDVEDEV, R. A., *The October Revolution* (New York, 1979).

MELGUNOV, S. P., *The Bolshevik Seizure of Power* (Santa Barbara, 1972).

MIKOYAN, S. (ed.), *The Memoirs of Anastas Mikoyan: The Path of Struggle* (Madison, CT, 1988).

MILIUKOV, P. N., *The Russian Revolution*, 3 vols. (Gulf Breeze, FL, 1978–1987).

MOOREHEAD, A., *The Russian Revolution* (New York, 1958).

PAGE, S. W., *Russia in Revolution* (New York, 1965).

PAYNE, R., *The Life and Death of Lenin* (New York, 1964).

PIPES, R., *The Formation of the Soviet Union: Communism and Nationalism, 1917–1923* (Cambridge, 1954).

_____, *The Russian Revolution* (New York, 1990).

POSSONY, S. T., *Lenin, the Compulsive Revolutionary* (Chicago, 1964).

RABINOWITCH, A., *Prelude to Revolution: The Petrograd Bolsheviks and the July 1917 Uprising* (Bloomington, IN, 1968).

RADKEY, O. H., *Agrarian Foes of Bolshevism: Promise and Default of the Russian Socialist Revolutionaries, March to October, 1917* (New York, 1958).

_____, *The Election to the Russian Constituent Assembly of 1917* (Cambridge, 1950).

_____, *The Unknown Civil War in Soviet Russia: A Study of the Green Movement in the Tambov Region in 1921* (Stanford, 1976).

REED, J., *Ten Days that Shook the World* (New York, 1989).

RESHETAR, J., *The Ukrainian Revolution, 1917–1920* (Princeton, 1952).

RESHETAR, M. S., JR., *A Concise History of the Communist Party of the Soviet Union* (New York, 1964).

ROSENBERG, W. G., *Liberals in the Russian Revolution: The Constitutional Democratic Party, 1917–1921* (Princeton, 1974).

SAUL, N. E., *Sailors in Revolt: The Russian Baltic Fleet in 1917* (Lawrence, KS, 1978).

SERGE, V., *Year One of the Russian Revolution* (New York, 1972).

SHAPIRO, L. B., *The Origin of the Communist Autocracy: Political Opposition within the Soviet State, First Phase, 1917–1922* (Cambridge, 1955).

SHUB, D., *Lenin* (New York, 1948).

SHUKMAN, H. (ed.), *The Blackwell Encyclopedia of the Russian Revolution* (Oxford, 1988).

SLUSSER, R. M., *Stalin in October: The Man Who Missed the Revolution* (Baltimore, 1987).

SMITH, E. E., *The Young Stalin* (New York, 1967).

SNOW, R. E., *The Bolsheviks in Siberia, 1917–1918* (Rutherford, NJ, 1977).

STEWART, G., *The White Armies of Russia* (New York, 1933).

SUKHANOV, N. N., *The Russian Revolution of 1917* (Princeton, 1984).

TUCKER, R. C., *Stalin as Revolutionary, 1879–1929: A Study in History and Personality* (New York, 1973).

ULLMAN, R. H., *Intervention and the War: Anglo-Soviet Relations, 1917–1921* (Princeton, 1968).

VARNECK, E., and H. H. FISHER, *The Testimony of Kolchak and Other Siberian Materials and Documents* (Stanford, 1935).

VON MOHRENSCHILDT, D., *The Russian Revolution of 1917: Contemporary Accounts* (New York, 1971).

WADE, R., *The Russian Search for Peace, February-October, 1917* (Stanford, 1969).

WHEELER-BENNETT, J. W., *The Forgotten Peace: Brest-Litovsk, March, 1918* (London, 1938).

WILDMAN, A. K., *The End of the Russian Army*, 2 vols. (Princeton, 1980, 1987).

WOLFE, B. D., *An Ideology in Power: Reflections on the Russian Revolution* (Stanford, 1969).

CHAPTER 18

Communist Russia
The Early Years

Building upon the foundation laid by Marx and Engels, Lenin conceived of the socialist state as only a step toward ultimate communism. During this interim period the state, under the dictatorship of the proletariat, would liquidate the capitalist class, do away with private ownership, and manage all production and distribution. Other European socialist revolutions would be necessary for the Russian experiment to succeed.

Lenin built upon much more than the vaporous theories of Marx and Engels. The theory grew out of Western European political and economic thought and practice, which were strange and foreign concepts to Russia. The nation's brief and primitive experience with capitalism made some modification of the theory inevitable before it could be applied to Russia. Lenin welded together the two pieces—the Western European and the Russian—to produce a whole that resembled both and yet differed from both in many ways.

The Theoretical Base

Karl Marx, the grandfather of modern communism, analyzed the nature and weaknesses of modern capitalism and predicted its inevitable collapse. He and his co-worker, Friedrich Engels, concerned themselves hardly at all, however, with the detailed nature of the society that should succeed capitalism. In 1917, Lenin drafted *The State and Revolution*, which expanded Marx's view of the course that society must follow after the defeat of the bourgeoisie.

According to Marx and Lenin, the state, born of the class struggle between workers and employers, is an instrument of suppression by which the ruling class—the employers, the "exploiters" under capitalism—keeps itself in power. Capitalism, however, contains within itself elements that lead to its deterioration and weakening, and at the right moment a movement of the industrial workers, or proletariat, led by a disciplined vanguard, the Communist party, can overthrow it.

Because the state, the theory continues, is an agency by which the exploiting class that owns society's productive property holds in subjugation the exploited class that works with, but does not own, the productive tools, the overthrow of capitalist society and the expropriation of the capitalists or owners will lead eventually to a classless society, communism, where there will be no exploitation; consequently, the state will no longer be necessary.

The birth of communism, however, will not follow immediately upon the passing of capitalism. Through a transitional stage—socialism—the state will continue as a "dictatorship of the proletariat" succeeding the "dictatorship of the capitalist class." The productive machinery of society will be social or national property under state control and operation. Limited private ownership may continue, but without the employment and exploitation of one person by another. No one will enjoy unearned income—profits, rents, or inheritances. All must work to live, and all who work will earn a reward determined by the principle "from each according to his ability, to each according to the quantity and quality of his work." The state will continue, not as a tool by which one class dominates another, but as an agency to protect the limited property rights of individuals and to control and distribute production. During the period of socialism the last resistance of the former exploiters will be broken.

Finally, with the arrival of the millennium of communism, classes will disappear; poverty will vanish; avarice, jealousy, dishonesty, and crime will cease; there will be no need for a bureaucracy or a standing army to restrain one class against another, and the state must and will "wither away." Then man will enjoy the complete freedom that is impossible as long as the oppressive and restrictive agency, the state, continues to exist.

Lenin and his colleagues assumed that socialist revolutions in Central and Western Europe would follow the Bolshevik seizure of power. Uprisings would be contagious and would produce a worldwide revolution. Indeed, they believed that revolution must topple at least some bourgeois governments in order for the one in Russia to succeed, and for a moment after the war, their hopes seemed justified. There were Communist uprisings in Hungary, Germany, Austria, Italy, Finland, and Poland. Some of them were momentarily successful. Quickly, however, the revolutionary fever subsided, leaving Russia alone to carry on the socialist experiment. The question whether socialism could exist in a single country surrounded by hostile capitalist states was long the subject of debate between

Trotsky and Stalin in their contest for power after Lenin's death in 1924. Trotsky protested that to attempt to make socialism work in one country was to betray the world revolution. Stalin insisted that a nation with Russia's size and resources could go it alone. He was willing to shelve, if not to forget, the open promotion of socialist revolutions abroad, at least until Russia should become strong enough to undertake the risks involved in such a policy.

Constitutional Beginnings

The Second All-Russian Congress of Soviets was in session in Petrograd at the moment of the Bolshevik Revolution. On the first day of the new era the Congress approved the list of cabinet ministers, called the Council of People's Commissars, with Lenin as president. It then elected a Central Executive Committee of a hundred members to serve in its stead when the Congress was not in session. The Congress of Soviets thus clothed itself with supreme authority in the nation, then delegated legislative power to its Central Executive Committee and administrative power to the Council of Commissars. In operation, the Council's authority included both executive and legislative responsibilities. The Central Executive Committee and the Congress of Soviets that reconvened from time to time could only rubber-stamp the Council's enactments.

In July 1918, the Fifth Congress of Soviets adopted a constitution outlining the governmental framework of the new state. The basic political unit was the city and village soviet to which delegates would win election by show of hands by all men and women over the age of eighteen, except members of the Romanov family, capitalists, former officials, members of the clergy, lunatics, and criminals. Each local soviet would elect delegates to a county soviet, which would send delegates to a district soviet, which in turn would choose representatives to a provincial soviet. The latter would send some of its members to attend the national All-Russian Congress of Soviets. The national Congress would contain one representative for each 25,000 city dwellers and one for each 125,000 rural inhabitants. This weighting of representation in favor of the cities reflected the Bolsheviks' confidence in industrial workers and their suspicion of peasants. The Congress would continue to choose the Central Executive Committee as it had been doing for the past year, and the committee in turn would name the Council of People's Commissars, the one to serve as an interim legislative committee, the other as executive cabinet.

From time to time non-Russian minorities received permission to form autonomous Soviet Socialist Republics, autonomous regions, or national districts within the Russian Soviet Federated Socialist Republic. With the end of Civil War, some arrangement was necessary to associate the liberated borderlands with the new state. In 1922 a modified constitutional document formally established the Union of Soviet Socialist Republics, and this structure continued until its termination in December 1991. By 1929 there were eleven member republics in all.

The Second Congress of Soviets of the Union of Soviet Socialist Republics in 1924 approved a constitution further defining the scope of government jurisdiction and clarifying the socialized economic system. Each constituent republic, such as the Russian Soviet Federated Socialist Republic, had its own legislature, but all were united under the All-Union Congress of Soviets as the supreme legislative authority for the entire nation. The 1918 and 1924 documents continued until 1936, when an even more expanded and modernized constitution replaced them. The 1922 document creating the Soviet Union lasted until its demise in late 1991, bringing this nation-state to an end.

In theory and constitutional phrasing, these legislative bodies represented the democratic authority of the new nation. In practice, the effective ruling bodies and organizations continued to be the Council of People's Commissars and the Communist party's Central Committee, Secretariat and Politburo. Legislative decisions served primarily only as confirmation and ratification of the decisions presented to them.

Rebuilding the Economy

With the triumph over the White armies and the end of the Polish War in 1920, the new regime faced the bleak prospect of restoring order and putting the nation back to work. There was little on which to build. The economy of no great power in 1914 was as backward as that of imperial Russia, although there had been much progress after the reforms of the sixties. The war itself had brought to no other belligerent such vast desolation as it had to Russia, and no other had torn itself apart in civil war after the global conflict that had cost it so sorely.

After assuming power, the Bolsheviks had moved quickly to nationalize land and key industries and to grant control over management to the laborers in each plant. Workers had expected, naïvely, that by appropriating to themselves the profits that had gone to factory owners they would receive bountiful wages and yet work shorter hours. Production fell off sharply and labor discipline disappeared under the workers' committees that directed each factory. Workers showed up when they pleased and left the bench whenever it suited them. When equipment wore out neither repairs nor replacements were available. People walked off with tools and paid themselves with finished goods or raw materials that they traded for food and clothing. Factories closed when machinery broke down or materials were gone. Industrial output had shrunk by 1920 to a fifth the prewar level and there were jobs for only half as many workers. Many drifted back to their villages to find the living they could not earn in the cities.

Agricultural output declined sharply as contending armies fought over some of the most productive areas and others fell under White control, as herds of livestock starved or were slaughtered for a last feast, as great estates that had always produced for market were broken up, and as peasants met government confiscation of surpluses by raising only what they could eat. The harvest of industrial crops—flax, cotton, sugar beets, tobacco—fell to less than half the prewar figure. Mines produced barely a fourth as much coal in 1920 as in 1913, and city dwellings went unheated through the severe Russian winter unless their occupants could find deserted houses to knock down for fuel. The collapse of the transportation system made impossible the effective distribution of what little fuel there was. The nation in 1920 produced only a seventh as many locomotives and 4 percent as many freight cars as before the war, and over half those in existence were not in working order. Real wages fell to a third the 1913 figure. The productivity of labor by 1920 was only a fourth as high as in 1913, partly because of the woeful undernourishment of workers. Epidemics of typhus and cholera swept the land. In addition, all through the period of civil war and intervention, the nation was under blockade, although there was nothing with which to pay for imports had there been any.

The situation in the areas under White rule was even worse than that in Communist Russia. Although the Whites controlled the agricultural districts, their confiscations discouraged production and the trampling armies made orderly farming impossible. The provinces under Communist rule contained most of the nation's industries, and there was, of course, no trade between the food-producing area that needed the output of factories and the industrial area that was desperately in need of grain. In 1921 a severe drought made the situation still worse. Over thirty million Russians were starving that year and the next, and there were five million victims of famine and its attendant diseases. The American Relief Administration, directed by Herbert Hoover, was feeding ten million Russians during August 1922, when the famine was at its worst.

By 1920, with victory in the Civil War in sight, the Bolshevik leaders pondered how to rebuild the nation's economy, how to make productive the desert they had conquered. At Trotksy's insistence they decided to apply the principles of War Communism to the problems of reconstruction. The Russian people, or all who were fit to work, became a labor army driven to work under military discipline. Citizens still in the army and others conscripted for labor service marched to tasks assigned them—clearing and planting fields, restoring buildings, repairing equipment, reopening mines, gathering raw materials, rebuilding roads, collecting food supplies. Every citizen had to carry a labor book, indicating his or her employment record and present place of work. The regime treated as deserters those who avoided work. It assigned those who shirked to punishment squads and put them on short rations. People resisted this militarization of labor. Peasant armies charged with weeding fields long unused in areas ravaged by civil war ran away to their own villages where there was plenty of weeding to do. Town workers resented military discipline in civilian work. Early in 1921 the number of urban strikes and rural revolts mounted. The peasant sailors at the Kronstadt naval base mutinied in protest against the grain requisitions their families had to undergo; they called for freedom of speech and association for workers and peasants and the parties that spoke for them. Bolshevik forces ruthlessly crushed the revolt.

The Kronstadt mutiny, which was in part an expression of peasant discontent and in part a demand for a shift of power from the Communist party to the soviets, which would represent all parties or at least all socialist parties, convinced Lenin that War Communism could not go on. He knew he would have to find another way to stimulate agricultural production, for the cities where his strength lay had to have food. During the chaotic days of the Provisional Government the peasants had broken up the great estates of landlord and church, and now each had plots of their own which were larger by a third than before the war. Never before had the peasant had such a proprietary outlook. They hated the collectivization that the Bolsheviks were considering and wanted to farm their own land for all they could get out of it. Lenin realized that the first need was to get as much land sown as possible in this plowing season of 1921 and knew that without tractors and farm machinery collectivization would fail. He could only retreat in the face of peasant determination. War Communism in all its phases would have to go. Collectivization of agriculture and socialization of industry could come later. There must be another breathing space if the government were to survive. The need now was to feed the nation.

The Tenth Communist Party Congress, in March 1921, agreed to Lenin's proposal that the government collect from the peasants a fixed tax in kind and leave them free to dispose of the surplus as they chose. The state would retain control of the "commanding heights"—the largest factories, transportation, banking, and foreign trade—thus preventing these strongholds of capitalist power from slipping into private hands that might seek to restore the old system. Small plants would revert to private ownership. Through a succession of orders, the government inaugurated and expanded its New Economic Policy, the NEP.

Peasants must pay a tax, at first in kind and later in money, amounting to a percentage of the produce they raised beyond their own needs. This crude income tax encouraged the peasant to produce as much as possible, because most of it could be kept or sold. Private retail trading once more became legal. To stimulate farm output, still more peasants might lease land from those who had more than they could handle, and by 1925 they were free to hire workers. The peasants responded slowly, perhaps suspiciously, to these enticements, but by 1927 agricultural production was approaching 1913 levels, although the size of the nation had shrunk considerably from secession of the western borderlands. Since there were only two tractors in all Russia in 1924, the remarkable agricultural achievement came from peasant toil and sweat.

All industrial units with fewer than twenty workers were restored to their former owners or leased to private operators. Larger plants remained under government management; these amounted to less than a tenth of the plants, but they employed 85 percent of the industrial workers. The state grouped the plants that it operated into combines or trusts, each seeking a profit, buying materials where it could get them, and selling its products to any who would buy. The administration invited foreign capital to invest in enterprise and brought in Western technicians to teach their skills to Soviet workers. With the legalization of private trading the government restored the use of money by stabilizing the ruble, issuing new currency with gold backing, and calling in old paper money in exchange for the new. A state bank to head the nation's credit system opened in 1921.

Lenin understood the risk he took in allowing this partial return to capitalism but felt confident that he could restrict it. Of course, there was never any relaxation of political control. Through the twenties there were steadily increasing limitations on Nepmen, as private traders and small producers were called. By 1923, private merchants carried on three-fourths of all retail trade; thereafter, their taxes steadily increased, the variety of goods they could sell was increasingly restricted, and they were eventually denied the use of the railroads for transmission of their wares. Their share of private trade transactions fell from three-fourths of the total in 1923 to one-fourth in 1928 and to less than 6 percent in 1930, after which they ceased to exist. Private industrialists felt the same pinch. They accounted for a fifth of the nation's industrial output in 1925, but less than 6 percent by 1930, and they, too, soon disappeared.

It was the government's hope that the New Economic Policy would win back the support of the peasants who had turned against it during the period of War Communism. Certainly, the position of the peasants had improved greatly. The prices the peasants received for their produce were high, the costs of the industrial goods they bought were low. Another year, however, brought declining farm income and rising industrial prices. The growing spread between the low prices the peasants received and the high prices they paid—the "scissors crisis"—forced the administration to fix prices of industrial goods and raise the prices it paid the farmers for the grain they shipped to the cities. Unfortunately, the peasants never quite made up the gap. Like the American farmers, they suffered throughout the twenties a disparity in prices that was distinctly to their disadvantage. It was partly in an effort to relieve the plight of poor peasants, partly because of the government's increasing difficulty in getting enough grain for the cities, and partly to fasten political control over rural areas that the leaders later abandoned the New Economic Policy.

By 1927, the Russian economy had nearly returned to prewar levels, as Western European nations were boasting full recovery. By that year, Russian agricultural production nearly equaled 1913 figures and industrial output had slightly exceeded them. Real wages for city workers had gone above their prewar level and the peasants certainly were better off than in 1913. The admitted retreat from communism in hope of a later drive toward socialism undeniably gave the Soviet Union a healthy working economy.

Religious Policy

The Russian Orthodox clergy had agitated mildly for separation of church and state in the closing days of the monarchy and had urged that only by restoration of the patriarchate could the church purify itself and recover its influence among the people. The tsar had proven deaf to such arguments. The Provisional

Government then had called a church assembly that chose Metropolitan Tikhon as the first patriarch since the time of Peter the Great. Tikhon's first act—he assumed office while the Bolsheviks were clearing aside the Provisional Government—was an attempt to halt the fighting and prevent further bloodshed. As a churchman he opposed the professed atheism of the revolutionaries, and his intervention was not likely to win Bolshevik approval.

The new government was antireligious, but its persecution of the church and the clergy during the Civil War was evidence primarily of its determination to wipe out an active center of resistance. The government seized clergy of all faiths and executed or exiled them, both as religious leaders and as counterrevolutionaries. This continued to be government policy as long as any member of the clergy revealed any disposition to harbor resentment against the new regime.

Early in 1918 the government published a decree ordering separation of church and state. Church land came under national ownership, as did all land. The decree permitted local soviets to lease nationalized property—buildings, vestments, and altar pieces—for use in church services to groups of twenty or more of the laity. The decree also forbade religious instruction in schools, public or private, and the government later prohibited religious teaching to groups whose members were less than eighteen years of age. Members of the clergy lost the right to vote and received no ration cards, making them dependent on their parishioners for food and shelter.

A thousand Orthodox churches and a number of mosques and Protestant churches were closed or used exclusively for nonreligious functions because many parishes could not muster twenty men brave enough to risk signing a contract with the local soviets. Precious ornaments and altar pieces were confiscated, to be sold for food during the famine in 1922. Orthodox and Roman Catholic churchmen who objected went on trial for "inciting the masses to civil war"; twenty-eight bishops and a thousand priests were executed and others exiled or imprisoned.

A number of the Russian Orthodox clergy decided to make their peace with the government and, denouncing Patriarch Tikhon, organized what they called "the Living Church." The Bolsheviks encouraged this schism, imprisoning the patriarch, turning over church buildings for the use of the schismatics, and removing bishops and priests to make way for the clergy of the Living Church. However, the government gradually withdrew its support when the laity refused to back the movement. Patriarch Tikhon, whom the government had threatened with execution, obtained his release from prison after vigorous protest from abroad. Many rebellious clergy recanted and deserted the Living Church, which evaporated when the Bolsheviks stopped supporting it. Tikhon died in 1925 and his successors went to prison as fast as they were named. In 1926 the newly chosen acting head of Russian Orthodoxy, Sergei, won a grudging toleration by promising, for himself and his church, to be loyal to the government and stand aloof from politics.

When the government failed to gain popular favor for the Living Church it turned to a propaganda campaign designed to win converts to atheism. It opened a publishing agency whose journal, *The Godless*, kept up a vitriolic attack on all religion. It established an antireligious seminary in the capital. It forbade the use of Christmas trees and decorations and celebrated the holiday with an anti-Christmas pageant that mocked belief in miracles and held all clergy up to scorn. It published the sworn testimony of aviators that there were no gods because they had scoured the skies and found none. It warned that the taking of communion promoted drunkenness and spread disease. It made "anti-God museums" of some churches, notably St. Basil's Cathedral in Moscow's Red Square, and the Kazan Cathedral in Leningrad. It sought to arouse the indignation of the faithful by displaying in the Kremlin Museum the gold eggs sprinkled with rubies, sapphires, and diamonds that church leaders had given to the tsars at Eastertime. Its most ambitious effort was the creation of the League of Militant Atheists, whose members wrote and preached that religion was unnecessary because science provided the answers to any questions one could ask.

By 1925, the assignment to wean the people away from the church went to the League of Militant Atheists. The results of the league's efforts were disappointing, and in 1929 the government renewed its pressure on all religion. It closed fifteen hundred churches on the ground that a socialist society had no need for them. Members of the clergy charged with sabotaging the Five-Year Plan went to prison, a hundred bishops were thrown into forced-labor camps, and hundreds of priests were shot or exiled to Siberia. Those who escaped seizure were prohibited from living in cities, and villagers who sheltered them were taxed for doing so. The government adopted the six-day week and severely punished anyone absent from work without a doctor's excuse; the effect was to prevent people from going to church unless the rest day just happened to fall on Sunday. Churches might not engage in any social or cultural activity—and could use the property they leased only for worship, not for religious instruction. Teaching in state schools now became for the first time deliberately antireligious.

When the new attack met with popular resistance, particularly in the villages where the authorities already had their hands full with collectivization, Moscow abandoned the policy and criticized overzealous party workers who had interfered with services or closed churches against the people's will. The Politburo listened to foreign threats to withhold the loans upon which some of the success of the Five-Year Plan would depend, but the government now could afford to be generous. It had so deprived religion of its means of existence that any threat to the regime from that quarter was impossible. By 1935 barely four thousand Russian Orthodox churches remained open of eleven times that many before the revolution; of fifty thousand priests only one out of nine still was active; four-fifths of the bishops were in prison or dead.

Persecution now gave way to a policy of toleration, as much to impress the outside world as to soften opposition at home. By 1935 materials for the preparation of the traditional Easter cakes became available in state retail stores, and the prohibition against the display of Christmas trees ended that year. The government even permitted the manufacture of wedding rings that only church ceremonies required. Children of priests received permission for the first time since the revolution to attend school. The 1936 constitution restored to the clergy the right to vote. The government even condemned recent efforts to ridicule Russia's conversion to Christianity in the tenth century, praising the work of the clergy in spreading literacy and denouncing the "frivolous attitude toward history" in which party stalwarts had interpreted the conversion as a reactionary step.

The government did not return to its policy of calculated persecution of religion, but many members of the clergy and laity suffered in the 1937–38 purge. During the purge, bishops were tried for sabotage and espionage for Germany. Priests were accused of inciting their flocks to practice terrorism. Many churches closed down when they lost their clergy members to the police; by the end of 1937, there were 1,100 fewer Orthodox and 240 fewer Catholic churches open than at the beginning of the year. When Stalin called a halt to the purge in 1939, the attack on the church came to a temporary end until the resurgence of persecution in the Krushchev period.

Education

Lenin sincerely wanted to promote literacy, for he looked upon education of the masses as the only way to expand production and bring a better way of life. Before the widespread use of radio and television, the regime could preach the message of communism to the masses and enlist their support only by teaching them to read. To make workers more productive and to reach them with its propaganda the government launched a program of adult education and sought to bring every child into the schoolroom.

Up to the age of four the child might be cared for in a nursery maintained by the factory where the mother worked. Each collective farm operated a nursery where peasant mothers left their children while they worked in the fields. Kindergartens, maintained by *kolkhozes* (collective farms) and industrial plants, cared for children too old for the nursery and too young for school, normally those between four and eight years old. There was no tuition for attendance at either nursery or kindergarten, for the right to place her child there was part of the mother's wage. Kindergarten training for every eligible child, however, was a goal still far away at the beginning of the First Five-Year Plan, where there were facilities to handle only one percent of the children of kindergarten age.

In 1930 the government decreed universal compulsory education beginning at the age of eight. The type of school and the length of compulsory attendance depended on whether the child lived in a rural or urban area. The peasant child completed a four-year elementary course that taught him or her to figure simple arithmetic problems and to read and write. At the end of the primary schooling, the child's education was completed. The village child normally went to work for a third of adult wages on the collective farm, becoming a member and assuming the rights and obligations of an adult peasant at the age of sixteen.

Moscow State University

The elementary school for the city child ran through seven years. To the reading, writing, and arithmetic of the four-year village school the urban school added a foreign language, history, science, and military training. When the child graduated from this seven-year elementary school, normally at fourteen, the student went to work; in fact, he or she had to do so at sixteen unless he or she continued in school.

One of Communist Russia's most outstanding achievements has been the conquest of illiteracy. By the beginning of World War I the zemstvo schools had achieved wonders in teaching most Russian children to read and write. Through seven long years of war, and foreign intervention, however, schools had closed, teachers had died, and most children under fifteen had had no opportunity to learn to read and write. The nation had slipped back into the slough of widespread illiteracy from which it had so recently emerged. By 1922 over half the people of European Russia and four-fifths of those in Asiatic Russia were illiterate. In the Moslem lands of southern Siberia less than 4 percent were literate as late as 1926.

Soon after the Civil War, the Communist party led a drive against illiteracy that fired the imagination particularly of young people. Children able to attend school for the first time were so eager to learn that it did not occur to them to object to unheated buildings or to sharing one pencil and one textbook with thirty or forty other pupils in a classroom. They went home and chided their ignorant parents into learning to read and write. Young members of the party went from house to house taking the names of illiterates and offering to teach those who would give their time. Less than half the population of the USSR was illiterate by 1928, and before World War II the rate had dropped below 20 percent for those over nine years of age. In 1913, the elementary and secondary schools of Russia accommodated about eight million students, and there were perhaps three hundred thousand in institutions of higher learning. The 1939 census showed thirty-one million in preparatory schools and another two and one-half million in universities and institutes.

In a reaction against the stern discipline and emphasis on fact and rote that had characterized tsarist schools, educational leaders of the USSR went to the other extreme of progressive education in the 1920s. Discipline, regarded as old-fashioned and reactionary, gave way to student government. Students, teachers, and janitors formed a collective, and elected officers and held meetings to decide policy. Pupils chose their own projects to develop, working on them in school or out as they chose. They went on tours to visit factories and government offices to such an extent that their visits threatened to interrupt the work in such places and the practice had to be discontinued. Boys and girls sat in the same classrooms for the first time. The teacher lost all control over the students and became an observer and advisor. "Polytechnical" education was fashionable— students alternated periods in school with days or weeks in factories and on farms—the "learning-by-doing" technique. So disappointing were the results of these fads, however, that in the early thirties there was a trend back to traditional methods. Progressive education came to an end, the teacher regained authority, projects gave way to learning a body of facts, girls and boys once again attended separate elementary and secondary schools, and students once more wore uniforms as they had in tsarist times. Titles, degrees, seminars, and examinations again came into use, after having been abolished in the 1920s.

Relations With the Non-Communist World

Lenin's fond hope that Communist revolution in the West would overturn several capitalist governments faded before the sobering reality that the Russian revolutionary success was unique and would remain so for years to come. If the world had turned Communist in 1918, Communist Russia would have had no foreign dealings in the traditional sense and so would have been rid of irksome foreign relations and the necessity for developing a foreign policy.

As soon as it became clear that the newborn Russia must live alone in a capitalist world, the government had to adjust to the inevitability of establishing formal relations with others whose survival Lenin had hoped not to have to face. This fact of international life made a tremendous impact upon the new Russia. There would be scarcely a moment when the nation's leaders could take their eyes off the world around them and devote their undivided attention to their own frustrating domestic problems; internally the new Russia, like the old, would react to pressures from outside its borders. Its leaders never could neglect the military and political strength of potential enemies near and remote. This so tended to slow down the revolutionary experiment or to divert the nation's energies away from it that, in a sense, the dreams of the founding fathers never were freely pursuable.

Many young Bolshevik visionaries keenly resented Lenin's compromise with principle—for example during the NEP period when he approved wage differentials, employment of one man by another, and private enterprise of a sort—but there was nothing else Lenin or his successors could do in the face of foreign hostility. He and those who came after him could not simply withdraw from the game of international politics. Isolation was out of the question; to indulge in it would court disaster.

Communist Russia, then, soon began to act like any other nation whose primary concern was survival. In 1920 the Western allies withdrew from Russia, lifted the blockade, urged Wrangel to stop fighting, and suggested that the border states settle their differences with the Bolsheviks. Their former support withdrawn or sharply reduced, several regions on the periphery attempting and succeeding in breaking away from the former Russian empire now recognized the Soviet government. This included Finland, Estonia, Latvia, Lithuania and eventually Poland. Establishment of diplomatic ties with contiguous states helped, but recognition by such weak neighbors on Soviet borders hardly constituted a diplomatic triumph. Germany and Sweden condescended to trade with Russia but refused to recognize its government initially.

There were obstacles in the way of Russia's restoration of normal relations with other powers. At its first meeting in March 1919, the Third or Communist International—the so-called Comintern—supported Communist efforts in Europe and Asia, linking them to the Comintern and to the revolutions and revolutionary threats between 1919 and 1929, and had called upon the workers of all nations to press their governments to withdraw their interventionist forces and recognize the Soviet regime. Representing nineteen nations, its thirty-five delegates, most of them residents in Russia, had gathered in Moscow shortly after a Communist uprising in Berlin and just prior to temporarily successful efforts to establish Communist regimes in Hungary and Bavaria. By 1922 the threat of Communist uprisings had faded, but the governments of the West were understandably wary of the Comintern, which by that time had had a second and then a third meeting of Communists from many lands. A second deterrent to normal relations between Russia and the capitalist powers was the fact that the Soviet regime had made foreign trade a state monopoly, a situation with which nonsocialist governments did not yet know how to cope. Much more serious stumbling blocks were Lenin's refusal to honor the government and private debts contracted in tsarist times with foreigners and the confiscation of foreign-owned property without compensation by the Soviet authorities. The repudiation of tsarist debts seemed to be most irritating to Russia's former allies, for it came into question every time the Bolsheviks broached the subject of restoring diplomatic or trade relations. The Soviet leaders recognized two objectives in the field of foreign relations: the responsibility to defend the nation and the experiment upon which they had embarked, and the assumed obligation to support workers in every country in the overthrow of capitalist governments. The two tasks were to be undertaken by two different agencies. The Comintern would lead the attack on bourgeois governments by disseminating propaganda, supporting Communist parties all over the world, taking advantage of strikes wherever they might occur, and subsidizing revolutionary activity whenever the need and the opportunity arose. Commissar for Foreign Affairs George Chicherin, a former aristocrat turned Bolshevik, would direct the nation's diplomatic affairs with other states toward maintaining peace and developing friendly relations. The two functions would go hand in hand. The pressure of native Communist parties on foreign governments would, presumably, so embarrass those governments that they would have no choice but to maintain peaceful relations with Russia. What the Bolsheviks only occasionally and dimly realized through the years is that the two agencies worked at cross purposes. Attempts by native Communist parties to embarrass their own governments irritated rather than smoothed relations with Russia. Such attempts were made time and again in Europe, Asia, and the Western Hemisphere. Almost invariably they failed in their purpose and had the effect only of convincing the non-Communist world that the Soviet government was wholly untrustworthy.

Delegates from thirty-four nations gathered at Genoa in April 1922, to hear suggestions for the economic recovery of Europe. Interpreting the New Economic Policy as a return to capitalism, Westerners expected Russia to recognize tsarist debts, compensate their nationals for confiscated property, and grant trade concessions. Chicherin did announce that his government would consider the payment of the nearly fourteen billion dollars that the tsars and the Provisional Government had borrowed, but he added conditions. The Soviet government must receive recognition as the legal government of Russia and must have extensive foreign credits. Finally, he shocked the representatives of the former allies by presenting them with a bill for sixty billion dollars in payment for the damage they had inflicted during the intervention. However, Russia would not press this claim for reparations if it could obtain loans with which to rebuild its war-torn land. The delegates could agree only that the nations represented would not interfere in each other's internal affairs.

Then German and Russian delegates met at nearby Rapallo and worked out an agreement between their two countries. The Soviet position constituted a manifest attempt to parry allied efforts to win access to the promising markets in the Soviet Union. The two countries mutually gave up all claim to reparations for war damage or compensation for nationalized property and agreed to restore diplomatic relations. Russia received assurance of an indefinite amount of credit for machinery and technical assistance; German army officers received permission to practice their profession in Russia and so evade the restrictions of the Versailles Treaty.

The Western powers had their revenge for Russia's diplomatic coup when the nations sent delegates to Lausanne later in the year to consider what should be done with the Straits, the key waterway coursing through Turkish territory that provided a maritime route between the Black and Agean Seas and giving Russia access to the Mediterranean. The Treaty of Lausanne permitted free use of the Straits by the merchant or war vessels of all nations in peacetime or during a war to which Turkey was not a party. The terms would not deter any nation wanting to attack Russia. Once again the most vulnerable point in the nation's defense perimeter lay exposed until such time as a navy could be built to defend it.

The other great powers were slow to follow Germany's lead in recognizing Soviet Russia. Britain's Conservative party had always been extremely hostile to bolshevism. When the British Labour party and the Liberals formed a cabinet in 1924, however, Prime Minister MacDonald fulfilled his party's pledge to recognize the Moscow government and sought to obtain in exchange a Soviet promise to pay Russia's war and prewar debts. When the Soviet leaders asked for a loan with which to pay the debts Britain demurred, and the negotiations dragged out inconclusively. The British move stirred the other powers to action. Italy, France, Norway, Sweden, Denmark, Austria, Greece, Mexico, and China extended recognition before the year was out, and early in 1925 Japan and Russia restored diplomatic relations. The United States remained intransigent, however, and officially refused to have anything to do with the Moscow government. American business interests, such as Ford, did sign economic agreements throughout the decade.

French fear of a German revival and British concern to prevent another Franco-Russian alliance to counterbalance Germany brought the European powers together at Locarno to search for peace. Russia received no invitation, repeating the pattern set in 1919 when the Paris Peace Conference met without it to establish the League of Nations and deal with the transition to the postwar period. Russia at that time was embroiled in its divisive Civil War. The Locarno conference guaranteed French and Belgian boundaries but did nothing to confine Germany to its eastern frontier. Since the League of Nations still denied membership to Germany, the Soviet government quickly exploited German pique at the exclusion. Just before Locarno the two reached a trade agreement awarding Russia a substantial loan, and six months after Locarno Germany and Russia promised neutrality if a third power attacked either. Soviet fears eased somewhat, and Germany, by its implied threat to line up with Russia, won admission to the league.

Although trade flourished between Britain and Russia after the restoration of diplomatic contact, relations between the two governments were anything but friendly. During the British election campaign in 1924, a London newspaper published purported instructions from Zinoviev urging a British Communist revolution. The letter later was proven a forgery, but it restored the Conservatives to power. A year later, Zinoviev praised British organized labor for spurning a settlement of disputes with management. He also predicted a serious mine strike and proposed financial aid to the strikers when it should come. The miners did walk out and a general strike ensued. Although the latter failed, the miners stayed off the job for months, and Russian workers volunteered nearly five million dollars for their support. Britons became indignant at this Russian interference in domestic affairs. An excuse for breaking off relations with Russia conveniently appeared when British detectives raided the London office of Arcos, the Russian trading firm, in search of secret documents stolen from the War Office. The stolen papers did not turn up, but the government insisted that other seized documents indicated the presence in England of a Soviet spy ring. Parliament voted to break off diplomatic relations. Russians, White and Red, accepted the Soviet government's contrived scare that Britain was preparing for war. The government was seeking desperately to generate patriotic backing for an economic plan that would call for extreme sacrifices. Peasants hoarded salt and grain, Muscovites were near panic with fear, and Russians asked foreigners when the war would come. Communists everywhere emphasized the ever-present menace of war throughout the world.

Russian leaders looked upon the League of Nations as an anti-Soviet bloc and were certain that Locarno was an attempt, as the British foreign secretary practically admitted it was, to arrange the peace and security of Europe not only without Russia but against it. Along its western frontier the peace settlement of 1919 left a *cordon sanitaire* of bitterly anti-Communist states who might, under Polish leadership and with French blessing, drive east at any time. The Poles, however, were fully awake to Soviet ambitions to push westward against Poland. Russia received an invitation to participate in framing the League of Nations' disarmament proposals, and Maxim Litvinov, Russia's vice-commissar for foreign affairs, proposed immediate demobilization and complete disarmament by liquidating all armed forces; destroying all weapons, warships, and military planes; abolishing military training; dismantling all war plants; removing all fortifications and military installations; sweeping away all general staffs and war ministries; and forbidding provision for military items in any state budget. All this he proposed should be done in a year or in no more than four years. After reading his "Fourteen Points" Litvinov sat down in a hushed house too shocked to grant him even polite applause. When the delegates recovered sufficiently three months later to consider Litvinov's proposals they all agreed, with the exception of Germany and Turkey who supported them, that the plan was "impracticable."

When nothing came of Litvinov's daring suggestions, the Soviet government resorted to more conventional ways of warding off attack. It concluded nonaggression pacts with Russia's neighbors—with Turkey, Germany, Lithuania, Afghanistan, and Persia in the 1920s, and with Finland, Estonia, Latvia, and even Poland by 1932. The treaties closed most, but not all, of the gaps in the nation's defense line; Romania and Japan would not listen to nonaggression proposals. Finally, Russia signed the Kellogg-Briand Pact in 1928 by which the powers piously promised not to resort to war as an instrument of national policy.

Soviet Interest in Asia

The joint Chinese-Russian protectorate over Outer Mongolia, established during World War I, deteriorated during the revolution when White forces seized the

Mongolian capital and used the area as a base for raiding Siberia. As White fortunes waned, Red troops scattered the counterrevolutionary armies and established a Soviet protectorate. In 1919, when Siberia and Manchuria were in hostile hands, the Bolsheviks nobly abandoned all rights over the Chinese Eastern Railway. When the Whites had been defeated the Russians came to realize that the short rail line over the Chinese Eastern to Vladivostok would be as valuable to Communist as to imperial Russia.

The Sino-Soviet Treaty of 1924 settled the outstanding issues between the two nations. Russia, tongue in cheek, recognized Mongolia as part of China, surrendered all concessions that the tsarist government had won from the Chinese, gave up the Boxer indemnity that the colonial powers had imposed in 1901, and renounced the right of extraterritoriality that every other power still retained and that the Chinese so resented. A half Chinese and half Russian board, under a Chinese chairman, was to operate the Chinese Eastern Railway.

The USSR became embroiled in the Chinese revolution that broke out anew in 1925 and that aimed to put an end to imperialist exploitation by Great Britain, France, Japan, and the United States. Because the Soviet government only recently had renounced its rights and concessions in China, it suffered none of the animosity against foreigners. The Chinese regarded Russia as the one sure enemy of imperialism and the one true friend of the peoples fighting for independence and dignity. Although not a Communist himself, the Chinese leader Sun Yat-sen sympathized with the Russian experiment and sided with the peasants and workers against the capitalists and landlords. There was a Communist wing in the Kuomintang that maintained a link between Moscow and the revolutionary party that he headed.

Although Moscow denied any official relationship with the Nationalist Government at Canton, as Sun Yat-sen's revolutionary movement now called itself, millions of rubles helped finance the Nationalist drive north to Shanghai and into the Yangtze valley. Michael Borodin, a Russian agent of the Comintern, went to China to advise the Nationalists on revolutionary strategy; General Blücher also arrived to serve as the major military adviser to the Chinese and brought a host of Russian army officers and technicians with him. Borodin advised Chiang Kai-shek, who took over the leadership of the Kuomintang soon after Sun Yat-sen's death in 1925, to order improved labor conditions and to divide the great estates among the peasants if he wanted popular support for his movement. However, at the insistence of the conservative wing of the party, Chiang rejected the advice and turned against the left wing and its Russian friend Borodin, executing thousands of Chinese and Russians, and emerging triumphant over all opposition and over the Chinese Communist party. Borodin and Blücher returned to Moscow in 1927, and Russia's influence waned.

Moscow had no intention of losing its rights to the Chinese Eastern Railway so vital to its position in East Asia. When threats accomplished nothing with Chiang Kai-shek, Russia launched a drive toward Harbin from both ends of the railway. The Chinese forces fell back in confusion and Chiang hastily agreed to a restoration of the dual control of the railroad provided in the 1924 agreement.

The ease with which the Russian Far Eastern army had driven off the Chinese may have spurred Japan to embark upon a campaign long planned to bring East Asia under its hegemony. Japan moved first into southern Manchuria, meeting no resistance other than feeble protests from China and a decision by the League of Nations to investigate this violation of a member's territory. In 1932 the Japanese occupied the rest of Manchuria, enthroned a puppet emperor, and proclaimed Manchuria, which they renamed Manchukuo, an independent state. Although the threat to eastern Siberia was unmistakably clear, the USSR was in no position to challenge the Japanese aggression. The unrest, confusion, and famine growing out of the First Five-Year Plan left the government no choice but to avoid war with a power as formidable as Japan. Russia later sold to Manchukuo its interest in the Chinese Eastern Railway, a humiliation that was compounded when Japan spurned a Russian proposal to sign a nonaggression pact.

Tightening Controls

From its infancy, bolshevism kept alive, or perhaps affected, an element of democracy in the movement, both at the top and in the rank and file. Occasionally the membership defied the dictates of the party's Central Executive Committee. This was increasingly so during the chaotic and anarchic months through 1917, when the authority of the Provisional Government waned and the nation in effect had no government. Democratic currents were most apparent among the party's leaders. Of course, they had to reckon with Lenin's strong will; he was stubborn and even petulant at times. Under Lenin's leadership, however, members of the party were relatively free to disagree with and criticize their leaders and even to attack party plans in the press after their adoption. There was no punishment for those who opposed Lenin so violently for his insistence that there was no alternative to accepting the German terms at Brest-Litovsk. Those who the following year protested against the drift toward overcentralization and the concentration of power in the hands of a few did so with impunity. The bitter attack on Lenin and Trotsky for using former officers in the new army brought no recrimination. His patience and his willingness to forgive and welcome back those who strayed away made Lenin the most admired of all Communists, and many who fled the country under Stalin looked back nostalgically to the relatively free times of his predecessor in 1917–1918.

The leadership tended to harden, however, with the coming of Civil War and foreign intervention. The first charge of the Cheka was to track down counterrevolutionaries and saboteurs—surely a reasonable undertaking for a new administration to order. What was sinister about it all—certainly the Bolsheviks were not unique here—was that the activities of the Cheka through the turbulent three years of civil and foreign war led to the steady erosion of whatever democratic scruples the Bolsheviks ever had.

The new nation had to withstand a siege by foreign foes and at the same time fight a deadly war, inside its defense perimeter, against Russians who chose to stand and fight, openly or covertly, a government they detested. Bolshevism's answer to the internal threat was the terror. At first the administration tended to see its enemies as specific groups—Socialist Revolutionaries or Mensheviks—or in general terms—capitalists, kulaks, clergy, landowners—and so the terror became an instrument of class war. Then it came to identify individuals as saboteurs of the revolution to be hunted down for subversion and even for intellectual dissent. It took the final step of gathering into its net not only obvious enemies of the regime but potential ones as well. There was a return to the Third Section's judgment of Herzen in his student days: "Not dangerous, but could be." When an end came to the Civil War the terror continued as a necessary part of the regime's pattern to keep the nation on the course its leaders charted. Terror was part of the system, even in Lenin's time.

Lenin was never a man of unlimited patience. In 1920, the so-called "workers' opposition group" demanded that labor unions operate the factories and protested against excessive centralization in the Communist party. Lenin carried a majority of the party congress with him in condemning "syndicalist and anarchist deviation" and threatened those who persisted in factionalism with losing their party membership. When the warning went unheeded Lenin demanded the expulsion of these "wavering Communists," and the party expelled a third of its members. His party purges were replenished by the influx of new recruits.

Battle Over the Succession

In 1919, the Central Executive Committee of the party organized three new agencies to handle the committee's work when it was not in session. The Political Bureau, or Politburo, which had fallen into disuse after the Civil War, was resurrected to deal with all major policy questions requiring immediate action. Lenin, Trotsky, and Stalin were among its five original members. From the beginning the Politburo concerned itself with both important and insignificant matters having to do with every phase of government. Every aspect of Soviet life came under the scrutiny of these top leaders. Anyone who made a decision was afraid to move without Politburo approval. The Organizational Bureau, or Orgburo, on which Stalin also served, was to exercise control over the party membership. The third agency, the General Secretariat, was to coordinate the work of the other two. Stalin interested himself primarily in organization and membership, and when he became general secretary in 1922 he took with him his knowledge of and control over the party workers. From then on, the Orgburo became unimportant and Stalin's authority steadily increased.

The secretary headed a huge staff, supervised party personnel, and guided propaganda work. His appointment of regional secretaries to direct activities of local cells gave him effective control of the party. Within a year Trotsky was complaining that Stalin's methods left the impression among most party workers that the general secretary made all decisions. The General Secretariat continued to supervise party membership, control most appointments, and carry out propaganda work, and Stalin's position as general secretary was primarily responsible for stilling all opposition to his rule.

Lenin suffered a stroke in May 1922, and two others in the succeeding year. While Lenin lay paralyzed and unable to work, Stalin teamed with the leftists Kamenev and Zinoviev to keep Trotsky from succeeding Lenin. Stalin and Trotsky had violently disagreed years before the revolution and again during the Civil War, and the Georgian was not one to forgive a hurt. (Kamenev, incidentally, was Trotsky's brother-in-law.) Trotsky's supporters suffered removal from important positions in government and party, and the little firebrand, left to stand alone, found himself accused of "petty-bourgeois deviationism." After the triumph over Trotsky, Stalin deserted his leftist friends and teamed up with the rightists in the Politburo to destroy Kamenev and Zinoviev. Their supporters were driven from the party and they, together with Trotsky with whom they had become reconciled, were removed from the Politburo.

The contest went on through 1927, Trotsky and the others accusing Stalin of suffering defeats in foreign affairs—the Communist failure in China and the rupture of diplomatic relations with Great Britain—and of reaction at home. Trotsky arranged secret meetings with his sympathizers, operated an underground press, and even organized street demonstrations against Stalin. The police trumped up the charge that Trotsky was conspiring with Whites to overthrow the regime, and the party expelled him along with Kamenev and Zinoviev. Early in 1928 Trotsky was exiled to central Siberia, later deported to Turkey and thence to Mexico, where, in 1940, one of Stalin's agents killed him. His supporters lost their party membership, although Kamenev and Zinoviev abjectly recanted and eventually returned to the party.

Lenin's decision to dismiss Stalin came too late, and the Georgian who had won control of the party organization was not to be brushed aside. Indeed, he climbed upward over Lenin's reputation, leadership, and the affection in which party members held him. Stalin's decision to rename Petrograd Leningrad was only the slightest manifestation of his determination to succeed the venerable leader. Embracing the cardinal principles that Lenin had proclaimed, Stalin allied himself first with the rightists who opposed Trotsky's succession, and then turned against them to wipe out both extremes.

By 1928, Stalin was firmly in control of the Communist party in spite of Lenin's deathbed warning that the Georgian was "too rude" and not to be trusted with power. This "grey blur, looming up now and then dimly and leaving no trace," this leader so long unnoticed who had seized control of the machinery to direct the party and the nation, had conquered all opponents.

Suggested Reading

AVRICH, P., *Kronstadt, 1921* (Princeton, 1970).
BALL, A. M., *Russia's Last Capitalists: The Nepmen, 1921–1929* (Berkeley, 1987).

BUNYAN, J., *The Origin of Forced Labor in the Soviet State, 1917–1921: Documents and Materials* (Baltimore, 1967).

CARR, E. H., *A History of Soviet Russia: The Bolshevik Revolution, 1917–1923* (New York, 1953).

———, *The Interregnum, 1923–1924* (New York, 1954).

———, *Socialism in One Country, 1924–1926*, 3 vols. (Baltimore, 1972).

CLEMEMTS, B. E., *Bolshevik Feminist: The Life of Aleksandre-Kollontai* (Bloomington, IN 1979).

COHEN, S., *Bukharin: A Political Biography* (New York, 1974).

DANIELS, R., *The Conscience of the Revolution* (Cambridge, 1960).

DEUTSCHER, I., *The Prophet Unarmed: Trotsky, 1921–1929* (New York, 1959).

———, *Stalin, A Political Biography* (New York, 1949).

DOBB, M. H., *Russian Economic Development Since the Revolution* (London, 1928).

FISCHER, L., *The Life of Lenin* (New York, 1964).

FISHER, H. H., *The Famine in Soviet Russia, 1919–1923: The Operations of the American Relief Administration* (New York, 1927).

JANSEN, M., *A Show Trial under Lenin: The Trial of the Socialist Revolutionaries, Moscow, 1922* (The Hague, 1982).

KRUPSKAYA, N., *Memoirs of Lenin* (London, 1942).

LENIN, V. I., *Selected Works* (New York, 1947).

LEWIN, M., *Lenin's Last Struggle* (New York, 1968).

MAGUIRE, R. A., *Red Virgin Soil: Soviet Literature in the 1920s* (Princeton, 1968).

MALLY, L., *Culture of the Future: The Prolekult Movement in Revolutionary Russia* (Berkeley, 1990).

MATTHEWS, M. (ed.), *Soviet Government: A Selection of Official Documents on Internal Policies* (New York, 1974).

McCAULEY, M. (ed.), *The Russian Revolution and the Soviet State, 1917–1921: Documents* (New York, 1975).

McNEAL, R. H., *Bride of the Revolution: Krupskaya and Lenin* (Ann Arbor, 1972).

MEYER, A., *Leninism* (Cambridge, 1957).

MIRSKI, M., *The Mixed Economy: NEP and Its Lot* (Copenhagen, 1984).

O'CONNOR, T. E., *Diplomacy and Revolution: G. V. Chicherin and Soviet Foreign Affairs, 1918–1930* (Ames, IA, 1987).

PAGE, S., *Lenin and World Revolution* (New York, 1959).

PAYNE, R., *The Life and Death of Lenin* (New York, 1964).

PIPES, R., *The Formation of the Soviet Union: Communism and Nationalism, 1917–1923* (Cambridge, 1964).

PORTER, C., *Alexandra Kollontai: The Lonely Struggle of the Woman Who Defied Lenin* (New York, 1980).

POSPIELOVSKY, D., *The Russian Church under the Soviet Regime, 1917–1982* (Crestwood, NY, 1984).

POSSONY, S. T., *Lenin, the Compulsive Revolutionary* (Chicago, 1964).

RESHETAR, J. S., JR., *A Concise History of the Communist Party of the Soviet Union* (New York, 1964).

SCHAPIRO, L. B., *The Communist Party of the Soviet Union* (New York, 1971).

———, *The Origin of the Communist Autocracy: Political Opposition within the Soviet State, First Phase, 1917–1922* (Cambridge, 1955).

SMITH, I. H., *Trotsky* (Englewood Cliffs, NJ, 1973).

SUTTON, A. C., *Western Technology and Soviet Economic Development, 1917–1930*, vol. I (Stanford, 1968).

SZEZSNIAK, B. (ed.), *The Russian Revolution and Religion: A Collection of Documents Concerning the Suppression of Religion by the Communists, 1917–1925* (Notre Dame, 1959).

TROTSKY, L., *The Revolution Betrayed* (Garden City, NY, 1937).

TUCKER, R. C., *Political Culture and Leadership in Soviet Russia—from Lenin to Gorbachev* (New York, 1987).

_____, *Stalin as Revolutionary, 1879–1929: A Study in History and Personality* (New York, 1973).

TUMARKIN, N., *Lenin Lives! The Lenin Cult in Soviet Russia* (Cambridge, 1983).

ULDRICKS, T. J., *Diplomacy and Ideology: The Origins of Soviet Foreign Relations, 1917–1930* (London, 1979).

ULLMAN, R. H., *Intervention and the War: Anglo-Soviet Relations, 1917–1921* (Princeton, 1968).

WARD, C. C., *Russia's Cotton Workers and the New Economic Policy: Shop Floor Culture and State Policy, 1921–1929* (Cambridge, Eng., 1990).

WHITE, S., *The Origins of Detente: The Genoa Conference and Soviet-Western Relations, 1921–1922* (Cambridge, Eng., 1985).

ZATKO, J. J., *Descent into Darkness: The Destruction of the Catholic Church in Russia, 1917–1923* (Notre Dame, 1965).

CHAPTER 19

Stalin's Revolution

The Fifteenth Communist Party Congress met in December 1927 to expel Trotsky and other opposition leaders from the party, thus blessing the triumph of Stalin over his personal enemies. Of far greater importance, it decided to begin an economic revolution aimed at socializing production.

Early in 1921, the administration had created the State Planning Commission, or Gosplan, to draft an economic plan for the nation. Originally consisting of forty economists, accountants, and engineers, the organization grew steadily until it came to number thousands of experts working in scores of branch offices all over the Soviet Union. Every year from 1925 on, the Gosplan suggested production figures and analyzed the nation's resources and potentialities. Then the 1927 congress ordered the State Planning Commission to prepare a plan for the expansion of the national economy over the next five years. Here began the ambitious, centralized and rigid system which came to be known over future decades as the "command" or "planned" economy.

The first of several such five-year plans went into operation on October 1, 1928. Gosplan suggested minimal and optimal programs, and the party leaders chose the second, the more ambitious of the two. It assumed that harvests would be normal through the period of the plan and that foreign credits and trade would increase appreciably. Neither assumption proved valid—the 1931 and 1932 harvests were poor and foreign trade dwindled when depression engulfed the world.

The First Five-Year Plan aimed at putting an end to private enterprise in industry, expanding industrial output (particularly that of basic industries), increasing electric power production six times over, mechanizing agriculture, and collectivizing a fourth of the nation's farms. The Second Five-Year Plan, to run through 1937, proposed to complete the collectivization of agriculture, to continue industrial expansion by giving increasing attention to consumer-goods industries while carrying on with the development of basic industries, to improve the transportation net, to move strategic industries east of the Urals, and, as in every one of the plans, to continue the improvement and modernization of the armed forces. The third plan, scheduled for completion in 1942, aimed at further growth of basic industries and promised much greater production of consumers' goods, especially clothing and food.

Socialized Agriculture

At the beginning of the First Five-Year Plan, four-fifths of Russia's population was rural. There were twenty-five million peasant households, half again as many as in 1917, for many had carved out small farms for themselves from the great estates. A very few held their farms all in one piece; the vast majority had several small plots scattered all over the township.

Here, in the conservative countryside, lay the heart of resistance to the nation's progress. Imported tractors assigned to cooperatives had little use and were left to rust out when they broke down. The peasant preferred to rely on a horse or human strength for the power needed to plant and harvest the crops. State-owned farms, or *sovkhozes*, had been organized on former imperial estates to set an example of good farming methods, but few farmers had changed their age-old ways of doing things. Ever since the revolution, the government had been encouraging peasants to throw their holdings together and pool their capital in a collective farm, or kolkhoz, a unit large enough to make practical the use of labor-saving machinery, but only one peasant household in sixty had joined a kolkhoz by 1928. The poor and "middle" peasants who made up the overwhelming majority raised five-sixths of the nation's grain, but they ate most of it and marketed only a tenth. The government had to find some way to increase their output.

Well-to-do peasants had grown still more prosperous during the years of the NEP, leasing more land and hiring labor as the government allowed them to do. They had some machinery, good buildings, herds of livestock, and enough money to lend to their neighbors at high interest rates. Their large farms produced much more than they could eat, and they sold the surplus not to the state but in the free market or fed it to livestock to reap a greater profit. There were under a million of these kulak families, but their relative affluence and their power as moneylenders and as renters of equipment and horses to their poor neighbors made them the object of bitter jealousy in every community.

There were several reasons why the party leaders decided to collectivize agriculture. Industry was largely under government operation, and the five-year plan proposed to nationalize the rest of it. To permit individualism in agriculture while pushing toward socialism in the rest of the economy would have been incongruous. The government proposed to abolish class in the cities; it could hardly allow the continued existence of poor, middle, and rich peasants in the villages. Individual enterprise, as the peasant worked it, was wasteful and inefficient. Large farm units using improved methods and modern equipment would produce much more, the planners reasoned, than the small individual plots. Farmers in 1928 were marketing only a third as much as before the war. As the flow of grain to the government was dropping, the urban population, much of which received its food through state-owned outlets, was rising. Collectivization would permit more effective use of labor and free thousands to fill the expanding needs of industry.

So ran the reasoning by which Stalin and his supporters justified the collectivization of agriculture. The real reason, however, was political rather than economic. Stalin was searching for a way to destroy the individualist enterprise of the peasant—poor, "middle," or prosperous—by forcing the peasant into a straitjacket of control. Peasants on a collective farm could be watched by a member of the Communist party put there to do so and to report unrest and potential subversion.

The government first tried persuasion to entice peasants into collective farms, favoring them with seed, credit, and the use of state-owned machinery. Some poor peasants, each with ten acres or so, did join, but these timid ventures could hardly relieve the grain shortage. The kulaks and many middle peasants went on as before, thus setting themselves in opposition to the government and to the rest of the farm community. Furthermore, they refused to sell their surplus grain to the state at a time when the cities were feeling the pinch of shortages and high prices. Communist squads from the cities went into the villages to seize the surpluses of the kulaks, and the government encouraged poor peasants to report their rich neighbors' hidden stores. Many kulaks burned their granaries and fled to the woods to carry on resistance, lynching the poor peasants who reported them and battling the Communist squads who went after them. When they were taken, Stalin had them shot or thrown into forced labor camps and confiscated their goods and lands. Through the fall of 1929 and the following spring the vengeful hunt continued. Many gave in to save their families and joined collective farms. But before they did so they killed their livestock and feasted, walking empty-handed like poor peasants into the kolkhoz. Between 1929 and 1933 the number of pigs and cattle in Russia fell off by nearly half and sheep and goats by two-thirds. Bitter kulaks even killed their horses, thus depriving the collective farm they joined of much-needed power. Some poor peasants, on the other hand, joined the kolkhozes willingly. Without equipment and with only an animal or two they had everything to gain by doing so.

Enraged at kulak resistance, Stalin stepped up the rate of collectivization. However, the drive to establish collective farms and populate them with peasants and kulaks fostered additional problems and suspicions which prompted Stalin to change his strategy. By the spring of 1930, well over half of all peasant families

Lunch in the fields during the harvest on Lenin's Way Collective Farm. Note the horse-drawn machinery.

were living in kolkhozes, but industry was not yet turning out farm machinery in sufficient volume to meet the needs of collective farms. Stalin suspected that many a resentful kulak had come into the kolkhoz with the intention of influencing its members to hide their grain and oppose the government. The peasants had joined the collectives, voluntarily or under duress, in such droves—ten million families in six weeks—that the resulting confusion threatened to disrupt the planting of the spring crop. In a letter to *Pravda*, Stalin, who earlier had ordered "the liquidation of the kulaks as a class," now criticized what he called "dizziness from success" and blamed over-zealous party members for forcing farmers into collective farms. Anyone who chose to leave the kolkhoz, taking animals and equipment, was now free to do so (at the risk, of course, of later confiscation of property and even death). Within two months, eight million families withdrew, leaving only six million families in the collectives.

A different kind of pressure to promote collectivization emerged. Peasants who operated their individual farms had to pay higher taxes than collective farmers and were not permitted to use state-owned machinery which the government, through its recently organized machine-tractor stations, rented at low rates to kolkhozes. Peasants who joined collective farms could keep their gardens and garden tools, a cow or two, and a few chickens for their personal use. This privilege broke the opposition of the middle peasants, and many moved back into the collective farms. By the end of the First Five-Year Plan, fourteen million families, over half the peasant population, were members of kolkhozes, but Stalin himself admitted that collectivization had cost seven million lives, a majority of them in the Ukraine. The police had deported another one or two million families of kulaks and middle peasants to labor camps in the Arctic Circle. Meanwhile, the destruction of livestock and grain, and the poor harvests that followed, brought famine as severe as that of the early twenties.

By 1936, nine-tenths of the peasants belonged to nearly a quarter million collective farms that cultivated practically all the arable land not belonging to the state farms. During the next two years the number of individual peasant farms fell to a million, and they contained less than one percent of the cultivated land of Russia. Nevertheless, the nation's leaders were still not content. When punitive taxes did not eliminate individual farmers, the government restricted the amount of land they could farm to an acre or two. Because the average collective farmer had that much in a garden plot, those who continued to go it alone hurt themselves. The state had triumphed over peasant individualism, but at a terrible cost. The nation had lost half its livestock, many farm buildings, and much equipment. The government had to import American tractors in 1933 to replace the fourteen million horses slaughtered by the rebellious peasants.

A kolkhoz theoretically was an association of peasants, averaging about eighty families, who turned over their equipment, livestock, and land (voluntarily, the government insisted) to a cooperative enterprise in which all shared the work and income. According to the government-drafted charter under which each collective farm operated, each member family might have a house and an acre or two for a garden, both of which were surrendered if the peasant family left the kolkhoz. Each family might also own one cow, two calves, two sows with their litters, ten sheep or goats, twenty beehives, and as much poultry as could be tended. All other livestock, buildings, and equipment belonged to the collective.

Each kolkhoz operated under an annual plan geared to the national plan. Although the soviet theoretically decided what to grow, in practice the choice was that of the chairman of the soviet, who was responsible to superiors for the delivery to the government of certain crops to meet the national goal. Farmers could dispose of the income resulting from labor on their personal plots as they pleased. In addition to working on their own land and with their own animals, peasants worked in the large fields and with the herds belonging to the collective enterprise. A part of the annual collective yield went to the state at fixed low prices as obligatory delivery of produce that the government accepted as rent for the use of nationalized land. Another fraction used to go to the machine-tractor station, as payment for the use of the combines and tractors that the kolkhoz rented during the year. A third was set aside as seed and fodder and reserve for poor harvest. What remained, approximately a third, went to the collective members on the basis of the labor contribution each had made to the crop. Part of the annual livestock increase similarly went to the government; the rest might be sold directly to consumers in the free market and the proceeds shared among the members. Of the crops and livestock, the government took a fixed quantity, thus leaving the collective farm to shoulder the burden of crop failures and disease. While slight modifications were introduced in later years, the kolkhoz or collective farm remains as one of the primary forms of agricultural organization and production. Efforts are being made in the decade of the 1990s to move toward private farm ownership, but the number of such farms barely threatens the established collective farm system.

Ninety percent of the land under cultivation in Stalin's time lay in collective farms that produced—so the government insisted—at least seven-eighths of the nation's agricultural commodities. The rest of the output came from the state farms, or sovkhozes. Two thousand of these state farms, which ran to five thousand acres or more, the government operated with hired laborers. The state took the entire output and paid the workers their daily wages. Fifteen percent of the milk, meat, and wool that the government received in the mid-1950s came from its own farms. Many of them specialized in dairy cattle or in the growing of sugar beets, cotton, grain, or vegetables. Others served as model or experimental farms.

In the twelve years following the adoption of the First Five-Year Plan, agricultural production moved out of the horse-and-wooden-plow stage into the stage of mechanization. In 1940 three-fourths of the nation's arable land was under the plow of a half million tractors, twenty times as many as were in use twelve years earlier. Over two hundred thousand trucks and nearly as many combines helped farmers in 1940, whereas there was none of either in 1928. Most of this gain disappeared during World War II. What equipment the army did not requisition or the Germans confiscate was worn out and not replaced.

During the First Five-Year Plan agricultural output in the USSR fell by a fourth. By 1940 it had climbed back to 1928 figures. Several growing seasons had passed before the land returned to full use. Agricultural output remained surprisingly low. Khrushchev admitted after Stalin's death that the 1952 totals were only 10 percent above the 1940 output. During that twelve years Russia's population had grown by almost 10 percent, partly from conquest and partly from natural increase. Yield per acre rose considerably after 1928, as improved techniques would insure, and the number of acres planted vastly increased. A concerted effort to expand the crop diversity and produce more animal fodder, however, left the quantity of bread and vegetables available to each citizen not much greater than before World War I. Exports of agricultural products continued throughout the decade of the 1920s, compounding the shortages throughout the nation. What improvement there was in food consumption resulted largely from fairer distribution. This was especially true of meat products. In spite of Russia's territorial growth in the intervening years, the nation possessed fewer cattle, sheep, and goats in 1953 than in 1939, although there were 75 percent more hogs.

Advances in Industry

If agricultural production was disappointing during the first three five-year plans, the nation made spectacular strides in industry. Soviet figures boasted of a thirteenfold increase in industrial output between 1928 and 1950. Western estimates placed it at about half the Soviet claim, but the progress was remarkable, nevertheless.

Soviet policy makers, recognizing that the military potential of the great Western powers rested on heavy industry capable of turning out huge quantities of weapons, concentrated through all the plans on the production of capital goods—power installations, transportation facilities, minerals, oil, steel, rubber, chemicals, and the like—to the neglect of consumer goods. Capital-goods production increased thirty times over in the quarter century following the adoption of the First Five-Year Plan—between the first plan and Stalin's death—while there was only an eightfold increase in the output of light industry whose products consumers use. Of the investment in plant construction during that period, only a fourteenth went into consumer-goods industry, a little more into agriculture, a fifth into transportation, and two-thirds into heavy industry. Here lies the key to the rapid growth of Russia's military potential and also the key to the fact that the indisputable economic achievements have brought little to consumers. Soviet leaders decided that such things as clothing factories would not be built until the nation possessed enough steel mills to insure its adequate defense. So unswervingly did they follow this policy that during the early thirties the nation exported huge quantities of grain in exchange for machinery while thousands were dying of starvation.

During the First Five-Year Plan the government made an effort to get foreign investors to build plants in Russia, offering them liberal concessions to do so. This continued the policy of Lenin's NEP, seeking foreign loans, trade, and industrial development. Very few accepted the invitation, and the USSR resigned itself to financing its own construction program. It did obtain equipment and the services of technicians from the United States, Great Britain, Germany, and France, some of it on short-term credit. By 1938 it had paid off its foreign debts, which reached a peak of a billion and a half dollars.

Much of the early construction of industrial plants went up in feverish haste, for Stalin expected the capitalist powers to unite in an effort to wipe out the socialist experiment. There were many costly mistakes and much work had to be done over. The government shared the German and American enthusiasm for establishing large units even in situations where smaller units would better have served Russian conditions and needs. By 1938, however, the planners realized the merit in fashioning industrial organization to the country's peculiarities. There was bitter criticism of "gigantomania," the obsession with large units, and Trotsky's followers received the blame for the mistake.

American, German, and British firms furnished much of the machinery that went into hydroelectric, steel, tractor, automobile, and other plants under construction during the First Five-Year Plan. Russians who stood at the elbows of their foreign tutors learned their lessons well, and by the late twenties the nation had its own engineers. Progress in basic industry, where the planners concentrated investment, was apparent from the fact that in 1928 the nation ran a poor fifth to the United States, Britain, France, and Germany in the production of coal, steel, and electricity, but by 1956—three years after Stalin's death—the USSR was producing as much coal, steel, and electricity as Britain, France, and West Germany combined.

Production of food, clothing, and the like fell far shorter of goals than did production of dams, steel plants, and war materials. Much of the clothing and other items of consumer use was of shabby quality. What commodities were manufactured were always in short supply. The shoe industry turned out one pair for every three citizens in 1929 and about the same number in 1945; by 1950 there was an average of one pair for every consumer.

The government's effort to modernize industry during the First Five-Year Plan was hobbled by a transportation system out of date and nearly worn out during the war and revolution. The greater demands made upon it after 1928 threatened to exhaust the system completely. When the Politburo realized that industrial progress might be hamstrung by the failure of the transportation facilities to carry the burden, it boosted investment in railroads and assigned to one of its members, Lazar Kaganovich, the responsibility for building a modern transportation net. The industrial accomplishments that followed, and indeed the operation of a planned economy, would not otherwise have been possible. However, the costs were high in human terms. Long hours, the use of forced labor, working in harsh conditions, and unbending central control combined to make this task an exhausting undertaking.

Stalin, in a notable speech in February 1931, declared that the pace could not be slowed. The nation, he said, was fifty to one hundred years behind the industrialized nations of the world. The Soviet Union had to catch up in a decade or face possible defeat and collapse in the event of another war. His prophetic remark proved true when Nazi forces invaded the Soviet Union in 1941.

The Worker and Employment

One striking aspect of Soviet economic development was the growth of the nonagricultural labor force. The number of men and women so employed rose from less than 6,000,000 in 1924 to 9,500,000 four year later and to 28,000,000 in 1938. This came about as farm areas, always overpopulated, were drained of young people and as the mechanization and collectivization of agriculture released still more workers to the cities. Unemployment offices closed down when the government announced in 1930 that there were no more unemployed. Soon there was a labor shortage, and the government resorted to pressure to force wives and youths to go to work when the rising cost of living was not sufficient inducement to do so. By 1940, women made up a third of the nation's labor force.

The pressing demand for labor, and the ease with which anyone could obtain employment, created in workers an inclination to drift from one job to another in search of better conditions. Directors bid against each other, particularly in the housing they could offer, for the services of workers. Ninety percent of the average plant's labor complement in 1935 had served the enterprise less than a year. Many did not stay long enough to complete training for the job. The government moved to reduce this labor turnover, forbidding wage increases for any skilled worker who left the job without permission of the plant director and suspending from industrial employment those who floated from one job to another. Those who quit their jobs could be evicted from the plant's housing facilities and their ration cards for food and clothing withheld. It became illegal to hire people who did not have a release from their previous employers. Tardiness and absenteeism without a doctor's consent came to be punishable by fines and loss of preferred jobs. After 1938 individuals who worked for a government enterprise had to carry a labor book showing their employment record, punishments, rewards, and reasons for leaving earlier jobs. For a director to hire anyone not presenting a labor book in good order was illegal. By 1940 those who left their jobs, except to attend school or because of health, could be sentenced to prison. Unexcused absence from work was punishable by freezing the worker to the job and imposing a fine of a fourth of one's wages.

During the early five-year plans, the working day in Russia was seven hours and the employee worked four days and rested the fifth. By staggering the rest days, a plant director could operate equipment at full capacity every day in the year. In 1940 the work week was six days, with the seventh, normally Sunday, the rest day. At the same time, the eight-hour day became standard to make the work week forty-eight hours long.

Until well into the period of the First Five-Year Plan, labor unions worked out job classifications and wage scales in negotiation with plant directors and industry leaders. After 1930 the government determined wage rates without consultation with trade union representatives. Wages were paid either on a piece-rate basis—so much for each unit of output—or by the hour, day, or week, in which case the worker must turn out so many units—an expected norm. Workers who exceeded the norm might receive a bonus; if the norm was not met, there was a reduction in wages.

The wages of the average nonagricultural worker rose steadily after 1928, but they did not keep up with rising prices. Real wages actually were less in 1953 when Stalin died than they were twenty-five years earlier. In terms of food prices in Moscow, the average worker in 1953 earned only nine-tenths of his 1928 wage.

One day in 1935, Alexei Stakhanov, a coal miner, by improving his methods, cut over 100 tons in 6 hours and earned for the day's work 225 rubles, more than the average miner's monthly wage. His record was later broken, but he gave his name to those who emulated his speedup methods. Stakhanovites became heroes, but many workers must have cursed them. The government thenceforth frequently raised the norm or standard day's output, not only for coal miners but among all types of workers, reasoning that if Stakhanov could cut 100 tons the average worker surely could cut 10 or more in the same time.

During the first decade of the Communist regime, trade unions functioned in some ways as they function in a capitalist economy. Their leader, Michael Tomsky, insisted that the unions must be independent, that they must fight for the interests of the workers against industry leaders and bureaucrats just as capitalist unions fought employers or cooperated with them to serve union needs. Through the NEP years, the Russian unions negotiated wage contracts and worked òut with the proper officials the job classifications for each industry. As Lenin had done before him in the trade union disputes of 1920, Stalin insisted that unions must be subservient to the state that hired their members, that they must serve state ends, and that in opposing the government and its agents in a socialist state they were opposing their own interests. This became the policy before the First Five-Year Plan got under way, and Tomsky was purged in favor of Shvernik, who accepted Stalin's position.

Ostensibly, union membership was voluntary, and nearly all workers belonged. Members enjoyed greater social-insurance benefits and other advantages unavailable to nonmembers. The basic unit, the union in factory or shop, belonged to a district organization, and so the pyramid rose through regional and republic associations to the All-Union Trade Union Congress, whose assembly spoke for all organized workers. Communist party influence was dominant at all levels. The unions administered the social security programs and payments for disability, old age, blindness, and the like; they maintained rest homes, children's camps, vacation resorts, libraries, clubs, and gymnasia. They did not negotiate wage contracts or press for improved working conditions and only "participated" in settling labor disputes. There was no right to strike.

Inmates of forced labor camps also constituted part of the nation's work force insofar as the products of their work contributed to the national output. The camps were under the direction of the Ministry of Interior (the NKVD) which was responsible for certain types of enterprise. Five percent of the lumber produced and a fifth of the railroad ties fashioned in 1941 were turned out in the camps of the NKVD. The prisoners of the secret police engaged in work on the Don-Volga canal, oil production in the Arctic, road construction, and even the manufacture of some consumers' goods. Political opponents of the government—kulaks (wealthy peasants), intellectuals, prisoners of war, and common criminals—made up the work force of the labor camps. The number of prisoners was a closely guarded secret, but in recent years more information gradually is becoming available, leading to more accurate Russian and Western estimates. At the height of the purges of 1937–1938, approximately seven to eight million citizens were arrested and an estimated one million were executed. The number of prisoners in the camps, known as the *gulag*, reached at least one and a half million and two million by 1940, although some estimates are substantially higher. This figure represents those in the camps under NKVD jurisdiction. Additional millions suffered in other categories of incarceration and ordinary jails. This level of terror needs to be added to the earlier persecution during the collectivization drive and the famine of the early 1930s. Estimates of deaths from those causes have been placed by responsible scholars at levels approaching fourteen million.

More arrests, imprisonment and executions occurred during and after World War II, to be added to the figures of the fatalities in the 1920s and 1930s. Over the entire Stalin period, scholars have concluded that the total suffering at the hands of Stalin's police state may have reached as many as thirty-five million. In addition to those executed, many more died of disease, starvation and neglect. This painful and horrifying record, emerging only in recent years in fragments, provides an overall picture of Stalin's excesses against his own people, which were of a magnitude that surpassed even that of Hitler and the Nazis. Today, the people of the former Soviet Union are trying to cope with this terrible heritage.

The consumer might obtain the needed goods through a network of state-operated retail stores in the cities, at cooperatives in the villages, and from the free town markets where collective farmers sold the surplus produce from their private plots. In the chief cities the government maintained large department stores that sold everything imaginable on the order of similar stores in the United States and England. The state set prices for all goods sold in government and cooperative stores, but produce was sold in the free market, where more was available, for whatever it could bring.

Prices rose sharply from the beginning of the First Five-Year Plan. Moscow food prices doubled during the course of the first plan and then increased four times over by 1935. On the eve of World War II the same prices were twelve times higher than in 1928, and by 1948 they were nearly thirty times higher. Almost every year thereafter the government reduced prices, preferring, after an earlier experiment with inflation, to cut prices rather than raise wages.

Real wages fell as prices rose, for money wages never kept pace with retail prices. The year 1928 was the best the Soviet wage earner would know for decades. In 1948, when prices were nearly thirty times as high as twenty years earlier, wages were less than eleven times as high as in the base year 1928. The average Moscow worker in 1953 had to work twice as long for a pound of bread as did the average New Yorker, five times as long for beef, six and seven times as long for milk and eggs, ten times as long for a cotton dress, and sixteen times as long for a woolen suit. A person had to put in thirteen working days to earn enough for a pair of leather shoes and nearly two months for a suit. In that same year, the worker had to work nearly twice as long as in 1928 for the same quantity of essential foods.

By 1954 prices had declined to the point where they were only fourteen times as high as those in 1928, whereas the average wage was about thirteen times what it was in 1928. Soviet workers had not quite reached the real-wage level they enjoyed at the beginning of the First Five-Year Plan. They had, of course, survived a very costly war and had paid for an industrial plant that promised much better living in the future.

Most housing was provided for urban residents either by the municipality or by factories whose dwellings were reserved for their employees. There were a few privately owned homes and some owned by cooperatives. If workers lived in government-operated or factory-maintained houses, the occupants paid a low rent, 2 or 3 percent of their income. Living space was always rationed, for the nation never overcame a serious housing shortage. Each five-year plan promised extensive construction, but each fell far short of its goal. Cities were flooded with people leaving the farms to work in rapidly expanding industries. As Moscow's population doubled to over four million between 1926 and 1939, the housing available to its citizens increased by only 70 percent. The average space allotted to each citizen was half the average available to Muscovites before the First World War. Of course, it was more equitably shared. By 1950, when the city's population had passed five million, the average person had 10 percent less space than in 1939. Typically, a family of four or five lived in one room, sharing the kitchen and bath with four or five other families.

Mass technological training, promising higher income in the future, sought to compensate the people for the tremendous sacrifices they were forced to endure to fulfill the economic goals of the five-year plans and the collectivization of agriculture. There was renewed hope for a brighter future.

The Dictatorship Perfected

The 1936 constitution—the "Stalin Constitution"—only slightly altered the machinery of the state. The legislative branch—the Supreme Soviet—consisted of two houses elected every four years: the Council of the Union where one delegate sat for each electoral district of three hundred thousand citizens and the Council of Nationalities where twenty-five deputies represented each constituent republic. Lesser political regions had reduced representation. The two houses were co-equal and bills had to pass both to become law. The Supreme Soviet chose a Presidium which met when the full body was not in session. This legislative branch had extensive designated powers: to order national elections, issue decrees, interpret law, name ministers and question their actions, appoint military commanders, declare war, ratify treaties, and send and receive ambassadors. In fact, the Supreme Soviet acted as a powerless "rubber stamp," accepting the proposals submitted for approval during its limited meeting schedule several times a year. Serious debate and meaningful votes did not exist in this one-party body that pretended to be democratic.

The Supreme Soviet chose the Council of Ministers, the highest executive branch of the government. The chairman of the Council of Ministers was comparable to the premier or prime minister in Western European states and somewhat akin to the president of the United States. Lenin filled the office from 1917 to his death in 1924, Rykov until 1930, Molotov until 1941, Stalin until his death in 1953, Malenkov for the next two years, Bulganin for three, Khrushchev for six (1958–1964), Kosygin for sixteen, Tikhonov from 1980 to 1985, Ryzhkov to 1991, and Pavlov for the final year of the Soviet Union. These chairmen were leading figures in the Communist party, including membership in the Politburo (or Presidium, 1952–1966), and coordinated their efforts according to the dictates of the party.

All men and women over eighteen might vote for delegates to local soviets, except those deprived of electoral rights by court sentence. Elections were direct, and voting for single candidates was by secret ballot. Only branches of the Communist party or approved groups might nominate candidates of any political party to put forward candidates for office.

Finally, the constitution of 1936 detailed certain "fundamental rights and duties," including the right to work, to "rest and leisure" and paid vacations, and to maintenance in old age and during sickness or disability. Freedom of speech, press, assembly, and organization ostensibly was inviolate, as was "freedom of religious worship and freedom of anti-religious propaganda." Citizens were to enjoy freedom from arrest, "except by decision of a court or with the sanction of a procurator," as well as inviolability of the home and privacy of correspondence.

The citizens' duties included obedience to law, the honest performance of public responsibilities, the maintenance of "labor discipline," protection of public property, and respect for "the rules of socialist intercourse." To defend the nation, not only as a member of the armed forces but as a civilian, was "the sacred duty" of every citizen, and "treason to the motherland" was "punishable with all the severity of the law as the most heinous of crimes."

The 1936 constitution created a political structure devoid of political power. The soviets, which a hundred million men and women went through the motions of electing, provided the appearance of a system of government. The real power lay with the Communist party, which followed the dictates of its Central Committee, which was appointed by the Politburo, and which in Stalin's time was the creature of the man who ran it all.

The Role of the Communist Party

Paralleling the hierarchy of soviets that constituted the governmental facade of the Soviet Union are the numerous primary organizations of the Communist party. Although the organization changed slightly over the years, the structure remained essentially the same from the beginning of the regime.

Theoretically, the "supreme organ" of the party was the All-Union Congress of the Communist Party, which was supposed to assemble at least every four to five years. The meetings lasted only a few days to hear, applaud, and unanimously approve leaders' reports. Here the leaders outlined new plans and goals, indicated shifts in party strategy or "line," and named new appointments to leading party posts. The congress also elected a Central Committee whose membership varied over the years from approximately one hundred to over three hundred. National and regional party secretaries, members of the Council of Ministers, important military and police officials, and leading intellectuals and Marxist theorists made up the Central Committee. The individual members were powerful in their own right, even though the Central Committee only met several times a year and dealt with the issues the Politburo presented to it.

In theory, the Central Committee elected the members of the Politburo and the general secretary. The practice was quite different. The general secretary selected members to the Politburo, which decided who should serve on the Central Committee. The Central Committee itself, however, was chosen by Stalin, the general secretary, the most powerful man in the USSR from 1928 to his death.

Branches of the Communist party appeared at every administrative and control level. The secretary on each level passed down directives and passed up reports; made appointments to key positions in the party, youth organizations, and labor unions; pushed economic production; carried on propaganda work; and, on the county and city level, kept records on every party member showing personal history, movements from one district to another, education, employment, punishments, and awards. The primary party unit, or cell, of the Communist party was the organization found in factory, shop, collective farm, army company, school, or government office.

Party membership first reached a million in 1929 and passed two million four years later. The purges of the thirties pared down the membership drastically, but the leaders always denied any interest in mere numbers. They urged subordinates to bring in only the best people, those with leadership potential in science, industry, the military, agriculture, and the arts, and they bid particularly for the young. Two-thirds of the party membership after the war were less than thirty-five years of age, and nearly a fifth were under twenty-five. The predominance of young people in the party membership was in part a result of the purges that fell most heavily upon old Communists and in part a reflection of the fact that Russia's population was youthful.

Communists occupied all important national and republican posts as well as sensitive spots in industry. The party or party-dominated organizations such as trade unions and cooperatives nominated candidates, only one for each office. There was never any opposition. Nearly 97 percent of the eligible voters went to the polls in the federal elections of 1937, and over 98 percent of them voted for the party candidates. The percentages were typical of Soviet elections. During the Stalin era women were visible in the Supreme Soviet and in several government positions including education, health, and diplomacy. Women, however, did not hold serious leadership positions in the Stalin era.

On the morrow of the November Revolution, the Bolsheviks organized the League of Communist Youth, the Komsomol, which exemplary young men and women from fourteen to twenty-three years of age might join. The aim was to enlist the nation's youth in support of the goals of the new society, to have the members report counterrevolutionary sympathies in the school or even in the home, help others their own age to understand the principles of socialism, and set before all an example of Communist discipline and youthful enthusiasm for the new society. They were very active and extremely effective in helping put over the collectivization of agriculture, the industrialization program of the First Five-Year Plan, the drive to stamp out illiteracy, and the crusade against religion. On the lower Amur River they build an industrial city, Komsomolsk, whose population rose rapidly to seventy thousand in 1939. Many joined the Young Pioneers, a similar organization for youths aged ten to sixteen. Children eight years of age joined the Little Octobrists. No other youth organization might exist. Progression from one age group to another leading to eventual membership in the parent organization, the Communist party, was normal.

The nation's leaders carefully scrutinized Communist party membership for loyalty, devotion, and personal conduct. Those who did not pass the test disappeared from the rolls and might suffer retirement from office, exile, imprisonment, or execution. The purge, usually of a mild and often bloodless sort, came to be the accepted way by which the party skimmed off the dross that floated to the top of its membership. The bloody purge—the "Great Purge"—came to be associated with the name of Stalin.

Late in 1934 Stalin's henchman and friend Sergei Kirov, party secretary in Leningrad after Zinoviev's disgrace, was assassinated under mysterious circumstances. Evidence supports the theory that Stalin himself ordered the assassination to remove a potential opponent; then he struck a pose of insane and hysterical resentment, lashing out to right and left, claiming that the deed was the work of a conspiracy led by Zinoviev and financed by foreign capitalists. The police shot a hundred former tsarist officials who were nowhere near the scene and could not possibly have been party to the plot.

Through a succession of carefully staged trials during the next four years top party leaders of both left and right who had opposed Stalin at one time or another paraded to the witness stand to confess plotting treason, assassination, sabotage, and conspiring with Poles, Germans, Japanese, and Trotsky to overthrow the regime. A grim nationwide search directed by Yezhov, the new head of the secret police, swept up hundreds of thousands of suspects in every walk of life—officials, army officers, industrial and labor leaders, teachers, artists, and ordinary citizens. The opportunity to hurl charges or whisper suspicions allowed many to settle personal grievances, and Stalin later admitted that many of the victims were innocent. Bukharin, Zinoviev, Kamenev, Rykov, Yagoda, and many "Old Bolsheviks" who had joined the party long before the revolution were executed. Tomsky cheated the executioners by committing suicide. Over three-fourths of the Central Committee of the Communist party were killed or imprisoned. Marshal Tukhachevsky and six other top-ranking army leaders received the death penalty for allegedly betraying military secrets to Germany and conspiring to restore capitalism, charges that were manifestly absurd. Officers of all ranks throughout the army suffered dismissal or worse. The purge destroyed many senior diplomats.

Stalin finally called a halt to the bloody business, but not before he had "purged the purgers." Yezhov himself was liquidated and replaced by Lavrenty Beria. The "Great Purge," or Yezhovshchina, sent thousands before firing squads and put untold numbers in labor camps or in exile in Siberian wastelands. Only in the Gorbachev period of the late 1980s was more statistical information published on the extent of the purges. The public was appalled at the scope of the repression.

By the time the Eighteenth Party Congress met in March 1939, the purge had subsided but not totally ended. The intellectuals in the Communist party, among

Joseph Stalin

them Lenin's followers who had opposed Stalin's "socialism in one country," had disappeared from the ranks. What remained was not the Communist party as Russia had known it but Stalin's party. Every citizen learned the bitter lesson that Stalin was the state and that to question his leadership or policies would be to invite the charge of treason. Still, the unjustified arrests and killings continued into 1940 and 1941. Even during World War II, many Soviet citizens suffered at the hands of their government.

The Stalin Cult

One consequence of the purges that dot the Stalin era was the elimination of party workers of middle age or beyond who had grown up with the revolutionary movement. Stalin surrounded himself with men of different temperament and background from those who had gathered around Lenin. The new toadies for the most part were party hacks rather than intellectuals, of whom Stalin, hardly an intellectual himself, was always suspicious. They had risen in the ranks because of their devotion to Stalin and their effectiveness in party work. Members of the Politburo ceased to be Stalin's partners and became simply his henchmen. Thus he compensated for a deep sense of inferiority that grew in the years when Lenin and Trotsky received the plaudits of the party faithful. The rank and file consisted of young men who knew nothing of the comparative freedom in the party that Lenin had allowed.

Many knew little of the Stalin-Trotsky contest, for the rewriting of the history books had deleted every mention of Trotsky's name. These young men could not remember when Stalin was not the ruler in the Russian land. They had learned, as all Russia had learned, that the party secretary would brook not the slightest opposition. Their generation had drunk in a constant stream of propaganda, through all the media of modern mass communication, which taught them that Stalin was all knowing and all wise, that his judgment was infallible, and that when things went wrong it was not his fault but that of the "wreckers, spies, and saboteurs" sent into the country by hostile capitalist governments. The press constantly attributed to him wisdom and genius in everything—from history, politics, government, military strategy, and economics to science, art, music, and literary criticism. Stalin dictated his own biography, which reeked with fulsome praise of his every thought and deed. He edited the *History of the Communist Party of the Soviet Union*, which attributed to him all the good that had come to Russia. Glowing tributes to him cluttered every public speech. Pictures of Stalin, sometimes along with those of Marx and Lenin, but most often alone, adorned public buildings; statues of him appeared in town squares. Cities all over the USSR bore his name—Stalingrad, Stalinabad, Stalinsk, Stalinir, Stalinogorsk, Stalino—as did streets, mountains, canals, collective farms, constitutions, and even automobiles.

The Rule of Terror

In 1922, Lenin abolished the Cheka, created to fight sabotage and counterrevolution, and reassigned its personnel and functions to a new agency, the State Political Administration or GPU, a branch of the Commissariat for Internal Affairs. Its job was to suppress counterrevolution, prevent espionage, and police the frontier. It had unlimited power to search dwellings and arrest suspects but was supposed to bring charges quickly or dismiss its prisoners. With the birth of the USSR in 1922 the GPU became the OGPU with jurisdiction over the entire Soviet Union.

Through its early years the OGPU concentrated its attention on former tsarist officials, merchants, the clergy, and members of non-Bolshevik political parties.

With the appearance of the Trotskyite opposition in the mid-twenties, the OGPU extended its activities over a wider range. Now it interested itself in subversion and heresy within the Communist party, watched foreign diplomats whom Trotsky's followers might contact, carried on espionage abroad and especially among émigré settlements, kept army personnel under surveillance, and guarded against sabotage in industry and transportation. Its prisoners when convicted went to concentration camps run by the OGPU With the adoption of the First Five-Year Plan the political police took on the task of rounding up kulaks and small businessmen who previously had escaped persecution. It also arrested non-Communist intellectuals suspected of opposing the socialization program. Between 1928 and 1933 many engineers and factory managers went to jail for failure to meet production goals, and perhaps a million kulak families and middle peasants who resisted collectivization were rounded up. Many were shot but the vast majority ended up in OGPU labor camps in northern Russia and Siberia to work in the forests and mines or on roads and public works. At the same time all criminals whose sentences exceeded three years, regardless of the crime they had committed, went to the forced-labor camps operated by the OGPU

In 1934 the OGPU became the Narodnyi Komissariat Vnutrennikh Del, the People's Commissariat of Internal Affairs (NKVD), under Genrikh Yagoda. Now it encompassed not only the political police but the regular police, fire departments, border guards, traffic officers, prison officials, and its own military force of infantry, cavalry, and tanks. The NKVD, on its own authority, could sentence prisoners to administrative exile or imprisonment for no more than five years, but it had to turn over to the regular courts all accused persons who, if found guilty, could receive a sentence of more than five years. The prisons released thousands taken during the First Five-Year Plan, and there seemed some likelihood that the power of the police system would decline.

All restraints fell away, however, after the assassination of Kirov in 1934. The NKVD arrested literally millions of suspects during the next four years. No one was safe from the knock on the door at night, the days of endless questioning, the threats to family and friends, the brutality of prison life, the deportation to Siberia. In a succession of public trials important officials of the Communist party confessed guilt to fantastic charges of treason and sabotage, but Khrushchev admitted in 1956 that the trials were staged, that the accused suffered cruel tortures, and that the confessions that shocked the world were made to obtain relief from further torture. Thousands without trial went before firing squads at Stalin's order. With the arrest of the NKVD head, Yagoda, and the appointment in 1936 of Nicholas Yezhov, the fury reached its height. Long after every possible threat to Stalin, the seizures and sentences continued.

The leaders eventually realized that the continuation of the purge was depriving industry, the army, government, and the party of scarce talent and leadership. The terror now turned against those who were making a career of it, and overzealous party workers and members of the NKVD were arrested and packed off by thousands to the labor camps to the cheers of those whom they had put their earlier. Stalin now donned the mask of savior of the people from mass terror and publicly condemned those who "suffer from a lack of concern for people" or who showed a "heartless attitude toward people." The purge subsided, but the fear it engendered never disappeared.

Even Lenin believed that terror was necessary to maintain the Communist revolution and promote its goals. He had no qualms about using force and publicly defended its utility. Like the period of the French Revolution when Robespierre and the Committee of Public Safety unleashed the "Reign of Terror" against the French population to preserve autocratic power, the Soviet regime never trusted its citizens to support it willingly. Explicit threats of the use of force against its adversaries or even those attempting to remain neutral set the tone of the new Communist era and created a society largely motivated and controlled by compulsion and inner fear.

Social and Cultural Trends

Rapid industrialization was accompanied by strains and stresses that older societies long since had conquered or with which they at least learned to cope; Russia's leaders still had to wrestle with not only economic, political, and technological problems but with social and cultural problems as well. Establishing a planned society enormously complicated their task. The persistence with which they explored new techniques to deal with such problems, however, often put to shame those who in relatively free societies muddled along in search of local solutions to local problems, all the while resenting the prod of a central government whose responsibility it was to consider the interests of the entire nation. The social problems that arose out of migration from region to region and from rural to urban areas, from industrial relocation, from rapidly growing industrial metropolitan centers, and a host of similar developments, complicated the task of those who had to chart the nation's course from year to year and from plan to plan. Had the planners been able to face their task without having constantly to prepare for problems beyond the Soviet frontier, their assignment would have been much simpler. Unfortunately for them, their paranoia in the period absorbed attention, energies, and scarce resources which might have been used more effectively and productively. The problems were largely of their own making, based on their hostility toward established capitalist systems and also their suspicion of the League of Nations of which the Soviet Union was not yet a member.

Because no aspect of Soviet life went unplanned and uncontrolled, the nation's cultural trends were only rarely the product of spontaneity among its citizens. Such trends were the fruit of a deliberate effort to mold artistic and philosophical endeavors to serve the needs of society, as the state planners decided those needs and plotted their fulfillment.

An atmosphere of intellectual freedom briefly existed during the later Lenin years and the initial Stalin period, as is reflected in the creative work in the Soviet theater and Soviet film industry. Sergei Eisenstein's genius as a director can be seen in his ground-breaking films, *Battleship Potemkin* and *Ten Days that Shook the World (October)*, through the use of skillful editing and the technique known as montage. Yet even his work fulfilled the government's objective to present the revolutionary events since 1900 in a positive Bolshevik light.

The formation of Prolekult (Proletarian Cultural and Educational Organization) after the Bolshevik seizure of victory provided the framework for the new Communist ideology to be spread across the nation. Gradually the heavy hand of the state over culture showed leading writers that their newfound literary freedom would not continue undisturbed. The poet Sergei Yesenin, suffering mental problems, committed suicide in 1925. Vladimir Mayakovsky, one of the most noted supporters of the new Bolshevik dream, eventually realized the realities of his support for a system of control. Writing that he had "stepped on the throat of his own song," he committed suicide in April 1930. Maxim Gorky, an associate of Lenin and an advocate of the repressed and unfortunate in society, supported the Bolshevik cause until the mid-1930s. His death in 1936 raised the possibility of homicide by poison at the hands of Stalin's supporters. The actor-director Vsevolod Meyerhold, put in charge of all theaters in the Soviet Union in the 1920s, disappeared in the thirties after publicly criticizing the Communist system for destroying art and culture. It later became known he died in a Soviet prison camp in the early 1940s.

The trend toward state and party control over the cultural realm gradually grew throughout the later 1920s, and by the early thirties the new system had been strengthened to oversee the creative efforts. RAPP, the Russian Association of Proletarian Writers created in 1928, was merged with the new Union of Soviet Writers formed in 1932. The new obligatory body, to which authors had to belong in order to publish, set forth the theory of "socialist realism" which required its members to reflect approximate reality but in a revolutionary and ideological context deemed satisfactory by the authorities. Writers had to produce works glorifying the five-year plans and other Communist projects or policies, and Stalin noted that "writers are to be engineers of human minds."

Some writers, artists, musicians and others emigrated to the West in order to continue their work in a freer atmosphere. A few, like Yesenin and Mayakovsky, took their own lives. Others, like film maker Eisenstein, followed the party line. In literature, the most successful figure who kept within the bounds of "socialist realism" and yet wrote several important works is Mikhail Sholokhov (1905–1984). His trilogy set in the Don River region earned him many national prizes (the Stalin prize in 1941, and the Order of Lenin three times) and the Nobel Prize for Literature late in his career. Yet overall, the cultural scene of the Stalin period in retrospect generally lacks an inspired and creative spirit. The repressive hand of party and state fell especially hard on many talented persons.

The Soviet Union took a general census in 1926 and another in 1939. The population in 1926 was 147,000,000, nearly 40 percent above the total in 1897—the year of the last imperial census—in a territory shrunken by loss of border areas after the revolution. By 1939 the same territory held over 170,000,000. The steady rise of urban and the decline of rural elements in the population distinguished the years since the inauguration of the First Five-Year Plan. One the eve of World War I about 15 percent of all Russians lived in cities. The percentage had grown to 18 by 1926, and to about 33 in 1939. More than any other great power, the USSR was a nation of youth. The Civil War, the famines, and the collectivization of agriculture took heavier toll among the old than among young people. By 1939 nearly two-thirds of the population were under thirty years of age, and nearly half of these were under twenty.

The 1918 constitution of the RSFSR pronounced "the equality of all citizens, irrespective of race or nationality," and the 1936 constitution repeated the promise. By 1939 the government had taken significant strides to educate the minorities in their own languages and dialects. Linguistic experts from Moscow developed written alphabets for forty nationalities who had known only a spoken language before the revolution. All this glossed over the fact that the Soviet government was deliberately pursuing a policy of Russification all over the USSR.

The minority group that suffered most during the Stalin years was the Ukrainian. This group had never been recognized by tsars or Communists as a separate nationality having its own language. Ukrainian nationalists during the Civil War had leaned heavily on foreign aid and direction, although most of the peasants had withheld their support from Bolsheviks, upper-class Ukrainian nationalist leaders, and foreigners with equal impartiality, and had joined the anarchist Makhno or some bandit or guerrilla leader. The Bolsheviks finally conquered the Ukraine in 1920, at a bloody cost.

During the NEP period, the Ukraine enjoyed relative quiet. Lenin permitted the Communist party of the Ukraine an identity of its own, even though it contained a number of non-Marxists and even Ukrainian nationalists, in the hope of pacifying the region and promoting national and party unity. The Ukrainian Communists invited the return of nationalist exiles, and vigorously pushed the use of the Ukrainian language, which until the nineteenth century was little more than a dialect.

Stalin deliberately incited resentment when in 1926 he removed the head of the Ukrainian Communist party and replaced him with Lazar Kaganovich, a non-Ukrainian, militant atheist and energetic Communist leader dedicated to carrying out Stalin's will. The entire countryside suffered persecution in the collectivization drive of the First Five-Year Plan. The Ukrainians defied and resisted collectivization far more stubbornly than did other Russians, and Stalin ordered Kaganovich and the GPU to harry them relentlessly into submission. He later admitted that the First Five-Year Plan had led to virtual war in the Ukraine. When drought combined with precipitate collectivization to produce a famine, Stalin refused to admit that the famine existed and withheld grain shipments into the area. This brought the forced starvation of a million Ukrainians, a planned atrocity that Stalin conceived as a way of disciplining the Ukrainian people. The purges of the thirties struck with particular ferocity at the Ukrainians. In 1938, Stalin appointed Khrushchev to complete the vicious persecution, and, after a period of continued repression, the new party leader in the Ukraine brought the bloody business to an end. Little wonder that hundreds of thousands of Ukrainians in the Red Army surrendered almost without a fight to the Germans in 1941. Villagers scattered flowers at the feet of the invaders and welcomed them as deliverers from Stalin's tyranny. German atrocities and German ruthlessness— nearly half of the forced laborers whom Hitler drafted for work in German factories were Ukrainians—quickly turned the people against their deliverers, although to the end of the occupation several bands of Ukrainians spent more time fighting Russians than they did fighting Germans. Despite Kaganovich's Jewish heritage, he sought to further weaken this religious group that had long been the target of the tsarist system and doomed to live in the so-called Jewish Pale. The pre-Communist history of Russia reveals excessive hostility to the Jewish population in the Ukraine and in Poland. Pogroms (the term for anti-Jewish riots) erupted periodically against this religious and social group. The pogroms at Kishinev and nearby areas in the Ukraine in 1903 are especially noteworthy for their ferocity against persons and property. The writer Maxim Gorky wrote a short story, *The Race Riot*, vividly describing these riots which often had the tacit support of the authorities.

Leon Trotsky, whose real name was Lev Bronstein, was of Ukrainian Jewish origins. Anti-semitism was one factor directing him toward radicalism against the regime. The Bolsheviks, while appearing to champion the rights of minorities including Jews, in fact sought to weaken the vitality and unity of this religious movement and targeted them for continued harassment during the Stalin years. Such ugly bigotry could be found toward other religious minorities, but the record of anti-semitism in the Ukraine was particularly severe. To compound the evil, the ravages of World War II and Nazi persecution of Jews in the Holocaust intensified the tragedy for Jews everywhere, but especially in the Soviet Union.

There had been only a small number of Jews in Russia before Catherine II, when the partitions of Poland brought most of the Polish Jews into the empire. At the time of the revolution, there were over five million Jews in Russia, although half of them went to Poland and the Baltic states as the borderlands became independent. Some of them, Mensheviks and others, fought with the Bolsheviks during the Civil War, for the possibility that the Whites would restore the old regime threatened them with a return to the savage persecution of tsarist times. Several leading Bolsheviks were Jews—Sverdlov, Radek, Zinoviev, Kamenev, and Trotsky—although the number was nowhere near as large as anti-Semitic opponents of the regime insisted.

Stalin referred to Jews as "little, physically unfit, cowardly, over-clever, excessively intellectual, selfish, and money-grubbing." His struggle with Trotsky surely deepened his resentment of Jews, particularly because most of them in the Communist party supported Trotsky, but it certainly did not create it. He detested Zionism, which he regarded as theocratic and pernicious, although many Russian anti-Semites in the nineteenth century had supported it.

Jews were to be found in cities all over Russia, as well as in the Pale in White Russia and the Ukraine where the tsars had concentrated them. At Kalinin's urging, Stalin in 1934 carved out an area larger than Palestine along the Manchurian border in Siberia, and made it the Jewish Autonomous Republic with Birobidzhan as its capital. Stalin naïvely expected it to become a homeland for Jews from all over the world. As a homeland even for Russian Jews it proved a miserable failure. No more than fifty thousand settled there, not to take up farming or build cities, but to work in the mines or to guard the frontier from the Japanese across the Amur river.

The Jews suffered disproportionately during the purges of the thirties, when a fifth of them were arrested and a fifth of the arrested ones were killed. After Stalin and Hitler divided Poland in 1939, the Jewish population of the USSR may have numbered five million. Fewer than half survived the war. Hitler killed over two million; another half million died in battle or of starvation behind either German or Russian lines.

International Tension

Until the rise of Hitler, Russian's problem of avoiding war was scarcely a problem at all. No nation in Europe wanted war, even though all were anti-Bolshevik. Many Europeans applauded the appearance of Hitler, hoping that he might undertake to eradicate bolshevism where they were unwilling to do so themselves.

Years before his coming to power Hitler published his program for a renascent Germany. *Mein Kampf* predicted that bolshevism was about to collapse. Germany, said Hitler, must take for itself the grain of the Ukraine, the oil of the Caucasus, the minerals or the Urals, and the timber resources of Siberia. That these were something more than wild dreams Russian diplomats learned in 1933 at the London Economic Conference soon after Hitler became chancellor. A Nazi delegate asked Westerners for a free hand for Germany in the Ukraine in exchange for the colonies it had lost in 1919.

In 1936 the Anti-Comintern Pact united Germany and Japan against the Third International. A year later Italy joined the other two in the Berlin-Rome-Tokyo Axis directed against the nation that provided a home for the Comintern and promoted the spread of communism.

The Kremlin's policy of seeking normal and friendly relations with all nations met with growing success after the emergence of Hitler and Japan's mounting pressure on China. In November 1933, the United States recognized the Soviet Union, the last major nation to do so. The move grew out of American business pressure for improved trade relations and more especially out of Washington's increasing concern over the Japanese threat in the Pacific. Six months later, the Soviet government received recognition from Czechoslovakia, Romania, and Bulgaria. Great Britain had restored diplomatic relations with Moscow, although there was little friendship lost between the two nations.

Ominous events in Germany threatened to undercut the tenuous equilibrium of European peace by the early and mid-1930s. The world depression weakened democratic systems everywhere and led to the collapse of the democratic Weimar Republic in Germany. Hitler came to power in 1933 and began his consolidation of power domestically and the build-up of German armed forces. France grew increasingly fearful of a revival of German militarism. Franco-Russian discussions in 1934 anticipated Russia's entry into the League of Nations to restore the league's falling influence after the withdrawal of Japan and Germany, sought a mutual-defense pact, and worked for cooperation between Russia and France's allies in Eastern Europe. In September 1934, Russia became a member of the league with a permanent seat on its council. France's efforts to secure Soviet support for guaranteed boundaries in Central and Eastern Europe, equivalent to the 1922 Locarno agreement confirming the border between Germany and its western neighbors, failed largely due to German and Polish opposition. In 1935, France and Russia agreed to stand together if either came under attack by another European power, obviously Germany. Immediately, Czechoslovakia and the USSR signed a similar agreement that Russia would come to the defense of the Czechs, but only if France had moved first to fulfill its mutual defense obligation to the Czech republic. Moscow's defensive alliance with France and Czechoslovakia would mean nothing, however, unless either Poland or Romania should consent to the passage of Russian troops through their territories, and neither country would agree to do this. French influence, strong as it always was in Warsaw, was not necessary to make Poles forget that it was the defeat of Russia, and not of Germany, that would bring them the richest territorial gain. Similarly, Romania might hope to profit from a Russian, but hardly from a German, defeat.

The Seventh Congress of the Comintern met in Moscow in 1935. Obviously on orders from the Kremlin, the congress voted to halt Communist revolutionary agitation against bourgeois governments and to support a "popular front" of liberal parties in every country against the mounting tide of fascism. Communists must join with socialists, laborites, democrats, liberals, or any others willing to combat fascist aggression. Although Communist support was embarrassing and even irritating to some political parties, Communist activity in popularizing the Soviet Union won Russia many friends in democratic countries.

The cynical Stalin never put much faith in the popular front, but felt that it could be of use in bargaining with Hitler. From the moment of Hitler's rise to power, Stalin preferred to believe that the Nazi leader was not serious in his fulminations against bolshevism and indeed that, when the time came to make a choice, Germany would be a more reliable ally than Britain or France. However, Stalin never fully trusted any man or any nation and could never be quite certain that his confidence in an alliance with Hitler would prove justified. Consequently, from 1933 to the moment of the German invasion of Russia in 1941, he played one potential ally against another in a desperate search for the security of his own regime.

From 1933 to 1945, Russia's management of foreign affairs was complicated by having to watch two fronts, one in Europe, the other in East Asia. The sale of its interest in the Chinese Eastern Railway in 1935 was the product of its concern to avoid involvement with Japan at a time when Hitler's ambition in the West was becoming increasingly evident. Russian statesmen hoped, however, that China might contest Japanese aggression and prevent it from moving against Russia. Their promotion of Chinese resistance had to recognize that after 1927 there were two Chinas, the Kuomintang and the Communists. When the two Chinas agreed to shelve their differences in the face of the common enemy, Russia fed military supplies into China, helping Chiang Kai-shek to some extent but contributing more to the Communists. In 1937 Moscow concluded a nonagression pact with the Nationalist government and stepped up the flow of equipment and military advisers to Chiang. Nine months earlier Japan had joined Germany in the Anti-Comintern Pact. Now Tokyo could argue that in pressing its campaign on the mainland it was fighting the battle of civilization against communism, for Chiang had come to terms with Moscow. Japanese generals tested Soviet military strength in several frontier battles along the Siberian-Manchurian border but were severely mauled by Russian armor; Japan agreed to a truce in 1939 that lasted for six years.

The Collapse of Collective Security

From the moment of Russia's entry into the League of Nations in 1934, Litvinov, foreign commissar since 1930, pleaded with the members to stand together in respect for world order, arguing tirelessly that "peace is indivisible," that a breach of the peace anywhere was a threat to the security of all nations. When Mussolini invaded Ethiopia the league condemned this rape of one member by another, but did nothing more.

In 1936 General Francisco Franco led a fascist military clique in a revolt against the legitimate government of Spain, a member of the league. Franco had no hope of success without foreign backing, but that was soon forthcoming as Germany and Italy sent guns, tanks, and troops to support Franco. Moscow sent planes, guns, food, and perhaps two thousand military technicians and advisers to back the Spanish government, but all in too modest a volume to influence the outcome of the civil war. Great Britain and the United States refused to intervene, and Russia sent so little help as to anger the Spanish Communists. Franco, with German and Italian sponsorship, won a decisive victory for fascism by 1939.

The vicious purges that went on in Russia while the Spanish civil war was in progress did nothing to improve Moscow's relations with the democracies. Although some Westerners had dealt gently with post-revolutionary Russia, the rigged trials and the mass persecutions now made cooperation with the brutal dictator in the Kremlin too distasteful to contemplate. Furthermore, the purge of the Red Army, with its liquidation of thousands of officers, seemed undeniably to have destroyed Russia's military effectiveness and so ended any value it may have had as an ally.

Hitler's absorption of Austria in March 1938 excited little concern in the West, but his move against Czechoslovakia, by all counts a peace-loving and democratic state, threatened to precipitate war. Czechoslovakia submitted to pressure from Great Britain and France to leave its destiny in their hands. Neither Czechs nor Russians were invited to the conference at Munich in September 1938. The British Chamberlain, the French Daladier, Hitler, and Mussolini concluded an agreement requiring that Czechoslovakia must surrender to Germany the Sudetenland, a border region that included the Little Maginot line, the loss of which made impossible the defense of what was left of Czechoslovakia.

Stalin knew that many conservative Britons and French longed to see Hitler turn east against the Soviet Union. When London and Paris gave in so obligingly to the neutralization of Czechoslovakia, Russia read the evidence to mean that the Western powers deliberately were seeking to usher Hitler into Eastern Europe, but Russia made it clear that two could play the game. If it could not find security against Hitler, Russia would find it with him. Stalin had felt confident all along of his ability to reach an understanding with Hitler. He had always been suspicious of Britain and France. Nevertheless, he let his diplomats play out the game to the end with the Western powers.

In March 1939, Hitler called in the president of Czechoslovakia and gave him one hour to sign over the rest of his country to Germany. Litvinov proposed a meeting to consider future action, but the British prime minister answered that the proposal was "premature." Next, Hitler insisted that Lithuania give him Memel, its only seaport. To refuse would have been disastrous, and another thousand square miles came under the Nazi flag. Mussolini joined in the territorial grab by taking Albania. Then it was Hitler's move again, and he declared that the city of Danzig, created by the League of Nations as an independent port city despite its former German status, must return to Germany.

Litvinov in April 1939, proposed to Britain and France an alliance to defend any country threatened by the fascist powers. Moscow insisted that the three powers must guarantee against fascist aggression all the states bordering on Russia's western frontier. Paris seemed interested in Litvinov's proposal but London obviously was not.

In May 1939, Litvinov, who symbolized Russia's hope to win Western confidence and cooperation, was dismissed as commissar for foreign affairs. He was succeeded by Stalin's close friend Viacheslav Molotov—"the best filing clerk in Petrograd," Lenin had once called him—who would hold the office for most of the next seventeen years. Litvinov's withdrawal from the Foreign Office signaled a shift in Soviet foreign policy. The Germans thought Molotov's appointment might indicate a withdrawal from the anti-Nazi stand the Russians had taken since Hitler's rise to power and a willingness to accept an offer of security from any nation that was ready to make it. The German analysis proved to be correct.

The obliteration of Czechoslovakia woke Britain to the need for positive action if Hitler's "artichoke policy" of devouring the small countries one by one were to be halted. However, the British prime minister, bitterly anti-Russian, held back from taking the one step—military alliance with the Soviet Union—that could stop the Nazis. Instead he guaranteed, piecemeal, the countries that might next appeal to Hitler's appetite. The British government guaranteed Poland from aggression when Warsaw rejected Hitler's insistence that he must have Danzig and the Polish Corridor. A few days later Greece and Romania received similar guarantees from both Britain and France. Chamberlain was overly sensitive to the reluctance of the border states to cooperate with Russia—Estonia and Latvia insisted they were in no danger and needed no assistance from the USSR; Romania refused to join a pact aimed against Germany; and Poland would have none of any defense arrangement that included Russia fearing the probable introduction of Soviet military forces on Polish territory—and did not press them for an alliance. Litvinov had sent an assistant to visit Turkey, Romania, Bulgaria, and Poland to plead for collective security but the conversations were disappointing.

Meanwhile, the British cabinet subjected correspondence between London and Moscow, regarding Russian proposals for an alliance, to irritating delays. Finally, Chamberlain gave in to parliamentary pressure that he stop stalling and enter into direct conversations with the Russians. Instead of going himself, as he had done on several occasions to meet Hitler, he sent a subordinate official in the Foreign Office, William Strang, but perhaps it was already too late. Two weeks before Strang left London, Molotov told the Supreme Soviet that there was no intention of breaking off trade relations with the fascist powers. The French cabinet interpreted this warning to mean that prospects for a triple alliance with Russia had died. That London had waited too long seemed apparent when Estonia and Latvia signed nonaggression pacts with Germany, thus forestalling any great-power attempt to bring the Baltic countries into a mutual security system.

Strang's talks with French and Russian officials in Moscow began in June and dragged on for weeks. The Kremlin proposed a three-power assistance agreement and also a guarantee of the Baltic states, Poland, Romania, and Turkey, from aggression either direct or indirect, but the British balked at guaranteeing the small powers against such aggression without their consent, which had already been denied.

The danger mounted through July that the Kremlin would lose all patience with Western procrastination and begin political as well as trade talks with Germany. Stalin suspected that London was trying to work out an agreement with Berlin. The common knowledge that a German mission was in England seeking a loan of a billion pounds sterling did nothing to allay Russian suspicions. Two days after learning of the German request for a British loan, Moscow announced the reopening of trade talks with Germany. The Kremlin had considered such a move for weeks, but took no step until the German arrival in London seemed to suggest the reason behind the delays in the talks in Moscow.

The announcement of the Nazi-Soviet trade talks stirred the Western delegates but slightly. They agreed to include the Baltic states in any guarantee against aggression but haggled over the definition of "indirect aggression." The three powers agreed to begin military staff talks aimed at pinning down the measures to be taken in the event of a threat to the guaranteed states. Stalin chose to assume that Britain and France in the end would reject any proposal. The British delegation had little authority to commit its government, and the talks were frequently interrupted by the need to refer to London for instructions. Poland and the Baltic states refused any guarantee and would not consent to the movement of Russian troops across their territories. The talks were dragging along when on August 23, 1939, Nazi Germany and Soviet Russia signed a ten-year nonaggression pact. A few hours earlier the British ambassador in Berlin, Sir Neville Henderson, told Hitler that if anyone had to sign an agreement with the Soviet Union he preferred that Germany rather than Great Britain do it. He soon got his wish.

Strange Alliance

Stalin addressed the Eighteenth Congress of the Communist Party in the spring of 1939 in the usual harsh terms about fascist aggression. However, the speech was more shrill in the derision it heaped upon Great Britain and France for their spinelessness. Soviet foreign policy, he pronounced, gave first place to "peace and the strengthening of business relations with all countries," a scarcely veiled appeal for cooperation with Germany. While the congress was in session, Hitler erased Czechoslovakia from the map and there was no more than formal protest from the Western powers. In April 1939, the Soviet ambassador in Berlin hinted that there was no reason why Russia and Germany should not live together peaceably. Later Hitler denounced the Munich accord and the Polish-German nonaggression pact and, for the first time in his career, spared bolshevism the "buckets of filth" he usually heaped on it. The German press began to show moderation toward Russia.

Through May and June there were talks looking toward an improvement in Soviet-Nazi trade relations; by early July there were hints that the attempt to do so might be fruitful. The Nazis had to hurry to establish bonds with Russia because the Nazi plan to attack Poland in August was already well under way.

As the fruitless talks with the Western powers dragged on Molotov informed Berlin that he was ready to discuss the differences between Russia and Germany. In August, Ribbentrop, the German foreign minister, asked to come to Moscow to arrange an agreement involving the whole area from the Black Sea to the Baltic. At that moment Voroshilov was trying vainly to get the Western military staffs to guarantee transit for Russian troops across Polish territory and to consent to the occupation of the Baltic ports to deter German aggression against Russia. The Westerners could promise nothing. Poland balked at the suggestion, as did the Baltic states, and without such consent from such minor powers, Russia's military cooperation with the others became impossible.

Whether he came to terms with the West or with Hitler, Stalin had everything to gain. If Britain and France had been willing to force Poland and the Baltic states to permit Russian armies inside their borders, Russia's neighbors would have come under Moscow rule. The establishment of mutually agreeable accords with Germany could gain economic and territorial strength for Russia. Stalin was gambling dangerously that Germany would honor the agreements, but within a year, he had erased the Baltic states and absorbed eastern Poland.

On August 19, representatives of the two dictatorships signed a trade agreement providing for a seven-year German credit to Russia of 200,000,000 marks in exchange for Germany's right to purchase raw materials from Russia to the value of 180,000,000 marks. Germany wanted oil, grain, cotton, flax, rubber, and various ores; Russia was to receive machine tools and military equipment. The Kremlin announced that Ribbentrop would fly to Moscow.

Ribbentrop landed in Moscow on August 23, 1939, and concluded with Russia a ten-year nonaggression treaty. The two powers agreed to avoid any aggressive act against each other and each promised to remain neutral if the other became involved in war with a third power. In a secret protocol attached to the nonaggression pact the signatories agreed on a line separating their spheres of influence in Eastern Europe. In the event of its political collapse, Poland would be divided along the Narev, Vistula, and San rivers, thus giving Russia nearly two-thirds of Poland and bringing it into the eastern suburbs of Warsaw. Russia received a free hand in Estonia, Latvia, and Finland. Germany declared itself uninterested in Bessarabia. This arrangement, which left Lithuania in the German sphere, was later altered to give Lithuania to Russia and move the Russo-German border in Poland back to the old Curzon Line.

German and Russian leaders were confident that the nonaggression pact ended any likelihood that Great Britain and France would defend Poland. However, the inevitability of World War II dated far back before August 1939. That Great Britain and France now should undertake the strategically impossible and militarily foolhardy burden of rescuing Poland without Russia's help when they had refused to succor Czechoslovakia with Soviet assistance never ceased to puzzle Moscow and Berlin. Conservative circles in both Western countries preferred to stand heroically, however futilely, against the Nazi tyranny without the Russian alliance rather than with it.

Communist parties outside Russia were caught off guard by the Soviet-German accord. For years they had faithfully carried out the Kremlin's order to support any bourgeois governments that would resist fascism. Only yesterday they had insisted that Poland must not go the way of Czechoslovakia. The contest of the thirties was one which lined up the "peace-loving democracies," which by Communist definition included the Soviet Union, against the anti-Comintern dictators. To make themselves completely ridiculous by veering round to opposing the war against Germany took a full week. On the very day that German troops crossed the Polish border the French Communists resolved that the "peace-loving democracies" must support the Poles. The painful reappraisal finally was worked out and the lackeys followed Moscow in condemning the Western powers for carrying on an "imperialist war." Not until the Nazi invasion of Russia nearly twenty-two months later did Communist parties the world over slip back to their position that the Nazis were aggressors against the "peace-loving democracies."

Within three days of the Nazi attack on Poland it was clear that the Polish nation would go under in weeks. Berlin immediately notified Moscow that, to wipe out Poland's resistance, the Wehrmacht would have to pursue the Polish army into the Russian zone unless the Red Army advanced to the demarcation line agreed upon previously. Moscow moved slowly, preparing a statement for world consumption that would make the Russian advance seem less than barefaced aggression. On September 16, Molotov announced that the Polish government had ceased to exist and that the Soviet government would rescue the defenseless Ukrainians and White Russians and grant them "protection." The Red Army crossed into Poland the next day, and organized resistance came to an end except in Warsaw which held out heroically for ten days. The Russians, not trusting the Germans to return any of the Soviet zone of Poland they might take, rushed through eastern Poland and overshot the demarcation line. The day Warsaw surrendered, Ribbentrop arrived in Moscow to sign the agreement defining the frontier. It moved the boundary a hundred miles east of Warsaw and conformed roughly to the Curzon Line. To compensate for this shift, most of Lithuania was transferred to the Russian sphere.

The zone of influence soon disappeared into the USSR. Local assemblies in eastern Poland, swept together for the purpose, petitioned for admission into the Ukrainian and Belorussian Republics, and the Supreme Soviet generously granted the request. Late in September, representatives from Estonia, Latvia, and Lithuania paraded to Moscow to sign mutual defense pacts allowing Russia to use air and naval bases in the Baltic states and to station troops there. Such hypocrisies fooled no one. In June 1940, when the disintegration of the French Army warned Russia to look to its own defenses, the Red Army occupied the three Baltic republics. In each case, a newly elected "people's government" asked for incorporation into the USSR Soviet troops occupied Lithuania; soon after they moved into northern Bukovina and Bessarabia, whose seizure by Romania during the Civil War the Bolsheviks had never accepted.

At the same time the Baltic states received the invitation to sign mutual-assistance treaties with Russia, Finland rejected a similar offer. The Soviet government then demanded that in exchange for land north of Lake Ladoga, the Finns turn over the Karelian Isthmus and allow Russia to fortify the Finnish islands in the Gulf of Finland which had been Russian bases under the tsars. Helsinki refused, the Red Army crossed the border, and Russian planes bombed the Finnish capital. Within the month, the League of Nations judged the USSR guilty of aggression and expelled it.

The Finnish people rallied to the defense of their government and to the support of Mannerheim, the former tsarist general who led their army. Britain sent planes, guns, and equipment, but in quantities too small to influence the outcome of the battle. Volunteers from the West joined the Finns, but Germany, which had given Russia a free hand in Finland, remained scrupulously neutral. In the Western press, Finland became the symbol of democracy, freedom, civilization, Christianity; Britain and France considered a declaration of war against Russia.

The Finns made a heroic stand and the Russian military leaders grossly underestimated the quality of their enemy and the determination of the Finnish people. Through December 1939 and the following January, the defenders repulsed every attack and took a heavy toll among Russian units sent against them. The Western press derided the vaunted Red Army and even prophesied that the little nation of four million would defeat the Communist colossus. Stalin never forgot the insults, and the memory of them contributed to his suspicion and mistrust of his Western allies throughout the war and postwar period.

Stalin, contemptuous of the Finns, had assumed that they would succumb to diplomatic pressure and had made no serious preparations for a military campaign. There was no formidable attack on the Mannerheim Line and what advances there were, except in the north against Petsamo, were poorly organized and weakly supported. In February 1940, the Soviet command, with orders to press the attack vigorously, went to Semen Timoshenko (whose forces had previously occupied eastern Poland when Germany and the Soviet Union partitioned their Polish victim in 1939, and who later served as the Soviet Union's Commissar of Defense between May 1940 and July 1941). In this Finnish "Winter War" of 1939–1940, heavy artillery fire obliterated the supposedly impregnable Mannerheim Line, and the Red Army, fought every step of the way by the Finns, advanced to Viipuri, the former Viborg. Helsinki had no choice but to accept Moscow's terms.

By the peace settlement concluded in March 1940, Finland turned over to the USSR a speck of land near Petsamo and the Karelian Isthmus including Viipuri, thus moving the Russo-Finnish frontier seventy miles farther away from Leningrad. Helsinki agreed not to admit a third power, obviously Germany, into the Åland Islands. Each signatory swore not to attack the other or to join an alliance against the other. Moscow asked no indemnity. There was nothing beyond the pressure of world opinion to prevent Russia's imposing more severe terms on the Finns.

The Finnish campaign uncovered a number of glaring weaknesses in the Red Army that Defense Commissar Timoshenko set about immediately to remedy: faulty administration, deficiencies in machinery under cold-weather operation, and the training of aviators. The measures taken to correct these problems, coupled with the growth in the number of Russian troops, served to prepare the Kremlin to meet the German challenge that was sure to come.

Uneasy Interlude

In the hope of postponing war until it was better prepared, the USSR scrupulously fulfilled its obligations under the nonaggression pact with Germany, delivering to Berlin the material it had contracted to send, but it is unlikely that Hitler ever changed for a moment in his determination to bring the wealth of the Ukraine and the Urals under German exploitation. Britain evidenced no loss of determination to carry on after the fall of the Netherlands, Denmark, Norway, Belgium, and France. In fact, its new government under Churchill showed far more spirit than before. Hitler decided to seek a quick victory over Russia before

Britain had grown any stronger and while Russia still was relatively unprepared. The purge of the Red Army and the poor showing in the Finnish campaign had made Hitler, like most Western political leaders, contemptuous of Russian strength. By August 1940, Hitler had made up his mind to invade Russia, and his general staff began work immediately on the plans.

Nazi-Soviet relations grew steadily cooler during the autumn of 1940. Berlin complained that the Russians were falling behind in deliveries of goods promised under the nonaggression pact. Moscow objected to the stationing of German troops in Finland. A Nazi force entered Romania and ostentatiously guaranteed its territory against Soviet aggression. Then, to buy the support of other Balkan countries, Hitler forced Romania to turn over Transylvania to Hungary and the Dobrudja to Bulgaria. In September 1940, Germany, Italy, and Japan signed the Tripartite Pact by which the three agreed to support each other if one should be attacked by any power not then involved in the European or the Asiatic war. The provision that the agreement was not aimed at Russia fooled no one.

Molotov went to Berlin in November 1940 to attempt to improve relations with Germany. Hitler volunteered to sponsor Russian admission into the tripartite accord formed two months earlier. He also offered to back a Russian drive into the Middle East toward the Indian Ocean, but Molotov would not be distracted. He asked that Bulgaria be assigned to the Russian sphere of influence. Hitler's revision of the Romanian, Hungarian, and Bulgarian frontiers came into question, and Molotov insisted on Russia's vital interests in the Balkans and in the Straits. He and Ribbentrop found little they could agree upon, and the conference ended in a spirit of only surface friendship.

In the spring of 1941, Hitler settled matters in the Balkans in a way not at all to Moscow's liking. German troops occupied Bulgaria and bound it into the Axis partnership. Yugoslavia fell to the Wehrmacht in two weeks and the Greek army capitulated in April. A month later the Nazis invaded Crete. It was not Britain, as Molotov had been fully aware, that the USSR had to fear at the Straits. With German troops in every Balkan country and in Finland, Hitler had outflanked Russia in the north and south.

Nevertheless, Stalin preferred to believe it possible to avoid war, and spurned warnings from Churchill and Roosevelt that the Nazis were planning to invade Russia. Believing it had no friends it could trust, Russia maneuvered desperately to prevent the unwanted eventuality of war. Expansion of the armed forces continued feverishly, and the correction of the weaknesses revealed during the Finnish War was due for completion by August. The forty-eight-hour week replaced the thirty-hour week for industrial workers. The government curtailed the output of consumers' goods and stepped up production of war matériel. Japan, tied down in China, agreed to a mutual neutrality pact in April.

Russia was not ready for war in June 1941, as the opening German campaigns quickly made apparent, but in the twenty-two months since the signing of the nonaggression treaty with Germany, its position had immeasurably improved. The western boundary had been pushed far back so that an invader would have to fight through a cushion of non-Russian territory before reaching the heart of the country. Absorbing the Baltic states and eastern Poland cost Russia in good will, but Hitler might have used those countries, unfriendly as they were to Moscow, as a springboard of attack. The Red Army was far larger and far stronger in the summer of 1941 than it had been two years earlier. Russian industry now was approaching a wartime footing, but had been far from it in 1939. The Finnish experience had provided many lessons and trained many unit leaders. After nearly two years of war, Britain was now ready to welcome Russia as a partner. International cooperation to beat back aggression was possible in 1941 but impossible in 1939. Even the United States, where neutralist feeling ran high in 1939 and where sympathy for the Finns had been especially strong, was now willing to assist Russia against Hitler. Nazi savagery in occupied Europe made the free world welcome even the Soviet Union as an ally in the struggle for the survival of their own democracies.

Suggested Reading

ADAMS, A., *Stalin and His Times* (New York, 1972).

BELOFF, M., *The Foreign Policy of Soviet Russia, 1929–1941* (New York, 1949).

BRZEZINSKI, Z. K., *The Permanent Purge* (Cambridge, 1956).

COHEN, S. F., *Bukharin and the Bolshevik Revolution: A Political Biography, 1888–1938* (New York, 1974).

CONQUEST, R., *The Great Terror: Stalin's Purges of the Thirties* (New York, 1968).

———, *The Great Terror: A Reassessment* (New York, 1990).

———, *The Harvest of Sorrow: Soviet Collectivization and the Terror-Famine* (New York, 1986).

———, *Stalin and the Kirov Murder* (New York, 1989).

DALLIN, D., and B. NICOLAEVSKY, *Forced Labor in Soviet Russia* (New Haven, 1947).

DEGRAS, J., *Soviet Documents on Foreign Policy*, 3 vols. (London, 1951–1953).

DE JONGE, A., *Stalin and the Shaping of the Soviet Union* (New York, 1986).

DYADKIN, E. G., *Unnatural Deaths in the USSR, 1928–1954* (New Brunswick, NJ, 1983).

EHRLICH, A., *The Soviet Industrialization Debate, 1924–1928* (Cambridge, 1960).

EUDIN, X. J. and R. M. SLUSSER, *Soviet Foreign Policy, 1928–1934: Documents and Materials*, 2 vols. (University Park, PA, 1967).

FAINSOD, M., *How Russia Is Ruled* (Cambridge, 1965).

GETTY, J. A., *Origins of the Great Purges: The Communist Party Reconsidered, 1933–1938* (New York, 1985).

GREY, I., *Stalin, Man of History* (Garden City, NY, 1979).

GROMYKO, A., *Memoirs* (New York, 1990).

HASLAM, J., *Soviet Foreign Policy, 1930–1933: The Impact of the Depression* (New York, 1983).

———, *The Soviet Union and the Struggle for Collective Security in Europe, 1933–1939* (New York, 1984).

HAZARD, J. N., *The Soviet System of Government* (Chicago, 1960).

HILGER, G., and A. G. MEYER, *The Incompatible Allies: A Memoir-History of German-Soviet Relations, 1918-1941* (New York, 1953).

HOCHMAN, J., *The Soviet Union and the Failure of Collective Security, 1934-1938* (Ithaca, NY, 1984).

HYDE, H. M., *Stalin: The History of a Dictator* (New York, 1972).

JASNY, N., *Soviet Industrialization, 1928-1952* (Chicago, 1961).

KAHAN, S., *The Wolf and the Kremlin* (New York, 1987).

KENNAN, G. F., *Russia and the West Under Lenin and Stalin* (Boston, 1961).

_____, *Soviet Foreign Policy, 1917-1941* (New York, 1960).

KHRUSHCHEV, N. K., *Khrushchev Remembers* (Boston, 1970).

KOSTIUK, H., *Stalinist Rule in the Ukraine: A Study of the Decade of Mass Terror, 1929-1939* (Munich, 1961).

KUROMIYA, H., *Stalin's Industrial Revolution: Politics and Workers, 1928-1932* (Cambridge, Eng., 1988).

LAQUER, W., *Stalin: The Glasnost Revelations* (New York, 1990).

LEVYTZKY, B., *The Stalinist Terror in the Thirties: Documentation from the Soviet Press* (Stanford, 1974).

McCAULEY, M., *Stalin and Stalinism* (New York, 1983).

McNEAL, R. H., *Stalin: Man and Ruler* (New York, 1988).

MARSH, R., *Images of Dictatorship: Portraits of Stalin in Literature* (London, 1989).

MEDVEDEV, R. A., *Let History Judge: The Origins and Consequences of Stalinism* (New York, 1971).

_____, *On Stalin and Stalinism* (New York, 1979).

MEYER, A. G., *The Soviet Political System* (New York, 1965).

MOORE, B., *Soviet Politics—The Dilemma of Power* (Cambridge, 1950).

NICOLAEVSKY, B. I., *Power and the Soviet Elite: The Letter of an Old Bolshevik and Other Essays* (New York, 1965).

O'CONNOR, T., *Diplomacy and Revolution: G. V. Chicherin and Soviet Foreign Affairs, 1918-1930* (Ames, IA, 1987).

READ, A. and D. FISHER, *The Deadly Embrace: Hitler, Stalin and the Nazi-Soviet Pact, 1939-1941* (New York, 1988).

RESHETAR, J. S., JR., *A Concise History of the Communist Party of the Soviet Union* (New York, 1964).

ROSSI, A., *The Russo-German Alliance: August 1939-June 1941* (Boston, 1951).

RUBENSTEIN, A. Z. (ed.), *The Foreign Policy of the Soviet Union* (New York, 1966).

SCOTT, D. J., *Russian Political Institutions* (New York, 1966).

SETON-WATSON, H., *From Lenin to Khrushchev: The History of World Communism* (New York, 1960).

SHAPIRO, L., *The Communist Party of the Soviet Union* (New York, 1960).

SHULMAN, M. D., *Stalin's Foreign Policy Reappraised* (Cambridge, 1963).

STALIN, J. V., *The Essential Stalin: Major Theoretical Writings, 1905-1952* (New York, 1972).

STEWART, D. H., *Mikhail Sholokhov: A Critical Introduction* (Ann Arbor, 1967).

TOWSTER, J., *Political Power in the USSR* (New York, 1948).

TUCKER, R. C. (ed.), *Stalinism: Essays in Historical Interpretation* (New York, 1977).

_____, *Stalin in Power: The Revolution from Above, 1928-1941* (New York, 1990).

ULAM, A. B., *Expansion and Coexistence: Soviet Foreign Policy, 1917-1973* (New York, 1974).

_____, *Stalin: The Man and His Era* (New York, 1973).

ULDRICKS, T. J., *Diplomacy and Ideology: The Origins of Soviet Foreign Relations, 1917–1930* (London, 1979).

URBAN, G. R. (ed.), *Stalinism: Its Impact on Russia and the World* (Cambridge, 1986).

WEINBERG, G. L., *Germany and the Soviet Union, 1939–1941* (Leyden, Neth., 1954).

WITTLIN, T., *Commissar: The Life and Death of Lavrenty Pavlovich Beria* (New York, 1972).

CHAPTER 20

World War, Cold War, and Reconstruction

By the early summer of 1941, Hitler's war campaign was successful on every front. The Nazis occupied France, Belgium, The Netherlands, Denmark, Norway, Czechoslovakia, Austria, Hungary, and western Poland and the Balkan nations to the southernmost tip of the Greek peninsula were in the German camp, either as allies or as conquered territory. Italy was an ally, Spain and Sweden benevolent neutrals. The north coast of Africa from the western tip to the Egyptian border was in German hands, and the British faced the loss of the Suez Canal. Great Britain and its empire stood alone. In effect, of course, the United States had already joined the conflict in the heavy commitment it had made to the support of Britain primarily through the Lend-Lease Program.

There can be no telling how long the war might have dragged on had Hitler been content to consolidate his gains and let his lone enemy, Britain, peck away at the perimeter. It is hardly likely that Stalin would have moved against him as long as Russia suffered no harm. The German general staff, however, had been perfecting plans for an attack on the Soviet Union ever since August 1940. Hitler had long since made up his mind about his next target. Indeed, he was undoubtedly impatient to move the assault and must have anticipated the coming crusade against bolshevism with greater relish than he felt toward any other goal. Hitler's decision to attack the Soviet Union remains his greatest strategic error and blunder of World War II, and this fateful decision led eventually to the overthrow of the Nazi system in Germany and occupied Europe. The Soviet Union did not collapse by the fall of 1941 as Hitler predicted, and this fact promised a long, drawn-out campaign of attrition. By the end of 1942 and early 1943, mounting evidence indicated the Red Army ultimately would begin the long march that would carry Soviet troops into Berlin.

The Nazi Invasion

On June 22, 1941, Hitler's armies crossed the Soviet border with 120 divisions, which rapidly expanded to 200. The three attacking forces fanned out toward Leningrad, Moscow, and the Caucasus. The assault came as such a surprise to Stalin that German bombers destroyed many Russian planes before they could get off the ground. Defense units at the border disintegrated, and the mechanized armies of the Wehrmacht swept into Russia at amazing speed. Twenty-five days after the invasion, German troops on the central front entered Smolensk, where a tank battle temporarily blocked their advance. Although von Bock, the German commander, claimed 300,000 prisoners, the Russian resistance was so stubborn that the German offensive slowed appreciably for two months. Then, when reinforcements brought his command up to 1,500,000, von Bock continued the drive toward Moscow. The first few miles passed easily, but again the defense stiffened and bad autumn weather set in to help the Russians. Muscovites dug trenches, threw up barricades in the streets, and prepared to defend the capital house by house. That the Germans would penetrate the city seemed so likely that the government moved 600 miles east to Kuibyshev on the Volga. On December 5, the attack stalled just 35 miles west and only 13 miles north of Moscow.

Meanwhile, the Germans on the northern front under von Leeb drove the defenders under Voroshilov back through Estonia and were approaching Leningrad by late summer. A Finnish army under Mannerheim captured Viborg and pushed down the Karelian isthmus to join hands with the Germans moving to the northeast. In September von Leeb launched an attack on Leningrad that the beleaguered defenders managed to beat off. He then moved eastward, but turned back to encircle Leningrad.

As the northern and central German armies were advancing eastward, von Rundstedt in the south was meeting with even greater success against Budenny. Before mid-August the southern German group had taken Odessa. A few days later the Russians destroyed the great Zaporozhe Dam in the Dnieper, rather than let it fall to the Nazis. Kiev held out for a while, but by mid-September the Germans were east of it, claiming six hundred thousand Russian prisoners. Days later the invaders overran the Crimea, although Sevastopol refused to surrender for nine months until pounded into submission by round-the-clock heavy artillery barrages. In November von Rundstedt captured Rostov and halted along the line of the Donets River. Budenny had done so poorly that Timoshenko

German soldiers discover a refugee living in the ruins of Stalingrad, 1942.

replaced him, while Zhukov took over command on the central front. Hitler was so enraged that his generals had not taken Leningrad and Moscow that he assumed command and dismissed von Bock, von Leeb, and von Rundstedt. Two months earlier he had proclaimed that Russia was finished as a military power. In November he announced the destruction of the enemy armies. Hitler felt the pressure to achieve what he had already stated to be a fait accompli.

With all their rapid advance, the Nazis were meeting a degree of resistance never before encountered. The people scorched the earth as they fell back or disappeared into the woods or swamps to form guerrilla bands, burning their haystacks and grain and driving their animals with them to leave nothing of value to the foe. When the Russian armies fell back they were replaced by partisan bands trained to operate in the enemy's rear, attacking supply lines and cutting communications. The stiffening of the Red Army and the stern discipline among the guerrillas were the product of the increasingly tight control over both elements by the Communist party.

The Soviet armies certainly were roughly mauled during the autumn of 1941. Stalin later confessed that Russian equipment and troop training were greatly inferior to those of the Nazis. The Kremlin admitted to a half million killed, another half million missing, and over a million wounded in the first ten weeks of the war. The German gains were costly too. When the Nazi juggernaut was stopped, for the first time by any army, it had failed to reach any of its objectives. In addition, the Soviet armies were still far from beaten. On December 6, the very next day after von Bock's offensive stalled just west of Moscow, General Zhukov ordered his own offensive. The American general, MacArthur, hailed the Russian resistance and counterattack as "the greatest military achievement in all history."

The temperature dropped to forty degrees below zero in the neighborhood of Moscow in early December. Because Hitler had expected to overpower the Red Army in a few weeks, the German troops had no winter clothing. German forces then re-formed their lines and re-grouped in fortified camps where the troops would have shelter from the bitter cold. However, the Russians, using mounted Cossacks, ski troops, and partisans, swirled around these hedgehog positions that bristled with German artillery. Many were overrun or bypassed, and the Germans had no choice but to withdraw a hundred miles and more from Moscow. The Soviet gains were less important than the lift they gave allied morale. Unfortunately, the cost had been frightful. Moscow admitted that the Red Army had suffered over four hundred thousand casualties in the first month of the counterattack.

Because Hitler found his goal to capture Moscow and Leningrad and destroy the Soviet armies in 1941 to be unattainable, he revised his military aims before the next summer's campaign. The German armies now must seize the Kharkov-Stalingrad-Baku-Batum region and deprive Russia of the industrial output, grain, and oil the area produced and cut the vital transportation artery, the Volga. Germany's primary objective was to cross the Caucasus Mountains to the southeast and seize the vital oil fields near Baku on the shores of the Caspian Sea. Several German armies regrouped and resupplied in preparation for the new spring offensive, spreading out in a multi-pronged attack. One army, the Sixth, had the assignment to move directly eastward to secure Stalingrad and the surrounding area on the German left flank, while other forces drove southeast toward the oil fields at Baku and the Caspian.

In June 1942, the Germans opened the drive toward Stalingrad that would cut the Volga communication artery. Thirteen days later they had crossed the Don and were entering Voronezh. The Russians fell back stubbornly, but by the middle of August the enemy was in possession of the entire bend of the Don and had crossed the river west of Stalingrad. On September 15, the Germans were on the banks of the Volga and Stalingrad's half million people literally had their backs to the water. The invaders were approaching their goal of cutting off Moscow from the industry, oil, and grain of the southeast.

Stalingrad was vital to both sides. The important industrial center turned out trucks and tanks. It guarded the great waterway over which sixty million tons

The GERMAN INVASION OF RUSSIA
1941 - 1942

— — — — — Line of deepest German penetration, 1941-1942

Borders of
U.S.S.R.
June, 1941

MILES

0   100   500

Sam H. Bryant

of goods moved in a normal year, but it would be difficult to capture. Here the river is more than a mile wide, and to bridge it in the face of stiff resistance would be difficult.

On September 15 the Germans attacked, and for the next month wave after wave advanced against Stalingrad. The Germans took most of the city but could not dislodge the Russians, who contested every building. The attack reduced the buildings to rubble that filled the streets, providing cover for the defenders and barricades against the assault. General Paulus, the German commander, attacked with over three hundred thousand men. Continued reinforcements from Siberia and other fronts joined and expanded the forces already defending this strategic location. On November 19 Zhukov ordered a counterattack that encircled Paulus and his Sixth German Army. The slaughter went on until the beginning of February 1943, when Paulus surrendered with fewer than one hundred thousand men.

The obliteration of the Sixth Army exposed the flank and hastened the withdrawal from the Kuban and Caucasus of the German armies that were under heavy frontal attack. Two weeks after Paulus surrendered the Russians re-entered Rostov. Zhukov's armies rolled on west from Stalingrad past the Don to the Donets and recaptured Kharkov. The Germans were back where they had started the summer before. Meanwhile, in the north Soviet troops opened a supply line to the starving defenders of Leningrad.

Russia had regained nearly two thousand square miles of territory. The land it took was bare, systematically stripped clean by the retreating Germans of what little the Russians had left and the fighting had not destroyed. The first two years of the war had cost the nation over four million soldiers killed or missing. Russia had borne almost the entire burden of the attack that Germany, with all its conquered territory, had mounted against the allies. In the midst of the Stalingrad campaign, Stalin reminded the world that two hundred forty Axis divisions were fighting on the Russian front whereas four German and eleven Italian divisions were facing the British in North Africa. The next year, 1943, brought about the final defeat of German and Italian forces in Africa under the command of Erwin Rommel, the "Desert Fox." The Anglo-American allied invasion of Italy in the spring led to Mussolini's overthrow and to essential allied victories against German forces in southern Europe. The tide of victory had turned in favor of the anti-German coalition, which Churchill characterized as the "Grand Alliance."

Russian Triumph

An important element contributing to Hitler's defeat was the loyalty of the Russian people. Some of it the Communist party forced by its effective and ruthless control over every Russian it could reach. German brutality accounted for the rest of it. Many Russians had little reason to be overjoyed with the Communist regime. Collectivization of agriculture, purges, shortages, and police cruelty had hurt many and made enemies of some who would stoop to treason if the opportunity came. However, Stalin had disposed of most potential traitors before 1941. Those ready to welcome the Germans as deliverers soon learned from the widespread and systematic Nazi atrocities that life under the invaders would be far less tolerable than under the Communists. The deliberate treatment of Slavs as inferior creatures, the torture and slaughter of civilians, the deportation of over four million to slave labor mills in Germany, the vandalism and wanton destruction of property, the desecration of churches, the looting of shrines and art galleries—such bestiality fired the patriotism of the Russian people. The loathsome German behavior caused the Russians to be brutal in their treatment of the few prisoners they took, but their harshness generated more cruelty in return. Over four million civilians were massacred in occupied Russia, half of them Jews whom the Nazis had determined to exterminate as a people.

The systematic persecution of the Russian people made inevitable the failure of Berlin's propaganda attempt to promote a liberation movement. Many bitter Soviet citizens joined the Nazis, yet most Russians living in exile supported Moscow. As uncompromising a foe of communism as Miliukov was, even he preferred Stalin to Hitler.

The loyalty of the people was most effectively put to the test by the government's decision not to evacuate most of the civilian population. Many factories were relocated east of the Urals, and their skilled workers went with them. People not needed in such transplanted industries, and particularly peasants, were commanded not to pull out but to form partisan bands and continue the fight against the Nazi rear. One-third of Russia's population was behind German lines in 1942. Some kolkhozes continued to function, often under German pressure, losing much of their produce to the conquerors, of course, but smuggling much of it to the guerrillas.

Those who lived in unoccupied Russia endured unbelievable hardship from the shortages brought about by the concentration on war production and the conquest of the agricultural and industrial south. The citizens of Leningrad, who were without fuel, whose clothing was in rags, and who constantly faced the threat of starvation, fought alongside the garrison in defense of their homes. Other cities followed Leningrad's example and held out against overwhelming odds. Kiev fought off the Germans for six weeks, Odessa for two months, Sevastopol for nine. Soviet military planning had ordered the defense of these strategic and sentimental strongholds.

Hitler insisted upon another German offensive in July 1943 at Kursk, but his generals could do little. Seven powerful Russian army groups surged forward all along the line from Leningrad to the Black Sea. By early October the Russians had bridged the Dnieper in three places and recovered Smolensk. On through the winter months the relentless pursuit continued. In January 1944, the siege of Leningrad came to an end after two and a half years, during which nearly a million citizens had died from enemy action, starvation, and disease. During the spring the Russians mopped up pockets of enemy resistance near the Black Sea. Malinovsky recaptured Odessa in April. The following month Tolbukhin stormed Sevastopol, and the Crimea was once more in Russian hands.

On June 6, 1944, as Soviet troops crossed the old Polish frontier at several points, an American-British task force landed in Normandy to open the "second front" that Stalin had impatiently been demanding since 1942. The bulk of the German forces remained on the eastern front as Hitler desperately attempted to stem the Russian advance. However, the Germans were fast losing men and equipment, and their military power was ebbing rapidly away. Many veterans of numerous earlier victories, obtained when they invaded Russia three years earlier, lay buried in the steppes or languished in prison camps.

In the summer of 1944, Red troops drove through the Baltic states and headed for East Prussia. Members of the Polish underground, impatient to throw off the Nazi yoke, came out of their hiding places to free Warsaw on their own. In spite of these efforts, the rising was savagely put down by the Nazis. Politically suspicious of the Polish underground, which was loyal to the Polish government in London, and preferring that Soviet forces should deliver Warsaw, Stalin did nothing to assist the Polish underground forces under the command of General Bor. German troops brutally suppressed the uprising in Warsaw, treated captured prisoners very harshly, and deliberately destroyed what was left of the city. Stalin's cynicism toward Poland again showed Russia's historical attitude and behavior toward its neighbor to the west, and this fact has not been lost on Poles even today.

From now on the Kremlin calculatedly used the Red Army to gain political as well as military advantage. Two Red Army groups penetrated Romania and captured Bucharest. Once freed from the Nazis, Romania made peace with Moscow and declared war against Germany the next day. The Red Army overran Bulgaria and forced the helpless little nation to accept the Kremlin's terms. Russian armies moved into Yugoslavia in October and, in cooperation with Tito's partisans, recaptured Belgrade. At the same time, other Soviet troops entered Hungary and early in November took Budapest, but German and Hungarian forces vigorously resisted, and the country was not completely subdued until the following January. As the other former Nazi allies had done, Hungary made peace with Moscow and declared war on Germany. Except for Greece, which the British occupied, Soviet troops had liberated the entire Balkan Peninsula and assured the predominance of Russian influence in the postwar period.

During the autumn of 1944 Soviet armies cleared the Baltic provinces and crossed into East Prussia. The Polish front, quiet for five months, came to life at the beginning of the following year. Zhukov liberated the ruins of Warsaw in January and the Red armies rolled on toward Silesia. In the spring of 1945, Soviet troops drove the Germans out of Vienna, and pushed into Czechoslovakia. The allied commander in the West, General Eisenhower, ordered his troops not to pass the Elbe River, leaving to the Russians the responsibility of taking Berlin. The meeting of Soviet and American units at Torgau on the Elbe in late April 1945, heralded the end of effective Nazi resistance. Zhukov's men took Berlin when one hundred thousand men surrendered on May 2, but Hitler committed suicide rather than face the humiliation of being taken prisoner. On May 7 the German High Command surrendered unconditionally. The Red Army had come to the end of the long road from Stalingrad fifteen hundred miles away. Soviet successes in the 1943–1945 period can be attributed to several primary factors: the continued and impressive growth of Soviet armed forces despite earlier high casualties; high German losses on the eastern front, which could not be adequately replaced; the eventual collapse of Germany's satellite allies; as well as the American and Western allied forces landing on the continent of Europe in 1943 and 1944 and their offensives toward Germany itself. The continued and expanded industrial output in the Soviet Union, plus the Lend-Lease aid from the United States, also provided the materials of war essential to eventual victory.

The Price of Victory

Much of the war damage in the USSR was the result of military action and therefore unavoidable. The Soviet scorched-earth policy during the 1941 retreat had devastated large areas. In addition, the Germans deliberately and systematically destroyed anything that stood in their way as they withdrew. They destroyed plants that turned out half of the nation's steel, freight cars, locomotives, cement, and electrical power sources, as well as 1,100 coal mines producing 100,000,000 metric tons, nearly two-thirds of the prewar output. They wiped out three-fourths of Russia's capacity to produce pig iron. Nearly 100,000 collective farms were ruined and ransacked, as were 1,800 state farms and almost 3,000 machine tractor stations. The invaders demolished or carried away almost a third of the 500,000 tractors that had worked the nation's farms in the spring of 1941, along with 50,000 combines, 1,000,000 seeding and threshing machines, and 4,000,000 pieces of other agricultural machinery. For several seasons to come much of the heavy farm work would have to be done by hand. The Germans slaughtered 7,000,000 horses, 17,000,000 cattle, 27,000,000 sheep and goats—a third of the 1941 herds—and 20,000,000 pigs, 70 percent of the prewar total. They wiped out 1,700 towns and 70,000 villages; they demolished 31,000 factories, 40,000 libraries, and 84,000 schools; they tore up 40,000 miles of railroad, and destroyed 90,000 miles of telegraph lines. Twenty-five million Soviet citizens found themselves homeless, and the crowded housing conditions reached the point in 1945 where, on the average, 30 persons had to share a four- or five-room dwelling. The devastation wrought by the Germans was particularly extensive and deliberate in the Ukraine and the Don basin, which produced half the nation's meat, grain, and vegetables, and where the concentration of prewar industries had been heaviest. Property damage amounted to $128 billion, a fourth of the prewar value of the nation's property. All this the enemy had destroyed. In addition, war expenditures and reduction of national income cost another $400 billion.

Human losses were equally staggering. Malenkov reported in 1947 that 7,000,000 Soviet citizens had died in action or as a consequence of the occupation. Well over 3,000,000 soldiers had fallen prisoner, and many would not return. Later statistics of wartime deaths from all causes provide an aggregate total of approximately 20,000,000 military personnel and civilians. When the decline in the birth rate during the war and the increase in the death rate caused by malnutrition and disease are taken into account, the population of the USSR was smaller in 1965 by 45,000,000 than it would have been had there been no war. How many millions were permanently crippled is not known. The magnitude of these enormous losses can scarcely be matched in human history.

Within two months of the fall of Berlin five out of six ruined farms were operating again. It would be years, however, before the shell holes were filled in, the fence lines mended, the abandoned military equipment cleared away, the buildings repaired. and the fertility restored to the soil. To build the herds and flocks back up to prewar levels would take still longer. Then in 1946, a disheartening drought, the worst in fifty years, struck an area wider than that affected in the disastrous year 1921.

Wartime Relations with the Allies

Britain welcomed the USSR as a partner against Hitler; now it was no longer alone. Although refusing to retract any of the bitter words he had spoken against communism since 1917, Churchill, a few hours after the invasion, offered Russia whatever technical and economic assistance it might need. He reaffirmed Britain's resolve never to negotiate with Hitler and sent Sir Stafford Cripps to Moscow to formalize the alliance into which Hitler's crossing of the Niemen had prodded the two governments. The United States State Department declared that the immediate threat to the free world came not from the USSR but from Germany. In late October, Russia received a billion-dollar Lend-Lease grant to purchase needed supplies in the United States. London had extended a credit of ten million pounds sterling six weeks earlier.

In mid-August 1941, Roosevelt and Churchill drew up the Atlantic Charter in which they rejected aggrandizement for their own governments, expressed the desire that there be no territorial changes without the freely registered approval of the people involved, and promised to respect the right of all peoples to determine the form of government under which they would live. Six weeks later, the USSR formally subscribed to the Atlantic Charter, Stalin apparently supposing that it must apply only to territorial changes that Hitler had carried through. On New Year's Day, 1942—by which time the Japanese attack on Pearl Harbor had brought America into the war—the United Kingdom, the United States, the USSR, and twenty-three other nations signed the Declaration of the United Nations, each pledging full resources to the defeat of the Axis and promising not to accept a separate peace.

In May 1942, Molotov visited London to conclude a long-term alliance, then flew on to Washington to plead for more Lend-Lease matériel and to argue for the opening of a second front in Western Europe during the summer to relieve pressure on the Red Army. In the first he was successful. Washington raised its Lend-Lease commitments to the Soviet government to three billion dollars. As for the second, he received something less than full satisfaction. The State

Department announced that "a full understanding was reached with respect to the urgent task of creating a second front in Europe in 1942." Stalin took this as a commitment to land on the continent before the year was out, whereas Roosevelt and Churchill meant it only as an expression of hope that a second front might prove feasible.

British and American shipments of war matériel to Russia did much for the time being to remove the coolness between Moscow and the Western capitals. The United States shipped to the Soviet Union $8.5 billion worth of supplies before the end of the war in Europe, and $11 billion worth after the fall of Berlin. To approximately 7,000 tanks, 13,000 planes, 400,000 trucks, 2,000 tons of steel, 11,000,000 pairs of shoes, and more, the British government added 5,000 tanks, 7,000 planes, and quantities of other supplies, and in doing so deprived other allied fronts of critically needed matériel. This was substantial help, surely, but only a small fraction of Russia's own output. By 1943 Russian industry was producing annually 30,000 machine guns, 3,000,000 rifles, and over 7,000,000,000 rounds of ammunition. Bitter that there was still no second front in October 1942, Stalin, choosing to ignore the fact that the United States was fighting a global war, told a news correspondent that "as compared with the aid which the Soviet Union is giving to the allies by drawing upon itself the main forces of the German fascist armies, the aid of the allies to the Soviet Union has so far been little effective."

The British, American, and Soviet foreign secretaries met for the first time in the Moscow Conference in October 1943. The three powers swore to accept only the unconditional surrender of the Axis, promised to restore the independence of Austria, declared that democratic government must return to Italy, and warned that Germans charged with committing atrocities would be tried and punished in the country where they had perpetrated such crimes.

In November 1943, Roosevelt, Churchill, and Stalin met in the Soviet embassy in Teheran, Iran. There Stalin learned details of the proposed allied landing in France the following spring and promised to coordinate a Soviet offensive with it. The three heads of state agreed on a common strategy as they liberated territory from the conqueror. They also repeated their determination to work together for an enduring peace in which "all the peoples of the world may live free lives untouched by tyranny and according to their varying desires and their own consciences." Such high resolve, reiterated at every conference during the war, led Westerners to expect an entirely different sort of peace than Stalin apparently had in mind. During the year then drawing to a close, he dissolved the Comintern, an act that did not liquidate the Communist parties over the world, of course, but one which Western leaders interpreted to mean that Moscow was renouncing world revolution. The dissolution of the Third International removed perhaps the worst irritant to East-West cordiality.

The exiled Czech government in London concluded a twenty-year alliance with the USSR in December 1943. This seemed to indicate to Churchill that Prague would cling to Moscow after the war, something he had feared and had tried to prevent by insisting all along that the British-American invasion of the continent should take place in the Balkans to prevent all Eastern Europe from falling under Russian domination. He won Stalin's consent that Greece should come under British influence and that Britain and Russia jointly should exercise influence in Yugoslavia. He had saved Greece and might yet save Yugoslavia from the Communist embrace.

Near Yalta on the Crimean coast the Big Three—Stalin, Churchill, and Roosevelt—met again in February 1945. Eisenhower's armies had begin their invasion of Germany itself and Red troops were in western Poland. Political questions were rapidly multiplying and some were already beyond compromise. As the allies converged on the Reich's borders there must be some agreement on the fate of Germany after the military victory and the nature of succession governments for the lands freed from Nazi control. Roosevelt and Churchill were also most anxious to bring the Soviet Union into the war against Japan as quickly as possible.

At Yalta there was a discussion of dividing Germany into several states, as Stalin had proposed at earlier conferences. In the end, the conferees agreed simply to occupy Germany for an indefinite time and arranged British, French, American, and Russian occupation zones. The occupying power would demilitarize each zone and liquidate Nazism. An Allied Control Commission sitting in Berlin, made up of the military commanders of the four zones, would settle problems among the occupying powers and arrange for the flow of food and reparations between the Russian and Western zones. The settlement was probably the best possible, since both East and West refused to let the other completely control Germany. Russia was fearful of being outvoted by the Western powers if all should undertake a joint administration of Germany. The allies feared that an economic breakdown might follow the cutting off of agricultural products in eastern Germany from the heavily industrialized Western zones; the interdependence of the two Germanies was unmistakably clear, surely as much to Stalin as to Westerners. The allies also feared a breakdown of the administration of Germany, if the Soviet Union should insist upon unanimous action. The settlement that left Berlin in the Russian zone assured the Soviet Union of a much smaller and industrially weaker enemy if the other occupying powers should undertake to rebuild Germany as a bulwark against it. Stalin insisted on reparations in kind and the Western powers accepted tentatively a figure of twenty billion dollars for all attacked nations, half of which should go to the USSR. The amount was reasonably small, and Russia's share constituted only a tiny fraction of the damages it had suffered. Stalin demanded reparations, also, from other countries in Eastern Europe and from Manchuria.

The joint statement at the close of the Yalta Conference announced that peoples liberated from the Nazi yoke would be encouraged to "form interim governmental authorities broadly representative of all democratic elements in the population and pledged to the earliest possible establishment through free elections of governments responsive to the will of the people." Poland's eastern boundary was to be the Curzon Line, and it would receive former German territory on its western border. The Provisional Government of Poland, set up under Russian

The Big Three at the Yalta Conference

sponsorship, was to be broadened to include democratic leaders from abroad, presumably those whom England and the United States had long recognized as the exiled government in London. This newly broadened Provisional Government must hold "free and unfettered elections as soon as possible on the basis of universal suffrage and secret ballot." Yugoslavia was to receive a similarly broad government.

Stalin agreed to join the war against Japan within ninety days after the end of the war in Europe. Both Roosevelt and Churchill, yet unaware of the potential force of the untested atomic bomb, were certain that Russia's entry into the Far Eastern conflict and its neutralization of Japan's powerful Kwantung army would save many thousands of British and American lives. In return for Stalin's promise, Russia would receive the southern half of Sakhalin, which it had lost in 1904, the Kurile Islands, and a sphere of influence in Manchuria. Finally, the three agreed that a meeting of the nations united in the fight against the Axis should gather at San Francisco to organize an international body to maintain the peace.

In July and August 1945, the British, American, and Russian heads of government met once more, this time in the Berlin suburb of Potsdam. Roosevelt had died three months earlier, and while the conference was in session the British electorate voted Churchill and his party out of office. Their successors, Truman and Attlee, had to deal with problems that had been growing since Yalta and added their own distrust and suspicions to those that their predecessors had begun to feel. To Russian concern over reparations and irritation at British support of royalist elements in Greece, the Western powers countered with dissatisfaction that there was no assurance of "free and unfettered elections" in Eastern Europe and that the Communist-dominated Polish government had taken over administrative control of former German territory including most of East Prussia and portions of eastern Germany.

The three powers agreed to create a Council of Foreign Ministers to draft peace treaties with the defeated nations. They announced that, although they did not intend to "destroy or enslave the German people," they would not allow "the production of arms, ammunition and implements of war, as well as all types of aircraft and seagoing ships." Chemical, metal, and machine industries might produce only to the extent that they contributed to peacetime needs. The occupying powers, through their Control Council sitting in Berlin, would eradicate every trace of Nazism and bring German war criminals to trial. Russia gained permission to satisfy its demand for reparations to assist in postwar economic reconstruction of the Soviet Union by removing machinery from its own occupation zone and, in addition, obtaining from the other three zones a fourth of the machinery that Germany would not need for peacetime production. In partial return for the industrial equipment removed from the western zones, Russia was to send food and raw materials into such areas. German assets in the Balkans, Finland, and the Russian occupation zone of Austria were to go to the USSR. The possibility of Russia's using the labor of German prisoners as reparations remained unsettled. The eastern tip of East Prussia would go to Russia, pending the final peace settlement, at which time the two Western powers promised to support Russia's permanent acquisition. The similar transfer to Poland of all other German territory east of the Oder and Niesse rivers, including Danzig, met with similar approval but likewise only until the conclusion of peace with Germany. Because Soviet troops were in control of the entire area the qualification was academic. Nine million Germans living in the territory now transferred to Russia and Poland were to be transplanted into the Western zones.

A few days after the adjournment of the Potsdam Conference and precisely three months after the victory over Germany, the USSR entered the war against Japan as it had promised at Yalta to do. Two days earlier the first atomic bomb had destroyed Hiroshima and the day after Russia's declaration of war a second atomic bomb fell on Nagasaki. Japan sued for an armistice before Russia had been in the Far Eastern war a week. Meanwhile, Red troops overran Manchuria and Korea and overpowered the Kwantung army. Before the Japanese surrender,

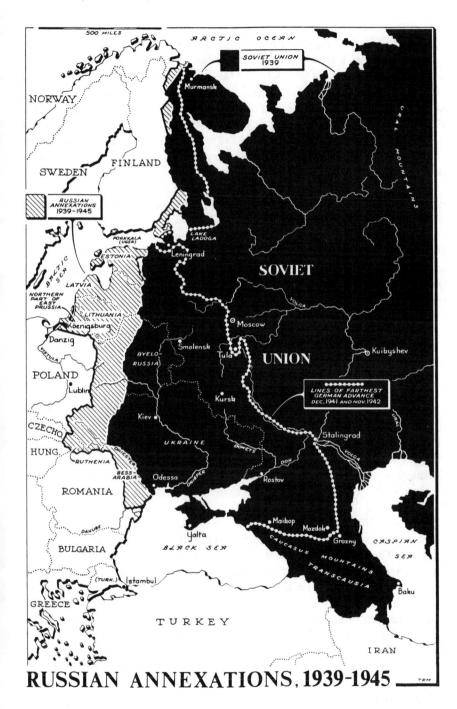

RUSSIAN ANNEXATIONS, 1939-1945

Russia and China concluded a thirty-year alliance that provided that the two signatories share the administration of the Chinese Eastern and South Manchurian Railways and that the two operate Port Arthur jointly as a naval base. Russia promised to withdraw its troops from Manchuria within three months and turn over the area to China. The signing of the treaty between the USSR and Chiang Kai-shek's Chinese government momentarily allayed Western suspicions that Moscow would back the Chinese Communists.

At the Moscow Conference in 1943 the allies had agreed on the creation of a postwar international body to promote peace and security for all nations. A year later American, Russian, British, and Chinese representatives worked out a proposal for such an organization. In April 1945, delegates representing fifty nations drafted a charter based on the earlier proposals. After two months of labor the United Nations was born.

The strength of the United Nations lay in the Security Council. Here the United States, the USSR, Britain, France, and China would occupy permanent seats, and the General Assembly would elect six other states for two-year terms. Questions of simple procedure might pass the Security Council with any seven votes, but on all other questions, or "substantive matters," the seven votes must include the votes of the five permanent members. Thus any permanent member's negative vote or veto would prevent any action detrimental to the country.

The Russo-Polish Tangle

One topic caused so many problems and controversies that it deserves special attention. Again and again, occurrences in Poland between 1939 and the end of the war affected relations among the "Grand Alliance" partnership and influenced the post-war atmosphere. This nation, caught geographically between Germany and the Soviet Union, was partitioned on paper between its hostile neighbors in the August 1939 Nazi-Soviet Pact. Poland's decisive defeat in September and October 1939 made this cynical agreement a tragic reality.

Soon after Hitler's armies invaded Russia, Moscow came to terms with the Polish government in exile in London, and diplomatic civility between the two returned. The Soviet government released Polish soldiers captured in 1939 to form an army, officered by Poles, to fight the common enemy. However, from the very beginning there was little cordiality among the Poles for the partnership that circumstances had forced on them. Moscow assumed that Polish divisions would take their place in the battle line as soon as they were ready, but the Polish government in London objected to the proposal that each division should enter the line separately. Many were bitter over the Russian invasion in 1939 and loudly insisted that Poland must regain its old frontiers. The age-old hatred of Poles for Russians did not soften because they happened to be fighting the same enemy. Cooperation proved to be impossible, and the Polish army with its commander, General Anders, was transferred to British administration.

After the withdrawal of General Anders's army, Moscow promoted the formation by Polish Communist refugees in Russia of a Union of Polish Patriots to work closely with the Soviet government. The exiled government in London now began to importune the Western allies to guarantee the prewar eastern frontier. As relations between Moscow and the London Poles steadily deteriorated, Hitler, in April 1943, announced that the German army had discovered a grave in the Katyn Forest near Smolensk containing the bodies of ten thousand Polish officers. Berlin, anxious to convince the world that the Russians had carried out the slaughter, as indeed proved to be the case, agreed to support an investigation by the International Red Cross, as the London Poles demanded. Moscow took this as an insult and broke off relations with the Polish government in exile. Only in 1990 did the Soviet government officially acknowledge its responsibility and offer apologies to the Polish people.

Efforts by the London Poles to get the Western allies to mediate with Moscow over the Russo-Polish frontier only irritated the Soviet government, which announced that the question was not open to discussion. Determined that the postwar government of Poland must be one sympathetic to Russia, Moscow allowed the Union of Polish Patriots and a number of leftist Poles living in Russia to proclaim themselves a "Committee of National Liberation," which amounted to another Polish government in exile, this one residing in Moscow. When Soviet forces moved into Poland in 1944, the Committee of National Liberation followed and with Russia's consent took over the administration of the liberated territory. The committee set up a temporary capital at Lublin southeast of Warsaw and came to be known as the Lublin government. In an attempt to prevent the country from falling under a Moscow-oriented administration, the Polish underground, led by General Bor, on order from the exiled Polish government in London, rose against the Germans in Warsaw just as the Russians were twenty miles from the city. Now the Red Army halted on the east bank of the Vistula and let the Germans put down the uprising, which they did with their customary brutality. Moscow's callousness in allowing the heartless massacre of the Warsaw patriots did nothing to improve Russia's relations with Britain and the United States.

The Satellites

Stalin's promises at Teheran and Yalta to Churchill and Roosevelt that Poland would be allowed to restore and develop democratic government initially assured his Western partners. However, with the Red Army's liberation of Poland in the closing months of 1944 and the installation of the Communist regime in Lublin, it soon became all too evident that Soviet promises of democracy and free elections were scarcely credible. Yet the West could do little other than to continue its efforts to persuade Stalin to honor his word. Soviet treatment of Poland thus became one of the major diplomatic and ideological battlegrounds as the cold war developed and set the pattern for the post-war era.

As the Red Army moved into Eastern Europe and the Balkans, liberating lands that had borne the Nazi yoke for five years, underground resistance movements emerged to organize provisional governments. In every country that endured German occupation, with the notable exception of Poland, the Communists dominated or at least shared in the leadership of the resistance movement. As Soviet troops drove back the Germans, they turned over the administration of the land to the partisans. If there were two resistance movements, as was the case·in Poland, the Communist movement disarmed or liquidated the non-Communists and handed the power of government to the Moscow-oriented group. Churchill and Roosevelt at Yalta and Truman and Attlee at Potsdam could only accept the fact that the Red Army was effectively in control of Eastern Europe and hope that Stalin would honor his promise of "free and unfettered elections."

After liberation, Moscow sponsored coalition governments, including Communists, socialists, and other leftist parties, in Poland, Hungary, Romania, Bulgaria, Yugoslavia, Albania, and Czechoslovakia. Although they permitted non-Communist parties to occupy cabinet posts, the Communists always kept for themselves the vital ministries of justice and interior, which controlled the nation's police system. Soviet troops remained in each country to buttress the authority of the new government, although they withdrew from Czechoslovakia late in 1945 and from Bulgaria two years later.

The growing popularity of the Communists was owing only in small measure to Russian sponsorship. In many countries, with the exception of Czechoslovakia and Bulgaria, there was need for land reform—for the partition of the great estates among the peasants. In much of Eastern Europe, with the same exceptions, the Communists had fought the reactionary tendencies of the prewar government most uncompromisingly. In every country but Czechoslovakia the upper classes—business magnates, estate owners, the higher clergy, officials, and even many workers and peasants—had dealt softly with fascism or openly supported it against the threat of proletarian revolution. The Communists, then, had a positive program which appealed to many. In fact, they might have had even wider popular support without Russian intervention than with it.

More or less gradually but steadily the Communists in the states of Eastern Europe eased non-Communists out of office. The governments of the so-called "people's democracies" settled the centuries-old land problem by breaking up the great estates among the peasants who, for the moment at least, were allowed to own the land outright. Small business continued under private ownership, but large factories, banking, transportation, and foreign trade came under government operation. It was the Russian New Economic Policy all over again. Each satellite, as the West came to call the people's democracies, traded primarily with the USSR. In fact, the Eastern European countries and the Soviet Union concluded trade agreements, as well as mutual-friendship-and-alliance treaties, as soon after liberation as the satellites formed governments to sign them. By 1947 over half of Russia's exports were going to the satellites, and they in turn were supplying a third of its imports.

When the United States in 1948 put forward the European Recovery Program, or Marshall Plan, to cushion Europe's adjustment from war to peace, Russia and its minions, suspecting some sinister scheme to control Europe, refused to accept the offer. Instead, Moscow organized a Council for Economic Mutual Assistance in 1949, the effect of which was to bind the satellite economies still more tightly to Russia.

The Comintern, which had voted to disband in 1943, in effect came back to life in the autumn of 1947, when Communist delegations from Russia, Poland, Romania, Bulgaria, Hungary, Yugoslavia, Czechoslovakia, France, and Italy organized the Communist Information Bureau, or Cominform for short. Its aim was to coordinate the work of its members and particularly to carry on a propaganda campaign against ''Anglo-American imperialism.'' However, the Yugoslav leader Marshall Tito refused to accept dictation of his foreign and trade policy from Moscow. The Cominform on Stalin's order expelled Yugoslavia in 1948, and thereafter Tito turned to the West for military and economic assistance.

The tightening of Soviet political and economic control over the satellites was Stalin's answer to the Marshall Plan and the Truman Doctrine—the policy of granting American military and economic aid to nations lying near the borders of the USSR and potentially under the threat of Russian encroachment. Although the United States took the first step, with full British support, it did so in growing concern over the extension of Russian influence in Eastern and Central Europe. Cooperation between East and West barely outlasted the war. By 1947 most of the nations of the world had chosen sides between two contesting power blocs, the one led by the United States, the other by the USSR.

With the Communist victory in China in 1949, Stalin had put together the most extensive empire the world had ever known, and had done so in a far shorter time than it had taken to build any earlier empire. Stalin's empire contained a greater variety of religions, languages, and ethnic groups than any earlier one. It had absorbed several cultures superior to that of Russia itself, but the vast agglomeration held together for only a few years. By the mid-1950s, it was beginning to break up. Some of the European satellites were defying the parent authority, albeit briefly and unsuccessfully, and by 1960 it was apparent that China would not only secede from the Moscow family but would carry others with it.

Growing East-West Tension

The division of Germany into four occupation zones soon produced vigorous disagreement over the future of the former enemy. The United States and the United Kingdom, anxious to be free of the burden of supporting the German economy by late 1946, promoted the economic recovery of the Western occupation zones. This, coupled with the effect of the Marshall Plan to economically resuscitate Western Europe against possible Soviet expansion, convinced Moscow that the Western powers were preparing another war, this one against the USSR, in which a revived Germany would serve as a tool and a springboard for the Western assault. Moscow's own hope to see Germany united under Communist domination slowly faded with the economic recovery of West Germany and its obvious sympathy for a Western political orientation. A Soviet protest that the Western powers were violating the terms of the Potsdam agreement on the occupation, when they promoted economic recovery in their own zones without Russian consent, went unheeded.

When the Western powers in 1948 extended German currency reform to their occupation sectors in West Berlin, Moscow retaliated by cutting off all contact between Berlin and the Western zones. Stalin ordered the Berlin blockade as a calculated threat to strangle the former capital and force the Western powers to cooperate with Russia in occupation policy. The Western powers surmounted the blockade; the Anglo-American "airlift" flew food and fuel into Berlin. After nearly a year of the expensive and dramatic operation, which the Western allies seemed willing to continue indefinitely, Moscow raised the blockade. A meeting of the Council of Foreign Ministers of the occupying powers settled the immediate issues, but the schism never closed between Russian-occupied East Germany and the Western zones, which soon with allied encouragement organized a German government as a separate state in 1949.

Frightened by the Berlin blockade and by the Communist seizure of power in Czechoslovakia in February 1948, the United States, Canada, and most nations of Western Europe in the spring of 1949 created the North Atlantic Treaty Organization and pledged to rearm, with American help, in defense against the further spread of communism. NATO created a unified force under a joint military command. West Germany joined NATO in 1955. The Soviet Union faced the threat, if it pushed its influence farther to the west, of a war in which its former enemies and allies would march together. As a counterbalance to NATO, the Communist nations of Eastern Europe signed the Warsaw Pact in 1955, committing themselves to measures for common defense and organizing a military system under Russian command.

The rift that had opened between the USSR and the United States even before the end of the war steadily widened through the postwar years. Fundamental disagreement between Moscow and the Western allies under American leadership appeared on every issue that arose. The two sides could not agree on what countries should win membership in the United Nations, on reparations, on occupation policy in Germany or Japan, on disarmament, on control of the Straits, on release of war prisoners, and on a number of other issues.

The hostility between the United States and the Soviet Union that surfaced at the council table was reflected in the press, on the stage, and in the pronouncements of political leaders in both countries. Russian newspaper articles and cartoons spewed forth venom against "Anglo-American imperialism" and particularly against American imperialism. American newspapers kept up their own attacks on "Soviet imperialism." Russian and American leaders exchanged the most heated charges, not all of which—on either side—were sane.

The Korean War

At the Potsdam Conference the powers agreed to divide Korea, once liberated from the Japanese, at the thirty-eighth parallel, into Russian and American occupation zone. The promised unification of Korea did not materialize, however, and the Republic of Korea, organized in 1948 under United Nations sponsorship, governed the peninsula south of the thirty-eighth parallel, whereas the "Democratic People's Republic of Korea," organized at the same time by Moscow, succeeded to the Soviet zone north of that parallel. Russia pulled its occupation troops out of North Korea and six months later the United States withdrew from South Korea. Both infant governments claimed to be the legal government of all Korea.

In June 1950, North Korean troops, armed with Russian tanks and planes, crossed the thirty-eighth parallel determined to force the unification of the peninsula under Communist rule. The defending South Korean army was rolled back and would quickly have been overwhelmed if left to its own resources. The United Nations Security Council, under American prodding, declared the North Korean invasion an act of aggression and called upon the members of the United Nations to join forces in defense of the victim. The resolution would surely have failed because of a Soviet veto but for the fact that the Russian delegation had walked out of an earlier session of the Security Council and had not yet returned.

After initial successes, the North Korea armies retreated northward across the thirty-eighth parallel and deep into their own territory due to the steady pressure of General MacArthur and his United Nations forces, which were predominantly American-manned and American-equipped. Then four Chinese armies joined their Communist ally and drove MacArthur back deep into South Korea. The seesaw went on to little advantage to either side for year, reaching a stalemate in June 1951, roughly along the thirty-eighth parallel. Then Moscow, who all along had been posing as the champion of peace and tarring the United States as the aggressor, proposed a cease-fire order and the initiation of conversations looking toward an armistice. For the next twenty-two months, the truce talks continued intermittently, painfully reducing one objection after another but failing to find agreement on whether prisoners of war should be forcibly repatriated, as the Communists insisted, or allowed to choose between repatriation and exile, as the United Nations insisted.

In April 1953, significantly the month after Stalin's death, the truce talks reopened after six months of stalemate. Soon afterward, the two sides agreed upon an armistice that accepted the United Nations proposal rather than the Communist view on repatriation. Prisoners who chose to return home might do so, whereas those who preferred exile were free to move to any country that would have them. The Korean War was over, although Communist and Western troops have continued to glare across the armistice line at each other ever since. No peace treaty has yet been signed, four decades later.

Postwar Reconstruction and Party Politics, 1945–1953

Reconstruction efforts were aided by several factors in the war's aftermath. Huge numbers of demobilized military personnel returned to their former occupations, added to large numbers of Soviet women already in the work force. German prisoners of war, in massive supply, could be utilized until their eventual return to their homeland in the 1950s. Soviet prisoners located in Soviet prisons and labor camps provided a further labor resource. One of those was Alexander Solzhenitsyn, the future novelist, who had been arrested in 1945 and sent to a labor camp for an eight-year term for a derogatory comment he made about Stalin in a personal letter.

The work week had been extended during the war, as the nation's economy had been mobilized for the war effort, and many factories were moved or built to the east in the Ural Mountain region beyond the war zone. Some economic and financial aid came from Western nations, although insufficient to meet Soviet requests, and the United Nations offered its assistance. Reparations and goods in-kind came from defeated Germany, which partially replaced destroyed equipment and industrial facilities.

The usual wartime controls of rationing and mobilization of the work force to undertake the government's projects made the reconstruction task more manageable. Underlying these efforts was the pattern of work and worker discipline established by Stalin in the thirties during the period of collectivization and increased industrialization. Five-year plans coordinated the reconstruction effort, and the Fourth Five-Year Plan ran from 1946 to 1950, followed by the Fifth Plan in the 1950s. Reaching production targets did not come easily, given the enormous challenges and problems, but substantial improvement had been made by the time of Stalin's death in 1953.

During this recovery period the Communist party, after 1945, reasserted its leadership and authority over the entire nation, especially in those regions which had been under German occupation during the war. Special efforts were undertaken to promote ideological obedience and party loyalty for those who might have been tainted with anti-Communist values. This included those who favored the freedom from Communist rule (as in the Baltic republics and the Ukraine) or who wished once again to own their own farmland. Special "agitprop" teams (agitation and propaganda) worked in those areas to restore the pre-invasion environment. Andrei Zhdanov, a member of the Politburo and widely assumed to be Stalin's heir apparent, had the responsibility for this task which he carried out with rigorous efficiency until his death in 1948. The Zhdanovshchina (Time of Zhdanov) gained a reputation for ruthless and repressive controls that shaped and dominated the immediate postwar atmosphere.

This period also shaped domestic conditions emerging from the worsening relations with the West in the early cold war period. Foreign correspondents found it difficult to report or even live in the Soviet Union, limited by censorship and even bans on travel outside major cities. Foreign broadcasts were interrupted, and marriages between Soviet citizens and foreigners eventually were banned. Zhdanov oversaw these policies as well. In addition, Soviet writers, musicians, artists, dramatists and others found their work coming under widespread criticism and outright censorship as the Communist party accused them of lack of ideological fervor and patriotic support for the motherland. Anna Akhmatova, a noted Soviet poet, was one of the most important intellectual victims, although she avoided prison or outright physical mistreatment. Sergei Eisenstein, the world famous film director of the twenties and thirties, had to make an abject written apology in 1946 to the Communist party for what the party told him were films lacking in ideological content. He died soon after, in 1948. These tragic instances underscored the domination of the party in the post-war period.

Above all, Stalin reigned supreme over party and nation. What later came to be known as the "cult of personality" grew throughout the Soviet Union during the postwar years. Statues and busts, banners, laudatory literature and art, and other examples too numerous to mention, portrayed Stalin as an all-wise and all-knowing national leader and statesman. Credit for planning and winning the war went to Stalin's alleged genius. On the occasion of his seventieth birthday in 1949, the effusive congratulations reached sickening heights. He had become a veritable god in an officially atheistic state.

In 1941 Stalin had assumed the office of chairman of the Council of Ministers in addition to his post as general secretary of the party. His leading associates by 1945–1946 had risen in the late 1930s after the purges removed the "Old Bolsheviks" of the Lenin era. Molotov served as foreign minister from 1939, Beria headed the secret police from 1938, and Zhdanov ran the party in Leningrad as well as overseeing the Zhdanovshchina. After Zhdanov's death in 1948, the next likely contender to be Stalin's heir apparent was Georgi Malenkov, an experienced senior party administrator. Nikita Khrushchev, party head of the Ukraine from the late 1930s, continued in that post after the war until Stalin brought him to Moscow to undertake major responsibilities at his side in the capital. All were powerful figures who served on the Politburo as major shapers of Soviet policy under the watchful eye of the general secretary.

Periodic meetings of the party congresses had not occurred for years, the last one taking place in 1939. Finally, the Nineteenth Party Congress met in the fall of 1952 after a thirteen-year interim. Stalin's authority seemed unshakable, although his age and health undoubtedly raised unspoken questions about the future and his eventual successor. Stalin took little part in the congress, although he did attend several sessions, leaving Malenkov to make the major pronouncements in his name. One curious event emerging from the meeting was the formation of a revised and enlarged Politburo, now designated the Presidium. Its expanded membership more than doubled as relatively younger and promising Communist officials made their appearance in new positions of responsibility. This included Leonid Brezhnev, a forty-five year old party head of one of the republics. He later came to power as the party chief in 1964, after his ouster of Nikita Khrushchev. Additional leadership changes were made at this time in the apparatus of the party's Secretariat, which further illustrated the growing pressures and revisions within the party. Observers and Kremlin watchers interpreted these changes as signalling the beginning of Stalin's intention to initiate a new purge of the party leadership by elevating younger men totally dependent on him for their authority. The future of such major figures as Malenkov, Beria, Molotov, and Khrushchev looked uncertain.

Already there had been signs of a slowly developing purge of middle- to senior-level Communist leaders. The purge of party personnel in what came to be referred to as the "Leningrad Affair" in the aftermath of Zhdanov's death in the late 1940s showed that the established and powerful could be undercut and removed. The dismissal (and execution) of a major party leader soon after provided another ominous sign for the future of party politics.

The re-emergence of growing anti-semitism in the Soviet Union and in several East European satellite states created further uneasiness in the late forties and early fifties. For many, the dangers proved to be very real, involving dismissal from jobs, social harassment, public criticism, and even arrest. Attacks on the alleged "Zionists" reached into the party ranks and even the higher echelons of party officials. Most Jews attempted to keep a low profile in hopes they could survive the anti-Jewish campaign of the period. The signs couldn't have been worse.

Suggested Reading

ARMSTRONG, J. A., *Soviet Partisans in World War II* (Madison, WI, 1964).

BIALER, S., *Stalin and His Generals: Soviet Military Memoirs of World War II* (New York, 1969).

BORTOLI, G., *The Death of Stalin* (New York, 1975).

CARRELL, P. *Scorched Earth: The Russian-German War, 1943–44* (Boston, 1970).

CHANEY, O. P., JR., *Zhukov* (Norman, OK, 1971).

CHUIKOV, V. I., *The Battle for Stalingrad* (New York, 1964).

CLARK, A., *Barbarossa, The Russian-German Conflict, 1941–1945* (New York, 1965).

CONQUEST, R., *Power and Policy in the USSR: The Study of Soviet Dynastics* (New York, 1961).

CRAIG, W., *Enemy at the Gates: The Battle for Stalingrad* (New York, 1973).

DALLIN, A., *German Rule in Russia, 1941–1945* (London, 1957).

DEANE, J. R., *The Strange Alliance: The Story of Our Efforts at Wartime Cooperation with Russia* (Bloomington, IN, 1973).

DEDIJER, V., *The Battle Stalin Lost: Memoirs of Yugoslavia, 1948–1953* (New York, 1971).

DOLGUN, A., *Alexander Dolgun's Story: An American in the Gulag* (New York, 1975).

DUNMORE, T., *Soviet Politics, 1945–1953* (New York, 1984).

ERICKSON, J., *Stalin's War with Germany*, 2 vols. (New York, 1975 and Boulder, 1983).

FEIS, H., *Churchill—Roosevelt—Stalin* (Princeton, 1957).

_____, *From Trust to Terror: The Onset of the Cold War, 1945–1950* (New York, 1970).

FISCHER, G., *Soviet Opposition to Stalin* (Cambridge, 1952).

FISCHER, L., *The Road to Yalta: Soviet Foreign Relations, 1941–1945* (New York, 1972).

GADDIS, J. L., *The Long Peace: Inquiries into the History of the Cold War* (New York, 1987).

_____, *Russia, the Soviet Union, and the United States: An Interpretive History* (New York, 1990).

GALLAGHER, M. P., *The Soviet History of World War II; Myths, Memories, and Realities* (New York, 1963).

GOURE, L., *The Siege of Leningrad* (New York, 1964).

The Great Patriotic War of the Soviet Union, 1941–1945 (Moscow, 1974).

HAHN, W. G., *Postwar Soviet Politics: The Fall of Zhdanov and the Defeat of Moderation, 1946–1953* (Ithaca, NY, 1982).

HAMMOND, T. T. (ed.), *Witnesses to the Origins of the Cold War* (Seattle, 1982).

HELLER, A., and F. FEHER, *From Yalta to Glasnost: The Dismantling of Stalin's Empire* (Cambridge, Eng., 1990).

HERRING, G. C., *Aid to Russia, 1941–1946: Strategy, Diplomacy, The Origins of the Cold War* (New York, 1973).

HODOS, G., *Show Trials: Stalinist Purges in Eastern Europe, 1948–1954* (New York, 1987).

INBER, V. M., *Leningrad Diary* (New York, 1971).

KAPLAN, C. S., *The Party and Agricultural Crisis Management in the USSR* (Ithaca, NY, 1987).

KENNAN, G. F., *Russia and the West under Lenin and Stalin* (Boston, 1961).

KHRUSHCHEV, N. K., *Khrushchev Remembers* (Boston, 1970).

KOCHINA, E. I., *Blockade Diary* (Ann Arbor, 1990).

LAUCK, J. H., *Katyn Killings, In the Record* (Clifton, NJ, 1988).

LIDDELL HART, B. H., *The Red Army* (New York, 1956).

LINZ, S. J. (ed.), *The Impact of World War II on the Soviet Union* (Totowa, NJ, 1985).

MASTNY, V., *Russia's Road to Cold War: Diplomacy, Warfare and the Politics of Communism, 1941–1945* (New York, 1979).

MOYNAHAN, B., *Claws of the Bear: The History of the Red Army from the Revolution to the Present* (Boston, 1989).

MULLIGAN, T. P., *The Politics of Illusion and Empire: German Occupation Policy in the Soviet Union, 1942–1943* (New York, 1988).

PAVLOV, D. V., *Leningrad 1941: The Blockade* (Chicago, 1965).

PETROV, V., *June 22, 1941: Soviet Historians and the German Invasion* (Columbia, SC, 1968).

SALISBURY, H., *The 900 Days: The Siege of Leningrad* (New York, 1969).

_____, *The Unknown War* (New York, 1978).

SCHWARTZ, H., *Russia Since World War II* (New York, 1961).

SEATON, A., *The Russo-German War, 1941–1945* (New York, 1971).

SETON-WATSON, H., *The East European Revolution* (New York, 1956).

_____, *From Lenin to Khrushchev: The History of World Communism* (New York, 1960).

SKRJABINA, E., *Siege and Survival: The Odyssey of a Leningrader* (Carbondale, IL, 1971).

THOMAS, H., *Armed Truce: The Beginnings of the Cold War, 1945–1946* (New York, 1987).

ULAM, A. B., *Expansion and Coexistence: The History of Soviet Foreign Policy, 1917-1973* (New York, 1974).

_____, *The Rivals: America and Russia Since World War II* (New York, 1972).

WERTH, A., *Moscow War Diary* (New York, 1942).

_____, *Russia at War, 1941-1945* (New York, 1964).

_____, *The Year of Stalingrad* (New York, 1946).

WOLFE, T. W., *Soviet Power and Europe, 1945-1970* (Baltimore, 1970).

ZAWODNY, J. K., *Death in the Forest: The Story of the Katyn Forest Massacre* (Notre Dame, 1962).

ZHUKOV, G. E., *Marshal Zhukov's Greatest Battles* (New York, 1969).

ZIEMKE, E. F., *Stalingrad to Berlin: The German Defeat in the East* (Washington, DC, 1968).

CHAPTER 21

Russia Under
Khrushchev and Brezhnev

In January 1953, nine Russian doctors were accused of conspiring with British and American agents to assassinate top Russian officials, particularly military and party leaders. Six of the nine were Jews alleged to be Zionists, and a bloodletting among Jews of every profession followed. Then the attack veered round to the Communist party, particularly in the Ukraine and to the security police whose supposed laxity had allowed the plot to develop. The terror of the thirties seemed to recur. "The old man has reached for the bottle again," one American observer told another, but this terror was short-lived. On March 5, 1953, Stalin suddenly died of a cerebral hemorrhage at the age of seventy-three. Many suspected that party leaders fearful for their own lives had assassinated him, although available evidence does not support this theory.

The man who had ruled in the Kremlin for a quarter century had molded the nation into "Stalin's Russia," a nation-state-empire whose lust for power and expansion differed only in insatiability and ruthlessness from others in modern times. In the eight years after World War II the Western world had learned by bitter experience how to deal with the formidable empire of satellites and allies that Stalin had assembled. There was no prospect of world peace. Aside from the neutrals who stood by helplessly, there were two armed camps, the one working relentlessly to expand the Communist empire, the other working doggedly to halt that expansion.

So accustomed had the non-Communist camp grown to its role of resisting Communist imperialism that Stalin's successors strove with little success to convince the rest of the world that the tyrant's death could produce any real change in Soviet policy. After its bitter war and postwar experiences with Stalin, the Western world was skeptical that Stalin's Russia could change. This skepticism made the United States and its allies slow to react positively to the opportunity for the relaxation of tensions. None could believe that the opportunity existed.

Slowly Western governments came to understand that much of the Stalin system died with him. The most brutal aspects he had created did not long survive. The fact that they did not was attributable to several factors. The Communist leaders who jousted for power after Stalin's demise quickly revealed a determination to alter the system that had kept them all in constant fear for their own lives. The Russian people sought unmistakably better living conditions and a relaxation of controls that had been their lot for three decades. Moscow soon lost its absolute control over the satellites and allies whom Stalin had managed to keep in line. The Communist world split in twain, and the cleavage forced the Soviet Union to seek rapprochement with Western Europe and the United States, the leader of its postwar enemies.

The Rise and Fall of Khrushchev

The death of Stalin threatened the Communist regime with crisis and possible destruction. Party leaders feared a widespread uprising of the people, now that the merciless old dictator could no longer visit his cruel vengeance upon men suspected of lack of enthusiasm for his rule. There was a real concern that the satellites might break away, and even that the nation's enemies in the West might take advantage of Russia's moment of weakness.

At the instant of Stalin's last breath, Beria (head of the secret police since 1938) quickly moved tanks and troops from his secret police command to Moscow and sealed off the capital. This ominous gesture alarmed Stalin's heirs. To assure that no secret police effort should again threaten to rule Russia, they arrested Beria and placed the political police under a committee. The former MVD became the KGB, or Committee of State Security, thus applying the principle of collective leadership—as old as Peter the Great—to the management of the dreaded security force. Beria was executed the same year, and his violent death marked the determination of the Communist party never again to let the secret police fall under the control of one man. The execution of Beria may have been the first move against Malenkov, with whom Beria was working hand in glove.

Even before Beria's execution, there were several gestures directed toward easing internal tension. The government dropped the charges in the ''Doctors' Plot,'' and announced the evidence had been fabricated as the start of a new purge era. Stalin's successors granted an amnesty, releasing prisoners serving terms for minor criminal offenses, and such amnesties became an annual affair. Political prisoners reaped the greatest benefits; in 1955 there was even an amnesty for those suspected of collaborating with the enemy during the war. A revision of the civil code was being undertaken soon after Stalin's death. It promised, when it appeared in 1958, a strict limitation on the power of the police to seize without warrant and imprison without trial, put an end to crimes by analogy, and strengthened the position of the defendant in criminal cases. Its reliability would depend upon who applied the code and how easily it could be set aside.

When the execution of Beria removed the immediate threat that another strong man might succeed Stalin, the members of the Presidium loudly proclaimed the principle of collective or collegial leadership, a principle soon discovered, by one of the logical distortions at which the Communists have proven themselves masters, to be a "law of Marxist-Leninist doctrine." A triumvirate—Malenkov, Beria, and Molotov—had assumed leadership immediately upon the announcement of Stalin's death, but Beria's contempt for the "principle" of collective leadership cost him his life.

Malenkov was immediately named the leader of the Soviet government and as premier headed the Council of Ministers or cabinet. He now moved to put himself in firm control as Stalin's successor. He was also named first secretary of the Communist party, thus occupying the two positions of strength that his predecessor had filled. He packed the Council of Ministers with his own men and chose to rely upon the top bureaucrats and directors of economic ministries, rather than upon the party men. Within ten days, however, the old stalwarts made it clear that they would have no new Stalin. They forced Malenkov to give up his party role, and Nikita Khrushchev controlled the party machinery thereafter as first secretary. These parallel national political offices and structures had existed since Lenin's time and were theoretically equal in status and authority. In reality, the party set the overall policies and goals; the government was responsible for their implementation.

When the party leaders returned home after Stalin's funeral, the new premier slightly relaxed controls on writers and intellectuals who took advantage of the freer atmosphere to speak after their long silence. Later he announced his plan for the rapid development of consumer goods industries and for reductions in taxes and prices, while promising that agriculture would supply a more bountiful living to all. His opponents, particularly those in the Communist party and the army, regarded Malenkov's announcement as a cheap bid for popular support. They felt it was militarily risky to curb the emphasis upon heavy industry, thus weakening the nation's defenses.

Khrushchev then charged Malenkov with ignorance of the capability of Soviet agriculture, pointing out publicly that the nation had ten million fewer cattle than in 1928 and that the number of livestock had fallen within the past year. He granted that there was no shortage of grain, but noted that there was a shortage of every other farm commodity. This obvious effort to embarrass Malenkov ignored the premier's plan to adopt personal incentives to stimulate agricultural output and painted the gloomiest of pictures, which Khrushchev implied only he knew how to correct. His own plan was to bring under cultivation millions of acres of virgin land in southern Siberia—more new farmland, in fact, than all the farmland in Britain, France, and Spain combined at the time, and more than the total in the USSR in 1928.

Malenkov stumbled along as premier for two years, steadily losing ground to the party secretary. Khrushchev removed Malenkov supporters from party offices all over the Soviet Union and even packed the Foreign Office with his friends, so that he and not the foreign minister would first learn of matters affecting Russia's foreign relations. Malenkov resigned in 1955, confessing his errors in analyzing the agricultural situation and emphasizing what Khrushchev called "consumerism." He admitted that the only way ultimately to increase the production of consumer goods is to concentrate first on heavy industry. His insistence that the premier should be one "with greater administrative experience" sounded strange, considering the administrative genius that he was.

Nicholas Bulganin, the new premier, was never more than Khrushchev's puppet. Molotov joined the new triumvirate, as he had the first. The real power among the three who assumed control in 1955, however, proved to be Nikita Khrushchev, who had moved unswervingly toward sole control almost from the moment of Stalin's death. He had served in Stalin's time as Communist party secretary in the Ukraine and then in a similar position in Moscow. He learned the lesson that Stalin's own earlier rise made clear, and he stored up that knowledge against the day when he would need a vast network of supporters. Within months of his appointment as party secretary Khrushchev was moving systematically in every republic to clear out the old guard who had done the bidding of the dead dictator and was installing, in all positions of responsibility in the party, new associates upon whose loyalty he could depend.

Only a year after Stalin's funeral, articles in the Soviet press began to emphasize Khrushchev's role, which the writers had invented, as an early stalwart in the Bolshevik Revolution. He began to make important speeches, to travel widely in the Soviet Union to keep in close touch with the party membership, and finally to visit foreign capitals, at first in company with Bulganin and later by himself, to show himself to non-Communists as an envoy of peace and good will.

The Twentieth Communist Party Congress met in Moscow in February 1956. It soon became apparent that Khrushchev was winning control of the party. He gave the address that opened the congress. Like Stalin before him, he took it upon himself to refine Communist theory, even daring to question Lenin's views on imperialism and revolution. Although condescendingly allowing that Lenin's analysis of war and world revolution may have been correct in his time, Khrushchev insisted that war with capitalism was not inevitable; that the imperialist powers might so come to respect the growing strength of the socialist nations that they would avoid a military challenge; and even that socialism might triumph without revolution by winning control of parliamentary bodies and legislating socialism. Thus emerged the policy of "peaceful coexistence."

If a potential new dictator had appeared in the guise of Nikita Khrushchev, the bones of the dead one did not long rest in peace. In a long tirade Khrushchev attacked the old leader for his abuse of power, accusing him of a horrifying list of crimes against individuals, particularly members of the Communist party, and of a variety of crimes against the state and socialism. Stalin was capricious, "sickly suspicious," despotic, and worked brutal torture upon all who opposed him. He destroyed men, "morally and physically," and practiced mass arrests, deportations, repressions, and terror. All this most Soviet citizens and much of the world knew, but Khrushchev added some trimmings that shocked his audience. In 1936 Stalin had urged Yezhov to speed up the work of his secret police, who were four years behind in their work of mass repression and terror. He had probably ordered Kirov's murder. Stalin was to blame for the heavy losses in the opening weeks of the German invasion, for he had not mobilized Soviet industry, and there was a shortage of tanks, artillery, and planes. He had become hysterical upon receiving word of Russian reverses; but he had insisted on directing military strategy and tactics, "planning operations on a globe." Khrushchev was taking the calculated risk that Russians would be so relieved at the dethronement of the despot that they would forget that Stalin's toadies, including himself, had sanctioned all his evil deeds and carried out all his terrible orders.

The Twentieth Party Congress confirmed Khrushchev's dominant position in the party. A majority of the members of the new Presidium were Khrushchev's creatures, as were the new party secretaries in the constituent republics and the largest bloc of members of the Central Committee. The number from the army and secret police declined. When the congress adjourned Khrushchev was effectively in command. He had taken over control of the party apparatus and had filled all important posts with his own men. His supporters in the Central Committee outnumbered those of any other man or group. There were some party leaders who resented the threat that a new Stalin would surface, and they could still marshal the courage to challenge Khrushchev before he had won the last full measure of power.

In an effort to reduce the influence of the industrial manager class for whom Malenkov spoke, Khrushchev decentralized control of Soviet industry by stripping the production ministries in Moscow of their authority and assigning control over production to a hundred local government or regional councils, the *sovnarkhozy*. Because such regional councils would fall under local party influence, where his control was manifest, Khrushchev could extend domination by the party, and so by himself, over the entire economy.

In December 1956, after Khrushchev's leadership had suffered the damaging effects of rebellion in Poland and Hungary, and when falling Soviet production was threatening the Sixth Five-Year Plan, opponents in the Central Committee carried through a vote to return to economic centralization by concentrating industrial administration once more in the ministries in Moscow. Khrushchev managed to gain a reconsideration, and the Central Committee then reversed itself and supported the leader's plan to break up the industrial ministries, decentralize economic administration, and scatter the managerial experts throughout the USSR, where Khrushchev's local party officials could watch them. It had been a close call.

In June 1957, Khrushchev's opponents attempted to oust him again. He faced the challenge from prominent figures in the Communist party leadership: Malenkov, economic expert Kaganovich, Molotov, and Shepilov (Molotov's successor as foreign minister in 1956). This clique demanded Khrushchev's resignation as party secretary. After a week of violent charges and countercharges, Khrushchev won the day. He continued as party secretary, and those who had attacked him—Malenkov, Molotov, and Kaganovich—lost their governmental and party positions for forming an "anti-party group" to promote factionalism. Khrushchev's purge was a bloodless but thoroughly effective one. His main opponents were sent to obscure jobs or remote locations, such as Molotov's appointment as Soviet ambassador to Outer Mongolia.

The Communist party, led by Khrushchev and directed on the local level by professional politicians whom the party secretary had named, disposed of two power groups that might challenge it—the secret police, shorn of power with the execution of Beria, and the industrial management group, which had lost its political power with the fall of Malenkov. Another power group remained as a potential challenge to Khrushchev—the army group led by Marshal Zhukov. The marshal, always politically maladroit, savored his new sense of political importance, after suffering humiliation by Stalin and then being elevated to the Central Committee by Khrushchev. Always jealous of his position in the Red Army and pleased with the hero worship that some army men accorded him, Zhukov now sought to reduce party influence in the army and to professionalize the armed forces. Khrushchev showed no patience with this attempt to free any segment of Soviet society from Communist party control. He dismissed the marshal from his government position as minister of defense, and drove him out of the Central Committee. Bulganin's removal as premier in 1958 was anticlimactic, for he had never shown any strength. Khrushchev succeeded to the premiership.

The Twenty-first Party Congress met in 1959; Stalin had been dead less than six years. Now the party was Khrushchev's party, although certainly in different ways, as earlier it had been Stalin's. The chairman of the Council of Ministers, or premier, was also general secretary of the Communist party. Khrushchev held the top positions in both the government and the party. His supporters dominated the Presidium. He controlled the Central Committee, which met only occasionally and which ostensibly chose the Presidium to carry on the day-to-day affairs that concerned the party. He expanded the membership of the party to nearly ten million by 1963, a third again as many as those enrolled in Malenkov's time. His power as party secretary gave him control of the Secretariat and the lesser offices in the party throughout the land. His position now seemed beyond challenge.

There was no one in Russia to defy Khrushchev when the Twenty-second Party Congress convened in October 1961. The challenge now came from outside the Soviet Union. Khrushchev bitterly attacked the Albanian Communist leader Enver Hoxha for purging the Albanian party of Moscow sympathizers and proposed to exclude Albania from the Communist bloc. Chou En-lai, the leader of the Chinese Communist delegation, resented Khrushchev's public attack on another

Communist bloc member and walked out of the congress. Khrushchev's subsequent bitterness toward the "anti-party group" was an unmistakable reference to Mao Tse-tung, whose views toward Khrushchev's relations with the other Communist powers closely paralleled those of Molotov.

The new dictator was a far different type from the dead Stalin. Rotund in appearance and uncouth in manner—he banged a shoe and his fists on his desk to disrupt a Spanish delegate's speech, as well as interrupted British Prime Minister Macmillan's speech to the United Nations General Assembly—he sought to cultivate popularity among the common people of his own and other lands. He traveled widely in Russia, posing as a man of the people, who felt at home with them and who understood their problems. His visit to an Iowa farm was calculated to leave Americans with the same impression—of an ordinary man whose interests ran to improving crop yields and developing new types of farm animals. His interviews with the press in New York and in Paris revealed the shrewdness of the Russian peasant but little of the polish expected of the premier of a powerful state. His wife, children, and grandchildren accompanied him on visits abroad to complete the picture of the ordinary man. There was none of the aloofness in him that kept the suspicious and paranoid Stalin away from contact with his own people as well as foreigners. Khrushchev seemed willing and even anxious to journey to the ends of the earth, to a summit conference, to a UN meeting, or on some tour of good will.

When, after Stalin's death, the party leaders "discovered" the "Leninist principle" of collective leadership, they assailed the "cult of personality" that Stalin had fostered. He was attacked with mounting vigor and resentment at every party gathering. Then in 1961, the leaders held him to be unworthy to occupy the same tomb with Lenin. For days the tomb was closed to the public while Stalin's body was removed and buried in a row of graves behind Lenin's mausoleum. The name of Stalin was no longer on the tomb, and only that of Lenin remained. Cities quickly changed their names to reflect the indignation that the nation had suffered from the cult of personality. Stalingrad became Volgograd, Stalinabad became Dushambe, Stalino became Donetsk, Stalinsk became Novokuznetsk. To carry out the new theme the city of Molotov restored its ancient name of Perm, and Voroshilovgrad became once again Lugansk. There was no move, however, to change the names of Leningrad, Sverdlovsk, Gorky, Kaliningrad, or Kuibyshev. That came later.

In 1963 the party was still insisting on the principle of collective leadership, and a new fiction appeared to explain its meaning. It did not mean, apparently, the leadership of the Communist party by any small group of three or four, or even the eleven of the Presidium. It meant the leadership of the nation by the party itself. The party spoke through its congress, which spoke through the Central Committee, which spoke through the Presidium.

Such strained reasoning could not hide the fact that a new personality cult was growing up around Khrushchev—perhaps not quite as fawning and craven as that which centered on Stalin, but unmistakable nevertheless. There was constant acclaim for his role as an old Bolshevik in the early history of the party, during the expansion of the prewar years, and as an active leader in World War II. He presumed to speak for the party in refinements of Communist theory. The press praised his work in promoting education, stimulating scientific research, developing agriculture, and even in encouraging the arts. Khrushchev was becoming what he had derided Stalin for being—the object of adulation.

In October 1964, a Moscow meeting of the Presidium, which gathered while he was vacationing on the Black Sea, forced Khrushchev to return to the capital and resign his party and government offices. Many things contributed to his downfall. He had been spectacularly successful in many ways and had failed dismally in others. In spite of his personal brand of brinkmanship in foreign affairs—the Cuban missile crisis with the United States in 1962 and his determination to expel Communist China from the world Communist movement—he had so managed to improve relations with the West that the outbreak of World War III (which may have happened had Stalin lived) was unthinkable.

Khrushchev had signed a limited nuclear test ban treaty with the United States in 1963, yet during his years in power, Soviet nuclear and space science had made enormous strides. The life of the consumer had grown far more tolerable, even though it still lagged well behind that of the Western European and American consumer. Controls over artists and intellectuals had loosened, if they had not by any means fallen away. The Soviet citizen no longer needed to live in constant fear of the secret police, as in Stalin's time. However, every one of these accomplishments had not been the work of Khrushchev alone but of his colleagues in the Presidium. That body, and the new leaders who would replace Khrushchev, would continue many of these constructive policies after his resignation. The policies that they would not continue were those for which he had been personally responsible.

Khrushchev resigned in the face of charges that he threatened to seize autocratic power and had revived the cult of personality; that he had driven many foreign Communist parties and nations into opposition to Moscow; that he had moved toward an accommodation with West Germany and considered sacrificing East Germany; that he had muddled the economy with his "harebrained" schemes—the virgin lands, the emphasis on the growing of corn, the decentralization of the production ministries; that his intemperate boasts (his claims that Soviet production would soon exceed that of the world's industrial leaders and that the Soviet standard of living would, by 1970, rise above that of the United States) had made the nation a laughing stock; that he had blanketed the land with a network of his favorite supporters; that his decisions and behavior were often inconsistent (such as his sudden shifts in domestic policy); and that he was not a successful administrator. Surely those who moved to dethrone him could not have forgotten that he had driven from office men like Molotov, Malenkov, Bulganin, Kaganovich, and Zhukov; nor could they have been unaware that their own turn might come next.

Leonid Brezhnev, who owed his continued presence on the Presidium to Khrushchev, succeeded his former mentor as first secretary of the Communist party in mid-October 1964. The new party chief, born in 1906, was an experienced administrator who had served as the party head in several republics and had held a significant position in the Communist party's supervision of the Soviet military. By 1964, he held the important-sounding post of president of the USSR, although in reality this was largely a ceremonial post. He relinquished the office on becoming party chief. Alexei Kosygin, born in 1904, assumed the position as premier or chairman of the USSR Council of Ministers. An experienced economist and government official, he had held substantial responsibilities in both the Stalin and Khrushchev periods. His major task was the implementation and oversight of economic policies.

Initially, the two men operated as nominal equals as part of collective leadership, but Brezhnev soon assumed the dominant leadership role of the party and nation. As evidence of his prominence, the post of president again was conferred upon him in 1977 with the ouster of the incumbent. A Brezhnev cult steadily grew, as the nation and party accorded him many honors, medals, titles and awards based on his alleged achievements before, during and after the Second World War. Following his death in 1982, growing criticism of these often unwarranted and sometimes illegal honors eventually led to many of them being rescinded posthumously.

Brezhnev's prominence and authority developed relatively quickly for several reasons. He placed associates in influential positions in Moscow and throughout the country, and he brought some of his inner circle to Moscow to assist his leadership there. His outgoing and expansive personality contrasted sharply with Kosygin's capable skills but reserved manner. In foreign policy Brezhnev usually made the trips to foreign capitals while Premier Kosygin oversaw the government and economy at home. In summit meetings, as with the Americans in the early 1970s both in Moscow and Washington, Brezhnev clearly played the leading role among the Soviet leadership. After a decade in power, however, his deteriorating health and increasingly unsatisfactory performance as a national leader revealed serious problems and challenges for the future. By 1977, when he became president for the second time in addition to his role as party head, he had been in power for twelve years, longer than any previous leader except Stalin. In addition to Brezhnev, there were other government officials in the Soviet Union who were over seventy and in poor health.

Few personnel changes in the elite leadership were made in the initial period of the Brezhnev era. The Presidium (renamed Politburo in 1966) remained remarkably stable during the rest of the 1960s, although death, resignations, and retirements by the early seventies brought several new faces to the group. One newcomer in 1973 was Andrei Gromyko, foreign minister since 1957, who provided expert knowledge about the United States based on his oversight of diplomacy as well as on his previous experience as the Soviet Union's ambassador to the United States many years earlier. Another rising figure in 1973 was Yuri Andropov, KGB head since 1967, who was promoted from "candidate" (non-voting) to "voting-member" status that year. This placed him at the apex of the party's system of power and showed his prominence in the party as well as his role in using the KGB to suppress dissent within the Soviet Union.

At the Twenty-third Party Congress in 1966 the party restored the older Politburo name in place of the Presidium designation, and also changed the party leader's title from First Secretary to General Secretary. Following the Twenty-fifth Party Congress in 1976, Brezhnev's health deteriorated seriously although he continued as both party head and president until his death in November 1982. His team was in place and the patterns of Brezhnev's style continued despite his faltering leadership. As relatively younger members were added to the Politburo, two of Brezhnev's final Politburo appointments became significant in 1978 and 1979 when Mikhail Gorbachev and Eduard Shevardnadze were added to the body as candidate members. However, their presence was countered by Brezhnev's long-time associate and loyal supporter, Konstantin Chernenko, whom Brezhnev quickly raised from initial candidate status (1977) to full member status in 1978, an extremely rapid promotion. The same could be said for the addition in 1978 of Nikolai Tikhonov (born 1905) who succeeded Kosygin in October 1980 as chairman of the Council of Ministers upon the latter's resignation due to poor health. Kosygin died two months later.

The general orientation of the Brezhnev era was to establish and continue policies emphasizing stability, consistency, and predictability. The new leadership also partially restored the reputation of Stalin, commending him for ideological correctness and many successes. His wartime leadership was admired, and articles and photos reappeared in the Soviet press. His grave was even enhanced by the appearance of the dictator's bust.

Economic reforms, including those of an experimental nature established in the late Khrushchev period, disappeared by 1966. A return to the command system of economic planning soon became evident, reintroducing the similar approach of the Stalin era when centralized economic oversight and regulations with policy making in Moscow characterized the period of the earlier five-year plans. Virtually all coordination affecting the utilization of resources, transportation, industrial and agricultural output; production quota levels; as well as the distribution and pricing of goods and services came from Moscow. Gosplan, the national Economic Planning Committee created in the 1920s, dominated and shaped the nation's future economic growth. The concept of national economic planning remained as the essential mechanism for both present and future.

A review of the period generally shows that the Brezhnev economic approach emphasized extensive additions of capital to build more factories, develop new and expanded transportation systems, expand irrigation projects, intensify the use of chemical fertilizer to increase crops, and make substantial investments in developing nuclear power as an energy source. Expensive plans even hoped to reverse the flow of Siberian rivers away from their northward course as a means to open semi-arid regions to the south. Even nature could be tamed!

While impressive due to their sheer magnitude, and a source of national pride for many who interpreted these efforts as evidence of a booming economy and a progressive nation, many of these expensive projects and ambitious efforts failed for several reasons. Shoddy workmanship and poor planning hindered results. Many schemes were more for "show" than anything else. Long-term effects of the overuse of chemicals and irrigation systems wore out the land and created serious health hazards for large areas and populations, especially in Central Asia. Inadequate maintenance and lack of parts and fuel frequently meant that equipment lay idle. Serious bottlenecks in transportation systems grew to critical levels, and worker morale problems added to the difficulties. More fundamental than these critical issues, the underlying economic assumptions of a command economy were not questioned. By infusions of capital over many years, several decades of apparent growth usually camouflaged the problems and inadequacies. The great economic decline of the 1980s, and in fact the collapse of the Soviet economy in recent years, has its origins in the Brezhnev era.

By the end of the Brezhnev era in late 1982, the Soviet economy had established a pattern of steady, if uneven, growth. However, the rate of increase of gross national product declined significantly from the previous decade, and in meaningful terms the economy was nearly at a no-growth level. Substantial future growth could not be expected, although the Eleventh and Twelfth Five-Year Plans (1981–1985, 1986–1990) still called for advances in all sectors of the economy: agriculture, industry, manufacturing, and consumer goods. Gorbachev, when he came to power in 1985, characterized the last half of the Brezhnev period as the era of stagnation which had to be reversed if the nation were to continue as one of the important world powers. (It is true that the one sector of the Brezhnev economy receiving extensive funding, with sustained major production output and steady growth, was the defense industry.)

The Brezhnev years lacked the flamboyance that had characterized the Khrushchev regime. The leaders seemed dull, tired, and unimaginative, except for an occasional slight shift in foreign policy—an effort at *détente* with the West, for example. The general secretary built up a powerful claque in the party, as his mentor, Khrushchev, had taught him to do. Stalin's reputation was sympathetically resurrected (even his wartime leadership) and some repression returned, though with something less than the brutal terror that Stalin had imposed. Brezhnev denounced the American president's call for respect for human rights as interference in Soviet domestic affairs. The persecution of Jews and intellectual dissidents went on with or without President Carter's profession of indignation.

With these cautious modifications, Brezhnev continued the policies already clearly in evidence in Khrushchev's time. Except for an occasional reckless undertaking in foreign affairs, Khrushchev and Brezhnev managed to carry Russia, at home and abroad, through the difficult post-Stalin years adroitly if not with finesse.

Production Plans and Accomplishments

Stalin's death brought immediate repercussions in the economy, as in all phases of Soviet life. The Fifth Five-Year Plan—to run from 1951 to 1955—had reflected Russia's promise to supply arms to its North Korean allies. The hopes of the long-suffering Russian people for a better life and more consumer goods fell victim to Stalin's reckless foreign ventures.

Malenkov moved quickly to end the Korean war, thus permitting the economy to return to a peacetime basis. In a bold effort to win popular support, the new leadership promised a rapid improvement in the standard of living. As if to assure the people that this shift in production goals would not weaken the nation in the face of Western military strength, Malenkov announced that the USSR had exploded its first hydrogen bomb in 1953.

Consumers received assurances of relief on the morrow of the Korean armistice, but only in general terms. There was none of the usual playing with statistics—the vow that production figures would rise by a certain percentage or that output would reach some specific level. Malenkov insisted not only on greater quantity but on better quality of goods. He agreed that there should be at least a minimum assortment of essential goods available everywhere in the Soviet Union. More capital must go into housing, schools, and hospitals. The government would deliver a plentiful supply of potatoes and vegetables. Within a month of Malenkov's avowal to satisfy consumer needs, Khrushchev, in his first major public speech, made a shockingly frank admission that Soviet agricultural output was depressingly low.

Malenkov fell from power after admitting the error of his concentration on consumer industry to the detriment of investment in heavy industry, which, so ran the old refrain familiar since 1928, was the only way ultimately to increase consumer goods. The administration that Bulganin now headed announced an altered budget early in 1955, one that "corrected" Malenkov's "mistakes." It reallocated investment capital from consumer goods industries to heavy industry and transportation. It ordered a sharp rise in military spending and a reduction in expenditures on new housing.

The Twentieth Party Congress, as were all such occasions, was a time to announce new economic goals as well as to indicate prospects in all fields of endeavor. The new Five-Year Plan—the Sixth—was to run from 1956 to 1960. It reaffirmed the emphasis upon capital goods; at the same time it promised more consumer goods. It would increase real wages of the average worker by a third and the real income of collective farmers by 40 percent, shorten the workday, and slightly increase housing construction. By making even small concessions, Khrushchev was telling the Soviet consumer not to abandon hope in improving the standard of living, although the primary task ahead, as always, would be to concentrate upon capital goods.

Soon after the congress adjourned, the administration modified the strict labor regulations in effect since before World War II. To be absent from work or to leave one job for another was no longer a criminal act. There was no reduction in labor discipline, but a transfer of responsibility for its maintenance from the courts to industrial managers. Workers must still carry passports or labor books recording their work elsewhere, without which no manager could employ them. Punishment for shoddy work became the responsibility of the factory director rather than the judge and might take the form of fines or even the reduction of social security benefits.

Khrushchev sought in several ways to stimulate agricultural production. In

1958 he ordered the machine-tractor stations to sell all their farm equipment to the collective farms. The rental of such equipment had always been a heavy charge upon kolkhoz income; the move must lighten the cost of mechanization. The MTS, or machine-tractor stations, were replaced by RTS, or repair and technical service stations, designed to keep kolkhoz machinery in repair, provide spare parts and fuel, and render technical advice to the collective farms on the use of farm equipment. The kolkhoz no longer needed to make compulsory delivery of grain and other produce to the state, and won some freedom in planning its own operations.

Khrushchev dealt sternly with the old problem of forcing peasants to spend time in the collective fields. Farmers who performed less than the required time in communal work faced reduction in the size of their private plots. He discouraged individual ownership of livestock, one of the peasant's few consolations, and urged the expansion of collective herds.

Party control of agriculture had never been effective when it operated through the MTS, the apparatus of planning. Khrushchev sought better control by combining two or three collective farms into one supercollective, ostensibly to permit more economical use of land and capital but in reality to permit the assignment of a sufficient number of Communist party members to each kolkhoz to maintain close supervision of the peasants. The party could now watch farm managers and remove inefficient ones. Propaganda work would become more effective. Soviet agriculture's backwardness may have resulted in some small measure from the regime's inability to popularize its goals in this, the most unsocialized, segment of the economy. After the removal of Khrushchev, Party Secretary Brezhnev insisted that consolidation of farms had gone too far, that many were too large to be manageable.

The sovkhoz or state farm, with its wage earners, was the rural equivalent of the city factory. After Stalin's death there was a phenomenal increase in the number of state farms and in their volume of production. Many of the new units were to be found in the virgin lands east of the Caspian Sea, over a hundred million acres of which went under the plow after 1954. By 1960 over a fourth of agricultural production came from state farms, and nearly half from collective farms. The collective-farm system stands indicted, however, from the fact that as late as 1985 over a fourth of the nation's food supply came from the peasants' private plots, averaging less than an acre in size, which made up only 3 percent of the land under cultivation. Of course, the collective fields and the state farms produced major large-scale crops such as cotton, flax, sugar, grain, and fodder. When fodder yields fell, the nation was forced to slaughter livestock. In 1964, thirty million animals were killed for want of feed.

In 1958 the government abandoned the Sixth Five-Year Plan launched two years earlier. It had been far too optimistic, and the planners had not seriously considered whether the nation could meet their ambitious goals. Party spokesmen tacitly admitted that planned industrial expansion had not been carefully contemplated—new plants had been injudiciously located or so poorly arranged as to make the cost of their operation three times the average in a particular industry. Perhaps a decision midway in the plan to emphasize research in space exploration forced a curtailment of investment in more prosaic enterprises.

In January 1959, Khrushchev announced to the Twenty-first Party Congress a Seven-Year Plan to cover the years 1959–1965. If the recent five-year plan was overambitious, the Seven-Year Plan seemed conservative to Western experts. The plan anticipated an annual industrial growth rate of 8.6 percent, well within the range of Russian accomplishment over the postwar years, or a rise in industrial output by 1965 to a level 80 percent above that in 1958. The emphasis was still on capital goods, scheduled to grow by 88 percent, whereas growth in consumer goods and agricultural output would rise by 65 and 70 percent. Of Khrushchev's predictions in consumer-goods output and agricultural production, Western observers were much more skeptical than of his goals in industry. In none of the five-year plans did the nation meet agricultural and consumer-goods goals, although it was usual in earlier plans that goals in heavy industry were substantially exceeded.

Halfway through the Seven-Year Plan it became apparent that agricultural goals were beyond reach. The vagaries of weather and climate, which make it difficult to predict crop yields in Russia, could not entirely account for the failure to meet farm production goals. In a towering rage Khrushchev accused local farm officials of deceiving the government and cheating the state, and he accused Ukrainian peasants of stealing half of the 1960 wheat crop from collective fields. He repeated the accusation a year later, adding the charge that low yields were a consequence of poor management or organization and noting that thousands of tons of potatoes, tomatoes, sugar beets, and other crops ready for harvest were rotting ungathered in the fields. Without admitting as much, he was identifying the great weakness of agricultural planning—the failure to offer sufficient incentive to stimulate production and provide the essential resources for harvesting and transportation.

Khrushchev boasted that the USSR would approach the United States in industrial output by the end of the Seven-Year Plan. He promised that the Soviet Union would surpass the American standard of living by 1970. At the moment of his saying so, however, the Russian economy was producing half the amount of goods and services as was the American economy. He was ever a man to make foolish promises, and those who drove him from power ridiculed him for it.

Khrushchev could make his foolish promises and be disarmingly candid, however, in admitting that certain obstacles might prevent the realization of the picture he drew of the Russian economy by 1970 or even 1980. He proposed a one-year moratorium on the construction of new plants, confessing that there were already a hundred thousand projects in various stages of completion, many of them two or three years behind schedule. This was an amazing confession, to the Russians and to the world, of shortages of labor, materials, and investment capital. He was equally forthright in admitting a persistent lag in agriculture, which consumed nearly half—44 percent in 1970—of the labor force, compared to the 5 percent that the American farmer represented in the U.S. labor force.

For the amount of capital invested in it, Soviet agriculture was one of the least efficient in the world. (Yet some areas, such as the grain regions of the south and west, were quite productive.) Farm machinery wore out much faster than did similar machinery in the United States, perhaps because of the poor quality of its manufacture but also because of inefficient operation and undermaintenance. The government's insistence on group action in tasks that individuals could better perform, not only unduly increased production costs but frequently actually reduced yields. Anyone who saw brigades of workers on kolkhoz land in Eastern Europe must have been shocked at the inactivity and indifference, as well as at the contrast between the scrubby growth in the collective fields and the strong, healthy plants in the individual plots. These difficulties, compounded by insufficient storage facilities and poor transport systems, caused a large portion of production to spoil before reaching consumers. Estimates of losses of 30–40 percent were common.

The Eighth Five-Year Plan (1966 to 1970) proposed to increase production in heavy industry by 50 percent and agricultural output by 45 percent. The goals proved to be excessively optimistic. The Ninth Plan, covering the years 1971–1975, planned greater emphasis on consumer goods than on heavy industry for the first time in all the plans. However, severe crop failures in 1972 and again in 1974, with their shock-wave effect on industry, made the goals unattainable. Again the consumer bore the burden of natural catastrophe, overoptimistic planning (or promising), and massive expenditures on space technology and the military.

The Tenth Five-Year Plan (1976 to 1980) proposed to increase efficiency and output of agriculture to make the nation self-sufficient—it had bought wheat from the United States and elsewhere in 1971 and 1974 and signed an agreement to purchase at least six million metric tons of American wheat and corn each year for five years beginning in 1976. The new plan suggested expansion of industrial output by 35 percent. It got off to a promising start with a record harvest in 1976 and another in 1977, but a staff member of Gosplan advised that "paying too much attention to consumer goods could make Soviet citizens greedy, egotistical, and dependent, and doctrinally weak on communism." People needed a strengthening of the socialist way of life, he urged, rather than more consumer goods.

The nature and goals of the Soviet economy—whether it was socialist in the Marxist sense, as Russia's leaders insisted it was; whether it was Communist, as Russia's leaders insisted it was becoming; whether it was a form of state capitalism; and whether its aim was political expansion, social reform, or improvement in the standard of living—have been debated over the years. Perhaps from the moment of Lenin's seizure of power, and certainly from the beginning of the First Five-Year Plan—and most clearly of all since Khrushchev's assumption of control in the mid-1950s—the primary aim of the rulers of Russia was economic control and expansion of production. Soviet leaders relentlessly marshaled the full and massive power of the state behind the achievement of this aim.

Economic growth rates, which economists have learned to measure with precision, have caught the fancy of Soviet and Western political leaders. These rates, in an economy characterized by private enterprise, are subject to fluctuations caused by many factors that are difficult to predict—consumer demand, attitudes of investors, labor-management relations, international tensions, and many other imponderables. The annual percentage increase in the gross national product may be subject, in a private enterprise economy, to considerable fluctuation as a result of the presence or absence of government pressure or leadership or lack of it. However, in a controlled and planned economy, such as that of the Soviet Union, growth rates are essentially the result of state action. Consumer interests, investment patterns, labor relations, and even to some extent international tensions are controllable and therefore supposedly predictable. Unfortunately, production output frequently fails to meet the specified targets.

Rapid industrialization, which is perhaps the real revolution that has occurred in Russia, has been the obsession of the regime since Lenin's time. Stalin used the need for rapid industrialization, if Russia were to survive against the more industrially advanced West, as the justification for the extermination of millions of kulaks and other "saboteurs" and the emasculation of labor unions which Lenin had begun. With the possible exception of the few months of the Malenkov administration, the Communist regime never hesitated to liquidate or at least impose drastic control over any institution that stood in the way of rapid industrialization. If the church, the family, the labor union, the peasant homestead, the small business enterprise, the school, the press, or the arts resisted the progress of the economy, then the regime destroyed that institution or so altered it as to make it serve the economic course that the leaders of the state had charted.

Industrial modernization and increased output remain as goals today, but the serious deterioration of economic conditions in the later 1980s and early 1990s has focused attention on essential food production for the population. Industrial productivity has declined significantly in recent years, with further reductions expected in the future. Until the problems associated with the disintegration of the Soviet Union are addressed and the issues related to the emergence of a decentralized entrepreneurial system comprised of privately owned businesses are resolved, industrial productivity seems destined to decline further regardless of what government policies dictate. It is evident that the capitalist system was easier to destroy in the time of Lenin and Stalin than to resuscitate in the era of Gorbachev and Yeltsin. Khrushchev expressed his optimism about the future, however, when he vowed that Russia would catch up with the West. His discovery that "peaceful coexistence" was a "fundamental principle of Leninism" led the premier to insist that not only was war not inevitable, but that the competition between the Communist and the capitalist worlds should be an economic contest to see which could outproduce the other. He voiced complete confidence that the Russian system would prove itself superior to the American—"we will bury you" is the way he put it to an American audience—and so would win converts, not only among the new nations emerging from colonial backwardness but among the old nations where socialism might triumph as a result of a peaceful parliamentary victory of socialist forces.

Western observers concede that the growth rate was high from 1928 to about 1965. Students of the Russian economy find several causes for this. Tight control over the allocation of building materials permitted expansion in productive rather than in nonproductive buildings (for example, the decision to build factories rather than hospitals or homes). For years there was no real work force problem; instead there was a sufficiency of labor because of the willingness of women to work. The historic backwardness of the economy permitted the government to quicken the rate of technological progress by forcing the substitution of new and efficient methods of production for old, inefficient, wasteful methods. In addition, the decision of the planners to concentrate investment on capital goods, rather than on consumer goods and agriculture, contributed dramatically to a high rate of economic growth. From the fact that the Soviet Union was half modern industrial society and half rural land, it did not follow that its growth rate must remain low. Indeed, the very combination of the modern and the backward allowed room for and even contributed to an amazingly high growth rate.

By 1966 the growth rate had slowed considerably; by the late seventies it was falling into line with or even dropping below that of more mature and stable, less volatile, non-socialist or semisocialist economies. Soviet economists excused the declining growth rate by citing the costly drive to develop Siberia, expensive antipollution measures, and the effort to get "more quality and efficiency on the job." The Tenth Five-Year Plan anticipated a continued slowdown in growth rate, as had the Ninth.

If the nation were to face a labor shortage, it would not be unlikely that the demand for industrial workers might force a drastic reorganization of agriculture. Further mechanization of farming and perhaps a radical change in operational methods could release millions for city work; a considerable reduction of the shocking inefficiency and waste in Russian agriculture was imperative. That the nation's leaders would ever admit their inability to solve the farm problem, however, seemed unlikely. They had lived with it for two generations and were not much nearer a solution in the late seventies than they were in 1917.

The remarkable industrial accomplishments of the USSR made the Soviet experiment attractive and appealing to new states emerging from colonialism. The fact that Russia faced and solved the problem of rapid industrialization—so necessary to provide the high standard of living that the emerging nations were impatient to enjoy—made an imitation of the Soviet experience seem desirable. Moscow took full propaganda advantage of the situation. The force of the argument that Russia had shown the way to all backward countries grew with the economic foreign aid programs of the USSR, all of which received far better publicity than did the more liberal programs of the West. However, the sluggish growth in the 1970s and early 1980s was an object lesson to the Third World, and many of the emerging nations began to turn away from the heavily socialized economies of the Soviet model. By the 1990s, the trend was toward free enterprise and open markets.

The Soviet Consumer

The oratory of Soviet leaders to assemblies of the party faithful always contained proud boasts of what the Russian economy produced. The Russian consumer, however, always had to be content with promises of what the future would bring. Western observers often wondered how long the Russian people would be willing to postpone consumption and how long the Russian worker might be content to sacrifice without suffering a sense of frustration and disillusionment with the regime. Perhaps the patience of the Soviet consumer should be attributed to the remarkable effectiveness of the propaganda media that convinced the people that a brighter future was surely on the way and might soon come about if only the Western powers would relieve international tension and promote peace.

Stalin always scorned the interests of consumers, insisting that the Soviet Union must catch up with and surpass the West in heavy industry and so become invincible to "capitalist encirclement." There may have been some conviction after the leader's death that only the domineering and ruthless Stalin with his merciless use of the machinery of terror could be completely indifferent to the sacrifices of the people. Surely the new administration in 1953 could not ignore the possibility of unrest and even revolt—the resentment against the dictatorship had been momentarily apparent at the time of the German invasion of 1941. Indeed, Malenkov had made a strong bid for popular support, and at the same time a tacit plea to remain calm, by promising to shift production goals from the time-honored emphasis on heavy industry to consumer goods industries.

The new regime's failure to achieve fully the reduction of international tension seemed to dictate a return to the old policy of asking consumers to wait a little longer for the fulfillment of their dreams while, in the interest of keeping the nation invulnerable to attack, the economy produced capital goods—steel, coal, electricity, chemicals, machine tools—and armaments and space satellites. Khrushchev's attack on "consumerism" and "cotton dress economics" forced the resignation of Malenkov for neglecting Russia's industrial and military strength.

Malenkov's fall signaled the decision of the party leaders, and particularly of Khrushchev, to emphasize the output of capital goods. At the same time, however, the Twentieth Party Congress repeated the old promise to consumers of better things to come. Khrushchev insisted that it would be possible to emphasize both heavy and light industry, as well as agriculture. The party faithful in 1959 heard Khrushchev announce the new Seven-Year Plan. The emphasis on capital goods investment was as clear as ever, but the premier assured his audience that now there would be none of the earlier neglect of consumer needs. There would be, he insisted, an increase of 70 percent in agricultural output by 1970. The low yields per acre of land and per worker-hour of labor made this optimistic prediction naïve. Whereas the Russian agricultural worker was producing 40 percent more in 1957 than in 1928, the output of the American farm worker had increased four times over in the same period.

In the autumn of 1961 *Pravda* published a detailed list of production goals that predicted an output of consumer goods several times as high by 1980 as in 1960—twice as much footwear, sugar beets, meat, and potatoes; three times as much textiles, milk, and vegetables; four times as much eggs, pork, beef, and horsemeat; and ten times as much fruit and household appliances. In 1977 Gosplan abandoned the 1980 goals. Khrushchev also promised adequate housing for city dwellers by 1970—in 1961 there was slightly less living space available than in 1917. There were three times as many "millions of square meters of housing space" as before the revolution, but the population of the city had more than tripled. The government announced pompously in 1962 that it was in the process of abolishing all taxes. What it apparently had in mind was income taxes, always a light burden on Soviet taxpayers and hardly an important source of revenue. The same promise was repeated in 1976. However, there was no mention of abolition of excise or sales taxes, on which the government depended not only for much of its revenue but as a readily adjustable means of equating demand for consumer goods to available supply.

The standard of living in the USSR rose noticeably after Stalin's time. There was more to eat, even if the monotony of the diet might bore a Westerner. There was less shortage of clothing, although much of it was of shoddy quality. Most Russians walked or rode bicycles or public transportation; some automobiles were in private use, and there were a few more repair shops and service stations to care for those on the road. Television sets were common and the average city family had a TV set or at least a radio.

The Russian knew little of the Western standard of living, having little opportunity for comparison. Only a few thousand Russians traveled outside the Soviet Union each year, most of them on official business. Russian tourists who traveled in other Communist countries found little to envy. For years the controlled press, radio, and television carefully protected the Russian people from learning what the standard of living in the West really was and grossly exaggerated the extent of poverty, undernourishment, discrimination, and other ugly conditions. The Russian people compared the amenities they enjoyed at the present time with the shortages they previously suffered; they judged the society in which they lived, not by the standards of some foreign society, but by the standards they knew in the past. They felt little envy toward some far-off land of which they knew nothing and in whose reports, written by some capitalist, they placed little confidence. These perceptions dramatically changed in the seventies when more travel, wider television coverage, and greater knowledge made Soviet citizens acutely aware of how low their standard of living actually was. Western tourists who visited the Soviet Union saw a standard of living far beneath their own and one which seemed considerably inconvenient. Many, however, expressed surprise to find living conditions by no means as bad as they had expected to see.

The Thaw

By 1956 the physical conditions of life and the atmosphere in the Soviet Union differed markedly from life in Stalin's time. The considerable relaxation of tensions inside Russia, the reduction of controls upon Soviet citizens, and efforts to improve cultural relations with the capitalist world were aspects of the "Great Thaw." There was evidence of something like a thaw in the bureaucratic system when the release of millions from slave labor camps followed Stalin's death, and particularly when Beria's removal heralded a sharp reduction in the power of the secret police. There was a thaw in the economic field signaled by Malenkov's concern to increase production of consumer goods, a concern which Khrushchev would never feel himself sufficiently powerful to ignore or defy. The Thaw appeared quickly in international relations. There was a thaw constituting almost an about-face in the cultural field.

In Stalin's time, Soviet poets, dramatists, novelists, musicians, painters, architects, and sculptors had slavishly done Stalin's bidding—that the artist must devote his or her talent to the "goals of socialist society," to the fulfillment of the five-year plans. The artist must present forcefully and optimistically to the world at home and abroad the image of the "new Soviet man." There must be no catering to bourgeois tastes, no show of interest in the life and emotions of the individual, except as they reflected the development of that "new Soviet man" whose concern was not one's own petty self but one's society, "marching toward socialism." The heroes of the artists, who composed in such a straitjacket, were oil field workers, lathe operators, collective farm leaders, coal miners, shock brigades in field and factory, and of course, Stalin.

Beria's arrest heralded a popular manifestation by Soviet citizens of a feeling of liberation. Poets, dramatists, literary critics, and essayists came forward, one after another, to insist that art since the war had been sterile and that no one in or out of the USSR had read the literature of the postwar years. No one ever would read it, one poet dared to say, so long as its theme was "the same old dam, the same old steam shovel." Ilya Ehrenburg, one of the leading writers of the Stalin era, wrote a novel entitled *The Thaw*. "An author writes a book," he suddenly dared to say, "not because he knows how to write, nor because he is a member of the Union of Soviet Writers, nor just to earn a living, but because he has something to say." Even the government for a while encouraged artists to paint and compose and write of human beings, not of plans and production goals, of dams and steam shovels. For once the government was following, not leading or driving, at least in the cultural field.

Some artists enjoyed the comfortable lives they had led when there was no need to think or criticize. Many who had grown up under Stalin could not imagine a creative life free of censorship and dictation. A noble few, however, led the attack on the governmental authority that had so long shackled them. They demanded that artists no longer be required to write and paint and compose works whose themes had to deal with "socialist realism"—dams and steam shovels.

They demanded an end to control of art by the party and called for the creation of literary organizations free of official restraint. A few editors of literary journals found the dignity and strength to support the rebels. Within months the Kremlin chose to curb the rebellion. It dismissed the editors who had agreed with the rebels, insisting that the rebels had gone too far. Anarchy and irresponsibility could not be tolerated. Yet the party, which itself had embarked upon a program of post-Stalin reform in many aspects of Soviet life, could hardly insist on a return to the blind, stupid censorship of earlier days. For two years literary forces critical of the regime marked time.

Khrushchev's speech in 1956 denouncing Stalin encouraged the literary rebels once again to attack censorship and dictation to Soviet artists. If the leaders themselves were denouncing the old dictator, whom Russia's youth had grown up to regard as a god, then the editors of the journals could not deny the hatred of the dead past to the writers who used their columns. Criticism of the old regime, however, came dangerously close to criticism of the new, and yet such defiance managed to appear in print. The poet Yevgeny Yevtushenko dared to write, "Certainly there have been changes; but behind the speeches some murky game is being played. We talk and talk about things we did not mention yesterday. We say nothing about the things we did ourselves." His 1961 poem, "Babi Yar," criticized Soviet anti-semitism and the continued reliance on repressive Stalinist methods. In 1962, the poet visited Britain, and a New York firm published a volume of his poems. *Not by Bread Alone*, a novel by Vladimir Dudintsev, defended the individual standing against the shackles of a collective society. It was an unmerciful castigation of the privileged bureaucrats, the career managers and factory directors, the grafters and the time-servers in Soviet society. The censorship reluctantly passed the novel, and it became the center of heated discussion among intellectuals young and old.

The 1956 rebellion of Soviet artists fared no better than that of 1953. Dudintsev was bitterly attacked in the party press and was hounded until he had to deny his own attitudes. Yevtushenko refused to recant, and his enormous popularity sustained him in his continued defiance of the administration. However, the Polish and Hungarian uprisings so frightened Khrushchev that he lost all enthusiasm for emancipation of the arts. The party called for unity at a time of international crisis and urged Soviet artists to take their places along the firing line, using the weapons of their trade in defense of the homeland. Early in 1957 the government called upon Soviet writers, particularly those who had led the recent rebellion, to gather in Moscow and admit to their recent errors. Many came and recanted, but many leading writers stayed away or came and said nothing in what came to be known as "the deed of silence."

The rebellion of the artists inspired university students all over Russia. In one of the most striking demonstrations since tsarist days, the students prepared wall newspapers and circulated appeals calling for punishment of greed and corrupt officials and for an end to cultural censorship. Such defiance inspired similar activism among factory workers and even members of the armed forces. The mounting threat of resistance, not against the system but against those in positions of leadership and management, brought quick reaction by the government. The University of Moscow expelled scores of students, an action that brought to mind the days of the Romanovs, and the rest were warned that further demonstrations would bring further expulsions. The students fell sullenly into line, and there were no more outward manifestations of hostility to the regime.

In the spring of 1957, shortly after the "deed of silence," Khrushchev invited the writing colony to Moscow for a garden party. In the blunt language to which he often resorted, the party secretary told the writers thai he would use force if necessary to curb their defiance. The Communist party, he insisted, must maintain its supremacy over the arts as well as over every other aspect of society; the nation could not afford to see its plans sabotaged by its artists. The recent uprising in Hungary, he told a stunned audience, had been inspired by a group of writers who had become the tools of foreign powers; the revolt might have been avoided if the Hungarian government had shot a few writers. If such a situation ever developed in the USSR, Khrushchev warned, shaking his finger, "his hand would not tremble."

The party secretary's threat to shoot Russian writers did not bring an end to the defiance of a few. Ilya Ehrenburg published a tirade against tyranny in any form, scarcely veiling its pointedness by declaring that it was essay on Stendhal, the critic of tyrants and dictators. Boris Pasternak, the greatest of Soviet poets, submitted to the editorial board of a literary journal for serial publication the manuscript of his novel *Doctor Zhivago*. The editors led him to believe that the novel would be published. Shortly thereafter he gave a copy of the manuscript to an Italian publisher who agreed to bring out the novel in an Italian translation. The editors of the Russian journal changed their minds, but the Italian translation came out and an English language version appeared in 1958. Pasternak was chosen to receive the Nobel Prize for literature, and immediately the novel's publication became an international incident. The Soviet government chose to regard the Nobel award for a manuscript rejected by Soviet critics and party officials as a deliberate insult, and Pasternak suffered the most scurrilous abuse. Scorned as a traitor, and fearing exile or arrest, he refused the Nobel Prize.

The uproar produced in the West by the badgering of Pasternak apparently surprised Khrushchev, who had not read *Doctor Zhivago*. When he did read it, he commented that the Russian editors had been fools for not publishing it. Still his writings, even his poetry for which he was most famous in Russia, continued to be banned from publication during the remainder of his life. The prohibition extended nearly three decades after his death. Only in 1988 did excerpts of *Dr. Zhivago* appear in the Soviet Union's literary press.

An interesting aspect of the Cultural Thaw, during the periods when it existed, was the government's enthusiasm for the exchange of Soviet artists with other nations both inside and outside the Communist bloc. The United States and the USSR sent and received pianists, orchestras, jazz bands, musical comedy groups, television programs, circuses and sports teams. The performances were remarkably free of the political differences that divided the two nations, and audiences in both countries seemed willing to judge the performers on their skills and talents. Occasional embarrassments did occur, however, when talented Soviet musicians and others used the foreign travel opportunity to defect and seek a greater creative atmosphere than they could find at home.

The Dissidents

Khrushchev had relaxed controls over artists and intellectuals only momentarily during the Thaw, and then had tightened them again after the Polish and Hungarian uprisings. His successors chose to continue the curbs on artistic expression, and their decision to do so produced a wave of intellectual defiance that had its roots in the immediate post-Stalin years. A parade of writers, some of promise and others of modest talent, found publishers abroad for their indictments of the regime's censorship and dictatorship over artistic expression, the mockery of justice in Soviet courts, the bestiality of life in labor camps, the cruelty of police action, and the denial of human dignity and human rights contrary, in fact, to the Soviet constitution.

Treatment of intellectuals quickly showed the conservative posture of the new Brezhnev-Kosygin period. One notable case involved the arrest and trial of Andrei Sinyavsky and Yuri Daniel, who wrote jointly under the pseudonym of "Abram Tertz." Their books provided a satirical view of life under a vaguely identified authoritarian regime, and Soviet officials tried for several years to locate the mysterious writer who slandered the Communist system. Finally they were caught, and the trial in 1965 showed Soviet writers and the world how cultural efforts would be treated if they portrayed ideas outside the established limits of "socialist realism." The court sentenced both men to substantial prison terms, and the following years saw a crackdown on a variety of groups and individuals who came to be labeled by the courts and government as "dissidents" (or even as traitors to the Soviet Union) for their slanderous views.

Freedom of speech scarcely existed, so far as independent comment was concerned. Yet gradually there arose a small cadre determined to express their views even in the face of certain retaliation by the authorities. Starting in 1967, supporters of human rights issues gathered in public, if only for a few seconds' duration, standing together at the statue of Alexander Pushkin in Moscow on Soviet Constitution Day. Even this minimal act triggered a police response, but the effort continued for several years.

Andrei Sakharov, the dean of nuclear scientists and the man who developed the Russian hydrogen bomb, eventually became the most notable of the Soviet dissidents, especially after the appearance in the West in 1968 of his lengthy essay *Progress, Coexistence and Intellectual Freedom*. His thoughtful and critical analysis brought him into immediate and sharp conflict with the Soviet authorities. Despite their efforts, Sakharov organized the Human Rights Movement, or Democratic Movement, in 1970, appeared at the trials of other dissidents, wrote manifestos, met with Western journalists, and was a general nuisance to the authorities. Fired from his important work as a leading Soviet physicist, he was stripped of the many honors and titles he had earned for his scientific achievements. The government, party, press and public accused him of slander and even treason against the Soviet Union, but he continued with his efforts despite deteriorating health and the effects of public harassment. Finally, in January 1980, the authorities arrested Sakharov and banished him to Gorky, several hundred miles east of Moscow. This city was off limits to Westerners, and the only communication with Sakharov was what could be conveyed through his wife. Under virtual house arrest, he remained in Gorky for nearly seven years until Mikhail Gorbachev permitted him to return to Moscow in December 1986. There he continued his human rights efforts right up to his death in December 1989. His stature and dedication are a tribute to all those who suffered under the Brezhnev regime.

Many scientists, writers, musicians, historians, and others joined Sakharov in publishing, on hidden presses or by typewritten copies, accounts of government violations of rights guaranteed in the constitution and proclaimed in the United Nations Declaration of Human Rights to which the USSR had subscribed. Stories of police beatings and tortures were widely disseminated and published abroad. Party leaders felt growing frustration at the attack that came from its finest minds, an attack not aimed at toppling the government but, perhaps more embarrassing and irritating still, at forcing the administration to abide by its own laws and constitution.

The many controls on dissident activity led to the creation of a new form of sharing information. *Samizdat*, or illegal publishing of written materials, provided the communication links among dissidents. These periodic reports contained news of arrests, house searches, prison camp conditions and the health of dissidents, and the like. They also contained essays and articles commenting on cultural, political and social issues. The *Chronicle of Current Events* became the most famous samizdat in the 1970s, until its final suppression late in the decade with the arrest, trial and recantation of two of its editors. Severe punishments were imposed for those producing, transmitting, or possessing these illegal materials. The KGB, Committee of State Security, became one of the most energetic government agencies to locate and destroy samizdat publications. The KGB focused on eradicating human rights groups established after 1975 as a result of the signing of the human rights section contained in the European Security Conference Treaty.

If Sakharov continued through the seventies as the most renowned and persistent champion of human rights to remain in the USSR, even defying the regime through Western television interviews, the best-known Russian dissident outside the country—he was expelled in 1974—was author Alexander Solzhenitsyn. He had served as a Red Army officer in World War II but spent a postwar decade in labor camps for intemperate language about Stalin. A beneficiary of the post-Stalin amnesty, he published *One Day in the Life of Ivan Denisovich*, an account of prison-camp life. It passed the censor, but later works—*Cancer Ward*, *The First Circle*, *August 1914*, and *The Gulag Archipelago*, a history of the slave-labor system since the Communist revolution—all were published abroad. While living in the USSR and (after his deportation) in the West, Solzhenitsyn persisted in challenging the regime, which made the Soviet authorities even more determined to quiet this independent writer. Others, like former general Pyotr Grigorenko, championed the rights of ethnic groups repressed over many years. He was imprisoned several times and was committed to a psychiatric prison hospital where his health deteriorated as a result of poor treatment and the use of mind-affecting drugs.

In the atmosphere of *glasnost* (openness) in the later Gorbachev era, several of Solzhenitsyn's critiques of Russia's past, present and future finally appeared in the Soviet press in 1990 and 1991. His conservative and traditional views had not altered appreciably from his earlier views. While it is true that a spiritual revival has reappeared and continues to grow, many within and outside the nation find his views to be too reactionary and, therefore, unrealistic as a contribution to a future agenda.

Whether the fight for human rights has been undertaken by people inside Russia (both because of and in spite of government policy) or by Russians in exile and by non-Russians sympathetic to the cause of human dignity and freedom, the impact has been mixed. However, the tenacity of those who struggled for this noble cause has prompted legal and political reforms which have improved the quality of human rights. Many analysts of Soviet society regard a return to the Stalinist police state system as impossible. The end of the awesome power of the Communist party in the early nineties has removed one major obstacle to democratic growth, and the collapse of the Marxist ideological system, which scarcely anyone could have countenanced or predicted in the Khrushchev and Brezhnev eras, offers new opportunities as well as difficult challenges.

Strains in the Communist Camp

The Communist empire in Eastern Europe after 1945 grew for the most part out of the conquests of the Red Army. In the early postwar years the empire held together from fear of Stalin and his cronies who ruled at the nod of his head in East Germany, Poland, Romania, Bulgaria, Albania, and Czechoslovakia. The one defiant Communist nation was Yugoslavia, which had been freed from Nazi rule by its own partisan bands under Marshal Tito. When Tito refused to allow Stalin to dictate his country's trade and foreign policies, Yugoslavia suffered expulsion from the Cominform, the community of Communist nations and parties that came to life in 1947 to succeed the old Comintern that Stalin had disbanded during the war. The satellites were held tightly in the Russian orbit by Russian control of the local Communist parties and by Soviet garrisons stationed in nearly every country bound to Moscow. They followed the Moscow line in a propaganda campaign against what they referred to as "Anglo-American imperialism." Yet most effectively of all, the satellites were bound to Moscow by an integration of their economies with that of the USSR.

The Communist empire grew enormously in 1949 with the triumph of the

Chinese Communists over all of mainland China. Stalin welcomed the new member of the family, to whose birth he had contributed far less than he wanted the Chinese now to believe. That the new China might ultimately challenge Russia for the leadership of the Communist world, Stalin surely never imagined.

The drift of the postwar world into two armed camps, between which there was little room for neutrality, moved humanity with frightening speed toward nuclear holocaust. The United Nations managed to localize the war in Korea, which raged for nearly three years. A month after Stalin's death the warring factions agreed to an armistice. The new leaders in the Kremlin moved quickly to reduce international friction and to heal the differences in the Communist family. The bitter animosity toward Tito that had produced frequent border clashes between Yugoslavia and the satellites came dramatically to an end. Moscow and Belgrade signed a commercial agreement ending six years of Yugoslav isolation from the Communist trade area. Khrushchev and Bulganin went to Belgrade in 1955 to woo Tito in his own capital, loudly deploring the rift that had parted the "ancient bonds of friendship" between the two countries, blaming it all on Stalin and Beria.

To the blandishments of his Moscow visitors Tito only partly succumbed. He granted that there was broad agreement on major international issues and received a sizable loan from Moscow and promise of Russian assistance in developing nuclear energy plants. Not the least of Tito's qualities that appealed to Moscow was the leadership he had come to assume among neutrals. Refusing to ally either with Russia or the West, Tito argued eloquently for a truce between the two power blocs and proclaimed the interest of all peoples in the preservation of peace.

The "new course" adopted by Stalin's successors led to some relaxation of control over the satellites. The Soviet leaders dissolved the Cominform, in part as a gesture to Tito and in part to impress other neutralist leaders. There was a rehabilitation of party leaders in the "people's democracies" who had sympathized with Tito in his struggle for independence. Collectivization of agriculture slowed down all over Eastern Europe and there were promises of expanded consumer goods output. There was an end, at least temporarily, to the attack on the church in the satellites, and clerical leaders earlier imprisoned won release.

The attempt to blame Stalin for Moscow's harsh policy toward the satellites and for the estrangement of Yugoslavia produced threatening repercussions. Titoists imprisoned for their anti-Stalin stand returned to power in Poland and Hungary. They immediately called for an end to Russian domination of their domestic policies while promising every assurance that if allowed to remain in power they would support the USSR in foreign affairs.

Moscow's efforts to return Yugoslavia to the fold, by absolving Tito of the charge of heresy and admitting that there were "several roads to socialism," stirred unrest in the satellites. In June 1956, Polish workers rioted against long hours and low wages. As the strike spread, however, the ancient hatred of Pole for Russian, the bitter memory of Russian action in 1939 and again in 1944, and resentment against a decade of Communist rule, turned the demonstration

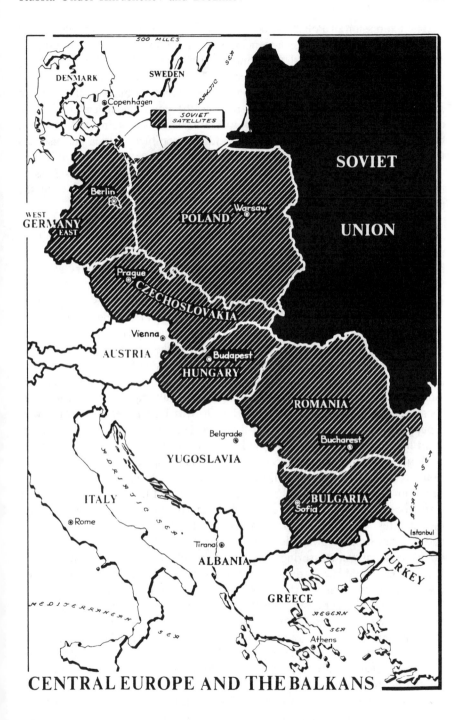

CENTRAL EUROPE AND THE BALKANS

into an expression of Polish nationalism that the de-Stalinization program and Tito's recent victory did much to inspire. That the discontent was widespread even the leaders of the Polish Communist party were ready to admit. The party removed the Stalinists from its Central Committee and freed from prison Wladyslaw Gomulka—a national Communist renowned for his sympathy for Tito and his hatred of Stalin—who now became the government leader. Several members of the Soviet Politburo flew to Warsaw to warn against such actions, but they backed down when the Polish leaders stood firm. Russia promised no further interference in Polish affairs, canceled Polish debts to the USSR, and transferred to the Warsaw government control over the movement of Russian troops whom the Polish leaders agreed should remain in Poland until the conclusion of peace with Germany.

The amazing success of the Poles in affirming their independence inspired discontent in Hungary. During the late summer of 1956 the Stalinists and the national Communists jousted for power in the Hungarian Communist party. The battle divided the party membership and then spread to the country at large. Students and workers rioted and fought the secret police, demanding Hungarian independence, freedom for non-Communist political parties, an end to collectivization, and the removal of all Russian troops from the country. Imré Nagy, the national Communist leader, adopted these goals as his own, and Moscow seemed willing once again to back down in the face of surging nationalist spirit. Then in November 1956, the Kremlin leaders decided to put down this growing threat that the Communist empire might fly apart. A force of two hundred thousand Russian troops and five thousand tanks brutally suppressed the Hungarian rising, deported thousands of Hungarians to Russia, and replaced Nagy with a puppet, Janos Kadar. A hundred thousand Hungarians fled to Austria, and from there some moved on to new homes in Western Europe and America.

Moscow thus took prompt measures to prevent the spread of nationalist revival to the rest of Eastern Europe. Poland and Hungary, however, had historically been more anti-Russian than had Czechoslovakia and Bulgaria. Perhaps in the difference between the Polish and Hungarian uprisings there was a lesson for the satellites. The Poles had never attempted the overthrow of communism and had insisted simply on practicing it in their own way. Poland only wanted to be independent while assuring Moscow of complete support in foreign affairs. Khrushchev could hardly do less than grant the Poles the right to follow their own road to communism, when a year earlier he had urged upon the Yugoslavs his conviction that there were "many roads to socialism." In Hungary, however, the uprising got completely out of hand. Students and members of the middle class clamored for the end of the Communist regime and would have welcomed Western intervention. The Hungarian revolt, then, failed because it went too far. The Polish revolt against Moscow's domination succeeded because of its limited goals.

The success of the Polish rising and the failure of the Hungarian rising in 1956 soon became apparent. Polish fear of a German military revival, coupled with Western refusal to regard the Oder-Neisse boundary of Poland as permanent, assured that Poland must remain within the Moscow orbit. The 1956 riots were soon forgotten. Gomulka stood forth as the symbol of Polish independence and nationalism. He even dared in 1960 to announce a five-year economic expansion plan that called for belt-tightening, heavy investment in capital goods, and little relief from the depressed standard of living. However, he was careful not to force collectivization upon the Polish peasant, and only a small percentage of farmland ever went into collectives.

The Hungarian revolt, on the other hand, got out of control and went beyond the point where there could be any compromise. Where there had been no Russian intervention in the Polish rising, Russian troops and tanks marched into Hungary, for Moscow could not stand idly by and permit the creation of a democratic government oriented toward the West. Not only did Russia savagely put down the uprising, but it installed a puppet regime completely subservient to Moscow, to be kept in power if necessary by Russian guns. Hungary succumbed to sovietization in a few years. By 1963 over nine-tenths of Hungarian farmland had been forced into collective farms, a rate more rapid than Stalin had imposed in the worst days of the First Five-Year Plan. The failure of the West to rescue Hungary in 1956 left the people with the despairing thought that there was no alternative to complete Soviet domination. Hungarians soon came to accept the regime that Russian guns had forced upon them.

The shift from Khrushchev to Brezhnev initially continued established relations within the Soviet empire in East Europe but Communist orthodoxy came under attack in the fact of economic problems and efforts to undertake meaningful

Soviet leaders on the stand of the Lenin mausoleum, November 7, 1975, celebrating the fifty-eighth anniversary of the October Revolution. Brezhnev and Kosygin are to the right of the microphones.

reforms. In 1968 Alexander Dubček, the new Communist leader of Czechoslovakia, embarked upon a daring effort to democratize society, reduce curbs on artists and intellectuals, and strengthen relations with the West. This threat of withdrawal from the Moscow orbit toward something approaching Yugoslav neutrality brought swift reprisal by Brezhnev. Soviet tanks rolled into Prague in August 1968 without warning, although serious violent conflict was avoided. Dubček was ousted, and the nation returned sullenly to its satellite role. Two years later wage and food-price riots in Poland forced the resignation of Gomulka, the anti-Stalinist who had led the party for fourteen years.

Internal unrest, particularly in the Ukraine, and threats of revolt among the East European allies provided all the excuse necessary—of course there were others—for the USSR to strive for military equality with the United States and its allies. Since Brezhnev and American presidents agreed that nuclear war would destroy both nations, the possibility that the West might assist democratic or secessionist moves in the satellites grew steadily more remote. Of the Red Army troops in service in 1973, two-thirds were stationed in Eastern Europe, most of them in the USSR, but available for swift action anywhere behind the Iron Curtain. The Brezhnev Doctrine, justifying military intervention as in Czechoslovakia in 1968, made clear that the Soviet Union would not countenance any threat, internal or external, to itself or any of its satellites. The Soviet empire, for the time being, seemed secure.

Soviet efforts to stabilize conditions in East Europe to its satisfaction were again seriously tested in Poland. In 1980 labor unrest and economic problems led to further changes in the party and government, and the authorities confirmed the right of a newly created labor union (Solidarity) to exist. Its success in mobilizing large segments of the population, not just the workers, raised the specter of a national revolt to overthrow the established regime and ideology. Polish leaders finally reacted in December 1981 by imposing martial law and banning the Solidarity organization. Reform leaders were arrested or went into hiding.

The Brezhnev regime supported the tough line of the Polish party and Communist government and achieved its goal of restoring comparative calm without the infusion of Soviet armed forces. However, it was widely assumed that if the local authorities had been unsuccessful in restoring order, Soviet forces would have undertaken the same form of intervention as they had in Hungary in 1956 and Czechoslovakia in 1968. Thus, the Polish case was an indirect application of the Brezhnev Doctrine. For the time being, for most of the decade, Poland remained quiet. Nevertheless, once martial law was lifted in 1989, Solidarity and the reform movement resumed its challenge to the status quo.

Communism in Asia

The most remarkable development after World War II was the rise to a position of influence by the Chinese Communist party. The expulsion of Chiang Kai-shek's

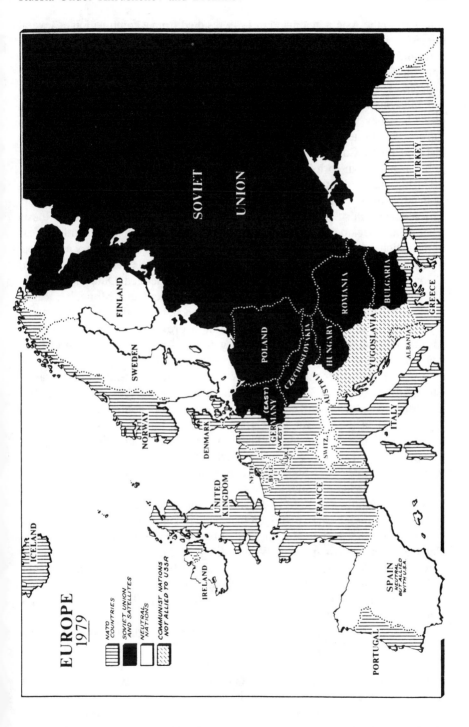

EUROPE
1979

NATO COUNTRIES

SOVIET UNION AND SATELLITES

NEUTRAL NATIONS

COMMUNIST NATIONS NOT ALLIED TO USSR

ICELAND

IRELAND

UNITED KINGDOM

NORWAY

SWEDEN

FINLAND

DENMARK

NETH.

BELG.

FRANCE

SPAIN
NEUTRAL BUT ALLIED WITH U.S.A.

PORTUGAL

SOVIET UNION

(EAST) GERMANY

(WEST) GERMANY

POLAND

CZECHOSLOVAKIA

AUSTRIA

SWITZ.

HUNGARY

ROMANIA

YUGOSLAVIA

BULGARIA

ALBANIA

ITALY

GREECE

TURKEY

forces from the Asiatic mainland in 1949 resulted from a combination of several domestic circumstances which included: corruption among Chiang's supporters; their indifference to the nation's welfare; and the conviction among Chinese that only the Communists would undertake overdue land reform and end graft in high places. Western powers were not paying close attention to the political activity in China but were preoccupied with returning peace to Europe as quickly as possible. They were uneasy about Russian aggression in Central and Eastern Europe. In addition, there was a naïve assumption among democratic statesmen that the Chinese Communists were only agrarian reformers who should join other political parties in forming a broadly representative government for China.

During Stalin's lifetime Communist China was too weak to threaten Russia's leadership of the Communist world. The treatment that the Chinese leaders suffered at Stalin's hands, however, may have embittered relations with Russia when China became sufficiently powerful to express its defiance without fear of retaliation. Mao Tse-tung received from Stalin precious little military equipment with which to carry on his war with Japan. With Japan's defeat Stalin recognized Chiang as the lawful ruler of China and acknowledged Outer Mongolia's independence. The Chinese Communists would not get Outer Mongolia; Russia wanted it. Then Stalin proceeded to strip Manchuria of the modern industry developed by Japan and making the northern province the most industrially advanced region in China, in callous disregard for his Chinese Communist friends who would need the factories to modernize the economy when they won the civil war. Russia later turned Manchuria over to Mao Tse-tung rather than to Chiang, to be sure, but Stalin regarded Manchuria as another satellite area like Eastern Europe to be milked to support the Russian economy.

Not until Chiang's defeat was certain did Stalin shift his full confidence and support to Mao. He advanced a $300 million loan to China in 1950, an insultingly small amount. Poland, with a twentieth of China's population, received substantially more. Then Stalin forced the Chinese Communists into the Korean War, which he had done so much to bring about, and then merely loaned China the weapons with which to fight the war and for which he expected repayment. The proud Chinese leaders, who felt they had won their own civil war with little help from Russia, had to hide their resentment for the moment, so weak was China after the exhausting war. With Stalin gone, his successors sought to tone down the ill will that he had created. A year later Khrushchev, Premier Bulganin, and long-time foreign trade specialist Mikoyan journeyed to Beijing to pay their respects to Mao. To sweeten their bid for his friendship, they agreed to increase economic assistance to China.

During the first short years of their rule in China, the Communists made enormous economic and political strides. By 1957 the nation had completed its First Five-Year Plan, which had seen the output of coal and cement double, that of iron and steel triple, and the production of electric power increase several times over. Overall figures were modest, but for a nation always bordering on starvation, with almost no industry and few technicians, and which almost without interruption since 1910 had endured revolution, dictatorship, warlordism, banditry, graft, plague, civil war, and invasion, the progress was tremendous. Much of China's economic and military strength was the product of Russian aid in equipment and technical advice. Indeed, strong Russian backing allowed the Chinese Communists freedom from foreign interference in establishing the new regime.

Although the economic and military strength of Communist China made remarkable gains, there was much evidence of strain in the economy. Soon there were such shortages that the government had to import grain. The goal for steel output for 1958 was twice that of the previous year, and the determination of the leaders to meet the goal led to the assignment of one hundred million Chinese to the production of iron and steel. Soon the leaders, dizzy with success, were talking about the early achievement of communism, hinting that the millennium would arrive in China long before it came to the Soviet Union. Such vain talk was greeted with derision in Moscow. In 1959 Khrushchev denounced the dreamers who tried to create communism overnight. After all, the struggle to achieve it in Russia had gone on for more than forty years, and the end was not yet in sight. The rift between Communist China and the Soviet Union widened from that moment forward. Mao showed little patience with the Russian point of view that war with the capitalist world was not inevitable. Russian talk of "coexistence" and "peaceful competition" met with a cool reception in Beijing.

The largest international congress of Communists ever assembled gathered in Moscow in 1960. It immediately became clear that, among the Communist parties of eighty-seven nations, different points of view were distinguishable. Many spurned Khrushchev's view that capitalism had changed, that peaceful coexistence was possible, that Leninist doctrine on the inevitability of war was out of date and required revision. The Soviet Union and its supporters among other Communists subscribed to Khrushchev's view that nuclear war would destroy civilization. The Russian leader argued that armed revolution must not be a reckless recourse, lest it precipitate world war. There must be negotiation of differences between the Communist and capitalist worlds, not only simply to avoid war but because as time passes communism will grow strong while capitalism grows weak. Capitalism ultimately must crumble away and communism triumph without the need to risk world destruction in nuclear holocaust.

Prior to 1961, twenty thousand Russian specialists—industrial managers, engineers, economists, statisticians, and key factory workers of various types— assisted the Chinese Communist regime to build bridges, dams, and factories and to train the Chinese workers who would operate the factories. Moscow took half of China's exports, which provided the foreign exchange with which to buy raw materials and to pay for technical assistance. After 1956, there were no new Soviet credits to the Chinese Communists and it became increasingly clear that further industrial expansion in China must take place without Russian support or encouragement. Before the end of 1961 all Russian economic aid to China came to an end.

Despite protestations in both Moscow and Beijing denying any real estrangement between the two, it was obvious by 1963 that the much vaunted unity of the

Communist world had broken down. China regarded the Soviet Union as a "have" nation, satisfied with the status quo and entirely too reluctant to advance the cause of communism through revolutionary or military action that might endanger the economic progress it had made. Russia, on the other hand, regarded China as entirely too prone to precipitate action that would destroy civilization. Indeed, Chinese Communist leaders bluntly said that a nuclear war would destroy capitalism, and perhaps many Chinese, but that at least three hundred million Chinese would survive it.

While the People's Republic of China lagged far behind other nuclear powers, it managed to develop a small arsenal as a scientific base for expansion of its hydrogen bomb potential. The successful detonation of a nuclear weapon in October 1964, at the exact time of Khrushchev's dismissal in Moscow, heightened the Soviet realization of the rising power of its southern neighbor. Further nuclear research, culminating in a Chinese hydrogen bomb, showed how crucial the China issue had become for Asia and for China's relations with other nations. The nation's most promising counterpoise to the threat of Soviet aggression, however, was its prospect of an alliance with the United States. Presidents Nixon, Ford, and Carter, regarding the Russian danger as the immediate one, moved deliberately if cautiously toward improved relations with the Chinese Communists.

Tensions between Moscow and Beijing intensified during the decade of the sixties, including occasional skirmishing on the Ussuri River frontier line in 1969. The two superpowers also disagreed on the objectives and support of the Communist efforts in Southeast Asia during the Vietnam War, although each gave some assistance to North Vietnam. Both the Soviet Union and China kept large military forces on or near their joint frontier, and reductions were not made until the latter part of the Gorbachev era. Another factor complicating Moscow's relations in the region came from the United States, which sought a rapprochement with Beijing. The official state visit of President Nixon to China in 1972 began a period of improved United States-China relations, and the two nations achieved full diplomatic recognition by 1979.

The most disruptive and costly foreign policy campaign in the Soviet Union's relations with Asia came in Afghanistan. This remote region, adjacent to the Moslem area of Soviet Central Asia, came under Communist control in the 1970s, but competition between Marxist factions soon led to further internal violence in the struggle for leadership. Policies of the new Taraki regime alienated many throughout the nation, and Amin, another Communist, seized power in September 1979. While the Soviet authorities initially favored Taraki, they shifted to Amin's side in the internal dispute. However, as domestic instability grew and Amin appeared to act too independently of Moscow's wishes, Soviet military forces invaded Afghanistan in December 1979, overthrew Amin by murdering him, and established a new regime under Babrak Karmal. Thus began what developed into a decade of Soviet intervention in Central Asia.

It later became known that the decision to send Soviet military forces in December and escalate the domestic confusion in Afghanistan was reached by only a few Soviet leaders. Several junior members of the Politburo at the time, specifically Gorbachev and Shevardnadze, years later revealed they were neither consulted nor involved in the matter. The goal of the invasion was victory over the anti-Communist rebels, the mujahedin. Soviet firepower, both on the ground and in the air, decimated great regions of the countryside, and massive numbers of refugees fled across the frontier to Pakistan for safety. American aid to the rebels counteracted Soviet aid for Karmal, and the war gradually settled into a war of attrition to see which side would eventually wear down and withdraw or surrender.

Soviet casualties were not reported in the Soviet press during the war which lasted until forces withdrew in 1989. Figures finally issued in 1989 reported that approximately sixteen thousand Soviet military personnel died in the Afghan War, thirty-seven thousand were wounded, and over three hundred were captured as prisoners of war. While the Soviet press during the war regularly referred to the USSR's participation as an instance of fraternal assistance to the government in Kabul, negative information gradually became available. Troops from other republics soon replaced Soviet Moslem troops due to their poor fighting ability and to possible complications affecting in the Central Asian Moslem republics. In addition, Moscow felt that regional Islamic fundamentalism and disillusionment with Moscow might lead to an anti-Communist religious crusade or moves toward independence from the Soviet Union. By the time of Brezhnev's death, the war had turned into a stalemate with no likelihood of victory for either side. The Soviet Union and its proxy government in Kabul never succeeded in suppressing the anti-Communist and anti-Soviet mujahedin, despite casualties. What was intended as a short-term intervention developed into a decade-long impasse, and only later did the Soviet government undertake serious efforts to terminate what came to be known as the "Soviet Vietnam."

Neighboring Iran also became a complication for Soviet foreign policy by the late 1970s. That nation, contiguous to both the USSR and Afghanistan, became embroiled in a domestic crisis by the later 1970s over the Shah's leadership and his policies of Westernization. His pro-West and anti-Communist stance also influenced Moscow to follow a cool policy toward its southern neighbor. In 1979, however, dramatic events transpired to provide new challenges and opportunities. The Shah left the country, never to return, and was replaced by the Ayatollah Khomeini, an influential Moslem cleric. The nation embarked on an anti-Western and pro-traditional campaign which culminated in the seizure by the end of the year of the United States embassy in the capital and its personnel as hostages. That issue between the Iranians and Americans was not resolved until early 1981.

Soviet opportunities in Iran seemed to improve as a result of Iranian-American tensions, and new relations were forged between the two governments. Economic ties were expanded, including the opening of an oil pipeline from Iran into the southern USSR. However, the rise of Moslem fundamentalism and the banning of the Iranian Communist party (the Tudeh) showed that the future would not always be a smooth one. During the eighties, relations between the two states saw a nominal improvement, but without major breakthroughs. One further complication affecting Soviet policy in the region was the outbreak of the Iran-

Iraq war, in which Moscow showed its fundamental commitment and support for Iraq.

Relations with Other World Regions

It became apparent soon after Stalin's death that the new leaders were intent upon easing the international tension that had mounted since the end of World War II. There was an armistice in Korea and a noticeable softening in the tone of Russia's anti-American propaganda. The Soviet delegation to the United Nations suddenly seemed less intractable than before.

Early in 1955 Stalin's foreign policy came under review and, in an effort to overcome the rigidity that it had imposed and to recover some maneuverability in foreign affairs, there was a quick reversal of positions to which Stalin had stubbornly clung. Russia ended its ten-year military occupation of Austria and guaranteed Austrian neutrality. The Soviet-held naval base in Finland was restored to the Finns. Moscow formally recognized the Federal Republic of Germany (West Germany) and gave up all claims to Turkish territory.

The prospects for world peace were better in early 1956 than at any time since Hitler's rise to power. There were many potential danger spots, but the hostile camps seemed more determined than at any time since 1945 not to be drawn into a world catastrophe. The gentler treatment of the satellites and the genial dealings with the non-Communist world that the Kremlin leaders had practiced after Stalin's death won many in Western Europe to the view that defense alliances and costly armaments were no longer necessary.

Khrushchev traveled to Yugoslavia to see Tito and spoke of "many roads to socialism." This affirmation for Moscow's apparent flexibility with its Communist neighbors heartened many, both in Communist societies and in the West. At the Twentieth Party Congress in February 1956, Khrushchev and other speakers appeared to advocate a more peaceful approach toward its international rivals. Khrushchev spoke of "peaceful coexistence" with other regions and nations, referring mainly to the United States and NATO in the West. He rejected nuclear war as a foreign and military policy option, in the higher cause of world peace and morality.

Then suddenly the situation radically changed. The ruthlessness with which Russia put down the Hungarian rising removed all possibility that the Western alliance might soon dissolve. The United States and its European allies were more firmly of one mind toward Russia than at any time since the Korean War.

By 1957 Khrushchev had triumphed over his rivals and was firmly in control of the administration. His position was unquestionably stronger than that of any man since Stalin. His triumph meant that in international relations, and particularly in dealing with the United States and its allies, Russia would be reasonable or intractable, predictable or uncertain, according to Khrushchev's will. He was well aware of what the people were thinking and of how far to go in the pursuit of any course. The leader was not, for example, able to ignore the interests of consumers, and the problem of adequately feeding the Russian people was a persistent concern. That Khrushchev could not make foreign policy decisions without reference to the wishes and interests of the other Communist states became abundantly clear, most especially when China manifested the ability to challenge Russia for the leadership of the Communist world. Furthermore, there had developed something like a world public opinion, of whose existence Soviet leaders were keenly aware, and indeed whose favor they actively courted.

In October 1957, Soviet scientists launched a space satellite called *Sputnik*; a month later they launched another. Aside from the scientific importance of the feat, the achievement was a great propaganda triumph. In Moscow there was a new air of confidence in the conduct of foreign affairs. The Kremlin could boast of winning the race to penetrate outer space. It must follow that Russia led the United States in science and implicitly in military strength.

In 1958 the Soviet premier precipitated an international crisis when he called for the evacuation of West Berlin by American, British, and French forces. Tension mounted with the approach of Khrushchev's deadline for the withdrawal of Western troops. A scheduled summit conference of American, Russian, British, and French leaders met in Paris in May 1960, primarily to deal with the German issue. French President DeGaulle hosted President Eisenhower, Prime Minister Macmillan, and the Soviet delegation headed by Khrushchev, but the summit broke up in acrimony and disarray over the U-2 spy plane crisis. This American high-altitude reconnaissance plane on a photographic espionage mission over the Soviet Union was shot down near Sverdlovsk, twelve hundred miles inside Russia. Khrushchev let the shocked world know that the plane's photographic equipment was intact, and that the captured pilot had admitted the espionage nature of his mission. President Eisenhower accepted blame for the affair and admitted that such flights had been going on for some time. Khrushchev wrung every bit of propaganda value out of the incident; he had known of the U-2 flights for some time. In Paris, the Soviet premier heaped insults upon Eisenhower and demanded an apology. The president refused to apologize, but did announce the suspension of reconnaissance flights over Russia.

In 1960 Khrushchev attended the meeting of the United Nations General Assembly, struck a pose as a true believer in Soviet-American friendship, and spoke to the assembly as the advocate of complete disarmament, an end to colonialism, and the dawn of peace, good will, and understanding. Then he demanded a reorganization of the UN Secretariat, proposing the *troika* principle— a three-man committee, one a Communist, one a non-Communist, and the third a neutral, with the right of any one to veto or prevent action by the secretariat. Unless such a reorganization came about, Khrushchev warned, Russia might withdraw from the United Nations, a candid admission that the Communists could no longer control it or even keep it from pursuing a course detrimental to their interests.

Khrushchev's continued threat in 1961 to settle the Berlin problem unilaterally by signing an agreement with East Germany posed a serious challenge to the vital question of allied access to Berlin through East German territory. His statements produced a feeling of desperation among Germans living under Communist rule. The rate of escapes into West Berlin rose sharply until the number reached three thousand a day. Faced with a critical loss of manpower, particularly of educated youth and skilled technicians—four million people had fled Communist Germany since 1945—the East German government, in August 1961, sealed off the border between East and West Berlin, first with troops and tanks, then with barbed wire barriers, and finally with a wall of cement blocks nearly thirty miles in length. At a moment of crisis, Russian and American tanks advanced toward each other and halted just short of the line separating East and West Berlin, then withdrew after a test of nerves. The world wondered how often the Soviet and the West could risk moments of extreme tension, bringing with them the danger that accident or miscalculation might touch off a nuclear war. When a Western diplomat was asked at the end of 1961 what was the most important achievement of the past year, he replied, "We survived."

What the Moscow press referred to as "war hysteria" in the United States may have alarmed the men in the Kremlin that war might well result from sustained Communist pressure on the West. The heightened armaments race imposed a great strain on the Soviet economy, and made more remote than ever the increase in consumer goods for which the Russians had been growing increasingly impatient. Muscovites fearful of war had rushed to the markets to store up food, thus adding to the shortages and irritation. Whatever the reason, Khrushchev showed signs of undertaking another "peace offensive." Asked about the unresolved question of Berlin sovereignty and the Big Four presence in the former German capital, Khrushchev answered, "It is a difficult question. It is not good for the time being to press one another." There was no doubt that the Kremlin had softened momentarily when Khrushchev sent birthday greetings to the pope!

Meanwhile, desperate attempts to escape over and under the Wall into West Berlin—only a few managed each day to break free—produced reckless shooting at refugees by East German police. The Wall, with all the sentiment West Germans and Western politicians and newsmen heaped upon it and the resentment that East Germans felt towards it, long remained the spot in the world where a flare of tempers might most easily precipitate a general war.

Khrushchev's clandestine build-up of missile bases in Cuba capable of launching nuclear attacks on American and Latin American cities was suddenly interrupted in late 1962 when President Kennedy threw a naval blockade around the island and proposed to turn back any ships carrying offensive weapons to Cuba. For a week the world waited for the clash between the giants that would precipitate nuclear desolation. Then saner judgment prevailed when Premier Khrushchev volunteered to dismantle the missile bases and withdraw the weapons that threatened the Western Hemisphere. President Kennedy accepted the Russian gesture as decisive in bringing the world back from the brink of disaster.

Shifts in Kremlin policy after Stalin's demise in 1953 seemed to be no more than tactical changes. Russia's goals—to isolate its most powerful enemy, the United States, and ultimately to make the world over in the Soviet image—

remained unaltered. To reach these goals, Soviet leaders developed a bewildering array of techniques. They exploited trade and economic assistance to win friends and to harness the economies of other states to the development of the Soviet economy: the European satellites were to link up with the USSR in a powerful economic bloc, permitting a division of labor and the integration of economic plans for the next twenty years. Communist Germany, possessing one of the largest industrial plants in Eastern Europe, was key to the program. Hence it was important to tie East Germany firmly to the Moscow orbit and halt the drain of its work force through Berlin into the West. Soviet leaders moved toward the realization of their ultimate goals by promoting revolts in colonial areas and by supporting subversion in older lands. They spent billions to achieve a formidable military posture that would encourage friends and frighten enemies. They pursued a diplomacy of alternating threats with conciliatory gestures, a diplomacy calculated to pit enemies against each other and confuse neutrals. Finally, the Soviet leaders poured forth an unending stream of propaganda aimed at convincing the world that the future—a future of hope and peace and plenty—belonged to the Communists and that to oppose communism and support capitalism was to work for a future of despair and war and famine. Suslov, a member of the Presidium, admitted all this when he told a meeting of social scientists in Moscow in 1962 that there would never be any peaceful coexistence with Western capitalists. The problem for Soviet leadership, he explained, was to avoid a general war, while pursuing the goal of winning the world to communism. In terms of tactics, he continued, this suggested an unceasing attack on Western positions through diplomatic pressure, propaganda, economic competition, political penetration, and subversion.

This complex of techniques on which the Soviet leaders relied to achieve their ultimate goals made international relations an extremely complicated game for Russia's opponents to play. Single issues between the USSR and the West might prove negotiable. Tension arising from one irritation might subside. Nevertheless, the basic issue that produced the tensions, irritations, and disagreements—the uncompromising hostility between the Soviet Union and the United States—ran too deep to solve in a few short years. If there was ever to be a solution, it would take the hard work of the West's most skillful, devoted, and patient statesmen, or it would take a threat to Russia's leadership of the Communist world. By 1969 the threat had materialized. Communist China had won the support of several Communist nations in its challenge for the leadership of the Marxist world. The Soviet Union found itself on the defensive in its own bailiwick for the first time since it had brought the Communist world into existence. Its position became even more insecure when détente deteriorated and a Sino-American accord loomed as at least possible. Brezhnev's relations with the United States also were adversely affected by intensified Soviet economic activity, ideological confrontation, and military support in the Western Hemisphere. The Soviet foothold in the Caribbean, in Castro's Cuba, continued unchanged from its Khrushchev era commitment, but now support was also extended into several other regions, notably Chile and Central America.

The election of Salvador Allende as president of Chile in 1970 brought a Marxist to power through the democratic process. Although United States-Soviet relations seemed to have improved, Allende's election and his domestic economic policies created opposition both within Chile and from the United States. The increasingly confrontational atmosphere finally resulted in the forcible overthrow by Chilean military of the Allende government in 1973—a coup d'état—and in the violent death of the president. The new military government of Chile reduced the Soviet connection and resumed closer relations with Washington.

Later in the decade, a rebellion in Nicaragua against the long-standing Somoza regime had support from a wide variety of opponents. This revolution in 1979 succeeded in ousting the old authoritarian government. It was replaced by a coalition of democratic parties, but the Sandinista movement, Marxist in outlook, soon dominated the post-Somoza regime and the Soviet Union gave its strong support to the new government. Anti-Sandinista forces in Nicaragua resisted the Marxist regime, and the United States gave extensive aid and support to these *contras*. By the early eighties, as the Brezhnev era was coming to an end, the Soviet Union and the United States seriously and doggedly competed for victory in this Central American region. This situation continued beyond 1982, the year of Brezhnev's death, and was not finally resolved until 1990 with the election of a non-Sandinista government. In neighboring El Salvador, Communist-led rebels attempted to overthrow the central government, and here again the Soviet Union and the United States competed through their surrogates for victory. By the early nineties, the situation had stabilized substantially in favor of the democratic movement.

Balance of Terror

The American monopoly of the atomic bomb lasted only until the summer of 1949 when foreign scientists detected a Russian explosion and Moscow later confirmed it. Disbelief turned quickly to resentment when Americans suddenly realized that they could no longer enjoy the sense of security that the monopoly had given them. Refusing to believe that Russian scientists and technicians could develop the capabilities necessary to produce the bomb, some Americans found comfort in assuming that the secrets of the bomb had been stolen by spies, especially by scientists in the pay of Moscow. Others wanted to believe that the Russians had captured German rocket scientists, as Americans of course had done, and that the Germans had produced the bomb for the Russians. Only slowly and grudgingly did Westerners finally listen to their own scientists—that the basic elements of research leading to nuclear fission had long been common property among scientists all over the world and that the results of fundamental research for years had been published in the journals for all to read. Russian scientists, like the Germans, French, Hungarians, Italians, British, and Americans, had contributed their share to the basic discoveries that made the bomb possible. Their results were published in Russian scientific journals, but few Western scientists bothered to learn the Russian language until after the revelation that Soviet scientists had indeed produced their own bomb.

Malenkov announced to the world in the summer of 1953 that Russia had exploded a hydrogen bomb. Within a year, Soviet scientists were producing rockets more powerful than those tested in the United States. By mid-1955 it was apparent that the United States and Russia had embarked on a race to launch an earth satellite and explore interplanetary space. The boosting power necessary to launch a satellite was, of course, applicable to weapons. In 1957 the USSR successfully completed the test of an intercontinental ballistic missile. Then two months later the first space satellite, the Russian *Sputnik*, went into orbit around the earth. Early in 1958 the American *Explorer* joined the Russian satellite in space.

The amazing achievement of the Russian scientists, which Western scientists were quick to appreciate, stunned American politicians and educators, if not American scientists. Because the cream of the German rocket scientists had surrendered to the Americans, it had to be admitted reluctantly that Russian scientists, products of the Russian education system, working in state-provided laboratories, had thus far won the race for space. There were loud cries that the American education system must be "brought up to date" and that there must be heavier reliance on mathematics and the physical sciences. Congress proved itself willing and anxious to vote for whatever funds were necessary to spur the development of rocket weapons and space exploration. That the Soviet Union had moved ahead was clear from President Eisenhower's admission that the Russians had been working on ballistic missiles since 1945, whereas the United States had begun serious work in intercontinental missiles only in 1953. Within weeks of the launching of the first *Sputnik*, and months before an American satellite would join it, the Russians launched *Sputnik II*. In 1959 there were two spectacular moon shots. A *Lunik* landed on the moon, and another *Lunik* circled the moon and photographed its dark side. In April 1961, the Russian "cosmonaut," Yuri Gagarin, orbited the earth in the first space flight by a man. Four months later another Russian cosmonaut landed safely after orbiting seventeen times around the earth. In 1962 America's Colonel John Glenn orbited the earth three times, and another American "astronaut" orbited six times later in the year. The men became national heroes immediately and world heroes as well. Meanwhile, the Russians took a tremendous leap forward when two of their cosmonauts circled the earth side by side, one making fifty orbits and the other sixty. By 1979 Russia and the United States each had scores of satellites in orbit.

With the perfection, both in Russia and in the United States, of intercontinental ballistic missiles, intermediate range missiles, anti-missile missiles, and ground-to-ground, ground-to-air, air-to-air, and under-sea missiles of all sorts, all capable of carrying nuclear warheads, the two military giants developed arsenals capable of incinerating each other and all the world with them. The United States established missile bases both at home and abroad. Khrushchev boasted of his ability to destroy American cities and warned the capitals of Europe that they would not survive if a nuclear war broke out because they permitted the establishment of American missile bases on European soil. Yet Khrushchev was well aware that he must avoid a nuclear war which, he frankly admitted, would wreck the Soviet Union as well as its enemies. The missile race proved costly to both sides and frightening to the rest of the world. Americans were assured in the summer of 1962 that the United States was ahead of Russia, but they were also told that a Soviet attack would wipe out most big cities and kill perhaps seventy million citizens. They did not know what to believe when their own secretary of defense admitted in 1962 that Russia was "substantially ahead" in some phases of military space development.

Almost from the firing of the last shot in World War II, East and West sought to negotiate a disarmament agreement. Aside from a drastic and perhaps unfortunate demobilization by the Western allies immediately after the war and an occasional modest reduction of armed forces by the Soviet Union in later years, no disarmament took place. With the development of nuclear weapons, any thought of disarmament in terms of conventional weapons seemed pathetically unrealistic.

The possibility of ever reaching significant agreement, either on disarmament or on the control of banning of nuclear tests, seemed remote. Neither side was willing to believe that the other was sincere. In this continuing air of distrust, each side was inclined to dismiss the other's proposals as insincere and untrustworthy. Each side sought to convince the world that the other was solely to blame for blocking disarmament or preventing a test-ban treaty. The problem of arranging a permanent cessation of nuclear tests became increasingly complicated when de Gaulle launched a series of tests aimed at bringing France to a position of nuclear parity and when Communist China exploded a nuclear bomb in 1964. The United States and the Soviet Union signed a limited "test-ban" treaty in 1963, but the problem for mankind was no longer a problem that two parties would settle alone.

Russia possessed, as did the United States, stockpiles of intercontinental ballistic missiles capable of launch from a distance of nine thousand miles and dropping within a mile of the target. Research was fast proceeding on both sides to perfect a missile that would intercept and destroy an intercontinental ballistic missile. Khrushchev boasted in mid-summer 1962 that Russia possessed an anti-missile missile so accurate that it could "hit a fly in space" and added that it was invulnerable to other anti-missile missiles. There was no disposition to deride the boast, for Western observers had learned long since to respect the capabilities of Soviet scientists. By 1967 Russia had erected a protective circle of anti-missile rocket launchers around Moscow. President Johnson sought to avoid a costly race in such protective devices by negotiation, but both Russians and Americans were suspicious that either could trust the other. President Nixon met with Brezhnev in Moscow in 1972, and the two agreed to limit missile defense systems. A later United States-Soviet summit in Vladivostok in 1974 sought to limit American and Soviet offensive nuclear weapons and set new ceilings of several categories of nuclear armaments.

Negotiations on SALT II (Strategic Arms Limitation Treaty) were intended to be a follow-up to SALT I, signed in 1972 and scheduled to expire in 1977. Important issues, complex technological details, and the search for symmetry acceptable to both sides delayed the final shaping of the treaty. Finally signed in 1979 in Vienna at a Carter-Brezhnev summit, SALT II became the basis of the immediate future arms balance. Major components of the treaty included limiting strategic launchers (land-based and sea-launched missiles plus bombers), limits on multiple warhead missiles (MIRV), and sharing information on testing and other technical data. The treaty never became law, as the United States Senate refused to ratify the treaty in the aftermath of the Soviet intervention in Afghanistan later in the year. Western concern over this Soviet action plus its continued deployment of intermediate-range weapons in East Europe created a negative atmosphere in which arms control efforts came to a virtual standstill. Important consultations did not resume until 1981 and only lasted to 1983. Only from 1985 did the broad topic of arms control take on continued commitment by both sides to act on these issues.

The political complexion of the United Nations, in which the world after 1945 had rested its hope for lasting peace, changed considerably in the postwar era. With the breakup of old empires and the emergence of new states, the membership rose to over a hundred and eighty nations by the nineties. Both East and West made a strong bid for the allegiance of the newly independent nations, but most of them proved to have a mind of their own. There was talk of an Afro-Asian bloc and of a neutralist bloc led by older states like Yugoslavia and India. Americans feared Communist influence in such blocs, whereas Russians charged the United States with succeeding in the evil influence of the old empires and in penetrating the very same blocs. The Soviet Union was forced to learn the lesson, which Americans found so painful to learn, that the United Nations could no longer be controlled by any great power. The veto was still available, but it had lost much of its effectiveness. Russia threatened more than once to pull out of the world organization, and some American politicians urged the United States to take the same course. The influence of the United Nations as a deterrent to war came to rest more on its ability to marshal world opinion than on any real power it possessed to control the actions of the great powers.

Thoughtful observers were reaching the conclusion that the only effective deterrent to a general war was the realization that the world had invented the means to destroy itself and that war would bring the end of civilization, if not of life itself. This forced both East and West to recognize that there was no alternative but to find some tolerable way of understanding and living with each other. This awareness during the Brezhnev era provided the basis for both the United States and the Soviet Union to seek behavior short of nuclear confrontation. While tensions certainly existed and continued, the patterns of "peaceful coexistence" prevailed into the early 1980s.

Suggested Reading

ALEXEYEVA, L., *Soviet Dissent: Contemporary Movements for National, Religious and Human Rights* (Middletown, CT, 1985).
ALLWORTH, E. (ed.), *Soviet Nationality Problems* (New York, 1977).
ANDREW, C., and O. GORDIEVSKY, *KGB: The Inside Story of Its Foreign Operations from Lenin to Gorbachev* (New York, 1990).
BARGHOORN, F. C., *Détente and the Democratic Movement in the USSR* (New York, 1976).
BERGSON, A. and H. S. LEVINE (eds.), *The Soviet Economy: Toward the Year 2000* (London, 1983).
BIALER, S., *The Domestic Context of Soviet Foreign Policy* (Boulder, 1981).
_____, *Stalin's Successors: Leadership, Stability and Change in the Soviet Union* (Cambridge, Eng., 1980).
BINYON, M., *Life in Russia* (New York, 1983).
BLOCK, S. and P. REDDAWAY, *Psychiatric Terror: How Soviet Psychiatry Is Used to Suppress Dissent* (New York, 1977).
BOUSCAREN, A., *Soviet Foreign Policy: A Pattern of Persistence* (New York, 1962).
BRADSHER, H. S. A., *Afghanistan and the Soviet Union* (Durham, NC, 1983).
BREZHNEV, L. I., *Leonid I. Brezhnev: Pages from His Life* (New York, 1978).
BRUMBERG, A., (ed.), *In Quest of Justice: Protest and Dissent in the Soviet Union Today* (New York, 1970).
BYRNES, R. F. (ed.), *After Brezhnev: Sources of Soviet Conduct in the 1980s* (Bloomington, IN, 1983).
CHALIDZE, V. N., *To Defend These Rights: Human Rights and the Soviet Union* (New York, 1974).
COLTON, T. J., *The Dilemma of Reform in the Soviet Union* (New York, 1986).
CONQUEST, R., *Power and Policy in the USSR: The Study of Soviet Dynastics* (New York, 1962).
CRANKSHAW, E., *Khrushchev: A Career* (New York, 1966).
DAWISHA, K., *The Kremlin and the Prague Spring* (Berkeley, 1984).
DERIABIN, P. and T. H. BAGLEY, *The KGB: Masters of the Soviet Union* (New York, 1990).
DODER, D., *Shadows and Whispers: Power Politics inside the Kremlin from Brezhnev to Gorbachev* (New York, 1986).
DORNBERG, J., *Brezhnev: The Masks of Power* (New York, 1974).
_____, *The New Tsars: Russia under Stalin's Heirs* (Garden City, NY, 1972).
DYCK, J. W., *Boris Pasternak* (New York, 1972).
EDMONDS, R., *Soviet Foreign Policy, 1962–1973: The Paradox of Super Power* (New York, 1975).
GARRISON, M., and A. GLEASON (eds.), *Shared Destiny: Fifty Years of Soviet-American Relations* (Boston, 1985).
GELMAN, H., *The Brezhnev Politburo and the Decline of Détente* (Ithaca, NY, 1984).
GERSTENMAIER, C., *The Voices of the Silent* (New York, 1972).
GIBIAN, G., *Interval of Freedom: Soviet Literature During the Thaw, 1954–1957* (Minneapolis, 1960).
GOURE, L. et al. (eds.), *Convergence of Communism and Capitalism: The Soviet View* (Miami, 1973).
GROMYKO, A. A., *Memoirs* (New York, 1990).

HAMMOND, T. T., *Red Flag over Afghanistan: The Communist Coup, the Soviet Invasion, and the Consequences* (Boulder, 1984).
HANAK, H., *Soviet Foreign Policy Since the Death of Stalin* (London, 1972).
HASLAM, J., *The Soviet Union and the Politics of Nuclear Weapons in Europe, 1969-1987* (Ithaca, NY, 1990).
HOLLOWAY, D., *The Soviet Union and the Arms Race* (New Haven, 1983).
HOLLOWAY, D., and J. M. O. SHARP (eds.), *The Warsaw Pact: Alliance in Transition?* (Ithaca, NY, 1984).
HOPKINS, M., *Russia's Underground Press: The Chronicle of Current Events* (New York, 1983).
JOHNSON, D. G., and K. M. BROOKS, *Prospects for Soviet Agriculture in the 1980s* (Bloomington, IN, 1983).
JONES, C. D., *Soviet Influence in Eastern Europe* (New York, 1981).
KAISER, R. G., *Russia: The People and the Power* (New York, 1976).
KELLEY, D. (ed.), *Soviet Politics in the Brezhnev Era* (New York, 1980).
KHRUSHCHEV, N. K., *Khrushchev Remembers* (Boston, 1970).
_____, *Khrushchev Remembers: The Glasnost Tapes* (Boston, 1990).
_____, *Khrushchev Remembers: The Last Testament* (Boston, 1974).
KHRUSHCHEV, S., *Khrushchev on Khrushchev: An Inside Account of the Man and His Era* (Boston, 1990).
KOHLER, F. D; M. L. HARVEY; L. GOURE; and R. SOLL, *Soviet Strategy for the Seventies: From Cold War to Peaceful Coexistence* (Miami, 1973).
LINDEN, C. A., *Khrushchev and the Soviet Leadership, 1957-1964* (London, 1967).
McCAULEY, M. (ed.), *Khrushchev and Khrushchevism* (Bloomington, IN, 1988).
MATTHEWS, M., *Education in the Soviet Union: Politics and Institutions Since Stalin* (London, 1982).
_____, *Soviet Government: A Selection of Official Documents* (New York, 1974).
MEDVEDEV, R. A. and Z. MEDVEDEV, *Khrushchev: The Years in Power* (New York, 1976).
_____, *A Question of Madness* (New York, 1971).
MERAY, T., *Thirteen Days that Shook the Kremlin* (London, 1959).
MILLER, R. F. and F. FEHER (eds.), *Khrushchev and the Communist World* (Totowa, NJ, 1984).
MORTON, H., and TÖKES, A., *Soviet Politics and Society in the 1970s* (New York, 1974).
NEWELL, R. S. and N. P. NEWELL, *The Struggle for Afghanistan* (Ithaca, NY, 1981).
ORLOV, Y., *Dangerous Thoughts: Memoirs of a Russian Life* (New York, 1991).
PETROFF, S. P., *Red Eminence: A Biography of Mikhail A. Suslov* (Clifton, NJ, 1988).
REDDAWAY, P. (ed.), *Uncensored Russia: Protest and Dissent in the Soviet Union: The Unofficial Moscow Journal, A Chronicle of Current Events* (New York, 1972).
RESHETAR, J. S., JR., *A Concise History of the Communist Party of the Soviet Union* (New York, 1964).
ROTHBERG, A., *The Heirs of Stalin: Dissidence and the Soviet Regime, 1953-1970* (Ithaca, NY, 1972).
RUBINSTEIN, A. Z., *The Foreign Policy of the Soviet Union* (New York, 1966).
SAKHAROV, A., *Alarm and Hope* (New York, 1978).
_____, *Memoirs* (New York, 1990).
SCAMMELL, M., *Solzhenitsyn: A Biography* (New York, 1984).
SHARANSKY, N., *Fear No Evil* (New York, 1988).

SHEVCHENKO, A. N., *Breaking with Moscow* (New York, 1985).

SHIPLER, D., *Russia: Broken Idols, Solemn Dreams* (New York, 1983).

SIMIS, K., *USSR, The Corrupt Society: The Secret World of Soviet Capitalism* (New York, 1982).

SMITH, G., *Doubletalk: The Story of the First Strategic Arms Limitation Talks* (Garden City, NY, 1980).

SMITH, H., *The Russians* (New York, 1976; rev. ed. 1984).

STEELE, J., *Soviet Power: The Kremlin Foreign Policy: Brezhnev to Andropov* (New York, 1983).

STRONG, J. W., *The Soviet Union under Brezhnev and Kosygin: The Transition Years* (New York, 1971).

TALBOTT, S., *Endgame II: The Inside Story of SALT II* (New York, 1979).

TATU, M., *Power in the, Kremlin: From Khrushchev to Kosygin* (New York, 1969).

ULAM, A. B., *Dangerous Relations: The Soviet Union in World Politics, 1970–1982* (New York, 1983).

———, *Expansion and Coexistence: The History of Soviet Foreign Policy, 1917–1973* (New York, 1974).

———, *Russia's Failed Revolutions: From the Decembrists to the Dissidents* (New York, 1981).

VEEN, H-J., *From Brezhnev to Gorbachev: Domestic Affairs and Soviet Foreign Policy* (New York, 1987).

VOLIN, L., *A Century of Russian Agriculture: From Alexander II to Khrushchev* (Cambridge, 1970).

WILLIS, D. K., *Klass: How Russians Really Live* (New York, 1985).

CHAPTER 22

Andropov to Gorbachev

With Brezhnev's death in late 1982, the Soviet Union entered one of its most interesting, challenging and significant periods in Russian history. The next decade revealed economic decline, domestic turmoil, calls for major reforms, the emergence of Mikhail Gorbachev as a dynamic and articulate leader, and culminated in the termination of the USSR as a nation-state in December 1991. The old system, already weakened, underwent a "shaking up" not seen since the confusing events of 1917 and the rise of the Bolsheviks to power.

Andropov and Chernenko

Early signs of these important trends were not immediately apparent. The Central Committee quickly elected Yuri Andropov to be the new general secretary, serving from November 1982 to his death in February 1984. At sixty-nine, Andropov was only slightly younger than the more senior party leaders. In addition, he had served on the Politburo since 1967 which linked him to most of the Brezhnev era. Moreover, as head of the Committee on State Security (KGB) from 1967 to May 1982, Andropov led the government's efforts to harass and prosecute members of the dissident movement.

Observers, hopeful for a more dynamic leader, noted Andropov's apparent better health and energy than his predecessor, his skills as an administrator, and his familiarity with a wide range of domestic and foreign issues. Even before Brezhnev's death, Andropov gave several speeches indicating the need to regain momentum in production output as well as in worker motivation and discipline. He promised reforms in the economy and in the party to improve efficiency.

Regrettably, the optimists soon discovered little change could be expected in the Andropov era. While the terminology and rhetoric of reform suggested change, the realities were not encouraging. A few leadership adjustments in the Politburo took place, such as the immediate promotion of Gaidar Aliev to full membership, as well as his selection as the deputy prime minister of the Soviet government. He came from a non-Russian republic, having served as first secretary of the Azerbaidzhan Communist party from 1969. Also, his age indicated a possible shift in orientation and outlook, as he was still in his fifties. Putting him as the number two man in the Soviet government might mean new or modified leadership in the Council of Ministers. His background and skills, however, rested on KGB experience, and his previous autocratic rule in Azerbaidzhan could scarcely be characterized as democratic. Several aged Politburo and Council of Ministers officials retired or were removed, and a new KGB chairman was named, but the main leadership, those holding substantial posts of power, generally remained in place. In addition, although some anti-corruption cases revealed some effort to control or punish wrongdoing in high places, many corrupt officials remained untouched.

Even more crucial to the potential legacy of the Andropov era was his health, which proved almost from the beginning to be a serious hindrance to his leadership. Although officially and apparently in stable health, rumors began to be heard in early 1983 to the contrary. His absence at events normally requiring his presence increased speculation about the mysterious ailments. He last appeared in public in August 1983, after which he was in such failing health that constant hospitalization and medical treatment were required. Speeches and announcements were given in his name, and he still ruled in absentia with the assistance of close colleagues. Yet clearly a crisis in leadership existed, and the problem led to the growth of factions within the party and the government preparing for another shift in power. Domestic reform, for all practical purposes, therefore came to a virtual halt; the domestic record of the Andropov period of seventeen months is quite limited. He died on February 9, 1984, at the age of seventy, and with him died the hope for reform in the immediate post-Brezhnev era.

His successor, Konstantin Chernenko, served as general secretary from February 1984 until his death in March 1985. His selection by the party apparatus underscored the need for a compromise. Rival factions competed for the succession. One side looked to Viktor Grishin, long-time party boss of Moscow since 1967. Grishin was a classic *apparatchik*. (This type of person is defined as a member of the party bureaucracy, often free from criticism or accountability, and motivated by the goal to maintain authority and privilege. The term suggests, in its common usage, a ''party hack'' or functionary.) Others, worried about the future leadership and health of the nation, sought younger leadership outside the well-entrenched Moscow apparatus. Mikhail Gorbachev, years younger than

Grishin and having comparatively short tenure in Moscow, looked like a good possibility. However, Gorbachev lacked extensive experience at the top and did not have sufficient support by early 1984 among his Politburo colleagues and the party's Central Committee. The conditions were not mature enough for his successful candidacy, although another year brought eventual victory over his rivals. Instead, the party sought a short-term candidate who could provide some continuity and stability. At seventy-two, when he began his tenure, Chernenko was the oldest general secretary in the entire Communist era. A firm believer in the leadership and policies of Brezhnev, whom he served loyally for a quarter of a century, Chernenko could not be expected to undercut the policies and legacies of his political and ideological mentor. He did have extensive experience within the Communist party apparatus, and therefore knew party procedures and personnel, but his experience as a leader was limited, and he lacked any foreign policy exposure. Few in the Soviet Union knew anything of their new party chief, and his appointment surprised many. Little could logically be expected of his tenure other than a cautious course of continuity and very limited shifts in policy. This included the emphasis on heavy industry, centralized economic planning and control, and the maintenance of domestic social tranquility by whatever means, including repressive measures. The strengthening of the Soviet military remained a high priority.

Chernenko, as in the initial Andropov pronouncements, advocated higher productivity, an increase in efficiency, and greater worker discipline and motivation. The rhetoric sounded impressive, but in fact this message essentially meant keeping the existing institutional structure and systems as well as the fundamental ideology. Any efforts sought only to make the lethargic system work better, and the results did not warrant any confidence that the economy and standard of living would be substantially altered or improved. What might come under Chernenko's eventual successor no one really knew. It does not appear that serious consideration was being given in 1984 to any extensive changes in doctrine and policy. We do know now that some in the party apparatus and the younger economic specialists felt the future could not continue unaltered. Gorbachev and the Georgian party chief, Eduard Shevardnadze, were people who held these beliefs, but they kept quiet and bided their time. For the time being, their views were kept out of public view in party discussions.

Chernenko's single year in power did not produce any important changes in economic policy and output. The one commodity for sale on international markets which did bring substantial income to the Soviet treasury was petroleum, a natural resource in ample supply in Soviet reserves. The USSR produced more petroleum at the well head per day than any other single oil producing nation including the members of OPEC (Organization of Petroleum Exporting Countries). This placed the Soviet Union in the position of serving world customers as a supplier of a non-manufactured natural resource. Therefore, oil sales, while large, did little for the improvement or modernization of the Soviet economy other than obtaining needed foreign exchange used to purchase grain and manufactured items from the West to meet immediate Soviet needs.

Waiting in line to buy shoes in Moscow, 1983

Two months after his election as general secretary, Chernenko, in April 1984, became president of the Soviet Union. This office at that time did not have the extensive authority of the president of the United States or the greatly expanded powers of the Soviet president (revised in early 1990). The additional position did give Chernenko more influence over many government functions including the USSR Supreme Soviet, the national parliament. He could have used that opportunity, if he desired to do so, to bring proposals for reform to that institution. Little in fact was done. It is noteworthy that Chernenko acquired the office of president within two months of becoming party head, while it took Brezhnev thirteen years and Andropov almost six months to add that post to their responsibilities.

Like Andropov, Chernenko made few changes in leading party and government personnel. Continuity clearly was the objective. One notable shift occurred with the death of Dmitri Ustinov, defense minister since 1976, a leading member of the Party Secretariat for many years and a Politburo member since 1965. His death in late 1984 removed a very senior figure whose presence gave stability. His successor as defense minister was not given Politburo membership, a step seen as a reduction in the influence of the Soviet military establishment.

It soon became apparent that Chernenko, like Andropov, faced serious health problems. He died on March 10, 1985, at the age of seventy-three. The last several months of his life required hospitalization, and effective leadership fell to his associates. This situation, emerging as a pattern for the late Brezhnev years and the interim Andropov phase, illustrated the difficulty of establishing effective political authority and avoiding caretaker regimes. While the chairman of the Council of Ministers, Premier Tikhonov, served continuously from 1980 to 1985 as head of the Soviet government, the lack of direction at the top of the Communist party hindered chances of coherent reform or even policy direction other than using established principles and existing inertia. Tikhonov, although an experienced administrator and a member of the Politburo, was born before Brezhnev, Andropov, and Chernenko. His age and subordinate role to the general secretary mitigated against effective leadership for the nation.

These domestic conditions and problems were paralleled by foreign policy problems in the immediate post-Brezhnev era. Both Andropov and Chernenko sought to present the Soviet Union to the world as a moderate, peaceful, and positive society. Yet the facts undercut this positive image.

Soviet participation in the Afghan war not only continued but increased in size, military operations, and the spread of devastation to the people and land of that Central Asia region. The official policy maintained support for the puppet Afghan regime in Kabul and called for victory over the anti-Communist Afghan opposition, the mujahedin. Costs and casualties mounted each year, although the Soviet media carried very few realistic news stories for Soviet readers.

Relations with the United States and its NATO allies substantially deteriorated during the period, as the West threatened and then prepared to place intermediate nuclear missile systems in Europe as a counterweight to the Soviet SS-20 systems already deployed in East Europe and in the western regions of the Soviet Union. Arms limitations talks with the Americans continued sporadically until the fall of 1983, when Western nuclear weapons began to arrive at their West European sites. The Soviet Union immediately withdrew from arms talks in November, and both sides continued the military build-up.

In the spring of 1983, President Reagan gave his famous "evil empire" speech in which he portrayed the Soviet Union in very negative terms. The same month he called for the creation of a "Strategic Defense Initiative" (SDI or "Star Wars" as the media labelled the concept) to protect the United States against an offensive Soviet nuclear attack. Finally, later in the year, the Soviet air force shot down an unarmed Korean airliner, which had strayed over Soviet territory on its flight from Alaska to Asia, killing all 269 passengers and crew. Although this incident occurred during Andropov's rule, no firm evidence existed to link the decision for the military response to Moscow. Nonetheless, all these events and controversies during the Andropov era increased Western concerns about the intentions and policies of the Soviet Union. This deteriorating and confrontational atmosphere also worried Kremlin leaders about the likelihood of even greater challenges in its international efforts. The short Chernenko interlude made little impact on Soviet relationships with the outside world.

By 1985, therefore, the Andropov-Chernenko period shows very uneven leadership, a faltering economy, and a confrontational foreign policy. Those who hoped for substantial improvements in some or all of these categories now realized the 1982–1985 period signified little more than lost time and meandering direction. In retrospect, these years served as little more than a brief passage in a transition from the lengthy stagnating Brezhnev era to the fresh approaches yet to evolve under the leadership of Mikhail Gorbachev. Whether he could make more progress on these vital issues remained to be seen when he came to power in March 1985.

The Gorbachev Years

Mikhail Gorbachev became the beneficiary of the challenges facing his nation, with his election as general secretary of the Communist party. His election, by the Central Committee, began a new era in the Soviet Union for the balance of the decade of the eighties and into the early nineties until his resignation as both party head and national president before the end of 1991.

The Central Committee's quick selection of the new party leader within one day of Chernenko's death indicates that decisions for the succession had been made during the last months of Chernenko's odyssey with death. To the Soviet population and world observers, the new party head represented comparative youth (he was fifty-four), good health, a quick and perceptive mind, and a willingness to confront the ills and inadequacies of his nation. He has often been compared favorably with Lenin as the brightest national leader since the founder of the Communist party died in 1924. Gorbachev's diagnoses of current problems and his vision of the future quickly created a favorable response, except among the party traditionalists and apparatchiks.

Gorbachev's background gave little indication of his later national stature and leadership. Born in 1931 in the Russian province of Stavropol just north of the Caucasus Mountains, he grew up in a small rural village. German forces occupied the region during part of the World War II period, and Gorbachev's father served in the Soviet army. As a teenager in the aftermath of the war, the young Gorbachev worked on farms before entering Moscow State University in 1951. He studied for a law degree, graduating in 1955, and joined the Communist party during his university days.

Following graduation, he returned to his home province to enter party service as his chosen career. First working with the Komsomol (the national youth branch of the Communist party which was established in 1918 and reached approximately forty-five million members by the mid-1980s), he transferred to party administration in the city of Stavropol and rose through various positions until he headed the party in the entire Stavropol province from 1970 to 1978. His record as an honest and effective administrator who generated results drew the attention of national party leaders who brought Gorbachev to Moscow in 1978 to oversee agricultural policy in the Secretariat. He became a member of the Central Committee in 1971, and at the age of forty-seven was elected to candidate

Mikhail Gorbachev

membership in the Politburo. The following year, he was raised to full member-ship as the youngest member of the most senior and powerful group of party leaders. From 1983 until his election as general secretary in 1985, Gorbachev assumed other important party responsibilities, including personnel and ideology assignments. During the Chernenko period, Gorbachev occasionally chaired Politburo meetings in the former's absence and provided greater leadership for the party.

These activities provided the experience and reputation required for his selection as party chief upon Chernenko's death. Following party procedures, the Central Committee (approximately three hundred members), rather than the entire party membership or the Soviet electorate at large, elected him general secretary. In 1988 he also was elected president, i.e., chairman of the USSR Supreme Soviet. A new office of president with substantial executive authority was created in early 1990, and the Congress of Peoples' Deputies elected Gorbachev as the first occupant of that post, to serve a five-year term. None of these elections involved the Soviet voters, and he never held a national post on the basis of such an election.

Nonetheless, he entered this new role as party head and national leader with zest and enthusiasm. It is evident that Gorbachev had already developed his own analysis of many Soviet problems before assuming power in 1985. Consequently he began almost immediately to discuss issues and possible reforms. The

Gorbachev agenda reflected his "new thinking" both in domestic and foreign policy, although they evolved, matured and changed in succeeding years. The years from 1985 to 1991 represent his determined and concerted efforts to bring his agenda into reality.

All too evident were the facts of the declining economy, the sluggishness of the party leadership, the lethargy and apathy of much of the population, and a variety of problems in Soviet foreign policy. To the astonishment of many within and outside the nation, Gorbachev proposed sweeping changes, new or revised priorities, an honest examination of the needs of the Soviet Union and the reasons for its malaise, and called for renewed efforts to create a nation in which progress, production, justice, and peace would result. His clear articulation of issues created a mood of excitement, anticipation, and hope, although some speculated the vision was so sweeping and the challenges so daunting that Gorbachev probably would fail. Understandably the traditionalists in the party and economy worried about the fashion in which Gorbachev was challenging the status quo.

To achieve his objectives, Gorbachev realized he had to give extraordinarily effective leadership and also convince the Soviet population to join him in facing and resolving such difficult tasks. He believed that the forceful methods of the Stalin-Brezhnev type could not be imposed with much chance of success, despite their utilization in the past. He therefore appealed to the aspirations and inner resources of his people to draw them along as partners in the cause of national renewal, but inertia, rigidity, and lack of support among many bureaucrats and administrators would make the task a difficult one. Thus he spoke directly to the people and travelled often across the Soviet Union to bring the message directly to those whose efforts would either result in success or failure. He certainly intended to use the machinery and authority of the Communist party to assist in the process, but he knew its membership had to be convinced of the validity of his agenda. His years as party head and national president provide a dramatic story of the successes and failures in Gorbachev's efforts to keep his nation from declining to what he referred to as a third-rate power.

Political Change

Of immediate importance in undertaking the daunting task, the Communist party had to be energized as an agent of reform. This required removing or shifting leading party personnel, from the Politburo down to party heads in the provinces. Gorbachev used his first two years in office to remove gradually most of the old guard from leading positions in the party. Romanov, one of his rivals for power who headed the party organization in Leningrad for many years, was dropped from the Politburo in the summer of 1985. Viktor Grishin, the party head of Moscow since 1967, was replaced in December 1985 by Boris Yeltsin, a younger provincial party leader from the Ural mountain region who soon became controversial and famous in his own right. The party leader of the Republic of

Kazakhstan since 1964 was removed from that position in 1986, as well as from the Politburo. Other younger party administrators from outside the Moscow region and the Brezhnev inner circle were added to the national leadership. Besides Yeltsin, Yegor Ligachev from Central Siberia served on the Politburo from April 1985 to July 1990.

Gorbachev also began the reshaping of the top personnel in the Soviet government, removing or retiring senior leaders. In 1985, Nikolai Ryzhkov, an industrial and economic specialist, replaced Premier Tikhonov, who was eighty years old. Ryzhkov served in this post until January 1991 and was added, as well, to the Politburo. Another notable appointment brought Eduard Shevardnadze, long-time party head of the Georgian republic, to Moscow to replace seventy-six-year-old Andrei Gromyko as foreign minister, a post he held since 1957. Nikolai Talyzin replaced Nikolai Baibakov as head of Gosplan (the State Economic Planning Committee) which he had led for two decades. Changes such as these brought in younger men, mostly in their fifties, to replace those in their seventies or older. The new Central Gorbachev team looked and acted vital and creative in assisting the new general secretary in his ambitious efforts.

In addition, for the fifteen Soviet republics, he began the gradual replacement of party first secretaries as well as the executive leadership of the regional governments. He also transferred or retired many province party secretaries. The one party group requiring a longer time to be purged of established and senior personnel was the Central Committee, but by the Twenty-eighth Party Congress in July 1990, that task had been completed sufficiently to ostensibly provide the support for his objectives. He also was responsible for the adoption of a new party program adopted at the Twenty-seventh Party Congress in 1986 to replace the 1961 program of the Khrushchev era.

Gorbachev, to his wider national audience, introduced the concept of *demokratizatsia*, the democratization of Soviet politics and society. To many this implied a more open, democratic political environment in the Soviet Union and even suggested the possibility of a pluralistic multiparty system. In fact, however, Gorbachev did not intend the end of the monopoly of the Communist party, but he did hope for more participation in decision making and for the development of a party and public committed to problem solving and energetic support for the improvements he felt had to be made.

One notable result of this new emphasis was the creation of a new national Congress of Peoples' Deputies, authorized in 1988 and elected in the spring of 1989. Although a substantial number of the 2,250 members still were appointed or elected by national interest groups, including the Communist party, approximately half were elected by the national electorate at large. The powers of the new body diminished the authority of the Communist party somewhat, although it still continued to hold extensive power in the new group.

The Congress of Peoples' Deputies elected from its midst a smaller (550 members) parliament, the reformed USSR Supreme Soviet, which acted as the primary sitting legislative body of the nation. The new Supreme Soviet elected in 1989, unlike the old body of the same name, began to manifest energetic debate and showed a vitality and independence in parliamentary activism not seen previously. The public could watch the televised sessions or read verbatim coverage in the Soviet press. Noted dissidents and spokesmen for democratic reform, such as Andrei Sakharov, took an active role in this new body.

A high point in the trend toward growing democracy resulted in the March 1990 decision to change article six of the Soviet constitution and thereby end the monopoly of the Communist party. Gorbachev had resisted the efforts to make such a change from the time the question began to be seriously debated in the fall of 1989, but he found the movement too strong for him to oppose the change successfully. The constitutional rule now offered for the first time the right of other political parties to form and to present candidates in elections at all levels. The next several years saw the emergence of a large number of popular fronts—organizations and embryonic political parties hoping to capitalize on the new opportunity for democratic activity. Their lack of experience and organization, funding limitations, absence of a popular power base, and often utopian or grandiose platforms led to mixed results. Confusion and inertia made it unlikely that substantial and relevant parties would develop quickly. Nonetheless, a dramatic new era began in Soviet politics. With time, a multiparty system seemed likely, if not inevitable.

At the same time these important alterations were taking place in the national legislature, Gorbachev moved to expand his own authority. Already head of the party, he supported the creation of a new office which would have extensive executive authority. After wide and open debate in the Congress of Peoples' Deputies, the new office of USSR president was created in March 1990. (A previous parliamentary post by the same name already existed as the nominal head of state, but with limited authority.) Powers of the new Soviet presidency went well beyond those of the American president. The Congress specified a five-year term, with a maximum of two terms. Although the legislation for the new post called for a nationally elected president, the severe domestic problems and national instability at the time led the Congress to undertake its own election for the first president in March 1990. Future elections were designated for popular vote in a national election.

Mikhail Gorbachev, not surprisingly, was elected president and began to use his increased authority to promote his reform agenda. With the right to rule by decree and even impose martial law under certain conditions, he consolidated and extended his authority well beyond his role as party chief. Reformers criticized this expansion of one-man rule, and periodically accused Gorbachev of dictatorial leanings and behavior. Foreign Minister Shevardnadze, one of the Gorbachev team, resigned in December 1990 and warned of the substantial dangers of rising dictatorship in the Soviet Union (although he did not explicitly accuse Gorbachev of such behavior previously).

Supporters of the old command system generally favored Gorbachev's increased powers and called on him in 1990–1991 to impose order on the nation by using martial law and by banning opposition parties. Their goal was to provide public stability in a nation deteriorating both socially and economically. Gorbachev continued to declare himself as a supporter of democratic values and attempted to find a middle ground between the rapidly multiplying factions. He sought to avoid using such extraordinary authority unless absolutely necessary. He favored an atmosphere of sufficient order and control to undertake and solidify his reforms within a democratic framework, but the proper balance generally eluded him.

Gorbachev used his authority from his earliest opportunity. Once firmly in power in 1985 as general secretary, Gorbachev moved immediately to address the Soviet economy as his most important challenge. Within a matter of weeks, he addressed the party and the whole nation about the problems resulting from what came to be known as the "era of stagnation" of the Brezhnev years, which continued during the short Andropov and Chernenko interlude. The evidence was mixed. Although productivity had generally been maintained and even grew in several categories, the overall level of economic growth over the past two decades indicated a serious and relative decline for the Soviet Union as a competitor both at home and abroad.

A Prescription for the Economy

By the time Gorbachev came to power, a number of negative phenomena, affecting the economy, existed in the Soviet Union: unsatisfactory agricultural productivity (requiring continued imports of foreign grain); mediocre worker productivity; the continuation of a command system in which bureaucratic Moscow attempted to coordinate and compel economic growth; overlapping departmental responsibilities often leading to inefficiency, cross purposes, and unacceptable results; a deteriorating transportation system, creating bottlenecks of shipments often consisting of perishable foodstuffs and resulting in excessive spoilage; and the lack of suitable Soviet trade opportunities and fiscal legitimacy in the world economy. Failing technology and out-of-date equipment further compounded the deteriorating economic conditions.

Gorbachev proposed a new approach which came to be known as *perestroika* (economic restructuring). His first task was to candidly explain the many problems and inadequacies in the economic system, well known to many but never publicly admitted so honestly and extensively by any previous Soviet leader. Immediately, Gorbachev's views created interest and support both inside and outside the Soviet Union. Such refreshing honesty and candor contrasted sharply with his predecessors. No longer declaring that the years under Communist rule were moving inevitably toward the utopian society promised for many decades, Gorbachev classified the Soviet Union as a society and economy in serious crisis. The command economy identified especially with Stalin and Brezhnev no longer could suffice. His early analysis hinted at reductions of bureaucratic systems, a modernized level of technology (including more computer-assisted manufacturing systems), and greater attention to consumer goods. Nevertheless, several elements of his plan maintained essentially the same principles of past leaders: private enterprise was not an alternative or acceptable system, public ownership of the agricultural sector remained the same, and his calls for more efficient labor discipline and worker motivation echoed similar admonitions of his predecessors. In fact, new enlarged bureaucratic structures were created in the Gorbachev era, such as Gosagroprom, a ministry created to oversee and coordinate the agricultural sector. This experiment was terminated in 1989 after it became apparent that the new super-ministry was compounding the problems rather than solving them.

By 1987 he went further in his critical assessment of structures and procedures. He now obtained the passage of the legislation for *khozraschot* (economic accountability), which established the principle that inefficient businesses must improve or face merging with other firms or outright closure. He called for the layoff of workers who were not needed or whose labor discipline fell below minimum standards. These threats, and the gradual implementation of this policy throughout portions of the Soviet industrial and manufacturing economy, eventually resulted in some improvement in what many agreed was a grossly inefficient system. Unfortunately, it also led to the appearance of unemployment which had been officially denied by the leadership in previous decades. By 1990–1991 the number of unemployed grew to worrisome levels forcing the introduction of unemployment plans and funding to assist those seeking work but unable to find it. Such conditions and support services had not existed officially since the early 1930s.

The many economic problems led the leadership in 1987 to take several small steps toward minimal free enterprise. Despite Gorbachev's coolness toward this approach as an essential condition of reform, a few opportunities gradually were introduced. The Supreme Soviet passed legislation permitting minor manufacturing, privately owned consumer services (such as restaurants, repair centers, and the like), and even some restricted private medical practice, but extensive controls over the number of persons allowed to be employed, plus the imposition of high taxation on profits, effectively kept these activities to a very limited-scale. Implementation of these national laws on enterprises were unevenly administered at the local level, and urban governments and party officials frequently interfered with these examples of small-scale capitalism.

An additional major obstacle and challenge to new entrepreneurs was the difficulty in obtaining materials to use in their manufacturing endeavors, because the state continued to absorb available facilities, funds, parts, and other essential resources. Nonetheless, the free enterprise efforts did continue and began to take hold despite these obstacles, and the growing outcry at high tax rates on business profits finally brought about some reduction in those percentages. This was, however, a far cry from what by 1990 and 1991 came to be spoken of as a "market economy" based on extensive capitalism which could exist outside the heavy hand of the Soviet government.

Soviet agriculture retained its traditional pattern of the state as the primary owner, employer, and producer and its existing practice of providing a small private plot to farmers. As in previous years, these small plots (totalling about 3 percent of all agricultural land) produced substantial amounts of certain types of foodstuffs, such as eggs, milk, vegetables (onions, garlic and potatoes), and fruit, which could be used in the village or sold at farmers' markets where the farmers earned the profits. Without this productivity, many foodstuffs would not have been as widely available. However, overall, large-scale state farms (sovkhozy) and collective farms (kolkhozy) continued to be the primary sources of agricultural output.

The Gorbachev era did experiment on a limited basis with leasing farms to one or more families. While it was not outright ownership, this approach did provide greater opportunity for some individual initiative. Most of these early leasing experiments were located in the Baltic republics, where good land and a more recent heritage of private farming had given positive results. Yet outright ownership was not permitted, and Gorbachev continued to oppose the growing pressure for the privatization of land by the national parliament in 1991. He quoted Lenin's views of private ownership as permitting exploitation of the land and people.

Declining production output and the unavailability of food for the public became the primary divisive issue in the Gorbachev era. A deterioration in the standard of living during his rule also substantially undercut his efforts and occasional successes. By 1990, food rationing was appearing in parts of the nation—primarily the major cities of Leningrad, Moscow, Kiev, and in cities in Siberia—to provide a minimum level of essential consumer products. Rationing, not seen since the Second World War and its immediate aftermath, attempted to guarantee scarce items to a wider public and did help somewhat in that regard. However, it added further to the public perception that Gorbachev promised a great deal but could not fulfill his assurances. By 1991 the situation had become much more serious and played a substantial role in the decision of Soviet republics to break away from the Soviet Union and try to meet the needs of their own populations. By the early nineties, republics refused to ship many products beyond their borders and tried to prohibit citizens from other republics from entering their own region in an effort to find and purchase scarce goods. Intra-republic shopping also was prohibited in many regions, as urban and rural areas within a single republic competed for scarce goods.

A wider variety of foodstuffs, in large amounts, could be found in the private farmers' markets. Here the prices were substantially higher than in the state food stores where subsidies kept costs lower but where empty shelves became the norm. To add to the public dismay and frustration at the shortages of food commodities, the government decreed the rise of food prices in the summer of 1990 in an effort to begin to bring food production costs into line with consumer prices. A wave of public criticism largely negated that plan from being implemented.

In the spring of 1991, the government again proposed price increases and this time introduced them on a number of items. Increases averaged 30 percent but specific consumer items rose as much as 250 to 300 percent. This government decision was adopted in part to reduce the federal deficit which had steadily mounted in recent years due to the large agricultural subsidies. Public confidence and morale was badly shaken, and most blamed Gorbachev for the increasing stresses and problems of the daily life they had to face.

These critical shortages of basic food commodities were partly the result of the failure to harvest corps at the optimum time and get them to proper storage and processing centers before spillage, damage, or spoilage could occur. Soviet harvests, while uneven from year to year, generally produced enough to provide adequate amounts for the Soviet population. However, it is widely known that extensive waste and damage occurred (and still does), leading to an estimated loss of at least 30 percent of vegetables, including potatoes, and fruit that never reached the general consumer. Broken equipment, lack of fuel, poor scheduling, and inadequate transportation have added to the damage and spoilage of much of the Soviet harvest. While the size of the Soviet Union compounded the difficulty of moving agricultural products, the material and human factors reflected an economic system in crisis.

The Soviet Union used to be a grain exporter to the world, but since the 1930s, this pattern generally has been reversed. Between 1960 and the present, extensive grain imports have been required to meet Soviet needs. These imports arrive from many sources including the United States, a primary supplier of grain. Interestingly, Gorbachev did not blame the socialist ideology of publicly owned farmland for contributing to the crisis, and he rejected the advocates of private farm ownership until almost the end of his public life. Even then, he never moved decisively to change the system of land ownership and production.

Another element of the Soviet economic system involved the inadequacies or irrelevance of a fiscal system which worked unevenly within the Soviet Union and very poorly in the international context. Gradually, the Soviet leadership realized the difficulties of a national system with inefficient and outmoded banking methods, a lack of investment capital, and a Soviet currency that had no credibility and convertibility in the world's financial arena. Consequently, arranging financial agreements and participating in world trade was difficult at best, although some minor advances have been made in recent years. Legislation to permit joint ventures now exists, allowing foreign investment in specific projects where ownership is shared with Russian counterparts. The results to date have been very mixed and generally discouraging to Western partners. Many projects have not moved ahead to completion, despite Western interest in entering Soviet markets. Some examples of successful foreign investments and business ventures do exist, notably the very visible and popular Western fast food and soft drink industries. However, the agreements leading to actual construction and operation of manufacturing facilities have taken years to complete, and the opportunities to revitalize fundamental Soviet industry still had a long way to go before the national economy could be significantly improved.

By the time Gorbachev assumed his additional position as president in March 1990, the deteriorating economic conditions compelled him to issue decrees demanding the provision of basic foodstuff and essential services to the Soviet population. While this approach sometimes worked in the past, it could not be relied upon as a long-term solution to the more fundamental problems in the

Russian crowds wait in line at the opening of the first McDonald's in the Soviet Union: Moscow, January 1990.

Soviet economy. One special problem emerged to compound economic shortages. Consumer goods, natural resources, and essential manufactured parts had to flow unhindered across all regions and republics. The large size of the nation made this integrated network a vital necessity. In the past, up to 80 percent of all domestic trade was between Soviet republics. As production output faltered or transportation systems created delays or bottlenecks, however, inter-republic and even intra-republic trade suffered as the producers sought to provide for their own local or regional needs first. Gorbachev attempted to keep the integrated economy moving, but his efforts frequently were ineffective or blocked by persons and conditions beyond his control.

A New Union

The pressure on Gorbachev to deal more effectively with economic challenges is directly related to the nationality and ethnic problems which finally led to the disintegration of the Soviet state in 1991. Simmering ethnic and regional unrest grew in an atmosphere of mistrust of Russian chauvinism and Communist rule from Moscow. The growth of regional self-awareness, a consciousness of the past, and also a vision of the future, became greatly intensified by the economic shortages facing Soviet citizens daily. This mixture seriously undercut the long-term Communist goal of creating a political union and assimilating more than one hundred distinct nationalities. Most of this effort came after 1917, although the process of "Russification" can be traced to much earlier in the imperial period with the acquisition of such areas as the Ukraine, Georgia, and Central Asia. The most recent annexations occurred in 1940 with the absorption of the three Baltic republics, Latvia, Estonia, and Lithuania. While previously part of the Russian empire, the three had been independent nations between the end of World War I and the early months of World War II.

Aside from memories and legends of political and territorial independence in the past, the current differences in language, culture, and religion exacerbated the stresses within the USSR. A growing cleavage developed between these Soviet republics and the central government in Moscow. Even the Russian Republic, the largest in size and population and also the most powerful militarily and economically, found itself at odds on many issues with the national authorities. These regional strains led to calls for independence in the three Baltic republics, Latvia, Estonia, and Lithuania, in 1989 and 1990, followed by similar efforts in 1990 and 1991 in Moldavia, Georgia, Azerbaidzhan, Armenia, and the Ukraine. By the end of 1991, all fifteen Soviet republics became independent nations, and the USSR ceased to exist as a nation-state.

While most of the so-called nationality controversy was between the republics and Moscow, inter-republic disputes added to the growing stress and danger of fragmentation. Religious and historic differences, sharpened by boundary disputes, created levels of antagonism difficult for Americans to understand. The bitterness of these relations are illustrated by the antagonism between Christian Armenia and Moslem Azerbaidzhan which led to occasional violence and bloodshed in early 1988, continuing into the next decade. Their dispute over the small Armenian enclave territory of Nagorno-Karabakh surrounded by Azerbaidzhan compounded the tenuous relationship. Similar hatreds can be seen among the peoples and regions of Central Asia, notably Turkmenia, Uzbekistan and Kyrgyzstan.

Previous Moscow administrations had been able to keep these Moscow-republic and republic-republic antagonisms in check. During the Gorbachev era, however, the new atmosphere of glasnost permitted the disputes to be publicly articulated and exacerbated. Many blamed Gorbachev for not preventing these antagonisms by strengthening local authorities or using military forces to keep order. Conversely, on those occasions when he did utilize regular army forces or Interior Ministry troops in several republics, as in 1990 and 1991, other voices criticized Gorbachev and Moscow for exerting Russian chauvinism and repressing ethnic nationalities.

Within most republics the growing self-awareness and the anti-Moscow opinion led to the formation of popular fronts. While not political parties in the formal sense, at least not originally, these organizations acted as a voice, expressing views about local and regional issues, and provided a useful forum for criticizing the central government and its policies. Prominent popular fronts included Sajudis (Lithuania) and Rukh (the Ukraine), and by 1990 several fronts matured into political parties with a slate of candidates running for local and republic offices.

Legalization of their status as the nucleus of non-Communist political parties was achieved in the February 1990 law removing the monopoly of the Communist party. By mid-1991, nearly half of the Soviet republics were under the direction of non-Communist governments. This included the Baltic republics and the Russian Republic. In the latter instance, the Russian voters elected Boris Yeltsin as president of the republic in June 1991. He had resigned from the Communist party the previous summer.

Tensions between the republics and the central government in Moscow plus the regional tensions between republics eventually proved irreconcilable. The centrifugal forces, by the fall and early winter of 1991, brought about the final collapse of the central government and the Soviet state. Gorbachev saw the support for the central regime eroding steadily, and he made a number of attempts in 1990 and 1991 to slow or reverse the worrisome trends. For example, in 1990 he created a new Council of the Federation whose members represented each republic. This group attempted to create consensus on issues affecting national unity and regional aspirations. Even though his authority and that of the central regime inevitably dissipated, he still sought to keep all republics working together for national purposes under the existing constitution. From these meetings as well as from the national parliament, a draft of a new union treaty gradually took shape.

One sign of Gorbachev's search for ways to keep the union together can be seen in his holding a national referendum on the question of national unity. The referendum took place on March 17, 1991 and asked voters if they wished to continue in a revised union structure, but nonetheless as a unified nation-state. The results could be interpreted according to one's purpose and objectives. The majority of those voting did in fact favor the continuation of the USSR, perhaps because the wording on the ballot appeared to many to provide only the choice between staying together as a political unit or facing the dangers and uncertainties of the collapse of the national structure. On the other hand, several republics did not participate in the vote, already declaring themselves independent of the Soviet Union. Gorbachev placed the most positive interpretation on the results of the voting, but many republic leaders and citizens doubted that the results had any significant impact. Events soon showed this to be the case.

Through the summer of 1991, the authorities continued revising the draft of a new union treaty. Even at the end of that period, after the final draft had been prepared, only nine of fifteen republics agreed to sign. The other six—the three Baltic republics, plus Armenia, Georgia, and Moldavia—refused to participate in these negotiations and preparations since they sought independence from the Soviet Union. The date of August 20, 1991 was set as the date of the official signing ceremony of the document, but the event disappeared in the face of the attempted coup against Mikhail Gorbachev (August 18–21, 1991). The plotters, worried about the growing political and economic problems, took action to prevent the signing of the document which would establish the new federal union. The coup and its aftermath are described in more detail in chapter 23.

Social Dilemmas

The changing political situation in the Gorbachev period complicated other important components of the Soviet Union's institutions and programs. During the Communist party's many years of existence, the authorities had promised extensive public benefits: free public education, free medical care, low-cost housing, subsidized food prices, paid maternity leave, equal job opportunities and fair wages without consideration of gender, guaranteed employment, old-age pensions, and various programs to aid the needy, the handicapped, the disabled, war veterans, and the like. There is little doubt that improvements in these important social issues have been implemented during the Communist era, and the record of these programs is noteworthy as compared to the very inadequate conditions of the tsarist era. These commitments continued for many years after 1917, although the evidence reveals great unevenness in the level of human services. This seems to partially confirm the observation of American humorist Will Rogers after a visit to the Soviet Union in the 1930s: "Communism was one-third practice and two thirds explanation."

Food prices, until 1990, remained remarkably stable thanks to high price subsidies and well-established price controls. Pensions gradually increased, reaching an average of 140 rubles monthly by the fall of 1991. Average salaries steadily increased in the 1970s and 1980s, rising at a faster rate than production output. Housing construction continued throughout the Brezhnev and Gorbachev eras, although Gorbachev's promise of an apartment for every Soviet family by the year 2000 clearly could not be achieved. Medical care, while useful in addressing essential health needs, lacked the components required of a modern and effective system: trained personnel, up-to-date equipment, adequate prescription drugs, sanitary hospitals, and even essentials such as disposable syringes and needles. In recent years, the latter had to be re-used which often had the terrible effect of spreading contagion from one patient to another. Diseases under control in other societies, such as viral hepatitis and diphtheria, continued to spread at a high rate in the Soviet Union. One very worrisome statistical fact is that the average life span of Soviet citizens was well below that of most industrialized societies, and in fact dropped to lower levels in the mid-1980s for several years.

Although the intentions of the Communist party were commendable, the average Soviet citizen did not enjoy the many amenities that Westerners and "select" Soviet citizens took for granted. This elite social entity, often referred to as the *nomenklatura*, lived in comparative comfort if not luxury, due to their presence on the officially sanctioned but unpublished list of leading party officials and other distinguished public figures. Estimates put the number of people on this list at approximately two million during the Brezhnev era. Thus, not surprisingly, all the other people felt cheated or left out of the promised good life, especially since they were increasingly aware of many of the privileges bestowed upon the Communist party elite. The special stores, hospitals, homes, and other benefits for the party's chosen few or for prominent figures in science, athletics, and the arts certainly permitted a lifestyle that met the aspirations of a small portion of the Soviet population but that were inaccessible to the public at large.

Unfortunately, for many years, few options existed for communicating or discussing public discontent. Press and media controls, the monopoly of the Communist party until 1990, and the strict judgments of the legal system kept most hostile views or questioning opinions in check. Thus, by the time Gorbachev came to power in 1985, the potential for more serious ferment was so evident to him that he moved quickly to permit a good deal of it to be expressed openly. This effort sought not only to admit problems but to serve as a means of encouraging the public to participate in the resolution of a variety of national issues. One example of this wider opportunity to speak critically on issues was the appearance of public opinion polls, which from 1987 have regularly sampled Soviets' opinions on many topics. Belatedly, the Soviet Union has embarked into this field of learning about public attitudes. Similarly, Soviet commentators (both in the press and in fields such as sociology) have explored public attitudes toward daily life, jobs, the leaders of the country, and the past. These studies and commentaries provide a deeper insight into the minds and psyches of ordinary citizens.

More and more, the attitudes in the 1980s reflected discouragement, frustration, and pessimism. Consumer goods were in short supply; municipal services (housing, utilities, education, health, and the like) did not perform as promised. Anti-social behavior increased substantially, raising both anger and concern. The increased use of illegal drugs, often imported by military forces returning from Afghanistan (who already suffered from drug addiction), made deeper inroads into Soviet society. Juvenile delinquency, although not absent during the Brezhnev years, seemed to spread, and no one clearly understood how to respond successfully to this phenomenon. A high level of delinquency was associated with alcohol abuse; most cases of robberies, rapes, other violent crimes, and prostitution also involved alcohol. Although the authorities attempted to respond to problems of drug or alcohol abuse, the situation continued and became even more widespread.

These and other worrisome conditions led to the creation of various government reforms to address the problems. One notable program, declared only a month after Gorbachev became general secretary, was a scheme to counter the abuse of alcohol. New standards were introduced: the minimum drinking age was raised from eighteen to twenty-one, liquor stores were open for a shorter amount of time each day, limits were set on the amount of bottled liquor that could be bought at one time, and even the size of bottles was modified. The government also responded by substantially increasing alcohol prices, which seemed to have the effect of increasing government revenues but not of contributing greatly to the reduction of consumption. The volume of liquor production was reduced for two years, but this caused greater consumer competition to purchase liquor when it was available and also motivated creative citizens to manufacture home-made alcoholic beverages (*samogen*). Samogen was manufactured without standards of quality control or health and safety tests. Its production also resulted in shortages of commodities such as sugar, which was used as a component in making this home brew.

Government efforts to promote abstinence or at least moderation appear to have had limited success. The public scoffed at the creation of temperance societies promoting the drinking of fruit juices and tea, although the media did support the Gorbachev plan for the first two years of his scheme. Finally, by 1988, the limits on production were substantially raised, and most agree that the overall effort to curtail alcohol abuse failed. The public never gave its full support to this cause, even though it had implications both for a person's physical health as well as his or her production and morale.

The need for housing persisted throughout the eighties. Although housing construction continued at a steady pace, the Soviet public experienced inadequate or substandard housing. Waiting lists for apartments remained as long as ever. The quality of recently built apartments consistently failed to meet required standards and expectations, and their shoddy quality, caused by hasty construction, soon resulted in widespread problems of maintenance and repairs. Large complexes of apartment buildings gradually spread across the suburbs of major cities, providing more housing opportunities but also giving the impression of mass impersonal habitations built to a master plan with little variation or creativity.

A related problem was the lack of the needed support services near these massive housing projects: schools, medical clinics, stores, recreational facilities, and the like. Nor were religious buildings constructed to serve the spiritual and social needs of Christians and other faiths who sought religious centers in their neighborhoods, despite promises of religious freedom in the 1936 and 1977 constitutions. In fact, a small number of religious congregations existed so the regime could maintain that religious freedom did exist. Opportunities were rigidly controlled and limited, however, and the anti-religious policies of the regime since its origin are well documented. Eventually, the national parliament passed a "freedom of conscience" law in October 1990, but its effects only slowly began to be felt across the nation. Houses of worship definitely did not meet the public need.

These unsatisfactory living conditions placed severe pressures and stresses on Soviet families. A sense of deadening boredom and a growing awareness of how far the Soviet Union lagged behind other leading industrial states created a growing cynicism and rebellious attitude. Increased coverage of these problems in the press and on television added to the frustration. These characteristics of modern Soviet life largely nullified or undercut the rosy and optimistic public statements the Communist authorities made about the harmonious and productive development of the Soviet population under Marxism-Leninism.

For many citizens, the struggle essentially became one of mere survival without seeking to make fundamental changes in the system. They believed their marginal life could probably not be improved and they attempted to hold on to what they had, while others turned to crime, especially the black market. Another response by a smaller segment was the increased vocal criticism of the government and party system whose ideological policies resulted in the unsatisfactory and depressing conditions. In recent years they sought to eliminate the Communist party in power, hoping that new leaders and non-Communist party agendas could make a difference.

Another option for many frustrated Soviet citizens alienated from their society (they felt that they worked for the system, not that the system worked for them) was the decision to emigrate, to start life anew in another environment. Although a wrenching process—leaving family, friends, heritage and a familiar way of life—millions of Soviet citizens left their homeland for Israel, Canada, the United States, and other countries in Europe. A few returned again to the Soviet Union, but most made the complete break and began to establish roots elsewhere.

Soviet Jews, although not the largest social or religious group in the USSR, were among the most prominent groups of those wishing to emigrate. Russia, with its long history of anti-Semitism both under the tsars and the Communists, continued the ugly patterns of bigotry, harassment, and persecution during the Gorbachev period, although he took steps to try to improve the situation. Gorbachev himself called for reconciliation and good will between diverse social and religious groups, but in recent years anti-Jewish publications and organizations (such as *Pamyat*) continued their vicious allegations against Soviet Jews. It is estimated that approximately three million Jews lived in the Soviet Union in the 1980s, but the exodus in recent years shows a steady hemorrhaging of this distinct group. During 1990, for example, approximately two hundred and fifty thousand Soviet Jews departed for Israel when government restrictions on emigration in the USSR were lifted or softened.

Emigration for Jews and other minorities has been and continues to be an issue affecting East-West relations. Those concerned about human rights have worked energetically for the removal of capricious or deliberate persecution. The rights of citizens to emigrate, guaranteed in international agreements signed by the Soviet Union but often unfulfilled in practice, see-sawed over the years from the Brezhnev through the Gorbachev eras according to the attitude of the Soviet authorities. Citizens who applied for exit visas usually had to wait for several years before permission was granted. In the meantime, they usually lost their main employment and other social service support, while enduring charges and taunts of traitor to the Soviet motherland from their neighbors and co-workers. These many thousands, seeking permission to emigrate, became known as ''refuseniks'' due to the official refusal to process and grant their emigration applications.

The picture began to change substantially in the late 1980s when greatly increased numbers of Jews and other Soviets legally departed. Most of the Jews, as noted, went to Israel, but the backlog of applicants would take years to process, given the outlook and practices of Soviet officials. The extent and speed of emigration was expected to increase substantially in the mid- and later-1990s, when a new law on emigration was to go into effect. This legislation, passed by the Soviet Parliament in June 1991, would have taken effect in 1993. It provided substantial guarantees of the right of Soviet citizens to leave or enter the nation if they wished. Soviet officials were given very limited authority to deny exit visas and other approval for those seeking to emigrate. However, in the aftermath of the termination of the Soviet Union as a nation in December 1991, which apparently negates this emigration law, it remains to be seen if the individual republics will adopt such policies for the citizens of their own territories.

One of the effects of emigration has been the loss of some of the most talented citizens. The bulk of those leaving or applying to emigrate include the younger and middle age groups, often with important skills and substantial education. Their absence will make the transition of the former Soviet Union even more difficult and uncertain in the decade of the nineties. Most of the older population will remain, unable physically and emotionally to leave their homeland and face the stress of new and strange surroundings. It could be that a good portion of the younger generation will stay, but only if they are convinced that their standard of living will increase and that their lives will have a reasonable chance of genuine improvement. At the present time they do not have that confidence. The future of the former Soviet Union largely depends on answers to difficult questions.

An unending flow of bad news continued to shake and erode public confidence. For example, the public uneasiness suddenly took a turn for the worse with the dramatic accident at the Chernobyl nuclear power plant in April 1986. This very serious event, with its dangerous effects on both the population and the environment, added to the sense of alienation of many Soviet citizens from the central authorities. The plant, north of Kiev in the Ukraine, failed to properly complete a routine test sequence on the night of April 25. This failure resulted in an increase in the amount of uncontrolled nuclear energy which destroyed one of the reactor facilities and spewed massive amounts of radioactive material into the atmosphere. Immediately, large areas of the Ukraine, Belorussia, and adjacent nations in eastern and northern Europe had to cope with the serious consequence of this catastrophe.

The incident revealed human misjudgment and errors made by the personnel at the reactor facility. The inability or the refusal to communicate rapidly the relevant information to the population in the affected areas, the inadequate medical attention, and the reluctance of the government to admit the seriousness of the accident were factors which contributed to the catastrophic effect of the incident. Only two months previously, the Soviet press boasted that a nuclear accident at this specific facility could not happen because of the modern technology and safety standards in place at Chernobyl. The course of events quickly showed how wrong such assurances were.

Gorbachev's concept of glasnost in this incident was shown to be more symbol than substance. Even in later years, the accident's consequences are still debated among nuclear specialists, health experts, journalists, and the public. While the exact number of people who will suffer long-term health problems is not yet clear, there seems little doubt that the ecological effects on land, livestock and people are extremely serious. Children have been especially affected by radiation, suffering thyroid cancer at very high rates as well as experiencing birth defects and other health problems. Present and future generations are the victims of this environmental nightmare. Although the accident occurred in the northern Ukraine, north of the capital city of Kiev, the contagion spread primarily to the north and west, affecting Sweden, Poland, Germany, and even Italy. Large areas of the western Soviet Union are now devoid of populations who were forced to leave, and the loss of usable agricultural land has been a serious blow to the nation in a region famous for its good farmland and agricultural output. Extensive funds have been appropriated and expended on "capping" the destroyed reactor, clean-up, medical treatment, population resettlement, and new housing. However, virtually all evidence shows that more funding and effective planning are needed to cope with the effects of this accident which, although it could have been far worse, stands as the most dangerous nuclear accident in the atomic age. The consequences of Chernobyl can be added to other conditions affecting the general health of the Soviet population, including poor diet, uneven medical care, alcohol abuse, and the spread of unsafe ecological conditions throughout much of the nation, both in the European and Asian sections of the Soviet Union.

The reporting of the Chernobyl accident highlighted the issue of news management and censorship in the Soviet Union. The first brief newspaper account did not appear until four days after the explosion in the reactor, and even radio warnings for the evacuation of nearby areas were not broadcast for many hours. Traditionally, accidents that caused loss of life, and other negative news, were not covered in the Soviet press. Extensive censorship and selective reporting were the norm, under the watchful eye of Glavlit, the Chief Administration of Literary and Publishing Affairs. News of political activity other than that of the Communist party was not approved and, therefore, rarely appeared. Individuals who protested the system or attempted to discuss the many problems which did exist in the nation could be accused of traitorous and heinous crimes against the nation. The harassment and vituperation of protesters were common practices in those instances, frequently supplemented by imprisonment in jail, labor camps, or prison psychiatric hospitals. Consequently, over many decades of the Communist era, editors and journalists developed and practiced a form of self-censorship, attempting to keep within the bounds of what Glavlit would permit to be reported.

The Gorbachev era started the transition away from this pattern of information control, and instances of free reporting in the spirit of glasnost have existed since 1985. This new atmosphere did not come immediately or totally, as the Chernobyl incident in April 1986 illustrates, but a trend did begin which eventually provided a wide variety of news stories that previously would have been rare or nonexistent. Topics covered with increasing frequency included: health problems, crime, divorce, ethnic unrest, economic problems, corruption, special privileges of the apparatchiki and the nomenklatura, and accidents (planes, trains, earthquakes, etc.) Journalists even provided more independent assessments of Communist ideology, the treatment of history in the tsarist and Communist periods, the excesses of the Stalin years, and the public disillusionment with life under communism. A major press freedom law finally was adopted in 1990, and Glavlit technically came to an end. Time will tell.

Open Communication

Gorbachev justified this candor by his belief that improving the motivation and commitment of Soviet citizens required a more open press and media. Admitting problems and challenges could be helpful in the search for a new effort to rebuild a nation dominated by an atmosphere of lethargy, stagnation, and the growing cleavage between the leadership and the people. Many citizens had already heard alternative news reports on foreign broadcasts beamed to the Soviet Union by the Americans, West Germans, and British. Efforts to "jam" these incoming broadcasts had some success, but news still filtered through. Eventually the authorities terminated their jamming efforts.

Soviet media personnel, long confined in the exercise of their craft, welcomed the relaxation of government controls. Restrictions still existed, but in reduced form. Proponents of political reform, plus those calling for ethnic and regional rights and even independence, used the new opportunities to appeal for their objectives. In addition to more press freedom, public meetings and demonstrations became new and unusual vehicles for people to comment actively on pressing national issues and citizens' concerns. These relaxed conditions stimulated the appearance and growth of popular fronts and eventually (by 1990) the formation of political parties to rival the Communist party.

Memories of how difficult it was in the past for individuals to express or communicate controversial views or talk about taboo subjects died hard. Nevertheless, gradually the atmosphere and reporting improved in the Gorbachev era, although certain strictures continued on such topics as pornography, state secrets, and materials promoting racial and ethnic hatred. New opportunities existed for people with creative minds in theater, film, art, and literature to develop their skills in a cultural scene dominated for so many years by the stifling hand of the state. Two leading Soviet poets became catalysts for renewed intellectual freedom. Yevgeny Yevtushenko and Andrei Voznesensky forthrightly demanded the end of the old system of control and urged their fellow writers to undertake a new literary and artistic renaissance. A steady flow of the new cultural vitality began the recovery process and nurtured the environment in which their efforts flourished, showing a creativity not seen since the twenties.

A wider variety of films began to appear for public viewing, including some that had been made ten or more years earlier but had not passed the censor's scrutiny. Previously forbidden subjects, such as drug and alcohol abuse, prostitution, discontented youth, and crime, began to be treated openly and graphically; more explicit sexual themes were also permitted. Some motion pictures dealt with political leaders or Soviet history, although sometimes in metaphorical or allegorical fashion. One noted film of this type is the movie *Repentance*, directed by the Georgian filmmaker, Abuladze. Its central character bore a striking resemblance to Lavrenti Beria, Stalin's head of the secret police. In the film he presents a benevolent face to the public while ruthlessly repressing honest citizens. It was a commentary on the Stalinist period.

In literature, novels such as Anatoly Rybakov's *Children of the Arbat* (1987) dealt with the period of the early 1930s and the role of Stalin as the national leader whose suspicious nature led to the notorious and devastating purges of the decade. Written in the early 1960s, at a time when its controversial interpretation would probably have prevented its publication, Rybakov kept the manuscript until the atmosphere of the Gorbachev period gave some assurance it could be published without retaliation. Some of the works of Valery Rasputin, a Siberian novelist, portray society and human relationships dominated by suspicion and fear. His *Pozar* (Fire) and other works present a message about the imperfections of human feelings, complemented by a strong concern for ecological issues and the misuse of his native Siberia exemplified by the damaging effects of Soviet industrial growth.

The Gorbachev era also gradually opened its cultural eyes to some of the prominent creative figures of the West, previously condemned as parasites or promoters of negative values. Art exhibits began to appear in major cities, where the works of Picasso and Matisse were shown for the first time. Soviet artists began to exhibit their own works which had been kept hidden for fear of public and official harassment. Slowly but surely the Soviet people were exposed to new thinking in the creative arts.

While many admired and welcomed the expanded freedoms of expression and news stories, others resisted the trends. Fearing confusion and possible rebellion, plus reflecting a revulsion against the experimentation and explicit nature found in the media and on the cultural scene, more traditional Soviet citizens and many in the established power structure denigrated the new freedoms as leading to intellectual confusion, moral anarchy, and social disruption. They warned of the breakdown of ethical values and the unity of the Soviet nation and its people. They feared the effects of criticizing national leaders, such as Stalin, and they fought back against the glasnost atmosphere. They stressed the depths of nationalist feeling in their emphasis on the sacrifices and victories of the Second World War. Pointing to the growing scholarly reinterpretation of the war against the Nazis, they worried that the heritage and legacy of those terrible days and years would be lost on the younger generation. These traditionalists also were especially disturbed by subject matter portraying, sometimes sympathetically, prostitution and other negative social behavior. This included portrayals of rebellious and bored youth, the drug scene, infidelity, and divorce. The perspective of the traditionalists still continues, and the final collapse of the Soviet Union as a nation-state added weight to their complaints about the destructive tendencies of the Gorbachev years.

On the other hand, the past tradition of hiding the imperfections did not make them disappear. The emergence of public opinion polls by the later 1980s provided the opportunity for many to comment on their own lives and on the state of the nation. By the use of careful questions and relevant sampling techniques, public opinion polls gave new information and insights never before available. The population previously represented a relatively passive citizenry, and the authorities had counted on this inertia. Now consumers, workers, men and women, youth and other social or occupational categories had the opportunity to express their opinions on domestic and foreign issues. These poll results gradually fill in gaps in the knowledge of the attitudes and values of Soviet people. Sociologist Tatiana Zaslavskaya is among the most prominent of the Soviet scholars evaluating the data collected from the polls.

The result of these many changes has been a much more interesting and vital Soviet media, cultural scene, and scholarly output. Although critics accuse glasnost of being the cause of many of the social ills existing at the present time, defenders argue that guided by the philosophy of openness and truth, the media serves only to communicate the news and not to create it. That healthy debate continues, as it does in other societies including the United States.

Foreign Policy

One of the most dramatic aspects of the Gorbachev period can be seen in Soviet foreign policy. While the Soviet Union still remained a superpower possessing nuclear weapons capable of imposing massive destruction (and this has continued in several republics in the post-USSR period after 1991), the Gorbachev years represented changes in Soviet strategic nuclear relationships with other nations. The period also saw significant re-examination of policy objectives, with some reduction in the Soviet Union's efforts to maintain or spread its control or influence abroad. By the latter part of the 1980s Communist systems in Eastern Europe became weaker and finally disappeared by 1990. Soviet support for its allies in other world regions declined or was otherwise modified, and the Soviet Union on many issues gave its support to the efforts of the United Nations in that organization's efforts to deal with crisis situations in many parts of the world.

These changes did not occur immediately upon Gorbachev's rise to power, but the overall record of adjustments in Soviet foreign policy and military planning was readily evident by the 1990s. There is little doubt of his intention to re-assess foreign policy, parallel to his re-examination of domestic policies. The initial statements of his new thinking, which related to foreign policy, can be seen as early as April 1985, a month after Gorbachev took office as party head. The issues he raised at that time were more thoroughly explored in his lengthy address to the Twenty-seventh Party Congress in February 1986.

His new thinking contained a number of elements to be reviewed and possibly altered. The most immediate was the question of arms control negotiations with the United States, in the context of the overall strategic nuclear balance. Other issues included Soviet support for Marxist movements in Third World countries (such as the Sandinista government in Nicaragua or the Castro regime in Cuba), efforts to improve relations with the People's Republic of China, a reduced role in Eastern European affairs (virtually ending the policy of the Brezhnev Doctrine), and more emphasis on domestic concerns (with a shift in some resources from defense expenditures to internal needs). The motivation and ultimate record were not always identical, but the picture over the six years of the Gorbachev era does show dramatic shifts and results.

Negotiations on arms issues began immediately with the United States, in fact, the day after his election as general secretary of the Communist party in March 1985. Most arms negotiations with the Americans had been broken off by late 1983, when the Soviet delegations left the negotiating table. However, by early 1985 the Chernenko regime planned to resume these negotiations and both sides agreed to meet again in March. Thus the new Gorbachev leadership came to power at this serendipitous moment.

The bulk of the negotiations sought to reach an accord on the category of INF (Intermediate Range Nuclear Forces). These weapons were designed to be used in Europe in the event of a conflict between the Warsaw Pact and NATO. Their range would not reach between the United States and the Soviet Union, but this class of deadly weapons did cover most of Europe and the western regions of the Soviet Union. Both superpowers eventually worked out the technical and political issues, and a treaty banning this class of nuclear weapons was signed in December 1987 in Washington. During the talks, the Soviet authorities attempted to keep some of their INF systems by offering to move them east of the Ural Mountains out of the range of Europe. They also attempted to include British and French nuclear weapons in the treaty. The United States refused to accept these approaches and called for a total "zero-zero" result, banning all weapons on both sides. In the end, the American position prevailed and the final treaty called for the physical destruction of these specified INF weapons by mid-1991, a feat achieved on schedule by both parties. The result gave Europeans a greater assurance they would not be the battleground in a nuclear conflict.

Talks also resumed in 1985 on another level of arms control negotiations known as START (Strategic Arms Reduction Treaty). The goal was to reduce the number of long-range strategic ballistic missiles capable of reaching targets between the United States and the Soviet Union. Several summit meetings gave impetus to the efforts of the American and Soviet negotiating teams. Gorbachev met President Reagan in Geneva in 1985 and in Reykjavik in 1986, and the two superpower leaders agreed on the principles of reductions to be achieved through more detailed negotiations. Although technical differences continued to slow the process of examining and resolving very complex issues affecting the national security of both states, a final treaty was completed and signed in May 1991 on the occasion of President Bush's visit to Moscow. If implemented as planned, the treaty calls for approximately 30 percent fewer strategic nuclear weapons by the end of the decade. More remains to be resolved in arms control efforts, but treaties like INF and START show that progress can be made when the two governments make serious commitments for meaningful reductions and when the negotiating teams work in a concerted way to reduce the danger of nuclear war while at the same time preserving and protecting the national interests of both sides.

Gorbachev made a major personnel move in 1985 to bring in a new foreign policy team to assist him in his new thinking. He tapped Eduard Shevardnadze to be his new foreign minister in June 1985, replacing Andrei Gromyko who had served in that post since 1957 in the Khrushchev years. Shevardnadze, a Georgian, had previously headed the Communist party in that republic and lacked any foreign policy experience, but his reputation as a skilled negotiator and a quick learner soon showed this appointment to be a very successful one, and he served Gorbachev in this capacity until his resignation in December 1990. He gained a high reputation with leaders of other nations for his careful and positive efforts. He also selected very able subordinates in the Foreign Ministry. Both Gorbachev and his foreign minister worked effectively together, and their good relations with the United States and other nations created an atmosphere in which major advancements in dealing with foreign policy issues could be achieved.

Some foreign relations were not always smooth, especially in the initial Gorbachev period. The war in Afghanistan, beginning in 1979, continued at an intense and destructive level through the first two years of the Gorbachev era. Soviet forces, aiding the Afghan government in Kabul, provided massive firepower against the rebels and the civilian population in that remote and barren nation. Gorbachev in fact increased the massive efforts, seeking military victory over the enemy. As the war dragged on, however, he referred to the conflict as a ''bleeding wound'' and eventually started the process for a Soviet withdrawal of combat forces. In 1987, he informed the Kabul government that future Soviet support could not be taken for granted.

He now accepted United Nations overtures to begin the process for a negotiated peace in Afghanistan, and a multi-nation agreement in early 1988 paved the way for the withdrawal of Soviet combat forces by mid-February 1989. Thus the USSR fulfilled its treaty obligations, although it still provided military aid to the Kabul government as the civil war dragged on. Only in the summer of 1991 did the United States and the Soviet Union, the two main outside suppliers to the two sides, agree to terminate the shipment of materials used in this destructive war.

Likewise, Soviet support continued to flow to its surrogate friends and partners in the Western hemisphere. The Sandinista government in Nicaragua depended on the Soviet Union for economic and military aid as did the Communist rebels fighting the central government in El Salvador. Gorbachev initially continued Soviet support, which made relations with Washington quite difficult. The United States, during most of the decade of the 1980s, supported the contras (the anti-Sandinista military forces) and also the El Salvador authorities in their internal conflict with Marxist rebels.

By the later 1980s, Soviet policy toward Central America specifically and the Third World in general showed signs of a shift away from confrontation. Gorbachev, in 1987, spoke of the need to allow troubled areas to find their own way and direct their future without the involvement of the superpowers. The Soviet Union began to reduce aid to its former allies, both in military as well as economic assistance. This included notifying Fidel Castro in 1989 and 1990 that the Soviet Union could not and would not be able to continue the level of support it provided Cuba in previous decades. (Three billion rubles, one-fourth of all Soviet foreign aid in 1989, went to Cuba.) Certainly part of the motivation for this shift was the result of the growing economic crisis inside the Soviet

Union, but Gorbachev's view also represented an altered perspective based on political, geo-political, and strategic considerations.

Along with these gradual changes in policy and commitment, the Soviet Union began the slow process of improving relations with the People's Republic of China. For nearly three decades the two Communist neighbors watched each other suspiciously. The rhetoric from both capitals was cool at best, and occasionally quite inflammatory and hostile.

Gorbachev's address to the Twenty-seventh Party Congress in February 1986 offered a broad opening to other nations, including China, for improved relations. He also indicated a possible shift in the Afghan war situation, which had been one of the points of disagreement in Sino-Soviet relations. In a major policy speech given in Vladivostok in July, he proposed a new Soviet orientation of Soviet policy toward East Asia and Southeast Asia, and China clearly would become an important element of this approach. China, seeing some possibility of changes in Soviet policy in Asia, continued to press for Soviet withdrawal from Afghanistan, the withdrawal of Soviet forces from Outer Mongolia, and the end of Soviet support for Vietnam in the continuing struggle for control over Cambodia in Southeast Asia.

Sino-Soviet talks resumed in February 1987 to discuss border disputes after nearly a decade of impasse on this subject. Following the 1988 Soviet agreement to eventually withdraw its forces from Afghanistan, relations between Moscow and Beijing steadily improved. Later that year, Gorbachev's speech in Krasnoyarsk in September 1988 continued the thaw in the relations of the two superpowers. Building on his earlier overtures to China, he proposed multilateral talks dealing with such Asian issues as the Vietnamese invasion and occupation of Cambodia, economic cooperation and trade, and more investment in the Pacific region. He also proposed a freeze on the introduction of more Soviet and American nuclear weapons in Asia and the western Pacific, the termination of several Soviet and American military bases in Southeast Asia, and he reiterated his call for a high-level summit with the Chinese. Gorbachev also made positive references to the Japanese for future cooperation, even though the two nations technically were still at war since a formal peace treaty ending World War II hostilities had not yet been signed. After the final withdrawal of Soviet combat forces from Afghanistan in early 1989, the stage was set for Gorbachev's official state visit to Beijing in May 1989, the first visit at such a high level in three decades. New agreements were signed on economic, cultural, and political cooperation, although strategic and regional issues still remained to be resolved in future meetings.

Soviet policy and behavior affecting the Communist regimes of East European nations underwent major changes in the late 1980s. By 1987, Moscow indicated its intention to follow a more hands-off policy toward that region which had been such an essential component of decades of Soviet policy. The historical record in the area since the end of World War II shows its great significance for the USSR: the creation of numerous Communist governments; the dispute with Tito in the late 1940s; Soviet intervention in Hungary (1956) and Czechoslovakia (1968); the creation of the Warsaw Pact; the declaration of the interventionist Brezhnev Doctrine to justify interference in the internal affairs of its nearby neighbors; the elaborate and interlinking economic agreements through Comecon/CMEA (Council for Mutual Economic Assistance) since its formation in 1949; and the extension of Soviet military strength during the post-war decades. All of these events came under Gorbachev's scrutiny in his reassessment in the new thinking Soviet foreign policy. Initially, he hoped to maintain the presence of Soviet military forces and Communist regimes in his neighbors to the west. However, by 1989 the Communist domination within those Soviet allies eroded almost completely. By the 1990s, those systems have for all practical purposes disappeared in the general collapse of the Soviet empire in Europe.

The signs of change were slow at first, articulated in general statements of the Soviet government and Communist party to follow a policy of peaceful cooperation with its neighbors. Gorbachev, in his book *Perestroika: New Thinking for the World* (written in the summer of 1987 and published in an English translation later that year) made explicit the right of states to make their own decisions. He gave assurances that the Soviet Union had no intention to intervene again in the affairs of other nations. He also began to refer to the concept of a common European home, suggesting new and improved relationships with the nations of Central and Western Europe as well. He confirmed this revised strategy on a state visit to Yugoslavia in March 1988, and the final joint statement of the two governments specifically included the provision banning intervention in the affairs of other nations. Interviews with the Western media in May confirmed this Soviet policy, and the point was reaffirmed at the Nineteenth Party Congress held in Moscow in early summer.

These signals culminated in the dramatic events of 1989 with the collapse of Communist governments in rapid succession. Poland made the initial break when a non-Communist government came to power in August and the Solidarity movement assumed major responsibilities in running that nation. When Gorbachev visited West Germany in mid-June, he was cheered as a force for peaceful change, and a similar reaction occurred with his visit to France in July where he again stressed the common European home theme. In his speech to the Council of Europe in Strasbourg on July 6, Gorbachev specifically rejected the concept of interference in the affairs of other states.

This policy was repeated in a meeting of Warsaw Pact governments held several days later in Bucharest, Romania. His visit to East Germany in late August, while nominally supporting the Honecker regime, occurred just on the brink of the dramatic events of October-December, when the Communist governments of East Germany, Hungary, Czechoslovakia, Bulgaria, and Romania were replaced by non-Communist governments or by interim Communist regimes destined to be short-lived. The dramatic image of the opening of the Berlin Wall in November 1989, and its eventual removal as the physical barrier not only between East and West Berlin but between West and East Germany, gave ample and visual evidence of the fundamental and stunning changes occurring in what had previously been the region deemed essential to Soviet influence and power.

Gorbachev continued to declare his intentions not to interfere with the domestic changes taking place in neighboring countries. He repeated this assurance on a state visit to Finland late in 1989. Thus the Brezhnev Doctrine of the 1960s became a major casualty of these important changes occurring in modern European history in the late twentieth century. The new conditions offered hope of reduced tensions in the post-World War II era, and it now became a common phrase to speak of the end of the cold war.

One evidence of the improved relations with Western powers can be seen in the summit meetings Gorbachev held with his American counterparts. Beginning in 1985 at Geneva, Gorbachev and Reagan continued these summits in 1986 in Reykjavik, 1987 in Washington, 1988 in Moscow and New York City, followed by meetings with President Bush in 1990 in Washington and 1991 in Moscow. In addition, Gorbachev and Bush participated in multi-government summits in 1990 in Helsinki and Paris and in 1991 in Madrid. These meetings, dealing with complicated issues and requiring extensive preliminary negotiations and preparation, nonetheless provided the opportunity for dealing with common concerns and interests of both superpowers. The benefits of regular summits gave hope that outstanding issues could be resolved in a positive way while protecting the national interests of each side. In July 1991, Gorbachev attended the "G-7" meeting in London, composed of government leaders of the seven major industrialized nations: Britain, Canada, France, Germany, Italy, Japan, and the United States. While not an official member of the G-7 group, the Soviet president's presence as an observer further indicated the Soviet Union's interest in closer relations with economically strong nations at a time when Soviet economic problems and needs required substantial international attention and financial assistance.

Additional evidence of more peaceful and cooperative Soviet intentions is seen in the Soviet moratorium on nuclear weapons testing. Gorbachev in the summer of 1985 announced a five-month moratorium, and he continued the testing ban until February 1987. He also called on the world to bring about a nuclear-free world by the year 2000, although few expected such a goal to be achieved. In a noteworthy speech to the United Nations in December 1988, he offered a unilateral reduction in Soviet armed forces of five hundred thousand troops by 1992.

In the aftermath of the collapse of Communist governments in Eastern Europe in 1989–1990, members of the Warsaw Pact began negotiations with the Moscow authorities for the removal of Soviet military forces from their territories. By early 1991, members negotiated the actual termination of the alliance, reaching final agreement in mid-1991 for its abolition. Likewise, the CMEA also was terminated in 1991, creating and forcing new relations between the Soviet Union and its former economic partners in East Europe. The unification of former East Germany with West Germany in 1990 had already initiated the removal of Soviet influence in the region.

Other examples of Gorbachev's new thinking in foreign policy include his visits to such Third World nations as India plus (in 1991) the first visit by a

Soviet president to South Korea and Japan. Gorbachev sought improved economic ties with both economic giants and also the resolution of a long-standing territorial dispute with Japan.

Recent years also have brought more Soviet support for the United Nations. Gorbachev and his government, having articulated this new commitment in the fall of 1987, exhibited substantial support. In recent years the Soviet Union cooperated far more frequently with the policies of the United Nations and with other leading members of the Security Council. This became especially apparent in the fall of 1990, following the Iraqi invasion of Kuwait. Soviet support for UN sanctions against Iraq and even for the use of force in early 1991 to free Kuwait from Iraqi control represented a clear shift in Soviet foreign policy in matters affecting the Middle East. Differences regarding policy goals in the area did continue, of course, because the USSR still had its own long-term interests in the region. Nor did Gorbachev permit the use of Soviet military forces in the allied coalition in the war against Saddam Hussein, the president of Iraq since 1979. However, these differences were not enough to undercut Soviet support of the UN response, and Foreign Minister Shevardnadze provided very important support for a strong UN plan to deal with the crisis. If the Soviet Union had cast its veto in the Security Council on one or more occasions in the summer and fall of 1990, the UN would have been blocked from taking any coordinated economic or military action to respond to the Persian Gulf crisis.

It is not too surprising, therefore, that the Nobel Peace Committee decided to select Mikhail Gorbachev as its recipient of the Nobel Peace Prize for 1990, for his many decisions and policies which reduced the tensions and dangers in so many demonstrable ways. His choice was widely hailed, although critics did point to his inability to improve the lives of his own people or to face successfully the serious economic and ethnic challenges within the Soviet Union.

Thus, it is important to note that Soviet foreign policy in the Gorbachev era experienced substantial alterations. The domestic problems of the Soviet Union effectively precluded any serious confrontations or meddling in the affairs of other states. The termination of the Soviet Union in December 1991 further weakened the capability or motivation of undertaking significant unilateral efforts unless absolutely necessary. However, even in the aftermath of the collapse of the USSR, Russia, as the largest single republic, still remains a major nuclear superpower. The potential for international confrontation and conflict still exists, but for the foreseeable near future, chances of dangers arising from the former member-states of the USSR seem unlikely. Fortunately, initial talks with the Russian government, headed by President Boris Yeltsin, signaled hope for further reductions and controls of thermonuclear weapons systems.

Suggested Reading

AGANBEGYAN, A. G., *Inside Perestroika: The Future of the Soviet Economy* (New York, 1989).

ÄSLUND, A., *Gorbachev's Struggle for Economic Reform: The Soviet Reform Process, 1985–1988* (Ithaca, NY, 1989).

BARADAT, L. P., *Soviet Political Society* (Englewood Cliffs, NJ, 1992).
BEICHMAN, A. and M. S. BERNSTAM, *Andropov, New Challenge to the West: A Political Biography* (New York, 1983).
BENNETT, P. R., *The Soviet Union and Arms Control: Negotiating Strategy and Tactics* (New York, 1989).
BLACK, C., *Understanding Soviet Politics: The Perspective of Russian History* (Boulder, 1987).
BOCHAROV, G. N., *Russian Roulette: Afghanistan through Russian Eyes* (New York, 1990).
BRZEZINSKI, Z., *The Grand Failure: The Birth and Death of Communism in the Twentieth Century* (New York, 1990).
COHEN, S. F. and K. VANDEN HEUVEL, *Voices of Glasnost: Interviews with Gorbachev's Reformers* (New York, 1989).
COLTON, T. J., *The Dilemma of Reform in the Soviet Union* (New York, 1986).
CROUCH, M., *Revolution and Evolution: Gorbachev and Soviet Politics* (Englewood Cliffs, NJ, 1989).
DAVIES, R. W., *Soviet History in the Gorbachev Revolution* (Bloomington, IN, 1989).
DAWISHA, K., *Eastern Europe, Gorbachev and Reform: The Great Challenge* (Cambridge, Eng., 1988).
DESAI, P., *Perestroika in Perspective: The Design and Dilemmas of Soviet Reform* (Princeton, 1989).
DODER, D. and L. BRANSON, *Gorbachev: Heretic in the Kremlin* (New York, 1990).
GATI, C., *The Bloc that Failed: Soviet-East European Relations in Transition* (Bloomington, IN, 1990).
GORBACHEV, M. S., *Perestroika: New Thinking for Our Country and the World* (New York, 1987).
GOSCILO, H. and B. LINDSEY (eds.), *Glasnost: An Anthology of Russian Literature under Gorbachev* (Ann Arbor, 1990).
HELLER, A., and F. FEHER, *From Yalta to Glasnost: The Dismantling of Stalin's Empire* (Cambridge, Eng., 1990).
HOUGH, J. F., *Russia and the West: Gorbachev and the Politics of Reform* (New York, 1988).
JACOBSEN, C. G. (ed.), *Soviet Foreign Policy: New Dynamics, New Themes* (New York, 1989)
JONES, A. and W. MOSKOFF (eds.), *Perestroika and the Economy: New Thinking in Soviet Economics* (Armonk, NY, 1989).
KAISER, R. G., *Why Gorbachev Happened: His Triumphs and His Failure* (New York, 1991).
KELLEY, D. R., *Soviet Politics from Brezhnev to Gorbachev* (New York, 1987).
LANE, D., *Soviet Society under Perestroika* (Boston, 1990).
MEDVEDEV, R. A., and G. CHIESA, *Time of Change: An Insider's View of Russia's Transformation* (New York, 1989).
MEDVEDEV, Z. A., *Andropov* (New York, 1984).
_____, *Gorbachev* (New York, 1986).
_____, *The Legacy of Chernobyl* (New York, 1990).
MORRISON, J., *Boris Yeltsin: From Bolshevik to Democrat* (New York, 1991).
MURAKA, D., *Gorbachev: The Limits of Power* (London, 1988).
NAYLOR, T. H., *The Gorbachev Strategy: Opening the Closed Society* (Lexington, MA, 1988).

OBERDORFER, D., *The Turn: From the Cold War to A New Era: The United States and the Soviet Union 1933–1990* (New York, 1991).

OWEN, R., *Comrade Chairman: Soviet Succession and the Rise of Gorbachev* (New York, 1987).

REMNICK, D., *Lenin's Tomb: The Last Days of the Soviet Empire* (New York, 1993).

SAIKAL, A. and M. MALEY (eds.), *The Soviet Withdrawal from Afghanistan* (Cambridge, Eng., 1989)

SAKHAROV, A., *Moscow and Beyond, 1986–1989* (New York, 1991).

SCHMIDT-HÄUER, C., *Gorbachev: The Path to Power* (Topsfield, MA, 1986).

SHLAPENTOKH, V., *Soviet Ideologies in the Period of Glasnost: Responses to Brezhnev's Stagnation* (New York, 1988).

SMITH, H., *The New Russians* (New York, 1990).

_____, *The Russians* (New York, 1984).

SOLOVYOV, V., and E. KLEPIKOVA, *Behind the High Kremlin Walls* (New York, 1986).

_____, *Boris Yeltsin: A Political Biography* (New York, 1992).

_____, *Yuri Andropov, A Secret Passage into the Kremlin* (New York, 1983).

SOLZHENITSYN, A., *Rebuilding Russia* (New York, 1992).

STEELE, J., *Soviet Power: The Kremlin's Foreign Policy: Brezhnev to Andropov* (New York, 1983).

TARASULO, I. J., (ed.), *Gorbachev and Glasnost: Viewpoints from the Soviet Press* (Wilmington, DE, 1989).

_____, *Perils of Perestroika: Viewpoints from the Soviet Press, 1989–1991* (Wilmington, DE, 1992).

TIMOFEYEV, L., *Russia's Secret Rulers: How the Government and Criminal Mafia Exercise Their Power* (New York, 1992).

WALKER, M., *The Waking Giant: Gorbachev's Russia* (New York, 1986).

WEEKS, A. L., *The Soviet Nomenklatura: A Comprehensive Roster of Soviet Civilian and Military Officials* (Washington, D.C., 1991).

WILLIS, D., *Klass: How Russians Really Live* (New York, 1985).

YELTSIN, B., *Against the Grain: An Autobiography* (New York, 1990).

YEVTUSHENKO, Y., *Fatal Half Measures: The Culture of Democracy in the Soviet Union* (Boston, 1991).

ZACEK, J. S. (ed.), *The Gorbachev Generation: Issues in Domestic Policy* (New York, 1989).

ZEMTSOV, I., *Chernenko: The Last Bolshevik: The Soviet Union on the Eve of Perestroika* (New Brunswick, NJ, 1988).

_____, *Policy Dilemmas and the Struggle for Power in the Kremlin: The Andropov Period* (Fairfax, VA, 1985).

ZEMTSOV, I., and J. FARRAR, *Gorbachev. The Man and the System* (New Brunswick, NJ, 1989).

ZICKEL, R. E. (ed.), *The Soviet Union: A Country Study* (Washington, D.C., 1991).

CHAPTER 23

Epilogue

By the latter half of 1990 and early 1991, we have seen how Gorbachev's leadership and options deteriorated substantially on the domestic scene. In retrospect, the origins of the coup of August 1991 can be more clearly seen as developing over a year's time.

The Twenty-eighth Party Congress (July 1990) met to discuss numerous economic and political questions. Gorbachev told his colleagues that the nation had to get the economic problems under control in the next two years, and he pushed for a series of reforms in the fall which came to be known as the ''Five-Hundred-Day Plan.'' Goals outlined in this plan included the gradual shift to the privatization of property and the creation of a market economy based on capitalist principles. Boris Yeltsin, increasingly influential as the leader of the Russian Republic, supported this plan. Unfortunately, Gorbachev failed to implement it as scheduled. In October 1990 he offered a compromise scheme which attempted to bridge the original, more radical, and speedy plan with a more traditional one developed by his finance minister, Valentin Pavlov.

In the meantime, as immediate economic problems had to be faced, the Soviet parliament extended Gorbachev's presidential powers to rule by decree in the later months of 1990 and into the following year. While many of his actions were intended to provide essential commodities and services, others had a more ominous tone, such as a January 1991 decree authorizing security searches of businesses and the seizure of financial records. By the spring of 1991, the introduction of higher prices by state fiat severely tested public support for the regime, since the availability of commodities still did not increase to any meaningful extent while the price of items that were available as much as tripled. Expanded rationing schemes were created and implemented, which helped somewhat, but hoarding became a primary daily objective.

The August Coup

Politically, the Soviet legislature in the spring of 1991 authorized the holding of a national referendum, and Gorbachev hoped this would give him increased support through a national mandate to rule a unified nation. However, as noted previously, the results were mixed in their implications for the future. By the summer of 1991, the reluctance and refusal of several republics to provide tax revenues to the central government created an increasingly impossible situation. A national structure existed, but with inadequate funds to pay for its operations. In addition, several republics by the late summer decided to embark on their own course and signed agreements with other republics without going through the usual procedure of central coordination and planning. By October and November 1991, in the aftermath of the failed coup, ten republics signed a treaty of virtually total control over their own economies, revenues, and natural resources. Moscow had become increasingly irrelevant.

Gorbachev's efforts to keep control of the deteriorating conditions led to several crucial personnel selections which eventually had important consequences. Most of the leaders of the abortive coup had been placed in key positions by Gorbachev in late 1990 and early 1991. Three important examples illustrate the situation. A comparatively moderate minister of the interior (the department overseeing internal security and public order) was replaced in December 1990 by a long-time conservative Communist who quickly declared the need for the restoration of law and order by whatever means were required. The new minister, Boris Pugo, was one of the primary leaders of the August 1991 coup. A new prime minister of the Soviet Union was selected in January 1991, following the resignation of Nikolai Ryzhkov due to health reasons and his failure to achieve economic improvement. The new leader, Valentin Pavlov, was a former finance minister whom Gorbachev picked to be Ryzhkov's successor. Pavlov consistently opposed the more radical economic reforms found in the Five-Hundred-Day Plan, and he was determined generally to follow the economic policies of the past. He also was one of the top leaders of the August 1991 coup a few months later.

Another example of Gorbachev's determination to select his own advisers and primary government leaders is seen in his selection of Gennady Yenayev to be his vice president. Gorbachev nominated Yenayev, head of the trade union organization, in December 1990, but the parliament defeated him in his bid for confirmation. Gorbachev, unhappy at the result, pressed the parliament to vote again and warned that a negative vote would represent a lack of confidence in his authority as president. The second vote resulted in a slim Yenayev victory. He held the position as vice president until he participated in the coup and was arrested after its collapse. Gorbachev, in the aftermath of the coup attempt, had to admit he had chosen several subordinates unwisely. This further undercut his authority and credibility in the latter months of 1991.

Gorbachev's selection and trust in those who eventually turned against him is puzzling. Attempting to understand how he made such a mistake, leading to the end of his own power and to the disintegration of the nation, will occupy scholars for some time to come. Gorbachev's own statements after the coup and his published accounts of this episode are far from clear in explaining his apparent lapse of judgment.

There are several elements that possibly provide reasons for the events of August 1991. Overall, Gorbachev chose experienced and capable senior administrators, well tested in their previous posts and responsibilities. The major exception is Yenayev, whom Gorbachev apparently planned to use as a spokesman for his policies, and who could represent Gorbachev at meetings that the president would not be able to attend. Second, this group of administrators was not seriously saddled by previous reform efforts that had not gone well. This provided the potential for moving ahead with a fresh agenda and leadership. Pavlov is the partial exception to this assessment, as he had been involved in the ongoing economic discussions and proposals of 1990. Third, they tended to represent a point of view held by a substantial wing of the party which could not be disregarded. Gorbachev may have felt that excluding them might lead to his ouster, so he sought to include them inside the decision-making process. He hoped they could be brought into the reform camp. Fourth, economic and political conditions had changed dramatically for the worse by the spring and summer of 1991. Independence movements had grown in number, size, and influence. Violence in the Baltics had broken out in January 1991, and national unity appeared to be in genuine peril. Economic conditions for 1991 and the future seemed to be in a state of paralysis with the potential for further deterioration and no likelihood of a satisfactory resolution. The plotters genuinely feared Gorbachev was losing control of the mounting problems, and their conspiracy against him reveals the growing belief that the Soviet Union was on the brink of catastrophe in 1991-1992. Finally, Gorbachev erroneously assumed that he had what political leaders throughout the world have a right to expect from their subordinates—their acceptance of his authority and support for his programs. Presidents do not expect treasonous behavior from their associates.

As evidence of the growing leadership crisis, one of Gorbachev's most trusted associates resigned in December 1990 in protest at the direction the nation was heading and at the growing possibility of dictatorship. Foreign Minister Eduard Shevardnadze, one of the major participants in Gorbachev's new thinking in foreign policy, resigned his post in a brief but spectacular public speech. He later resigned from the Communist party and shifted his efforts and interests to the democratic movement in the nation.

Continued nationality problems further compounded the growing crisis. Lithuania in March 1991 was the first to declare full independence from the USSR, although it was unable to achieve its objective immediately. Other republics adopted a position short of independence, declaring their sovereignty over natural resources, finances, and the economy and making their laws equal to those of the national regime. More popular fronts and republic political parties emerged in 1990 and 1991, adding to the public discontent and confusion. Authorities used forceful tactics in Lithuania and Latvia in January 1991, causing fatalities and expanding public hostility toward Moscow. Top Communists moved away from the party. For example, even before Shevardnadze's withdrawal from the party in 1991, Boris Yeltsin dramatically resigned from the party in July 1990 at the Twenty-eighth Party Congress and walked out of the meeting. In June 1991 Russian voters elected him overwhelmingly as president of the Russian Republic, thus becoming a rival with Gorbachev for national leadership.

These elements formed the background for Gorbachev's negotiations with republic leaders in his attempt to develop a new union treaty for the nation. As stated in chapter 22, drafts were corrected and negotiated over many months, from late 1990 through the spring and summer of 1991. The date of August 20, 1991, was selected as the date for the formal signing of the new federal structure. That date triggered the conspirators' effort to block the treaty, impose firm national control, and remove Gorbachev as the national president. The coup, starting on August 18, included major figures in the government: Prime Minister Pavlov, Minister of the Interior Pugo, Minister of Defense Yazov, KGB head Kryuchkov, and USSR Vice President Yenayev. The evidence suggests their discussions about taking strong measures began as early as December 1990, with the primary goal to prevent the signing of the union treaty and to restore the authority of the Communist party.

When the conspirators seized power in the capital on August 19, 1991, a series of published decrees revealed their agenda: all non-Communist parties were banned, as were public demonstrations; the press was put under state control, and many newspapers were forbidden to publish; the parliamentary bodies were abolished; martial rule prevailed. They arrested Gorbachev at his Black Sea vacation home on the night of August 18th and informed the nation that he had resigned due to overwork and illness. While initially successful in Moscow, the coup soon collapsed by August 21, thanks to the refusal of most military commanders to obey the plotters and use force against the populace opposing the coup. Boris Yeltsin's dramatic presence and brave speeches heartened the anti-coup public response. Only three persons died violently in those dangerous days. The resistance seen by the West on television came mainly from Moscow. People who lived in other cities, such as Kiev and Leningrad, did not have the same degree of defiant opposition to the plotters, because for many Soviet citizens, life during those several crucial days seemed unaffected.

Gorbachev's rescue by his loyal followers restored him to power again, and he immediately distanced himself from his disloyal associates. He still did not give satisfactory support for the reforms that many demanded, impatient in the face of further delays in signing the treaty. His efforts to defend the Communist party and its ideology in the aftermath of the coup further discredited him, and public pressure forced him to resign as general secretary of the Communist party

Russian President Boris Yeltsin opposes the August 1991 attempted coup in Moscow.

on August 24, 1991. His continued position as national president also appeared to be in serious jeopardy.

In the aftermath of the coup's failure, one plotter (Pugo) committed suicide and the other major figures were jailed while awaiting trial for treason. Certainly there was much to be fearful about in looking to the future. The economy and relations with the republics did not improve by the end of the year. A new governing group, the State Council, was established under Gorbachev's direction, but their decisions led primarily to further disintegration of the nation. The Council accepted the complete independence of Latvia, Estonia and Lithuania on September 6. Most of the other republics passed their own resolutions of independence in the immediate post-coup days, and the collapse of the balance of the USSR seemed only a matter of time. In one of the most important of these events, the great majority of the Ukrainian electorate voted on December 1 for complete independence from the Soviet Union, and also elected Leonid Kravchuk as its new president.

The Commonwealth of Independent States

Gorbachev still attempted to hold some of the republics together in a loose federation of remaining states, and plans for another union treaty were completed in November. However, the growing economic crisis, the discrediting of the Communist party's leadership after seven decades of one-party rule, the abolition of the national Communist party in the aftermath of the August coup, and virtually uncontrollable regional activism doomed Gorbachev's dogged efforts to keep the fragmented union together. His failure to achieve this goal led to his demise as the national president by the end of the year. His resignation speech as president was broadcast on Soviet television on December 25, 1991.

December also brought about the creation of the political arrangement intended to serve as the successor of the USSR. Three republics (Russia, Belorussia or Belarus, and Ukraine) formed the nucleus of the Commonwealth of Independent States on December 8, and the addition of other republics created an expanded eleven-member CIS on December 21. The three Baltic republics already had separated from the union, and of the remainder only Georgia did not participate. The CIS was a loose federation of totally sovereign states, committed to continuing economic ties, friendly relations, and military coordination. The founders spoke of their new creation as a possible modified version of the European Economic Community of Western Europe. A common military command was needed, at least for the immediate future, while final arrangements would be worked out regarding defense policies as well as the control of military forces and nuclear weapons.

It is an extraordinary event to see a nation disappear with a minimum of violence and bloodshed. By comparison, the similar disintegration of the nation of Yugoslavia beginning in 1991 was accompanied by a violent civil war and high civilian losses. Whether Gorbachev or any other leader might have succeeded in maintaining the union will be debated for years to come. The immediate task was to see if the component republics of the former Soviet Union could in fact exist as viable economic entities with stable governmental systems to serve the needs of their populations. There seems little doubt that the political collapse of the Soviet Union would have been substantially delayed if economic conditions had not deteriorated throughout the nation during the Gorbachev years. Separation might have come eventually, but in a slower and measured fashion. This, in fact, is what Gorbachev proposed as an ultimate possibility but would have required approximately a decade to achieve. As it turned out, the process took no more than two years in the absence of legal procedures and coordinated negotiations. Old procedures and structures disappeared without adequate preparation for the new uncertain future. Social, economic, and political systems collapsed. No one could predict what lay ahead.

In his 1991 resignation speech, lasting only ten minutes, Gorbachev summarized many achievements of his more than six years as the leader of the USSR: domestic reforms, glasnost, perestroika, greater democracy, a new period of opportunity for the Soviet people, a turning away from the totalitarian model and the Stalinist heritage, and a substantial reduction in international tension and competition. He spoke only briefly about the recent events preceding his fall—economic decline, domestic turmoil, the August coup, and the break-up of the Soviet Union. Overall, he concluded that his years in office had been quite successful in achieving the goals he sought. Yet considering that the nation had just disappeared as a viable state, the virtual absence of any comment on that profound reality appears quite extraordinary. Apparently he decided to end his public career on a positive note rather than again outlining the dreams and efforts which ultimately had proved so elusive.

Out of the wreckage of the old USSR the new Commonwealth of Independent States (CIS) entered 1992 with a combination of hope and trepidation. Virtually each republic had its own strong executive president with substantial powers (for example, Yeltsin in Russia, Kravchuk in Ukraine, and Nazarbayev in Kazakhstan). Whether their regional leadership could provide the answers to fundamental problems and develop public support remained to be seen. Immediate questions had to be resolved, such as the direction and ownership of the military system. This quickly divided the Russian and Ukrainian governments; for example, each contended for dominance over the former Soviet naval fleet stationed in the Black Sea. Control over tactical and strategic nuclear weapons also challenged the new leaders.

Promises of economic cooperation in the CIS, although agreed on paper, did not translate readily into the shipments of essential foodstuffs, raw materials (such as petroleum, coal, and iron ore), and manufactured goods across the borders of the former Soviet republics. This led to a slowing down of production, to factory shutdowns, and to rising unemployment. Furthermore, payments for these resources could not be made due to the falling production, creating additional economic hardship for production facilities and hence the work force.

In January 1992, the partial removal of price controls on food and other commodities caused rapid inflation which in turn led to a further loss of purchasing power and increased public frustration. Support for the new post-Communist era began to disappear quickly as the morale of the population eroded. The currency and banking system, never ideal in the late Soviet period, steadily deteriorated as the ruble lost purchasing power and credibility. It stood at an exchange rate of approximately $1.60 to the ruble in 1989, but the value dropped to sixteen cents in 1990 and to a penny in 1991. By the spring of 1992, the rate was over 400 rubles to the dollar; by the end of 1992 the figure was approximately 450 to the dollar; and by mid-1993, the rate was 1,100 rubles to the dollar. As prices increased for virtually everything (often in the range of 600–1,200 percent), wages were tremendously increased throughout 1992 in an attempt to keep up with the inflationary pressures. Such fiscal policies only fueled the effects of inflation, despite occasional (and sometimes successful) efforts to contain the fiscal hemorrhaging throughout the Russian nation. Not all occupations benefitted from these increases, and the pressure on people living on fixed incomes or pensions became especially severe.

Political instability appeared in an unfolding series of crises and controversies. Ethnic and nationality disputes between CIS republics continued and increased throughout 1992, notably between Russia and Ukraine and between Russia and Georgia. There was speculation that Moldova (formerly Moldavia) might join neighboring Romania, its former national homeland, but some Moldovans wished to remain independent. In addition, Russians living in Moldova fought to avert this option. To protect Russian citizens there, as a result, Russian military forces became actively involved in Moldovan affairs.

The violence between Armenia and Azerbaijan over Nagorno-Karabakh continued without pause throughout 1992, despite several efforts by other CIS republics to arrange a ceasefire and bring the two sides together in negotiations to resolve the bitter dispute. Violence in the Central Asian region toppled the president of the Tajik Republic in September 1992, in a struggle between the pro-Communist faction, the pro-democratic forces, and Islamic fundamentalists. No quick solution to this regional trauma could be seen on the horizon.

In Georgia, civil unrest in December 1991 led to a civil war that toppled the elected president in January 1992 and brought about the eventual return of former Soviet Foreign Minister Eduard Shevardnadze to his homeland as the leader of the post-civil war government there. His formal election in the fall of 1992 added to his legal and constitutional status, but the domestic controversies and violence continued and even intensified despite his efforts to seek a resolution between the various factions. A section of the Georgian Republic, along the Black Sea coast, attempted to secede in the latter half of 1992, renewing domestic violence between Georgian forces and the break-away rebels in Abkhazia. The presence of Russian military forces further complicated the Georgian problem.

As previously noted, Ukraine and Russia differed not only over control of military facilities and equipment, but also over trade issues between the two regions. Both republics created military forces to protect their interests from their potentially aggressive neighbors. An overriding issue with international strategic implications involved the control of long-range nuclear weapons. Negotiations with the United States over the applicability of the START I treaty, signed in the summer of 1991 when the USSR still existed, only slowly gained acceptance by both the successor states. Russia hoped to be the sole strategic nuclear power in the CIS, but the Ukranian government balked at losing its weapons which provided status and influence in the international arena. Further planned reductions in strategic nuclear armaments were contained in the subsequent START II treaty, which Presidents Bush and Yeltsin signed in Moscow in January 1993. However, the actual implementation of these major arms control agreements depended largely on Ukraine's acceptance of the provisions, and President Kravchuk did not feel bound by what his Russian counterpart had negotiated.

It became clear that the future of the CIS could not be taken for granted. When created in December 1991, four of the former Soviet republics (Estonia, Georgia, Latvia, and Lithuania) did not join. Continued problems, both economic or otherwise, further tested the loose federation. Of the initial eleven members, the Azerbaijan parliament refused to ratify the CIS agreement, thus signalling its withdrawal from the group. Disputes over currencies, access to resources, border checkpoint problems, nationality and ethnic differences, and the question of Russian dominance or excessive influence in the CIS made continuing cooperation and toleration extremely difficult to achieve.

The role of Russia must remain the central question in judging the ultimate success or failure of the post-Soviet period. Its huge geographic size, large population (approximately one hundred-fifty million people), military strength, industrial development, and its heritage as the dominant nation in relations with contiguous regions cannot be discounted as we look to the future. While some

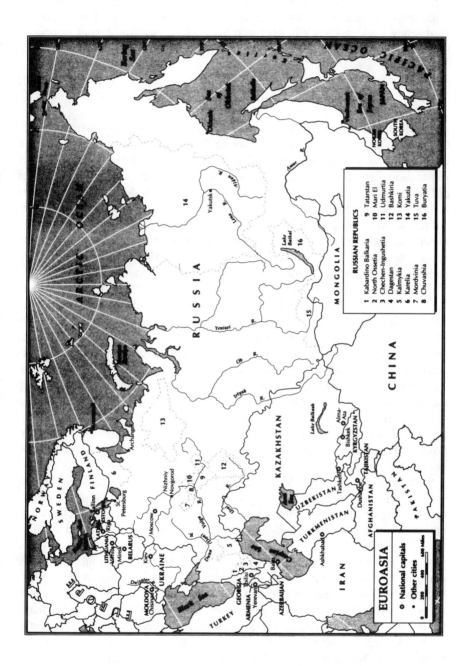

conditions seem well beyond the ability of individuals to shape or change, the leadership question now dominates the debate about Russia's future. Just as Gorbachev made his mark in his more than six years as the Soviet leader, so Boris Yeltsin became the focus of attention in the period from 1991 onward.

Boris Yeltsin

Yeltsin's background has been noted previously. A long-time member of the Communist party, he came to Moscow in 1985 from a position as a regional Communist party head in Sverdlovsk in western Siberia. Born in 1931, Yeltsin was the same age as Gorbachev, although their educational and party experiences did not follow a similar pattern. Named party head of the Moscow organization in 1985, and added to the powerful Politburo, he was removed from both bodies within two years after criticizing Gorbachev for moving too slowly on reforms as well as after actively cutting into the authority and privileges of the party nomenklatura and apparatchiki. Many assumed his fall from power in disgrace had ended the ebullient politician's opportunities for national leadership.

In 1990 Yeltsin's career took a new turn when he became the chairman of the Russian parliament. In mid-year, he publicly resigned from the Communist party. Then, in 1991, while the Soviet Union still existed, he became president of the Russian Republic. His popularity with ordinary citizens grew, and he championed many of the same objectives as the growing number of reformers and critics of the Communist system. By the summer of 1991, Gorbachev found Yeltsin to be a formidable opponent, and the effects of the August 1991 coup increased the latter's stature and leadership. He became the catalyst for the breakup of the USSR and the formation of the Commonwealth of Independent States in December. With Gorbachev's resignation that month, and the dissolution of the Soviet Union, Yeltsin became the singular figure to lead the nation into the uncertain future.

Starting in January 1992, Yeltsin faced the challenges and realities of dealing with the myriad of problems facing the independent Russian Republic and of establishing relations with the other former Soviet republics (as well as with major foreign powers, such as the United States). The core of Yeltsin's domestic future depended on the outcome of a power struggle with contending parties, factions, and political institutions. Throughout 1992, this confrontation played out between the Russian president and the two major Russian parliamentary bodies: the Supreme Soviet and the Congress of Peoples' Deputies. Elected in the period when the Soviet Union still existed and the Communist party dominated the political scene, both parliamentary groups contained many individuals loyal to the old regime and its policies. Representatives of new parties in the two legislative bodies, although non-Communist, had their own agendas to achieve, and they frequently contended with Yeltsin's policies. These new conditions caused Yeltsin to perform a juggling act—seeking compromise when victory was not possible but striving to hold on to his reform policies and his promises of improvements in economic conditions by the fall of 1992.

His cabinet contained supporters of the move toward a free market economy in which the privatization of land, industry, and businesses would steadily evolve with the passage of time. Would time permit these fundamental adjustments to occur before Yeltsin's opponents or the realities of daily existence so weakened him that his authority was eroded or possibly even terminated?

By early 1993 Yeltsin still continued in power as the Russian president, but in a weakened condition. As the economy continued to falter in nearly every sector, his opponents became increasingly hostile and confrontational. They could not succeed in ousting Yeltsin who, after all, had been overwhelmingly elected president in 1991 in the first free popular election in Russian history. A strong current of supporters believed in his democratic outlook and reform efforts. Consequently, his opponents zeroed in on his cabinet and those leading advisers who looked more vulnerable as likely targets.

Of the several associates leading and then forced to leave the political scene, Yegor Gaidar became the most visible. An economist and advocate of free market reforms, he held several cabinet economic posts until Yeltsin named him as acting prime minister in June 1992. His tenure in that post, and especially after Yeltsin nominated him in the fall to be the prime minister, became the test of Yeltsin's power. In acrimonious debates and negotiations through the fall, the balance of power see-sawed back and forth between the two sides. In early December, the anti-Gaidar group in the two legislatures succeeded in blocking Gaidar's nomination and forced Yeltsin to remove his associate. A more cautious member of the cabinet, former Energy Minister Viktor Chernomyrdin, was selected as prime minister. This contentious issue and its outcome weakened Yeltsin's influence by the turn of the new year.

As the opposition grew, with a myriad of new parties and factions, one group slowly emerged as a legitimate and effective catalyst for the anti-Yeltsin effort. It also offered a new policy agenda. The Civic Union, led by Arkady Volsky, represented the industrial sector, the defense industries, and many who had sympathy for the economic policies of the former Soviet Union, characterized by heavy government involvement in directing the economy, massive subsidies, keeping facilities under state ownership, and the like. As Yeltsin's promises of economic success faltered, the Civic Union by late 1992 grew as a significant and potential rival. Their preferred approach, slowing the pace and extent of the Yeltsin program, may become the pattern for the future if Yeltsin is unable to maintain his leadership role in the nation. Another figure of potential leadership is Yeltsin's vice president, Alexander Rutskoi of the People's party, who is likely to be a future candidate for Russian president in the next election.

Still Yeltsin may succeed over the next several years. Previous political obituaries of this colorful and dynamic Russian have been premature. His term as president continues until 1996, if this element of the democratic process is allowed to continue unhindered. His skills in defending his fundamental objectives are well known to his supporters and detractors, and his tactical shifts or even retreats may not be fatal to his cause. He consistently declared that the general direction of political, economic, and social reform would not be altered or cancelled. Like Gorbachev, he has been forced to learn the limits of what can be done and to pace how fast change can occur with what the system and society will tolerate.

Whether he will ultimately fall from power as did Gorbachev is not evident in mid-1993 as these lines are written. Continued problems and crises facing Yeltsin and the Russian people created increasing anger and frustration in 1992–1993. The dangers of potential plots and coups could not be discounted totally, although their likelihood in the near future appears relatively remote. For now, the military and legal authorities and their forces support the president and the existing political system. Yet the calls for a more conservative leadership, emphasizing a highly nationalistic foreign policy and authoritarian style at home, have grown significantly. This outlook is found especially among those who favor a strong Russian military force with nuclear weapons, an active and even expansionist foreign policy, support for Russian rights in other former Soviet republics, opposition to democratic reform and political pluralism, resurgent nationalism, and (for some) deeply rooted anti-Semitism.

Movements of this persuasion have grown throughout 1992 and 1993, as seen in the formation of organizations such as Nashi (Ours) and the National Salvation Front, a coalition of conservatives, nationalists and even some Communists. The existence of dedicated supporters of the former Communist party hostile to Yeltsin and the democratic process has now led to the creation of new versions of a Marxist political movement. Conditions such as these understandably create growing concern among the reformers in the center who must struggle with the myriad of daily problems facing them as well as with the antagonism of their opponents.

No matter from what vantage point, whether in Russia or from other nations, observers generally agree that the future success of whatever economic agenda is followed will require from three to five years at the very minimum before any meaningful improvement can be expected. The fact that Yeltsin's optimistic assurances in early 1992 for noticeable improvements by the fall of that year have not been realized compound his problems, undercut his credibility, and also reflect the extent of the challenges to be overcome. In the face of the mounting and what appear to be nearly intractable difficulties, Yeltsin said in the spring of 1993 that the transition period before Russian conditions could become stabilized and productive would require not only years, but even decades. That prediction seems closer to the reality of the situation. The world waits to see the outcome, with both interest and concern.

Economic improvement, of critical importance, is not the only issue. An even more fundamental question is the source of political authority. A good deal of the political confusion has been generated by the deeper problem of where primary political authority is located. Is it found in the legislative or executive branch of the national government? Is one dominant over the other? Are they more equal, as in a "separation of powers" arrangement similar to that found under the United States Constitution? What is the proper balance? Also, what is the structure and relationship within the Russian Federation, giving authority to the national government but also supporting the rights of the component republic regions within the Federation?

These crucial decisions currently are being debated and the outcome is far from clear at this time. Contentious reactions on this issue have created a paralyzing degree of immobility in the national government, with President Yeltsin on one side and the Russian parliamentary system (under its chairman, Ruslan Khasbulatov) on the other. Answering these concerns through a new constitutional arrangement, drawn from the lessons of practical experience and the dedication to particular political theories and structures, must come soon in order to move ahead toward the resolution of vital national issues and needs. Meanwhile, the economic and social crisis deepens.

One attempt to begin to break this impasse occurred in a national referendum in late April 1993. Even the number of questions and their wording took several months to resolve amid acrimonious debate and discussion. Whether to even have such a public vote divided the political leaders and bodies, and deciding in advance whether the results would be binding or merely a statement of public opinion also lacked substantial consensus. The final list of questions to which Russians (even those living in other former Soviet republics were eligible to vote) were to give their response included: Do you support Yeltsin? Do you favor the direction of economic reform? Do you wish an early election for president of Russia? Do you wish an early election for the Congress of Peoples' Deputies? The Yeltsin camp favored a "yes" response to the first, second, and last questions and a "no" response to the third question; his opponents favored just the opposite outcome. Whether the ballot results would have relevance for the future divided the Russian people. Many thought the referendum would be only one more distraction and predicted its results would be meaningless to the resolution of their daily problems. Others took the opportunity more seriously to express their views, positive and negative, toward the issues and leaders included on the ballot.

Considering the cynicism and apathy of many Russians about the current political scene, the number of voters participating was impressive. Of the 107,000,000 citizens eligible to vote, over 64 percent participated in the referendum balloting. The results showed substantial, although not overwhelming, support for Yeltsin and his policies. On the question measuring public confidence in Yeltsin as Russian president, over 40,000,000 gave an affirmative response while approximately 27,000,000 voted against him.

A second question gave the electorate the opportunity to judge the government's economic and social policies since early 1992. The "yes" responses, supporting Yeltsin's efforts and overall results, outnumbered the "noes" by a margin of 36,000,000 to 30,000,000 votes. The Yeltsin camp hoped for public support and pressure that would lead to early parliamentary elections, and this fourth question decisively passed (over 46,000,000 "yes" votes to approximately 21,000,000 "no" votes) in the most lopsided result of the referendum. Only on the third question did the Yeltsin forces suffer a reverse. On the issue of

calling an early election for Russian president, over 32,000,000 answered ''no,'' while 34,000,000 answered in the affirmative. This was the closest of the totals of the votes cast.

Still, as parliamentary leader Khasbulatov interpreted the results afterward, ''the referendum decides absolutely nothing.'' Results of questions one and two had no legal bearing on the continuation of the government and the policies it might undertake in the future. Also, based on a ruling of the Russian Constitutional Court, the public responses on the last two questions were not legally binding and hence early elections for president and parliament were not required to take place. Hence the political system continued unchanged into the middle of 1993, although the Yeltsin regime and others prepared drafts for a new national constitution, and plans were made for the holding of a constitutional convention in June to develop such a document. Thus the effort to define and create political institutions continued unresolved.

Coping with Change

In a deeper sense, the loss of a national identity and consensus, which has placed severe stresses on the citizens of the CIS, will continue to do so. The loss of identity could be seen in the February 1992 Winter Olympics held in France and in the Summer Olympics in Spain. Soviet athletes participated, but since the USSR no longer existed, they competed under the designation of the

"Unified Team," an ironic title considering what had just happened to their homeland. The hammer and sickle flag could not be flown nor the Soviet national anthem played even when athletes won gold medals. Instead, when these gold medalists stood on the podium to receive their awards and the accolades of the audience, the Olympic flag was raised and the "Olympic Hymn" played in their honor. The stoic faces of these gifted athletes masked the emotions that lay underneath. The resurgence of a sense of moderate Russian nationalism may take years to evolve, and the ugly manifestations of feelings of superiority and jingoism can undercut the valuable elements of a sense of national identity.

Even the traditional icons of the Communist period have disappeared or been dramatically altered. The Communist party of the Soviet Union, banned in the fall of 1992, has not been allowed to reconstitute itself in its former configuration, despite efforts to restore its legal status. *Pravda*, founded by Lenin in 1912, served for decades as the national newspaper of the Communist party. Its daily circulation fell from a high of thirteen million copies to less than two million by early 1992. It stopped publication briefly that same year due to financial exigencies, although it currently exists with a small circulation. *Pravda* no longer officially or legally represents the outlawed party, but consistently presents an anti-Yeltsin and anti-reform viewpoint, especially on the question of economic privatization. It also criticizes Russian foreign policy, accusing Yeltsin and Foreign Minister Andrei Kozyrev of slavish obedience to the United States and Western interests. *Izvestia*, another long-time newspaper representing the former Soviet government in the Communist era, is now under independent journalistic control and no longer presents the "party-line." Statues of Lenin and other leaders in the Communist pantheon of heroes now lie prostrate in parks for children to climb on, or have been taken to junk yards in their disgrace. Some are even advertised for sale as an odd form of souvenir for the curious.

The renaming of cities to restore their pre-Communist designation continues. The most notable example, in the summer of 1991, was the renaming of Leningrad to be St. Petersburg. Lenin's city, the site of the Bolshevik revolution, now returned to its historic name from the tsarist era beginning with Peter the Great. Gorky became Nizhini Novgorod once again, Sverdlovsk became Yekaterinberg, Frunze was designated Bishkek, and Kuibyshev was dropped in favor of the historic name of Samara. There were many more. It truly represented a new era.

On the other hand, "communism" is not dead in the country. Loyal and dedicated rank-and-file party members throughout Russia periodically hold rallies, fly the hammer and sickle flag of the former Soviet Union, and noisily defend Lenin, Stalin, and the heritage of the Communist period. They portray Gorbachev as a weak party leader who permitted the collapse of the Soviet Union. They also demonstrated in favor of the defendants put on trial for undertaking the coup against Gorbachev in August 1991, and vilified Yeltsin as the symbol and cause of their current discontent and national problems.

Although the Russian Constitutional Court ruled in November 1992 that the former Communist party of the Soviet Union would not be permitted to exist again, it also decreed that Communist political organizations at the local level would be allowed, with their right to develop new coordinating committees at the national level. Thus the potential for new versions of the Communist party does exist, and by the late spring of 1993 at least six new "Communist" parties had emerged in the Russian Republic. Their strength and influence, although currently small in number and limited in influence, will have to be another factor to be considered in the emergence of the shaping of the "new" Russia of the future.

Seven decades of structure and context have been removed. Bewilderment, uncertainty, frustration and anger add to daily hardships. No guarantees or assurances exist for the political and economic future of the former USSR, now composed of Russia and its neighbors. Each major region is thrown back on its own creativity and resiliency to cope with existing problems. Suspicion, confrontation and further territorial fragmentation offer little evidence of their resolution in the near term. On the other hand, out of the collapse of the political, economic and ideological Soviet system could emerge the values, leadership, and vision for the future which may give this Russian nation and its people the opportunity to rise again. Certainly Russia has shown the ability to recover after facing staggering challenges and crises in its long history. Now one more "Time of Troubles" has been added to those preceding it. If history provides the precedents and potential, the Russian people will be successful once more. Tolstoy, while writing *War and Peace*, quoted a French proverb in one of his letters that "happy nations do not have a history." Russia certainly has been unhappy for much of its existence, but its history is a rich mosaic of creative achievement.

To predict the future is always fraught with uncertainty. Perhaps we can conclude with the metaphor provided by Nicholas Gogol, the famous Ukrainian author of the nineteenth century. He used the image of the troika, the sleigh pulled by three horses harnessed evenly with each other. One is pulling directly ahead, while the horses to the right and left are harnessed with their heads pulled toward the side and thus their energies are to pull to the right and left. Gogol spoke of Russia as a troika, pulling in several directions at once but moving ahead nonetheless:

> And Russia, are not thou too flying onwards like a spirited troika, that nothing can overtake? The road smokes beneath you, the bridges tremble, everything retreats and is left behind. The onlooker is left amazed at the God-like marvel. Is it lightning thrown from heaven? What is the meaning of this terrifying onrush? What mysterious force is hidden in this troika, never seen before? Ah, horses, horses, what horses! Is the whirlwind hidden under your manes? They hear the familiar song over their heads—at once in unison they strain their iron chests and scarcely touching the earth with their hooves are transformed into straight lines flying through the air—and the troika rushes on, full of divine inspiration. But whither, Russia, are you flying? Answer me. She gives no answer. The ringing of the bells melts into music; the air, torn to shreds, whirs and rushes like the wind, everything flies past, and the other states and nations draw aside and make way for her.

One reality is sure. Russia has survived many challenges, and we should assume it will continue to play a notable role in the future. Only its precise characteristics are still clouded or fuzzy, but Russia, like the troika, rushes onward towards a new historical destiny.

Suggested Reading

GERON, L. (ed.), *Who's Who in Russia and the New States* (London, 1992).
GORBACHEV, M., *The August Coup. The Truth and the Lessons* (New York, 1991).
LOORY, S. and A. IMSE, *Seven Days that Shook the World: The Collapse of Soviet Communism* (Atlanta, 1991).
MILLER, J., *Mikhail Gorbachev and the End of Soviet Power* (New York, 1993).
REMNICK, D., *Lenin's Tomb: The Last Days of the Soviet Empire* (New York, 1993).
SOLOVYOV, V., and E. KLEPIKOVA, *Boris Yeltsin: A Political Biography* (New York, 1992).
STERN, G. (ed.), *Atlas of Communism* (New York, 1991).
WILSON, A., and N. BACHKATOV, *Russia Revised: An Alphabetical Key to the Soviet Collapse and the New Republics* (London, 1992).

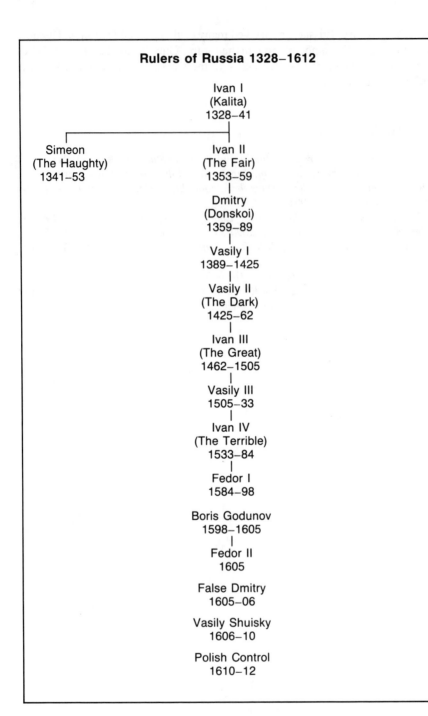

Rulers of Russia 1328–1612

Ivan I
(Kalita)
1328–41

Simeon
(The Haughty)
1341–53

Ivan II
(The Fair)
1353–59

Dmitry
(Donskoi)
1359–89

Vasily I
1389–1425

Vasily II
(The Dark)
1425–62

Ivan III
(The Great)
1462–1505

Vasily III
1505–33

Ivan IV
(The Terrible)
1533–84

Fedor I
1584–98

Boris Godunov
1598–1605

Fedor II
1605

False Dmitry
1605–06

Vasily Shuisky
1606–10

Polish Control
1610–12

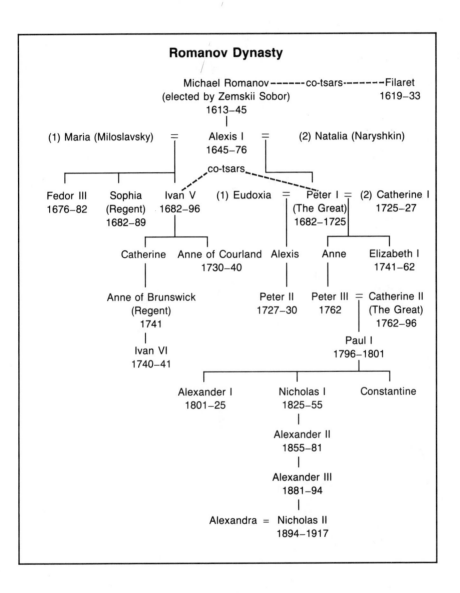

Romanov Dynasty

Michael Romanov ------ co-tsars ------ Filaret
(elected by Zemskii Sobor)   1619–33
1613–45

(1) Maria (Miloslavsky) = Alexis I = (2) Natalia (Naryshkin)
1645–76

co-tsars

Fedor III   Sophia   Ivan V   (1) Eudoxia = Peter I = (2) Catherine I
1676–82   (Regent)   1682–96   (The Great)   1725–27
1682–89   1682–1725

Catherine   Anne of Courland   Alexis   Anne   Elizabeth I
1730–40   1741–62

Anne of Brunswick   Peter II   Peter III = Catherine II
(Regent)   1727–30   1762   (The Great)
1741   1762–96

Ivan VI   Paul I
1740–41   1796–1801

Alexander I   Nicholas I   Constantine
1801–25   1825–55

Alexander II
1855–81

Alexander III
1881–94

Alexandra = Nicholas II
1894–1917

Index